David Bowie

David Bowie

No shit, just facts

part 1

Wim Hendrikse

Aspekt Publishers

David Bowie - No Shit, just facts part 1

© Wim Hendrikse
© 2016 Aspekt Publishers

Amersfoortsestraat 27, 3769 AD Soesterberg, Nederland
info@uitgeverijaspekt.nl – http://www.uitgeverijaspekt.nl

Cover design: Maarten Bakker / Aspekt Publishers
Cover picture: Ton van der Horst
Interlining: Aspekt Publishers

ISBN: 9789461538932
NUR: 660/669

All rights reserved. No part of these pages, either text or image may be used for any purpose other than personal use. Therefore, reproduction, modification, storage in a retrieval system or retransmission, in any form or by any means, electronic, mechanical or otherwise, for reasons other than personal use, is strictly prohibited without prior written permission.

01. INTRODUCTION BY JEAN-PAUL HECK AND THE AUTHOR.
02. SOME QUOTES.
03. SINCE WHEN AM I A BOWIE FAN?
04. WHY DID I WRITE THIS BOOK?
05. ACKNOWLEDGEMENTS.
06. THE CRACKED ACTOR DOCUMENTARY.
07. HOW TO USE THIS BOOK.
08. CHRONOLOGY / BIOGRAPHY / COLLECTORS GUIDE.
09. SELECTED BIBLIOGRAPHY
10. BACK.

INTRODUCTION BY JEAN-PAUL HECK

Stars are bigger and brighter, but above all more distant and untouchable on poster or album cover.
When I was a 13-year-old boy, my father gave me an LP of David Bowie. I thought it had something to do with a comic book.
When I had a close look at the cover of Hunky Dory I thought 'Strange name for a woman'.
A kind of female Pierrot with long blond hair and pink painted lips.
But a woman could never sing Life on Mars? the way it was done here. Besides that a song title like Queen Bitch would be completely out of its place.
Hunky Dory still is my favourite Bowie record, although the records I bought in the years that followed, Low, Ziggy Stardust (which I bought a little later) and Station to station, came very close to that one.
I have never been a blind Bowie fan, because his work was to prickly and above all the last 20 years sometimes a little to precarious.
You should not be a fan of David Bowie, David Bowie thinks himself.
Sometime he described his music as a storm that passes you by. Some go on the run; others let themselves drag along with the elements that go with it.
Two years ago I had the privilege to interview David Bowie for the music magazine Aloha.
And then something happened what I had never experienced before. A storm started in my head and for the first time in my life I worried whether I could ask a good question.
For a lot of people Bowie is a phantom, something unreal but o so beautiful.
As a possessed man I started digging in one of the unpacked removal boxes, which stood on the attic for the last few months, to find my old Bowie collection.
Alright, I had all his classic songs on CD for a long time, but refused to put these at stake. They would only break the magic. With an almost mathematic precision I examined the lyrics on the cover. Who was the producer and who were the musicians? This time it wasn't a professional ritual, but a compulsive curiosity.
A few weeks later I shook his hand in New York. He was short, smiled his charming smile and opened his mouth. There was the magic voice captured in words. Very easily we worked through my questions and almost shameless openhearted he told his sometimes painful story. As happy as a just born foal I took the New York subway and underground I listened as some kind of FBI agent to the result. A few months later the man of the voice gave a concert at a beach festival at the Belgian coast (Ostend, 7-7-2002). Surrounded by bodyguards David Bowie stepped out of his dressing room. He looked at least 20 centimetres taller than in New York. Ten minutes later the singer opened his mouth and got 40.000 muddy en deadly tired festival goers as quiet as a mouse with an a capella version of Life on Mars?
This book is a great ode to a man who deserves an own encyclopaedia.

Jean-Paul Heck (Music Journalist for music magazine Aloha and newspaper De Telegraaf. Winner of the Jip Golsteijn prize 2004).

INTRODUCTION BY THE AUTHOR

I think this is the most complete and best researched book about Bowie so far.
The last 9 years I listed and listened to 100 officially released CD's, 300 officially released CD-singles, looked at 200 hours of video and 100 hours of VCD, read 100 books and 80 fanzines.
Besides the officially released CD's and CD-singles, I listened to a lot of unofficially released stuff: About 800 audiotapes and 2.500 CD's and CDR (the so called Bootlegs).
All these CD(R)'s, VCD's, Video's etc. are part of my private collection. They are marked *in Italic* in the right column of the Chronology / Collectors guide.
Besides the descriptions of about 1.000 concerts, 3.500 bootlegs, 755 songs and the Albums and Singles

Discography, I listed about 90 cover albums, 2.900 cover versions, 200 songs that inspired Bowie and 220 songs that were inspired by Bowie.
Name anything about Bowie's musical career and it's mentioned in the book.
I tried to make this book as detailed as possible. It's a work of love, done by a super-fan.

Bowie is a very important pop star. In the seventies and eighties he influenced almost everyone in the music business with his innovative music and stage acts.
He is most known for his bizarre and decadent unisexual and bisexual behaviour.
He is loved, hated, called a cheat and a sexual tourist. Kenny Everett called him "The second greatest thing next to God." Some called him a hero. Some called him an anti-hero. He was manipulative and manipulated.
He constantly amazed with his prodigious talents and changed direction every album. Before the fans and record company got used to an image, he had already changed like a chameleon.
His story deals with drugs, sex, brilliant highs and infuriating lows. He is a performer who created character playing by using stage personas. He can be seen in movies. He is active on the Internet. He is innovative. He is a workaholic.
Marc Bolan was the inventor of Glam Rock, but Bowie conquered it.
Bowie grew up from an insecure schoolboy that peed on the floor in Stockwell Infants School to a self-confident performer, who doesn't need the characters anymore.

He took saxophone lessons with Ronnie Ross and formed various R & B bands:
The Kon-Rads their first performance was stopped when the power was cut off.
The Hooker Brothers were formed by David and George Underwood (who had beaten David so hard on the eye that it was permanently damaged).
The King Bees drove to their gigs in a Bedford Dormobile.
The Manish Boys had to leave Luton on the run for motorcyclists.
Mr. Toller (a promoter) told them they were obscene and warned them not to come back.
Bowie did almost everything to get media attention. November 1964 he was interviewed for the BBC TV as spokesman for the International League For The Prevention of Cruelty to Long Haired Men.
The Lower Third held auditions in La Discotheque in Soho. For his audition David played Rip it up from Little Richard on his saxophone, while Steve Marriot did the vocals.
With The Buzz David played for the first time with John Hutchinson (who later demoed various songs like Space oddity with him and joined Feathers).
In Chelmsford Bowie "collapsed" on stage.
The Riot Squad had a theatrical stage show. They used a lot of paint on their face and were an important influence on Bowie's later career. This is overseen by almost every biographer, probably because there is not much we known about this group.
The slogan they used: One day we will live next door to you and your lawn will die!
During the song Little Toy Soldier (inspired by Venus in Furs – Velvet Underground) Bowie whipped sax player Bob Evans.
He made singles with The King Bees, The Manish Boys and The Lower Third, but they all flopped.
June 1967 he released his first album (David Bowie).
A few months later he met Chimi Youngdong Rimpoche and became a Buddhist for some weeks.
He "starred" in the short film "The Image" hanging at the gutter, while they poured water over him.
He toured a few months with the Lindsay Kemp Mime Company, performing Pierrot in Turquoise.
He made love to Lindsay Kemp and also to Natasha Kornilof. When both found out, the tension in the group was measurable.
June 1968 he did some solo performances as support act for Marc Bolan and Tyrannosaurus Rex. When he sang Silly boy blue, an American didn't quite get the meaning of the song (he thought it had an anti-communist theme) and shouted: "No politics!"
Feathers was an acoustic trio.

The red haired Hermione Farthingale (real name Hermione Dennis) was his first real love. They danced a minuet for the BBC play The Pistolshot. He was really depressed when she left him.
He recorded six solo singles that flopped, before he had his first single hit in 1969: Space oddity.
David met his later wife Angie (Mary Angela Barnett). She had a big influence on him.
At the Maltese song festival the bisexual Angie drew a lot of attention, when she was seen in the corridor with a topless teenage girl and walked down the stairs the next morning in a see-through dress.
During the years 1970 to 1972 Bowie was concentrating on song writing and released the albums The man who sold the world (April 1971) and Hunky Dory (December 1971).
The original LP sleeve of The man who sold the world (David wearing a dress) is now a collectors-item.
After the concert in Beckenham (19-3-1970) Angie and David stayed all night with Clare Shenstone and her brother. The next day they woke up late and had to hurry for their own wedding at 11.00 h.
May 1970 Tony DeFries became David's new manager and they started working on their plan to make David Bowie the biggest star the world had ever seen.
Angie taught David to provoke. They experimented with role-playing, wearing each other's clothes and shared their bed with the same boyfriends and girlfriends.
DeFries advice was very simple: If you want to be a star, act like a star. Spend a lot of money and people will think you're a big star. And I handle the money (something David would regret later).
Rodney Bingenheimer arranged a huge party for Bowie at the Los Angeles house of Warhol star Ultra Violet. David wore a Mr. Fish dress, sat on a waterbed and played a selection from The man who sold the world.
His comments for KSAN-FM Radio: "My last LP was, very simply, a collection of reminiscences about my experiences as a shaven-headed transvestite."
The cast of the Warhol play Pork attended a concert at Hampstead. When Bowie introduced them to the other people, Cherry Vanilla stood up and popped out a tit.
By 1972 he had created the character that would make him a superstar: Ziggy Stardust.
The MainMan publicity machine (which included almost the complete cast of Pork) started working full speed. Almost everything was allowed to draw as much attention as possible.
"I'm Gay!" Bowie said in an interview with Michael Watts for Melody Maker.
One week later in New Musical Express: "I'm not ashamed of wearing dresses."

Bowie really burst on the scene in June 1972 with the album The Rise and Fall of Ziggy Stardust and the Spiders From Mars. The album was a mix of Friedrich Nietzsche, Jean Genet, Greta Garbo, Fritz Lang, Jimi Hendrix (real name Jimmy James), 2001-A space Oddissy, A clockwork orange, Lindsay Kemp, Judy Garland and many more.
The album and the 1972 / 1973 concerts with The Spiders from Mars were unique.
The follow up albums Aladdin Sane (April 1973) and Pin Ups (October 1973) went straight to number one.
Between recordings, shows etc. Bowie produced albums for Lou Reed, Iggy Pop and Mott the Hoople.
It was a crazy time and as long as the Ziggy tour lasted, the crazier the crowd went.
In Sunderland there were six fans in wheelchairs (aping disablement). They acted as if they were cured by Messiah Bowie and stood up of their wheelchairs.
In Oxford Mick Rock took the famous photo of Bowie simulating fellatio on Mick Ronson's guitar.
Kenny Everett announced him in London as: "The second greatest thing next to God."
The press reported: A STAR IS BORN.
In Nashville the war veterans thought a homosexual communist was coming to town.
His wife Angie was making fun (nude) in the hotel pool with bodyguard Anton Jones.
In Tokyo Angie threw some policemen out of their seats. A riot started and she had to leave Japan in a rush.
The tour ended in London (3-7-1973) and Bowie announced: "This is the last show we'll ever do." The retirement speech was just a publicity-stunt and gave him time to think over his next move.
In 1973 for 19 weeks he had 5 different albums in the charts at the same time.
When a naked girl climbed through an open window in Haddon Hall, this was the last drop and the Bowie's decided to move to Oackley Street.

Bowie was still married to Angie, but at the end of 1973 he started visiting Ava Cherry very regularly (they became lovers and did some recordings, that were finally released in 1995). Begin 1975 Bowie, Angie, their son Zowie and Ava Cherry lived together in New York.
Later in the year Bowie rented a house in Beverly Hills and had an affair with a black actress named Winona Williams.
Bowie created the futuristically destitute metropolis of desperation Hunger City, for his album Diamond Dogs (April 1974), which produced the smashing hit single Rebel rebel. The show had dancers, moving bridges and a huge cherry picker, which suspended him over the audience during Space oddity.
He created new characters: Halloween Jack (1974) and The Thin White Duke (1976). He was the first white Soul Singer and turned up drunk for the recordings for Soul Train.
Sometimes he even forgot he was David Robert Jones!
He released a string of singles and the albums David Live (October 1974), Young Americans (March 1975) and Station to station (January 1976).
In 1976 David and Angie set up a new home in Switzerland and David went on tour again. The Station to station tour had a set, which reeked of Fritz Lang and Third Reich authoritative bleakness, combined with a cinematic flair that came with his first starring role in the film The Man Who Fell To Earth.
After the first concert in Seattle there was an after party in Bowie's hotel room. The party ended in an orgy, directed by Bowie.
In Rochester he and Iggy Pop were arrested for possession of marijuana.
In Stockholm he said: "As I see it, I am the only alternative for the premier of England. I believe Britain could benefit from a fascist leader. After all, fascism is really nationalism."
May 1976 he arrived at Victoria Station in London. A photographer caught him in mid-wave and declared he made a Nazi-salute. I have a piece of film that proves Bowie was just waving.

From the early days on, Bowie has never been a regular "guy next door."
He turned himself into a media monster, but was able to keep most of his private life hidden to the fans and press.
In 1974 cocaine almost turned him into a rock casualty. In 1976 he drank heavily.
September 1976 he moved to Berlin and got control over his cocaine addiction. He collaborated with Brian Eno and created the trilogy Low (January 1977), Heroes (October 1977) and Lodger (May 1979).
Bowie and Iggy Pop often had breakfast in the gay bar Anderes Ufer. In the discotheques they got to know transsexuals (like Zazie de Paris), fashion models (like Rosalia di Kulessa), and painters (like Artur Vogdt). The work of Berthold Brecht and Kurt Weill fascinated Bowie. He drank heavily and was a regular visitor to a bar called Joe's Beer House.
He started dating Romy Haag (a Dutch transsexual, who owned the nightclub Chez Romy). Her revue was an inspiration for the Boys keep swinging video.

January 1977 he celebrated his 30th birthday at the Roxy in Berlin.
Bowie joined Iggy Pop for his Idiot World Tour as a keyboard player and collaborated on the Iggy albums The Idiot and Lust for life.
After the tour Bowie took Bianca Jagger to Spain for a short holiday.
September 1977 he did some remarkable TV-performances with Marc Bolan and Bing Crosby. Both died shortly after the recordings.
January 1978 he took his son Zowie from Switzerland to Berlin. One day later his wife Angie did a suicide attempt (overdose sleeping pills).
In 1978 he toured again and surprised everybody by his collaboration with Eugene Ormandy and the Philadelphia Orchestra for the album Peter and the wolf.
The Low and Heroes World Tour was very successful and produced the live album Stage (September 1978). In Boston the police removed two topless girls. In Marseille the PA blew up, guitar player Carlos Alomar ordered everybody to leave the stage and a riot started.

December 1978 he visited the premiere of his new film Just a gigolo and the party at the Roppongi disco with a woman called Dewi Sukarno.
A few days later he was in the company of a charming Japanese girl.

After the brilliant album Scary monsters (September 1980) and the smash hit Ashes to ashes (who doesn't know the brilliant video with Bowie as Pierrot), Bowie surprised everyone by playing Joseph Merrick in the play The Elephant Man.
In February that year a divorce settlement with Angie was finalised.
In 1981 he recorded a duet (Under pressure) with Queen. He starred in the BBC play Baal (broadcast 2-3-1982) and recorded the soundtrack for it.
In 1982 he filmed The Hunger and Merry Christmas Mr. Lawrence.
In the eighties he entered mainstream music and started to make money. He pleased a lot of new fans and disappointed a lot of his older fans with the album Let's dance (April 1983), produced by Nile Rodgers (best known from Chic).
Actress Lee Ping appeared in the video China girl and stayed his lover for the most of 1983. The scene with Bowie and Lee Ping making love naked on the beach, was banned in a lot of countries.
Iggy Pop wrote the song China girl in 1976 for Mitsu (half Norwegian / half Tai). Later she died of an overdose.
The single Let's dance gave Bowie a number one hit all over the world. The accompanying Serious Moonlight World Tour made him rich and "released" him for quite a few years from his cult-status. He said: "Bowie now plays Bowie."
In San Bernardino he played for 300.000 people and received a fee of USD 1 million.
In the eighties he made some more albums that sold very well, but killed his creativity: Tonight (September 1984) and Never let me down (April 1987).
January 1985 his half-brother Terry Burns committed suicide.
Bowie sang duets with Tina Turner (Tonight) and Mick Jagger (Dancing in the street).
He played in a three more films: Into the night, Absolute beginners, Labyrinth.
The title track for the film Absolute beginners was musically one of the highlights of the second part of the eighties.
The soundtrack Labyrinth (July 1986) produced the single Underground.
He collaborated again for Iggy Pop's album Blah-blah-blah.
In 1987 he set out for the Glass Spider World Tour. It was a very theatrical show with a dance team and Peter Frampton as a member of the backing band.
Melissa Hurley (one of the dancers) became Bowie's new girl friend.
June 1987 lightning engineer Michael Clark was killed when he fell from a scaffold 90 minutes before the start of the concert.
In Rome there were riots outside the stadium and tear gas floated over the stage.
In Paris he was drunk and forgot a lot of words. He just made up new ones. Strangely enough it worked out very well. A good concert.
Wanda Lee Nichols accused Bowie of raping her at a Dallas hotel. She was photographed covered in bite marks. February 1990 a grand jury in Dallas dismissed the case.
In London (1-7-1988) Bowie did his first live appearance with Reeves Gabrels. It was the start of a collaboration that lasted 11 years.

Wim Hendrikse, Axel 8 July 2004.

SOME QUOTES:

"I have always been camp since I was about seven" (1972. Bowie in his own words – Miles 1980).

"I shall be a millionaire by the time I'm 30" (1969).

"There's a lot of madness in my family, real fucking madness. It worries me sometimes, because I don't know whether it's in my genes and if I'll end up that way, too" (1969).

"I'm gay, and I always have been, even when I was David Jones" (Melody Maker, January 1972).

"I'm not sure if that's really me coming through in the songs" (Rolling Stone, 9-11-1972).

"When I write songs sometimes a month later I don't understand it. That's why I enjoy listening to my early stuff" (1972).

"I find that I'm a person who can take on the guises of different people that I meet. I can switch accents in seconds of meeting someone. I've always found that I collect. I'm a collector, and I've always just seem to collect personalities and ideas" (1973).

"I cannot breathe in the atmosphere of convention. I only find happiness in the realms of my own eccentricity" (David Bowie Fan Club Magazine, Issue 1, 1973).

"I consider myself responsible for a whole new school of pretensions" (1976).

"I steal from everybody" (1976).

"One reason I hate interviews is I hate seeing quotes of mine in print haunt me later. Hell, I'm a terrible liar. I change my mind all the time" (1976).

"It's true, I'm a bisexual. But I can't deny that I've used that fact very well. I suppose it's the best thing that ever happened to me. Fun too" (1976 to Cameron Crowe).

"Bisexual? Oh lord no. Positively not. That was just a lie. They gave me that image so I stuck to it pretty well for a few years" (1976 to Chris Charlesworth).

"I don't make changes to confuse anyone. I'm just searching. That's what causes me to change. I'm just searching for myself" (1978).

"Girls are always presuming that I've kept my heterosexual virginity for some reason. So I've had all these girls try to get me over to the other side again. I always play dumb" (February 1976. Bowie in his own words – Miles 1980).
"The Thin White Duke was a very nasty character indeed" (September 1977. Bowie in his own words – Miles 1980).

"A good friend pulled me off the settee one day, stood me in front of a mirror and said "I'm walking out of your life because you're not worth the effort." Somtimes you can't see how far you've sunk until you're slapped in the face with it. After that humiliation, I went to my wardrobe closet and locked all my characters inside" (January 1978).

"You start to approach the very thing that you're scared of. It had tragically afflicted particularly my mother's side of the family. There seemed to be any number op people who had various mental problems and varying states of sanity. There were far too many suicides for my liking, and that was something I was terribly fearful of. I felt that I was the lucky one because I was an artist and it would never happen to me. As long as I could put these psychological excesses into music and into my work, I could always be throwing it off" (1993).

"Not knowing where you're going is what makes it exiting for me. It leaves a permanently open landscape" (1996).

"The seventies for me started the twenty-first century. It had such a lot to do with breaking absolutes down" (January 1997).

"The reinvention thing, I don't buy into that at all. I think there's a real continuity with what I do, and it's just about expressing myself in a contemporaneous fashion. I'm probably the chameleon of rock because what I do is all about ch-ch-changes! The clichés are a stack high" (1997).
"In art you can crash your plane and walk away from it. If you have that chance, you should take it. The worst thing would be to maintain a particular kind of celebrity and commercial success for the entire career, and then look back and think of all the things that one could have tried and could have done, and think – why didn't I do that?" (2000).

SINCE WHEN AM I A BOWIE FAN?

I'm a Bowie-fan since 7-2-1974 shortly after 19.00 h.
My interest in pop music started a little earlier, the second half of 1972.
The first song I can remember as a favourite of mine is All the young dudes by Mott the Hoople (although by then I didn't know the song was written by Bowie).
Shortly after this one came Happy x'mas – John Lennon & Plastic Ono Band, Elected - Alice Cooper, Gudbuy t' Jane – Slade, Block Buster – The Sweet, School's out – Alice Cooper.
End 1972 I started to make my own Hit Parade (I still do).
The first Bowie single that entered my Hit Parade was The Jean Genie on 3-3-1973 and reached number 6.
My smash hits during that time were Hello Hooray – Alice Cooper and Cum on feel the noize – Slade.
In Holland the Bowie-mania started in 1974. In fact, I completely missed the Ziggy Stardust period. I remember Aladdin Sane being the Album of the week in Radio Veronica's LP top 20. A week later the album entered at nr. 20.
The album cover hung attached to the window of record store Sonora in the Noordstraat in Terneuzen. The cover (with the flash across his face) really intrigued me. But I didn't have a record player (I was almost 15 years old and didn't have that much pocket money) so I did not buy the album.
Then came the moment I saw Bowie for the first time on TV. As every week I sat in front of the television to watch the popular Dutch TV programme Toppop. They showed the Rebel rebel clip with Bowie in his pirate outfit.

From that moment, 7-2-1974 between 19.00 h. and 20.00 h., I became addicted to Bowie's music. Rebel rebel is still a favourite of mine.
It's funny, if you talk to other Dutch Bowie fans that are my age, 9 out of 10 will tell you the same story.
When Diamond Dogs was released on 14-4-1974 I rushed to the music store and bought the album (although I still did not have a record player). A few days later I bought Billion dollar babies – Alice Cooper.
In may 1974 I went to Belgium on summer camp. In a store I saw (for a nice price) the album David Bowie. One of the guys had brought a record player to the camp, so we could listen to the album over and over, until

one of the teachers asked us to listen to something else.

I still have a soft spot for the early Bowie songs. I have heard them so many times and their lyrics still can make me smile.

Back home I bought a record player and listened for the first time to the album Diamond Dogs. That was the second time Bowie really hit me. From that day on I was a Bowie-freak and started collecting all his albums.

The next day I went to Sjiep (another record store in the Noordstraat in Terneuzen). The owner was a Bowie fan too and he advised me to buy Hunky Dory.

I had just finished school and did not have a job, so I had plenty of time to listen to Bowie music.

The next day I returned to the store and bought The rise and fall of Ziggy Stardust and the Spiders from Mars, a Mott the Hoople album, Killer – Alice Cooper, Transformer – Lou Reed.

The next day I returned and bought The man who sold the world. I also had the Ronson album Slaughter on 10th Avenue in my hands and doubted to buy it or not. My budget did not allow me to buy this one, so I had to put it back.

From that day on I followed all the news concerning Bowie and rushed to the store as soon as a new album was released. Young Americans was a bit disappointing, but Station to station was great again and Low became one of my all time favourite albums.

The instrumentals on Low were created from a purely visible approach, placing dots on a tape and then adding and erasing, based on what looked good to the eye, before transcribing it to musical notation.

In 1983 my Bowie addiction stopped. He did not loose me as a fan, but Let's dance was such a downer. I heard the single and could not believe my ears. Was this Bowie? Was this my hero? I was so disappointed I didn't even buy the albums Let's dance and Tonight. I bought them years later, to complete my CD collection, but I still hate Let's dance.

Tin Machine made the change and I got more interested in his music again. Black tie white noise was good, but not one of his best.

Bowie became an Internet pioneer. His BowieNet is very successful. He created the company Ultrastar, that designs ISP's with a personal flavour. He went into banking by BowieBank.

He did a live concert on Internet.

Outside was a killer. It really addicted me again and I started collecting concert tapes etc.

Pimm Jal de la Parra's book The Concert Tapes helped me a lot. I became a member of BowieNet and the Dutch Bowie Fanclub The Voyeur and contacted other fans.

Now a day a lot of fans know me and contact me to trade Bowie and Bowie-related audio.

Bowie has always been an innovator and inspired a lot of musicians and artists.

I thank everybody who provided me with information and made it possible to write this book.

Hendrikse
http://home.hetnet.nl/~wimenchristine/index.html

WHY DID I WRITE THIS BOOK?

In 1995 I did not have the intention to write a book. I had written 3 novels, but could not find a publisher. So my confidence as a writer wasn't that big anymore.

As I collected all the Bowie audio it became harder and harder to prevent buying and copying things twice, so I started making all kinds of lists.

The lists became longer and longer and I started to ad more dates and details to the lists.

As I read more and more Bowie books, all the published errors in dates and tour schedules started to annoy me. I compared all the lists, dates etc. and started to make my own.

It's funny, but when I listen to interviews with Bowie and read books and articles about him, I can't help myself and immediately start correcting the wrong dates.

I made my own Bowie chronology. By publishing this book I can give other collectors / writers the opportunity to use it as a reference.

As I write this I have just re-read the booklets of the 2CD The rise and fall of Ziggy Stardust and the Spiders from Mars 30th anniversary edition and the Ziggy Stardust tour dates in the 2CD Ziggy Stardust the motion picture 30th anniversary Special edition. In these booklets, approved by the record company and Bowie, I found a lot of wrong dates. This is a pity, because most of the fans assume the dates are all correct and start using these errors, making confusion a little bigger.

I made the chronology / collector guide as a hobby. But I am glad I can share it with you.

Is it complete? No, but I tried to be as complete as possible.

Is this book 100% without errors? I hope it is!

If you think you see an error in this book, please let me know, so I can check it.

ACKNOWLEDGEMENTS

First of all I like to thank my wife Marie-Christine for her support and patience during the years I worked at this book. She had to put up with long stretches of antisocial behaviour on my part. Sometimes she sighed and asked me: "Is this all you can think of, Bowie, Bowie and Bowie? Don't you get tired listening to this music over and over again?" But she always supported me. Thanks darling!

Second I like to thank Caro Rigter. He really makes beautiful paintings and drawings and was so kind to let me use some of them for my book.

Third Jitske Kingma, for all her advises.

I also like to thank all the people I traded with during the years. They provided me with a lot of information. With some people I only traded once, others frequently. I will list them alphabetically:
Paul Aarts, Alex Alexander, Davy Boshoven, Maurice Brals, Frank van den Boomen, Liam Buckley, J.P. Caille, Ricardo De Campos, Julien Carpezat, Francesco Cipresso, Derek Carroll, Chris Carter, Leiulf Clausen (thanks for the research), Steve Coleman, Ges Creaton, Giacomo De Crecchio, Gert van Dompseler, Hans van Dijk, Geoff Eadson, Michael Eikmans, Eric Ekkerman, Masato Ide, Daniel Fitch, Robert Flinterman, Christian Frifelt, Luc Germain, Ernesto Giacomelli, Brian Gibson, Edward Glowinski, Michel Goes, Marcel de Groot, Sudour Guillaume, Keith Gullidge, Remco Havenith, Erik Heibloem, Terry Hermon, Hans Hoek, William Hoffman, Adris Hoyos, Louis Iosub, Svein Iversen, Marshal Jarman, Daniel Jaspers, Albert Johnston, Ian Jones (thanks for using so many CD's), Steve Knight, Willemien Kort, Maarten Kwant, Wim de Leeuw, Cindy Lesquillier, Marc Levy, Arno Lieftink, Max Luinge, Nel Maat, Luc Machiels, Simone Metge, Jürgen Mahrle, Regina Moens, Lars Nielsen, Jack Noordhoek, Thom Oderkerk, Rob Ormeling, Ruud den Ouden, Mickael Pernel, Paolo Pontini, Eric Potasse, Marko Pyhtila, Pieter Raspe, David Read, Camillo Ressl, Caro Rigter, Frank Riteco, John Robertson, Roland (Starbuck), Philippe Sanmiguel, Adam Schanke, Cor Schreuders, M. Schuurman, Robert Stok (thanks for all the trades and lists Robert!), Raymond Stolp (thanks for all the video's and the analysis), Roeland Suurmond, Michael Umbach, Elisabeth Vas Visser, MarcWeinreder, Teil Wise, Victor Zantman, Marco van Zelst.

Thanks to everyone I forgot!

THE CRACKED ACTOR TV DOCUMENTARY (BY ALAN YENTOB)

(Thanks to Raymond Stolp for his analysis)

The Cracked Actor TV documentary (first shown on BBC TV on 26 January 1975) is one of the most interesting rock-documentaries ever filmed.
The most fascinating part is the contradiction between word and picture. Bowie talks about the way he got control over his life: "I'm me now." The image shows us a totally paranoid, coke-addicted man, who has no control at all over his life.
The documentary is full of inventive and creative masterpieces.
It's a great moment, when Bowie looks at the fly in his milk. He compares the fly with his own stay in America, absorbing as much as possible.
The symbolic way the mask is removed from his face and the relief on Bowie's face.
Almost every part of the documentary tells us Bowie will be the next drug casualty.
The way the Diamond Dogs tour changes in the Soul-tour is another way in which Bowie tries desperately to drop the mask.
One Bowie fan hits the nail right on the head when he says: "He intentionally keeps himself a mystery."
Bowie comments on his fans: "They're finding maybe nothing to do with me, but the idea of finding another character within themselves. I mean, if I've been at all responsible for people finding more characters within themselves than they had, then I'm pleased, because that's something I feel very strongly about; that one isn't totally what one is being conditioned to think one is. That there are many facets of the personality, that a lot of us have trouble finding, and some of us do find to quickly."
Bowie's mime, his role-playing, the A-lad-insane flash over his face, they are all very symbolic for Bowie's struggle to find his real identity.
Bowie doesn't show what is behind the mask, but he tells us the truth about the confusion he is dealing with.
He describes Ziggy as a monster he had to kill. Did Bowie kill Ziggy, or did Ziggy make Bowie's death wish come true?
Years later Bowie told the maker, Alan Yentob, he had watched the film again and again, because it told the truth.
Cracked Actor ends with the words: "I'm me now" but the pictures tell us something totally different. A great ending for a 'reality show', in which the actor can't see the difference between fiction and reality.
In 1979 and in 1997 Yentob interviewed Bowie again.
In 1979 the shadow of the Cracked Actor documentary still hangs over a very nervous Bowie.
He still insists he has found a certain rest and peace in his life, but the viewer knows better.
In the 1997 documentary we see a totally different Bowie. Yentob ends the documentary with the words: "I didn't believe you when you said to me before, that you were being "me". But now I would believe you."
It is no coincidence the documentary was titles Changes.

HOW TO USE THIS BOOK

The Chronology / Biography / Collectors Guide lists all events on date. You want to know what Bowie did on 20 November 1983? Go through the list until 20 November 1983 and you will find out he performed in Sydney that day.
For every concert very characteristic parts are mentioned, like things Bowie said. This makes the (audio of the) concerts recognisable for the collectors
At the right side of each page I listed the existing audio and video of the concerts and TV-performances.

CHRONOLOGY / BIOGRAPHY / COLLECTORS GUIDE

In this part of the book I listed all the events, LP's, CD's, Bootlegs, Concerts, Audio, Video etc. chronologically.

For the ones that want to collect all the existing Bowie audio: When you don't count the re-releases and count the 2CD's as 1, it is possible to collect about 100 officially released albums and more then 330 officially released singles.

I haven't got much vinyl myself, but do have almost all the official CD-releases. In the seventies a lot of fans started to trade tapes of Bowie-concerts (I collected some 800 myself).

Besides the official releases there are a lot of unofficial releases, the so-called Bootlegs. In the early days things were simple. There were only fabric made Bootlegs, the so-called Silver Discs. They were sold by mail-order and fabricated in countries that legally allowed to make these albums. In other countries they were pressed illegal and they were even harder to get.

Nowadays everyone who has a CD-burner (who hasn't?) can transfer the audio to CDR and start distributing them. With a Scanner and a Photo-programme you can make great cover-scans.

Fans taped about 1.100 Bowie-concert. Until now I collected about 815 of them on CD and CDR. The amount of circulating CD's and CDR's increases every day. When I count the 2CD as 2, I have about 2.500 myself, so I guess there must be about 3.500 by now.

If you want to collect them, go search the Internet, type Bowie CDR Trade and be amazed how much sites you can find. If you don't want to search that hard and have a hit right away, just type:
http://home.hetnet.nl/~wimenchristine/index.html

The dates of events are listed at the left side of each page. Dates of live performances are <u>underlined</u>. When there is any video or audio of the event, it is listed at the right side.

I choose this way to list everything, to prevent as much searching as possible.

Every time I read a Bowie book, it took me hours to search in the back of the book to find the sources the writer used, or go through other lists to find the audio that exists of a concert or TV performance. During the 9 years it took me to write this book, I listened / or watched the ones in Italic (these titles are part of my private collection).

Between parentheses under the title of the bootleg CD you find the label and number of release.

For TV appearances and radio-broadcasts listed in the left side, you find numbers between parenthesis that refer to the song(s) on the bootleg(s).

```
CD     = Compact Disc Album
CDS    = Compact Disc Single
CDR    = Compact Disc Recordable
VCD    = Video CD
LP     = Vinyl Album
Single = Vinyl 7"
Flexi  = Flexi-disc
PCS    = Promo Cassette
Tape   = Audio Cassette
DAT    = DAT Tape
NT     = No (audio) Tape
Video  = VHS Videotape
DVD    = Digital Video Disc
```

DATE / EVENT	AUDIO / VIDEO	TITLE

1836 The Alamo. Texan adventurer Jim Bowie died. His brother Rezin invented the Bowie-knife (sharpened at both ends, with a strong finger guard between the blade and the hilt). Jim made it popular by using it during a fight on a Mississippi sandbar in 1827.

1871 Book published: The coming race - Edward Bulwer - Lytton.
This science fiction novel inspired Bowie to write Oh! You pretty things.

1882 Book published: The joyful wisdom - Friedrich Nietzsche. The section 'The Madman' was an inspiration for the song All the madmen.

1891 Book published: The picture of Dorian Gray - Oscar Wilde (Modern Library. Boni and Liveright Inc.). Wilde was inspired by a visit to a painter's studio in 1884. The book inspired Bowie (he used the idea for a video). In the book (page 157) Dorian Gray appears at a ball as Anne de Joyeuse, wearing a dress.

1905 Book published: Also sprach Zarathoestra - Friedrich Nietzsche (Van Looy). In 1985 Published by Wereldbibliotheek, ISBN 90-284-1505-X. The Uebermensch was inspiration for The Supermen.

1912 Doncaster, Yorkshire, birth of Haywood Stenton Jones.

1921 Walter Grammatte paints the canvas: Selbstbildnis in Hiddensoe (inspiration for album sleeve Heroes in 1977).

1923 Book published: The elephant man and other reminiscences - Sir Frederick Treves (Cassell).

1923 Book published: The Prophet - Kahlil Gibran (New York: Knopf) (Dutch translation: Mirananda 1990, ISBN90-62710597-9) (inspiration for The width of a circle).

1930 Book published: Vile Bodies - Evelyn Waugh (In 1977 republished by Little, Brown). ISBN 0-316-92616-7. Inspiration for the songs Aladdin Sane and The pretty things are going to hell. In the book they also talked about queers, cousins in lunatic asylums and a woman dressing and behaving like a man.

1932 Film Freaks, directed by Tod Browning. Inspiration for the album Diamond Dogs and name checked in the title track.

19-12-1933 Haywood Stenton Jones marries Hilda Louise Sullivan.

1946 Howard Stenton Jones and Margaret Burns set up home in Stansfield Road, Brixton, along with Terry (Margaret's son from a previous relationship).

26-5-1946 Mick Ronson was born in a nursing home on Beverly Road in Hull.

8-1-1947 9 a.m. David Robert Jones born at 40 Stansfield Road, Brixton, London SW9. The mite: "He's been here before. It's his eyes. They're so knowing."

21-4-1947 Muskeganr (Michigan), James Jewel Osterberg was born. Later he called himself Iggy Pop (in homage to neighbourhood junk friend Jim Popp).

DATE / EVENT	AUDIO / VIDEO	TITLE

26-6-1947 Hilda Louise Jones granted decree nisi.

11-8-1947 Decree nisi made absolute.

12-9-1947 Haywood Stenton Jones marries David's mother, Margaret Mary Burns at Brixton Register Office. Terry came to live with his mother from this day on.

1949 Book published: Journal du Voleur - Jean Genet (Librairie Gallimard). In 1964 published in English translation by Grove Press inc. (this was the one Bowie read). In 1973 published as The Thief's Journal by Jean Genet (Black Cat Edition, ISBN 0-394-17811-4). The book inspired Bowie to write The Jean Genie. On page 57 he talks about An Occasional Dream. On page 67 Genet tells about wearing dresses.

1950 Book published: 1984 - George Orwell. In 1984 Published in Holland as pocket edition by Uitgeverij De Arbeiderspers. ISBN 90 295 3371 4 / CIP. The book inspired Bowie to write a musical in 1973/1974. George Orwell's widow refused her permission. Most of the songs he had written were used for the LP Diamond Dogs. This masterpiece made me a Bowie fan for life!

Mrs. Jones: "The post war years were no party for anyone, and we were no exception. When David was about 3 years old, he put on make-up for the first time" (In other words -Kerry Juby 1986).

25-9-1950 David's aunt Una was sent to Park Prewett, near Basingstoke. In this mental hospital she was diagnosed as schizophrenic.

12-11-1951 David began his education and went to Stockwell Infants School. He was very nervous and peed on the floor (Alias David Bowie - Peter & Leni Gillman1986).

Second part of 1951 Mick Ronson (5 years old) got piano lessons from Trevor Bolder's grandma. Ronson and Bolder found out in 1972, when they recorded The rise and fall of Ziggy Stardust and the Spiders from Mars.

1953 Book Published: Seven years in Tibet - Heinrich Harrer (Rupert Hart-Davis Ltd). In 1956 The book was published by Pan Books Ltd. as a pocket edition. The book inspired Bowie to write a song for the Earthling album.

January 1953 David moved to 106 Canon Road, Bromley, Kent.

1953 Father Jones bought a television to see the coronation of Queen Elizabeth 2.

Summer 1953 David's cousin Kristina spends two weeks with the Jones family in Bromley.

1954 Book published: The world in the evening - Christopher Isherwood.
The book holds a two-page sketch on Camp. As fas as I know the first time anyone ever wrote about Glitter/Camp as a (life)style.

1954 The Joneses moved to 23 Clarence Road in Bromley. David looked at TV series as The Flowerpot Men and The Quartermass Experiment. David went to a local council school Raglan Infants. He sang in school choirs and joined the local Wolf Clubs.

DATE / EVENT	AUDIO / VIDEO	TITLE

June 1955 The Joneses moved to 4 Plaistow Grove, Bromley.

1955 David, aged eight, and his mother spend 2 or 3 weeks with his uncle in Yorkshire (who had a farm). In an interview with George Tremlett Bowie lied and told him he moved with his half brother Terry Bruns to live for a long time with his uncle in Yorkshire.

20-6-1955 David Jones became admission number 603 at Burnt Ash Junior School (he remained there until 24-7-1958) in Rangefield Road, Bromley. Mrs. Pat Mountford (one of the teachers): "One of the teachers, George Lloyd, told me that David was quiet, artistic and self-effacing. Not a great personality, but a sensitive and imaginative boy" (Alias David Bowie - Peter& Leni Gillman 1986).

November 1955 Terry Burns left to join the Royal Air Force.

1956 Book published: A walk on the wild side - Nelson Algren (Farrar, Straus and Cudahy, cat. nr. 56-8623). One of the characters (Kitty Twist, who shaved her eye-brows and did a hustle here and a hustle there), inspired Lou Reed to write Walk on the wild side for the album Transformer.

1956 The movie Somebody up there likes me inspired Bowie for a song title in 1974 / 1975.

8-5-1956 London. Sloane Square. Royal Court Theatre. Look back in anger. Play by John Osborne. Later the play was filmed with Richard Burton. Inspired Bowie for a song title in 1979.

11-5-1956 His teeth were X-rated, by school dentist Graeme King.

26-5-1956 Book published: The Outsider - Colin Wilson (Houghton Mifflin) (inspiration for album Outside). Published in 1978 by Picador (Pan Books), ISBN 0 330 25391 3.

David Bowie: "I saw a cousin of mine dance when I was very young. She was dancing to Elvis 'Hound Dog' and I had never seen her get up and be moved so much by anything" (this was in September / October 1956). The original version of Hound Dog was recorded by Willie Mae 'Big Mama' Thornton in 1953. Elvis Presley covered the song in 1956 and scored a no. 1 hit.

Christmas 1956 John Jones took his son to Catford Town Hall, where they saw Tommy Steele perform. After the show they went backstage. His cousin Kristina visited them for Christmas and agreed to swap her single Hound Dog for David's Love me tender (Alias David Bowie - Peter & Leni Gillman 1986).

1957 Book published in US: On the road - Jack Kerouac. 1958 Published in UK by Andre Deutsch. 1972 Published by Penguin Books. ISBN 0 1400.3192 8. His brother Terry gave him a copy and in various interviews Bowie mentioned this book as an important early influence.

1957 The movie Wild is the wind. Dimitri Tiomkin wrote the title-track (sung by Johnny Mathis). In 1976 Bowie covered the song for the album Station to station.

15-4-1957 David and his cousin Kristina went to the cinema, to see The Hunchback of Notre Dame.

<u>1957</u> David performed Elvis and Chuck Berry numbers at 18th Bromley Wolf Club Boy Scouts attached to St. Mary's Church. He had joined the club in September 1957.   NT

DATE / EVENT	AUDIO / VIDEO	TITLE

Marjorie Lloyd ran the Club.

Christmas 1957 Bromley area. David and a boy called Smith went carol singing. They collected GBP 2/2 for the Bromley Blind Club funds.

1958 Book published: The Subterraneans - Jack Kerouac (Grove Press. In 1966 reprinted by Zebra Books. Z-1006S). The book inspired Bowie to write the track Subterraneans for the Low album (see January 1977 for more details). The book also inspired Bowie to write lyrics for various songs. Somebody had a "lacerated" brain (Rock 'n' roll suicide). Gold in the morning would slip away and a guy asked "Whatsamatter with you?" (Slip away). I don't want to go out, I want to stay in (Modern love). The chips are down (Red sails). Somebody has no eyes (Teenage wildlife). One guy is called Sam (Scream like a baby?), the other one Paddy (The heart's filthy lesson?). I think this book inspired Bowie even more than Kerouac's 1957 book On the road (which he read first).

<u>1958</u> Bromley, St. Mary's Church. He sang in the St. Mary's Church Choir (Also in the choir were George Underwood and Geoffrey MacCormack).
Mrs. Baldry (who was in charge of the choir): "He was no spectacular singer. You'd never have picked him out as the boy that sings wonderfully."   NT

14-7-1958 David was interviewed by the Borough Education Officer at Bromley Technical High School.

24-7-1958 David left Burnt Ash School.

<u>August 1958</u> Isle of Wight, with the 18th Bromley Wolf Club Boy Scouts Summer Camp.   NT
David Robert Jones and George Underwood.
They performed just three songs:
1. Gambling man (Woody Guthry, 1948).
2. Putting on the style (Lonnie Donegan, 1958).
3. Cumberland gap (Lonnie Donegan, 1958).

September 1958 Book published: The idiot - Fyodor Dostoevsky (translated from Russian to English by Constance Garnett) (Bantam Books SC4). The writer died in 1881.
The book was the inspiration for the album title The Idiot for Iggy Pop's 1977 album.
Ippolit says to Myshkin (page 406): "I want to look you in the eye."
Myshin cries: "What is the matter with you?" (inspiration for Slip away?).
Aglaia says to Myshkin: "Sacrifice yourself" (inspiration for Tin Machine?).

September 1958 David attends Bromley Technical High School, Oakley Road, Keston.

November 1958 Terry Burns came home from the RAF. His mother told him there was no place for him. John Jones did not want Terry to live with them anymore.

1959 Book published: Absolute beginners - Colin MacInnes (MacGibbon & Kee). In 1986 published by Penguin Books, ISBN 0-14-002142-6.

DATE / EVENT	AUDIO / VIDEO	TITLE

1959 A teacher asked David what he wanted to be when he grew up. David: "The British Elvis" (Living on the brink -George Tremlett 1996).

Summer 1959 a girl called Liza Fisk kissed David Jones. Liza Fisk: "I stuck his hand in my pants and told him I loved him. For a twelve-year-old he was quite passionate" (Loving the alien - Christopher Sandford 1996).

1959 / 1960 David discovers the world of free-form Jazz, Italian bistros and Beat "happenings" in frequent excursions to London with his half-brother Terry.

Around 1960 David saw Anthony Newley's TV Show The World Of Gerny Slade. He was very impressed (Virgin Radio Interview, September 2002).

1961 Book published: A Stranger in a strange land - Robert L. Heinlein (G.P. Putnam's Sons). In the book they talk about Lobotomy (All the madman), Heathens, Goon squads and A bit afraid of you (Fashion).

March 1961 David's left eye damaged in a school fight with George Underwood (over a girl called Deirdre). Bowie was treated in Farnborough Hospital. One of his eyes is permanently damaged. The doctor found out the sphincter muscles were damaged and left David with a pupil that remains open, neither dilating nor contracting with light (Living on the brink - George Tremlett 1996). David Bowie: "I got the punch because I had my eye on George's girl friend. The girl almost cost me my eye. There was some thought I'd lose it, which was particularly alarming since I was an artist at the time" (David Robert Jones: The discography of a generalist - David Jeffrey Fletcher 1979). Mrs. Sheila Cassidy (the school secretary): "My recollection is that they were in fact good pals and it was a simple argument over a girl. George didn't intend any real harm, but he had a ring on that caught David's eye" (Alias David Bowie - Peter & Leni Gillman 1986).

Easter 1961 Exmouth. David took part in a table-tennis competition.

Summer 1961 Spent holiday with his parents in a caravan at Great Yarmouth.

1961 David got a plastic alto saxophone. He brought round meat, to pay back his father.

1962 Margaret Burns (David's grandmother) died.

1962 David had some part-time jobs: delivering meat and working at the local record-shop (where he was fired for daydreaming).

David's school teacher Mr. Lane about him dyeing his hair: "It was probably only food dye or something removable. The next day he would put the colour right when asked to" (A chronology - Kevin Cann 1983).

As an assignment they had to make themselves business cards. David used the name Luther J. for the card.

Begin 1962 London. Roundhouse in Soho and The Marquee. Performances of (Alexis Korner's) Blues Incorporated. 17-3-1962 Opening of Ealing Jazz Club. Brian Jones joins Blues Incorporated. From 7-4-1962 on Mick Jagger is a few months singer of Blues Incorporated. Begin May 1962 they get a

| DATE / EVENT | AUDIO / VIDEO | TITLE |

regular Saturday evening at the Marquee Club. Bowie saw them in The Marquee, where they played songs like Dust my broom - Elmore James, Got my mojo working - Muddy Waters, Ride 'em on down - Muddy Waters, Bad Boy - Billy Boy Arnold, Around and around - Chuck Berry (Stone alone - Bill Wyman and Ray Coleman 1990).

May to August 1962 David took saxophone lessons with Ronnie Ross (6 Irving Way in Orpington). Charlie Parker was a big influence. He took 8 lessons (every two weeks) and paid GBP. 2,— a lesson.

16-6-1962 The Kon-Rads formed (they had met at Vic Furlong's record shop). Their name is taken from the Jess Conrad introduction as "My Conrads."

Vic Furlong: "He was always a bit of a dreamer in that I'd give him a job to do, come back in about an hour and he was still chatting, the job unfinished, so he had to go" (In other words - Kerry Juby 1986).

<u>16-6-1962</u> Bromley, Technical High School.   NT
The evening was opened by disc jockey Alan Dell.
The Kon-Rads (line-up 1 from June 1962 to August 1962).
David Jones (Vocals, Tenor Sax).
Dave Crook (drums).
Alan Dodds (Guitar).
Neville Willis (Guitar).
George Underwood (Vocals).
Their signature tune was In the Mood by Glenn Miller.
A short set of instrumental songs.
They are forced to stop when the power is cut off.

The other members of the Kon-Rads gave David the nickname: Old Odd Eyes.

22-6-1962 Kentish Times. Article: Nearly 4.000 at school fete.

Former classmate Michael Todd: "The women he went out with were beyond my reach. He always went out with older women. When you're fifteen and she's eighteen, it's a big deal. David was a great womaniser in high school (Stardust - Henry Edwards and Tony Zanetta 1986).

<u>Summer 1962</u> Bromley, Church Hall, Bromley Common.   NT
Rehearsals. (Many rehearsals where held here).
Fans had to pay 2 shillings to watch the performances.

Summer 1962 David played baseball for the Dulwich Bluejays.

<u>1962 Bromley</u>, Chiselhurst Caves in Kent.   NT
The Kon-Rads (line-up 2 from August 1962 to Dec. 1962).
David Jones (Vocals, Tenor Sax).
David Hadfield (drums).
Alan Dodds (Guitar).
Neville Willis (Guitar).
George Underwood (Vocals).

4-10-1962 Little Richard joined The Rolling Stones on stage. At the end he jumped on top of a piano

DATE / EVENT	AUDIO / VIDEO	TITLE

and sang his last song (Stone alone - Bill Wyman and Ray Coleman 1990). Bowie imitated his hero years later when he jumped on top of a piano to sing Golden years.

<u>17-11-1962</u> Cudham, Cudham Villiage Hall.　　　NT
The Kon-Rads. They received GBP. 15,— for the gig.

The Kon-Rads.
Third line-up (December 1962 to September 1963):
David Jones (Vocals, Tenor Sax).
David Hadfield (drums).
Alan Dodds (Guitar).
Neville Willis (Guitar).
Roger Ferris (Vocals).
Rocky Shahan (Chaudhari) (Bass guitar).
Christine Patton (Backing vocals).
Stella Patton (now named Gall) (Backing vocals).

Songs the three Kon-Rads line-ups played:
A night with Daddy G (Curch Street Five, 1961).
A picture of you (Joe Brown and The Bruvvers, 1962).
Baby it's too late (Rehearsed and demoed without Bowie).
China doll (Glad Rags).
Hey baby (Bruce Chanel, 1962).
I didn't know how much (Rehearsed and demoed without Bowie).
I never dreamed (own composition).
I thought of you last night (Rehearsed and demoed without Bowie).
I'm over you (Rehearsed and demoed without Bowie).
In the mood (Clarinet getaway) (Jimmy O'Bryant's Washboard Wonders, 1925).
It's only make believe (Conway Twitty, 1958).
Judgement day (Rehearsed and demoed without Bowie).
Now I'm on my way (Rehearsed and demoed without Bowie).
Sweet little sixteen (Clarence Garlow, 1954).
The better I know (Rehearsed and demoed without Bowie).
The young ones (dream lover) (Bobby Darin, 1959).

David suggested to change the bands name in the Ghost Riders, but the other band members did not agree.

Background singer Stella Patton: "What made them stand out from most of the groups in the area was that they were good musicians and they weren't satisfied unless their sound was perfect. They had a very professional attitude right from the start. David was always playing to the crowd, he was a good showman and went down well" (Alias David Bowie - Peter & Leni Gillman 1986).

1963 Book published: The man who fell to earth - Walter Tevis (Bantam Books). ISBN 90 274 1481 5.

DATE / EVENT	AUDIO / VIDEO	TITLE

1963 Book Published: The seed and the sower (Merry Christmas Mr. Lawrence) - Laurens van der Post (The Hogarth Press). Published by Penguin Books in 1966, 1973, 1977 and 1983. ISBN 0 14 00.2402 6.

David and his friend Sweeney Todd sometimes went to the Bromley Court Hotel for the Saturday-night jazz club.

<u>May 1963</u> Bromley, Technical High School.　　　　　NT
George and the Dragons.
Two shows for the Christmas pageant (in the afternoon for
the pupils, in the evening for the parents).
They share the bill with The Little Ravens, featuring
12-year-old Peter Frampton on guitar.
The show raised GBP. 50,—.

In his young years Bowie ran over himself with an automobile. He was cranking the car with it in gear and it ran against him, damaging both his legs. David Bowie: "I was under a doctor's care during much of my youth, not because I was sickly, but because I was accident-prone. I broke a hand and then after it healed, I broke a thumb on the same hand. And this was while I was planning to be an artist" (David Robert Jones: The Discography of a generalist - David Jeffrey Fletcher 1979).

<u>18-5-1963</u> Lebanon Gardens Biggin Hill, Hillsiders Youth　　NT
Club.
Dave Jay and the Kon-Rads.
The name Jay was inspired by Peter Jay and the Jaywalkers.
George Underwood did the vocals for the songs It's only
make believe and A night at Daddy Gees.

<u>May 1963</u> West Wickham, Ravensbourne Art School,　　NT
Justin Hall.
Dave Jay and the Kon-Rads.

<u>May 1963</u> Orpington, Civic Hall.　　　　　　　　NT
Dave Jay and the Kon-Rads.

<u>25-5-1963</u> Bromley, Technical High School, (2 shows).　　NT
Dave Jay and the Kon-Rads.

July 1963 David left Bromley Technical High School with O-levels in Art and Woodwork. His mother found him a job as an electrician's mate in Beckenham. He left after only 8 weeks. He then endured a month of manual labour around Bromley, before finding work as a tea-boy-trainee artist in the advertising agency Nevendy Hirst (part of the design Group Ltd) at Old Bond Street W1, London. He kept this job until December. There worked a guy called Ian. He advised David to buy some Johnny Lee Hooker records.

<u>August 1963</u> the Kon-Rads (without Bowie) demoed:　　1 CDR　　*Kon-Rads Rehearsals*
1. The better I know (2.51).　　　　　　　　　　　　　　　*(No label, no number)*
2. Now I'm on my way (3.31).　　　　　　　　　　2 CD　　*Ziggy's final farewell 1973*
3. Baby it's too late (2.38).　　　　　　　　　　　　　　　*(Rattle Snake RS 131/32)*

DATE / EVENT	AUDIO / VIDEO	TITLE

4. I'm over you (0.35).
5. Judgement day (1.43).
6. I didn't know how much (1.57).
7. I thought of you last night (1.57).
The last two songs (without Bowie) had an unnoticed single release in Canada.

30-8-1963 Kon-Rads do audition in Decca Studios, Broadhurst Gardens, West Hampstead. They played and recorded: I never dreamed (a Bowie /Roger Ferris / Alan Dodds composition). The recording (that concerned an air crash) was not released. Roger Ferris did the main vocals. David the harmonies.

<u>September 1963</u> Bromley, Bromley Court Hotel, Bromel   NT
Club. Peter Melkins owned the club.
They were the interval act for 3 or 4 weeks.
The Hooker Brothers (Dave's Reds and Blues).
They play blues (but not very well).
David Jones (Vocals, Sax, Guitar).
George Underwood (Vocals, Rhythm Guitar, Harmonica).
Viv Prince (Drums).

One of the songs they played:
Blues in the night (often called My mother dun told me).

<u>September 1963</u> West Wickham, Ravensbourne College of   NT
Art. The Hooker Brothers (The Bow Street Runners).
They used the name The Bow Street Runners only once.
There was a band in Harrow (with Mick Fleetwood and
Mike Patto, which was called Bo Street Runners). I think
they used the name of this band to get the gig.

20-9-1963 Bromley Times. Advert for the Kon-Rads gig in Orpington at 21-9-1963.

<u>21-9-1963</u> Orpington, Civic Hall.   NT
Tickets: 5p.
The Kon-Rads (without David).

3-11-1963 David was at The Hammersmith Odeon and saw a package tour of Little Richard, Everly Brothers, Bo Diddley and the Rolling Stones.

End 1963 The Kon-Rads without David where support act for the Rolling Stones.

December 1963 David Jones joins Bromley R & B group The King Bees. David writes to washing machine tycoon John Bloom for help. He refers him to agent Les Conn, who signs the group. The name came Slim Harpo's song I'm a King Bee from 1957.

David Jones (Vocals, Tenor Sax).
Roger Bluck (Lead guitar).
George Underwood (Guitar, Harmonica, Vocals).
Dave Howard (Bass).

DATE / EVENT	AUDIO / VIDEO	TITLE

Robert (Bobby) Allen (Drums).

Some of the songs they played:
Can I get a witness (Marvin Gaye, 1963).
(I believe I'll) Dust my broom (Robert Johnson, 1936).
Got my mojo working (Ann Cole, 1957).
(I'm your) hootchie coochie man (Muddy Waters, 1954).
Liza Jane (David Bowie).
Loui Louie (go home) (Richard Berry, 1956).

They auditioned and rehearsed at Ronnie Pressman's flat in Albion Street.

Les Conn: "He had natural charisma. He was as broke as any of the kids in those days but he walked around like a star. He had that star quality right from the very first minute I met him."

Christmas 1963 David and his group send Christmas cards to friends. David's name on the card was Dave Jay.

1964 David was spending his weekends in the Bromley Wimpy Bar.

1964 A Hull group called Peter King and the Majestics changed their name into The Rats.

1964 Partisane Review. Article by Susan Sontag: Notes on Camp.
What Susan Sontag wrote could have been with the future image of Ziggy Stardust in mind: "Camp sees everything in quotation marks. To perceive Camp in objects and persons is to understand Being-as-Playing-a-Role. It is the fullest extension, insensibility, of the metaphor of life as theatre. The androgyne is certainly one of the great images of Camp sensibility. What is most beautiful in virile men is something feminine. Camp taste is above all, a mode of enjoyment, of appreciation - not judgement. Camp is generous. It wants to enjoy."
In 1969 the article was published in her book Against interpretation (Laurel Edition 0083).

Begin 1964 David worked for a company that send him out to clean people's houses etc.

25-1-1964 Petts Wood, Memorial Hall.
The Kon-Rads (without David).

<u>14-4-1964</u>, Soho (London), Jack of Clubs at 10 Brewer Street W1 (owned by Jack Isow).   NT
John Bloom's wedding anniversary party. A very loud gig. Stopped after 10 minutes (they received GBP 20,—).
Davy Jones with the King Bees (Their debut gig)
Only two numbers: Got my mojo working (Muddy Waters / Jimmy Smith), Hoochie coochie man (Muddy Waters).
Attended by a.o: Adam Faith, Lance Percival (who was drunk), Lord and lady Woolfson.
As car to drive at gigs they used a Bedford Dormobile.

<u>15-5-1964</u> London, Marquee Club.   NT
Davy Jones with the King Bees.

DATE / EVENT	AUDIO / VIDEO	TITLE

May 1964 Recording of Liza Jane and Louie Louie go home at Decca Studios in West Hampstead.

Second half of May 1964. David went to record shop Imhofs in London. A friend of his told him about Bob Dylan and gave him the Dylan albums: Bob Dylan and Freewheelin' Bob Dylan (The Pitt Report - Ken Pitt 1983).

17-5-1964 London, Cafe des Artistes.   NT
Davy Jones with the King Bees.

21-5-1964 London, Roundhouse.   NT
Davy Jones with the King Bees.

4-6-1964 Record Retailer. Review of Louie, Louie go home by Davie Jones and The King Bees (Vocalion V9221).

4-6-1964 Evening News. Article: Bloom goes into pops. Davy Jones: "I was wondering how I could get the group launched without any money. Then I hit on the idea of writing to Mr. Bloom and asking him to help. Back came a telegram telling me to contact Leslie Conn, the artists' manager. So that was the start of it."

5-6-1964 Bromley Times. Article: David Jones' rocker.

5-6-1964 Davy Jones and the King Bees were signed to Vocalion (a subsidiary of Decca).

5-6-1964 Release Liza Jane (2.18) / Louie Louie go home (2.12) - Davie Jones with the King Bees (Vocalion Pop V. 9221).

5-6-1964 Bowie went to Giacondo Café in Denmark street (known as Tin-pan-alley) and dragged Dana Gillespie into Francis Day & Hunter (the record shop next door) and wanted her to listen to his single (Interview Dana Gillespie for Dutch Fanzine The Voyeur).

6-6-1964 RM. Review of Louie, Louie go home by Davie Jones and The King Bees (Vocalion V9221).

6-6-1964 Melody Maker. Advert for the concert in London, 7-6-1964.

6-6-1964 BBC1's Juke Box Jury at 17.40 hours. They played the record Liza Jane. Only David was shown on camera (the other band members were present in the studio). In the jury: Diana Dors, Jessie Matthews (who played in Mrs. Dales Diary), comedian Charlie Drake and promoter Bunny Lewis. Only Charlie Drake voted the record a hit.

7-6-1964 London, Bedsitter, 120 Holland Park Avenue,   NT
London W11. At 21.00 hours.
Davy Jones with the King Bees.

13-6-1964 Disc. Review of Louie, Louie go home by Davie Jones and The King Bees (Vocalion V9221).

17-6-1964 Evening Argus. Review (by Annie Nightingale) of Louie, Louie go home by Davie Jones

DATE / EVENT	AUDIO / VIDEO	TITLE

and The King Bees (Vocalion V9221).

<u>19-6-1964</u> UK TV. ITV. Ready, Steady, Go! (a Rediffusion Network Production).
Liza Jane (live).
Presented by Keith Fordyce and Cathy McGowan.
Also on the bill: The Crickets, The Animals, Troy Dante and the Infernos. NT

20-6-1964 RM. Article: D. Jones and Co.

<u>21-6-1964</u> UK TV. ITV. Ready, Steady, Go!
Liza Jane (recorded around Granada and Tyne Tees). NT

July 1964 Coxheath, at the house of Paul Rodriguez, meeting David and The Manish Boys. Started rehearsing. NT

<u>27-7-1964</u> UK TV. BBC2. The Beat Room at 19.35 hours. Introduced by Pat Campbell.
Liza Jane.
Davy Jones with the King Bees.
Also on the bill: Kenny Lynch and the Echoes, Elkie Brooks, Georgie Fame, The Beat Girls. NT

Later that year the Hull Times reported Mick Ronson as a member of the King Bees. As Mick Ronson was a member of the Crestas, this is not very likely. Maybe he just guested for a few concerts.

18-8-1964 Chatham Standard, first performance of Davy Jones and the Manish Boys announced. Bookings can be made at: Hunton 473. The article also announced The Manish Boys to appear on the TV programme "Opportunity Knocks." A lie David told the reporter?

<u>19-8-1964</u> Twickenham (London), Eel-Pie Island Jazz Club. NT
Davey Jones and the Manish Boys.
The name is taken from the Muddy Water's song Mannish boy.
David Jones (vocals, sax).
Johnny Flux (guitar, vocals).
Bob Solly (organ).
Woolf Byrne (sax, trumpet, guitar, harmonica).
Paul Rodriguez (bass, vocals).
Johnny Watson (bass, vocals).
Mick White (drums).

Live repertoire Manish Boys:
Believe to my soul (Albert King).
Big boss man (Stack O'Dolars) (Sleepy John Estes, 1930).
Can't nobody love you (Solomon Burke).
Don't try to stop me (?).
Duke of Earl (The Dukays, 1961).

DATE / EVENT	AUDIO / VIDEO	TITLE

Hello stranger (Barbara Lewis, 1963).
(I'm your) hootchie coochie man (Muddy Waters, 1954).
I ain't got you (Jimmy Reed, 1954).
I pity the fool (Bobby Bland, 1961).
If you don't come back (The Drifters, 1963).
Last night (instrumental group composition, never rec.).
Little Egypt (The Coasters).
Live at the Apollo 1962 medley (James Brown, 1962).
Liza Jane (The King Bees, 1964).
Loui Louie (go home) (Richard Berry, 1956).
Love is strange (Mickey and Sylvia, 1956) (Mickey Baker and Sylvia Vanderpool).
Mary Ann (Ray Charles, 1956).
Night train (Jimmy Forrest, 1952).
So near to loving you (Bowie composition. Only rehearsed, never performed for an audience).
Stupidity (Solomon Burke, 1962).
Take my tip (own composition).
That lucky old sun (Frankie Laine, 1949).
Try me (James Brown, 1962).
Watermelon man (Herbie Hancock, 1963).
What 'd I say (Ray Charles, 1959).
You can't sit down (Paul Revere and The Raiders).

March 1970 Bowie commented on the Manish Boys: "We were too loud on stage. We used feedback and didn't play any melodies. We just pulverized the sound, which was loosely based on Tamla Motown. We had an ardent following of about a hundred Mods but when we played out of London we were booed right off the stage. We weren't very good" (Black Book - Barry Miles 1980).

Paul Rodriguez: "David played for us the album James Brown Live at the Apollo (1962) and it was as if heaven was opened up to us."

<u>Second part of August 1964</u> London, Bricklayers Arms on Old Kent Road.
Davey Jones and the Manish Boys.   NT

28-8-1964 Kent Messenger. Article: Manish Boys to record.

<u>30-8-1964</u> Suffolk, Ipswich.   NT
Davey Jones and the Manish Boys.

<u>2-9-1964</u> Twickenham (London), Eel-Pie Island Jazz Club.   NT
Davey Jones and the Manish Boys.

<u>9-9-1966</u> Braintree.   NT
Davey Jones and the Manish Boys.

<u>September 1964</u> Bromley, Chiselhurst Caves.   NT
Davey Jones and the Manish Boys.

DATE / EVENT	AUDIO / VIDEO	TITLE
September 1964 Luton. Davey Jones and the Manish Boys. They left on the run for motorcyclists. They did not like the "poofters."	NT	
19-9-1964 London, The Scene. Davey Jones and the Manish Boys.	NT	
21-9-1964 Chatham, Invicta Ballroom. Davey Jones and the Manish Boys.	NT	
23-9-1964 Kent, Medway County Youth Club. Davey Jones and the Manish Boys.	NT	
26-9-1964 London, Acton Town Hall. Davey Jones and the Manish Boys.	NT	
27-9-1964 London, The Flamingo Club. Davey Jones and the Manish Boys.	NT	
29-9-1964 Isle of Worth. Davey Jones and the Manish Boys.	NT	
2-10-1964 Boreham Wood, Lynx Club. Davey Jones and the Manish Boys.	NT	

6-10-1964 Regent Sound Studios in Denmark Street recording by The Manish Boys of Hello stranger, Duke of Earl and Love is strange. Never released. Produced by Mike Smith.

7-10-1964 Twickenham (London), Eel-Pie Island Jazz Club. Davey Jones and the Manish Boys.	NT	
9-10-1964 London, Finchley. Davey Jones and the Manish Boys.	NT	
10-10-1964 Newmarket. Davey Jones and the Manish Boys.	NT	
13-10-1964 London, Putney. Davey Jones and the Manish Boys.	NT	
17-10-1964 Lee-On-Solent, Tower Ballroom. Davey Jones and the Manish Boys.	NT	

17-10-1964 Local group top ten in magazine Mirabelle (for teenage girls) 6th place The Manish Boys. Also in the top ten: The Rats.

25-10-1964 Lee-On-Solent, Tower Ballroom.	NT	

DATE / EVENT	AUDIO / VIDEO	TITLE

Davey Jones and the Manish Boys.

<u>31-10-1964</u> Bromley. NT
Davey Jones and the Manish Boys.

2-11-1964 The Evening News and Star (London newspaper) Headlined: For those beyond the fringe (interview with David as president of The International League for the preservation of Animal Filament. Article by Leslie Thomas).

<u>6-11-1964</u> London, Marquee Club. NT
Davey Jones and the Manish Boys.

Dana Gillespie: "During the break of the sound-check I was standing in front of the mirror, brushing my waist length hair. David took the brush out of my hand and started brushing my hair and asked me if he could walk me home that night. I remember when David would come and stay the night, I would have to sneak him up to the top floor. The first time he met my father, he actually thought he was a girl" (The Starzone Interviews - David Currie 1987). Later on, Dana Gillespie (full name Dana Richenda Antoinette de Winsterstein Gillespie, sized 44-26-37 inch) would become England's water-ski champion.

<u>7-11-1964</u> Bedford. NT
Davey Jones and the Manish Boys.

<u>8-11-1964</u> Twickenham (London), Eel-Pie Island Jazz Club. NT
Davey Jones and the Manish Boys.

<u>12-11-1964</u> BBC. The Beat Room. Long Hair interview, by Cliff Michelmore. *CD* *The London Tapes (World productions of compact music WPOCM 0589 D 020-2)*
Spokesman for The International League For The Prevention of Cruelty to Long Haired Men.
Bowie: "For the last two years we've had comments like "Darling" and "Can I carry your handbag?" and it just has to stop." LP The other Bowie (Piar Records) (Piar Records A/B)
  Video *Stolp Tapes no. 1 (2 min)*
  Video *Various 26, 2 min.*

<u>13-11-1964</u> Hastings, The Witch Doctor. NT
Davey Jones and the Manish Boys.

<u>14-11-1964</u> Maidstone, Agricultural Hall. NT
Davey Jones and the Manish Boys.

17-11-1964 Chatham Standard. Article: Happy Blues Group.

<u>20-11-1964</u> Bromley, Justin Hall. NT
Davey Jones and the Manish Boys.

24-11-1964 Chatham Standard. Article: Long suffering. About The International League For The Prevention of Cruelty to Long Haired Men. Davy Jones: "Most of us are well-behaved and law-abiding citizens."

DATE / EVENT	AUDIO / VIDEO	TITLE

December 1964 Released in US: Spoonful / I've got my eyes on you baby - The Rats (Laurie).

December 1964 Bromley, Chiselhurst Caves. NT
Davey Jones and the Manish Boys.

December 1964 Luton. NT
Davey Jones and the Manish Boys.

1-12-1964 Wigan, ABC Cinema (2 shows). NT
Davey Jones and the Manish Boys.
Support group for Gene Pitney, Gerry and the Pacemakers,
The Kinks, Marianne Faithfull and Bobby Shafto.
Every performance of The Manish Boys was 15 minutes
and started at 6.30pm and 8.50pm.

2-12-1964 Hull, ABC Cinema (2 shows). NT
Davey Jones and the Manish Boys.
Support group for Gene Pitney, Gerry and the Pacemakers,
The Kinks, Marianne Faithfull and Bobby Shafto.
Every performance of The Manish Boys was 15 minutes.

3-12-1964 Evening News and Dispatch. Advert for the show in Edinburgh that same evening.

3-12-1964 Edinburgh, ABC in Lothian Road (2 shows at NT
17.30 and 20.50 hours).
Davey Jones and the Manish Boys.
Support group for Gene Pitney, Gerry and the Pacemakers,
The Kinks, Marianne Faithfull and Bobby Shafto.
Every performance of The Manish Boys was 15 minutes.

4-12-1964 Stockton-On-Tees, Globe Cinema (2 shows). NT
Davey Jones and the Manish Boys.
Support group for Gene Pitney, Gerry and the Pacemakers,
The Kinks, Marianne Faithfull and Bobby Shafto.
Every performance of The Manish Boys was 15 minutes.

5-12-1964 Newcastle (2 shows). NT
Davey Jones and the Manish Boys.
Support group for Gene Pitney, Gerry and the Pacemakers,
The Kinks, Marianne Faithfull and Bobby Shafto.
Every performance of The Manish Boys was 15 minutes.

6-12-1964 Scarborough (2 shows). NT
Davey Jones and the Manish Boys.
Support group for Gene Pitney, Gerry and the Pacemakers,
The Kinks, Marianne Faithfull and Bobby Shafto.
Every performance of The Manish Boys was 15 minutes.

DATE / EVENT	AUDIO / VIDEO	TITLE

<u>13-12-1964</u> Bedford (2 shows).   NT
Davey Jones and the Manish Boys.

15-12-1964 Chatham Standard. Article: Thank you, Gene Pitney!

1964 / 1965 Mick Jagger used to sign notes with the name Little Boy Blue. Inspiration for Silly boy blue, or is this to far-fetched?

January 1965 Release Restless / Take my tip (2.08) - Kenny Miller (Stateside SS405). B-side written by David.

1965 Released by the Kon-Rads (Without Bowie): Baby it's to late / I'm over you (CBS 204812) I didn't know how much / I thought of you last night (Decca 32060).

Early 1965 Mick Ronson and the Crestas performed at The Duke of Cumberland at Ferriby. Ronson touched his guitar and the microphone stand at the same time and got a shock that threw him of the stage, still holding the guitar and stand. Eric Lee kicked the guitar away and Johnny Hawk got him in the recovery position. Mick was taken to hospital, but one or two days later he was already back on stage (Mick Ronson: The spider with the platinum hair - Weird and Gilly, 2003).

February 1965 Released in UK: Spoonful / I've got my eyes on you baby - The Rats (Columbia).

February 1965 David and the band went to the BBC studios to watch Donovan perform for Ready Steady Go! David managed to get an interview with co-host Cathy McGowan. David told her they would be in Ready Steady Go! the next week (this was a lie, but they published it).

<u>1-2-1965</u> Maidstone, Star Ballroom.   NT
The Monday Spin disc show.
Davey Jones and the Manish Boys.

8-2-1965 The Manish Boys recorded I pity the fool and Take my tip at IBC Studios at 35 Portland Place. Lead guitar on I pity the fool by Jimmy Page. 2 Versions of Take my tip. 1st Version Bowie sings: Bider in the sky (this version became the single release). 2nd Version Bowie sings: Spider in the sky. Produced by Shel Talmy.

3-3-1965 David at home interviewed by the Daily Mirror.

<u>4-3-1965</u> Bournemouth.   NT
Davey Jones and the Manish Boys.

4-3-1965 The Daily Mail. Article by Douglas Marlborough: Get your hair cut BBC tells pop man. About David being banned from appearing in Gadzooks! It's all happening on 8-3-1965 because his hair was too long (just a publicity-stunt made up by manager Less Conn and the BBC producer).

4-3-1965 Daily Mirror. Article: Row over Davy's hair.

4-3-1965 Daily Telegraph. Article: Pop singer gets Haircut ultimatum.

4-3-1965 Radio Times. Article about Gadzooks! It's all happening and the performance of Davy Jones

DATE / EVENT	AUDIO / VIDEO	TITLE

and the Mannish Boys (it should be Manish Boys).

5-3-1965 Kent Messenger. Article: Long Hair.

5-3-1965 Release I pity the fool (2.09) / Take my tip (2.16) - Davy Jones and the Mannish Boys (Parlophone R 5250). Jimmy Page plays lead guitar. Original in 1961 by Bobby "Blue" Bland (real name Deadric Malone).

6-3-1965 The Daily Mirror. Article: Long-hair Davy's TV reprieve. Producer Barry Langford: "Kids today don't want this long-hair business. For his own sake, Davy should have a hair cut." Davy Jones: "I want to prove that the length of my hair doesn't matter. It's the performance that counts."

6-3-1965 The Sun (front page). Article: Long-haired Davy beats TV ban.

6-3-1965 RM. Review of I pity the fool - The Manish Boys (Parlophone R 5250).

6-3-1965 Disc Weekly. Review I pity the fool - The Manish Boys (Parlophone R 5250).

6-3-1965 Melody Maker. Advert for the concert in Bromley 10-3-1965.

8-3-1965 The Evening News published a photograph of David.

8-3-1965 Kent Messenger Gazette. Article about Davy Jones who gets a net over his head for a set after trimming his long blond hair by hairdresser Sylvia Halliday.

<u>8-3-1965</u> UK TV. BBC2. Gadzooks! It's all happening.   NT
At 19.00 hours. Introduced by Alan David and Christine Holmes.
I pity the fool.
Davey Jones and the Manish Boys.
Other guests: Peter Cooke, Dorris Henderson, The Three Bells, The Mike Leander Combo featuring The Beat Girls, Adrienne Poster.

<u>8-3-1965</u> London, The Mayfair Hotel.   NT
Birthday party for Shel Talmys wife Jenni.
Davey Jones and the Manish Boys.

9-3-1965 The Daily Mirror. Article: Fee (about payment of The Manish Boys).

<u>10-3-1965</u> Bromley, Bromel Club (Bromley County Hotel).   NT
Davey Jones and the Manish Boys.

11-3-1965 Bromley Advertiser (front page). Article: 14 In. Hair on TV.

11-3-1965 Daily Mail. Disc pick. Review of I pity the fool - The Manish Boys (Parlophone R5250).

12-3-1965 Kent Messenger. Article: TV Ban lifted. Woolf Byne (sax) told the reporter they were searching for a good second hand 12-seater Commer van. You can call Hunton 473 for more info.

DATE / EVENT	AUDIO / VIDEO	TITLE

13-3-1965 Disc Weekly. Article about the concert on 8-3-1965 at the Mayfair Hotel.

13-3-1965 Pop Weekly. Review of I pity the fool - The Manish Boys (Parlophone R 5250).

<u>20-3-1965</u> Norfolk (Cromer), Olympia Ballrooms.   NT
Davy Jones and the Manish Boys.
The promoter (Mr. Troller) told them they were obscene and warned them not to come back. He thought Johnny Flux danced in a disgusting manner.

23-3-1965 Chatham Standard. Article: The Manish Boys are indignant.

26-3-1965 Kent Messenger. Article: Manish Boys Ban. (About being banned to perform in Norfolk again).

March / April 1965 David performed with various bands on a casual basis (a.o. The T-Bones, Sonny Boy Williamson).

April 1965 Giaconda coffee bar at 9A Denmark Street WC2 in London (David's regular haunt). In this coffee bar an audition for The Lower Third in La Discotheque in Wardour Street (Soho) was announced.
Mark Feld (Marc Bolan) worked briefly in the cloakroom at La Discotheque, where he earned most of his money from tips.

Phil May (Pretty Things): "He was always at The Marquee, wanting to talk music. David came backstage and asked for my home phone number. I didn't want everyone to hear it, so I took the address book out of his hand to write it down. I couldn't help noticing that in the left-hand column, where my name should have been, he'd written in "God" (Loving the alien - Christopher Sandford 1996).

April 1965 The Lower Third holds auditions for a sax player in La Discotheque in Soho.

In 1963 The Lower Third was known as Oliver Twist and The Lower Third. In April 1965 they moved to London and rented a flat in Pimlico for GBP. 12,— a week. Denis Taylor: "David came along with Steve Marriott. We did an old rock 'n' roll number called Rip it up (Little Richard), Marriott sang it and David played alto-sax" (The Starzone Interviews - David Currie 1987).

First line up of The Lower Third:
David Jones (vocals, guitar, tenor sax).
Denis 'Tea-Cup' Taylor (lead guitar).
Graham Rivens (bass guitar).
Les Mighall (drums).

Denis Taylor: "We had a guitar making as much noise as possible, a drummer trashing hell out of the drums, and the bass player looking moody. It really worked."

1-4-1965 Australian Post. Article: Too much hair for the BBC.

DATE / EVENT	AUDIO / VIDEO	TITLE

4-4-1965 UK TV. ITV. Thank you lucky stars. Recorded in Birmingham. Calvin James (George Underwood) mimed his single Some things you never get used to. After the recording George Underwood was mobbed by hundreds of screaming teenage fans (David Bowie 1962 -1968 - Alex Alexander and Pete Foulstone 2002). Broadcast 10-4-1965.

<u>8-4-1965</u> Minster, Working Men's Club.   NT
The Lower Third. Started at 20.00 h.

9-4-1965 The Scottish band King Bees released a single called You're holding me down / I've gotta buzz (Coral 62492). This single has nothing to do with Bowie. A lot of people got confused by the similarity in group name.

9-4-1965 Bromley Times. Article about Calvin James (George Underwood) being mobbed by screaming fans.

<u>10-4-1965</u> Sheerness, Sheerness Conservative Club.   NT
The Lower Third. Started at 20.00 h.

<u>11-4-1965</u> Minster, Working Men's Club.   NT
The Lower Third.

15-4-1965 Single released by Calvin James (George Underwood): Some things you never used to / Remember (Columbia DB 7516). The name Calvin James was given to George Underwood by producer Mickie Most (his son was called Calvin).

<u>17-5-1965</u> Romney, Grand Hotel (Littlestone).   NT
Davie Jones and The Lower Third. Started at 20.00 h.
Phil Lancaster: "We generally finished the set with a number from the Planet Suite - Mars (Mars the bringer of war - Gustav Holst), it was great, really loud with lots of feedback" (The Starzone Interviews - David Currie 1987).

Second line up:
David Jones (vocals, guitar, tenor sax).
Denis 'Tea-Cup' Taylor (lead guitar).
Graham Rivens (bass guitar).
Phil Lancaster (drums). Roger Seamark painted The Lower
Third sign on his bass drum.
Neil Andersen (sometimes he did the vocals).

Denis Taylor: "During a weekend when Mighall had gone home to Margate, girlfriend problems evidentially got the most of him and he never returned to London." Graham Rivens: "When Phil came along he had an unusual style and looked like Keith Moon" (The Starzone Interviews- David Currie 1987).

Repertoire:
And I say to myself (Bowie).
Baby loves that way (Bowie).
Bars of the county jail (Bowie).

DATE / EVENT	AUDIO / VIDEO	TITLE

Boom boom (John Lee Hooker, 1960).
Born of the night (own composition).
Can't help thinking about me (Bowie).
Chim Chim Cheree (Julie Andrews and Dick van Dyke).
Glad I've got nobody (Bowie).
I lost my confidence (own composition).
I want my baby back (Bowie).
I'll follow you (Bowie).
Louie Louie (go home) (Richard Berry, 1956).
Mars, the bringer of war (Gustav Hols, 1953).
Rip it up (Little Richard, 1956).
Shakin' all over (Johnny Kidd and The Pirates, 1960).
That's where my heart is (Bowie).
The London Boys (Bowie).
You've got a habit of leaving (Bowie).

May 1965 Central Sound Studios in Denmark Street owned by Freddie Winrose. Recording Born of the night / I lost my confidence by The Lower Third. Produced by Shel Talmy.

20-5-1965 Morden (Surrey). RG Studios. Recording by The Lower Third: Youthquake clothing of America - US Radio jingle, written by Bowie and Denis Taylor. It's a lie (to advertise Puritan), originally written by Denis Taylors brother-in-law and re-written by Bowie.

21-5-1965 Kent Messenger. Article: Medway Sound by the Manish boys.

21-5-1965 Kent Messenger. Article: Maidstone's professional beat group breaks up.

<u>28-5-1965</u> Bournemouth, Pavilion Ballroom.   NT
Davie Jones and The Lower Third.

<u>30-5-1965</u> Bournemouth, Pavilion Ballroom.   NT
Davie Jones and The Lower Third.

Phil Lancaster: "We were rehearsing one afternoon in Bournemouth. Pete Townshend came walking into the dance hall and we were going through Dave's stuff. Pete said, "Whose stuff is that you're doing?" So David replied, "It's mine," to which Pete replied, "That's a bit of a cheese-off, it sounds a lot like mine!" (The Starzone Interviews - David Currie 1987).

June 1965 Released in UK: New Orleans / I've got to see my baby - The Rats (Columbia).

June 1965 Bristol TV. Discs A Go Go. New Orleans, Chicago calling - The Rats

3 and 4-6-1965 Bournemouth Evening Echo. Adverts for the concert on 4-6-1965 in Bournemouth.

<u>4-6-1965</u> Bournemouth, Pavilion Ballroom.   NT
19.45 to 23.00 hours. Tickets: 5p.
Davie Jones and The Lower Third.
Support acts: Jacqueline Rivers and the Boy Friends, Roger and The Rallies.

DATE / EVENT	AUDIO / VIDEO	TITLE

5-6-1965 Queensborough, Borough Hall. NT
Davie Jones and The Lower Third.

9-6-1965 Morden. R.G. Studios. Recording demos: That's were my heart is, I want my baby back, Bars of the county jail. Produced by Shel Talmy.

11-6-1965 Evening Argus. Advert for the concert on 11-6-1965 at the Starlight Rooms in Brighton.

11-6-1965 Brighton, Starlight Rooms (Starlight Club). NT
Tickets: 2/6p.
Davie Jones and The Lower Third.

12-6-1965 Manchester, King's Head. NT
Davie Jones and The Lower Third.

13-6-1965 London, Roebuck Club. NT
Davie Jones and The Lower Third.

13-6-1965 An audition for Ralp Horton was arranged at the Roebuck Public House on the Tottenham Court Road, London with the view of becoming their manager. Horton lived at 79A Warwick Square, Victoria.

14-6-1965 Leeds, White Bear Tavern. NT
Davie Jones and The Lower Third.

19-6-1965 Edgbaston (Birmingham), Happy Towers NT
Ballroom.
Davie Jones and The Lower Third.

23-6-1965 Tadcaster, Fairlight Gardens. NT
Davie Jones and The Lower Third.

The band's Atlas van broke down on the way home from the show and they replaced it by and ambulance they bought for GBP. 145,— in Brixton. Denis Taylor: "The big ends just blew out of it and we had to dump it there" (In other words - Kerry Juby 1986).

25-6-1965 Bournemouth, Pavilion Ballroom. NT
Davie Jones and The Lower Third.

26-6-1965 Bromley, The Bromel Club (Bromley Court NT
Hotel). Support for Moody Blues.
Davie Jones and The Lower Third.

27-6-1965 Bournemouth, Pavilion Ballroom. NT
Davie Jones and The Lower Third.

Ralph Horton took some 8mm film when the group was messing about on the seafront of Bournemouth (The Starzone Interviews - David Currie 1987).

DATE / EVENT	AUDIO / VIDEO	TITLE

2-7-1965 Bournemouth, Pavilion Ballroom.	NT
Davie Jones and The Lower Third.

3-7-1965 Melody Maker. Real thing. Letter by J.A. Bolton from London (advises to listen to Davie Jones and The Lower Third instead of the Who).

4-7-1965 Bournemouth, Pavilion Ballroom.	NT
Davie Jones and The Lower Third.

10-7-1965 Melody Maker. Bit Much. They published a letter by Bowie stating they had lost a gig because the promoter told them they were too good. "Prestige is all very well, but must we spend hours rehearsing just to be told to lower our standards?"

25-7-1965 Sheerness. Sheerness & District MCC,	NT
Conservative Club.
Davie Jones and The Lower Third.

31-7-1965 Isle of Wight, Ventnor, Winter Gardens.	NT
Davie Jones and The Lower Third.
Support for Johnny Kidd and the Pirates.
Neil Anderson performed a solo spot.
They were announced by Patrick Kerr (the host of Ready Steady Go!). Ralph Horton did some 8mm film.

3-8-1965 IBM Studios in Portland Street. Recording You've got a habit of leaving and Baby loves that way. Phil Lancaster: "I used David's tweed jacket to hang over my bass drum to improve the sound" (The Starzone Interviews - David Currie 1987).

7-8-1965 Isle of Wight, Ventnor, Winter Gardens.	N1
Davie Jones and The Lower Third.
Support for The Pretty Things, Cliff Bennett and Rebel Rousers.

14-8-1965 Record Mirror. Article (with pictures) about Davie Jones.

14-8-1965 RM. Review of You've got a habit of leaving / Baby loves that way - Davy Jones (Parlophone R 5315).

19-8-1965 London, 100 Club in Oxford Street.	NT
Radio Caroline Show. 19.30 to 23.30 hours.
Davie Jones and The Lower Third.
Also on the bill: The Strollers, The Legends, Danny Williams.

20-8-1965 Release You've got a habit of leaving (2.32) / Baby loves that way (3.03) - Lower Third (Parlophone R 5318). Recorded at IBM Studios in Portland Street at 3-8-1965.

21-8-1965 Melody Maker. Advert for the concert on 19-8-1965 at 100 Club in London. They were a

DATE / EVENT	AUDIO / VIDEO	TITLE

bit late with the advert!

<u>26-8-1965</u> London, 100 Club in Oxford Street.   NT
Radio Caroline Show.
Davie Jones and The Lower Third.
Also on the bill: Peter Jay and the Jaywalkers, Gemini,
Patsy Ann Noble.

31-8-1965 Morden. R.G. Studios. Three-hour session. Unknown what was recorded.

August / September 1965 First contact between Bowie and Pitt.

<u>4-9-1965</u> London W1, Marquee Club, 90 Wardour Street.   NT
Phone: GER 8923.
Part of The Inecto Show (sponsored by Inecto Shampoo).
Taped by pirate Radio London (never broadcast).
Davie Jones and The Lower Third. Fee: GBP 15,—.

<u>7-9-1965</u> London, 100 Club.   NT
Davie Jones and The Lower Third.

<u>11-9-1965</u> London, Marquee Club.   NT
Part of The Inecto Show (sponsored by Inecto Shampoo).
Taped by pirate Radio London (never broadcast).
Davie Jones and The Lower Third. Fee: GBP 15,—.

14-9-1965 David signed a one-year contract with Sparta. Promised David an advance of GBP 10,— against a 50-50 share of royalties each time a recording of one of his songs was released.

<u>14-9-1965</u> London, 100 Club.   NT
Davie Jones and The Lower Third.

15-9-1965 Horton telephoned Kenneth Pitt, to request assistance. Pitt turned the offer down to manage The Lower Third.

15-9-1965 Davy Jones changed his name in David Bowie, on Pitt's advice, who knew another Davey Jones, who played in Lionel Bart's musical Oliver. Ralph Horton and Patrick and Teresa (two dancers on Ready, Steady Go!) gave David a hairdo and turned him into a mod.

<u>18-9-1965</u> London, Marquee Club.   NT
Part of The Inecto Show (sponsored by Inecto Shampoo).
Taped by pirate Radio London (never broadcast).
Davie Jones and The Lower Third. Fee: GBP 15,—.

<u>21-9-1965</u> London, 100 Club.   NT
Davie Jones and The Lower Third.

<u>25-9-1965</u> London, Marquee Club.   NT
Part of The Inecto Show (sponsored by Inecto Shampoo).

DATE / EVENT	AUDIO / VIDEO	TITLE

Taped by pirate Radio London (never broadcast).
Davie Jones and The Lower Third. Fee: GBP 15,—.

<u>28-9-1965</u> London, 100 Club. NT
Davie Jones and The Lower Third.

October 1965 R.G. Jones Studios. Recording of demo Silly boy blue (2.59) with The Lower Third (had different lyric).
Demo of That's a promise (working title: Baby) (2.21).

2-10-1965 Boyfriend. Head Tales. Article about Davie Jones Haircut (including pictures before and after the cut). Davy Jones: "It took me about two years to grow. I had it cut little by little. When it was long I was much more conscious of my hair and was always washing it. I consider myself just to be fashion conscious, not a mod or anything."

2-10-1965 Fabulous. Article (with picture) about Davie Jones who designs and shows clothes for John Stephen, of the famed Carnaby Street clan.

<u>8-10-1965</u> London, Marquee Club. NT
Billed as: David Bowie and The Lower Third.
Support act for Gary Farr and the T-Bones.

9-10-1965 Melody Maker. Article about David Bowie and The Lower Third performing at the Marquee.

<u>2-11-1965</u> BBC audition. Never broadcast, not suitable Tape
for the BBC.
Chim Chim Cheree (Mary Poppins).
Davie Jones and The Lower Third.

<u>5-11-1965</u> London, Marquee Club. NT
19.30 to 23.00 hours.
David Bowie and The Lower Third.
Shared the bill with The Summer Set.

6-11-1965 Melody Maker. Advert for the concert at the Marquee club on 5-11-1965 (1 day to late).

15-11-1965 Agreement with Ray Cook. GBP 1.500,— invested. In return 10% of monthly earnings above GBP 100,—.

19-11-1965 Cook paid outstanding bills (GBP 70,—).

<u>19-11-1965</u> London, Marquee Club. NT
David Bowie and The Lower Third.
Shared the bill with The Summer Set.

20-11-1965 Cook paid GBP 25,— to Horton, to buy a microphone.

26-11-1965 New Musical Express. Advert for David Bowie and The Lower Third performing at the

DATE / EVENT	AUDIO / VIDEO	TITLE

Marquee.

6-12-1965 Cook gave GBP 410,— to buy a set of amplifiers and speakers (Living on the brink - George Tremlett 1996).

<u>10-12-1965</u> London, Marquee Club.   NT
David Bowie and The Lower Third.
Support act for Gary Farr and the T-Bones.

10-12-1965 Mable Arch. Pye Studios. Recording of Can't help thinking about me, And I say to myself.

<u>24-12-1965</u> London, La Discotheque.   NT
Billed as Xmas Eve with the Lower Third.

24-12-1965 New Musical Express. Advert for Bowie.

Late 1965 Marble Arch Studios, recording of The London boys by The Lower Third (working title: Now you've met the London boys). Recording got lost.

<u>31-12-1965</u> Paris, Golfe-Drouot Club (owned by Henri   NT
Leproux). David Bowie and the Lower Third.
The show is filmed and later shown on French
ORTF TV.
They were support-act for Arthur Brown.

1966 The band Craig (ex King Bees without Bowie) release the singles A little bit of soap and I must be mad.

<u>1-1-1966</u> Paris, Montmartre, Bus Palladium.   NT
David Bowie and The Lower Third.

<u>2-1-1966</u> Paris, Golfe-Drouot Club.   NT
David Bowie and The Lower Third.

<u>6-1-1966</u> London, Gaiety Bar, Victoria Tavern, 10A   NT
Strathearn Place, Hyde Park (Financed by Raymond Cook,
GBP 100,—) from 12.00 to 14.30 hours.
Launch party for Can't help thinking about me.
David Bowie and The Lower Third.
Attended by John Lennon's father.

7-1-1966 Walhamstow Independent. Article by Adella Lithman: Teen and around.

<u>7-1-1966</u> London, Marquee Club.   NT
David Bowie and The Lower Third.

8-1-1966 Les Conn offered Mark Feld (Marc Bolan) to Kenneth Pitt. Pitt declined.

<u>12-1-1966</u> Newmarket, Community Hall.   NT

DATE / EVENT	AUDIO / VIDEO	TITLE

David Bowie and The Lower Third.

14-1-1966 Release Can't help thinking about me (2.47) / And I say to myself (2.29) (Pye 7N.17020). David dropped a promo copy of the record into Paul McCartney's recording studio in Soho Square (he got no reaction from McCartney).

14-1-1966 New Musical Express. Bowie on front cover (ad for Can't help thinking about me).

14-1-1966 Bromley Times. Article: Pop-singer changes his image. New name and new hair style.

<u>15-1-1966</u> Harrow, Alexander Tavern.   NT
David Bowie and The Lower Third.

<u>17-1-1996</u> Carlisle, Holly Bush.   NT
David Bowie and The Lower Third.

<u>19-1-1996</u> Birmingham, Cedar Club.   NT
David Bowie and The Lower Third.

22-1-1966 Music Echo. Advert for Can't help thinking about me - David Bowie (Pye 7N 17021).

28-1-1966 Cook paid GBP 300,— to Horton (last instalment).

<u>28-1-1966</u> Stevenage, Town Hall.   NT
David Bowie and The Lower Third.

29-1-1966 Disc Weekly. Advert for Can't help thinking about me - David Bowie (Pye 7N 17021).

<u>29-1-1966</u> London, Marquee Club.   NT
David Bowie and The Lower Third.
Morning Show.

29-1-1966 Bromley, Bromel Club, evening.
Cancelled
David Bowie and The Lower Third.

Horton told the band the wages would not be paid, there was no money left. The band refused to perform, leaving David in tears because it was his hometown (In other words - Kerry Juby 1986).

29-1-1966 Melody Maker. Article: Cancelled gig, breakdown of The Lower Third.

End January 1966 Ralph Horton placed an advert in Melody Maker: Musician required to accompany a singer.

February 1966 Bowie writes song Going Down.

February 1966 Interview for Melody Maker

1-2-1966 Horton and David asked Cook another GBP.1.500,—. He paid GBP 300,— at once. They told

DATE / EVENT	AUDIO / VIDEO	TITLE

him they were negotiating to take over Wimbledon Stadium (a lie).

4-2-1966 Bromley Times. Pop Scene. Article: Ex-Bromley schoolboy's debut under new name.

3,4 and 5-2-1966 79A Warwick Square, Victoria (Ralph Horton's home) and The Marquee. Auditions for The Buzz. A London DJ suggested the name The Buzz. John Eager (drums) auditioned on 3-2-1966 at The Marquee and got the job on 6-2-1966. John Hutchinson got Bowie's number from Jack Barry (manager of The Marquee). He auditioned at 5-2-1966. John Hutchinson: "David asked me to play a Bo Diddley beat, just sussing out if I could play" (The Starzone Interviews - David Currie 1987). Organist Derek Boyes was recommended by (his friend from Scarborough) John Hutchinson. He was considering a job playing to the transatlantic passengers on the Queen Elizabeth when he met John Hutchinson.

7-2-1966 Bowie forms new group The Buzz.
First line-up:
David Bowie (vocals, guitar, sax).
John Hutchinson (lead guitar).
Derek 'Chow' Boyes (organ).
John Eager (drums).

<u>7-2-1966</u> London, Start rehearsals.   NT

8-2-1966 Recording of Little bombardier.

<u>10-2-1966</u> Leicester, Mecca Ballroom.   NT
David Bowie and the Buzz. Advertised as David Bowie and the Lower Third.
Support act for: Graham Bond Organisation, Jimmy James and the Vagabonds, Boz and The Sidewinders.

Repertoire The Buzz:
And I say to myself (Bowie).
Breakout (Mitch Ryder and the Detroit Wheels, 1966).
Can't help thinking about me (Bowie).
Come see about me (Nella Dodds, 1964).
Dance dance dance (Bowie composition, never recorded).
Do anything you say (Bowie).
Girl from Minnesota (early Bowie composition?).
Good morning girl (Bowie).
Harlem shuffle (Bob and Earl, 1963).
Hold on I'm coming (Sam and Dave).
Hung up (early Bowie composition?).
I dig everything (Bowie).
I'm not loosing sleep (Bowie).
It doesn't matter anymore (Buddy Holly, 1959).
It's getting back (Bowie composition, never recorded).
It's so easy (Buddy Holly and The Crickets, 1958).
Jenny Jenny (Little Richard, 1956) (covered by Mitch Ryder and the Detroit Wheels in 1965 as Jenny take a ride).

DATE / EVENT	AUDIO / VIDEO	TITLE

Join the gang (Bowie).
Land of 1.000 dances (Chris Kenner, 1962).
Maid of Bond Street (Bowie).
One more heartache (Marvin Gaye, 1966).
Over the wall we go (Bowie).
See-saw (Don Covay and The Goodtimers, 1965).
Send you money (early Bowie composition?).
Shake (Sam Cooke, 1965).
Silly boy blue (Bowie).
Stay (Maurice Williams and The Zodiacs, 1960).
Take it with soul (Bowie composition, never recorded).
Take my tip (Bowie).
That's a promise (Bowie).
The Fairground (early Bowie composition?).
The London Boys (Bowie).
There is a happy land (Bowie).
We are not your friends (We are Hungry Men) (Bowie).
What kind of fool am I? (Anthony Newley).
You better tell her (early Bowie composition?).
You'll never walk alone (when you walk through a storm)
(Classic from the musical Carousel in 1945. They covered
the version of Johnny Kidd and the Pirates).

<u>11-2-1966</u> London, Marquee Club.   NT
David Bowie and the Buzz.
The concert was (by mistake) advertised as The Lower
Third.
Support act: Boz and the Sidewinders.

19-2-1966 Boyfriend. Heads and Tales. Article about Bowie.

<u>22-2-1966</u> Regent Sound Studios.   Tape
Recording demo Do anything you say.
David Bowie and the Buzz.
Tony Hatch was there to listen to the new song.

26-2-1966 Melody Maker. Article by Anon: A message to London from Dave. Bowie stated he was helping his producer Tony Hatch to write a musical score and the numbers for a TV show. Bowie about Buddhism: "Also I want to go to Tibet. It's a fascinating place y' know. I'd like to take a holiday and have a look inside the monasteries. The Tibetan monks, Lamas, bury themselves inside mountains for weeks and only eat every three days. They're ridiculous and it's said they live for centuries."

26-2-1966 Melody Maker. Advert for the concert in Eastbourne on 28-2-1966.

<u>26-2-1966</u> Chelmsford, Corn Exchange.   NT
David Bowie and the Buzz.
Support act: Coltrane Union.
Exhausted at the end of the gig, David collapses on stage.

DATE / EVENT	AUDIO / VIDEO	TITLE

28-2-1966 Eastbourne, Club Continental, 123 Terminus Road. Tickets on advance 4p. Tickets on night 5p.
David Bowie and the Buzz.
The concert was advertised as Dave Bowie.

NT

28-2-1966 Interviewed by Disc and Music Echo for an article called: From Dave.

3-3-1966 UK TV. ITV. Ready Steady Go!
Recorded at Rediffusion House, Kingsway.
Broadcast 4-3-1966.
Can't help thinking about me (the band mimed and David sang live).
David Bowie and the Buzz.

Tape — quality 10, 3 min.
Video — quality 10, 3 min.

Ray Cook gave Ralph Horton GBP 250,— to help buy Can't help thinking a bout me into the Hit parade. Came 34th in The Melody Maker.

5-3-1966 Birmingham, Cranes Record Shop. Bowie signed records. He was photographed with Pauline Williams and Mary McGulkin (staff of the shop).

7-3-1966 Pye Studios at Marble Arch. Recording of Good morning girl / Do anything you say, by Bowie and the Buzz. Produced by Tony Hatch. Each member received GBP. 9,— as session fee.

First part of March 1966, Crawley.
David Bowie and the Buzz.

NT

First part of March 1966, Bournemouth.
David Bowie and the Buzz.

NT

11-3-1966 Walthamstow Independent. Article: Pop Group's TV Hopes Dashed.

11-3-1966 Evening Argus. Advert for the concert in Brighton on 12-3-1966.

12-3-1966 Brighton, One-O-One Club (formerly The New Barn), 75A West Street. Tickets 2/6.
David Bowie and the Buzz. By mistake advertised as Dave Bowie & The Lower 3rd.

NT

18-3-1966 High Wycombe, Target Club (Co-Op Memorial Hall).
David Bowie and the Buzz.

NT

March 1966 Southampton.
David Bowie and the Buzz.

NT

March 1966 Nottingham.
David Bowie and the Buzz.

NT

March 1966 Peterborough.

NT

DATE / EVENT	AUDIO / VIDEO	TITLE

David Bowie and the Buzz.

March 1966 Newmarket. NT
David Bowie and the Buzz.

25-3-1966 Harrow, Alexander Tavern. NT
David Bowie and the Buzz.

31-3-1966 Horton telephoned Pitt again to ask for his assistance.

1-4-1966 Release first solo-single: Do anything you say (2.32) / Good morning girl (2.14) (Pye 7N. 17079).

2-4-1966 RM. Review of Do anything / Good morning girl (Pye 7N. 17079).

2-4-1966 MM. Review (by Dusty Springfield) of Do anything you say (Pye 7N. 17079).

2-4-1966 Carlisle, Holly Bush. NT
David Bowie and the Buzz.

3-4-1966 Edinburgh. Rehearsals. NT
David Bowie and the Buzz.
Only rehearsals, the concert was Cancelled

4-4-1966 Dundee, College. NT
David Bowie and the Buzz.
Drummer John (Ego) Eager recalls being pulled off his drum stool by screaming girls (The Pitt Report - Kenneth Pitt 1983).

5-4-1966 Glasgow, Greens Playhouse. NT
David Bowie and the Buzz.
Support for Johnny Kidd and the Pirates.

6-4-1966 Hawick. NT
David Bowie and the Buzz.

8-4-1966 Bromley times. Article: First solo disc for Davie.

9-4-1966 Thetford, Guildhall. NT
David Bowie and the Buzz.
Performed two 45-minute slots.

10-4-1966 London, Marquee Club. NT
David Bowie and the Buzz.
First of the Bowie Showboat gigs (sponsored by Radio London). From 15.00 to 18.00 hours.
a.o. You'll never walk alone (Rodgers and Hammerstein classic), the way Johnny Kidd and the Pirates performed it.

DATE / EVENT	AUDIO / VIDEO	TITLE

Attended by Jonathan King and Kiki Dee.

16-4-1966 Fabulous. Article about Bowie at the Marquee.

17-4-1966 London, Marquee Club.   NT
David Bowie and the Buzz.
Bowie Showboat gig.
Ken Pitt present during performance.
The concert ended with You'll never walk alone.

17-4-1966 5-Year management-contract with Pitt. Agreed at Horton's flat in Warwick Square.

24-4-1966 London, Marquee Club.   NT
David Bowie and the Buzz.

End April 1966 the first Official David Bowie Fan Club was formed by Shirley Wilson, Sandra Gibling and Violet Neal. Shirley Wilson once accompanied the band to a gig in the ambulance. When they stopped at the traffic lights David let his hand flop out of one of the black glass windows. Some of the people looked with hands to their mouths, with eyes wide open (The Pitt Report - Kenneth Pitt 1983).

1-5-1966 London, Marquee Club.   NT
David Bowie and the Buzz (Bowie Showboat gig).

8-5-1966 London, Marquee Club.   NT
David Bowie and the Buzz (Bowie Showboat gig).

15-5-1966 London, Marquee Club.   NT
David Bowie and the Buzz (Bowie Showboat gig).

16-5-1966 Pitt paid GBP 125,— for a converted ambulance.

22-5-1966 London, Marquee Club (15.00-18.00 hours).   NT
David Bowie and the Buzz (Bowie Showboat gig).

25-4-1966 Chester.   NT
David Bowie and the Buzz.

29-5-1966 London, Marquee Club (matinee).   NT
15.00 to 18.00 Hours.
David Bowie and the Buzz (Bowie Showboat matinee gig).
Also on the bill: The Soul System and a top ten guests D.J.

29-5-1966 Blackpool, South Pier (evening).   NT
David Bowie and the Buzz.
Promoters: George Cooper and Herry Dawson.
Host-compere-singer Long John Baldry.
Support for Crispian St.Peters, Dave Antony's Moods,
The Mark Leeman Five.

DATE / EVENT	AUDIO / VIDEO	TITLE

After the show they drove back home in the ambulance, Kenneth Pitt at the passengers seat and the boys lay on mattresses in the back. They stopped for a meal at the Blue Boar Inn.

1-6-1966 Mick Ronson moved to 110 Gloucester Ave, Chalk Farm, London. From 25-5-1966 to 23-6-1966 he joined the band The Voice, managed by Micky Most.
6-7-1966 To end July 1966 he performed with The Wanted.

5-6-1966 London, Marquee Club.   NT
David Bowie and the Buzz (Bowie Showboat gig).

6-6-1966 Pye Studios. The Buzz recorded a demo of I dig everything and I'm not loosing sleep. Halfway through the session producer Tony Hatch decided to rearrange the tracks with session musicians instead of The Buzz on 5-7-1966.

12-6-1966 London, Marquee Club.   NT
David Bowie and the Buzz (Bowie Showboat gig).

13-6-1966 Ramsgate, Coronation Ballroom (Pleasurama).   NT
David Bowie and the Buzz.

14-6-1966 Cambridge, Corn Exchange.   NT
David Bowie and the Buzz.

15-6-1966 Hutch left The Buzz and was replaced by Billy Gray ('Haggis') (a 16-year old guy from Kilmarnock, Scotland). Hutch was tired of being broke. He also couldn't get on with Ralp Horton. He returned to Yorkshire and then went to Montreal to work as a maintenance engineer for Air Canada at Dorval Airport.

17-6-1966 Catford.   NT
David Bowie and the Buzz.

18-6-1966 Kenneth Pitt send an acetate disc of I dig everything to Vicki Wickham (editor of Ready, SteadyGo!). She didn't like the record.

18-6-1966 Thetford.   NT
David Bowie and the Buzz.

19-6-1966 Brands Hatch, Racing Track (Charity Show).   NT
David Bowie and the Buzz.

22-6-1966 Bognor Regis, The Shoreline Club.   NT
David Bowie and the Buzz.
They shared the bill with Long John Baldry and Bluesology (featuring a very young Elton John on keyboards).

23-6-1966 Lowestoft.   NT
David Bowie and the Buzz.

DATE / EVENT	AUDIO / VIDEO	TITLE

<u>24-6-1966</u> Dunstable, California Ballroom. NT
David Bowie and the Buzz.

25-6-1966 Marriage of John Hutchinson. Hutchinson: "David tried to talk me out of it! He didn't come to the wedding" (The Starzone Interviews -David Currie 1987).

<u>27-6-1966</u> Great Yarmouth. Britannia Theatre. NT
The Summer Sunday Spectacular.
David Bowie and the Buzz.
Support for Freddie and the Dreamers, Oscar, Geneveve,
Wolf and Griff, The Stuart Taylor Trio.

<u>2-7-1966</u> Warrington, The Red Lion Hotel. NT
David Bowie and the Buzz (First time with Billy Gray
as a member of the band).
Second line-up (June 1966 to 2-12-1966):
David Bowie (vocals, guitar, sax).
Billy Gray (guitar).
Derek 'Chow' Boyes (organ).
Derek 'Dek' Fearnley (bass).
John 'Ego' Eager (drums).

<u>3-7-1966</u> London, Marquee Club. NT
David Bowie and the Buzz.

5-7-1966 Pye Studios. Bowie recorded I dig everything (2.45) / I'm not loosing sleep (2.52) with studio-musicians.

9-7-1966 Melody Maker. Pop Parade. Records reviewed by Jack Hutton.

<u>15-7-1966</u> Essex, Loughton Youth Centre. NT
Members: 4p. Guests: 5p. Single David Bowie (Major Tom
David Bowie and the Buzz. 6052-205)

<u>30-7-1966</u> Bishop's Stortford, Rhodes Centre. NT
Presented by Limelight Promotions. Tickets 7/6p
David Bowie and the Buzz.
Support act: The U-NO-WHO

Begin August 1966 Bowie wrote three songs: Funny Face, Funny Bunny, Pussy Cat. The songs would be part of a film made by Mithras films. The project was cancelled and the songs remain unreleased.

<u>12-8-1966</u> Leicester, Latin Quarter. NT
David Bowie and the Buzz.

<u>13-8-1966</u> Boston, Gliderdrome. NT
David Bowie and the Buzz.

DATE / EVENT	AUDIO / VIDEO	TITLE

19-8-1966 Release I dig everything (2.45) / I'm not loosing sleep (2.52) (Pye 7N. 17157).

<u>21-8-1966</u> London, Marquee Club (first of 6 Sunday afternoon shows, known as the Bowie Showboat). David Bowie and the Buzz (sponsored by Radio London). Attended by Maurice Hatton and Carl Davis of Mithras Films.   NT

After the show Bowie gave an interview from the stage.
Radio London: "You work here with a backing-group, The Buzz. Did you always work with them?"
Bowie: "As David Bowie, yes. I always worked with them, about 6 months."
Radio London: "Why do you say As David Bowie?"
Bowie: "Before that I was somebody else."

<u>21-8-1966</u> London, Marquee Club. From 19.30 to 23.00 Hours. David Bowie and the Buzz. Bowie Showboat (sponsored by Radio London).	1 CDR	Various Singles - 1 (No label, no number)
	CD	The London tapes (World Productions WPOCM 0589D020-2)
	2 CD	God knows I'm good (BEEB 1/2)
	1 CD	God knows I'm good (Invasion Unlimited IU9753-2)

Interviewed on stage for Radio London (1.15). During the interview Bowie stated he was helping his producer Tony Hatch to write a musical score. He also stated this during an interview for Melody Maker on 26-2-1966. The musical would be called: Kids on the roof, based on the idea of the musical Oliver (starring Lionel Bart). He was also writing some songs for a TV show called Peacock's Farm (about a young man called Peacock who runs a boutique). Both projects were cancelled but a part of the songs were used for Bowie's first album and the idea for Kids on the roof was an inspiration for the song Diamond Dogs in 1974.

26-8-1966 Kent Messenger. Article: David makes his bow at Big 'L'. They wrote: "The group has re-shaped it's act, spending as much as eight hours a day rehearsing."

<u>26-8-1966</u> Ramsgate, Coronation Ballroom (Pleasurama).   NT
David Bowie and the Buzz.
The Big L Disc Night.
David tried to address the audience through a console, in a ghostly, echoing voice. The microphone failed.
Parts of the act were performed to prepared backing tapes.

<u>27-8-1966</u> Greenford (Wembley), Starlite Club.   NT
David Bowie and the Buzz.
Parts of the act were performed to prepared backing tapes.
They dropped this way of working after this concert.

<u>28-8-1966</u> London, Marquee Club.   NT
David Bowie and the Buzz.

DATE / EVENT	AUDIO / VIDEO	TITLE

Bowie Showboat (sponsored by Radio London).

September 1966 The contract with Pye ended.

<u>4-9-1966</u> London, Marquee Club.   NT
David Bowie and the Buzz.
Bowie Showboat (sponsored by Radio London).

6-9-1966 Bowie went to see Pitt and talk about his future.

<u>11-9-1966</u> London, Marquee Club.   NT
David Bowie and the Buzz.
Bowie Showboat (sponsored by Radio London).

<u>18-9-1966</u> London, Marquee Club.   NT
David Bowie and the Buzz.
Bowie Showboat (sponsored by Radio London).

<u>23-9-1966</u> London, Marquee Club.   NT
David Bowie and the Buzz.
Support act for Gary Farr and The T-Bones.

<u>25-9-1966</u> London, Marquee Club.   NT
David Bowie and the Buzz.
Bowie Showboat (sponsored by Radio London).

<u>2-10-1966</u> London, Marquee Club.   NT
David Bowie and the Buzz (Bowie Showboat).

<u>9-10-1966</u> London, Marquee Club.   NT
David Bowie and the Buzz (Bowie Showboat).

<u>16-10-1966</u> London, Marquee Club.   NT
David Bowie and the Buzz (Bowie Showboat).

18-10-1966 Morden (Surrey). R.G. Jones Studios. Recording of Rubber band (2.05), The London boys (3.20), Please Mr. Gravedigger. With The Buzz (minus Billy Gray) and 2 session musicians. First recording of Rubber Band (inspired on family-stories of David's grandfather in the army). The master tape of Please Mr. Gravedigger later got lost.

21-10-1966 Maurice Hatton (Mithras Films) confirmed Kenneth Pitt he was going to make a film with Bowie. He only had to raise the finance. Project was later cancelled.

<u>23-10-1966</u> London, Marquee Club.   NT
David Bowie and the Buzz (Bowie Showboat).

24-10-1966 K.Pitt went with 3 tracks (recorded 18-10-1966) to Decca (Deram) at Decca House on the Albert Embankment. He had a meeting with Hugh Mendl and MikeVernon. They bought the songs for GBP 150,—. Agreed to pay an advance of GBP 100,— for an album.

DATE / EVENT	AUDIO / VIDEO	TITLE

27-10-1966 Bowie and Kenneth Pitt had a meeting with Hugh Mendl and Mike Vernon at Decca House. They discussed plans for an album.

29-10-1966 Bognor Regis, Shoreline Club.　　　　　NT
David Bowie and the Buzz.
Shared the bill with: Action, Bluesology, Long John Baldry.

30-10-1966 London, Marquee Club.　　　　　NT
David Bowie and the Buzz (Bowie Showboat).

5-11-1966 RM. Most Promising. David Bowie voted at place 18 with 91 points.

6-11-1966 London, Marquee Club.　　　　　NT
David Bowie and the Buzz (Bowie Showboat).

8-11-1966 Ken Pitt goes to New York and meets Andy Warhol and Lou Reed, and brings Bowie back acetate of influential Velvet Underground album and an album by the Fugs.

10-11-1966 Kenneth Pitt went to see Walt Maguire of London Records and made him listen to Rubber band.

13-11-1966 London, Marquee Club (19.30-23.00 hours).　　　　　NT
David Bowie and the Buzz (Bowie Showboat).
Derek Fearnley: "The kids didn't want David's songs. They didn't understand them. The songs were too pretty for them. All they wanted was soul."
The band scrawled We Hate Soul along the side of the ambulance (The Pitt Report - Kenneth Pitt 1983)

14-11-1966 Decca Studios (Studio no. 2). Recordings of She's got medals (2.23), Uncle Arthur (2.07). She's got medals is a slang euphemism for male genitals. It is also a simile for courage.

16-11-1966 London. Olympic Studios. The Rolling Stones record Let's spend the night together. Bowie covered the song for his 1973 album Aladdin Sane (Stone alone - Bill Wyman and Ray Coleman 1990).

19-11-1966 Cromer, Olympia Ballrooms.　　　　　NT
David Bowie and the Buzz (Billy Gray's final gig).
The tour ambulance broke down.

24-11-1966 Recording Join the gang (2.17), We are hungry men (working title We are not your friends) (2.58), There is a happy land (3.11), Did you ever have a dream (2.06) at Decca Studios (Studio 2). Join the gang was written one or two months earlier at the open-air cafe at Clapham Common. Gus Dudgeon thought the sitar at the front was totally manic, bloody brilliant.

25-11-1966 The band had a meeting with Ralph Horton. They decided to break up after the gig in Shrewsbury, because of the band's very bad financial situation. Even the offer to play for free couldn't keep the band together (The Pitt Report - Kenneth Pitt 1983).

DATE / EVENT	AUDIO / VIDEO	TITLE

<u>26-11-1966</u> Gosport, Community Centre.　　　　　NT
David Bowie and the Buzz (Their debut as a quartet).
Bowie made his appearance from a dustbin.
Before the show they gave away copies of the single
Rubber band.

<u>27-11-1966</u> Maids Head, King's Lynn.　　　　　　NT
David Bowie and the Buzz.

December 1966 Released in US Rubber band (2.05) / There is a happy land (3.11) (Deram 85009).

December 1966 Decca House spreads a flyer to the media stating that Bowie lives in Bromley with his parents and his dog Leo, listening to Stravinsky (usually "Ragtime for eleven instruments"). He adores Vaughan Williams, Dvorak, Elgar and Holst. His record collection includes lots of Glenn Miller, Stan Kenton and Gary McFarland.

2-12-1966 Released in Europe Rubber Band (2.05) / The London Boys (3.20) (Deram DM. 107).

Denis Taylor: "I was coming out of the Gioconda. David called me over. He had an acetate in his hand. We went into a record shop and played it, it was Rubber band, which I thought was a fantastic record and I told him so" (The Starzone Interviews - David Currie 1987).

<u>2-12-1966</u> Shrewsbury, Severn Club.　　　　　　NT
David Bowie and the Buzz.
After this gig they broke up. Although the band continued
to record with Bowie for his first album.

3-12-1966 Disc. Article about Bowie claiming that Carnaby Street manufactures military gear he designed 18 months ago. I think (with the military background in Bowie's family and songs like Rubber band, She's got medals etc.) he could be right.

3-12-1966 RM. Review of Rubber band (2.05) / The London Boys (3.20) (Deram DM 107).

3-12-1966 RM. Article about the Jacket Bowie designed that Neil Christian wore on "Tale of two streets."

7-12-1966 Bowie signs a publishing contract with David Platz of Essex Music for GBP 500,—. It was a blunder, Pitt already had an offer of GBP 1.000,— from Platz.

8-12-1966 Recording Maid of Bond Street (1.43), Silly boy blue (3.51), Sell me a coat (2.59), Little bombardier (3.25) in Decca Studios (Studio 2).

12-12-1966 Bowie recorded Come and buy my toys (2.07) in Decca Studios (Studio 2).

13-12-1966 Re-recording of Please Mr. Gravedigger (2.35) (version 2) in Decca Studios (Studio 2). The first take of 16-10-1966 has got lost. Gus Dudgeon: "I just love 'Gravedigger'! The bottom end on the thunder is fantastic! What I remember is Bowie standing there wearing a pair of cans with his collar turned up as if he was in the rain, hunched over, shuffling about in a box of gravel" (Strange fascination - D. Buckley 1999).

DATE / EVENT	AUDIO / VIDEO	TITLE

24-12-1966 New Musical Express. Le Reviews. Review of Rubber band / The London Boys (Deram DM 107).

In 1966 Bowie and The Lower Third earned GBP 2.204,— from performances.

1967 Audition for role of David Copperfield in The Touchables.

1967 Book published: I am still the greatest says Johnny Angelo - Nik Cohn (Secker & Warburg). A fictional tale concerning the rise and fall of a pulp hero. Violence, glamour and speed, splendour and vulgarity. Later they made a cult film of it: Peeping Tom. The book was an inspiration for Bowie to create Ziggy Stardust.

Early 1967 Mick Ronson joined The Rats. John Cambridge turned down the offer to become their drummer.

4-1-1967 The Speakeasy in Margaret Street, London opened it's doors. It would become one of the places very frequently visited by Bowie to "collect" new ideas. This was also the place where he met his later wife Angie.

17-1-1967 Bowie phoned Kenneth Pitt: "Ken, I'm worried about Ralph. May I come up and talk about it?" (The Pitt Report - Kenneth Pitt 1983).

19-1-1967 End of contract with Ralph Horton.

21-1-1967 Bill Wyman and Peter Frampton went into town (London). They met two girlfriends and Peter Frampton had his first sexual experience. Some time later he phoned Bill Wyman, he had found strange, small animals in his pubic hair (Stone alone - Bill Wyman and Ray Coleman 1990).

26-1-1967 Recording of The gospel according to Tony Day (2.48), The laughing gnome (3.01) at Decca Studio No.2. For the final session The Buzz were augmented by members of The London Philharmonic Orchestra.

30-1-1967 Release Over the wall we go (2.48) / Everyday of my life - Oscar (Reaction 591012). A-side written by David. Oscar late came known as Paul Nicholas. He performed the song on TV in the Ken Dodd Show.

9-2-1967 Prince of Wales Theatre. Bowie and some members of Pitt's family went to see Cilla Black and Frankie Howerd.

10-2-1967 Pitt wrote a letter to John Jones he would do his best to get David's career going along the right lines.

25-2-1967 Recording of Love you till Tuesday (3.09) (Tune later used for BBC Game Show Blankety Blank), When I live my dream (3.22) and Rubber band (version 2) (2.17). Last day of recordings for the album David Bowie.

25-2-1967 Trend. Article about The Riot Squad (without David Bowie), who released the single Gotta be a first time.

DATE / EVENT	AUDIO / VIDEO	TITLE

March 1967 Ken Pitt sent demo tape and lyric sheet to producers for a short film musical that would be composed by Carl Davis (nothing more was heard of the project).

1-3-1967 David, Kenneth Pitt and his cousin Hilary went to the London Palladium, to see Cliff Richard in the pantomime Aladdin.

9-3-1967 Bowie joins the Performing Rights Society. Ken Pitt lists for him a total of 29 songs, including a novelty item called "The Laughing Gnome," his next single.

<u>13-3-1967</u> Tottenham (London), The Swan. Tape
Rehearsals with The Riot Squad.
Little toy soldier, Silly boy blue, Silver treetop school for boys.
Line-up:
David Bowie (vocals, guitar, tenor sax).
Rod Davies (guitar).
Croke Prebble (bass).
Bob Evans (sax, flute).
George Butcher (keyboards).
Derek Roll (drums).

The Riot Squad did about 20 shows between March and June 1967. Most of the dates are unknown. This is something that puzzles me quite some years now. Their stage act was very unusual, so this must have drawn the attention of quite a few people. Slogan they used: One day we will live next door to you and your lawn will die! Former Riot Squad member Graham Bonnet left for a solo career (he had a hit with 'Supergirl'). Later he sang with Ritchie Blackmore's Rainbow. In 1966 bassist Mike Martin had jumped ship to Georgie Fame's Blue Flames, before hooking up with Jimi Hendrix.

5-4-1967 Decca Studios, 163-165 Broadhurst Gardens,   CD   *Ultra Rare Trax Vol.1 (The*
London, Bowie and The Riot Squad recorded Little toy   *Genuine Pig TGP-CD-108)*
soldier (3.11) (working titles: Sadie, Sadie's song, part of   *(2 songs)*
chorus was borrowed from Venus in furs) and Waiting for
the man (4.06). Producer Mike Vernon and engineer Gus
Dudgeon helped Bowie with the sound effects for Little
toy soldier. Lou Reed lifted a part of the lyrics and the
song title from the poem Venus in furs by Sacher Masoch,
which was written in 1886 (David Bowie 1962 -1968 -
Alex Alexander and Pete Foulstone 2002).

<u>13-4-1967</u> London, Tiles Club, 79-89 Oxford Street. NT
David Bowie supported by The Riot Squad.
Also present: D.J. Chas Stevens.
The Riot Squad used a lot of face paint and they had a theatrical stage show (Very important influence on Bowie's later career. Overseen by almost every biographer).
They used a flashing red lamp. During the song Little toy soldier (inspired on Venus in furs) Bowie whipped sax player Bob Evans.

DATE / EVENT	AUDIO / VIDEO	TITLE

Some of the songs they played:
America (The Shark Girls, from West Side Story, 1957).
Dirty old man (The Fugs, 1966).
It can't happen here (Mothers of Invention, 1966).
Little toy soldier (Bowie).
Silly boy blue (Bowie).
Silver treetop school for boys (Bowie).
Waiting for the man (Velvet Underground, 1966).

Earlier that day Bowie traipsed up and down Oxford Street advertising the evening show, wearing a large sandwichboard. After the gig there was a photo session for the Riot Squad's promoter. Gerald Fearnley made the photos (brother of Dek Fearnley who played in The Buzz).

14-4-1967 Release The laughing gnome (3.01) / The gospel according to Tony Day (2.48) (Deram DM. 123).

<u>14-4-1967</u> London, Marquee Club.   NT
David Bowie solo.

25-4-1967 Bowie signs a 1-year management contract with Ken Pitt. It gave Pitt 25% of Bowie's earnings.

May 1967 Recording demo Social girl / Everything is you. Demo was privately sold in 1996.

May 1967 Recording demo Silver treetop school for boys. The demo later was send to Steve Rowland and got lost.

May 1967 Bowie Signs contract and gets advance from Decca to make LP.

May 1967 Bowie occasionally attends the Dance Centre in Floral Street, London WC2.

May 1967 Bowie often visited Tony Visconti in his flat at 108 Lexham Gardens, London W8. Marc Bolan was often present during these visits. They went to a cinema in Chelsea, to see Roman Polanski's film A knife in the water.
Tony Visconti started his musical career in the duo Tony and Siegfrid (his wife). He worked for the Richmond Organisation in New York. Denny Cordell (producer of Procol Harum and Moody Blues) persuaded him to come to London and work for Decca's Deram label.

May 1967 BBC session with The Riot Squad (Without Bowie). They recorded Penny Lane (2.56), A little bit me, a little bit you (2.23). Both songs featured on the covers compilation Hits 67.

May 1967 Brian Jones (Rolling Stones) introduces Nico to the American cult group Velvet Underground. She would become their singer (Stone alone - Bill Wyman and Ray Coleman 1990).

1-5-1967 Start of 1 month of performances at Golfe Drouot in Paris by The Rats. They arrived two days late because their van broke down in Grantham, Nottinghamshire.
After completing the French gigs they returned home broke and Mick Ronson was thown out by his father (Mick Ronson: The spider with the platinum hair - Weird and Gilly, 2003).

DATE / EVENT	AUDIO / VIDEO	TITLE

5-5-1967 Demo's of Everything is you, Summer kind of love and Going down were send to A&R man John Burgess (Manfred Mann's producer). A demo of Love you till Tuesday was send to Peter Grant of RAK Records.

13-5-1967 Bowie and Pitt went to the Piccadilly Theatre to see the musical Oliver, starring Lionel Bart.

Second half of May 1967 Bowie took a tape of There is a happy land to Lewis Rudd, Head of Children's programmes at Rediffusion Television.

June 1967 H. Williams (an employee of Norman's Garage in Vauxhall Bridge Road) bought the Buzz's old ambulance for GBP. 10,—.

1-6-1967 Release LP David Bowie (Deram DES. 18003). The cover photo was taken by Gerald Fearnley (the brother of Dek) at 13-4-1967. David Bowie was one of the first British artists to issue an album without having first had a hit single.

1-6-1967 Bowie went to see film director Franco Zeffirelli at 65 Dean Street in Soho, to discuss singing and composing songs for his new film Romeo and Juliet. They agreed Bowie should write some music and then Zeffirelli would decide. On 8-8-1967 he got a letter he was not the one Zeffirelli was looking for. It turned out he had chosen Donovan to write the music.

3-6-1967 Decca Studios (Studio no.3). Re-recording of Love you till Tuesday (version 2) (single-version) (2.59), re-recording When I live my dream (Version 2) (3.52) (used for the film Love you till Tuesday). Ivor Raymonde wrote the arrangements for the songs. Produced by Mike Vernon, engineered by Bill Price.

7-6-1967 Bowie and Pitt went to see Zeffirelli's film The Taming of the Shrew.

10-6-1967 Released in Belgium: Love is always (2.29) / Pancho (2.11) - Dee Dee (Palette PB 25.579). Lyrics A-side by Bowie. Music by Albimoor and Glround. B-side co-written by Bowie.

10-6-1967 Disc and Music Echo. Advert for the single Love you till Tuesday.

11-6-1967 Pitt took John Jones, David and his belongings to 39 Manchester Street, Marylebone W1 (his home) in his tiny Fiat 500. From that day on David stayed in the spare room on the top floor. One of Pitt's books he read: A picture of Dorian Gray by Oscar Wilde (first published in 1891). Ken Pitt: "The routine was that at about noon when he surfaced, he would telephone the office to say he was up and ask what we were doing for lunch. There wasn't much to do at the flat, really, we were rarely there. It was quite remarkable how he kept alive. He was all coffee and cigarettes. I remember once we went through an Eastern cooking time. It did dreadful things to my digestion! I have various tracks that no-one else had heard of, and he's probably forgotten about them as well" (The Starzone Interviews - David Currie 1987).

24-6-1967 RM. Article by Derek Boltwood: Bowie the 19-yr-old epistle writer.

27-6-1967 Michael Armstrong offered Bowie a role in A Floral Tale (a camp satire on Orpheus in the Underworld, about a pop singer who appears naked on stage, plays a love scene with another man and at the end of the play is torn to pieces by his fans). The project was cancelled. Rumoured: Bowie wrote

| DATE / EVENT | AUDIO / VIDEO | TITLE |

7 pieces of music for the project. Later that day he went to a reception at Chappell's music shop in NewBond Street. Bowie got very drunk and took home (to Kenneth Pitt's flat) a sixteen-year-old girl. When Bowie had to throw up, Pitt send the girl home (The Pitt Report - Kenneth Pitt 1983).

28-6-1967 Interviewed by Bob Dawbarn of Melody Maker.

Bowie used to have dinner (always spaghetti) at the Ristorante Anacapri in Dorset Street.

6-7-1967 Kenneth Pitt wrote a letter to film director Bryan Forbes, with Bowie's LP, to suggest Bowie would play a role in his new film Please Sir (The Pitt Report - Kenneth Pitt 1983).

7-7-1967 Release The laughing gnome / If I were a richman - Ronnie Hiltop (HMV Pop 1600). A-side written by Bowie.

7-7-1967 Bromley Times. Article: Plaudits for Bowie.

8-7-1967 Jackie. Pop Gossip. Article about the new line-up of The Riot Squad.

14-7-1967 Release Love you till Tuesday (2.59) / Did you ever have a dream (2.06) (Deram DM. 135).

Record Mirror, Peter Jones: "This boy is really something different. It's a stand-out single."
Record Retailer: "This boy shows again his ability as singer and writer. A performance which could easily make it."
Disc, Penny Valentine: "This is a very funny rather bitter little love song."
Melody Maker, Chris Welch: "Very funny, and deserves instant recognition."
Record Mirror: "This boy really is something different."

14-7-1967 Bowie and Pitt went to Holland Park Studios to see John Bryan and Robert Freeman. They asked them for an audition for Bowie for the role of David Copperfield in their film The Touchables. They were not interested (The Pitt Report - Kenneth Pitt 1983).

22-7-1967 Melody Maker. Article by Syd Barrett (Pink Floyd): Blind Date. About Love you till Tuesday: "It's a joke number. Everybody like jokes. Very chirpy, but I don't think my toes were tapping at all."

29-7-1967 FAB 208. Article by Christine Osbourne: On Our Wavelength.

August 1967 Release Album David Bowie in US.

24-8-1967 Bowie and Pitt went to the Criterion Theatre to see Loot (a play written by Joe Orton).

September 1967 Tibet Society's Headquarter in Hampstead. Bowie met Chime Yong Dong Rimpoche at a lecture of Christmas Humpreys (he was a black judge, who was the chairman of the Tibet Society). In an interview with George Tremlett he explained his later visits to Rimpoche: "I just sit there, asking questions, and he usually answers them with another question. In fact, he's teaching me to find my own solution."

1-9-1967 Recorded Let me sleep beside you (3.25), Karma man (3.02), at Advision Studios in New Bond Street, London, with Tony Visconti. The Decca selection board suggested a safer title: Let me be

DATE / EVENT	AUDIO / VIDEO	TITLE

beside you. Bowie refused and 18-9-1967 Decca turned the single down.

2-9-1967 Cashbox selected Rubber Band / Love you till Tuesday as Newcomer Pick.

11-9-1967 Border Films send Bowie a contract for the film The Image.

12-9-1967 Director Michael Armstrong took Bowie to Oxford Circus to buy him a pair of jeans to wear in the film The image.

13 to 16-9-1967 Filming for "The Image", for Border Films, directed by Michael Armstrong. Filmed in black and white by Ousama Rawi, edited by Julian Hindson, music by Noel Janus. William Mason painted the portrait of Bowie. Bowie received GBP. 30,—. Earlier in the year Michael Armstrong gave his script of A Floral Tale The British board of film. The censors disapproved the script and the project was cancelled (David was supposed to play a major part). Years later Bowie commented on "The Image": "My first true film appearance was in a movie called The Image, an undergound black and white avant garde-type thing done by some guy. He wanted to make a film about a painter doing a portrait of a guy in his teens, and the portrait comes to life and, in fact, turns out to be the corpse of some bloke. I can't remember all the plot, if indeed it had a plot, but it was a 14-minute short and it was awful" (A rock 'n' roll odyssey - Kate Lynch 1984).	*Video*	*Stolp Tapes no. 1 (13 min)*

15-9-1967 Released Silver treetop school for boys / I've lost a friend and found a lover - The Slender Plenty (Polydor 56189). A-side written by Bowie.

15-9-1967 Chelsea News. Article: Not only his singing gets them.

15-9-1967 Chelsea News. Article by Barbara Marylin Deane: Today I feel so happy…
Deane wrote: "David is contented with contentment. He is a happy loving person with a gentle nature. He is the only person who I have met who brings nursery rhymes and fairy stories to the forecourt of my mind."
Bowie: "I believe in loving a person impersonally. In this way you can learn to love everything. All emotion can lead to sickness in the mind."

18-9-1967 Deram's selection panel turned down the single Let me sleep beside you.

End September 1967 David wrote a script called The Chamion Flower Grower. He send it to the BBC. They turned it down. The play was about Woody, who had won a free weekend in London in a Championship at a local flower show. He arrives in a hotel with all hippy flower children. They start a comedy dialogue (The Pitt Report - Kenneth Pitt 1983).

30-9-1967 Photo-session for magazine Fab 208.

DATE / EVENT	AUDIO / VIDEO	TITLE

30-9-1967 FAB 208. Article: Bowie bows to age. David Bowie: "The people who are the powerful ones are about twenty-five. Teenagers are the customers. These people turn out what the young want. The teenagers buy what's in the shop, but they don't put it there and they don't get the money and it's the money that is power!"

October 1967 Recording demo C'est la vie.

October 1967 John Cambridge joined The Rats.

13-10-1967 David went to see Ned Sherrin in Bywater Street in Chelsea, to discuss a part in the film The Virgin Soldiers (to a book, written by Leslie Thomas).

4-11-1967 Jackie. Article: Photographer's Nightmare.

7-11-1967 Bowie and Pitt flew to Holland (cost: GBP. 37,14 for two return flight tickets). They stayed 3 nights at the Motel Naarden, Amersfoortsestraatweg 92, Naarden. They were invited by Jan Corduwener of Phonogram Records.

9-11-1967 Dutch TV. Fanclub.   Video
Love you till Tuesday (mimed).
Broadcast on 10-11-1967.

<u>19-11-1967</u> London, Dorchester Hotel, Park Lane.   NT
Stage Ball on behalf of the Catholic Stage Guild and the
British Heart Foundation.
David Bowie with Bill Saville Orchestra, 10-minute spot.

November / December 1967. Dance Centre in Floral Street. Bowie took dance lessons (not mime) from Lindsay Kemp.
Bowie's dance partner Robin Whitecross (a girl from Portsmouth) remembers: "We formed a kind of duo. We were about as tall, and Lindsay gave us always an idea and we had to improvise on that. Lindsay shouted: "David and Robin! Two birds! David and Robin! Wind!"
We moved our arms and bodies to picture the wind. We improvised and taught to use our bodies without being afraid" (David Bowie - Jerry Hopkins 1985).
Bowie: "So I became his pupil. He was the master and I was the student. I was into ballet and mime and I got into the company and wrote some of the plays with him and realized Lindsay Kemp was a living Pierrot "(Living on the brink - George Tremlett 1996).

2-12-1967 Released Silver treetop school for boys (2.10) / Sugar chocolate machine - The Beatstalkers (CBS 3105). A-side written by Bowie. Silver treetop school for boys was inspired on a newspaper report about the boys of Lancing College smoking pot (The Pitt Report - Kenneth Pitt 1983).

<u>18-12-1967</u> London. Piccadilly 1 Studio, 201 Piccadilly.   2 CD   *God knows I'm good (songs*
Rec. Top Gear, Dave Lee Travis, BBC Radio Session.   *1,2,3,4 and 5) (BEEB 1/2)*
Produced by Bernie Andrews.   1 CD   *God knows I'm good (songs*
Broadcast 24-12-1967 and 28-1-1968.   *1,2,3,4 and 5) (Invasion*
1. Love you till Tuesday (3.01).   *Unlimited IU 9753-1_*
2. Little bombardier (3.31).   CD   *The rise and rise of Ziggy*

DATE / EVENT	AUDIO / VIDEO	TITLE
3. In the heat of the morning (2.47). 4. Silly boy blue (3.27). 5. When I live my dream (3.37). Steve Peregrin Took (T.Rex) played Pixiephone (at Marc Bolan's suggestion he named himself after the Hobbit Peregrin Took in Tolkien's The Lord Of The Rings. His real name was Stephen Ross Porter). The Arthur Greenslade Orchestra (16 musicians) was the backing band. Bowie received 10 guineas for the recording. Other acts on the bill: Jimi Hendrix, Traffic, Family and Ice.	 CD CD CD CD 4 CD 1 CDR CD CD	*Stardust vol. 1 (songs 1,2,3,4, and 5) (Savage Hippo Records)* *Mega Rare Trax vol. 1 (1,3) (Seagull Records CD 022)* *Emerged from shadows (all 5 songs) (EBD 001)* *Starman in session (5 songs) (Silver Rarities SIRA 93)* *The complete BBC master recordings (No label, no nr.)* *The complete BBC files vol. 1 (Old Gold Records OGCD 075)* *Ziggy in Wonderland (1,3) (PROCD 89 001-2)* *Five years (1,3) (Triangle records PYCD 047)*

22-12-1967, Tiddy Dolls Restaurant, just around the corner of Shepherd Market. Kenneth Pitt and David dined with Bernie Andrews from BBC Radio and thanked him for the Top Gear session on 18-12-1967.

22-12-1967 Bromley Times. Article: Local Pop Singer on Radio.

24-12-1967 BBC Radio. Broadcast Top Gear, recorded 18-12-1967.

25-12-1967 Bowie gave Pitt as a Christmas present the children's book The Farmer's Boy.

Lindsay Kemp: "It had been arranged through NEMS' office that we should meet. I'd heard the voice of an angel. I expected a very pimply youth to be standing there. There in fact was an angel. Love at first sight. We weren't lovers from the beginning, it took about 30 seconds" (In other words - Kerry Juby 1986).
Kemp was 35 year old and born in Liverpool. He had been a ballet dancer, male stripper, chorus boy and actor. His partner, a big, shaven-headed man called Jack Birkett, also had been ballet dancer and male stripper. By 2003 his sight had become very bad.

<u>28-12-1967</u> Oxford, New Theatre (Playhouse). David Bowie and the Lindsay Kemp Mime Comp. David's (as Cloud) mime debut in Pierrot in turquoise.	NT	

29-12-1967 Oxford Mail. Article by Don Chapman: Miming promise.

29-12-1967 Financial Times. Article by B.A. Young: Pierrot in Turquoise. Young wrote: "Mr. Bowie is a young pop-singer whose songs tend to follow ambition beyond the boundaries of his talent."

Winter 1967 Hull, Fairview Studios (the font room of Keith Herd). The Rats recorded The rise and fall of Bernie Gripplestone (with a chord sequence lifted from Eleanor Rigby by the Beatles).

End December 1967 Recording demo Threepenny Pierrot (also called Threepenny Joe) (1.56).

DATE / EVENT	AUDIO / VIDEO	TITLE

1968 UK TV. "My way" excerpt. — Video — 1 min.

Early 1968 recorded demo's April's tooth of gold, Mother Grey. An acetate of April's tooth of gold (2.32), backed by When I'm five (demo) (3.18) circulates. — 1 CDR — *April's tooth of gold*

2-1-1968 The whole company drove in a Transit they rented from Nick the Maltese (driven by Natasha Kornilof, Russian from father's side) to White Heaven, where they stayed in a Farmhouse. Bowie shared Lindsay Kemp's bed. Later that night he went to Natasha Kornilof's room. Kemp and Kornilof had a row when they found out (Living on the brink - George Tremlett 1996).
Lindsay Kemp: "It's horrible to wake up when you expect someone to be there and they're not, they're wrapped up in bed with some woman, and then you hear the music coming through the wall" (Alias David Bowie - Peter & Leni Gillman 1986).

<u>3-1-1968</u> Cumberland, Whitehaven, Rose Hill Theatre. — NT
(owned by Nicky Seker, a friend of Kemp).
Pierrot in Turquoise. Started at 20.00 hours.
David Bowie and the Lindsay Kemp Mime Comp.
Cloud: David Bowie.
Harlequin: Jack Birkett.
Pierrot: Lindsay Kemp.
Columbine: Annie Stainer.
Piano: Michael Garrett (he also was the Musical Director).
Décor and costumes: Natasha Kornilof.
Bowie helped Natasha Kornilof to paint the front cloth.

<u>4-1-1968</u> Cumberland, Whitehaven, Rose Hill Theatre. — NT
Pierrot in Turquoise. Started at 20.00 hours.
David Bowie and the Lindsay Kemp Mime Comp.

Bowie: "I gained an extraordinary amount of being with Lindsay. He introduced me to things like Cocteau and The Theatre of the Absurd, Antonin Artaud and the whole idea of restructuring and going against what people generally expect" (Black Book - Barry Miles 1980).

<u>5-1-1968</u> Cumberland, Whitehaven, Rose Hill Theatre. — NT
Pierrot in Turquoise. Started at 20.00 hours.
David Bowie and the Lindsay Kemp Mime Comp.
Bowie received a fee of GBP. 40,— for 3 performances.

11-1-1968 Stage. Article: Pierrot in Turqoise. David Bowie, the show's inventive composer, makes several striking appearances as Cloud, a multi-purposed and multi-guised character.

13-1-1968 Jackie. Article about Bowie's acting in The Image.

Mid January 1968 Bowie did auditions at the BBC for The Pistol Shot (a play by Chekhov).

28-1-1968 BBC Radio 1 Repeats Top Gear. Recorded 18-12-1967.

DATE / EVENT	AUDIO / VIDEO	TITLE

<u>30-1-1968</u> Shepherds Bush. BBC Studios. Filming "The Pistolshot" for BBC-2.
David dances minuet with Hermione Farthingale (her real name was Hermione Dennis).
Bowie wore a wig and they both wore "classic" clothes.
Broadcast 20-5-1968 and 24-12-1968.
Afterwards Bowie chatted with Hermione in the BBC canteen and escorted her towards Shepherds Bush tube station (In other words - Kerry Juby 1986).

NT

February 1968 Bowie recorded a prototype rock-musical called: Ernie Johnson (someone who throws a party to mark his intended suicide, planned for the next day). Ernie Johnson has a racist conversation with a tramp. He sings a song to himself in the mirror and he buys a new tie, to hang himself.
Songs he used for the musical:
Tiny Tim (borrowed heavily from Sweets for my sweet).
Where 's the Loo (early version Queen Bitch).
Season folk (influenced by Jimmy Webb).
Just one moment sir (the racist tramp song).
Various times of day (Early morning (with multi-dubbed lyrics).
Noon-Lunchtime (with 'raindrop' percussion).
Evening (doo-wop style).
Ernie boy (a monologue in 3 parts, in text a foretaste of Modern Love).

3-2-1968 Jackie. Article: Eye spy!

5-2-1968 Bowie went to see Florence Norberg at 59 George Street, a voice production consultant, to get some advice.

Begin February 1968 Geoffrey Heath (a song publisher) suggested David Platz (Essex Music) Bowie to write the English lyrics to a French song called Comme d'habitude (sung by Claude Francois). Written by Claude Francois, Gilles Thibault and Jacques Revaux.
Heath send a copy of the song, now called Even a fool learns to love, to Frank Sinatra's A & R man, but didn't enclose the English lyric. So they ordered Paul Anka to write the lyrics. And that's the way Comme d'habitude' became the million seller 'My way' (The Pitt Report - Kenneth Pitt 1983).

26-2-1968 Bowie and Mrs. Joan Barlay (secretary to Decca records overseas department head Marcel Stellman) flew from Heathrow Airport to Hamburg.

<u>27-2-1968</u> German TV. ZDF. 4-3-2-1 Musik fur junge leute filmed in Hamburg. Broadcasted 16-3-1968.
1. Love you till Tuesday.
2. Did you ever have a dream.
3. Please Mr. Gravedigger.

Tape   quality 10, 10 min.
Video   quality 10, 10 min.

March 1968 Release My people were fair and had sky in their hair… but now they're content to wear stars on their brows - Tyrannoraurus Rex. On Bowie's advise Marc Bolan asked George Underwood to do the artwork for the album sleeve.

DATE / EVENT	AUDIO / VIDEO	TITLE

<u>6-3-1968</u> London, Mercury Theatre, Notting Hill Gate.   NT
Pierrot in Turquoise. Bowie received GBP. 4,—.
David Bowie and the Lindsay Kemp Mime Comp.
Director for the performances Jean-Pierre Voos.
Musical director: Michael Garrett.
Stage manager: Robert Anthony.
Attended by David's parents.

<u>7-3-1968</u> London, Mercury Theatre, Notting Hill Gate.   NT
Pierrot in Turquoise. Bowie received GBP. 4,—.
David Bowie and the Lindsay Kemp Mime Comp.

8-3-1968 Bromley times. Article by D.J.B. about Bowie performing in Pierrot in Turqoise.

8-3-1968 Evening Standard. Article by Annabel Farjeon.

<u>8-3-1968</u> London, Mercury Theatre, Notting Hill Gate.   NT
Pierrot in Turquoise. Bowie received GBP. 4,—.
David Bowie and the Lindsay Kemp Mime Comp.

<u>9-3-1968</u> London, Mercury Theatre, Notting Hill Gate.   NT
Pierrot in Turquoise. Bowie received GBP. 4,—.
David Bowie and the Lindsay Kemp Mime Comp.

<u>10-3-1968</u> London, Mercury Theatre, Notting Hill Gate.   NT
Pierrot in Turquoise. Bowie received GBP. 4,—.
David Bowie and the Lindsay Kemp Mime Comp.

<u>11-3-1968</u> London, Mercury Theatre, Notting Hill Gate.   NT
Pierrot in Turquoise. Bowie received GBP. 4,—.
David Bowie and the Lindsay Kemp Mime Comp.

12-3-1968 Decca Studio in West Hampstead recording of In the heat of the morning (2.56), London Bye Ta Ta (2.36), Angel angel grubby face.
On acetate disk: Angel angel grubby face / London bye ta ta (2.36) (on auction at Christie's 1993).
Master tapes of In the heat of the morning and London bye ta ta were completed on 10-4-1968.
The master tape went missing not long afterwards.

<u>12-3-1968</u> London, Mercury Theatre, Notting Hill Gate.   NT
Pierrot in Turquoise. Bowie received GBP. 4,—.
David Bowie and the Lindsay Kemp Mime Comp.

<u>13-3-1968</u> London, Mercury Theatre, Notting Hill Gate.   NT
Pierrot in Turquoise. Bowie received GBP. 4,—.
David Bowie and the Lindsay Kemp Mime Comp.

14-3-1968 Stage. Article in Week in the theatre: Pierrot in Turqoise.
They wrote: "David Bowie, singing mind-bendingly off-beat songs of his own compositions, also as the

DATE / EVENT	AUDIO / VIDEO	TITLE

elusive Cloud, shows up as an effective mime."

<u>14-3-1968</u> London, Mercury Theatre, Notting Hill Gate. NT
Pierrot in Turquoise. Bowie received GBP. 4,—.
David Bowie and the Lindsay Kemp Mime Comp.

<u>15-3-1968</u> London, Mercury Theatre, Notting Hill Gate. NT
Pierrot in Turquoise. Bowie received GBP. 4,—.
David Bowie and the Lindsay Kemp Mime Comp.

<u>16-3-1968</u> London, Mercury Theatre, Notting Hill Gate. NT
Pierrot in Turquoise. Bowie received GBP. 4,—.
David Bowie and the Lindsay Kemp Mime Comp.

16-3-1968 German TV. ZDF. 4-3-2-1 Musik fur junge leute. Recorded 27-2-1968.

17-3-1968 Grantham, Cat Ballou. The Rats support act for The Jeff Beck Group.

Second half of March 1968 Bowie auditioned for the films Alain and Oh what a lovely war.

22-3-1968 Release Silly boy blue (3.06) / One minute woman - Billy Fury (Parlaphone 45681). A-side written by Bowie.

25-3-1968 Palmers Green (London), Intimate Theatre. Dress rehearsal. David Bowie and the Lindsay Kemp Mime Comp.

<u>26-3-1968</u> Palmers Green (London), Intimate Theatre. NT
Pierrot in Turquoise. Bowie received GBP 7,10.
David Bowie and the Lindsay Kemp Mime Comp.

<u>27-3-1968</u> Palmers Green (London), Intimate Theatre. NT
Pierrot in Turquoise. Bowie received GBP 7,10.
David Bowie and the Lindsay Kemp Mime Comp.

<u>28-3-1968</u> Palmers Green (London), Intimate Theatre. NT
Pierrot in Turquoise. Bowie received GBP 7,10.
David Bowie and the Lindsay Kemp Mime Comp.

<u>29-3-1968</u> Palmers Green (London), Intimate Theatre. NT
Pierrot in Turquoise. Bowie received GBP 7,10.
David Bowie and the Lindsay Kemp Mime Comp.

<u>30-3-1968</u> Palmers Green (London), Intimate Theatre. NT
Pierrot in Turquoise. Bowie received GBP 7,10.
David Bowie and the Lindsay Kemp Mime Comp.

April 1968 Release Deborah / Child star - Tyrannosaurus Rex (Regal Zonophone 3008). Rumoured Bowie did the handclaps on the A-side (there is no proof, could have been anyone. Probably just a rumour, spread when the song was re-released in the 80's, to influence the sales).

DATE / EVENT	AUDIO / VIDEO	TITLE

The name Tyrannosaurus Rex was taken from Ray Bradbury's short story A Sound Of Thunder (included in his 1952 collection R Is For Rocket).

5-4-1968 Bowie and Gunther Schneider went to see Cabaret at the Palace Theatre, Cambridge Circus. Based on Berlin Diaries (written by Christopher Isherwood). Starring Judy Dench. The stark white light was used by Bowie for his 1976 tour. Afterwards they had dinner at the Via Maria in Blandford Street.

10-4-1968 Decca Studio in West Hampstead. They completed the master tapes of In the heat of the morning and London bye ta ta (recorded 12-3-1968).

27-4-1968 Recording of Everything is you (2.22) by The Beatstalkers (Bowie and Tony Head did the backing vocals, they both received GBP. 9,—). Song written by Bowie. Released 21-6-1968.

Begin May 1968 Bowie had a meeting with Marylin Fox (of the BBC programme Jackanory).

Begin May 1968 Bowie had a meeting with Monica Sims (head of children's programmes at the BBC).

Date / Event	Audio / Video	Title
12-5-1968 London, Piccadilly 1 Studio, 201 Piccadilly. Recording Top Gear for BBC Radio 1 (247 m). Broadcast 26-5-1968 at 14.00 hours, repeated 20-6-1968. With the Tony Visconti Orchestra (14 musicians, including Herbie Flowers on bass, Barry Morgan on drums, probably John McLaughlin on guitar and some session musicians). Backing vocals: Steve Peregrin Took (T.Rex). Produced by Bernie Andrews. Engineers were Pete Ritzema and Alan Harris. 1. London bye ta ta (broadcast 26-5-1968 and 20-6-1968) (2.34). 2. In the heat of the morning (broadcast 26-5-1968 and 20-6-1968 (2.35). 3. Karma man (broadcast 26-5-1968 and 20-6-1968) (2.59). 4. When I'm five (broadcast 26-5-1968 and 20-6-1968) (3.03). 5. Silly boy blue (broadcast 20-6-1968) (4.36). When I'm five was used for the film Love you till Tuesday.	CD 3 CD CD CD CD 4 CD 1 CDR 1 CDR Single Tape	The rise and rise of Ziggy Stardust vol. 1 (song 4) (Savage Hippo Records) Bowie at the Beeb (1,2,3,5) Emerged from shadows (4) (EBD 001) Ziggy in Wonderland (2) (PROCD 89 001-2) Bowie at the Beeb, 8 track sampler (For demonstration only) (EMI) (2) The complete BBC master recordings (No label, no nr.) The complete BBC files vol. 1 (Old Gold Records OGCD 075) (4) Anthology (4) (BOW 1999) Te Amo Hasta Martes (4) quality 10, 15 min.

18-5-1968 Melody Maker. Advert for the concert on 3-6-1968 at The Royal Festival Hall.

19-5-1968 Covent Garden (London), Middle Earth Club. Try out for the concert in Royal Albert Fest. Hall (3-6-68). Charity event for Gandalf's Garden Benefit. From 15.30 to 23.00 hours. Tickets: 12/6. Advertised as 'David Bowie In Mime'. 20 Minute solo mime (Yet-San And The Eagle) to the soundtrack Silly Boy Blue. Other acts on the bill: John Peel, Tyrannosaurus Rex, Junior's Eyes, Ginger Johnson, Haps Hash and the   NT

DATE / EVENT	AUDIO / VIDEO	TITLE

Coloured Cast, Edgar Broughton Blues Band, Tibetan Mind, Christopher Logue, Exploding Galaxy, Mandala Jazz Group, Third Ear Band, Flame, Tyres, Tales of Justice.

20-5-1968 BBC 2 (Ch.33). Theatre 625, at 21.05 hours. The Pistolshot shown (first time). — Video

26-5-1968 Top Gear session broadcast at 14.00 hours. Recorded 12-5-1968.

30-5-1968 Bowie had another meeting with Ned Sherrin, to discuss a part in the film The Virgin Soldiers.

30-5-1968 BBC. Radio 1 (247 m). "Late night extra", broadcast at 22.00 hours. Interview. — NT

<u>3-6-1968</u> London, Royal Festival Hall. General Manager of the Hall was John Denison C.B.E.). Promoter: Blackhill Enterprises. Sang 1 song (Silly boy blue), combined with mime (Yet-San And The Eagle). Support-act for Marc Bolan and Tyrannosaures Rex. Roy Harper and Stefan Grossman (who opened the show) were also on the bill. Bowie received GBP 20,—. Presented by John Peel (he was drunk). An American thought it was not right Silly boy blue had an anti-communist theme. He stood up and shouted: "No politics" (A chronology - Kevin Cann 1983). — Tape — quality 10, 20 min.

4 To 6-6-1968 Bowie worked on a cabaret act. Songs he wrote (unavailable): Dat Dere, It's alright with me.

7-6-1968 Günter Schneider took David to see the musical Sweet Charity. Afterwards they discussed Bowie's appearance in two of his German TV shows later in the year (19-9-1968 and 11-11-1968).

14 To 27-6-1968 International Times. Article: Rex Set. About the concert in the Festival Hall at 3-6-1968. David Bowie, although one or two drags were heckling him, received the longest and loudest applause of all the performers, and he deserved it. It was a pity that he didn't have a longer set. Advert: David Bowie needs acoustic guitarist good singing / speaking for exciting project, must be alive. 460-6489.

17-6-1968 Bowie auditioned for the musical Hair.

20-6-1968 Top Gear session repeated. Recorded 12-5-1968.

21-6-1968 Released Rain coloured roses / Everything is you (2.22) - Beatstalkers (CBS 3557). B-side written by Bowie. He also did the backing vocals.

23-6-1968 David had to do a second audition for the musical Hair. After the second audition he was

DATE / EVENT	AUDIO / VIDEO	TITLE

turned down.

Ken Pitt: "Those were warm summer days and he derived comfort from leaving off his clothes, sometimes sitting cross-legged on the floor encircled by blaring hi-fi speakers, sometimes just loping around the flat, naked, his long, weighty penis swaying from side to side like the pendulum of a grandfather clock" (The Pitt report - Kenneth Pitt 1983).

12-7-1968 A costume fitting for the film The Virgin Soldiers at theatrical costumier Bermans.

15-7-1968 Mayfair Gymnasium, Paddington Street, London. Rehearsal for film the Virgin Soldiers.

16-7-1968 Twickenham Film Studios. Test for the film the Virgin Soldiers. Bowie was offered a very small role. When you look at the film, don't blink your eyes or you'll miss his appearance.

August 1968 He moved to 22 Clareville Grove, Chelsea (South Kensington), where he shared an attic room with Hermione Farthingale. Hutch visited them very frequently.

<u>1-8-1968</u> London, Marquee Club.　　　　　　　　　NT
Solo performance, 20 min.
Support for The Groop and The Beatstalkers.

<u>August 1968</u> Kenneth Pitt's office. Audition for Sidney　NT
Rose with cabaret act.

<u>August 1968</u> London, Astor Club, Audition for cabaret act　NT
for Harry Dawson and Michael Black. Act took 27 min.
Love you till Tuesday, Life is a circus (When the circus left town), The laughing gnome, When I'm five, When I'm sixty-four (Beatles), Yellow submarine (Beatles, 1966), a poem by Roger McGough called At lunchtime - a story of love, All you need is love (Beatles, 1967), When I live my dream, Even a fool learns to love.
Other songs used during his rehearsals: Can't get used to losing you (Andy Williams, 1963), Goin' back (Dusty Springfield, 1966), The joker (Randy Newman), On the other side of the tracks (Bobby Hebb, 1966), Sunny (Bobby Hebb, 1966), Trains and boats and planes (Burt Bacharach, 1965), What kind of fool am I? (Anthony Newley).
Harry Dawson: "Ken, it's a marvellous act but it's too good." That was the end of cabaret (In other words - Kerry Juby 1986).

August 1968 Bowie formed Turquoise. They performed only once, 14-9-1968 at the Roundhouse. David Bowie (vocals, acoustic guitar and mime). Tony Hill (acoustic guitar, vocals). Hermione Farthingale (acoustic guitar, vocals and mime). Tony Hill came from the group 'The Misunderstood'. On 14 September 1968 he left Turquoise and joined 'High Tide' (a group that David was later to support).

September 1968 Inspired by Stanley Kubrick's movie 2001: A Space Odyssey, Bowie writes Space

DATE / EVENT	AUDIO / VIDEO	TITLE

Oddity. A lot of musicians went to see the movie. The Rolling Stones had seen the film on 16-5-1968 (Stone alone - Bill Wyman and Ray Coleman 1990).

5-9-1968 Günter Schneider (the producer of Musik fur junge leute) suggested Ken Pitt to make a half our special. The idea for the promo-film Love you till Tuesday was born.

14-9-1968 Melody Maker. Advert for the concert on 14-9-1968 at The Roundhouse.

14-9-1968 London, The Roundhouse.   NT
Turquoise.
Played at midnight a 30 min. set. Received GBP. 15,—.
First and last performance with Tony Hill (replaced by John Hutchinson).
Benefit concert (promoted by Peter Jenner + Andrew King of Blackhill Enterprises). Started at 21.30 hours and went on till dawn. In aid of the Neighbourhood service (free legal advice, housing advice, provide adventure playgrounds).
Other acts on the bill: Scaffold, Pete Brown and his Battered Ornaments, Ron Geesin, Terry Reid's Fantasia, Junior's Eyes, Principal Edwards's Magic Theatre, Spider and the Stable, Pete Drummond, Geth Semane, Moonlight & Sun.

15-9-1968 Covent Garden (London), Middle Earth Club.   NT
Feathers.
They shared the bill with Flame.
In the dressing room David met photographer Ray Stevenson for the first time. He was the only photographer that photographed Feather's appearances.

David Bowie (vocals, acoustic guitar).
John Hutchinson (acoustic guitar, vocals).
Hermione Farthingale (acoustic guitar, vocals).
Feathers shared the bill with Flame.
Backstage David met photographer Ray Stevenson (who made a lot of early photo's in 1968 and 1969).

Some of the songs they played:
A hundred years from today (Frank Sinatra / Doris Day).
(At) Lunchtime (a story of love) (Bowie).
Back to where you've never been (Bowie).
Ching-a-ling (Bowie).
Dans le port d'Amsterdam (Jaques Brel).
Lady midnight (Leonard Cohen, 1969).
Life is a circus (Djin).
Love song (Leslie Duncan, 1969).
Next (Jaques Brel).
Sell me a coat (Bowie).

DATE / EVENT	AUDIO / VIDEO	TITLE

Space oddity (Bowie).
When I'm five (Bowie).

<u>16-9-1968</u> London, Wigmore Hall.   NT
Feathers.
Support act for The Strawbs.
Tony Hill's last gig.

<u>19-9-1968</u> German TV. ZDF 4-3-2-1- Musik fur junge   Video   quality 10
leute.
Love you till Tuesday (with parts in German).
When I live my dream (the last 8 lines in German).
He received GBP 140,—.
David had flown with Pitt to Hamburg. They stayed at the
Hotel Eggers, Rahlstedterstrasse 78 (close to the ZDF
studio).

26-9-1968 Bowie and Pitt arrived in London.

Autumn 1968 Lindsay Kemp offered Bowie a role in Pussin Boots (Bowie turned it down).

8-10-1968 Bowie and Pitt had a meeting with Malcolm J. Thomson, discussing the making of a promotional film.

24-10-1968 Recorded by Feathers (never released): Back to where you've never been. Trident Studios in Wardour Street (Soho).

29-10-1968 to 4-11-1968 Filming "The virgin soldiers"   *Video*   *Stolp Tapes no. 1 (1 min)*
(small part for Bowie). He received his short back and
sides haircut. Afterwards Bowie was photographed by
Kenneth Pitt, wearing his uniform.

10-11-1968 Ken Pitt's birthday. He and David flew to Munich. They stayed at the Hotel Cristallo, Hirtenstrasse 20.

11-11-1968 German TV. ZDF. Fur Jeden Etwas Musik.   Video   quality 10
David sang 1 song, the rest was a mime piece to
Stravinsky's Circus Polka.
He received DM 2.566,— for the performance.

12-11-1968 Bowie and Pitt arrived in London and had another meeting with Malcolm J. Thomson to discuss the making of their film (financed by Pitt).

16-11-1968 Melody Maker. Advert for the concert in Hampstead on 17-11-1968. Advertised as Turquoise (not correct).

<u>17-11-1968</u> Hampstead (North-London), Country Club in   NT
Haverstock Hill (something like a garage behind a row of
shops).

DATE / EVENT	AUDIO / VIDEO	TITLE

Feathers. They earned GBP. 6,—.
Support act for Jon Hiseman's Colosseum.
Also on the bill: The Third Ear Band and Doris Henderson.
A few of the songs they played:
A hundred years from today (Frank Sinatra or D.Day).
Lady midnight (Leonard Cohen).
Life is a circus (Djin).
Next (Jaques Brel).
(Port of) Amsterdam (Jaques Brel).
Ching-a-ling.
When I'm five.

27-11-1968 Recording Ching-a-ling - Feathers (2.41). Mixed and finished on 4-12-1968. Trident Studios, Soho.

Late 1968 Ray Stevenson did a photo shoot with Marc Bolan and Steve Took (Tyrannausorus Rex) in the garden of Hermione Farthingale's family home.
Tony Visconti: "I set it up, but they never even spoke to David or thanked Hermione for the use of her parents' garden. The rivalry was always there."

5-12-1968 Birmingham, Art Lab.
Cancelled.

<u>6-12-1968</u> London, Drury Lane Arts Lab (run by Jim   NT
Haines, who lived in the back and Jack Henry Moore).
Feathers. They performed for free.

<u>7-12-1968</u> Brighton, Sussex University in Falmer.   NT
Feathers. They earned GBP. 50,—.

11-12-1968 The Times. Article by Sheila More: The Restless Generation: 2 (the second in a 3-part series, in which she looks at the philosophy of the pop world). David Bowie: "My father tries so hard. But his upbringing was so different that we can't communicate. He and all his friends were in the army during the war, an experience I can't imagine, and he takes naturally to iron discipline. Discussing religion embarrasses him, and to get emotional about something, well that's only fit for the servants quarters, like mental illness."

14-12-1968 Birmingham, Arts Lab (Moseley Balsall Heath Institute).
Cancelled.

24-12-1968 UK TV. BBC 2. The Pistol Shot repeated.

<u>24-12-1968</u> Falmouth, Magician's Workshop (Cornwall).   NT
20 Minute solo performance (he earned GBP. 25,—).
Support for Steve Miller Band.

Christmas 1968 at the house of Gerry Gill at Higher Broad Lane in Poole (near Redruth).

DATE / EVENT	AUDIO / VIDEO	TITLE

<u>26-12-1968</u> Falmouth, Magician's Workshop (Cornwall).   NT
20 Minute solo performance (he earned GBP. 25,—).
Support for Keef Hartley.

1969 Major Tom. A German promo film. Bowie's part was recorded in 30 minutes. Suzanna Mereen and Samantha Bond co-starred.

1969 Music Now! Interview by Kate Simpson.

January 1969 Book published: Against interpretation - Susan Sontag (Laurel Edition 0083). Includes the article: Notes on camp (published in 1964, in the magazine Partisan Review). The book is reprinted in 1994 by Vintage Books.

<u>4-1-1969</u> London, Round House.   NT
Feathers (support for the Who and Scaffold).
First time Angie saw David.
At that time Angie was working at a travel agency.
There were only 2 employees. The other one was a girl
called Dinxie.
Angie: "It was rough at times. On one occasion I found a
body outside. I called the police and was then told that I was
not required to work there any longer" (In other words -
Kerry Juby 1986).

10-1-1969 Pitt paid an advance of GBP 2.650,— to Thomson (budget was GBP 7.500,—).

11-1-1969 Released Little boy / When I'm five (3.00) - The Beatstalkers (CBS 3936). B-side written by Bowie.

13-1-1969 Bowie had a meeting with Timothy Hest at the Dance Centre, to discuss following 6 or 7 movement lessons.

22-1-1969 Films LUV TV-commercial for Lyons Maid (30 seconds). Made by Ridley Scott. David earned 25 Guineas. Filmed at 7 Eccleston Square, London. Luv Luv Luv. Let me give it all to you. Let me know that some day. You'll do the same for me. Luv Luv Luv.	*Video* *Video*	*Stolp Tapes no. 1 (1 min)* *Various 26 (20 sec.)*

During this time Bowie also worked now and then in a lithography firm near Russell Square.

26-1 to 7-2-1969 Hampstead Heat. Filming for "Love you till Tuesday." Bowie wore a wig. The steel-grey suit was from Just Men by Nikki. Chrsitie's auctioned auctioned the suit 8-9-1994.	*Video*	*Various 10*
29-1-1969 Trident Studios. Recording When I live my dream (German) (3.51), Love you till Tuesday (German) (3.06). Lyrics translated by Lisa Busch.	*CD*	*TV Rebel (NICO SDRM 671288)*

DATE / EVENT	AUDIO / VIDEO	TITLE

1-2-1969 Clarence Studios in Greenwich. Recording Ching-a-ling (2.02) and Sell me a coat (2.53) for the Love you till Tuesday film. — ***Video*** — ***Various 10***

2-2-1969 Morgan Studios, 169 High Road, Willesden. Recording song "Space oddity" (5.07) (first time full-version recorded). The silver lurex suit David wore was supplied by Calvin Mark Lee (who worked in a boutique). Bowie vocals, John Hutchinson guitar, Dave Clegg bass guitar, Tat Meager drums, Colin Wood organ and mellotron. Produced by Jonathan Weston.

3-2-1969 Clarence Studios in Greenwich. Filming of Rubber band and Love you till Tuesday. — *Video* / Video — *Various 10* / The video archives 1964-1976

4-2-1969 Clarence Studios in Greenwich. Filming of Let met sleep beside you and When I live my dream (3.20). — *Video* / Video — *Various 10* / The video archives 1964-1976

5-2-1969 Clarence Studios in Greenwich. Filming of The Mask (pantomime) (5.03). — *Video* / Video — *Various 10* / The video archives 1964-1976

6-2-1969 Clarence Studios in Greenwich. Filming Video clip for Space Oddity by Thomson. — *Video* / Video — *Various 10* / The video archives 1964-1976

7-2-1969 Clarence Studios in Greenwich. Filming of When I'm five. — *Video* / Video — *Various 10* / The video archives 1964-1976

Around 8-2-1969 Hermione Farthingale was doing a film called Song of Norway. She did a ballet in the film and fell in love with another player. She left David (who was heart broken).

<u>11-2-1969</u> Brighton (Sussex), Sussex University. Feathers without Hermione. — NT

<u>15-2-1969</u> Birmingham, Town Hall. Support for Tyrannosaurus Rex with a solo mime called: Yet-San and the Eagle. The 6-day Tyrannosaurus Rex tour was called: For the lion and the unicorn in the oak forest of faun tour. — NT

<u>17-2-1969</u> Croydon, Fairfields Halls. Support for Tyrannosaurus Rex with a solo mime called: Yet-San and the Eagle. — NT

20-2-1969 Bowie auditioned for musical "Hair." Despite the fact he also auditioned 2 times in June 1968 the producers recalled him.
He and Dana Gillespie (who was hanging around with a band called Ashton Gardner and Dayke) were both turned down.
A few months after the auditioning David and Angie went to see Dana Gillespie in the play Catch my soul. Afterwards Bowie introduced Dana Gillespie to Tony DeFries (interview Dana Gillespie for The Voyeur).

DATE / EVENT	AUDIO / VIDEO	TITLE
<u>22-2-1969</u> Clairville Grove. Demo taped in David's bedroom. 1. Space oddity (5.30). 2. Letter to Hermione (3.16). 3. Love song (original by Lesley Duncan) (5.45). 4. When I'm five (2.53). 5. Life is a circus (4.06). 6. Janine (4.22). 7. An occasional dream (2.45). 8. Conversation piece (3.27). 9. Ching-a-ling (3.01). 10. Lover to the dawn (4.48).	CD	*The Beckenham oddity (9 songs) (MDCD 010)*
	CD	The Beckenham oddity (Early Years 02-CD-3318)
	CD	*A letter to Hermione (9 songs) (Flashback World Productions Flash 08.89.0105)*
	CD	Outta space (9 songs) (World Productions of Compact Music WPOCM 00490D049-2)
	CD	Ching-a-ling (Spinkx Records SXCD 009)
	CD	The best of David Bowie (Dixie Live DLCD 4057)
	CD	Sussex University Live 1969 (Black Panther ABP-032)
	CD	Greatest hits live (Alpha Record AR7104)
	CD	Anthology (3) (BOW 1999)
	CD	Rec. live at Sussex (9 songs) (DV More Records M.T.T. 10.11)
	CD	The duke (9 songs) (Never End ACT*7)
	CD	Life is a circus (10 songs) (CD/003)
	CD	Ultra Rare Trax Vol.1 (The Genuine Pig TGP-CD-108) (1, 4,6,8)
	CD	A semi-acoustic love affair
	LP	The Beckenham oddity (Leisure Records 005 A/B)
	LP	Letter to Hermione (Flashback World Productions Flash 08.89.0105 - 33 A/B)
<u>22-2-1969</u> Manchester, Free Trade Hall. Attendance: 2.529. Support for Tyrannosaurus Rex with a solo mime called: Yet-San and the Eagle. According to Bowie fan Geoff Ward, the background music during the mime was very loud. Marc Bolan joined Bowie for Space Oddity. Marc Bolan: "David opened wearing a blouse and ballet pumps, and acted out a twenty-minute piece about Chinese troops' rape of Tibet. The first couple of minutes weren't easy. I mean, it was "What a poof," you know?" (Loving the alien - Christopher Sandford 1996).	NT	

DATE / EVENT	AUDIO / VIDEO	TITLE

<u>23-2-1969</u> Bristol, Colston Hall.
Attendance: 2.121.
Support for Tyrannosaurus Rex with a solo mime
called: Yet-San and the Eagle.

NT

28-2-1969 The producers of the musical Hair recalled Bowie to do a fourth audition. And again they turned him down.

March 1969 Bowie moved in with Mary Finnigan at 24 Fox Grove Road, Beckenham, Kent. He was introduced to her by her neighbours (the flat above) Barry and Christina Jackson. Barry had been to school with David and George Underwood.
Mary Finnigan heard him play his guitar in the flat above when she was sunbathing in her garden. She asked everybody to come down for coffee, which they drank in the sunshine. One of the things Bowie brought with him was a 12-string guitar (a present from Pete Townsend). The whole flat, and garden, within a very short space of time, was wired for sound (Dutch Fanzine The Voyeur, September 2001. The David Bowie Story by M. Finnigan).
Bowie was working at Legastat in London (a photocopying office) (In other words - Kerry Juby 1986). They used to smoke a lot of marijuana during the time they lived together. John Paul Jones (Led Zeppelin) had introduced him to smoking marijuana (In his own words - Miles 1980).

March 1969 Pitt played a demo of Space oddity to Atlantic Records (they turned it down).

<u>1-3-1969</u> Liverpool, Philharmonic Hall, Hope Street.
Support for Tyrannosaurus Rex with a solo mime
called: Yet-San and the Eagle. The other support act was an
Australian sitar player called Vytas Serelis. Somebody
called him "One of the rarest of God's creatures."

NT

3-3-1969 Bowie and Pitt went to the Criterion to see the one-man play Brief Lives (played by Roy Dotrice), based on the diaries of John Aubrey.

<u>8-3-1969</u> Brighton, Brighton Dome.
Attendance: 2.100.
Support for Tyrannosaurus Rex with a solo mime
called: Yet-San and the Eagle.

NT

<u>11-3-1969</u> London, University of Surrey.
Guildford Arts Festival.
Feathers (duo with Hutch). They earned GBP. 35,—.
Bowie announced John Hutchinson: "This is Hutch. He is
my friend. I found him in the classified ads in Time Out,
under macrobiotics."

NT

<u>14-3-1969</u> Guildford, Town Hall.
Feathers (duo with Hutch).

NT

<u>16-3-1969</u> Lincoln, Assembly Rooms.
Feathers (duo with Hutch).

NT

DATE / EVENT	AUDIO / VIDEO	TITLE

24-3-1969 Bowie did a rehearsal for Michael Armstrong's film The Dark. He took home the script and didn't like it.

9-4-1969 Bowie phoned to the owner of Sir Christopher Wren pub, near St. Paul's Cathedral, to discuss the start of Contemporary Folk evenings on Tuesdays.

9-4-1969 Bowie meets Mary Angela Barnett at the Speakeasy Club, Margaret Street, London at a King Crimson press reception (led by Robert Fripp). Support act for King Crimson was Donovan. They had dinner at Jaspers in Sloane Square.
A few days later she moved in with David and Mary Finnigan in at 24 Foxgrove Road in Beckenham. Their phone number: 01-6503432.
David and Angie were perfectly honest to each other. She told him she was dispelled from school for a lesbian relation with a girl called Lorraine.
Soon she found out David fucked a lot of girls. Within a week Angie also slept with Mary Finnigan (David Bowie - Jerry Hopkins 1985 and Backstage passes - Angela Bowie and Patrick Carr 1993). Angela also played a few times conferencier in the Folk Club. Angie and Mary did handclaps for the recording of Space oddity. Later Mary Finnigan found a song or poem in David's room called "Beautiful Angie" (never published) (In other words - Kerry Juby 1986).
Angela: "He was a right stud. A stallion. He could poke a hole in the wall (Stardust - Henry Edwards and Tony Zanetta 1986).

Bowie in an interview to Playboy: "Angela and I knew each other because we were both going out with the same man. Another one of her boyfriends, a talent scout for Mercury Records, took her to a show, where I happened to be playing. He hated me. She thought I was great. Ultimately she threatened to leave him if he didn't sign me. So he signed me. I married Angela and we both continued to see the mutual friend."

14-4-1969 Pitt gave Simon Hayes (Mercury) a private screening of the film Love you till Tuesday.

<u>29-4-1969</u> Ealing, College of Technology. NT
Lunchtime Show.

April / May 1969 Bowie and John Hutchinson made an audition tape at Mercury's Knight Bridge (9 songs). Calvin Mark Lee dispatched the tape to Mercury's office in New York.

April / May 1969 Hermione started writing David again. Later (begin 2000) when Bowie read his old letters, he realised that they could have come together again, if he had approached her again.

<u>4-5-1969</u> Beckenham, The Three Tuns Public House NT
(the oak panelled dining room). Attendance: 25.
David sang and played tapes when he wasn't performing live. The opening night was attended by a band called Comus (led by Roger Wootton). They would become, more or less, the Arts Lab resident band.
In the early days The Three Tuns was called 'The Pig & Spoke. In 2003 it is known as 'The Rat & Parrott and can be found at: 157 High Street, Beckenham, Kent BR3 1AE. Chas Lippeatt handled the Art Lab PA system and film unit.

DATE / EVENT	AUDIO / VIDEO	TITLE

He used to tape record the evening music for a free lending library sponsored by the Arts Lab, so somewhere there must be original tapes of these events!
Roger Wootton: "He wasn't particularly impressive live, the audience weren't particularly impressed with him. The club itself was mainly hippies. There were lots of drugs around and the Three Tuns used to stink of dope every week" (In other words - Kerry Juby 1986).

<u>6-5-1969</u> Hampstead, Three Horseshoes.   NT
Lunchtime Show.

9-5-1969 Bowie went to see Alan Folnander at 61 Kinnerton Street, to discuss a Rowntree Kit-Kat commercial.

<u>9-5-1969</u> Hampstead, Three Horseshoes.   NT

10-5-1969 UK TV. BBC 2. Colour me Pop.   Video
London, Hounslow, The White Bear Public House.
Together with Tony Visconti.
Guest appearance with the Strawbs. David mimed to one of their songs 'Poor Jimmy Wilson'.
Broadcast 14-6-1969 at 22.55 hour.

<u>11-5-1969</u> Beckenham, The Three Tuns Public House.   NT
Attended by 50 people.
George Underwood designed the poster.
Regular performers at the "Arts Lab": Steve Harley, Ricki Sylvan, Mick Ronson, Keith Christmas, Tony Visconti, Tucker Zimmerman, Dave Cousin, Ron Geeson, Bridget St. John, poetry by Lionel Bart, Peter Frampton, Strawbs. On a couple of evenings Chime Rimpoche came down to give talks on Buddhism.

<u>18-5-1969</u> Beckenham, The Three Tuns Public House.   NT
Attended by 90 people.

<u>22-5-1969</u> London, Wigmore Hall.   NT
Support act: Tim Hollier (an Arts Lab regular).

<u>25-5-1969</u> Beckenham, The Three Tuns Public House.   NT
Attended by 120 people.
Guest appearance by Tuck Zimmerman (Bob Dylan's cousin).

June 1969 Rolf Vasellari, Dorfstrasse 44, Basle started the Swiss David Bowie Fan Club.

<u>1-6-1969</u> Beckenham, The Three Tuns Public House.   NT

DATE / EVENT	AUDIO / VIDEO	TITLE

8-6-1969 Record Retailer. Advert for Bowie's first album. Management: Kenneth Pitt Management Limited, 35 Curzon Street, London, W.1 Tel: 01-499-7905/6.

10-6-1969 Disc and Music Echo. Article: Hear David Bowie - he's something new.

14-6-1969 UK TV. BBC 2. Colour me Pop.
Recorded 10-5-1969.

<u>15-6-1969</u> London, Marquee Club.   NT

Mary Finnigan: "David used to get drunk and on many occasions I had to pick him up and carry him home from London, absolutely pissed out of his brain. He drank barley wine which is quite strong stuff and he'd smoke a few joints as well" (In other words - Kerry Juby 1986).

20-6-1969 Bowie signed for Mercury (in July Philips took over Mercury). An advance of GBP 1.250,— for an album. The contract had arrived from Chicago on 16-6-1969.

20-6-1969 Trident Studios in Soho. Recording: Space oddity (Full length 5.14, edited 4.33), Wild eyed boy from Freecloud (4.48 and 4.57).
Producer Gus Dudgeon. Paul Buckmaster played strings and flutes. Tony Cox (from the folk group Pentangle) on drums, Rick Wakeman on mellotron and Herbie Flowers on bass (it was his first professional session and he was paid GBP 7,10).
Gus Dudgeon: "When I listened to the demo of Major Tom I thought it was incredible. I couldn't believe that Tony Visconti didn't want to do it" (Changes - Chris Welch 1999).
In later years Gus Dudgeon would complain he never got paid the agreed GBP. 100,— for his work.
Ken Pitt about Space oddity: "The technicians stopped whatever they were doing and stood to listen. Minutes after David finished the song they were all humming it" (The Pitt Report - Kenneth Pitt 1983).
Tony Visconti: "The people at Deram said to me "We've got this young man David Bowie and no one quite knows what to do with him. You seem to be the expert on weird people. We'd like you to meet him.""

July 1969 International Times. David interviewed by Mary Finnigan. Bowie: "Part of my motivation in doing a hit parade number is to promote the arts lab along with it, but without elitist attitudes."

5-7-1969 Hyde Park. Rolling Stones free concert. The single Space oddity was played to 250.000 people.

11-7-1969 Release in US: Space oddity (3.26) / Wild eyed boy from Freecloud (without the first verse) (3.14) (Philips BF 1801).
11-7-1969 Release in UK: Space oddity (4.33) / Wild eyed boy from Freecloud (4.48).
11-7-1969 Release in Europe: Space oddity (4.33) / Wild eyed boy from Freecloud (with additional spoken intro) (4.57) (Philips 1801).
The single becomes a number 5 hit in the UK charts in November 1969.

Bowie about Space oddity: "Home for David Bowie and Major Tom is the world we inhabit. What we want to know is what our heroes have for breakfast. Major Tom is a loser, he's nothing if not a human being. We drew this parallel that the public image of a spaceman at work is of an automat on. I know astronauts were like that, they had to be like that" (David Robert Jones: The discography of a generalist - David Jeffrey Fletcher 1979).

DATE / EVENT	AUDIO / VIDEO	TITLE

In 1993 Bowie commented on Wild eyed boy from Freecloud: "Things and songs seemed to mean more to me than people. This feeling of isolation I've had ever since I was a kid was really starting to manifest itself through songs like that" (3 Part BBC Radio 1 documentary).

<u>15-7-1969</u> Hounslow, White Bear Public House.   NT

16-7-1969 Begin recording Album Space oddity at Trident Studios. First session fro 14.oo to 17.00 h. Second session from 19.00 h. to 24.00 h.

<u>18-6-1969</u> Beckenham, The Three Tuns Public House.   NT

<u>24-7-1969</u> Malta, Song Festival at the Hilton Hotel   NT
in Sliema (Valetta), organised by John B. Cassar.
Bowie and Pitt had Hotel room 142.
When I live my dream (sang to an orchestral accompaniment by Norrie Paramor, made up by musicians from the British Army, The United States Navy and the Spanish embassy).
Bowie was voted second after the Spanish entrant Christina. Patricia Paay (a Dutch singer who was also there for the festival) said 27-7-2002 on Dutch TV she had "something" with David during the festival.
Bowie wore the same steel-grey suit as used for the Love you till Tuesday film shoot in January 1969. Only the jacket was re-cut. The suit was auctioned at Christie's 8-9-1994.

<u>Between 24 and 30-7-1969</u> Bowie gave an impromptu   NT
solo performance aboard of the USS Saratoga for the
crew of the ship whilst in port. Every singer of the Maltese
Festival contributed one or more songs.

30-7-1969 All the contenders of the Song Festival flew to Rome and then had a six hour drive to the Hotel Reale.

<u>31-7-1969</u> Pistoria, Monsummano-Terme, Theatro Premio.   NT
Italian Song Festival, called Carosello Internazionale Del Disco. He performed When I live my dream and they presented him with a prize for the Best Produced Record. Malcolm Carr (a London businessman) passed by Bowie, Angela and a topless teenage girl in the corridor that night (Loving the alien - Christopher Sandford 1996).
The next morning Angela came down the stairs, while she wore a diaphanous, full-length, see-trough dress, so transparent that one immediately saw that she wore beneath it the briefest of panties and nothing else (The Pitt Report - Kenneth Pitt 1983).

July / August 1969 Disc. Article by Penny Valentine: David Bowie-amazing sound!

DATE / EVENT	AUDIO / VIDEO	TITLE

She wrote about Space oddity: "I have a bet on in the office that this is going to be a huge hit. David Bowie has always been talented but had a nasty knack of sounding like Tony Newley. Mr. Bowie now sounds like the Bee Gees in their best record - New York Mining Disaster."

3-8-1969 Returned home after the song festivals.

3-8-1969 Beckenham, The Three Tuns Public House.   NT
During the evening Mary Finnigan told him: "Oh, by the way, while you were away I had a message, your father is not very well." Bowie went ashen and screamed: "Why didn't you tell me earlier?"
He finished his set and rushed to his father.
It was the last time he saw his father alive.
Mrs. Margaret Jones: "David handed the statuette to his father. His father told him he knew he would succeed in the end. He died not long afterwards" (In other words - Kerry Juby 1986).

5-8-1969 Haywood Stenton Jones dies from lobar pneumonia.

7-8-1969 David informed the Bromley and Christlehurst Registry Office of his father's dead. He also handled the funeral arrangements.

11-8-1969 Haywood Stenton Jones buried at Elmers End Cemetery.

Some time during the second half of 1969 Bowie and Finnigan edited a weekly newsletter called "Growth."
In the issue of 16-8-1969 they wrote: Growth is people, Growth is revolution, Growth grows at its own speed, expands according to the energy input it receives, is open to all, but closed to old ideas, cliches, destructive elements and grey thoughts.

16-8-1969 Beckenham, Growth Summer Festival at   NT
Croydon Road, Beckenham Recreational Ground.
Attendance: 5.000. Entrance was free.
Space oddity was done in a reggae version (Backstage passes - Angela Bowie and Patrick Carr 1993).
He also sang Buzz the fuzz (Biff Rose, 1968), I feel free (Cream, 1966).
Bowie was in a very bad mood and insulted various people, who worked voluntarily at the festival.
Other performers: Juniors Eyes, Gas Works, Strawbs, Miscarriage, Keith Christmas, Amory Kane, Bridget St. John, Tony Visconti, John Peel.

John Peel about Bowie: "Not a joke exactly but a chap who was full of extraordinary ideas and notions, none of which seemed very likely to ever come to fruition."

22-8-1969 Wolverhampton, Catacombes Club.   NT
Matinee. 20-Minute performance, received GBP. 20,—.

DATE / EVENT	AUDIO / VIDEO	TITLE

<u>22-8-1969</u> Wolverhampton, Catacombes Club.　　　NT
Evening. 20-Minute performance, received GBP. 20,—.

23-8-1969 Bowie and Pitt flew to Amsterdam, where they were met by Jan Corduwener, who took them to the Hotel Ardina, Keizersgracht 268 in Amsterdam.

23-8-1969 Interview by Jojanneke Claassen for the newspaper "Het Parool." Appeared in the newspaper of 30-8-1969.
In the evening Bowie, Pitt and Jojanneke Claassen went to a club called Napoleon. After some time they first walked back to the hotel, but David and Jojanneke returned to the Napoleon.

24-8-1969 Interviews for "Radio Hilversum" and for "Radio Veronica."

25-8-1969 Dutch TV. Doebidoe. Playback Space oddity.　　Video
Broadcast on 30-8-1969.

27-8-1969 Kenneth Pitt flew back to London. David and Calvin Mark Lee decided to stay one day longer.

<u>28-8-1969</u> BBC. Radio1 Club. Recorded at the Leas Cliff　　Tape
Hall in Folkestone.
Broadcast 1-9-1969.

30-8-1969 Het Parool. Article by Jojanneke Claassen: David Bowie's grote liefde is zijn Arts Lab (Bowie's big love is his Arts Lab).

September 1969. Melody Maker. Article by Chris Welch (about the Arts lab).

<u>13-9-1969</u> Bromley, Library Gardens.　　　NT
Bromley's first ever open-air pop concert. Four-hour event
organised by Ravensbourne College of Art student
Geoffrey Bradbury.
Attendance: 1.000.

September / October 1969 David used his father's Fiat 500 for some months. After a row with his aunt Pat he returned the car to his mother.

October 1969 Bowie and Angela went to live in Flat 7, 42 Southend Road, Beckenham (Haddon Hall). The rent was GBP 7,— a week.

October 1969 German TV. Music fur junge leute.　　Video
Taped in West-Berlin, presented by Günter Schneider

October 1969 The Virgin Soldiers shown in various British Cinemas.

<u>1-10-1969</u> Downham, Folk Club (inside The Bal Tabarin).　　NT
Open Air concert.

DATE / EVENT	AUDIO / VIDEO	TITLE

2-10-1969 UK TV. BBC. Top of the Pops.
Recorded in Lime Grove, Shepherds Bush (Studio G).
Johnny Stewart booked Bowie.
Bowie drove his mother to the studio, so she could be present during the recordings.
Space oddity (Broadcast on 9-10-1969 and 16-10-1969).
Between recordings he was interviewed by Penny Valentine for the 11 October edition of Disc.

Tape — quality 10, 4 min.
Video — quality 10, 4 min.

8-10-1969 Coventry, Coventry Theatre.
Support for Humble Pie. Received GBP 50,—.
Bowie was booked by Humble Pie manager Andrew Loog Oldham (former manager of the Rolling Stones).
Bowie played an acoustic set (20 min) and was booed by the Humble Pie fans.
Other support act: Dave Edmund's Love Sculpture.
Bowie stayed at the Leofric Hotel.

NT

9-10-1969 UK TV. BBC. Top of the Pops.
Space oddity (Recorded 2-10-1969).

Tape — quality 10, 4 min.
Video — quality 10, 4 min.

9-10-1969 Leeds, Town Hall. 20 Minutes.
Support for Humble Pie. Received GBP 50,—.
Bowie played an acoustic set.
Other support act: Dave Edmund's Love Sculpture.

NT

10-10-1969 Birmingham, Town Hall. 20 Minutes.
Attendance: 1.543.
Support for Humble Pie. Received GBP 50,—.
Bowie played an acoustic set.
Other support act: Dave Edmund's Love Sculpture.

NT

11-10-1969 Broadcasting House. Interview for BRT-radio by Ward Bogaert (he represented Belgium at the Maltese Song Festival in July). Broadcast 1-1-1970.

11-10-1969 Melody Maker. Article by Chris Welch: A mixture of Dali, 2001 and the Bee Gees. Bowie about the Arts Lab: "We started our lab a few months ago with poets and artists who just came along. It's got bigger and bigger and by now we have our own light and sculptures etc. And I never knew there were so many sitar players in Beckenham."

11-10-1969 Disc. Article by Penny Valentine. Interview, 2-10-1969 between recordings for Top of the Pops.
Valentine wrote: "David Bowie is 22 years old, thin, with a halo of fair hair, a delicately soft face and two odd eyes. One is pale kitten blue and the other green and it makes it rather disconcerting to talk to him. It is a gentle mixture of Bob Dylan and Donovan with 90% himself. He says he sings like Dylan would have done if he'd been born in England and he's an absolute charmer. His charm is so overpowering that it has given him more freedom to achieve his ideals than you would have thought in his day and age."
Bowie about the song Janine: "A bit hard to explain without sounding nasty. It was written about my

DATE / EVENT	AUDIO / VIDEO	TITLE

old mate George and is about a girl he used to go out with. It's how I thought he should see her."
About Wild eyed boy from Freecloud: "The boy lives on a mountain and has developed a beautiful way of life. He loves the mountain and the mountain loves him. I suppose in a way he's rather a prophet figure. The villagers disapprove of the things he has to say and they decide to hang him. He gives up to his fate, but the mountain tries to help him by killing the village. So in fact everything the boy says is taken the wrong way, both by those who fear him and those who love him, and try to assist."

<u>11-10-1969</u> Brighton, Brighton Dome. 20 Minutes.   NT
Attendance: 2.100.
Support for Humble Pie. Received GBP 50,—.
Bowie played an acoustic set.
Other support act: Dave Edmund's Love Sculpture.

<u>12-10-1969</u> Beckenham, The Three Tuns Public House.   NT
Ward Bogaert recorded David announcing Roger Kany, who then went on to read his poem about the sex life of traffic signs (The Pitt Report - Kenneth Pitt 1983).

<u>13-10-1969</u> Bristol, Colston Hall. 20 Minutes.   NT
Attendance: 2.121.
Support for Humble Pie. Received GBP 50,—.
Bowie played an acoustic set.
Other support act: Dave Edmund's Love Sculpture.

16-10-1969 UK TV. BBC. Top of the Pops.   Tape   quality 10, 4 min.
Space oddity (Recorded 2-10-1969)   Video   quality 10, 4 min.

<u>17-10-1969</u> Exeter, Tiffany's.   NT
Attendance: 1.000.
Support for Humble Pie. Received GBP 50,—.
Bowie played an acoustic set.
Other support act: Dave Edmund's Love Sculpture.

18-10-1969 Melody Maker. Article by D. Detheridge: Caught in the act.

<u>19-10-1969</u> Birmingham, Rebecca's Club.   NT
Support for Humble Pie. Received GBP 50,—.
Bowie played an acoustic set.
Other support act: Dave Edmund's Love Sculpture.

<u>20-10-1969</u> BBC Radio Session, Dave Lee Travis Show,   CD   *Kiss away the darkest*
Top Gear. Broadcast 26-10-1969.   *day / Liquor & Drugs*
Recorded at Studio 2, Aeolioan Hall, New Bond Street,   CD   *Liquor and drugs*
London.   CD   *The rise and rise of Ziggy*
David Bowie with Juniors Eyes.   *Stardust vol. 2 (songs 1,2,3,)*
1. Unwashed and somewhat slightly dazed (broadcast   *(Savage Hippo Records)*
26-10-1969) (3.54).   CD   *Chameleon Chronicles vol. 3*
2. Let me sleep beside you (not broadcast) (3.21).   *(1,2,3) (Living Legend*
3. Janine (not broadcast) (3.00).   *Records LLR-CD 050)*

DATE / EVENT	AUDIO / VIDEO	TITLE
4. Interview by Brian Mathew (1.28).	3 CD	Bowie at the Beeb (2,3)
	CD	Bowie at the Beeb, 8 track sampler (For demonstration only) (EMI) (2)
	CD	Ultra Rare Trax Vol.1 (The Genuine Pig TGP-CD-108) (1, 2)
	CD	Stardust memories (1,2,3) (Retropop 159081)
	CD	BBC Sessions 1969-1972 (2,4)
	CD	Outta Space (1,2,4) (World productions of compact music, WPOCM 00490d049-2)
	2 CD	God knows I'm good (3songs) (BEEB 1/2)
	CD	God knows I'm good (3songs) (Invasion Unlimited IU9753-1)
	CD	Ziggy in Wonderland (PROCD 89 001-2)
	CD	Kiss the vipers fang (3 songs) (EBD002)
	4 CDR	The complete BBC master recordings (No label, no nr.)
	1 CDR	The complete BBC files vol. 2 (Old Gold Records OGCD 076) (3 songs)
	CD	The Jean Genie (vol 1.) (1,2) (Ban-004-A)
	CD	Starman (1,2) (Oil Well RCS 0117 CD)
	CD	White light white heat (1,2) (The Swinging Pig Records TSP-CD-053)
	CD	At the Beep (1,2) (Archive Productions AP 89004)
	CD	Rebel rebel (1,2) (Oil Well RCS 021)
	CD	Live Vol. 1 (1,2) (Joker JOK-001-A)
	CD	Mega rare trax vol. 1 (1,2) (Seagull Records CD 022)
	CD	Ziggy in Wonderland (2) (PROCD 89 001-2)
	CD	Five years (1,2) (Triangle Records PYCD 047)
	CD	Kooks (1,2) (Turtle Records TR-36)
	CD	The London Tapes (1,2,3) (World productions of

DATE / EVENT	AUDIO / VIDEO	TITLE
		compact music WPOCM 0589 D 020-2)
	CD	Dynamic Live (1,2)
	CD	BBC Bowie (1,2)
	CD	The best of David Bowie (1,2)
	1 CDR	Battle for Bowie (2,3,4) (No label, no number)
	1 CDR	A London Show
	LP	White light white heat (1,2) (The Swinging Pig Records TSP 053A/B)
	LP	Kiss away the darkest day (Igor/Jonas Production A-8148)
	Single	Junior Eyes (SR 69) (1,2)

21-10-1969 London, Queen Elisabeth Hall. 20 Minutes.   NT
Support for Humble Pie. Received GBP 50,—.
Bowie played an acoustic set.
Other support act: Dave Edmund's Love Sculpture.

22-10-1969 Interview by Bill Gates for Radio 3XY Melbourne.

23-10-1969 Edinburgh, Usher Hall. 20 Minutes.   NT
Support for Herman's Hermits and the Troggs.
Bowie played an acoustic set.
John Cambridge: "After a few drinks, he told me that, for a whole week, his phone had rung at the same time every afternoon. When he answered it, there was no one there. He was convinced it was his father, calling him from the beyond" (Loving the alien - Christopher Sandford 1996).

24-10-1969 Sunderland, Empire. 20 Minutes.   NT
Support for Herman's Hermits and the Troggs.
Bowie played an acoustic set.

25-10-1969 Manchester, Odeon Theatre. 20 Minutes.   NT
Support for Herman's Hermits and the Troggs.
Bowie played an acoustic set.

25-10-1969 Disc & Music Echo. Article about LP David Bowie (Space oddity).

26-10-1969 Liverpool, Empire Theatre. 20 Minutes.   NT
Attendance: 2.550.
Support for Herman's Hermits and the Troggs.
Bowie played an acoustic set.

26-10-1969 Broadcast the Dave Lee Travis Show, recorded 20-10-1969.

28-10-1969 Bowie and Pitt flew to West Berlin. They stayed at the Plaza Hotel, Kurfurstendamm. After

DATE / EVENT	AUDIO / VIDEO	TITLE

dinner they went to a few clubs.

29-10-1969 German-TV, 4-3-2-1 Musik fur junge leute. Recorded in West Berlin. Broadcast 22-11-1969. Space oddity (play back).

November 1969 Bowie auditioned for Sunday, bloody Sunday.

2-11-1969 Bowie and Pitt flew to Switzerland, where they stayed for two night at the Hotel Exelcior, Dufourstrasse 24, Zurich (room 37).

2-11-1969 Swiss TV. Hits a go go.   Video
Produced by Mani Hildebrand (who represented
Switzerland at the Maltese Song Festival in July 1969).
Space oddity (play back).

4-11-1969 Bowie and Pitt were flying home from Zurich.
Bowie: "One of the engines is on fire."
Pitt: "So it is," and returned to the book he was reading (The Pitt Report - Kenneth Pitt 1983).

4-11-1969 Release LP David Bowie (Space oddity) (Mercury-Philips SBL 7912).
With different tracks than the first release. The UK release has a version of Unwashed and somewhat slightly dazed, closing with Don't sit down.

Penny Valentine wrote in Disc: "David Bowie is a lasting talent. Space oddity is not to be all and end all of his talents, he has been around writing some very good songs for the last four years. Unheralded, and to great extent, unnoticed, except by the Bowie believers and devotees."

In Music Now! they wrote: "Those lyrics are but heavy. Deep, thoughtful, probing, exposing, gouging at your innards. This album seems to serve as an intimate discussion between old friends. This is more than a record. It is an experience. An expression of life as others see it."

<u>7-11-1969</u> Perth, Salutation Hotel.   NT
Promoters: Andy Lothian and Derek Nicol.
Backed by Juniors Eyes. Received GBP 100,—.
During Wild eyed boy from Freecloud, to Bowie's surprise,
screaming young girls rushed the stage.

Junior's Eyes:
Mick Wayne (guitar).
Tim Renwick (guitar).
John Lodge (bass guitar).
John Cambridge (drums).

7-11-1969 Interview by phone for New Musical Express from Perth by Gordon Coxhill (published 15-11-1969).

<u>8-11-1969</u> Kilmarnock, Grand Hall.   NT
Promoters: Andy Lothian and Derek Nicol.
Backed by Juniors Eyes. Received GBP 100,—.

DATE / EVENT	AUDIO / VIDEO	TITLE

<u>9-11-1969</u> Dunfermline, Kinema Ballroom. NT
Promoters: Andy Lothian and Derek Nicol.
Backed by Juniors Eyes. Received GBP 100,—.

<u>10-11-1969</u> Glasgow, Electric Garden. NT
Promoters: Andy Lothian and Derek Nicol.
Backed by Juniors Eyes. Received GBP 100,—.

11-11-1969 Stirling, Albert Hall.
Cancelled.

12-11-1969 Aberdeen, Music Hall.
Cancelled.

13-11-1969 Hamilton, Town Hall.
Cancelled.

<u>14-11-1969</u> Kirkaldy, Adam Smith Hall. Matinee. NT
Promoters: Andy Lothian and Derek Nicol.
Backed by Juniors Eyes. Received GBP 100,—.

<u>14-11-1969</u> Edinburgh, Frisco's (Caley). Evening. NT
Promoters: Andy Lothian and Derek Nicol.
Backed by Juniors Eyes. Received GBP 100,—.

14-11-1969 Interview by Ben Lyon for BBC Radio 1 Club. Recorded in BBC's Glasgow Studio.

<u>15-11-1969</u> Dundee, Caird Hall. NT
Promoters: Andy Lothian and Derek Nicol.
Attendance: 2.500.
Backed by Juniors Eyes. Received GBP 100,—.

15-11-1969 New Musical Express. Article by Gordon Coxhill (tel. Interview on 7-11-1969): Don't dig too deep, pleads oddity David Bowie.
Bowie: "I've been the male equivalent of a dumb blonde for a few years, and I was beginning to despair of people accepting me for my music. It may be fine for a male model to be told he's a great looking guy but that doesn't help a singer much, especially now that the pretty boy personality cut seems to be on the way out. I dearly want to be recognizes as a writer, but would ask them not to go too deeply into my songs."

17-11-1969 Ken Pitt's apartment at 39 Manchester Street in London. Bowie interviewed by George Tremlett (for the magazine Jackie).
Bowie: "I shall be a millionaire by the time I'm 30 and I'll spend the rest of my life doing other things" (Living on the brink - George Tremlett 1996).

17-11-1969 After Tremlett left, there was a second interview, with Tim Hughes of Jeremy magazine.

<u>18-11-1969</u> Croydon, Egg Croydon Workshop (Arts Lab). NT

DATE / EVENT	AUDIO / VIDEO	TITLE

<u>19-11-1969</u> Brighton, Brighton Dome. NT
Attendance: 2.100.

<u>20-11-1969</u> London, Purcell Room (Royal Festival Hall). Tape
Attendance: 350. An evening with David Bowie.
Support acts: Juniors Eyes and Comus. Started at 19.30 h.
A very good show. No press invited (forgotten by
Calvin Mark Lee). David's last word when he left the
building: "Fuck it!" (David Bowie - D. Thompson 1986).
Played Space oddity acoustic. Gus Dudgeon was in the
audience and thought it didn't go down very well (In other
words - Kerry Juby 1986).
Bowie was backed by Comus (friends from Beckenham).

<u>21-11-1969</u> Devizes, Poperama. NT
Promoter: Mel Bush. Received GBP. 150,—.

<u>22-11-1969</u> Gravesend, General Gordon. 1st Show 20 min. NT
Received GBP. 30,—.

<u>22-11-1969</u> Gravesend, General Gordon. 2nd Show 20 min. NT
Received GBP. 30,—.

<u>23-11-1969</u> Gillingham, Aurora Hotel. 1st Show 20 min. NT
First show started at 23.00 h. Received GBP. 30,—.
The crowd (a rough bunch) did not like Bowie's act.

<u>23 11 1969</u> Gillingham, Aurora Hotel. 2nd Show 20 min. NT
Second show started at 1.00 h. Received GBP. 30,—.
The crowd was drunk and rowdy.
Bowie had to play Buddy Holly covers, backed by the
support bands. When he played Spaced oddity at the end
it was not appreciated by the audience, they started
throwing beer bottles and lighted cigarettes. Angie started
to punch the guy that threw the cigarettes and the police
came to arrest her. It took David 4 hours to get her out of
jail (The Starzone Interviews - David Currie 1987).

24-11-1969 Sunderland, Empire Theatre.
Cancelled.

27-11-1969 Bowie had a meeting with Miriam Brinkman. She was casting agent for the film Sunday,
Bloody Sunday.

28-11-1969 Bowie had a meeting with director John Schlesinger at Vic Films, 33 Bruton Street,
London. He didn't get the role (Murray Head did).

<u>30-11-1969</u> London, Palladium. Rehearsal for Save Rave NT

DATE / EVENT	AUDIO / VIDEO	TITLE

69. Backstage an interview for Jeremy by Tim Hughes.

<u>30-11-1969</u> London, Palladium (charity concert in aid of the Invalid Children's Aid Association).
Save Rave '69. (started at 19.15 hours). He sang Space oddity and was presented to Princess Margaret.
Other artists: Dusty Springfield, Marmelade, The Mojos, Tiny Tim, The Settlers, The Equals.

    NT

    Video

Bowie visited various Beckenham antique dealers, like Pepsy's Antiques in Kelsey Road (owned by Mrs. Anne Gayle).

December 1969 Filmmaker Tony Palmer met Bowie to discuss the possibility of working on film Groupie girl.

December 1969 Hull, Fairview Studios. The Rats recorded Telephone blues (original by John Mayall) / Early in the spring (based on a guitar riff by Junior's Eyes guitarist Tin Renwick that Mick Ronson had heard).

<u>5-12-1969</u> Irish Radio Telefis Eireann. "Like now."   NT
Produced by Bill Keating. Received GBP. 50,—.

6-12-1969 Music Business Weekly. Article: Over ambitious Bowie is a disappointment.
They wrote about the album Space oddity: "A disappointing album which does not live up to the promise of the single Space oddity, which is included. Bowie seems to be a little unsure of the direction he is going in."

7-12-1969 The Observer. Article by Tony Palmer: Up-to-date minstrel.
Palmer wrote: On stage he is quite devastatingly beautiful. With his loofah hair and blue eyes, he pads around like every schoolgirl's wonder movie star. He smiles; you melt. He apologizes that his repertoire is mostly his own songs, which he admits sound all very much the same.

Half December 1969 Bowie, Pitt, Trevor Richardson and Tim Hughes went to see the world premiere of Vesalii Icones at the Queen Elizabeth Hall, London. Peter Maxwell wrote the play (danced by William Louther).

17-12-1969 Bowie had lunch with Claudio Fabi, to discuss recording Ragazzo Solo, Ragazza Sola.

20-12-1969 Morgan Studios. Recording Ragazzo Solo Ragazza Sola (5.15).
Produced by Claudio Fabi. He also taught Bowie the lyrics.

20-12-1969 Music Now! Interview by Kate Simpson.
Bowie: "The only importance in singles is to go and show people I write different stuff. Every single is going to be different. I'm bored with Space oddity, it's only a pop song after all."
Bowie: "This country is crying out for a leader. God knows what it is looking for, but if it's not careful it's going to end up with a Hitler. This place is so ready to be picked up by anybody who had a strong enough personality to lead."

22-12-1969 Bowie and Pitt had a meeting with film-maker Tony Palmer, to discuss a role in his film

DATE / EVENT	AUDIO / VIDEO	TITLE

Groupie Girl.
In the evening they went to Chelsea, where Nina (of the duo Nina and Frederik) cooked them dinner.

Christmas 1969 Angie was in Cyprus, visiting her parents. David played a new song, The prettiest star, over the phone and told her it was written for her (Backstage passes - Angela Bowie and Patrick Carr 1993).

27-12-1969 Fabulous Magazine. Bowie and Angie on front page.

1970 Released in Germany: In the beginning Volume One (compilation) (Deram).

1970 Book published: The sound of the city: the rise of rock and roll - Charlie Gillett (Outerbridge & Dienstfrey). New edition printed in 1983. ISBN 90-6213-745-8.
Gives a lot of info about songs that inspired the young Bowie. Bowie mentioned on page 246, 307, 370, 386, 390, 391, 392 and 428.

January 1970 The Hype was formed.

January 1970 Jeremy Magazine. Article by Tim Hughes and Trevor Richardson: Bowie for a song. Interview took place on 8-1-1970.
They wrote: It's just not David's scene. The disco stops and a single sharp spot stabs its way through layers of multi-coloured light show. He works hard. People keep right on talking. No one seems involved. It's all over and David joins us at the bar. A marauding groupie gropes him in the crush. "Who was it? I ought to get a fee for that."

January 1970 Rave. Article about Bowie.

January 1970. Advision Studios. Recording 2 versions of Lightning Frightening. Version 1 (3.35), Version 2 (3.55).

January 1970 Released in Italy: Ragazzo Solo, Ragazza Sola (5.15) / Wild eyed boy from Freecloud (4.52) (Philips BW 704 208). Italian lyrics written by Mogol.

January 1970 Boris Bergman wrote the French lyrics for Space oddity: Un Homme a Disparu Dans le Ciel.

1-1-1970 Belgian Radio. BRT. Broadcast the 11-10-1969 interview by Ward Bogaert.	Tape	
8-1-1970 London, Speakeasy. Tony Visconti (bass guitar), John Cambridge (drums) and Tim Renwick (guitar) backed David. Bowie also did a poem by Mason Williams. There was no crow-response at all. Most of the people just ignored Bowie and kept right on talking. Tim Hughes and Trevor Richardson (from Jeremy Magazine) interview Bowie that day. They are also backstage at the Speakeasy.	NT	

DATE / EVENT	AUDIO / VIDEO	TITLE

8-1-1970 Recording The prettiest star (Marc Bolan on guitar) (3.09) and a part of London bye ta ta (second recording), including some guitar by Marc Bolan (real name Mark Feld) and backing vocals by Sue & Sunny and Lesley Duncan (2.33). The all-black backing band was called Gass.

Bowie: "I like Marc's guitar on it because he made a lot of mistakes. It was my first slipped disc, as we lost the master tape when we moved" (David Robert Jones - The discography of a generalist - David Jeffrey Fletcher 1979).

Producer Tony Visconti about Marc Bolan: "He was dying to prove that he could play. So he came in with his little amp, and he'd learned the song and practiced really hard. And David was really chuffed, because he loved Marc. He was probably more in love with Marc than Marc was in love with him. So Marc did his solo and everybody applauded. Suddenly Marc's wife, June, turned viciously on David and said "We're gonna go now, Marc is too good to play on your record!" And I was stunned. It was the first time I realized there was any rivalry between them" (Glam! Bowie, Bolan and the Glitter Rock Revolution - Barney Hoskyns 1998).

Visconti: "This was the only time they could have played together. It was the only time their egos allowed it. If David Bowie had appeared on any of his records, believe me, Marc would have been the first to talk about it" (Moonage daydream - Dave Thompson 1987).

Tony Visconti: "They never actually recorded together apart from Prettiest Star. I was there the whole time and even the albums I was absent on, I can promise you that Marc Bolan never walked in on any session. During the Young Americans days David stayed up all night with Marc. They did have plans to work together, probably that night. Just casual plans to work together, but they never came to fruition." (The Starzone Interviews - David Currie 1987).

Bowie in 1989: "There was a lot of rivalry between Marc and myself. We had a sparring relationship. We both knew we were going to do something in the future, but he was a few rungs up. He was really starting to happen. I don't think we were talking to each other that day. I can't remember why, but I remember a very strange attitude in the studio. We were never in the same room at the same time. You could have cut the atmosphere with a knife."

Between 13-1 and 15-1-1970, Trident Studios, recording London by ta ta was finished.

DATE / EVENT	AUDIO / VIDEO	TITLE
14-1-1970 Lewisham, Old Tiger's Head. The Old Downham Folk Club had merged with the South East London Tech Folk Club to form this new venue. Other artists on the bill: The Gasworks, Ralp McTell and Marc Ellington.	NT	
18-1-1970 Beckenham, The Three Tuns Public House.	NT	
29-1-1970 Scottish TV. Grampian. Cairngorm Ski Night. Booked by Neil Warnock. Broadcasted 27-2-1970. London bye ta ta with a studio orchestra and a dance routine with Angie and Lindsay Kemp. Bowie received GBP. 35,—.	Tape Video	quality 10, 3 min. quality 10, 3 min.
30-1-1970 Aberdeen, Johnston Hall (University). Promoter: Andy Lothian. Solo performance.	NT	

31-1-1970 Edinburgh, Gateway Theatre. Rehearsal for The Looking glass murders.

DATE / EVENT	AUDIO / VIDEO	TITLE

Late January 1970 John Cambridge went to Hull to convince Mick Ronson (who worked as a grounds man for Hull council) to join The Hype.

January / February 1970 Release LP The Zig-Zag Festival (US-Mercury SRD-2-29). 1 Track by Bowie: Space oddity.

February 1970 Pitt arranged work for an advert for Wall's Sausages (Bowie turned it down).

February 1970 Release Album Space oddity in US.

<u>February 1970</u> Thomas A Beckett Public House.   NT
Rehearsals.

<u>1-2-1970</u> TV. Recording "The looking glass murders."   VCD   *Pierrot in Turqoise (The*
Edinburgh, Gateway Theatre.   *Looking Glass Murders)*
Directed by B. Mahoney. Original title was Another World.   *(No label, no number)*
A TV adaptation of Pierrot in Turquoise (25 min.).   Video   *Various 25 (26 min)*
Bowie played Cloud.
Broadcasted 8-2-1970 on Scottish TV.

<u>3-2-1970</u> London, Marquee Club.   NT
Last gig with Juniors Eyes.
Special guests: Time Box.
129 People were present. Among them was Mick Ronson.
Tony Visconti had met Ronson during the sessions for
Michael Chapman's "Fully Qualified Survivor" album
(Black Book - Barry Miles 1980).
Ronson met Bowie after the concert. They went to his flat
and they jammed. Bowie asked: "Hey, do you wanna come
down to this radio show and play with me?" (The
Starzone Interviews - David Currie 1987).

4-2-1970 Bowie had a meeting with film executive Rex Sheldon, to discuss writing the theme music for the film Silver Lady. Later that day he did an interview for Penny Valentine for the magazine Disc.

<u>5-2-1970</u> London. Paris Cinema Studios. Lower Regent   CD   *The day and the moon*
Street. BBC Radio. John Peel, The Sunday Show.   *(first 13 songs) (Manic*
Produced by Jeff Griffin.   *Depression MD CD 016)*
With the Hype. Broadcast 8-2-1970.   CD   *A semi-acoustic love affair*
1. Amsterdam (2.56).   *(first 13 songs)*
2. God knows I'm good (3.10).   *(Gold Standard)*
3. Buzz the Fuzz (2.24).   CD   *Radio Hype (first 13 songs)*
4. Karma man (3.04).   *(GS-96006)*
5. London bye ta ta (2.37).   2 CD   *God knows I'm good (songs*
6. An occasional dream (2.51).   *1,2,4,5,6,12) (BEEB 1/2)*
7. The width of a circle (4.50).   CD   *God knows I'm good (songs*
8. Janine (3.37).   *1,2,4,5,6,12) (Invasion*
9. Wild eyed boy from Freecloud (4.10).   *Unlimited IU 9753-1)*
10. Unwashed and somewhat slightly dazed (4.54).   CD   *The rise and rise of Ziggy*

DATE / EVENT	AUDIO / VIDEO	TITLE

11. Fill your heart (2.23).
12. The prettiest star (2.38).
13. Cygnet committee (7.56).
14. Memory of a free festival (not broadcast) (3.17).

Waiting for the man (original by Velvet Underground in 1966) was destroyed when cutting the tape.
First time The width of a circle was recorded (it was a very extraordinary version).

Line-up The Hype:
David Bowie (vocals, guitar, electric piano).
Mick Ronson (lead guitar).
Tony Visconti (bass guitar).
John Cambridge (drums). On 30-3-1970 replaced by John Cambridge.

Mick Ronson: "I didn't know anything, none of the material, I just sat and watched his fingers. I didn't really know what I was doing, but I suppose it came across OK, I don't know? Maybe it sounded horrible, I really don't know." (The Starzone Interviews - David Currie 1987).

Afterwards George Tremlett interviewed Bowie.

The width of a circle (A monster who was sleeping by a tree. I saw the monster was me) was inspired by Nietzsche's Jenseits von Gut und Bose. He also mentioned the Lebanese philosopher Kahlil Gibran. His 1926 book The Prophet was one of Bowie's inspirations. This was the first philosophic book I ever read.

	CD	*Stardust vol. 1 (all the songs, except 14)* (Savage Hippo Records)
	CD	*Paris bye Ta Ta (first 13 songs) (The Early Years 02-CD-3327)*
	CD	*Chameleon Chronicles vol. 3 (1,2,7,9) (Living Legend Records LLR-CD 050)*
	3 CD	*Bowie at the Beeb (1,2,7,10, 13 and 14)*
	CD	*Bowie at the Beeb, 8 track sampler (For demonstration only) (EMI) (1)*
	4 CDR	The complete BBC master recordings (No label, no nr.)
	1 CDR	The complete BBC files vol. 1 (Old Gold Records OGCD 075)
	CD	*Rare Tracks 1* (No label, no number)
	1 CDR	A London Show
	1 CDR	Live in Cleveland and rare track! (Tradepoint) (6)
	1 CDR	*Janine* (No label, no number)
	LP	No more sleeping with Ken Pitt (Citizen Kane Records 001) (13 songs)
	LP	We were so turned on (Daffy Poduction / Citizen Kane 001 A/B) (13 songs)
	LP	Janine (Fancy Records PCS 70)
	LP	London studios (Citizen Kane Records 001)

8-2-1970 Scottish TV. Broadcast "The looking glass murders." Recorded 1-2-1970.

9-2-1970 Bowie had a meeting with John Sherrard of Le Treport Productions, at Upper Montagu Street in London, to discuss a role in the film Perspective.

13-2-1970 Pitt received Brian Howerd's script (just ideas) for the stage play The Fair Maid of Perth. Howerd was director of Harrogate Theatre in North Yorkshire. Bowie started to study it, but the project was cancelled.

13-2-1970 Voted Brightest Hope for 1970 in Disc and Music Echo's Valentine Pop poll.
DJ Tony Blackburn (not one of Bowie's favourites) handed Bowie the award. He accepted with barely a glance and gave the award to Ken Pitt (The Pitt Report - Kenneth Pitt 1983).
A party in Café Royal, Regent Street in London.

DATE / EVENT	AUDIO / VIDEO	TITLE

14-2-1970 Disc. Article by Penny Valentine: A new star shoots upwards.
Bowie: "I suppose I want success, but not for the reason people think. I want to establish myself so that I can fulfil other desires by using success as a springboard and then swiftly dis-establish myself."

16-2-1970 Daily Sketch. Article by Anne Nightingale.
She wrote: Stardom comes quickly these days. He could be the giant heart-throb that Scott Walker was."

22-2-1970 Chalk Farm (London), Round House. NT
Event called: Implosion. Promoter: NEMS. *Video*   Stolp tapes no. 23 (1 min)
Debut with The Hype (in full costume, with Mick Ronson on guitar). Kenneth Pitt had suggested the band's name. Support act for Country Joe and the Fish and Noel Redding's Fat Mattress.
The earned GBP. 10,— (only the expenses).
Marc Bolan attended the concert, in blue jeans and a floppy hat, watching with open mouth.
It was their first costumed gig. Mick Ronson was Gangsterman, wearing a gold lame double-breasted suit and fedora. Tony Visconti was Hypeman, dressed in a mock Superman costume with leotard, crocheted silver knickers and a big red cape with a collar. John Cambridge was Cowboyman. Bowie was Rainbowman, dressed in lurex, pirate boots and diaphonous scarves pinned to his clothes.

Photographer Ray Stevenson: "That was the time of scruffy jeans and denims. But I always thought you should do the opposite of what everyone else did" (Alias David Bowie - Peter & Leni Gillman 1986).

Tony Visconti: "It was the predecessive performance to glam rock. Angie suggested that instead of going on in jeans, which every group did in those days, "Let me sew together some costumes." We went on stage dressed outlandishly like this, and half the place absolutely roared with enthusiasm, and the other half was completely stunned" (People stared at the make-up on his face - Per Nilsen 1985).

Bowie: "It came off as no more than everyone dressing up. I was in silver lame and blue and silver cloak and blue hair and the whole thing, glitter everywhere. The whole thing was on that scale… and we died a death" (Glam! Bowie, Bolan and the Glitter Rock Revolution - Barney Hoskyns 1998).

Genet once wrote: "The only criterion of an act is its elegance."
Oscar Wilde once wrote: "In matters of great importance, the vital element is not sincerity, but style."

Repertoire Hype included:
Dans le port d'Amsterdam (Jaques Brel).
Buzz the fuzz (Biff Rose, 1968).
Fill your heart (Biff Rose, 1968).
Madame George (Van Morrison, 1969).
Waiting for the man (Velvet Underground, 1966).

23-2-1970 London, Streatham Arms. Secret gig by NT
The Hype under the pseudonym Harry the Butcher.

27-2-1970 Scottish TV. Grampian. Cairngorm Ski Night.
Recorded 19-1-1970.

DATE / EVENT	AUDIO / VIDEO	TITLE

<u>28-2-1970</u> Basildon, Arts (Centre) Theatre.   Tape   quality 7
Promoter: NEMS.
With the Hype. Tickets: 7p. Received GBP. 51,—.
The Hype billed as: David Bowie's New Electric Band.
Support acts: The Tide and Iron Maiden.

March 1970 Zigzag Magazine. Interview with Marc Bolan.
Marc Bolan: "Sexually, I believe that one should love what one loves, and I quite enjoy the Greek idea of two warriors going to war and mentally being very close. They don't actually screw each other on the battlefield, but mentally they were really into each other. I really dig David. I like his songs and we have a very good head thing… but we don't make love. To make love wouldn't be repulsive to me. It would just be a bit of a bore with bums, and it'd hurt."

March 1970 Release LP The world of David Bowie (compilation) (Decca SPA 58).

March 1970 Terry Burns stayed some weeks at Haddon Hall.

1-3-1970 Mick Ronson moved into Haddon Hall.

<u>1-3-1970</u> Beckenham, The Three Tuns.   NT
With the Hype.

<u>3-3-1970</u> Hounslow, White Bear (Arts Lab).   NT
With the Hype.

<u>5-3-1970</u> Beckenham, Three Tuns Public House.   NT
Solo performance.

6-3-1970 Release The Prettiest Star (3.09) / Conversation piece (3.05). Marc Bolan plays guitar on The Prettiest Star. (Mercury MF 1135).

Music Business Weekly: "A lazy, gentle swinging number with strings and some nice fuzzy guitar embellishing Bowie's croaky voice."
Disc: "He comes up with a lovely, gentle, gossamer piece about the great love of his life. This has the most compact, catchy melody I've ever heard."
Daily Mirror: "Not to sure that David Bowie will make it this time. It hasn't got the gimmick of his last."
New Musical Express: "It could do very well indeed."
Record Mirror: "Chart cert."

<u>6-3-1970</u> Hull, Hull University.   NT
Attendance: 900. With the Hype. Received GBP. 125,—.
Benny Marshall (The Rats) joined the band on harmonica during Unwashed and somewhat slightly dazed.
After the show David and Angie stayed overnight at the home of John Cambridge's parents.
John Cambridge remembers his father coming to him and crying: "He's smoking me cigs!" (The Pitt Report -

DATE / EVENT	AUDIO / VIDEO	TITLE

Kenneth Pitt 1983).

<u>7-3-1970</u> London, Extension Building, Little Titchfield Street (Regent Street Polytechnic). With the Hype. Received GBP. 100,—. Promoted by Polytechnic Entertainments. Tickets: 10p. Started at 19.30 h. Support acts: Bridget St. John, Alan Skidmore Quintet. Gavin Petrie wrote in Disc: David Bowie, in ten-league boots and groovy gear, presented his new backing group Hype. The show was a disaster. The volume on Mick Ronson's lead guitar was so high and not only did he block out David's singing but also completely over-powered John Cambridge's drums. The volume also cleared the seats in direct line with his speaker. — NT

<u>11-3-1970</u> London, Round House. Atomic Sunrise Festival. With The Hype. — NT

<u>12-3-1970</u> London, Royal Albert Hall (charity show). Acoustic solo performance, 20 min. Received GBP. 50,—, despite the fact it was a charity evening for Mental Health Charity (MENCAP), organised by Michael Sugrue. — NT

<u>13-3-1970</u> Sunderland (Fillmore North), Locarno Ballroom. Attendance: 1.500. With the Hype. Received GBP. 125,—. — NT

<u>14-3-1970</u> Guildford, University of Surrey. Solo performance. Received GBP. 100,—. — NT

19-3-1970 In the afternoon. Kensington Antique Market. Angie choose her wedding dress and David a pair of black satin trousers.

<u>19-3-1970</u> Beckenham, Three Tuns Club. Solo performance (David's stag night). After the concert they went to Clare Shenstone and her brother (friends they had met through Calvin Mark Lee). They had dinner at her house and stayed there all night. Later Angie said this was the first time she slept with a man and a woman both at the same time, but she really enjoyed it. The next morning they woke up and had to hurry to be on time for their wedding at 11.00 h. (David Bowie - Jerry Hopkins 1985). — NT

20-3-1970 Marriage David and Angie at Bromley Registry Office. Only 5 people were present: Liz Hartley, Roger Fry (David's roadie), John Cambridge, Clare Shenstone and Mrs. Margaret Jones. They exchanged Peruvian bangles (a present from Angie's brother).
After the marriage they had a few drinks at the Swan and Mitre Public House. Later on they went to Haddon Hall, to have a party and watch television.

DATE / EVENT	AUDIO / VIDEO	TITLE

21-3-1970 Articles in Beckenham and Penge Advertiser and The Beckenham Journal.

23-3-1970 Trident Studios. A new acetate of Memory of a free festival was made. The first attempt to record The Supermen. John Cambridge could not play a part of The Supermen. After the session he was replaced by Mick Woodmansey (who played in The Roadrunners and The Rats).

Mary Parr (who lived a few doors from Trident Studios): "David Bowie had a delicate, spooky quality. Over a glass of gin in the pub, he outlined his plans for the next year. I invited him to join me in Wardour House. The night was like 'groupie heaven' and when I woke up, he was playing his guitar."

24-3-1970 London, Wembley, LWT's Studio 5. Recording Oh baby / Universal love by Dib Cochran and the Earwings. Bowie was not involved in this project. Released August 1970.
Tony Visconti: "It was myself, Marc Bolan, John Cambridge and Rick Wakeman. I'm not sure if Steve Took or Mickey Finn played on it. Mick Ronson watched the six hour session. This was a period when Marc became very jealous of David and David stayed away from him."
Rick Wakeman: "It was a one-off, a bit of a laugh, and we had a lot of fun" (Bolan - The Rise and fall of a 20th century superstar - Mark Paytress, Omnibus Press 2002).

Date / Event	Audio / Video	Title
<u>25-3-1970</u> London. Playhouse Theatre Studio in Northumberland Avenue. Produced by Bernie Andrews. BBC Radio Session. Sounds of the Seventies. Andy Ferris Show on 6-4-1970 and David Symonds Show on 11-5-1970. The Backing group was billed as The Tony Visconti Trio.	2 CD	God knows I'm good (2,3,4) (BEEB 1/2)
	CD	God knows I'm good (2,3,4) (Invasion Unlimited IU9753-1)
	3 CD	Bowie at the Beeb (4)
1. The Supermen (3.12) (broadcast 6-4-1970 + 11-5-1970).	CD	Outta space (2,3,4) (World productions of compact music WPOCM 00490D049-2)
2. Waiting for the man (5.43) (broadcast 6-4-1970 and 11-5-1970).	CD	Lost in our vaults until now (No label, no number)
3. The width of a circle (5.38) (broadcast 6-4-1970 and 11-5-1970).	CD	Ziggy in Wonderland (PROCD 89 001-2)
4. Wild eyed boy from Freecloud (4.42) (spoken word after Fly at 1.48) (broadcast 11-5-1970). First recording of The Supermen.	CD	The rise and rise of Ziggy Stardust vol. 2 (songs 1,2,3,4) (Savage Hippo Records)
	CD	BBC Sessions 1969-1972 (2)
Extra-ordinary version of Waiting for the man!	CD	Ultra Rare Trax Vol.1 (The Genuine Pig TGP-CD-108) (4)
	CD	Rebel rebel (4) (Oil Well RSC 021)
	CD	Live Vol. 1 (4) (Joker JOK-001-A)
	CD	Kiss the vipers fang (songs 2, 3 and 4) (EBD002)
	CD	Stardust memories (2,3,4) (Retropop 159081)
	CD	Starman in session (2,3,4) (Silver Rarities SIRA 93)
	4 CDR	The complete BBC master recordings

DATE / EVENT	AUDIO / VIDEO	TITLE
	1 CDR	The complete BBC files vol. 2 (Old Gold Records OGCD 076) (2,3,4)
	CD	Chameleon Chron. vol. 3 (2) (Living Legend Records LLR-CD 050)
	CD	Changesthreeandahalf (Grace AZL1-1989)
	CD	ChangesthreeBowie (PD 81989)
	CD	The Jean Genie (vol 1.) (4) (Ban-004-A)
	CD	Starman (4) (Oil Well RSC 017 CD)
	CD	White light white heat (4) (The Swinging Pig Records TSP-CD-053)
	CD	At the Beep (4) (Archive Productions AP 89004)
	CD	Mega rare trax vol. 1 (4) (Seagull Records CD 022)
	CD	Ziggy in Wonderland (4) (PROCD 89 001-2)
	CD	Five years (4) (Triangle Records PYCD 047)
	CD	Kooks (4) (Turtle Records TR-36)
	CD	Dynamic Live (4)
	CD	BBC Bowie (4)
	CD	The best of David Bowie (4)
	LP	White light white heat (4) (The Swinging Pig Records TSP 053A/B)
	LP	David! Break the barriers (2,3,4) (Hole Records 20187/HW 0045 A/B)
	LP	Lost in our vaults until now (Elephant Records Elp 012)
	LP	Thin White Duke meets Ziggy (3)
	LP	The unofficial Wembley Wizard Box File (3)
	Single	The width of a circle / The wild eyed boy from Freecloud (Major Tom 6052-202)
	Tape	quality 9, 15 min.

28-3-1970 Melody Maker. Interview by Raymond Telford (David was interviewed mid-march 1970): Hype and David Bowie's future.

DATE / EVENT	AUDIO / VIDEO	TITLE

Bowie: "I deliberately chose the name Hype in favour of something that sounded perhaps heavy, because now no one can say they're being conned. I suppose you could say I chose it deliberately with tongue-in-cheek.
We've had these costumes made by various girlfriends which make us look like Dr. Strange or the Incredible Hulk. I was a bit apprehensive about wearing them at the Roundhouse gig because I didn't know how the audience would react. If they think it's a huge put-on the whole thing will backfire, but they seemed to accept it which was nice."

<u>30-3-1970</u> West Croydon (Broad Green), Star Hotel.   NT
With the Hype (John Cambridge's last gig, replaced by
Woody Woodmansey).
Support act: Ugly Room.

31-3-1970 Bowie told Pitt he wanted to manage himself.

April 1970 Plans to make a documentary by Tony Palmer about The man who sold the world-sessions and life at Haddon Hall (were shelved).

April 1970 Olav Wyper (Philips / Mercury) arranged a meeting between Bowie and DeFries at his office at Godfrey Davis and Batt.

April 1970 Disc. Article by Penny Valentine: A new star shoots upwards.

2-4-1970 Scarborough, Penthouse.
Cancelled.

4-4-1970 Stockport, Poco-A-Poco Club.
Cancelled.

6-4-1970 Andy Ferris Show. Broadcast Sound of the Seventies, recorded 25-3-1970.

<u>12-4-1970</u> Harrogate (Yorkshire), Harrogate Theatre.   NT
(First show, at 16.30 h.).
Solo, 30 minutes. Support for Keef Hartley Band.
Bowie used Hartley's PA equipment.

<u>12-4-1970</u> Harrogate (Yorkshire), Harrogate Theatre.   NT
(Second show, at 19.30 h.).
Solo, 30 minutes. Support for Keef Hartley Band.
Bowie used Hartley's PA equipment.

3,14+15-4-1970 A short version of Memory of a free festival (part 1, 3.59) (part 2, 3.31) was recorded (for the American market) in the Advision Studios in 23 Gosfield Street (they had moved). Released 12-6-1970.

14-4-1970 Bowie had a lunch with Brian Howerd and discussed working on The Fair Maid of Perth. After lunch he went to see Frank Nesbit at Elstee Film Studios and discussed the possibility to work on the music for his film Dulcima.

DATE / EVENT	AUDIO / VIDEO	TITLE

18-4 to 30-4-1970 Soho (London). Trident Studios. First part recording The man who sold the world.

27-4-1970 Pitt received a letter from David. He asked him to confirm within 7 days he was no longer his manager.

<u>27-4-1970</u> Stockport, Poco-A-Poco Club (School Union Show). With the Hype.
Show organised by Stockport Grammar School featuring David Bowie and The Hype, Barclay James Harvest, High Tide and Purple Gang.   NT

May 1970 Haddon Hall. Recording The Shadowman (Demo 1, working title: The man) (3.47) and Tired of my life (3.05).

May 1970 Creem. Article by Dave Marsh: The incredible story of Iggy and the Stooges.

7-5-1970 Meeting David, Pitt, DeFries in Pitt's apartment. They decided to end Pitt's management-contract. DeFries became his manager. He was financially supported by Laurence Meyers of Gem Productions.
Short after this meeting a new contract was made by Gem (DeFries / Myers). 20% For Gem and 80% minus all expenses for Bowie. Myers reserved a sum of GBP 5.000,— to spend.

DeFries commented on the first time he saw David: "He came wandering in very unshaven, hollow-cheeked, bleary-eyed and nervous, chewing his fingernails and sat in my office looking like a refugee. I felt sorry for him. When David wants people to do things he usually gets people to feel sorry for him. I thought: Poor little chap, he's got himself into a terrible mess" (David Bowie - The Archive - Chris Charlesworth 1981).
DeFries' parents were peddlers. As a child DeFries had been a market boy in Petticoat Lane.

<u>10-5-1970</u> US TV. Ivor Novello Awards.
London, Talk of the Town.
In memory of the actor-composer Ivor Novello, who died in 1951. Bowie was awarded Best Song.
Produced by Jack Lynn.
Space oddity (with the Les Reed Orchestra) (4.11).
Live on screen in New York's Carnegie Hall and at Filmore East. 5 Hours later there was a delayed replay.
Laurence Myers was present.
Also on the bill: The Rolling Stones, Lulu, John Lennon & Yoko Ono, Malcolm Roberts, Blue Mink, Sandie Shaw, Dusty Springfield, Mary Hopkin, Matt Monroe, Peter Sarstedt, The Beatles, Ringo Star and company, Ginger Baker's Air Force.
Ken Pitt didn't allow Angie Bowie to attend the evening. Angie was pissed and called him "A pig" (The Starzone Interviews - David Currie 1987).

	AUDIO/VIDEO	TITLE
	1 CDR	*Diamonds in space* (No label, no number)
	1 CDR	*TracksTwoBowie* (No label, no number)
	2 CDR	*TracksBowie* (A Dutch Connection)
	CD	*Anthology* (BOW 1999)
	VCD	*VideotrackOne* (No label, no number)
	VCD	*I keep a good friend... Vol.2* (No label, no number)
	Video	

11-5-1970 BBC Radio. David Symonds Show. Broadcast Sounds of the Seventies, recorded 25-3-1970.

DATE / EVENT	AUDIO / VIDEO	TITLE

12-5 to 22-5-1970 Advision Studios in Gosfield Street. Second part recording Album The man who sold the world.

Tony Visconti: "We just laid down the chords, the arrangements, the guitar solos, the synthesizers and David would be in the lobby, holding hands with Angie."

Bowie in 1998: "I really did object to the impression given in some articles that I did not write the songs on The man who sold the world. You only have to check out the chord changes. No one writes chord changes like that."

21-5-1970 Scarborough, The Penthouse. NT
Attendance: 308. With the Hype.

June 1970 Trident Studios. Recording of Holy holy (3.13). Only available on vinyl. This is not the same as the bonus track (2.18) on the Ryko CD The man who sold the world.

June 1970 First version of All the madmen (5.38) was recorded. It was mixed in August 1970. Also a demo version (4.45) was recorded.

12-6-1970 Released in US: Memory of a free festival Part 1 (3.59) / Memory of a free festival Part 2 (3.31) (Mercury 6052 026).

16-6-1970 Cambridge, University, Jesus College May Ball. NT
Solo performance.

4-7-1970 Bromley (Shortlands), Queens Mead Recreation NT
Grounds. Free concert.

5-7-1970 London, Round House. NT

8-7-1970 Scottish TV. Crampian TV. Cairngorm Ski Night. *Video* *Various 25 (26 min)*
Shows The Looking Glass Murders.
Later the tape was wiped by Crampian (to controversial).

17-7-1970 Southend, The Cricketers Inn (Fickle-Pickle NT
Club).

1-8-1970 Southen-On-Sea, East Woodbury Lane. NT
Shelter Charity Show.

August 1970 Trident Studios. Recording of All the madmen (version without the central spoken passage).
In August another version of All the madmen (recorded in June 1970) was mixed. Album mix (5.38) and alternate mix (4.39). Another demo of The Supermen (demo 2) (3.01) recorded.

August 1970 Release Oh baby / Universal love - Dib Cochran and the Earwings (Marc Bolan guitar, Visconti lead vocals and bass, John Cambridge, Rick Wakeman piano (on Oh baby) (Bell Label 1121). Bowie did not play the saxophone, he stayed home the day the songs were recorded in March 1970.

DATE / EVENT	AUDIO / VIDEO	TITLE

September / October 1970 Mike Weller (a friend from the Arts Lab) made a drawing for the cover of The man who sold the world. It showed Cane Hill's main entrance block. In front was an unshaven figure with a rifle. He called the drawing Metrobolist.
David gave the recordings and Weller's artwork to Robin McBride who took it to Chicago.

After McBride left, Bowie went to Philips office and arranged a photo-session (famous photo's of David wearing a dress, designed by Mr. Fish).
A year before Mick Jagger was also photographed wearing a dress.

23-10-1970 Bowie signed a 50-50 publishing contract with Chrysalis for GBP 5.000,—. It included 100 song titles over 5 years.

November 1970 Release in US Album The man who sold the world (Mercury 61325).
There was a bad communication Mercury - Philips. For the cover in the US the drawing was used, in Europe the dress-photo (a parody of a painting by Dante Rosetti).

Nicholas Pegg suggest in his book The Complete David Bowie, the song Saviour Machine was inspired by Joseph Sargent's 1969 film thriller The Forbin Project, with the publicity tag line: "We built a super computer with a mind of it's own and now we must fight it for the world!"

<u>November 1970</u> Stockport, Poco-A-Poco Club.   NT
Trevor Bolder replaces Tony Visconti on bass after this show. Also on the bill are Barclay James Harvest and Tony Hill's High Tide. Tickets: 50p.

12-11-1970 Released Ragazzo Solo / Sheila - The Computers (Numero Uno ZN 50016). Music A-side written by Bowie.

November / December 1970 Bowie attends show by Phillip Glass at the royal College of Art (Eno was also in attendance).

December 1970 Recording demo Oh! you pretty things (3.07) at Radio Luxembourg's Studios.
As Bowie was not a great piano player, he had to play the music in 4 times. After each part he got cramp in his fingers. The producer had to glue the pieces together. Part of the lyrics was inspired on Bulwer-Lytton's book The Coming Race.

Bob Grace took the demo to Mickie Most, who thought it suitable for Peter Noone.
Bob Grace: "We always recorded the demo's in the studio of Radio Luxembourg because they were so cheap. The guitar solo's could not be to high and not to long, because otherwise the radio broadcast would be disturbed" (David Bowie - Dave Thompson 1986).

December 1970 Release US Promo single: All the madmen (3.14) / Janine (3.19) (Mercury DJ 311, later re-released as Mercury 73173).

8-12-1970 Pitt went to see DeFries in Gem offices. He asked GBP 2000,— to end his contract. DeFries told him he would look at the figures.

15-12-1970 Changes. Article by Janet Marlin and Leee Childers: Going apeshit from St. Marks to Staten Island with Iggy and the Stooges.

DATE / EVENT	AUDIO / VIDEO	TITLE

1970 / 1971 When Bowie was at home in Haddon Hall he used to look at The Alwin Nicholas Dance Company on the television.

They often visited the trendy gay discotheque the Sombrero. They met outrageously dressed queens, fashion models and all kinds of weird people.
One of the frequently visitors was Freddi Buretti. He wore extravagant costumes and acted he was the most desirable boy in the club (although he had a girlfriend called Daniella Parma).
Bowie: "Daniella was a fantastic-looking Anglo-Indian girl who was a friend and try-out for all Freddie's new designs. She had short peroxided white hair and she had cut various shapes into the back like ice-cream cones and flags and then dyed them red or pistachio or whatever. She just looked oh-so stunningly tomorrow (Internet chat 1998).

1971 Curious (UK). Article: Transvestites, queen drag and the fairies.

1971 Demo for Life on Mars? (sold at Philips in 1988 for GBP. 90,—).

1971 Book published: The great beast: The life and magick of Aleister Crowley - J. Symond (MacDonald).

1971 Book published: The elephant man: A study in human dignity - Ashley Montagu (Outerbridge & Dienstfrey).

Early 1971 Bowie offers the song Star to a band out of Princes Risborough, called Chameleon.

Early 1971 Release compilation LP Dimension of Miracles (Mercury). 1 Bowie track: The width of a circle.

January 1971 Released Fourth hour of my sleep (written by Tucker Zimmerman, who used to perform regularly at The Three Tuns Pub in Beckenham) / Power of darkness (written by Mick Ronson and Benny Marshall) - Ronno (Vertigo Records). Produced by Tony Visconti.

January 1971 Trevor Bolder replaced Tony Visconti.

17-1-1971 Release Holy holy (3.13) / Black country rock (3.32) (Mercury 6052 049).

Tony Visconti about Black country rock: "David did it as a joke. I thinned his voice with equalisation to get it sound more like Bolan's. The fascination these two men had with each other's career is obvious."

<u>20-1-1971</u> UK TV. Granada. Holy holy. Bowie wore a dress.	Tape Video	quality 10, 3 min. quality 10, 3 min.
27-1-1971 Bowie visits America to promote The man who sold the world and meets Andy Warhol in New York. At the airport interviewed and searched (a delay of 45 minutes). Bowie wore a long blue coat. He was met by Oberman and his parents and stayed at Oberman's home in Washington. Oberman: "Everyone disembarked, and there was no	Video	At the factory, 4 min.

DATE / EVENT	AUDIO / VIDEO	TITLE

David. I was waiting with my parents for almost 45 minutes and was pretty positive he hadn't missed the plane. I waited and waited and finally he got off."
There were only interviews with a small newspaper and a local station.

He went to Electric Circus (a club in New York) to see the Velvet Underground. After the show he went backstage and asked John Cale if he could speak to the singer. The singer came and Bowie thought he talked to Lou Reed. He did not know Reed left the Velvet Underground on 23-8-1970 and was replaced by someone who had the same kind of hair as Reed (Dough Yule).

An old lady stopped him at Broadway and 57th Street to enquire which animal was used to make his woolly greatcoat. "Teddy bear" Bowie replied (Black Book - Barry Miles 1980).

Date / Event	Audio / Video	Title
29-1-1971 Interview by Janice Schaat.	Tape	quality 7, 15 min.
End January 1971 Washington.	NT	
February 1971 Bowie signs for RCA.		
February 1971 New York. In New York he visited his cousin Kristina.	NT	
February 1971 Philadelphia.	NT	
February 1971 Philadelphia. 94WY Radio. Interview (7.27).	1 CDR	*Friars - Aylesbury - 25th September 1971* (No label, no number)
February 1971 Chicago, Quiet Knight Club. Acoustic set. Could not play in US due to visa problems. This was the only "official" performance.	Tape	quality 10, 60 min.
February 1971 Los Angeles. After they flew to Los Angeles, Rodney Bingenheimer (Mercury's promoter in southern California) showed him round. Bowie stayed at a mansion in Hollywood hills owned by Tom Ayres (manager of the Sir Douglas Quintet) and at the midtown Holiday Inn. Demoed Moonage daydream, using Ayres recording equipment. He also recorded a demo of Hang on to yourself (he used Gene Vincent's guitar) (2.16). They borrowed Ayres Cadillac and took a tour to: KMAC Radio at Long Beach. CIMS Radio at Santa Anna. KET Radio in Los Angeles Topanga Canyon Corral.	NT	

DATE / EVENT	AUDIO / VIDEO	TITLE

Hamburger Hamlet on Hollywood Boulevard (Hollywood High School).
Whisky A-Go-Go.
Tim Hardin's Greenwich Village Club.

Rodney Bingenheimer invited a nymphet who loved famous men. After dinner Bowie took her up to his room (Stardust - Henry Edwards and Tony Zanetta 1986).

Chris Van Ness wrote in the Los Angeles Free Press: "What happens to a flower-child when all of the world around him is going slightly crazy and power struggles are taking over everything, including his music, is that he harnesses his genius, conforms to the insanity, outpowers the loudest group around, and does it all just a little better than anybody else."

6-2-1971 Sounds. Article by Penny Valentine.
Valentine wrote: It is amazing, that completely out of the blue his new album, which has taken nearly a year to release after a year of comparative silence and no success as we've come to understand it, is being acclaimed in America. Bowie has been forced out to spend three weeks there this month just to talk about it.

<u>14-2-1971</u> Bingenheimer arranged a huge party (at the home of Paul Feigen in Los Angeles).	1 CDR	*Hendrikse various vol. 5* (No label, no number)
That same evening they also visited Warhol star Ultra Violet's party (at Dianne Bennett's house). David was wearing a Mr. (Michael) Fish dress.	1 CDR	*Friars - Aylesbury - 25th September 1971* (No label, no number)
He sat on a waterbed and played a selection from The man who sold the world. After all and the first part of All the madmen was recorded (2.11).	CD Tape	OST Mayor of the Sunset Strip quality 7, 2 min.

The remastered version of All the madmen was released on the OST Mayor of the Sunset Strip on 16-3-2004.
Rodney Bingenheimer: "He wasn't coming on like a girl. He was grabbing girls right and left."

<u>February 1971</u> San Francisco.	NT	
February 1971 Interview in the studio of San Francisco's KSAN-FM Radio.	Tape	

Bowie says: "My last LP was, very simply, a collection of reminiscences about my experiences as a shaven-headed transvestite."

February 1971 FM Radio interviews (Chicago and San Jose) Bowie talks about LP The man who sold the world.	Tape	
<u>February 1971</u> Texas.	NT	

18-2-1971 Rolling Stone. Article by John Mendelsohn: The man who sold the world.
Mendelsohn wrote: "An experience that is as intriguing as it is chilling, but only to a listener sufficiently together to withstand its schizophrenia."

DATE / EVENT	AUDIO / VIDEO	TITLE

February / March 1971 Terry Burns left Cane Hill. Some days later he was on the doorstep of his aunt Pat. She took him to Haddon Hall. David and Angie refused to let them stay the night, they were expecting guests for dinner.

10-3-1971 Radio Luxemburg Studios.   CD   *Freddi & The Dreamer*
1. Lady Stardust (3.35).   *(3 songs) (Switch On! Devil*
2. Right on mother (2.08).   *KWSK 99-04)*
3. Moonage daydream (3.48).   CD   *The complete Arnold Corns*
                                                                                Sessions (BOW71) (3 songs)
                                                      CD   *Ultra Rare Trax Vol.1 (The*
                                                                        Genuine Pig TGP-CD-108) (1)

20-3-1971 Disc and Music Echo. Interview published.
Bowie: "I became disillusioned after Space Oddity. The album was released at the same time and did absolutely nothing. No one even bothered to review it and I'm personally convinced that some of the tracks were really good. I just decided to leave London and come to live down here. In fact, the only thing that gave me faith again was being asked to go across to America."

March 1971 Trident Studios. Recording demo How lucky you are (Miss Peculiar) (3.32). Demo Andy Warhol (only the preceding chat (0.58) is left, the rest of the tape is erased).

End March 1971 London, The Marquee.
The Rolling Stones ended their tour with a TV-concert. Inspiration for Bowie to do the same in October 1973?

Spring 1971 New York. La MaMa Theatre. Pork (a play, directed by J. Ingrassia, based on tapes provided by Andy Warhol).

April 1971 Gentlemen's Quarterly. Article by Jan Hodenfield: Iggy Stooge, I'll stick it deep inside.

April 1971 Pitt wrote to DeFries and Myers. He would be exercising his option to extend David's contract to its fifth and final year. They simply ignored the letter.

April 1971 Release in UK LP The man who sold the world (Mercury 6338 041).
The cover shows him wearing a woman's dress. In the US it was replaced by a cartoon drawing in November 1970.
Bowie: "It's the most drug-oriented album I have ever recorded, for I was going through hell at the time" (David Robert Jones: The discography of a generalist - David Jeffrey Fletcher 1979).
John Cambridge: "Nobody really smoked a lot of dope at that time. I wasn't into it and David never really and Mick Ronson never. It was really casual and if I was offered I'd say, 'Nah,' and it was the same with David, he wasn't really bothered. Now and again he'd just have a drag and that would be it" (Alias David Bowie - Peter & Leni Gillman 1986).

April 1971 Released in Germany LP The man who sold the world with a different track: Saviour machine / The Supermen (reprise).

1-4-1971 Rolling Stone. Article by John Mendelsohn: David Bowie? Pantomime rock?
Bowie: "What the music says may be serious. But as a medium it should no be questioned, analysed or

taken so seriously. I think it should be tarted up, made into a prostitute, a parody of itself. It should be the clown, the Pierrot medium. The music is the mask the message wears. Music is the Pierrot and I, the performer, am the message."

17-4-1971 Melody Maker. Article by Chris Welch: Why does David Bowie like dressing up in ladies clothes?
Bowie about Oh, you pretty things: "I don't know if Peter Noone knows what it means, it's all about Homo Superior. Herman goes heavy. He's going to be a slightly more adult entertainer."

Bowie: "I went to America to promote The man who sold the world and, as I was going to Texas, I wore a dress. One guy pulled out a gun and called me a fag. But I thought the dress was beautiful" (In his own words - Miles 1980).

23-4-1971 Interviewed at Chrysalis music publishers' offices by George Tremlett.

23-4-1971 Trident Studios. Recording The Shadowman.

23-4-1971 Trident Studios Recording of Rupert the Riley (Nick King All Stars), piano riff lifted from Let's spend the night together - Rolling Stones.
First version: Bowie on lead vocal (3.09). Second version: Lead vocal Micky King, Bowie backing vocal (3.13).
Demo Miss peculiar (first version How lucky you are), with vocals by Micky King (3.36).

24-4-1971 Daily Mirror. Half-page story and two-column photograph.

<u>29-4-1971</u> London, Roundhouse.   NT

30-4-1971 Release Oh! you pretty things (3.07) / Together forever - Peter Noone (RAK 114). A-side by Bowie (he also did backing vocals). A Top twenty hit single.

Peter Noone in 1983: "When we recorded that, David had some trouble playing it through completely, so we recorded it in three sections. There were actually three breaks in that piano track, something that Mickie Most helped to arrange."

Beginning of May 1971 Bowie to hospital, because he had a flesh wound. He stalled his car outside Lewisham Police Station whilst driving to London. In an attempt to crank the engine into life he forgot he had left the car in gear. The vehicle lurched forward and the starting handle badly gashed in his leg. He had to stay in hospital for a week (David Bowie Theatre of Music - Robert Matthew - Walker 1985). This is the incident Bowie referred to in interviews when he stated to have broken both his legs.

7-5-1971 Release Moonage Daydream (3.52) / Hang on to yourself (2.51) - Arnold Corns (B & C CB.149).

28-5-1971 David and Angela's son Duncan Zowie Haywood Jones Bowie is born in Bromley Hospital (8 pound and 8 ounces). Birth wasn't easy and Angie cracked her pelvis. David was at home, listening to a Neil Young album, when he got the happy news. They hired Suzie Frost as a nanny.

29-5-1971 Bowie wrote Kooks.
Later he commented on the song: "It just shows how slushy and sentimental a songwriter can get."

DATE / EVENT	AUDIO / VIDEO	TITLE

But on 20-6-1971 he said: "I was listening to Neil Young and they told me my wife had had a baby Sunday and so I wrote this song for small Z" (David Robert Jones: The discography of a generalist - David Jeffrey Fletcher 1979).

May / June 1971 Top of the Pops. Oh! you pretty things by Peter Noone. Bowie on piano.

June 1971 Electric Circus. Performance by Iggy Pop, covered in glitter and gold and silver spray-paint.

June 1971 Londonderry Hotel near Hyde Park Corner. Meeting Steinberg, McBride, DeFries, Bowie. They agreed the Mercury contract would end. Mercury had to be repaid all their costs.

<u>June 1971</u> Portsmouth, South Parade Pier. NT
Warm up for Glastonbury.

June 1971 Sounds. Article: John Peel, commenting on the Sunday evening "In concert" radio recording at London's Paris Studios.

3-6-1971 BBC Radio Show recorded. Broadcast 20-6-1971.

<u>4-6-1971</u> Trident Studios. CD *Freddi & The Dreamer*
1. Looking for a friend (rough mono mix) (3.24). *(3 songs) (Switch On! Devil*
2. Man in the middle (mono mix) (4.08). *KWSK 99-04)*
3. Looking for a friend (mono mix) (3.20). CD *The complete Arnold Corns Sessions (BOW71) (3 songs)*

17-6-1971 In Trident Studios with Arnold Corns. CD *Freddi & The Dreamer*
Arnold Corns was originally a group of students at *(Switch On! Devil KWSK*
Dulwich College who had been playing for some time *99-04)*
under the name Runk.
Recording Man in the middle (4.08), Looking for a friend (3.19).

<u>20-6-1971</u> BBC Radio. John Peel, In Concert. CD *A crash course for the ravers*
Recorded 3-6-1971 at BBC Paris Cinema Studios in Lower *(No label, no number)*
Regent Street in London. CD *Wild-eyed boy (9 songs)*
Also on the bill: Mike Heron (ex-Incredible String Band). *(Retropop 159082)*
1. Queen bitch (3.15). CD *The rise and rise of Ziggy*
2. Bombers (2.43). *Stardust vol. 2 (9 songs)*
3. The Supermen (2.43). *(Savage Hippo Records)*
4. Looking for a friend (3.01). 2 CD *God knows I'm good (songs*
5. Almost grown (original by Chuck Berry in 1959). Lead *2,3,4,5, and 6) (BEEB 1/2)*
vocals by Jeff Alexander (2.06). CD *Ziggy in Wonderland (2,4,5,6)*
6. Kooks (2.47). *(PROCD 89 001-2)*
7. Song for Bob Dylan. Lead vocals G. Underwood (4.30). 3 CD *Bowie at the Beeb (2,4,5,6,9)*
8. Andy Warhol. Lead vocals Dana Gillespie (3.08). CD *Bowie at the Beeb, 8 track*
9. It ain't easy (original by Ron Davies in 1970) (2.40). *sampler (For demonstration*
10. Oh! you pretty things (not broadcast) (3.13). *only) (EMI) (6)*
Attendance: 380. CD *Kiss the vipers fang (9 songs) (EBD002)*

DATE / EVENT	AUDIO / VIDEO	TITLE
A quiet version of Queen bitch. Bowie played piano on Bombers. The only time Looking for a friend and Almost grown were played live.	CD	*Hazy Cosmic Jive (2,3,4,5,6) (Invasion Unlimited IU9753-2)*
	4 CDR	The complete BBC master recordings (No label, no nr.)
	CD	*Pinups 3 (9) (BOWPU03)*
	1 CDR	The complete BBC files vol. 2 (Old Gold Records OGCD 076) (first 9 songs)
	CD	*The complete Arnold Corns Sessions (BOW71) (4)*
	CD	*Freddi & The Dreamer (4) (Switch On! Devil KWSK 99-04)*
	CD	*Canal+ Canada (10)*
	CD	*The Jean Genie (vol 1.) (2,4,5, 6) (Ban-004-A)*
	CD	*Starman (2,4,5,6) (Oil Well RSC 017 CD)*
	CD	*White light white heat(2,4,5,6) (The Swinging Pig Records TSP-CD-053)*
	CD	*At the Beep (2,4,5,6) (Archive Productions AP 89004)*
	CD	*Rebel rebel (2,5,6) (Oil Well RSC 021)*
	CD	*Live Vol. 1 (2,5,6) (Joker JOK-001-A)*
	CD	*Mega rare trax vol. 1 (2,4,5,6) (Seagull Records CD 022)*
	CD	*Five years (2,4,5,6) (Triangle Records PYCD 047)*
	CD	*Kooks (2,5,6) (Turtle Records TR-36)*
	CD	*The London Tapes (4) (World productions of compact music WPOCM 0589 D 020-2)*
	CD	*Dynamic Live (2,4,5,6)*
	CD	*BBC Bowie (2,4,5,6)*
	CD	Happy Birthday Mr. Bowie
	LP	*Ziggy 2 (Tune in 002 - Dragon Fly Rec.) (8 songs)*
	LP	*Caught in the act (MIM Records MIM-XXX/400) (1,4)*
	LP	*London by ta ta (No label, no number)*
	LP	*White light white heat (2,4,5,6) (The Swinging Pig Records*

DATE / EVENT	AUDIO / VIDEO	TITLE
	LP	TSP 053 A/B) Goodbye to the Brixton son (1, 4)
23-6-1971 Pilton (Worthy Farm) Glastonbury Fayre Fest. The tapes of the performance are unreleased and owned by Jake Riviera (David Bowie - Dave Thompson 1986). The festival was held Sunday 20-6-1971 to Thursday 24-6-1971. Bowie entered the stage at dawn. Bowie sang: Oh! you pretty things, Kooks, Changes, Amsterdam, The Supermen, Memory of a free festival and Song for Bob Dylan. Dana Gillespie: "People were waking up and they didn't expect music at this hour. When David began Memory of a free festival, the sun came over the hill and lit him up and everybody warmed to him. He was a huge success. He really won people over."	2 CD Single Tape	*The Electric Score* *(Studio versions)* *(No label, no number)* David Bowie (Major Tom 6052-202)

Around 25-6-1971 Start recording sessions for Hunky Dory at Trident Studios.

End June 1971 Dana Gillespie took Angie to her parents villa at the Lago Maggiore in Italy, to recover from the birth of her son. They were making love when Dana's mother popped up in the doorway of the bedroom.
The next day they went to see the band I Giganti (who had a hit with an Italian cover of Space oddity). They took two of the band members to the villa. When the boys left, Dana made love to one of them, while he lay on his back in the middle of the road, while Angie and the other guy kept an eye on traffic from the left and the right (Backstage passes - Angela Bowie and Patrick Carr 1993).

June / July 1971 Carnaby Street. Interview in a pub. Bowie and Freddi Burretti turned up in dresses.

9-7-1971 Trident Studios. Recording first version It ain't easy (2.53). Backing vocals: Dana Gillespie. Before the recordings of Hunky Dory were finished!
August 1971 the song is released on a GEM promo LP with one side of Bowie songs and one side of Dana Gillespie songs.

| 28-7-1971 Hampstead, Country Club (Haversock Hall). Acoustic. Ronson on guitar, Rick Wakeman on piano. Attended by about 28 people and the Cast of Pork. They all sat in a semicircle on the floor. Leee Black Childers: "He introduced us from the audience and Cherry Vanilla stood up and popped out a tit for the other 28 people" (In other words - Kerry Juby 1986). In the play Cherry Vanilla played Pork from New York. She was a groupie that showed one of her breasts every time she saw a rock star. Wayne (later he would become Jayne) County bowed in his best Southern belle fashion. Afterwards they all went to The Sombrero and Cherry Vanilla practically attacked Mick Ronson sexually on the | NT | |

DATE / EVENT	AUDIO / VIDEO	TITLE

dance floor.

August 1971 500 Promo-LP's of Hunky Dory / Dana Gillespie stuff were pressed.
Interesting songs: Early versions Kooks (3.13), Eight line poem, It ain't easy (2.53).

August 1971 DeFries flew to New York with an acetate of 5 songs from Hunky Dory (a.o. Changes, Kooks, Oh! You pretty things, Eight line poem) to meet Dennis Katz of RCA on the Avenue of the Americas in Manhattan.
Agreed a contract for USD 37.500,— an album.

1-8-1971 Bowie signs for GEM.

<u>1-8-1971</u> London, Marquee Club.   NT
David Bowie / Mick Ronson (acoustic duo).

2-8-1971 Premiere (first of 26 nights) "Pork" at the   *Video*   *Various 14 (3 min)*
Round House in London.

The cast of Pork included: Kathy Dorritie (Cherry Vanilla), Wayne (later Jane) County, Anthony Zanetta, Leee Black Childers, Gerri Miller, Jamie de Carlo Andrews. The play was directed by Tony Ingrassia.
Posted notices warned: "This play has explicit sexual content and offensive language. If you are likely to be disturbed, please do not attend."
Bowie visited the play together with Dana Gillespie, Angela, Mick Ronson.
The cast of Pork rented a place they called Pig Mansions.
Cherry Vanilla gave an interview to a journalist from Rolling Stones, while giving a blowjob to some guy she'd picked up (Man enough to be a woman - Jayne County with Rupert Smith 1995).
When Pork closed in London, Cherry Vanilla asked DeFries a few copies of Hunky Dory. DeFries gave her and Leee Black Childers each a box of fifty. They gave them to DJ's in the New York scene and influential friends.
Angie Bowie: "You could see it lightning the fuses of all sorts of ideas in his head as he sat there watching those people, every one of them as sharp as you could want a performance artist to be" (Backstage passes - Angela Bowie and Patrick Carr 1993).
Leee Black Childers: "I think glitter really took of when John Vaccaro (who formed The Ridiculous Theater with Charles Ludlam in 1966 / 1967) came across this little place in Chinatown. He bought it all, giant shopping bags of glitter in all colours. Baby Betty, who was playing a thalidomide baby, had glitter coming out of her pussy, so it was because of John Vaccaro that glitter became synonymous with outrageousness" (Glam! Bowie, Bolan and the Glitter Rock Revolution - Barney Hoskyns 1998).

<u>11-8-1971</u> Hampstead, Country Club (Haversock Hall).   NT
David Bowie / Mick Ronson (acoustic duo).

14-8-1971 Sounds. Article by Steve Peacock: Confessions of a disillusioned old rocker.

28-8-1971 Last night of Pork. Bowie was backstage and went with the cast to the Hard Rock Café afterwards. From the Hard Rock Café Bowie went to the Sombrero and talked to Tony Zanetta.

One day Mick Ronson had to do a string arrangement for a band called Milkwood. He was afraid he would wake up late and asked Bowie's mother (who was coming to Haddon Hall the next day) to wake

DATE / EVENT	AUDIO / VIDEO	TITLE

him up in time. So the next day she shouted at Mick to get up. Half asleep he assumed he woke up very late and jumped naked out of his bed and rushed past a very surprised Margaret Jones (Mick Ronson: The Spider with the platinum hair - Weird and Gilly, 2003).

29-8-1971 Tony Zanetta visited David and Angie in Haddon Hall. They had dinner, listened to David's music and talked about the future. They ended up in bed having a threesome. Tony Zanetta came back to the flat of the Pork cast and was kind of embarrassed (Man enough to be a woman - Jayne County with Rupert Smith 1995).

September 1971 Recording demo Only one paper left.

September 1971 Holland. Free shows in small bars and public houses.   NT

September 1971 Belgium. Free shows in small bars and public houses.   NT

September 1971 Northern France. Free shows in small bars and public houses.   NT

Begin September 1971 DeFries, Bowie, Angela and Mick Ronson stayed at The Warwick Hotel in New York.
Bowie and Angela saw Elvis Presley perform at The Madison Square Garden.

They met Lou Reed at Ginger Man Restaurant (afternoon), surrounded by A&R men and journalist Lisa Robinson.
In the evening in Max's Kansas City Bowie was introduced (by Lisa Robinson and Danny Fields) to Iggy Pop.
The next morning Bowie and DeFries met with Iggy Pop to discuss working together (Iggy came by on his way to the methadone clinic).
Leee Black Childers: "I think Bowie's infatuation with Iggy had to do with Bowie wanting to tap into the rock 'n' roll reality that Iggy lived" (Glam! Bowie, Bolan and the Glitter Rock Revolution - Barney Hoskyns 1998).

8-9-1971 Iggy Pop signs management deal with Tony DeFries.

9-9-1971 New York. Bowie signs contract with RCA.
Delivered acetate disc of Hunky Dory.
RCA arranged a reception at Max's Kansas City (bar and nightclub close to The Factory, on Park Avenue South off Union Square, owned by Mickey Ruskin). Some guests: Lou Reed, Iggy Pop.
One of the waitresses at Max's was Debbie Harry. She was always stoned and regularly dropped cheeseburgers in people's laps (Man enough to be a woman - Jayne County 1995).

9-9-1971 Trident Studios. Recording It ain't easy (2.57).

10-9-1971 Met Andy Warhol at The Factory.   *Video*   *Stolp tapes no. 23 (1 min)*
They rang a bell labelled 'Do not ring' and the door was opened by Warhol's assistant Paul Morrissey.

DATE / EVENT	AUDIO / VIDEO	TITLE

10-9-1971 Aylesbury, Friars Club.
Cancelled.

14-9-1971 Trident Studios. Recording The Shadowman (unfinished) (demo 2) (3.44).

17-9-1971 First payment of RCA USD 56.250,— (37.500 for Hunky Dory and 50% for next album).

21-9-1971 Recording Sounds of the 70's. Bob Harris. Broadcast 4-10-1971. Repeated 1-11-1971.

<u>25-9-1971</u> Aylesbury, Borough Assembly Rooms (Friars), managed by David Stopps.	CD	*Close to the golden dawn (Switch On!)*
Support act: America. Started at 19.30 hours. Promoter: Lol Coxhill. Received GBP. 150,—.	1 CDR	*Friars Aylesbury September 25th 1971*
The show is filmed. MainMan will later lose the film.		*(No label, no number)*
Nice recording of an intimate performance. Bowie tells in a funny way about his trip to America the next day.	1 CDR	*Friars - Aylesbury - 25th September 1971*
"This is a song about a friend of mine in America, Lou Reed. He is funny, outrageously funny. It's called Queen Bitch."	Video	*(No label, no number)*

David Stops: "DeFries was a bit of a hustler. That night when we paid David, I had to pay the last bit of it in 50p coins. DeFries counted it in the dressing room and came back to tell it was 50p short."

27-9-1971 Bowie received an advance from GEM (GBP 2.000,—).

End 1971 GEM increased its share from 10% to 20% from David's performances.

October 1971 Released in US. Promo-single. Eight line poem / Bombers (RCA, BOWPROMO 1A1/1B1).

4-10-1971 Bowie received second advance from GEM (GBP 2.000,—).

<u>4-10-1971</u> BBC. Sounds of the 70's. Bob Harris. Recorded 21-9-1971, repeated on 1-11-1971.	CD	*Oh! you Pretty Thing (6 songs) (Savage Hippo Records SH111)*
Recorded at Studio1, Kensington House, Shepherd's Bush, London (The first and only BBC-recording in stereo).	2 CD	*God knows I'm good (1,7) (BEEB 1/2)*
Bowie only joined by Mick Ronson.	CD	*God knows I'm good (1,7) (Invasion Unlimited IU9753-1)*
1. The supermen (2.48).		
2. Oh! you pretty things (3.19).	CD	*Ziggy in Wonderland (1) (PROCD 89 001-2)*
3. Eight line poem (2.56).		
4. Kooks (3.27).	CD	*The rise and rise of Ziggy Stardust vol. 3 (6 songs) (Savage Hippo Records)*
5. Fill your heart (2.46).		
6. Amsterdam (3.36).		
7. False start (0.12) Andy Warhol (2.33).		
	3 CD	*Bowie at the Beeb (1,2)*
	CD	*Pinups 3 (5) (BOWPU03)*
	CD	*Pinups 4 (6) (BOWPU04)*

DATE / EVENT	AUDIO / VIDEO	TITLE
	CD	Nobody's Children (5 songs) (EBD003)
	1 CDR	Battle for Bowie (7) (No label, no number)
	4 CDR	The complete BBC master recordings (No label, no nr.)
	1 CDR	The complete BBC files vol. 2 (Old Gold Records OGCD 076) (1,2,3,4)
	1 CDR	The complete BBC files vol. 3 (Old Gold Records OGCD 077) (5,6,7)
	CD	BBC sessions 1969-1972 (7)
	CD	The Axeman Cometh (complete) (DB003)
	CD	Stardust memories (1) (Retropop 159081)
	CD	The Jean Genie (vol 1.) (1,) (Ban-004-A)
	CD	Starman (1) (Oil Well RSC 017 CD)
	CD	White light white heat (1) (The Swinging Pig Records TSP-CD-053)
	CD	At the Beep (1) (Archive Productions AP 89004)
	CD	Rebel rebel (1) (Oil Well RSC 021)
	CD	Live Vol. 1 (1) (Joker JOK-001-A)
	CD	Mega rare trax vol. 1 (1) (Seagull Records CD 022)
	CD	Five years (1) (Triangle Records PYCD 047)
	CD	Kooks (1) (Turtle Records TR-36)
	CD	Rare and well done (7 songs) (No label, no number)
	CD	Dynamic Live (1)
	CD	BBC Bowie (1)
	CD	Under the table (6 songs) (Savage Hippo SH 111)
	LP	White light white heat (1) (The Swinging Pig Records TSP 053A/B)
	LP	Die Bowie (1)
	LP	The unofficial Wembley Wizard Box File (1)

DATE / EVENT	AUDIO / VIDEO	TITLE
	LP	Ziggy 1 - My radio Sweetheart (1)
4-10-1971 London, Seymour Hall (Seymour Place).	NT	

14-10-1971 Hull, Kingston Upon Hull Royal Infirmary. Denise Irvin gave birth to Mick Ronson's son Nicholas.

15-10-1971 Release Walnut whirl / Right on mother (2.41) - Peter Noone (RAK 121). B-side by Bowie (he also played the piano and sang backing vocals).

November 1971 Release Jeepster / Life is a gas - Marc Bolan and T.Rex (Fly Bug 16).

November 1971 Creem. Article by Andrew Lycett: David Bowie: A rock oddity.

November 1971 London, Rainbow Theatre. Alice Cooper made his UK debut, with a shocking visual spectacle.

| November 1971 South East London, Underhill Rehearsal Studios. Rehearsals by The Spiders. Willie Palin, who had come to London for six weeks and wanted to earn some money before returning to the farm where he used to work, had a job in the studio and became their roadie. | NT | |

1-11-1971 Sound of the Seventies repeats the recordings of 21-9-1971.

8-11-1971 London. Trident Studios.
Recording Starman (4.38), Hang on to yourself (2.38).
Starman was included on the Ziggy album because RCA needed a single.
Outtakes recorded during Ziggy Stardust sessions: Only one paper left (Sept. 1971), It's gonna rain again.
Woody Woodmansy had complained that the drum-sound on Hunky Dory sounded like a bunch of cornflake boxes. They send the tea boy out to buy as much different shaped cornflake boxes he could get. For Woody they set up a full drum kit of cornflake boxes and no drums. You can imagine the laughter when he entered the studio (Strange fascination - David Buckley 1999).

11-11-1971 London. Trident Studios.
Recording Ziggy Stardust (electric 2.35) (acoustic (3.36), Star (2.47), Sweet Head (take ?, 4.14) (take 4, 4.52).

11 or 12-11-1971 London. Trident Studios.
Recording Amsterdam (2.55).

12-11-1971 London. Trident Studios.
Recording Moonage daydream (4.37), Soul love (3.33), The Supermen (2.41), Lady Stardust (3.21).
The Supermen was released in July 1972 as part of the 3LP Revelations - A musical anthology for Glastonbury Fayre.

DATE / EVENT	AUDIO / VIDEO	TITLE

15-11-1971 London. Trident Studios.
Recording Five years (4.42).
This day also an early running order for the album Ziggy Stardust was assembled (it included the later substituted Amsterdam, Round and round, Velvet goldmine, Holy Holy).
Working title for the album: Round and round.

End November 1971 David, Angie, Zowie, Woody Woodmansey and Mick Ronson spend a week in Cyprus.

15-12-1971 A provisional tape of the LP Ziggy Stardust is made.

17-12-1971 Release LP Hunky Dory (RCA LSP.4623).

Bowie in 1976 for BBC Radio: "The crack in the sky, the hand coming through the crack in the sky. A lot of the songs in fact do deal with some kind of schizophrenia, or alternating id problems. Oh! you pretty things was one of them. According to Jung, to see cracks in the sky is not, is not really quite on. Yes, I hadn't been to an analyst. No, my parents went, my brothers and sisters and my aunts and uncles and cousins, they did that. They ended up in a much worse state, so I stayed away. I though I'd write my problems out."
In Oh! you pretty things Bowie refers to Edward Bulwer - Lytton's 1871 science-fiction novel The Coming Race.
Song for Bob Dylan refers to the story of Pallas Athena, who jumped from Zeus' brow: "The same old painted lady from the brow of the super brain." In 1993 he did another song about Pallas Athena.

RCA / MainMan Radio Promo: LP catalogue ad (the background song is Kooks) (1.00).

17-12-1971 Released in Spain: A pedir de boca (Hunky Dory) (RCA).
The photograph for Hunky Dory sleeve was taken by Brian Ward and hand-coloured by George Underwood.

17-12-1971 Agreement GEM-Mercury. GEM paid Mercury USD 17.884 for the master tapes of Space oddity and The man who sold the world. Mercury was paid back for all the costs in the past. GEM leased the master tapes to RCA for USD 20.000 and still owned the tapes.
A great move by DeFries, he freed himself from Mercury and got the master tapes and even earned a little money!

25-12-1971 Disc and Music Echo. Article: Forget the "Spacey" David and enjoy this offering.

28-12-1971 Lou Reed arrives in London.
David Bowie was very busy and his wife Angie took care of Lou and Betty.

1972 Release LP A clockwork orange (Soundtrack) - Var. Art. (Warner Bros.). Later re-released on CD (Warner Bros. 7599-27256-2). Includes Ninth Symphony and Pomp And Circumstance, as used for the 3-7-1973 concert.

January 1972 UK. Limp Documentary. Tape quality 8, 10 min.
Phone interview. Played Don't be afraid and Bombers.

Early January 1972 Photo's for the cover of Ziggy Stardust shot in Heddon Street, Piccadilly (by Brian

DATE / EVENT	AUDIO / VIDEO	TITLE

Ward).

6-1-1972 Rolling Stone. Article by John Mendelsohn: Hunky Dory.
Bowie about Life on Mars?: "That's my favourite on it. I wrote it around the same chord pattern as Frank Sinatra's 'My way.' I couldn't believe those lyrics. You know, I'll get pissed my way - Really Evil. I love the arrangement on Life on Mars? I would rather have put that out as a single than Changes, but I decided to leave it up to RCA."

7-1-1972 Release Changes (3.33) / Andy Warhol (3.58) (RCA 2160).
Chosen by Tony Blackburn as record of the week.

<u>11-1-1972</u> BBC Radio Session. John Peel, Sounds of the Seventies (at BBC Kensington House).
Broadcast 28-1-1972. Repeated 31-3-1972.

1. Hang on to yourself (broadcast 28-1-1972 and 31-3-1972) (2.48).
2. Ziggy Stardust (broadcast 28-1-1972 and 31-3-1972) (3.16).
3. Queen bitch (Begin: Well, I'm up on the eleventh floor) (Broadcast 28-1-1972 and 31-3-1972) (3.03).
4. Waiting for the man (Contains: Dark grey building, up three flights) (Broadcast 28-1-1972 and 31-3-1972) (5.25).
5. Lady Stardust (broadcast 31-3-1972) (3.16).

AUDIO / VIDEO	TITLE
CD	*The rise and rise of Ziggy Stardust vol. 3 (songs 2,3,4 and 5) (Savage Hippo Records)*
2 CD	*Starman over the rainbow (songs 3,4) (Savage Hippo Records SH118)*
CD	*Nobody's Children (songs 2,3, 4 and 5) (EBD003)*
2 CD	*God knows I'm good (songs 1 and 5) (BEEB 1/2)*
3 CD	*Bowie at the Beeb (1)*
CD	*Hazy cosmic jive (songs 1,5) (Invasion Unlimited IU9753-2)*
1 CDR	*Battle for Bowie (1) (No label, no number)*
4 CDR	The complete BBC master recordings (No label, no nr.)
1 CDR	The complete BBC files vol. 3 (Old Gold Records OGCD 077)
CD	*Missinglinksone Ziggy (4) (Icon One)*
CD	*The Vintage David Bowie (4) (ZIG 1)*
CD	Dynamic Live (1)
CD	BBC Bowie (1)
1 CDR	*Used up and empty (1) (No label, no number)*
LP	Oh! You Pretty thing (Spaceheat SH2799 A-8207 A-1/83 S111)
LP	Goodbye to the Brixton son (FA001)
LP	Die Bowie (Lines Production LTD. LP 70 A/B)
LP	The passenger (Emir Gema DBIP 111 291-A/B LP-70-A/B)
LP	Used up and empty (1)
LP	Ziggy 1 - My radio Sweetheart

DATE / EVENT	AUDIO / VIDEO	TITLE
	7"/45 Tape	(1) Five years (1) quality 9, 15 min.

11-1-1972 Studio T1. Recorded mono mix of Waiting for the man (4.55).

13-1-1972 London. Stanley Kubrick's film A Clockwork Orange opens. Soon after the release Bowie and Mick Ronson saw the film.

18-1-1972 BBC Radio Session, Sounds of the 70's, Bob Harris. Broadcast 7-2-1972. Maida Vale Studios 5, Delaware Road. 1. Queen bitch (2.56) (opens with: Oh yeah! Hmm, I'm up on the eleventh floor. After the first line Bowie says: Louder). 2. Five years (4.19) (Contains: I had to cram so much, everything in there). 3. Hang on to yourself (2.51) (Contains: She'll come to the show tonight, praying to the light machines). 4. Ziggy Stardust (3.23) (Contains: Played it left hand, but played it to far). 5. Waiting for the man (5.08) (not broadcast on 7-2-1972) (Contains: Grey dirty building, up three flights).	2 CD CD CD CD 4 CDR 1 CDR CD 2 CD CD	Starman over the rainbow (songs 1,5) (Savage Hippo Records SH118) The Year of the spiders (songs 1,2,3,4,5) (Switch On! Devil KWSK 99-03) The rise and rise of Ziggy Stardust vol. 3 (songs 1,2,3,4 and 5) (Savage Hippo Records) Nobody's children (5 songs) (EBD003) The complete BBC master recordings (No label, no nr.) The complete BBC files vol. 3 (Old Gold Records OGCD 077) Stardust memories (1,3,4,5) (Retropop 159081) God knows I'm good (songs 1,2,4, and 5) (BEEB 1/2) Ziggy in Wonderland (2,4) (PROCD 89 001-2)
Hang on to yourself from 18-1-1972, not from 11-1-1972 as mentioned on official release CD Bowie at the Beeb.	3 CD CD CD CD CD CD CD CD CD CD	Bowie at the Beeb (1,2,4,5) Bowie at the Beeb, 8 track sampler (For demonstration only) (EMI) (3) Hazy Cosmic Jive (1,2,4,5) (Invasion Unlimited IU9753-2) BBC Sampler 1969-1972 (3) Chameleon Chron. Vol. 3 (4) (Living Legend Records LLR-CD 050) Rebel rebel (2,3,4,5) (Oil Well RSC 021) Live Vol. 1 (2,3,4,5) (Joker JOK-001-A) The Jean Genie (vol 1.) (2,3,4, 5) (Ban-004-A) Starman (2,3,4,5) (Oil Well RSC 017 CD) White light white heat (2,3,4,5)

DATE / EVENT	AUDIO / VIDEO	TITLE
		(The Swinging Pig Records TSP-CD-053)
	CD	*At the Beep (2,3,4,5)*
	CD	*Mega rare trax vol. 1 (2,4)*
		(Seagull Records CD 022)
	CD	*Five years (2,4)*
		(Triangle Records PYCD 047)
	CD	*Kooks (2,4,3,5)*
		(Turtle Records TR-36)
	CD	*Starman in session (4)*
		(Silver Rarities SIRA 93)
	1 CDR	*Battle for Bowie (4)*
		(No label, no number)
	CD	*Dynamic Live (2,4,5)*
	CD	*BBC Bowie (2,4,5)*
	2 CDR	*Cyberstation (5)*
		(StationToBowie)
	1 CDR	*Used up and empty (2)*
		(No label, no number)
	CD	Happy Birthday Mr. Bowie
	LP	Lost and forgotten (1,5) (Halloween Jack Production LTD. Gema A-8206 S111)
	LP	White light white heat (2,3,4,5) (The Swinging Pig Records TSP 053A/B)
	LP	BBC Show (1,2,4,5)
	LP	Die Bowie (1)
	LP	Used up and empty (2)
	LP	The unofficial Wembley Wizard Box File (5)
	LP	Ziggy 1 - My radio Sweetheart (1,4,5)
	7"/45	Bowie does Reed (5) (Major Tom 6052-204)
	7"/45	Five years (2)
	7"/45	Spiders from Mars (DB-TAP 008-PRO) (5)

18-1-1972 Recording session 1: Demos Rock 'n' roll suicide, Suffragette city. New version Ziggy Stardust (3.13). Recording session 2: Demo Starman.

<u>19-1-1972</u> London, Royal Ballroom on Tottenham High Road. Rehearsal.   NT
During rehearsals they decided to call the band The Spiders.

19-1-1972 Royal Ballroom, interview by George Tremlett.
Bowie: "This new act will be theatrical and a kind of entertainment. Quite different to anything anyone else has tried to do before. There's not much outrageousness left in pop music anymore. There's only

DATE / EVENT	AUDIO / VIDEO	TITLE

me and Marc Bolan."

20-1-1972 Disc. Article by Rick Atkinson: All that glitter.

21-1-1972 Maida Vale Studios. Recording demo John I'm only dancing (2.43). Broadcast in reworked version on 21-9-1972.

22-1-1972 Melody Maker. Article by Michael Watts: "Oh you pretty thing."
Michael Watts wrote: David's present image is to come on like a swishy queen, a gorgeously effeminate boy. He's as camp as a row of tents, with his limp hand and his trolling vocabulary. 'I'm gay,' he says and I have always been, even when I was David Jones'. But there's a sly jollity about how he says it, a secret smile at the corners of his mouth. He knows that in these times it's permissible to act like a male tart, and that to shock and outrage, which pop has always striven to do troughout it's history, is a balls-breaking process."

A few days later a worried Mrs. Ronson called Haddon Hall, looking for reassurance that her beloved son Mick hadden't fallen into the den of iniquity (Backstage passes - Angela Bowie and Patrick Carr 1993).

Mick Ronson: "My family in Hull took a lot of flak about it because they'd never even heard about it up there. It came like throwing paint over the car and paint up the door and stuff like that, which really annoyed me" (In other words - Kerry Juby 1986).

Angela invited various Vogue models to Haddon Hall. When the Spiders looked down from the balcony they saw about eight gorgeous females undressed (Mick Ronson: The Spider with the platinum hair - Weird and Gilly, 2003).

28-1-1972 BBC Radio Session. John Peel, Sounds of the Seventies. Recorded 11-1-1972.

29-1-1972 New Musical Express. Article by Danny Holloway: David Bowie - I'm not ashamed of wearing dresses.
Bowie: "What kind of cult would I develop? Gay lib? Spaced-out queen?"

29-1-1972 Sounds. Article by Penny Valentine: Bowie coming back to life.

29-1-1972 Iggy Pop joined Bowie in England. He stayed at The Royal Garden Hotel in Kensington.

<u>29-1-1972</u> Aylesbury, Borough Assembly Hall (Friars).   NT
Tickets: 60p. Support act: Grand Canyon.
Concert attended by Roger Taylor and Freddie Mercury.

Rumoured Mott the Hoople recorded Suffragette City in February 1972. They only listened to Bowie's demo and (according to drummer Buffin) decided not to record it (David Bowie - Dave Thompson 1986).

2-2-1972 New running order for the album Ziggy Stardust is prepared.
Amsterdam, Velvet Goldmine and Holy holy replaced by It ain't easy, Suffragette city and Rock 'n' roll suicide. The last 2 songs are last minute compositions. On the eventual finished track order Round and round was later replaced by Starman (also a last minute composition).

DATE / EVENT	AUDIO / VIDEO	TITLE

3-2-1972 Coventry, Lancaster Arts Festival.
Cancelled.

4-2-1972 London. Trident Studios. Recording master takes of Starman (4.16), Suffragette city (3.25) and Rock 'n' roll suicide (2.58).

7-2-1972 BBC Radio Session, Sounds of the 70's, Bob Harris. Recorded 18-1-1972.

8-2-1972 UK TV. BBC 2. Old Grey Whistle Test. Not a real BBC session.	CD	*Wild-eyed boy (1,2,3)* (Retropop 159082)
1. Oh! You pretty things (slightly edited album version) (3.08).	2 CD	*God knows I'm good (1,2,3)* (BEEB 1/2)
2. Queen bitch, recorded 3-6-1971 (edit to 2.23).	CD	*MissinglinksoneZiggy (1,2,3)* (Icon One)
3. Five years (3.15).		
4. Queen bitch (take 1) (0.32).	CD	*The Axeman Cometh* (5 songs) (DB 003)
5. Queen bitch (take 2) (2.58).		
6. Oh! You pretty things (Alternative take. Never broadcast on radio, but aired on BBC TV in 1982) (3.38).	CD	*Hazy Cosmic Jive (1,2,3)* (Invasion Unlimited IU9753-2)
	CD	*The Vintage D. Bowie (1,2,3)* (ZIG 1)
Bowie was dressed in a jumpsuit and played piano during Oh! You pretty things.	1 CDR	*Ziggy TV (100% 13) (5 songs)*
	CD	*Toys from the attic (5 songs)*
Bowie and the band watched the show at home in Beckenham.	CD	*Happy Birthday Mr. Bowie*
	CD	*Legendary Lost Tapes Vol.1 (1,2,3,)* (VigOtone 178)
	VCD	*Various 1 (10.23 min.)*
	VCD	*Bob's Eggs [+extras] (6)* (No label, no number)
	VCD	*I keep a good friend....(2)* (No label, no number)
	VCD	Videobits Volume 1 (2) (No label, no number)
	LP	Bowiestudio 70-75
	Tape	quality 10, 6 min.
	Tape	quality 9, 10 min.
	Video	*Stolp tapes vol. 10 (7 min)* (Songs 1 and 3)
	Video	25 Years of Ziggy Stardust
	Video	*Various 10 (songs 1,2,3)*
	Video	*Stolp tapes vol. 21 (3 min)* (Song 2)
	Video	*Various 15 (3 songs)*
	Video	*Various 26 (11 min)*
10-2-1972 Tolworth (London), Fox at the Toby Jug. Opening date of Ziggy Stardust tour. David wore a dress. Opening music: Ode to joy (a moog take by Wendy Carlos). The clothes and the speech of the Ziggy character were	NT	

DATE / EVENT	AUDIO / VIDEO	TITLE

heavily influenced by the film A Clockwork Orange. Vince Taylor was another influence.
In 1993 Bowie acknowledged about A Clockwork Orange: "I got most of the look from Ziggy from that. The jumpsuits I thought were just wonderful, and I liked the malicious, malevolent, vicious quality of those four guys. I picked out all these florid, bright, quilted kind of materials."
His hair was done by Suzy Fussey (who later would become Mick Ronson's wife). From a French Vogue and two German Vogues she got the idea for the model and a German hair dye called Red Hot Red and an enormous amount of peroxide were used to give the red a hot cast (Stardust - Henry Edwards and Tony Zanetta 1986).

The Spiders From Mars:
Mick Ronson (lead guitar).
Trevor Bolder (bass guitar).
Mick 'Woody' Woodmansey (drums).

11-2-1972 High Wycombe, Town Hall.   NT
Attendance: 714.

11-2-1972 Terry Burns married Olga at Croydon Register Office. Olga was a daughter of a Durham miner. She was an epileptic, who was already seven years in Cane Hill.

12-2-1972 Melody Maker. Article by Michael Watts: Night of the Iggy.

12-2-1972 London, Imperial College, Great Hall.   NT
Entrance: 50p. Support act: Sutherland Bros.
During encores Bowie tried to step out across the audience's shoulders (Iggy Pop imitation). The crowd was too sparse and he fell to the floor.

20-2-1972 Crawdaddy. Article: Hunky Dory.

23-2-1972 Chichester, Chichester College.   NT

24-2-1972 Wallington, Public Hall.   NT

25-2-1972 Eltham (South London), Avery Hill College,   NT
Disco-bar Armada. Entrance: 60p.

26-2-1972 Sutton Coldfield, Belfry Hotel (Mayfair Suite),   NT
On A446, Near Sutton Coldfield.

28-2-1972 Glasgow, City Hall.   NT
                                     Video   quality 4, 5 min. (Suffragette City).

DATE / EVENT	AUDIO / VIDEO	TITLE
29-2-1972 Sunderland, Locarno Ballroom. Attendance: 1.500. Six fans in wheelchairs (aping disablement). When Bowie (The Messiah) started to sing, they acted as if they were healed and stood up out of there wheelchairs.	NT	
1-3-1972 Bristol, University. Attendance: 920. After the show, a group of fans carry David around the hall on a lap of honour.	NT	
4-3-1972 Portsmouth, Guildhall. Attendance: 2.017.	NT	
7-3-1972 Yeovil, Yeovil College.	NT	
11-3-1972 Southampton, Guildhall.	NT	
14-3-1972 Bournemouth, Chelsea Village.	NT	

17-3-1972 Birmingham, Town Hall.
Cancelled.

Second part March 1972 interview by Mick Rock for Rolling Stone.

24-3-1972 Gasbag. Article: Bowie: Pseud or Sage?

31-3-1972 BBC, Sounds of the Seventies, repeated broadcast of 28-1-1972.

April 1972 Mick Jagger wrote the lyrics for the song Angie after the birth of Keith Richard's daughter Angie.
End 1973, when Mick Jagger had an affair with Angie Bowie, someone spread the rumour Mick Jagger had written the song for her.

April 1972 Video shot for Moonage daydream.
Mick Rock in 1998: "It was shot on a Bowlex 16mm camera. It was a collage of live footage. I can't remember if it's ever been publicly shown."

1-4-1972 Melody Maker. Article by Michael Watts: Lock up your daughters, Iggy's here.

14-4-1972 UK TV. ITV's Lift off with Ayshea. Presented by Ayshea Brough and an old owl puppet called Ollie Beak (it was a kids TV programme). Starman (3.20). Broadcast 21-6-1972.	1 CDR Tape Video	*Ziggy TV (100% 13)* quality 9, 5 min. quality 10, 3 min.
14-4-1972 UK TV. BBC. Centre Studio 8, Top of the Pops. Starman (3.32). Broadcast 5-7-1972. Robin Lumley plays piano with the Spiders.	CD CD	*Look back in anger* (No label, no number) *Ziggy in Wonderland* (PROCD 89 001-2)

DATE / EVENT	AUDIO / VIDEO	TITLE
	CD	*1980 Floorshow (Chapter One CD 25155)*
	CD	*Demo's & Outtakes (A Dutch Connection)*
	1 CDR	*Ziggy TV (100% 13)*
	2 CDR	*Cyberstation (StationToBowie)*
	CD	*Legendary Lost Tapes Vol.1 (VigOtone 178)*
	Tape	*5 min.*
	Video	*Various 10 (3 min)*
	Video	*25 Years of Ziggy Stardust*
	Video	*Stolp tapes no. 22 (2 min)*
	Video	*Stolp tapes vol 10 (4 min)*
	Video	*Various 25 (4 min)*
	Video	*Various 26 (4 min)*

14-4-1972 Release Starman (4.16) / Suffragette city (3.25) (RCA 2199). In Suffragette city Bowie calls his friend Droogie. This is one of the characters from the film A Clockwork Orange.

14-4-1972 Release in Spain: Starman (4.16) / John, I'm only dancing (RCA 3-10798).

<u>17-4-1972</u> Birmingham, Town Hall.   NT
Attendance: 1.543.
Mick Rock meets and photographs Bowie for the first time.

<u>20-4-1972</u> Harlow, Playhouse.   NT
Matthew Fisher (Procol Harum) first time on piano.

<u>21-4-1972</u> Manchester, Free Trade Hall.   NT

29-4-1972 High Wycombe, Town Hall.
Cancelled.

<u>30-4-1972</u> Plymouth, Guildhall.   NT

May 1972 Trident Studio. Bowie and Mott the Hoople recorded: 1. All the young dudes (3.58). 2. It's alright (4.24). 3. Sweet Jane (with Lou Reed) (3.14).	CD	*Trident Sessions 72 (3 songs) (CRB S.A. Spain)*
	CD	*The legendary lost tapes (3 songs) (No label, no number)*
	1 CDR	*Ziggy rarities... to victory (No label, no number) (1)*

6-5-1972 Disc. Article by Rosalind Russell: David Bowie - Bent on success.

<u>6-5-1972</u> London, Kingston Polytechnic.   2 CD   *David Bowie with Lou*
Support act: J.S.D. Band.   *Reed (complete concert)*

DATE / EVENT	AUDIO / VIDEO	TITLE
I feel free (5.20) and Got to get a job (7.09) on RarestOneBowie. Got to get a job was inspired by Marva Whitney and James Brown's song You got to have a work. Angie studied some time psychology at Kingston College. Bowie says: "I'm David Bowie. These could be The Spiders from Mars. This is some of our music." They played I feel free (original by Cream, 1966) with a long instrumental part. "We shall continue with a number written by somebody I admire very much. An American songwriter called Lou Reed." Followed by White light white heat. At the end of the show: "With this banjo we'll do one more for you tonight. It's a Lou Reed number called Waiting for the man."	CD 1 CDR 1 CDR 2 CD CD CDR 2 CD 2 CDR 1 CDR LP LP Tape Tape	*(DB72-5-4 & DB72-7-8_ RarestOneBowie (1)* *MoreRareBowie (1)* *(No label, no number)* *Live at the Kingston Polytechnic 1972* *(No label, no number)* *Soul asylum (BLY 003/004)* *Gotta get a job (A Dutch connection CD 060572)* *Ziggy rarities… to victory (No label, no number) (2 songs)* *72 Joint Live* *I feel free (Old Gold Records OGCD 400A/B)* *I can't explain* *Live Kingston Polytechnic vol 1 + 2 (Poly 1+2 A/B)* *Live in England 1971 (Wizard WRMB 504/5 A/B)* quality 7, 80 min. quality 8, 90 min.
<u>7-5-1972</u> Hemel Hampstead, Pavilion. Attendance: 1.041. Tickets: 75p. Support act: Lee Riders.	NT	
<u>9-5-1972</u> BBC Radio Show, Sounds of the Seventies. All songs previously broadcasted. Not a new session. Repeated 5-11-1972. Ziggy Stardust, Five years, Queen bitch, Hang on to yourself, Suffragette city, Moonage daydream, Waiting for the man, Rock 'n' roll suicide, Supermen, Oh! you pretty things, Andy Warhol, Lady Stardust, White light, white heat (original by the Velvet Underground in 1967).	LP Tape	*BBC Show (complete) (Avenue Records SRL BN 2378 A/B)* quality 9, 50 min.
<u>11-5-1972</u> Worthing, Assembly Hall. Attendance: 900. Tickets: 50p. According to fan Alan Edwards, Bowie sat on the shoulders of Mick Ronson. Ronson played on and carried the singing Bowie into the crowd.	NT	
<u>12-5-1972</u> London, Polytechnic of Central London, 115 New Cavendish Street W1. Doors open at 7.30 p.m. Tickets: 60p. Support act: Good Habit.	NT	
<u>13-5-1972</u> Slough, Technical College. Attendance: 750.	NT	

DATE / EVENT	AUDIO / VIDEO	TITLE

14-5-1972 Olympic Studios. Recording of All the young dudes and One of the boys - Mott the Hoople. Recordings for the album All the young dudes continue to July 1972 (continued in June at Trident Studios)

16-5-1972 BBC Radio Session. Sounds of the 70's. Broadcast 23-5-1972. Repeated 25-7-1972. Originally billed: John Peel with Top Gear, Sounds of the Seventies. Nicky Graham on piano. 1. Hang on to yourself (2.49) (Contains: Comes to the show tonight, praying to the light machine) (Broadcast 23-5-1972 and 25-7-1972). 2. Ziggy Stardust (3.20) (Contains: Well, he played it left hand, but made it too far) (Broadcast 23-5-1972 and 25-7-1972). 3. White light White heat (Contains: White light makes me sound like Lou Reed) (3.49) (Broadcast 23-5-1972 and 25-7-1972). 4. Suffragette city (3.28) (Broadcast 23-5-1972 and 25-7-1972). 5. Moonage daydream (4.53) (Broadcast 25-7-1972).	CD	*The Year of the spiders (songs 1,2,3,4 and 5) (Switch On! Devil KWSK 99-03)*
	4 CD	*The Rise and Rise Of Ziggy Stardust Vol. 4 (songs 1,2,3,4 and 5) (Savage Hippo Records)*
	2 CD	*God knows I'm good (5 songs) (BEEB 1/2)*
	CD	*Emerged from shadows (songs 1,2,3,4 and 5) (EBD 001)*
	4 CDR	*The complete BBC master recordings (No label, no nr.)*
	CD	*BBC Sessions 1969-1972 (2)*
	CD	*Hazy Cosmic Jive (5 songs) (Invasion Unlimited IU9753-2)*
	CD	*Stardust memories (songs 3,4) (Retropop 159081)*
	3 CD	*Bowie at the Beeb (5 songs)*
	CD	*The Vintage David Bowie (3) (ZIG 1)*
	CD	*Starman in session (1,3,4,5) (Silver Rarities SIRA 93)*
	1 CDR	*Used up and empty (2) (No label, no number)*
	1 CDR	*Missing Link 1 (3) (No label, no number)*
	CD	*Happy Birthday Mr. Bowie*
	LP	*Lost and forgotten (1,4,5) (Halloween Jack Production LTD. Gema A-8206 S111)*
	LP	*Oh! You Pretty thing (Space Heat SH 2799)*
	LP	*Goodbye to the Brixton son (FA001)*
	LP	*Stardust from the 70's (BO-16)*
	LP	*BBC Show (1,4,5)*
	LP	*Thin White Duke meets Ziggy (5)*
	LP	*Used up and empty (2)*
	LP	*The unofficial Wembley Wizard Box File (3,4,5)*
	LP	*Ziggy 1 - My radio Sweetheart (3,4)*
	7"/45	*Bowie does Reed (3)*

DATE / EVENT	AUDIO / VIDEO	TITLE
	7"/45 Tape	(Major Tom 6052-204) Spiders from Mars (DB-TAP 008-PRO) (3) quality 9, 20 min.
19-5-1972 Oxford, Polytechnic. Attendance: 1.000.	NT	
20-5-1972 Oxford, Polytechnic. Attendance: 1.000.	NT	
22-5-1972 BBC-Network-Session, Johnny Walker Lunchtime Show. Broadcast 5,6,7,8+9-6-1972. Recorded at Studio 2, Aeolian Hall, New Bond Street, London. 1. Starman (4.04) (Broadcast 6,7,8 and 9-6-1972). Used a remixed backing tape of the Trident original. 2. Space oddity (4.16) (Spoken words: I'm just a rocket man) (the song was not broadcast). 3. Changes (3.28) (not broadcast). 4. Oh! you pretty things (full band rendition) (2.58). (Broadcast 5-6-1972). Starman was broadcast over four consecutive days as Johnnie Walker's single of the week.	CD 2 CD CD CD CD CD 3 CD CD 2 CD 1 CDR 4 CDR 1 CDR CD CD CD CD CD	The Year of the spiders (4 songs) (Switch On! Devil KWSK 99-03) God knows I'm good (1,2,3) (BEEB 1/2) God knows I'm good (2) (Invasion Unlimited IU9753-1) The rise and rise of Ziggy Stardust vol. 4 (songs 1,2,3,4) (Savage Hippo Records) Hazy Cosmic Jive (songs 1,3) (Invasion Unlimited IU9753-2) BBC Sessions 1969-1972 (2) Bowie at the Beeb (4 songs) Bowie at the Beeb, 8 track sampler (For demonstration only) (EMI) (3,4) Starman over the Rainbow (songs 3 and 4) (Savage Hippo Records SH118) Bättle for Bowie (2) (No label, no number) The complete BBC master recordings (No label, no nr.) The complete BBC files vol. 3 (Old Gold Records OGCD 077) (4 songs) Kiss the vipers fang (all 4 songs) (EBD002) Look back in anger (1) (No label, no number) The Jean Genie (vol 1.) (1) (Ban-004-A) Starman (1) (Oil Well RSC 017 CD) White light white heat (1) (The Swinging Pig Records TSP-CD-053)

DATE / EVENT	AUDIO / VIDEO	TITLE
	CD	At the Beep (1) (Archive Productions AP 89004)
	CD	Rebel rebel (1) (Oil Well RSC 021)
	CD	Live Vol. 1 (1) (Joker JOK-001-A)
	CD	Mega rare trax vol. 1 (1) (Seagull Records CD 022)
	CD	Ziggy in Wonderland (1) (PROCD 89 001-2)
	CD	Five years (1) (Triangle Records PYCD 047)
	CD	Kooks (1) (Turtle Records TR-36)
	CD	Starman in session (1,3) (Silver Rarities SIRA 93)
	CD	Dynamic Live (1)
	CD	BBC Bowie (1)
	CD	Happy Birthday Mr. Bowie
	LP	White light white heat (1) (The Swinging Pig Records TSP 053A/B)
	Video	Stolp tapes no. 3 (1 min)

23-5-1972 BBC Radio. Sounds of the 70's. Recorded 16-5-1972. Repeated 25-7-1972.

23-5-1972 BBC. Maida Vale Studio 5. Recording Sound of the seventies. Bob Harris Show. Broadcast 19-6-1972.

25-5-1972 Bournemouth, Chelsea Village.   NT

27-5-1972 Epsom, Ebbisham Hall.   NT
Entrance: 50p. Doors open at 7.30 p.m.
Matthew Fisher (Procol Harum) last time on piano.
Presented by Bob Harris (Sounds of the 70s).
Attended by music journalist Mick Brown. He wrote: "A unique mixture of the exciting, disturbing, amusing and bizarre. The audience went wild."

June 1972 Released in Spain: La ascendia y caida de Ziggy Stardust y las aranas de Marte (LP Ziggy Stardust) (RCA).

June 1972 Released LP Vince Is Alive, Well and Rocking in Paris - Vince Taylor.

2-6-1972 Newcastle upon Tyne, City Hall.   NT
Attendance: 2.168 (Hall was half-empty).
Bowie had arrived by plane.
Robin Lumley replaced Matthew Fisher on piano.
Neil Tennant (later Pet Shop Boys) got Bowie's autograph

DATE / EVENT	AUDIO / VIDEO	TITLE

on a Ziggy picture that had showered the audience during Suffragette City, when he sang: "Wham bam, thank you mam."
Standing ovation after the concert.

3-6-1972 New Musical Express. Review Ziggy Stardust by James Johnson.

<u>3-6-1972</u> Liverpool, Stadium.   NT

<u>4-6-1972</u> Preston, Guildhall (Public Hall).   2 CDR   *Preston 4 June 1972*
Attendance: 700 (only 1/3 of the hall for 2.146 people).   *(BowieHobby)*
A very good concert. The ones that stayed at home made   1 CDR   *The rise of Ziggy Stardust*
the mistake of their live.   *and the Spider from Mars*
                                                                           (Old Gold Records OGCD 014)
                                                              1 CDR   *Slow voice on a wave phase*
                                                                           (Downunder discs)
                                                              Tape   quality 7, 75 min.

6-6-1972 UK Release LP The Rise and fall of Ziggy Stardust and The Spiders from Mars (RCA LSP.4702).
Cover and inner sleeve photos by Brian Ward. Two girls assisted him. After the photo's were taken Bowie walked off with a hand planted squarely on each girls' arse (Loving the alien - Christopher Sandford 1996).
Sleeve designer: Terry Pastor.

<u>6-6-1972</u> Bradford, St. George's Hall.   2 CDR   *Bradford 6 June 1972*
Attendance: 1.911.   *(BowieHobby)*
"Thank you, that was Song for Bob Dylan. This one's   Tape   quality 7, 80 min.
called Starman." Nice versions of I feel free (Cream, 1966)
and White light light white heat (Velvet Underground,
1967).

<u>7-6-1972</u> Sheffield, City Hall.   NT
Attendance: 2.292.

<u>8-6-1972</u> Middlesborough, Town Hall.   NT
Attendance: 1.247.
Support act: J.S.D. Band.

8-6-1972 Rolling Stone. Article by Mick Rock: David Bowie is just not serious.
Bowie: "So often it's not my point of view I'm putting across. I'm more like a focal point for a lot of ideas that are goin' around. Sometimes I don't feel like a person at all. I'm just a collection of other people's ideas."

June 1972 Bowie, Angela and Mick Ronson landed on Heathrow after a weekend visit to New York. Bowie had a meeting with RCA and the three of them saw Elvis Presley perform at Madison Square Garden. Bowie was in full Glam get-up, perched in the front row.
The intro-music to the Elvis show was: 2001 A space odyssey. This most likely inspired Bowie to use the same intro-music for his later Ziggy concerts.

DATE / EVENT	AUDIO / VIDEO	TITLE

RCA secretary Barbara Fulk: "I was rushed to the Park Lane Hotel to bring Bowie a hairdryer. It was like a medical alert. Angela was wearing something made of lace and no bra. Bowie was nude asleep on top of the bed. Then Angela started flirting with me and I rushed out."

10-6-1972 RCA report: Bowie will produce the new albums of Mott the Hoople and Lou Reed.

10-6-1972 Leicester, Polytechnic.   NT
Attendance: 1.630.

13-6-1972 Bristol, Colston Hall.   NT
Attendance: 1.886.
Support act: J.S.D. Band.

15-6-1972 Bowie flew to Manchester, to record a TV appearance for Granada.

17-6-1972 Sounds. Article by Steve Peacock: Rock on Ziggy.

17-6-1972 Oxford, Town Hall.   NT
Mick Rock made the famous photo of Bowie simulating fellatio on Ronson's guitar, while he was playing his solo during Suffragette City.

19-6-1972 Southampton, Civic Hall. "That was Five years. This is a new one… someone can construct a film… you wanna sit down… okay… an image maker from America... called Andy Warhol."	1 CDR	Southampton 19 June 1972 (BowieHobby)
	Tape	25 min.
19-6-1972 BBC. Sounds of the seventies. Bob Harris Show. Recorded 23-5-1972 at Maida Vale Studio 5. Nicky Graham on piano.	CD	Ziggy 1 - My Radio Sweetheart (No label, no number)
1. Andy Warhol (3.13) (Ends with: I only look at the pictures myself).	2 CD	God knows I'm good (3,4) (BEEB 1/2)
2. Lady Stardust (3.20) (Ends with: Wrong song).	CD	The Year of the spiders (Switch On! Devil KWSK 99-03)
3. White light white heat (3.57) (Contains: Gonna take me outta my brain). 4. Rock 'n' roll suicide (3.17).	2 CD	Starman over the Rainbow (songs 1,2 and 3) (Savage Hippo Records SH118)
	CD	Ziggy in Wonderland (4) (PROCD 89 001-2)
	CD	Hazy Cosmic Jive (3,4,) (Invasion Unlimited IU9753-2)
	3 CD	Bowie at the Beeb (1,2,4)
	CD	Bowie at the Beeb, 8 track sampler (For demonstration only) (EMI) (2)
	CD	Nobody's children (4 songs) (EBD003)
	CD	The rise and rise of Ziggy

DATE / EVENT	AUDIO / VIDEO	TITLE
	CD	Stardust vol. 4 (songs 1,2,3,4) (Savage Hippo Records)
	CD	The Jean Genie (vol 1.) (4) (Ban-004-A)
	CD	Starman (4) (Oil Well RSC 017 CD)
	CD	White light white heat (4) (The Swinging Pig Records TSP-CD-053)
	CD	At the Beep (4) (Archive Productions AP 89004)
	CD	Rebel rebel (4) (Oil Well RSC 021)
	CD	Live Vol. 1 (4) (Joker JOK-001-A)
	CD	Mega rare trax vol. 1 (4) (Seagull Records CD 022)
	CD	Five years (4) (Triangle Records PYCD 047)
	CD	Kooks (4) (Turtle Records TR-36)
	CD	Demo's & Outtakes (4) (A Dutch connection)
	CD	A crash course for the ravers (No label, no number) (3,4)
	1 CDR	Used up and empty (4) (No label, no number)
	1 CDR	The complete BBC files vol. 4 (Old Gold Records OGCD 078) (4 songs)
	CD	Dynamic Live (3,4)
	CD	BBC Bowie (3,4)
	CD	The best of David Bowie (3)
	LP	White light white heat (4) (The Swinging Pig Records TSP 053A/B)
	LP	Zigg 1 - My radio sweetheart (Tune In 001)
	LP	BBC Show (1,2,3,4)
	LP	Used up and empty (4)
21-6-1972 UK TV. BBC. Lift Off With Ayshea. Recorded 14-4-1972. Starman (3.20).		
21-6-1972 Dunstable, Civic Hall. Attendance: 1.000. Started at 20.00 hours. Tickets: 65p. Support: Flamin' Groovies. Mick Rock filmed the concert. Parts of the film were used for the video to promote the CDS Ziggy Stardust which was	NT	

DATE / EVENT	AUDIO / VIDEO	TITLE

released in April 1994 (taken from Santa Monica 1972).

<u>24-6-1972</u> Guildford, Civic Hall. NT
Attendance: 1.200.

<u>25-6-1972</u> Croydon, Fox at Greyhound, Park Lane. NT
Attendance: 1.500 (sold out).
Support act: Roxy Music.
A thousand people are turned away at the door.

26-6-1972 Barnes. Olympic Studios.
John I'm only dancing (2.46) master recorded.

30-6-1972 High Wycombe, Royal Grammar School.
Cancelled.
Jonathan Kelly (who was to be the support act) became the main-act.

30-6-1972 DeFries changed the name of his company Minnie Bell in MainMan.

June / July 1972 Second part of recordings album All the young dudes - Mott the Hoople at Trident Studios.
Ian Hunter: "David used to tell people I was the head of a motorcycle gang and he had this very heavy deal about us. He sucks, like Dracula. He sucks what he can get and then he moves on to another victim" (Alias David Bowie - Peter & Leni Gillman 1986).

June / July 1972 Release 3LP Revelations - A musical anthology for Glastonbury Fayre (Revelation REV 1/2/3).
Bowie's version of The Supermen is an alternative studio version (2.41), recorded 12-11-1971. The real live version is never released.
In 2001 the 3LP was released in Japan as a 2CD called: The Electric Score.

Summer 1972 David had a dept of GBP 29.062 to GEM.
Myers pulled out and DeFries took over. DeFries and Myers made a deal: Myers had to be paid USD 500.000,— from David's future earnings. DeFries got all the master tapes of the recordings.
David had to sign a new contract (that replaced the GEM contract). DeFries wanted 50% of David's earnings.

1-7-1972 Melody Maker. Article by Michael Watts: Caught in the act. Waiting for the man.
Watts wrote: "Campness has become built-in to his public persona. I mean that however, in a far from derogatory sense. The main preoccupation of David's work is not directly with gay sexuality, though that element is there, as with a flourishing theatricality and dramatic sense."

1-7-1972 Weston-Super-Mare, Winter Gardens.
Cancelled.

<u>2-7-1972</u> Torbay, Rainbow Pavilion. NT

<u>5-7-1972</u> BBC TV. Top of the Pops. 2 CDR *Cyberstation*
Starman (2.12). Recorded 14-4-1972. *(STATIONTOBOWIE)*

DATE / EVENT	AUDIO / VIDEO	TITLE

Ian McCulloch (Echo and the Bunnyman) and Pete Shelley (The Buzzcocks) were very impressed. The performance changed their lives (Strange fascination - D. Buckley 1999).

<u>8-7-1972</u> London, Royal Festival Hall.
Attendance: 3.000.
Support acts: Marmelade, J.S.D Band.
Friends of the earth (Save the Wale charity show).
Kenny Everett announced David: "The second greatest thing next to God."
Afterwards Melody Maker reported: A STAR IS BORN.
First British performance of Lou Reed.
Sound problems during the show. Bowie comes on stage and says: "I'm David Bowie and these are The Spiders from Mars. We can have a wonderful system in a minute. This is something about you" and they start Hang on to yourself.
After Moonage daydream Bowie says: "He's still playing and he is now in England and this is his very, very, very first appearance anywhere in England. Ladies and gentlemen: Lou Reed!"
With Lou Reed:
1. White light white heat (4.48).
2. Waiting for the man (5.38).
3. Sweet Jane (5.39).
At the end of the concert people got posters and photographs.

    CD   *David Bowie with Lou Reed (complete concert) (DB72-5-4 & DB72-7-8)*
    CD   *Cocaine adds life (Seagull Records CD 037)*
    1 CDR   *When stars collide (Old Gold Records OGCD 405)*
    1 CDR   *Save the whale (No label, no number)*
    1 CDR   *Ziggy rarities... to victory (No label, no number) (3)*
    1 CDR   Live in London
    2 LP   Live in England (WRMB 505)
    Tape   quality 7, 75 min.

The first few weeks after the concert Bowie and Lou Reed were inseparable. They had a lot of fun and frequently visited Soho by night, with it's drunks, hookers, strippers and night clubs (Lou Reed - Victor Bockris 1994).

9-7-1972 The Guardian described Bowie as 'a remarkable performer'.
The Times described him as 'T.S. Eliot with a rock and roll beat'.

12-7-1972 Gay News. Article by Peter Holmes: Gay rock - David Bowie in concert at the Royal Festival Hall.
Peter Holmes: "David Bowie is probably the best rock musician in Britain now. One day, he'll become as popular as he deserves to be. And that'll give gay rock a potent spokesman."

<u>14-7-1972</u> London, King's Cross Cinema.
A few journalists attended the evening.
This was a warm up show for the Aylesbury concert.
Mick Ronson played the base guitar on 1 song: Andy Warhol. A nice concert, but a pity of the bad sound quality of the circulating tapes. Unfortunately none of the circulating tapes includes Hang on to yourself.

    1 CDR   *The queen of King's Cross (Old Gold Records OGCD 015)*
    Tape   quality 6, 50 min.

<u>15-7-1972</u> Aylesbury, Friars Club (Borough Assembly Hall). Attendance: 2.000 (sold out instantly).

    1 CDR   *Aylesbury 15 July 1972 (BowieHobby)*

DATE / EVENT	AUDIO / VIDEO	TITLE
25 American journalists flown over to see him in concert: a.o. Lilian Roxon, Henry Edwards, Lisa Robinson of After Dark. They all stayed at the Inn On The Park. The total costs were about USD 25.000,—. Concert filmed by Mick Rock (16 mm). First time live: I can't explain. Bowie wore a jumpsuit and high-heeled red boots. Bowie walks on stage and says: "Alright, I'm David Bowie and this is some of our rock." He announces I feel free: "This is a song from a long time ago. It is written by Jack Bruce and Keith Brown. It's called I feel free." During Suffragette City Bowie did his famous fellatio act on Mick Ronson's guitar (Mick's parents were very shocked when they saw the photographs (that were taken on 17-6-1972) in the papers).	1 CDR 2 CDR 2 CDR 1 CDR Tape Tape	*I can't explain (A Dutch Connection CD150772)* *Aylesbury 15 July 1972 (2) (BowieHobby)* *Aylesbury Nights (Old Gold Records OGCD 016A/B)* *Press to play* quality 5, 75 min. quality 7, 75 min.

15-7-1972 New Musical Express. Article: Bowie Zowie.
They wrote: Anybody still unconvinced that David Bowie will sweep all before him should have witnessed the end of his remarkable concert last Saturday (8-7-1972).
Marc Bolan on Bowie: "I believe the ultimate star is the star who makes it by just being themselves."

15-7-1972 Melody Maker. Article by Ray Coleman: A star is born.
He wrote about the 8-7-1972 concert: When a shooting star is heading for the peak, there is usually one concert at which it's possible to declare: "That's it, he's made it."

15-7-1972 Disc. Article by Rosalind Russell: Bowie's back-up men.

15-7-1972 London. King's Cross Cinema.
First UK show of Iggy and The Stooges.
A young John Lydon (Johnny Rotten of the Sex Pistols) attended the gig.

16-7-1972 Dorchester Hotel (London). Day of Bowie-interviews, arranged by DeFries.
Iggy Pop walked round with silver hair and eye-shadow. Lou Reed interrupted one of David's interviews by kissing him full on the mouth. Angie Bowie was bitten in the stomach by Reed's road manager Ernie. Angie put her teeth in the left breast of columnist Lilian Roxon (BlackBook - Barry Miles 1980).
Angie Bowie: "A mere hug and a thank you is not as demonstrative of your affection as a good hard bite on the tit" (Alias David Bowie - Peter & Leni Gillman 1986).

<u>18-7-1972</u> Aylesbury, Friars Club. Attendance: 2.000. Support act: J.S.D. Band. Filmed by Mick Rock. Last time Robin Lumley on piano. "Good evening, my name is David Bowie and these are the Spiders from Mars and we're gonna rock and roll tonight. Alright?" "Our new single on RCA Records and tapes. This is called	1 CDR CD CD CD CD	*This boy (A Dutch Connection 180772)* *Who'll love Aladdin Sane in Tokyo* *A semi-acoustic love affair (1 song) (Gold Standard)* *Radio Hype (1 song) (GS-96006)* *Immersed in Crowley's uniform (1 song)*

DATE / EVENT	AUDIO / VIDEO	TITLE

John, I'm only dancing."
"This is a song for pleasure" and they start This boy (2.26) First and last time they played this song live (original by The Beatles in 1963).
"Alright Mr. Reed, your numbers now," and Waiting for the man and White light white heat follow.
"Thank you very much Aylesbury." They end with Round and round (first time live).

		(No label, no number)
	2 CDR	*Did you see the suits & the platform boots?* *(Downunder Discs)*
	2 CDR	*Aylesbury Nights (Old Gold Records OGCD 016A/B)*
	1 CDR	On the road
	1 LP	On the road (1 A/B)
	Tape	quality 7, 50 min.

20-7-1972 Rolling Stone. Review LP Ziggy Stardust by Richard Cromelin.
He wrote: "Flamboyance and outrageousness are inseparable from that campy image of his, both in the Bacall and Garbo stages and in his new butch, street-crawler appearance that has him looking like something out of the darker pages of "City of Night." It's all tied up with the one aspect of David Bowie that sets him apart from both the exploiters of transvestisism and writer/performers of comparable talent - his theatricality."

22-7-1972 New Musical Express. Article by Charles Shaar Murray: David at the Dorchester.

22-7-1972 Melody Maker. Article by M. Oldfield: Up Pops Iggy.

25-7-1972 BBC Radio. Sounds of the 70's. Recorded 16-5-1972. Repeated from 23-5-1972.

28-7-1972 Release Single All the young dudes (3.26) / One of the boys (5.34) - Mott the Hoople (CBS S.8271). A-side written and produced by Bowie (he also did the backing vocals and rhythm guitar). A few years before the leader of the band, Guy Stevens, has changed the band's name from Silence into Mott the Hoople, inspired by a novel by William Manus (David Bowie - Dave Thompson 1986).

29-7-1972 New Musical Express. Article by Charles Shaar Murray: Back at the Dorchester.

End July 1972 MainMan office moved to Gunter Grove, Kensington.

July / August 1972 London, CBS Studios. Iggy and the Stooges record LP Raw Power.

August 1972 Records & Recordings. Article by Duncan Fallowell: Twinkle twinkle superstar.

August 1972 Crawdaddy. Article by James Graig: The rise and fall of Ziggy Stardust and the Spiders from Mars.

August 1972 Phonograph Record. Review LP Ziggy Stardust by Jim Bickhart.
Bickhart wrote: "The songs, beginning with the doom-portending "Five years," create a tale in which a number of Bowie's beliefs and fantasies are placed in full view."

<u>First two weeks of August 1972</u>. Theatre Royal in Stratford East.
Rehearsals for Ziggy Stardust tour.
Lindsay Kemp helped with the stage presentation.
Nicky Graham joins the backing band on piano.

NT

DATE / EVENT	AUDIO / VIDEO	TITLE

8-8-1972 Sunday News. Article by Lilian Roxon: A rock happening: David's debut.

11-8-1972 London. Trident Studios. Second part of recording LP Transformer - Lou Reed. Influenced by a lot of drugs they worked very fast.
Mick Ronson later described the sessions as "A bloody shambles" (Changes - Chris Welch 1999). The songs Walk on the wild side, Vicious, Make up and New York Telephone conversation were based on Nelson Algren's novel A walk on the wild side. Andy Warhol had asked Lou Reed to write the songs for a Broadway musical. The idea was dropped, but Reed had written some of the best songs he ever did. The in December 2001 released DVD Transformer shows parts of the recordings.

Bowie later commented on the Reed and Pop sessions: "When you get caught up in that wave of euphoria and become well known, you are sure it's only going to last for a limited amount of time. So you cram as much work into it as possible. I was also writing and working up ideas for future shows before it all suddenly disappeared" (Changes - Chris Welch 1999).

During the night time (from 3.00 to 7.00 h.), when Bowie had left, Queen was allowed to use the Trident Studios (Freddie Mercury The Definitive Biography - Lesley-Ann Jones 1997).

11-8-1972 Release Hang on to yourself (2.51) / Man in the middle (4.08) - Arnold Corns (B & C CB.189).

<u>13-8-1972</u> Guildford, Civic Hall, Mott the Hoople.　　　　　NT
David joins Mott the Hoople on stage for an encore
(All the young dudes).
Attended by Lou Reed.

Bowie to journalist Andrew Tyler: "I think what I do and the way I dress is me pandering to my own eccentricities and imagination. It's a continual fantasy. Nowadays there is really no difference between my personal life and anything I do on stage. I'm rarely David Robert Jones anymore. I think I've forgotten who David Jones is."

<u>19-8-1972</u> London, Rainbow Theatre. Afternoon.　　　　　Tape
Rehearsal. Filmed by Mick Rock.

19-8-1972, London, Rainbow Theatre. Afternoon. Promo video of John I'm only dancing shot by Mike Rock during rehearsal for the evening show.

<u>19-8-1972</u> London, Rainbow Theatre. Evening. Attendance: 3.000. Support acts: Roxy Music and Lloyd Watson. Started at 19.30 hours. Tickets: 75p. Promoter Mel Bush paid GBP 1.000,—. Pianist Matthew Fisher played the intro Ode to joy. First time Nicky Graham on piano. Choreographed by Lindsay Kemp. Dance-group was called: The Astronettes (dressed in fishing net suits, chosen by Lindsay Kemp), miming every song in the background. During the "Rainbow" shows they played Lady Stardust and Life on Mars? for the first time live. During Lady Stardust Marc Bolan's face was projected on the backcloth.	2 CDR 2 CD 2 CDR 2 CDR 2 CDR	*London 19 August 1972* (BowieHobby) *Starman over the Rainbow* (Savage Hippo Records SH 118) *The Ziggy Stardust Show* (Old Gold Records OGCD 423A/B) *Raw Rainbow* (tape version) (No label, no number) *David Bowie at the Rainbow* (No label, no number)

DATE / EVENT	AUDIO / VIDEO	TITLE

A good version of Wild eyed boy from Freecloud. In Starman Bowie sang a few lines from Over the rainbow. Starman was broadcast on Japanese TV.
Show was attended by: Lou Reed, Mick Jagger, Alice Cooper, Rod Stewart, Andy Warhol, Elton John.
Lou Reed described the show as: Amazing, fabulous, incredible, the most amazing he had ever seen (Lou Reed - Victor Bockris 1994).

	Tape	quality 6, 90 min.
	Video	*Various 20 (5 min)*
	Video	quality 7, 25 min.

19-8-1972 Record Mirror. Article: Bowie sell-out!
They wrote: "A stunning production spectacle with a breathtaking finale."

19-8-1972 Melody Maker. Article by Michael Watts: The rise and rise of Ziggy Stardust.
Full-page ad in the same issue: David Bowie is Ziggy Stardust Live at the Rainbow.
Bowie: "I'm not content just to be a rock-and-roll star all my life. All I want to do is investigate and present the result."

<u>20-8-1972</u> London, Rainbow Theatre (Finsbury Park).
Attendance: 3.000. Support band: Roxy Music.
Promoter Mel Bush paid GBP 1.250,—.
Pianist Matthew Fisher.
During Lady Stardust Marc Bolan's face was projected on the backcloth.
Choreographed by Lindsay Kemp. Dance-group was called: The Astronettes.

Tape
Video

20-8-1972 New Musical Express. Charles Shaar Murray about the Rainbow concerts: "A thoroughly convincing demonstration of his ascendancy over any other soloist in rock today."

<u>27-8-1972</u> Bristol, Locarno Centre, Electric Village.
Attendance: 2.000. Tickets: GBP 1,25.
Support act: Gnidrolog, Thin Lizzy.

	CD	*Cocaine adds life (1 song)*
		(Seagull Records CD 037)
	CD	*Who'll love Aladdin Sane in Tokyo (1 song)*
		(Moonraker 449)
	1 CDR	Bristol 72
		(No label, no number)
	Tape	50 min.

31-8-1972 MainMan opened an office at East 58th Street in New York. Tony Zanetta became the Company President.

<u>31-8-1972</u> Bournemouth, Starkers, Royal Ballroom.   NT

September 1972 Pre-Ziggy radio interview. Bowie reveals the upcoming album "Round and round."
Broadcast: Starman, He's a goldmine, Bombers and Something happens (2.11).

1 CDR   *Hendrikse various vol. 5*
         (No label, no number)

September 1972 US Phone interview with songs.   Tape   quality 7, 25 min.

137

DATE / EVENT	AUDIO / VIDEO	TITLE

Begin September 1972 recording of Let's spend the night together (3.03). The original was recorded by the Rolling Stones in 1967.

1-9-1972 Release John, I'm only dancing (2.43) / Hang on to yourself (2.38) (RCA 2263).

1-9-1972 Doncaster, Top Rank Suite, St. Leger Festival. Attendance: 2.000.   NT

2-9-1972 Manchester, Hardrock Concert Theatre. Attendance: 3.000. It was the opening of the theatre. D.J. for the evening: Andy Peebles. Bowie stayed at the Excelsior Hotel near Manchester Airport.   1 CDR   The Hardrock Manchester

3-9-1972 Manchester, Hardrock Concert Theatre. Attendance: 3.000. Bowie stayed at the Excelsior Hotel near Manchester Airport. They appear in denims. "Our costumes are at the cleaners," David told a fan afterwards.   NT

3-9-1972 In the morning announcement by DeFries: American tour within 2 weeks.

4-9-1972 Liverpool, Top Rank Suite. Attendance: 2.000.   NT

5-9-1972 Sunderland, Top Rank Suite. Attendance: 900.   NT

6-9-1972 Sheffield, Top Rank Suite. Attendance: 2.500.   NT

7-9-1972 Stoke-On-Trent, Hanley Top Rank Suite. Attendance: 1.200. Last time Nicky Graham on piano.   NT

7-9-1972 The Scene. Article by Jim Girard: From McCartney to Ziggie: History of David Bowie - Almost.

8-9-1972 Release LP All the young dudes - Mott the Hoople (CBS 01-465754-14). The band's name was taken from Willard Manus' book by the same name.

9-9-1972 Bowie signs for RCA in New York.

9-9-1972 Record Mirror. Article by J. Arthur: Hard rockin' Mr. Bowie.

September 1972 London, Stratford, East Theatre. Rehearsals.   NT

DATE / EVENT	AUDIO / VIDEO	TITLE

15-9-1972 New York, RCA office. Gustl Breuer met DeFries and had to take care of Bowie in the US. DeFries stayed at the Plaza Hotel.

Prior to the American tour Bowie said to Mick Rock: "I get worried about dying. At the moment it's this terrible travel thing. I keep thinking we're going to crash. Last month it was being killed on stage. Not here so much. In America, I know that one day a big artist is going to get killed on stage. And I know we're going to be very big. And I keep thinking it's bound to be me. Go out on my first tour, get done in at my first gig, and nobody will see me. And that would make me wild" (A rock 'n' roll odyssey - Kate Lynch 1984).

17-9-1972 Arrived with Queen Elizabeth 2 in New York. Accompanied by George Underwood and his wife. Breuer welcomed them in behalf of RCA and escorted them to Central Park's Plaza Hotel. Gustl Breuer: "Mr. Bowie had very red hair and, I think, blue fingernails. He was friendly and shy and amazed at the skyline, and a wife, Angela, who looked like a gentle Barbra Streisand and who was very much in command of the whole situation" (Alias David Bowie - Peter & Leni Gillman 1986).

18-9-1972 The band arrived at Kennedy Airport in New York and stayed at The Plaza Hotel. In the evening there was a party at The Plaza attended by George Underwood and his wife Birgit, Mick Rock and his wife Sheila.

19-9-1972 Mike Garson recruited. He was introduced by Annette Peacock (he played in the song I'm the one on her solo album) and recommended by RCA's London boss Ken Glancey. Garson used to play in a tiny New York jazz club called Poopy's Pub. As audition song he played Changes in a cocktail lounge style.

20-9-1972 They left on a 2 days journey to Cleveland. Spend the night at Erie in Pennsylvania. On the bus they had a lot of fun and bodyguards Stuie George and Tony Frost told dirty jokes and teased Suzy Fussey. When it became dark Angela and Anton Jones seemed to play a game of feel-me touch-me (Stardust - Henry Edwards and Tony Zanetta 1986).

21-9-1972 Cleveland Plain Dealer. They wrote: "Bowie is a self-proclaimed bisexual who appears on stage in feminine garb, but he is not the violent anti-sexual sham of his contemporary, Alice Cooper."

DATE / EVENT	AUDIO / VIDEO	TITLE
<u>21-9-1972</u> BBC Radio. Not a BBC session. Reworked versions of the original album tracks. 1. John I'm only dancing (3.02). 2. Star (3.17). 3. Lady Stardust (2.43). Reworked version of songs recorded 21-1-1972 at Maidenvale Studios. DJ Talking with Rick Wakeman.	CD CD 4 CD LP Tape	*The Rise and rise of Ziggy Stardust Vol. 4 (songs 1,2,3) (Savage Hippo Records)* *Nobody's children (EBD003)* The complete BBC master recordings Lost and forgotten (Halloween Jack Production LTD. Gema A-8206 S111) quality 10, 10 min.
<u>22-9-1972</u> Cleveland, Public Auditorium (Public Hall). Public Auditorium was housed in the same building as the Music Hall (the two halls were devided by a stage curtain). Attendance: 3.200. Sold out. Started at 19.30 hours.	CD 1 VCD	*Va Va Va Voom (Savage Hippo Records SH120)* 8MM Ziggy (No label, no number)

DATE / EVENT	AUDIO / VIDEO	TITLE

Support act: Lindisfarne. Tickets: USD 5,00.
Promoted by WMMS Radio and Belkin Productions.
Mike Garson's first gig. The gig was very loud, he had to
play with earplugs.
Show later broadcast by WMMS FM Radio.
The promoters (The Belkin Brothers) had to agree 90% of
the earnings was for DeFries / Bowie. From the stage you
could see a sea of lit matches and lighters in the audience.
After the show a party was held at Hollander Hotel. Jane
Scott of Cleveland Plain Dealers was present. She wrote:
"Bowie is a one-man multi-media with an incisive
perfectionist touch and the sensitivity of an artist. I think
a star has been born."
Bowie interviewed for Rolling Stone by Timothy Ferris.

Leee Childers about the Cleveland gig: "The grand piano was two feet too short. DeFries said, 'Cancel the gig'. So I cancelled the gig and they got the piano that was the right size and the gig was back on" (In other words - Kerry Juby 1986).

The Plain Dealer. Article by Jane Scott.
She wrote about the Cleveland gig: "Tickets sold out within days. Police escorted three suspected pot users from the hall and chased away ten youths who had climbed up the side of the building, trying to get in through an upper window."

23-9-1972 In the Greyhound bus Ronson played guitar and a little jam started. Bowie wrote The Jean Genie. They made an overnight stop in Nashville.

23-9-1972 Disc. Article by Gavin Petrie: Ziggy Stardust.

23-9-1972 Disc. Article by Rosalind Russell: David Bowie, the man who saved the music world.

23-9-1972 Disc. Article by Andrew Tyler: Just and old poser.

<u>24-9-1972</u> Memphis, Ellis Auditorium.   NT
Attendance: 4.335. Sold out.
After the show a party at the Memphis Downtowner Motor Inn.

25-9-1972 Memphis Commercial Appeal. Article, written by Joe E.Dove.
He wrote: "They loved it. They screamed. They yelled. They danced on their seats and begged for more."

25-9-1972 Press-Scimitar.
They wrote: "In their rapt attention, the audience exhibited a strange and somewhat puzzling attraction to Bowie."

<u>28-9-1972</u> New York, Carnegie Hall.   *CD*   *RarestOneBowie (1 song)*
Attendance: 2.886 (sold out). Promoter: Ron Delsener.   *CD*   *Pinups 4 (1 song)*
Support-act: Ruth Copeland.   *(BOWPU04)*

DATE / EVENT	AUDIO / VIDEO	TITLE

Taped by RCA for a possible album.　　　　　　　　　1 CDR　　　　　*MoreRareBowie (1 song)*
There were 100 press cards for 400 requests.　　　　　　　　　　　*(No label, no number)*
Many free tickets, so there was no profit at all.　　　　Tape　　　　　quality 10
In the audience: Ex-Pork cast, Cherry Vanilla, Andy
Warhol, Truman Capote, Anthony Perkins, Alan Bates,
Todd Rundgren, New York Dolls, Lee Radzi Will (sister
of Jackie Kennedy).
After Rock 'n' roll suicide Geri Miller dashed on stage to
present David gladioli.
My death (5.49) was released on RarestOneBowie.
Backstage interviewed by Scott Osborne for US TV, News
Service, broadcast 29-9-1972.
They stayed at The Plaza Hotel (New York).
David had flu and went to bed before the end of the party.
Iggy Pop told him stories about revolutionary guys in
Detroit he knew in Michigan when he was young. This was
an inspiration for Bowie to write Panic in Detroit.
Angie danced with a Marilyn Monroe look-a-like and
Cherry Vanilla danced with the transvestite Wayne County
(David Bowie - Jerry Hopkins 1985).
Cyrinda Foxe (who can be seen dancing in Bowie's video
clip Jean Genie): "We'd spy through those huge old Plaza
Hotel keyholes, and we'd watch the bodyguards giving it
to some groupies. After they were through David would
occasionally take over, and I would sit in a chair sometimes
and talk to him while he was having sex. I'd watch
television and sit in a chair, because he wanted somebody
to talk to, so I was good for that" (Stardust - Henry
Edwards and Tony Zanetta 1986).

29-9-1972 US TV. News Service. Interview by Scott Osborne (28-9-1972 backstage).
Bowie describing himself: "Partly enigmatic, partly fossil."

29-9-1972 Newsday, article by Bob Caristgau.
Caristgau about Bowie: "An English fairy."

29-9-1972 New York Times, article by Don Heckman.
Don Heckman: "David had overcome the suspicions aroused by the publicity overkill. He delivered a performance of beautiful coordinated physical movements and well-planned music."

29-9-1972 Daily News. Lilian Roxon wrote: A STAR IS BORN.
"I always wanted to write this and now I can."

29-9-1972 New York Post. Article by Al Aronowitz: The super pop event.

29-9-1972 The Sun. Article by Gordon Coxhill: Superstarman.

<u>29-9-1972</u> Washington, J.F. Kennedy Center.　　　　　　　NT
Attendance: 5.300.

DATE / EVENT	AUDIO / VIDEO	TITLE

Concert recorded by RCA.

30-9-1972 New Bowie - MainMan contract. The contract was dated 31-9-1972!

October 1972 After Dark. Article by Henry Edwards: The rise of Ziggy Stardust.

October 1972 Let it rock. Article by Ian Hoare: You're so wonderful, gimme your hands.

October 1972 Phonograph Record Magazine. Article by Ron Ross: David Bowie's glamorous career.

October 1972 Changes. Article by Lenny Kaye: Smiling & Waving & Looking so fine.

October 1972 First part of recording Aladdin Sane in Nashville. Recorded a.o. Zion (A lad in vain) (6.15). The instrumental song was never finished, but appeared on a lot of bootlegs.

Bowie: "It's much more of a realism for me to think that this is all me, that there's nothing else in here. It's all outside. I prefer that way of existence."

1-10-1972 Boston, Music Hall.	CD	This is your life (PD 81997)
Attendance: 4.225.	4 CD	Sound and vision box
Recorded by RCA for a possible live album.	2 CD	David Live
3 Tracks released on Sound and Vision Box 1990 and bonus tracks on David Live:	2 CD	Aladdin Sane 30th Anniversary Edition (4 tracks)
John I'm only dancing (2.40), Changes (3.18), The Supermen (2.44).	CD	From the vaults of MainMan (1 song) (U.R. 001)
My death (5.27) released on various bootlegs.	CD	Absolutely Rare (1 song) (No label, no number)
Changes (3.18), The Supermen (2.44), Life on Mars? (3.25) and John I'm only dancing (2.40) in 2003 released on Aladdin Sane 30th Anniversary Edition.	CD	Ziggy with soul (1 song) (Dancing Horse DH-001)
	1 CDR	Ziggy rarities… to victory (No label, no number) (4 songs)
After the concert Bowie and his bodyguards went to a gay bar.	1 CDR	Dollars in drag (The Amazing Kornyfone Records Label TAKRL 1935) (1 song)
	Tape	

Begin October 1972 New York. Mercer. Bowie attended a New York Dolls concert.

6-10-1972 New York. Recording The Jean Genie (4.02). Inspired by Jean Genet's book A thief's journal.

6-10-1972 Re-release maxi-single Do anything you say (2.32) / I dig everything (2.45) / Can't help thinking about me (2.47) / I'm not losing sleep (2.52) (Pye 7NX.8002).

7-10-1972 Chicago, Chicago Public Auditorium.	2 CDR	Chicago 7 October 1972 (BowieHobby)
Attendance: 4.000.	1 CDR	Live Chicago Auditorium '72 (No label, no number)
Bowie announced My death and the audience kept very silent and just applauded polite after the song.		
Before Moonage daydream Bowie says: "This is a number	1 CDR	Chicago Glam (Old Gold

DATE / EVENT	AUDIO / VIDEO	TITLE

by Ziggy." In the first line he sings: "Well, I'm an ace invader."
They performed Jean Genie for the first time live.
During the intro of the song Bowie mentions Iggy Pop as an inspiration for the song.

2 CDR

Tape

Records OGCD 090)
Wowing the windy city (KLTA CD13 1/2) quality 7, 80 min.

7-10-1972 Melody Maker. Article by Roy Hollingworth: Can Bowie save New York from boredom?

7-10-1972 Sounds. Article by Chuck Pulin: Ziggy in NYC.

7-10-1972 Disc. Article by Lisa Robinson: David's the darling of the city.

8-10-1972 Sunday News. Article by Lilian Roxon: A rock happening: David's debut.

<u>8-10-1972</u> Detroit, Fisher Theatre.   NT

9-10-1972 Newsweek. Article by Hubert Saal: The Stardust Kid.

<u>9-10-1972</u> Indianapolis.   NT

<u>10-10-1972</u> St. Louis, Kiel Auditorium (Music Hall).   NT
Attendance: 110 (in a 11.000 seat arena).
Bowie asked the crowd to come close to the stage. He sat on the edge of the stage and between the songs he told the audience stories about himself, his band and his impressions of America (In other words - Kerry Juby 1986).

<u>11-10-1972</u> Kansas City, Auditorium (Memorial Hall).   NT
Attendance: 250.
Bowie was drunk and fell of the stage (he kept on singing). In Kansas he met Hunt and Tony Sales (who would join him in 1977 in Iggy Pop's backing band and in 1989 in Tin Machine).

14-10-1972 New Yorker. Article by Ellen Willis: Bowie's limitations.
Willis wrote: A week ago, I went to see Bowie's New York debut at Carnegie Hall and ended up standing on my seat.

<u>14-10-1972</u> Denver.   NT

<u>15-10-1972</u> Salt Lake City, Memorial Hall.   NT

16-10-1972 Chicago.
Cancelled.

16-10-1972 Bowie stayed at The Beverly Hills Hotel in Hollywood. Bowie now had a travelling crew of 46. They stayed about 6 days. The hotel bill that was send to RCA was about USD 20.000 (In other words - Kerry Juby 1986).
Cyrinda Foxe (who later married David Johansen of the New York Dolls) slept a few nights with

DATE / EVENT	AUDIO / VIDEO	TITLE

Bowie. She fed him croissants when he woke up in the afternoon. Iggy Pop and Mike Garson's wife and two children had also arrived. One day Leee Black Childers came into Bowie's room. Everybody was sunbathing but Bowie was in bed, with the covers pulled up to his chin, watching TV. Childers told him what a beautiful day it was. Bowie replied: "Oh really? In that case open the window."

17-10-1972 Boston Phoenix. Article by Ben Gerson: Bowie's Martian Spiders spin new world.

18-10-1972 DeFries arrived at The Beverly Hills Hotel.

20-10-1972 RCA report: Three shows of the American tour are recorded for a live album before Christmas.

<u>20-10-1972</u> Santa Monica, Civic Auditorium. Sound-check in the morning.	NT	
<u>20-10-1972</u> Santa Monica, Civic Auditorium.	CD	*Santa Monica 1972*
Attendance: 3.000.	2 CD	*Aladdin Sane 30th Anniversary Edition (16)*
Bowie stayed in the Beverly Hills Hotel.		
DeFries asked promoter Jim Rismiller what David should get paid. Rismiller said USD 4.000,— and DeFries agreed.	CD	*Santa Monica '72 (No label, no number)*
Taped by RCA for a possible live album.	CD	*Moonage daydream (Musique Sabot Stereo DB72)*
Ronson's backup singing was off key.		
Beautiful version of Space oddity.	CD	*Rock 'n' roll suicide (Great Dane Records GDR CD 8909)*
"This is a painter from New York. Terrific. That's my impersonation and it's about a man called Andy Warhol."	2 CD	*Rock 'n' roll suicide (The Swinging Pig Records TSP-CD-041-2)*
Bowie sings the song fully concentrated.		
Before My death Bowie says: "Playing to you courtesy of a piece of palm tree that I ate. I asked for lobster tail and they brought me palm tree, piece of palm tree. Yeah, really. That's all."	CD	*Rock 'n' roll suicide (ALEGRA CD 9035)*
	CD	*Soft in the middle (No label, no number)*
They close down with Rock 'n roll suicide after a great concert.	CD	*The 1972 American Tour (Golden Stars PRCD 1038)*
After the concert a party given by Wolfman Jack.	CD	*Changes (Lobster LOB CD 031)*
David took a tall, young woman to the bathroom and stayed there for almost the rest of the night.	CD	*Five years (6 songs) (Triangle Records PYCD 047)*
1. Intro (0.15).	CD	*Thin White Duke Live (P910028)*
2. Hang on to yourself (2.47).		
3. Ziggy Stardust (3.24).	CD	*Ziggy Stardust (I miti del rock)*
4. Changes (3.32).		
5. The Supermen (2.57).	CD	*Live 1972 (Teichiku Records TECX-25754)*
6. Life on Mars? (3.28).		
7. Five years (5.21).	CD	*The Jean Genie (vol. 2) (Banana BAN-004-A)*
8. Space oddity (5,22).		
9. Andy Warhol (3.58).	CD	*Spaced out (PB81998)*
10. My death (5.56).	CD	*Greatest hits live (Alpha Record AR7104)*
11. The width of a circle (10.39).		

DATE / EVENT	AUDIO / VIDEO	TITLE
12. Queen bitch (3.01).	2 LP	David Bowie (Berkeley 1806 A/B 1807 A/B)
13. Moonage daydream (4.38).	2 LP	David Bowie (Trade Mark of Quality TMQ 72011 A/D)
14. John, I'm only dancing (3.36).	2 LP	David Bowie (The Amazing Kornyfone Records Label TAKRL 2965 72011 A/D)
15. Waiting for the man (6.01).		
16. The Jean Genie (4.02).		
17. Suffragette city (4.25).		
18. Rock 'n' roll suicide (3.17).		
	LP	In person
	LP	Space oddity
	LP	In America (Trade Mark of Quality TMQ 71062 DB 531)
	LP	In America (K&S Records 006 DB 531 A/B)
	2 LP	The Bowie wonder (Space Records HH BOW 1/4)
	2 LP	Live in concert / Adults only (Moon Child Recs. 0050)
	2 LP	Live at the Santa Monica Civic
	LP	Soft in the middle / Good enough to eat (The Amazing Kornyfone Records Label TAKRL 1915)
	LP	Bump and grind (Aftermath records 9#9 TAKRL 1915 A/B)
	2 LP	The 1972 American Tour (The Amazing Kornyfone Records Label TAKRL 2965)
	LP	That's advertisement (Gema 66.23058-01/Brixton Boys 66.23058-01-1/2)
	2 LP	Make up and rock 'n' roll (Audio Recording Corp. ARC 2001)
	LP	Ziggy plays guitar live '72 (Ugolini LO 1 DB A/B)
	2 LP	Rock 'n' roll suicide (The Swinging Pig Records TSP 041-2 A/D)
	2 LP	Double David Bowie (None or Great Live Concert GLC)
	2 LP	Width of a circle (TMQ 71062 DB 531)
	2 LP	Ziggy in concert (Berkeley 1806 A/B 1807 A/B)
	LP	Golden years of Bow (Gold Records DB 6791) (4 songs)
	Single	Alabama song
	Tape	quality 9, 80 min.
	Video	3 min.

DATE / EVENT	AUDIO / VIDEO	TITLE
	Video	Various 14 (1 min)

21-10-1972 Sounds. Article by Steve Peacock: Under the image.

21-10-1972 Santa Monica, Civic Auditorium.   Tape
Attendance: 3.000.

21-10-1972 Los Angeles (Santa Monica). Rodney Bingenheimer and Tom Ayres opened the E Club on Sunset Boulevard. Bowie visited the club in full Ziggy regalia. Glam was born in Hollywood!

23-10-1972 Los Angeles Times. Article by Robert Hilburn: David Bowie rocks in Santa Monica. Robert Hilburn: "Bowie is a new singer-songwriter, whose album contains all the humour, intelligence, irony and personal vision that one expects from our best musical minds."

24 and 25-10-1972 Bowie mixes Iggy and The Stooges album Raw Power at Western Sound Studios in Hollywood. Everything was recorded on 3 instead of 24 tracks, so there was not much to mix.

27-10-1972 San Francisco, Winterland Auditorium.   NT
Attendance: 4.300 (sold out). Promoter: Bill Graham.
Support act: Sylvester.
When DeFries inspected the venue he told promoter Bill Graham a wall had to be build along the side of the theatre, so nobody could see Bowie before he entered the stage, or otherwise the gigs would be cancelled (Stardust - Henry Edwards and Tony Zanetta 1986).
In Los Angeles Mick Ronson had been sun bathing and swimming in the pool. From the chlorine in the water his peroxide hair had turned to a kind of green.

28-10-1972 San Francisco, Winterland Auditorium.   NT
Attendance: 1.100. Promoter: Bill Graham.
Support act: Sylvester.

28-10-1972 San Francisco, in front of The Mars Hotel). Video of Jean Genie shot by Mick Rock. Dancing model: Cyrinda Foxe.

30-10-1972 Time. Article by Dave Thompson: Vaudeville rock.

31-10-1972 Seattle, Paramount Theatre.   NT
Almost no public (only 400 people showed up).
They stayed at Bayside Hotel.

October 1972 A special edition released of The rise and fall of Ziggy Stardust and the Spiders from Mars.

Bowie about himself and Lou Reed: "I really don't know what we're doing, if we're the spearhead of anything, we're not necessarily the spearhead of anything good. But people like Lou and I are probably predicting the end of and era and I mean that catastrophically. Any society that allows people like Lou and I to become rampant is pretty well lost" (A rock 'n' roll odyssey - Kate Lynch 1984).

DATE / EVENT	AUDIO / VIDEO	TITLE

3-11-1972 Re-released LP The man who sold the world (RCA LSP 4816).

<u>4-11-1972</u> Phoenix, Celebrity Theater.   NT

5-11-1972 Los Angeles Times Calendar. Article by Robert Hilburn: David Bowie arrives with a burst of Stardust.

5-11-1972 BBC Radio Show repeated. Recorded and broadcast for the first time 9-5-1972.
Andy Warhol, Lady Stardust, White light, white heat, Rock 'n' roll suicide.

6-11-1972 Billy Murcia (New York Dolls) overdosed on alcohol and Mandrax and died. His death inspired Bowie to write the songs Watch that man and Time.

9-11-1972 Rolling Stone (UK). 2 Articles by Timothy Ferris:
1. Are you man enough for David Bowie and The iceman, having calculated, cometh.
2. David Bowie in America.
Timothy Ferris wrote: "Bowie keeps moving, strikes poses reminiscent of a dozen earlier rockers and behaves much of the time like a puppet. He looks the way he says he feels, like and actor playing the role of a rock star. The thesis of the role is that freedom on stage is an illusion paid for by freedom."
About DeFries: "A lawyer-like paunch, who smokes fat black cigars. He has a pallid skin and a long pointed nose, like a character from Dickens."
Bowie: "I'm a pretty cold person. A very cold person, I find. I can't feel strongly. I get so numb. I find that I'm walking around numb. I'm a bit of an iceman."

11-11-1972 Advertisement for Space oddity and The man who sold the world: "Make room for 2 Bowie Albums."

11-11-1972 Dallas, Majestic Theatre.
Poor ticket sales.
Cancelled.

12-11-1972 Houston, Music Hall.
Poor ticket sales.
Cancelled.

13-11-1972 Oklahoma City.
Poor ticket sales.
Cancelled.

<u>14-11-1972</u> New Orleans, Layola University.   NT

14-11-1972 Bowie wrote Time (8 days after Billy Murcia of the New York Dolls died).

17-11-1972 Re-released LP Space Oddity (RCA LSP.4813).

<u>17-11-1972</u> Fort Lauderdale, Pirates World, The Jai Alais   2 CD   *Drive in Saturday (Rag Doll*
Fronton. Attendance: 200.   *Music RDM-942013A/B)*
A sharp stud of his costume into his boot. After the show   CD   *Look back in anger*

DATE / EVENT	AUDIO / VIDEO	TITLE
the foot looked like a mess of blood and raw flesh. After Ziggy Stardust they have to tune their instruments for the second time. Bowie says: "Let me tell you that we're all totally out of tune. But we're gonna play." "I've a new song for you I'd like to do very much. I wrote it on the train from L.A. to Chicago before I came down here and tried to write it on the train journey from Chicago to here. I'm not quite sure if I've learnt it yet. We'll see now, won't we." Drive-in Saturday (6.08) follows. The crowd loves it. "This is a number that was written by a band. This is a New York band's number and the band was called the Velvet Underground." Waiting for the man follows.	1 CDR 2 CDR 2 CDR 2 CDR LP Tape	(No label, no number) Ziggy rarities… to victory (No label, no number) (1 song) Live Miami 1972 (complete) (No label, no number) I'm an alligator (Old Gold Records OGCD 424A/B) Crashing out with Sylvian Bowiestudio 70-75 quality 8, 80 min.

In the hotel he got drunk and shaved of his eyebrows (later he told he was pissed because Mott the Hoople turned down Drive-in Saturday).

18-11-1972 The Times Herald. Article by Dennis Dyroff: David Bowie, Strange Man, Hits Musical Big Time.

<u>18-11-1972</u> Atlanta.   NT

19-11-1972 Nashville. Gustl Breuer, Mick Ronson and Woody Woodmansey went to see The Guarneri Quartet play Beethoven.

<u>20-11-1972</u> Nashville, Municipal Auditorium.   NT
Attendance: 4.424.
Right-wing demonstration outside the venue.
Over-enthusiastic Cherry Vanilla told a lot of lies in an interview (about making tapes to entertain prisoners of war in Hanoi etc.). The war veterans were not amused.
People thought a homosexual communist came to town.
Because of all the curious people, the concert was attended very well (David Bowie - Dave Thompson 1986).

In a closed (but not deserted) bar of the Hotel Angela gave frottage to a female fan. Later that night she made fun (nude) in the pool of the Hotel with bodyguard Anton Jones (a green eyed Jamaican black). The Hotel management complained and the next day Tony DeFries put her on a plain via New York to London (Backstage passes - Angela Bowie and Patrick Carr 1993).

21-11-1972 Nashville Banner about Bowie: "I don't like queers."

21-11-1972 Nashville Tennessean.
They wrote: "Bowie really is not a bad rock musician, if one can consider him such."

22-11-1972 Mott The Hoople flies from London airport Heathrow to Los Angeles for a 5 week American tour.
Leee Black Childers welcomes them in Los Angeles in behalf of their management MainMan.

DATE / EVENT	AUDIO / VIDEO	TITLE

22-11-1972 New Orleans, The Warehouse.   NT
Attendance: 3.500. Tony DeFries attended the concert.
It was freezing cold in The Warehouse and the heating did
not work. Bowie got pissed and the guitars wouldn't stay
in tune.

23-11-1972 Tony DeFries joins Mott the Hoople in Los Angeles for the start of a 5 week American tour. At that moment their single All the young dudes is in the American top 40. The album of the same name is also in the charts.

23-11-1972 Louisville.   NT

24-11-1972 Release The Jean Genie (4.03) / Ziggy Stardust (3.13) (RCA 2302).

24-11-1972 Released in US, Italy and Spain. Promo single: The Jean Genie (3.59) / Hang on to yourself (3.28) (RCA 74-0838).

24-11-1972 Release Single Walk on the wild side (4.14) / Perfect day (3.56) - Lou Reed (RCA 2303). David's former saxophone teacher Ronnie Ross played on David's invitation the sax solo (he received the standard fee of GBP 9,—). The backing singers were called: Thunderthighs (Casey Synge, Karen Friedman, Dari Lalou and Juanita Franklin).
In 1975 the Thunderthighs had a hit with the song Central Park Arrest.

24-11-1972 Cincinnati.   NT

25-11-1972 Cleveland, Entertainment Arena (Music Hall).   2 CD   *Aladdin Sane 30th*
Attendance: 10.000 (Sold out).   *Anniversary Edition (1 track)*
A very good concert in a great sound quality!   CD   *Ziggy's invasion of America*
"I'd been asked to ask the people who have… good   *(Stardust 721125)*
evening everybody… Then I should ask if people who   1 CDR   Cleveland music '72
were standing could sit down. I'd appreciate it and a lot of   CD   *Cleveland Music Hall (76 min)*
other people would. Thank you. I'm sure you will."   *(No label, no number)*
During Space oddity: "Can I hear me Major Tom."   1 CDR   Live in Cleveland and rare
Andy Warhol has some nice guitar parts.   track! (Tradepoint) (9 tracks)
Drive-in Saturday (4.55) in 2003 released on Aladdin   4 CD   *The North American Tours*
Sane 30th Anniversary Edition.   *(Pearls Before Swine PBS*
Attended by Chrissie Hynde (The Pretenders), who talked   *1037 / 1038 / 1039 / 1040)*
to Mick Ronson at the backstage after-party.   Tape   quality 8, 75 min.

26-11-1972 Cleveland, Public Hall.   NT
Attendance: 10.000 (Sold out).
There was a small party in Bowie's suite. A black groupie
joined him to his bedroom.

28-11-1972 Pittsburgh, Syria Mosque (Stanley Theatre).   NT
Attendance: 3.500.   Video

29-11-1972 Mott the Hoople at Philadelphia, Tower Theatre   CD   *Miscellaneous of cats*
WMMR Radio. With Bowie on stage for the encores.   *(No label, no number)*

DATE / EVENT	AUDIO / VIDEO	TITLE

Attendance: 2.000. Support act: Brownsville Station.
On the day of the Mott concert Bowie's car broke down.
He and his bodyguards Stuey and George took a 200 dollar
cab. They were just in time. Ian Hunter: "I'd like to
introduce you to the guy who wrote the song: David
Bowie!" Bowie says: "I'd like to do a number for ya called
All the young dudes."

1. All the young dudes (4.02).
2. Honky Tonk women (original by Roling Stones in 1969)
(Bowie backing vocals) (8.44).
The whole Bowie entourage and Mott the Hoople stayed at
the Warwick Hotel. Bowie was very tired, but joined the
others for a visit to the local all-night hamburger café.

	1 CDR	With Mott the Hoople 1972 (No label, no number)
	1 CDR	All David's dudes (Mott the Hoople)
	2 CD	All the way from Stockholm to Philadelphia Live 71/72 (Mott the Hoople) (Angel Air)
	2 CD	"Live and otherwise" (The best of Mott the Hoople + Ian Hunter Live and Studio)
	LP	Mott the Hoople live with David Bowie
	Tape	quality 9, 80 min.

<u>30-11-1972</u> Philadelphia, Tower Theatre.   NT
Attendance: 2.575 (sold out).
Promoter Rick Green. Originally scheduled for Friday the
13th. But Bowie's management refused this date.
Just before the start of the concert a figure with a red haired
Ziggy haircut took place in the fifth row. Some (even
promoter Green) thought it was Bowie, but it was DeFries
girlfriend Melanie.

December 1972 Release Backside - Strawbs (credited to Ciggy Barlust and the Whales from Venus).

December 1972 MainMan moved to 240 East 58th Street in New York. It contained also an apartment for Tony DeFries and Melanie McDonald.

December 1972 Released in US Space oddity / The man who sold the world (RCA 74-0876).

December 1972 Release Promo EP. Space oddity / Moonage daydream / Life on Mars? / It ain't easy (RCA EP 45-103).

December 1972 Release 3LP 20 Fantastic Hits by Original Artists Volume 3 (Arcade ADDE 5). Incudes: The Jean Genie and All the young dudes.

December 1972 Release in Japan: Space oddity / It ain't easy (RCA 552252).

December 1972 Released in Portugal: Starman (edit) (3.58) / Hang on to yourself (2.38) / John I'm only dancing (2.43) / Suffragette city (3.25) (RCA TP-656).

December 1972 Newsday. Article by Robert Christgau: Growing up grim with Mott the Hoople. Christgau wrote: All the young dudes is the most exciting piece of White rock-and-roll released all year. It recalls The Stones at their peak.

December 1972 Music Scene. Article by Gordon Coxhill backstage in September 1972 at the Top Rank Suite: "Whereas most pop stars attract their share of groupies David, for some unaccountable reason, attracts boys to the front of the stage and into his dressing room. Some of the boys can get quite bitchy

DATE / EVENT	AUDIO / VIDEO	TITLE

so nobody is allowed backstage."

December 1972 Rolling Stone. Article by John Mendelsohn.
"Bowie is definitely and original. The album Hunky Dory is his most engaging album musically."

<u>December 1972</u> UK TV. Top of the Pops.   1 CDR   Ziggy TV (100% 13)
The Jean Genie (5.36).

Winter 1972 Bowie became fascinated with Robert Heinlein's in 1961 published book A stranger in a strange land. 17-2-1973 MainMan would do the announcement he was starring in the film Stranger in a strange land.
Bowie: "We just devised that as a ploy. Tony didn't want to go to the trouble of asking for movie roles. So we did the announcement and the scripts suddenly started pouring in."

1-12-1972 Philadelphia. Mott the Hoople visited Skin Clothing on Lexington and 62nd Street. It is the shop where Iggy Pop buys his stage gear.

<u>1-12-1972</u> Philadelphia, Tower Theatre.   NT
Attendance: 2.575 (sold out).
The Spiders stayed at The Warwick Hotel. There were stories of naked Spiders knocking on every hotel room.

2-12-1972 Sounds. Article by Patrick William Salvo: Changing face of David Bowie.

<u>2-12-1972</u> Philadelphia, Tower Theatre.   NT
Attendance: 2.575 (sold out).
Last encore. David slipped and almost fell of the stage (half on, half of the stage). He kept singing while he crawled back on the stage. To let it look as a part of the act Bowie hung backward on the edge of the stage, singing upside-down.
Two little girls hugged Bowie.
After the show Bowie found out he was missing a silver bracelet. David Douglas (the writer of Presenting David Bowie) realised he had seen a flash of metal as the two girls hugged Bowie. He rushed after them and found them outside. He promised them 3 free tickets and a personal meeting with Bowie (which never transpired) and got the bracelet to return to Bowie (it can be seen on the cover of Young Americans) (Presenting David Bowie - David Douglas 1975).

3-12-1972 Valley Forge. Bowie's sound crew joins Mott the Hoople. Tony DeFries has finished Bowie's American tour and will be non-stop with Mott the Hoople for the rest of their American tour.

Begin December 1972 David and Angela went to Max's Kansas City in New York. Here they met Bebe Buell (Todd Rundgren's 18 year old girlfriend).
The next night Bowie and Bebe Buell had dinner at the Indian restaurant Nirvana overlooking Central Park.

DATE / EVENT	AUDIO / VIDEO	TITLE

The next evenings they went to Kenny's Castaways, to hear the New York Dolls and in another venue Thelonius Monk.

First part of December 1972. New York, RCA Building. Aladdin Sane sessions and video of Space oddity was shot.
Recording All the young dudes (outtake 1) (2.58), completed at Trident Studios in January 1973 with Ken Scott.

8-12-1972 Release LP Transformer - Lou Reed (RCA Victor LSP 4807).

9-12-1972 Adverts for the UK dates in December and January: "Bowie's Back!"

9-12-1972 Angie Bowie calls Ian Hunter to invite him to a party with Bowie and Spiders after finishing recording Aladdin Sane within about 2 weeks.
Bowie's bodyguards Stuart and Zee join Mott the Hoople for the rest of their tour after an incident in St. Louis.

10-12-1972 New York. Warwick Hotel.
Bowie plays Ian Hunter songs he wrote for the next album (Aladdin Sane).
Bowie got a Japanese bell tent top on with huge bell trousers and clogs. They listened to Drive in Saturday, his version of All the young dudes, Aladdin Sane (that had no vocals yet).
Bowie tells Hunter he wants 4 sax players on stage for the next tour. They have to wear white wide-lapel suits and have Mafia frizzled hairdos, with glitter stuck on.
They get a cab and eat at the Stage deli (Diary of a rock 'n' roll star - Ian Hunter, Panther 1974).

11-12-1972 New York, RCA Studio 3. Press conference party.
After the press conference Bowie leaves New York.

Mid-December 1972 From US to Britain on the ship Ellinis (during the voyage he wrote lyrics for Aladdin Sane).

16-12-1972 New Adverts for the UK December and January concerts: "RCA Welcomes Bowie Back from his triumphant tour of the U.S."

19-12-1972 Bowie's bodyguard Stuey left the Mott the Hoople tour and returned to London to join Bowie.

23-12-1972 Melody Maker. Article by Lorraine Alterman: Bye, bye, Bowie.
Alterman wrote: "David Bowie was certainly the main man of 1972, just as we predicted when we front-paged him back in January."

23-12-1972 London, Rainbow Theatre.   Tape
Attendance: 3.000. Support act: Quiver.
Featuring the Lindsay Kemp Mime Company.
Let's spend the night together for the first time live.
Steve Peacock: "I realised that most of Bowie's new found audience didn't know anything further back than Hunky Dory, and where there mainly for cheap thrills, camp charisma, and a performance centred around the media

DATE / EVENT	AUDIO / VIDEO	TITLE

creation of gay rock" (Loving the alien - Christopher Sandford 1996).

23-12-1972 London. MainMan is having a small party for Bowie, The Spiders and Mott the Hoople, because they made the latter part of 1972 successful.

Date / Event	Audio/Video	Title
<u>24-12-1972</u> London, Rainbow Theatre. Attendance: 3.000. Support act: Quiver. Featuring the Lindsay Kemp Mime Company. Bowie asked fans to do a donation to Dr. Barnardo's. The next day a lot of toys were given to several hospitals. They start with Let's spend the night together (3.33). At the end of the song Bowie starts a kind of improvisation (in 1990 he would do the same with Young Americans). "Are you still in school? That turns me on. Education is wonderful." Halfway Life on Mars? Bowie stops and the audience helps him to finish the song.	1 CDR	*London 24 December 1972 (BowieHobby)*
	1 CDR	*Christmas with Ziggy (Old Gold Records OGCD 017)*
	1 CDR	*Live at the Rainbow Theatre December 29th 1972 (No label, no number)*
	1 CDR	*Ziggy plays guitar vol. 2 (No label, no number)*
	CD	*Bowie back live at the Rainbow*
	1 CDR	*London 24.12.1972 (No label, no number)*
	LP	*David Bowie at the Rainbow complete concert (Label:ll)*
	Tape	quality 7, 60 min.
	Video	*Various 26 (4 min)*

Christmas 1972. Stayed at Haddon Hall.

25-12-1972 Bowie called Ian Hunter in Northampton. He wanted to see him very urgent. Hunter and his wife Trudy drove to Haddon Hall. It was just a joke to see how fast he could get them in Haddon Hall. Hunter and his wife left and drove to their flat in Wembley (they were not happy). (Diary of a rock 'n' roll star - Ian Hunter, Panther 1974).

26-12-1972 New York, Hempstead. Lou Reed radio performance. Also a 5 minute interview about Bowie and Ronson producing his album. They also asked him about Dough Yule (who replaced him in the Velvet Underground since 23-8-1970). Answer: "I hope he is dead."	CD	*American Poet (Lou Reed) (Burning Airlines PILOT 83)*

Marc Bolan: "With no disrespect to David, it's much too soon to put him in the same class as me. I'd give Slade that credibility but, without being arrogant or unfair, I certainly wouldn't give it to David. He's still very much a one-hit wonder, I'm afraid. I've always thought Mott the Hoople were bigger than David. I think maybe he's been sucked into something that's unhealthy for him. You can't create an image, it's only what you are. The whole pop star machine thing is a heavy one to handle. Maybe David can cope with it. I suppose I managed."

<u>28-12-1972</u> Manchester (Stretford), Hardrock Concert Theatre. Attendance: 3.000. He again does the improvisation part during Let's spend the night together. "What sign are you? I'm a Capricorn, nice to meet you." "This one is relatively new. It's called John, I'm only	1 CDR	*Manchester 28 Dec 1972 (BowieHobby)*
	1 CDR	*Last stand 1972 (Old Gold Records OGCD 018)*
	1 CDR	*Live Manchester Hardrock 1972 (No label, no number)*

DATE / EVENT	AUDIO / VIDEO	TITLE

dancing."
Attended my Mick Ronson's sister Maggi. Angie took her in a plane (her first flight) to Manchester.

1 CDR
Tape

Live Machester 1972
(No label, no number)
quality 6, 60 min.

Rumours say, in the dressing room someone put acid in a bowl of punch. The journalist of the local newspaper was the most of the evening convinced of the fact he was a dog (David Bowie - Dave Thompson 1986).

<u>29-12-1972</u> High Wycombe, Town Hall.   NT

1972 The early American interview. A tape of David's thoughts on America during the fall '72 Ziggy Stardust tour.   Tape

1972 Radio Luxembourg interview. Bowie talks about suddenly finding some success and recognition with Ziggy Stardust after many years.   Tape

End 1972 The first Dutch David Bowie fan club was founded, complete with a magazine called "Stardust."
Wouter (Wally) van Middendorp: "I'd read an English newspaper about Bowie. The first album I bought was Space oddity. In the beginning you've got a lot of problems making the magazine. Later in 1974 more members joined the club because the promotion of Bowie in Holland was extremely high during David's stay in Amsterdam" (Dutch Fanzine The Voyeur, August 2000).

End 1972 / Begin 1973 the drummer of Queen asked Bowie to produce them. Bowie was interested, but didn't have the time to do it.

1973 Book published: The wild boys - William Burroughs (Grove Press Inc.) ISBN 0-394-17819-X. Inspired Bowie to use the cut up technique to write lyrics.

Bowie: "The Wild Boys, by William S.Burroughs, was a really heavy book that had come out around 1970. It was a cross between that and Clockwork Orange that really started to put together the shape and the look of what Ziggy and the Spiders were going to become. They were both powerful pieces of work, especially the marauding boy gangs of Burroughs's Wild Boys with their Bowie knives. I got straight on to that. I read everything into everything. Everything had to be infinitely symbolic" (Rolling Stone Raves - A. Bozza and S. Dahl 1999).

1973 Released in France: David Bowie Coccinelle Varietes (same as The world of David Bowie) (Decca 210.039).

1973 Released in France: David Bowie Mille-Pattes Series (same as Images 1966-1967).

1973 Released in Spain: El Rey Del Gay-Power (same as Images 1966-1967) (Decca DCS 15044/45).

1973 Superpop - A Disc special. Article by A. Tyler: David Bowic.

1973 Book published: The Songs of David Bowie - Wise Publications.

DATE / EVENT	AUDIO / VIDEO	TITLE

1973 David Bowie Fan Club Magazine, Issue 1 (MainMan). Filled with nonsense and photo's.

Early 1973 A MainMan office was opened in Los Angeles. It was run by Leee Black Childers, a blond haired photographer who had quite a few nude photo's of Bowie (Backstage passes - Angela Bowie and Patrick Carr 1993).

January 1973 Stereo Review. Article by Steve Simels: David Bowie: No honey, it's not one of those.

Nicky Chinn (producer of the Sweet's Blockbuster, that used the same riff as Jean Genie: "I remember being introduced to Bowie at Tramp, and he looked up at me completely deadpan and said: "Cunt!" And then he got up and gave me a hug and said: "Congratulations"" (Glam! Bowie, Bolan and the Glitter Rock Revolution - Barney Hoskyns 1998).

1-1-1973 UK TV. The Old Grey Whistle Test, Presented by Bob Harris.
He asked guest Kim Fowley to define the difference between David Bowie and Alice Cooper.
Kim Fowley replied: "Bowie is Rommel and Cooper is Einstein. Bowie is an innovator, Cooper an imitator."

5-1-1973 LWT South Bank Studios. Recording for the Russell Harty Show. Broadcast 17-1-1973.

The Ziggy Stardust World Tour.
David Bowie and The Spiders from Mars:
David Bowie (vocals, guitar, harmonica).
Mick Ronson (lead guitar).
Trevor Bolder (bass guitar).
Mick 'Woody' Woodmansey (drums).
Mike Garson (piano).

Date / Event	Audio / Video	Title
<u>5-1-1973</u> Glasgow, Greens Playhouse (Apollo). Matinee. Attendance: 3.181. Support-act: Quiver.	CD	*Trident Sessions 72 and Glasgow Green's Playhouse* (CRB S.A. Spain)
1. Hang on to yourself (2.45).		
2. Ziggy Stardust (2.56).	CD	*The legendary lost tapes* (No label, no number)
3. Changes (3.36).		
4. The supermen (2.35).	Tape	quality 6, 60 min.
5. Five years (3.44).	Tape	quality 8, 60 min.
6. Life on Mars? (3.23).	Video	5 min.
7. John I'm only dancing (2.25).		
8. Moonage daydream (4.36).		
9. Suffragette city (2.28).		
10. Width of a circle (10.26).		
11. Rock 'n' roll suicide (3.02).		
<u>5-1-1973</u> Glasgow, Greens Playhouse (Apollo). Evening. Support-act: Quiver.	Tape	quality 6, 60 min.

6-1-1973 Melody Maker. Article by P. Bosworth: Bowie: Is it all for a Lark?

6-1-1973 Sounds. Article by David Clark: Bowie the cosmic job.

DATE / EVENT	AUDIO / VIDEO	TITLE
<u>6-1-1973</u> Edinburgh, Empire Theatre. Matinee. Support-act: Quiver. During Let's spend the night together Bowie says: "When I saw you walking down the street, I said what's you name and she said what's your name. What's your game, have you got a name? I'm a Capricorn. I dropped my handkerchief on the ground. I've been here rather ages. I said are you still at school? Yeah? I said do you believe in education? Will you educate me?"	1 CDR 1 CDR Tape	*Will you educate me? (Old Gold Records OGCD 019)* Zodiac Ziggy (KTLA CD37) quality 6, 60 min.
<u>6-1-1973</u> Edinburgh, Empire Theatre. 2nd Show. Support-act: Quiver.	Tape	quality 6, 60 min.
<u>6-1-1973</u> Edinburgh, Empire Theatre, 3rd Show (evening). Support-act: Quiver.	1 CDR Tape	*Will you educate me? (Old Gold Records OGCD 019)* quality 6, 60 min.
7-1-1973 Los Angeles Times Calendar. Article by Robert Hilburn: David Bowie rated top recording Artist of '72.		
<u>7-1-1973</u> Newcastle upon Tyne, City Hall. Attendance: 2.168. Support act: Quiver. A great show! Freelance photographer Ian Dickson took a lot of photo's (unauthorised). They appeared 2 weeks later on the cover of Disc Magazine. Decca used the cover shot for the Re-release of the LP The world of David Bowie.	1 CDR 1 CDR Tape	*A Newcastle daydream (Old Gold Records OGCD 117)* *So softly a super god cries (KTLA CD38)* quality 6, 60 min.
<u>9-1-1973</u> Preston, Guildhall. Attendance: 2.146. Support act: Quiver. A short (65 min), but very good concert. Announcing John I'm only dancing: "This is an old one… for us anyway." During Starman Bowie forgot the words and there was a long instrumental part in the middle of this encore song. "Ok this is our very last night on tour. So we'll do a few extra numbers. Alright?"	1 CDR 2 CDR Tape Tape	Let's spend the night together (Old Gold Records OGCD 020) *Did you see the suits & the platform boots? (Downunder Discs)* quality 7, 60 min. quality 8, 70 min.
<u>17-1-1973</u> UK TV. LWT. Russell Harty Show. Interview and 3 songs (Recorded 5-1-1973 at LWT South Bank Studios). 1. Drive in Saturday (4.13). 2. Interview (12.09). 3. My death (original French version by Jaques Brel) (3.48). 4. John I'm only dancing. Bowie told: My next role will be a person called Aladdin Sane.	2 CDR CD CD 1 CDR 1 CDR CD	The final stand (Old Gold Records OGCD 215A/B) *A crash course for the ravers (No label, no number) (1)* *The Axeman Cometh (1) (DB 003)* *Russell Harty 17-1-1973 (No label, no number) (1,2,3)* *Ziggy TV (100% 13) (1,2,3)* Hours… My death (3)

DATE / EVENT	AUDIO / VIDEO	TITLE
Russell Harty: "Do you believe in God?" Bowie: "I believe in an energy force, but I wouldn't like to put a name to it." Russell Harty: "Do you indulge in any form of worship?" Bowie: "Life. I love life very much indeed." Bowie wore his Freddi Burretti-designed suit, the jacket of intricately patterned worsted, with ruby velvet trim and cream lining. The suit was in 1998 sold by Christie's for GBP. 2.600,—. Other guests in the show: Georgie Fame, Elton John and Alan Price.	CD CD VCD VCD Tape Tape Video Video Video Video	(DCCD 2000) *Heaven or maybe Hell (3)* (Artie Fartie CD001) *Legendary Lost Tapes Vol. 1* *(1) (VigOtone 178)* *Various 1 (6.03 min.) (1,2)* *Bob's Eggs [+extras]* (No label, no number) quality 10, 7 min. 20 min. *Various 10 (song 1 and interv)* *Stolp tapes, vol. 10 (6 min)* *25 Years of Ziggy Stardust* *Various 26 (7 min)*

18-1-1973 Daily Express. Article. A gold disc on the way for Bowie's third million selling album.

20-1-1973 Disc. Article by Gavin Petrie: Bowie is End of an Era.

20-1-1973 Disc. Article by Rick Atkinson: All that glitters.

20-1-1973 London. Trident Studios. Recording of John I'm only dancing (sax-version) (2.41). The music for Panic in Detroit (4.25) and Lady grinning (3.46) soul was recorded. Bowie added the vocals on 24-1-1973.

21-1-1973 Daily Mirror stated "Ziggy" had sold a million copies (in fact it was only 200.000 in Britain and USA together).

19 to 25-1-1973 Tottenham (London), Royal Ballroom.   NT
Rehearsals.
Added to the backing band:
Brian Wilshaw (saxophone, flute).
Ken Fordham (saxophone).
Geoffrey MacCormack (percussion, backing vocals).

21-1-1973 Honolulu, International Sports Centre. Performance of the Rolling Stones. Mick Jagger jumps round with a crystal mask, in a parody on Bowie.

22-1-1973 Daily Mirror. Article by Deborah Thomas: King of Rock & Rouge.

24-1-1973 London. Trident Studios.
Bowie finished LP Aladdin Sane after recording lyrics for Panic in Detroit and Lady grinning soul. John Hutchinson visited them in the studio. David said: "If you can go with us we leave for New York next week" (The Starzone Interviews - David Currie 1987).
Bowie: "I've written a new song which is called Time. I wrote about time, and I played it back, and my God, it was a gay song! And I'd no intention of writing anything at all gay" (In his own words - Miles 1980).
Bowie: "I ran into a very strange type of paranoid person when I was doing Aladdin Sane. Very mixed up people and I got very upset. I was just looking around seeing what was in my head" (In other words

DATE / EVENT	AUDIO / VIDEO	TITLE

- Kerry Juby 1986).

24-1-1973 Times. Article by Michael Wale: David Bowie: Rock and theatre.

25-1-1973 Bowie leaves from Southampton by boat Queen Elizabeth 2 for New York.

27-1-1973 New Musical Express. Article by Charles Shaar Murray: Goodbye Ziggy and a big hello to Aladdin Sane.
Bowie: "I would like to get one thing straight: It's not an additional Spider. The Spiders are still Trevor, Mick and Woody. We've just got in some back-up men and tenor saxes and piano and voices. I read in some of the papers that the Spiders were expanding - no way. It's three Spiders, back-up musicians and me."

30-1-1973 They arrived in New York on the Queen Elizabeth 2.

February 1973 Music Scene (UK). Small article about Bowie.

February 1973 Stereo Review. Article by Steve Simels: Bowie and Hoople and Reed.

1-2-1973 Pierre Laroche designed the sleeve image for Aladdin Sane.

3-2-1973 Evening Standard. Article by Ray Connoly: Wowie, Bowie.

6-2 to 12-2-1973 New York City, RCA Studios. Rehearsals. John Hutchinson and Bowie went to a performance of jazz bassist Charlie Mingus (Bowie used his album title Wham-bam-thank-you-mam in Suffragette City). John Hutchinson: "Harry Belafonte was upstairs and he came down to ask us to keep the noise down. He was very nice about it all, though" (The Sarzone Interviews - David Currie 1987).	NT	

13-2-1973 Daily Planet. Article by Alan Newman: The return of Ziggy Stardust.

13-2-1973 New York, Radio City Music Hall. Rehearsal.	NT	
14-2-1973 New York, Radio City Music Hall. Attendance: 5.884 (Sold out). Support act Fumble was cancelled. Bowie descended on stage in a cage 17 meters above the stage and did 7 costume changes. Mike Garson joins Bowie on piano. Large banners at the backcloth, depicting a black zig-zag similar to Aladdin Sane's trademark lightning bolt, lit by flashing strobes (had a passing resemblance to the Nazi's SS symbol). Bowie played a sax solo in Soul love. During Rock 'n' roll suicide a guy jumped on the stage and	2 CDR 2 CD 2 CDR 2 CDR Tape	New York 14 February 1973 (BowieHobby) Soul Asylum (2 songs) (BLY 003/004) St. Valentine's day massacre (Old Gold Records OGCD 011A/B) A lad Insane New York 1973 (The Dutch Connection CD 140273) quality 8, 90 min.

DATE / EVENT	AUDIO / VIDEO	TITLE

kissed Bowie. Bowie said: "Ah, mon amour, j'etouffe."
Show attended by: Andy Warhol, Truman Capote, Todd Rundgren, Bette Midler, Allen Ginsberg, Salvador Dali, Johnny Winter and Frankie LaRocka (David Johansen Group).
Bowie fainted at the end of the show and Bette Midler dashed backstage to see if there was anything she could do to help. Bowie explained: "It's alright. I haven't been eating enough" (Living on the brink - George Tremlett 1996).

15-2-1973 New York. Before the show interviewed by Michael Watts.

Date / Event	Audio / Video	Title
<u>15-2-1973</u> New York, Radio City Music Hall. Attendance: 5.884 (Sold out). Support act: Fumble. Tickets: USD 7,50. My death was superb. It had a great film running on the backcloth (the cosmos running at high speed towards the audience). Bowie starts The Supermen on his own. After the first part of the song the band joins in. Attended by Johnny Winter and Todd Rundgren and Salvador Dali.	2 CDR 2 CD 2 CDR 2 CDR 2 LP LP LP LP Tape	*New York 15 February 1973 (BowieHobby)* *Soul Asylum (BLY 003/004) complete concert* Amazed & Amused (Old Gold Records OGCD 496A/B) Live NYC 15-2-1973 (No label, no number) Aladdin Sane watch that man (MIW Records 7 MW 7 A/IV) The cracked actor (SNJ 38 MW 7 A/III) Ziggy Stardust '73 (MW 7 A/II) Into the Labyrinth (L ZL 036 MW 7 A/III) quality 9, 90 min.
<u>16-2-1973</u> Philadelphia, Tower Theatre. Attendance 2.575 (Sold out in hours). Support act: Fumble.	NT	

17-2-1973 Announced that he will star in film of Robert Heinlein's "Stranger in a strange land," but not for at least 18 months.

17-2-1973 Philadelphia Evening Bulletin. Article by William Mandel: Bowie creates a musical experience.

Date / Event	Audio / Video	Title
<u>17-2-1973</u> Philadelphia, Tower Theatre. Attendance 2.575 (Sold out in hours). Support act: Fumble.	NT	
<u>18-2-1973</u> Philadelphia, Tower Theatre. Attendance 2.575 (Sold out in hours). Support act: Fumble.	NT	

DATE / EVENT	AUDIO / VIDEO	TITLE

19-2-1973 Philadelphia, Tower Theatre.
Attendance 2.575 (Sold out in hours).
Support act: Fumble.　　　　　　　　　　　　　　　NT

20-2-1973 Philadelphia, Tower Theatre.
Attendance 2.575 (Sold out in hours).
Support act: Fumble.　　　　　　　　　　　　　　　NT

23-2-1973 Nashville, War Memorial Theatre.　　　　NT
Support act: Fumble.

24-2-1973 Melody Maker. Article by Michael Watts: Stranger in a strange land.

24-2-1973 Melody Maker. Article by Michael Watts: Bowie's last tour?

24-2-1973 New Musical Express. Article by Charles Shaar Murray: Gay guerrillas and private movies.

26-2-1973 Memphis, Ellis Auditorium.　　　　　　　NT
Attendance: 5.000. Support act: Fumble.

27-2-1973 Memphis, Ellis Auditorium.　　　　　　　NT
Attendance: 5.000. Support act: Fumble.

28-2-1973 South End. Article by Tom Leavens: Making of a Pop Star 1973.

March 1973 Magazine Rock Scene. Article called: A visit with David Bowie.

March 1973. The Image had a handful of screenings at the Jacey Cinema at Trafalgar Square between two other films (I am sexy and Erotic Blue).

March 1973 Release 20th Century boy / Free angel - Marc Bolan and T.Rex (Wax Co. Marc 4).

1-3-1973 Detroit. Detroit Hilton. Afternoon. Interviews.

| 1-3-1973 Detroit, Masonic Temple Auditorium. Attendance: 4.856. Support act: Fumble. Bowie talks a lot, introducing the new songs on Aladdin Sane. The show is good, but to short. After the show a small party. Bowie introduced to Michael Des Barres (member of group Silverhead) and B.P. Fallon. | 1 CDR

1 CDR
CD

1 CDR

Tape | *Detroit 1 March 1973* (BowieHobby)
Last Panic (MA 990074)
American Daydream (Switch On! 2001-12-1)
Panic in Detroit (Old Gold Records OGCD 022)
quality 7, 70 min. |

3-3-1973 Record World. Article by Robert Feiden: David Bowie brings back style to rock and roll.

3-3-1973 Los Angeles Times. Article by Robert Hilburn: Second Bowie concert for overflow crowd.

3-3-1973 Sounds. Article by Jerry Gilbert, Martin Hayman and Steve Peacock: Bowie: Man and the mask.

DATE / EVENT	AUDIO / VIDEO	TITLE

3-3-1973 Chicago, Aragon Ballroom.
Attendance: 5.500. Support act: Fumble.
They stayed in the Beverly Hills Hotel. Andy Warhol and his entourage stayed in the same hotel.
In his Hotel room Bowie filmed 2 women making love.

NT

9-3-1973 Bowie saw Lori Mattix (who later became Jimmy Page's girlfriend) and Sable (2 famous Californian groupies) at the Rainbow Restaurant. Stuey invited them to spend the evening with Bowie. If you want to read the full details of the evening, read the book Alias David Bowie, written by Peter & Leni Gillman.

10-3-1973 Los Angeles, Long Beach Arena.
Attendance: 6.200. Support act: Fumble.
Promoter: Pacific Presentations.

These songs can be found on most bootlegs (it is not the right song order, but the order they were broadcast):
1. My death (6.26).
2. Aladdin Sane (4.14).
3. Five years (3.37).
4. Width of a circle (10.57).
5. Ziggy Stardust (3.01).
6. Changes (3.38).
7. Panic in Detroit (4.06).
8. Time (5.29).
9. Suffragette city (3.24).

	1 CDR	*The all American Bowie (from LP) (No label, no number)*
	1 CDR	*The all American Bowie (No label, no number)*
	1 CDR	*The all American Bowie (Old Gold Records OGCD 002)*
	1 CDR	*Long Beach Arena 1973 (No label, no number)*
	1 CDR	*Live Long Beach 1973 (No label, no number)*
	CD	*Ziggy 1: My radio Sweetheart (Tune in 001/ Dragonfly records Ziggy A/B)*
	LP	*Ziggy 1: My radio Sweetheart (Tune in 001/ Dragonfly records Ziggy A/B)*
	LP	*Gimme your hands (Rocksolid Records Ziggy A/B)*
	3 LP	*When gravity fails (Slaughtered Lamb Ziggy A/B Ziggy II A/B DB 6142 A/B)*
	4 LP	*Unofficial Wembley wizard box file (Moonbeam Records Duke 001 A/H)*
	LP	*The all American Bowie (TMOQ 71074)*
	Tape	*60 min.*

11-3-1973 Los Angeles, Hollywood Palladium.
Attendance: 2.200. Support act: Fumble.
There was a dinner party for Ringo Starr and Klaus Voorman.

Tape

12-3-1973 Los Angeles, Hollywood Palladium.
Support act: Fumble.

Tape

DATE / EVENT	AUDIO / VIDEO	TITLE

12-3-1973 Los Angeles Times. Article by Robert Hilburn: Rock theatre of David Bowie at Long Beach.

Mid March 1973 Los Angeles. Long Beach Arena. Bowie attended a Bette Midler show.

17-3-1973 New Musical Express. Article by Ian MacDonald: The revolution is here… doesn't anybody want it.

22-3-1973 DeFries made a new touring-deal with RCA that ran 5 years from 1-1-1973.

23-3-1973 Los Angeles Free Press. Article by Peter Jay Philbin: In Long Beach: David Bowie sings.

29-3-1973 Rolling Stone. Article by B. Kirsch: Midnight special shines with Bowie and choreography.

29-3-1973 Rolling Stone. Article by Stephen Davies: Performance: David Bowie, Radio City Music Hall.
Davies wrote: "Curtains parted to reveal a giant screen, on which was projected an animated film of the cosmos rushing at light-year speed at the viewer. A cage 50 feet above the floor of the stage, in the middle of which was standing a sternly staring Bowie, clad in a black silver garment, the first of what would be five different costume changes that night. It was a truly amazing sight."

<u>End March 1973</u>. London, Central Studios.   NT
Rehearsals for Japanese tour.

April 1973 Re-release LP The world of David Bowie (compilation) (Decca SPA 58).

April 1973 Released John I'm only dancing (sax mix) (2.41) / Hang on to yourself (2.38) (RCA 2263). Same B-side as the single release on 1-9-1972.

April 1973 Released in Japan Promo: Time / Panic in   LP   Hard Meat and Limp Hits
Detroit (special version) (RCA).

<u>Begin April 1973</u>. Travelling to Japan on the SS Oronsay.   NT
He gave an impromptu solo acoustic performance for the
ships passengers and crew.

5-4-1973 4 p.m. Bowie landed at the port of Yokohama aboard the SS Oronsay. He stayed at the Imperial Hotel.

6-4-1973 The other musicians arrived by plane.

6-4-1973 Release Promo single Drive-in Saturday (3.59) / Round and Round (2.39) (RCA).

6-4-1973 Release Promo single Drive-in Saturday (4.29) / Round and Round (2.39) (RCA 2352).

Drive-in Saturday is about a future in which people don't have sex anymore and have to relearn it and they watch old films.

Bowie about his Japanese concerts: "In Japan we were faced with an audience that we presumed didn't

DATE / EVENT	AUDIO / VIDEO	TITLE

understand a word of what I was saying. There I was more physical than on any other tour I've ever done and I carried it back here (England) again. Literally, I activated the whole thing with my hands and my body. I needn't have sung half the time" (A rock 'n' roll odyssey - Kate Lynch 1984).

Added to the band for the Japanese leg of the tour: John Hutchinson (rhythm / 12-string acoustic guitar). Aynsley Dunbar (additional drummer and former member of Aynsley Dunbar's Retaliation).

8-4-1973 Tokyo, Shinjuku Koseinenkin Kaikan. Sold out.	CD	*Miscellaneous of cats (DBJP-72)*
Son Zowie attended his first Bowie concert. Great crowd response at the start of Space oddity.	CD	*Who'll love Aladdin Sane in Tokyo (No label, no number)*
But Bowie's voice sounded a little weak during the song. During Rock 'n' roll suicide the background singers keep on repeating You're wonderful. Bowie point at people in the crowd and shouts: "And you… and you… and you!"	CD	*Who'll love Aladdin Sane in Tokyo (Moonraker 449)*
He thanked the crowd in Japanese. After the show the Japan Times described David as the most exciting thing to hit rock music since The Beatles.	2 CDR	*Ziggy strikes Hiroshima (Old Gold Records OGCD 023A/B) (8 songs)*
Bowie stayed in Imperial Hotel during his stay in Tokyo. He was visited by Kansai Yamamoto with a new collection	1 CDR	*The rising son (10 songs) (KTLA CD42)*
of stage costumes.	1 CDR	First Landed Japan (MP3)
	LP	*Who'll love Aladdin Sane in Tokyo (Silver American Records Salp 1973 A25132)*

The Japan Times about Bowie's Tokyo performance: Musically he is the most exiting thing that has happened since the fragmentation of the Beatles, and theatrically he is possibly the most interesting performer ever in the pop music genre.

9-4-1973 Tokyo. Show by Tomasa Boru (Kabuki Theatre).
Bowie attended the show and met Boru backstage.

10-4-1973 Tokyo, Shinjuku Koseinenkin Kaikan. Sold out.	NT	

11-4-1973 Tokyo, Shinjuku Koseinenkin Kaikan. Sold out.	CD	*Ziggy goes to east (Trystar)*
The crowd went wild. During the intermission the police	1 CDR	When cultures collide (Old Gold Records OGCD 500)
arrived and set up folding chairs along the front of the stage. Bowie wanted them to leave. When they refused	1 CDR	Ziggy in Japan
Angie threw some out of their seats. A riot started and the	2 CDR	*Far East Freak Out (Little Wonder)*

police left the theatre. A policeman was hurt and charges were made against Angie and Tony Zanetta.
Back in the Imperial Hotel Angie and Zanetta got into a fight with an American tourist, who made remarks about Angie's breasts. They had to leave Japan in a rush and were never allowed to come back to Japan (David Bowie - Dave Thompson 1986).

DATE / EVENT	AUDIO / VIDEO	TITLE

12-4-1973 Release LP Aladdin Sane (RCA LSP.4852).
Fastest selling album since Beatles heyday with 100.000 advance orders and goes straight to number one in the UK. Cover photo taken by Brian Duffy.
Brian Duffy: "Elvis Presley once had worn a ring marked with a lightning flash. I showed David a rice-cooker made by National Panasonic and which bore that company's distinctive logo, a lightning flash. That was what David wanted."
Pierre Laroche did the make-up. The photograph was air-brushed by Philip Castle.

12-4-1973 Nagoya, Kokusai Tenji Kaikan. Sold out.	NT	
14-4-1973 Hiroshima, Yubinchokin Kaikan. Sold out.	CD	*Ziggy in Japan* not complete
As always the audience responds almost hysterically when Bowie announces Starman.	2 CDR	*Live at Yubinchokin Kaikan '73* (No label, no number)
The round reflector Bowie wore on his forehead during that period was designed by Pierre Laroche (he also styled the Aladdin Sane LP cover).	2 CDR	*Ziggy strikes Hiroshima* (Old Gold Records OGCD 023A/B)
	LP	*Ziggy in Japan* (Duck Production DW 37387)
	Tape	quality 7, 80 min.
	Tape	quality 9, 80 min.
15-4-1973 Tokyo, Shinjuku Koseienkin Kaikan. Sold out.	1 CDR	*quality 5, 25 min.*
15 Minutes applause after the first encore Rock 'n' roll suicide. Bowie came back to do Round and round (original by Chuck Berry in 1958).	2 CDR	*Ziggy strikes Hiroshima*
	CD	*A cat from London* (You J-003)
	1 CDR	*Earl's Court disaster volume 2* (7 songs) (Old Gold Records OGCD 025)
	Tape	quality 6, 25 min.
16-4-1973 Hyogo (Kobe), Kobe Kokusai Kaikan. Sold out.	1 CDR	*Hyogo and Osaka* (KTLA CD43)
During Let's spend the night together he missed a few lines. This version "stayed" close to the original by The Rolling Stones.	Tape	quality 7, 25 min.
17-4-1973 Osaka, Koseinenkin Kaikan. Sold out.	1 CDR	*"I'm much too fast"*
A short tape / CD of a less quality. As far as I can hear (the quality is so-so) it is a good concert.	1 CDR	*Hyogo and Osaka* (KTLA CD43)
	Tape	quality 6, 25 min.
20-4-1973 Tokyo, Shibuya Konkaido. Sold out. A very good concert!	CD	*Suicide attack* (Zeus Z2009001)
During Ziggy Stardust: "He was the Nazz, to God given task." Moonage daydream had a great guitar solo.	1 CDR	*Tokyo was rockin'* (A Barfing Spaniel Recording BS 168)

DATE / EVENT	AUDIO / VIDEO	TITLE
The set closes to a fifteen-minute ovation.	2 CDR	*Far East Freak Out (Little Wonder)*
	4 CD	*Watch that man in Tokyo (BOW 5162/63/64/65)*
	Tape	25 min.

21-4-1973 New Musical Express. Article by Nick Kent: This is America Special.

21-4-1973 Bowie leaves Japan (by boat from Yokohama to Nahodka).   NT
On board of the boat he sang Amsterdam and Space Oddity.

26-4-1973 The sun. Article by Mike Nevard: David Wowie.

From 23-4-1973 to 30-4-1973 on the Trans Siberian Express from Vladivostock to Moscow.
He was accompanied by Geoffrey MacCormack, Leee Black Childers and Bob Musel (correspondent for the American news agency UPI). Leee Childers had flown to Khabarovsk and caught up in Irkutsk (Siberia).
The 10-day journey had 92 stops across Siberia. For the passengers Bowie did an acoustic set, that included Amsterdam and Space oddity.
In Khabarovsk Leee Black Childers took a photograph of a Russian soldier. The soldier tried to take his camera. Bowie started filming the incident. More soldiers arrived and people from the train stopped them, allowing Leee and Bowie to get back on the train (In other words - Kerry Juby 1986).

30-4-1973 They arrived in Moscow (the day before the May Day Parade) and stayed at the Intourist Hotel (middle of town).
After a few days in Moscow he catches the Orient Express to Paris.

May 1973 Released in Germany: In the beginning vol. 2 (Deram material) (Decca NDM 770).

May 1973 Music Life. Bowie on front cover and an article.

May 1973 Entertainment Magazine. Article by Henry Edwards: The king of glitter rock.

Begin May 1973 Promo stunt in Berlin. The train stopped at Bahnhof Zoo to talk with journalists and a handful of fans for almost an hour.

3-5-1973 They arrived in Paris and stayed at The GeorgeV Hotel, were Bowie met Jacques Brel.
He gave a press conference for the French journalists.

4-5-1973 Arrives back in London after world tour and a journey of 8.000 miles overland.
David missed the boat-train and took the hovercraft from Boulogne. He was now arriving at Charring Cross instead of Victoria Station.
At the way home Roy Hollingworth for Melody Maker interviewed him.

5-5-1973 A Party at Haddon Hall, attended by T.Visconti, Mary Hopkins, Lindsay Kemp, Mick Ronson, George Underwood, Freddi Burretti, Sue Fussey, Ken Scott, Mary Finnigan.

DATE / EVENT	AUDIO / VIDEO	TITLE

Bowie and Visconti visited Peter Cook and Dudley Moore backstage at "Behind the fridge."

10-5-1973 Bowie visits Ken Pitt in Manchester Street.
Kenneth Pit: "When he got up to make some coffee I joined him in the kitchen, but it was as if he had never been away; he knew exactly where to find the coffee, the crockery and the spoons (The Pitt Report - K. Pitt 1983).

<u>8 to 11-5-1973</u> London, Central London Studios.   NT
Rehearsals.

12-5-1973 Evening News. Article by John Blake: Superstar David Bowie tales to Evening News. Back from Russia with love.

12-5-1973 London Evening Standard. Article: Firm sue David Bowie over pop songs.
Bowie is being sued in the High Court by London music publishers Essex Music International over three pop songs Ching-a-ling, Mother grey, April's tooth of gold. Essex claim that under a 1967 agreement Bowie should have made a songwriter assignment to them of the three pops. They also allege that he broke his contract by entering into an agreement for his services with Chrysalis Music.

A pity Bowie was sued in 1973. The three songs are still unreleased by 2004.
Only April's tooth of gold circulates on the Internet.

12-5-1973 Evening News. Article by John Blake: Kinky king of rock.

12-5-1973 Melody Maker. Article by Roy Hollingworth: Ch-ch-ch-changes - A journey with Aladdin.
Bowie: "I've gone through a lot of changes on my way back from Japan. After what I've seen of the state of the world, I've never been so damn scared in my life. If I wrote about it, it would probably be my last album ever because I wouldn't be around very long after finishing it."

12-5-1973 Melody Maker. Article by Chris Welch: Bowie A-Z.
Bowie: "This decadence thing is just a bloody joke. I'm very normal. I never thought Ziggy would become the most talked-about man in the world."

12-5-1973 New Musical Express. Article by Charles Shaar Murray: Aladdin Sane.

12-5-1973 London, Earls Court, backstage. A promo video was shot for Life on Mars?

<u>12-5-1973</u> London, Earl's Court Arena.	1 CDR	Earl's Court disaster vol.1 (Old Gold Records OGCD 024)
Attendance: 18.000 (a.o. Ken Pitt).		
Show started at 20.30 hours. Tickets: GBP 1,50.	1 CDR	Earl's Court disaster vol.2 (Old Gold Records OGCD 025)
Promoters: Mel Bush, MainMan and RCA Records.		
The audience saw and heard nothing.	2 CDR	Earl's Court concert 1973 (A Dutch connection DCCD 120573)
The gig ended in complete chaos.		
People stormed to the stage. Four drunken Australians		
danced naked in the aisles and one of them ripped a	2 CDR	Ziggy Riot Show
woman's blouse of. Another one urinated in the aisle	Tape	quality 8, 85 min.
(Black Book - Barry Miles 1980).	Tape	quality 7, 90 min.
At one stage Bowie stopped the show and asked the	Tape	quality 7, 75 min.
audience to "stop being silly."	Video	8 min.

DATE / EVENT	AUDIO / VIDEO	TITLE

Halfway the concert the band left the stage because of the riots.
Bowie did Aladdin Sane for the first and last time during this tour.
Comments in The New Musical Express:
Aladdin Distress.

Bowie cancelled second show. DeFries says: Neither David nor myself will make any further comment on the matter.

Leee Black Childers and Wayne County lived in an apartment down on the West Side near the Docks. Puerto Ricans hunted down one night Wayne County. He freaked out, drank a bottle of wine and phoned Bowie in London and screamed: "They tried to kill me! They came after me with knives." Bowie calmed him down and the next day DeFries moved them into a duplex on 58th street. Rent: USD 1.200,— a week, paid by MainMan (Man enough to be a woman - Jayne County 1995).

15-5-1973 By train from Station Kings Cross to Aberdeen. He arrives at Aberdeen Station after ten hours and stays at the Imperial Hotel.

Date / Event	Audio/Video	Title
<u>16-5-1973</u> Aberdeen, Music Hall. Sound check at 17.00 h.	NT	
<u>16-5-1973</u> Aberdeen, Music Hall. Matinee, at 19.00 h. Attendance: 1.500. A good concert and a great (Scottish) crowd response. The recording is not good, and as far as I can hear Bowie does not say much or anything extra-ordinary.	1 CDR Tape Tape	*Aberdeen quicksand (56 min)* *(For collectors only) (Old Gold* *Records OGCD 406)* 90 min. 80 min.
<u>16-5-1973</u> Aberdeen, Music Hall. Evening, at 21.00 h. Attendance: 1.500. Bowie stayed at the Imperial Hotel.	Tape	90 min.
<u>17-5-1973</u> Dundee, Caird Hall. Attendance: 2.680. On his way to the waiting limo after the show, David is nearly trapped by a mob of fans. Bodyguard Stuey George saves the day.	NT	
<u>18-5-1973</u> Glasgow, Apollo (Green's Playhouse). Matinee. Attendance: 3.131. The crowd responds hysterically on Bowie. "Get those light on" before Lets spend the night together. "Hello Glasgow. There is one word for an audience like you. It's an Americanism and it's called Hot Shit. You really are." After Rock 'n' roll suicide: "We love you Glasgow. Thank you, we love you."	2 CDR 2 CDR 3 CDR 2 CDR 2 CDR 2 CDR	*Glasgow, Apollo, 1st Show,* *18-5-1973 (BowieHobby)* *Then we went to Glasgow* *(Downunder Discs)* *Hot Shit! (Old Gold Records* *OGCD 026/A/B/C)* *A Glasgow afternoon* *Green's Playhouse Glasgow* *18 5 1973* *(No label, no number)* *Apollo Theatre (1st Show)*

DATE / EVENT	AUDIO / VIDEO	TITLE
	1 CDR Single Tape	(KTLA CD44 1/2) Glasgow 73 *The Myth (medley Quicksand/ Life on Mars? / Memory of a free festival (CD Various Singles - 1)* quality 7, 85 min.
<u>18-5-1973</u> Glasgow, Apollo (Green's Playhouse). Evening. Attendance: 3.100. There was some crowd violence. A very good concert with a lovely medley. Bowie commenting on the concert: "We had I think, four couples making it in the back row which was fabulous. It's the first time I've heard of that happening. There was also a whole row of seats physically torn out of the floor, which sounds like the fifties to me. Can you imagine how much energy has to be used to tear out a theatre seat?"	2 CDR 3 CDR 2 CDR 2 CDR 2 CDR Tape	*Glasgow, Apollo, 2nd Show, 18-5-1973 (BowieHobby)* *Hot Shit! (Old Gold Records OGCD 026/A/B/C)* *A Glasgow evening* *A lad in Edinburgh* *Apollo Theatre (2nd Show)* (KTLA CD48 1/2) quality 7, 85 min.

19-5-1973 Melody Maker. Article by Roy Hollingworth: Drive out Saturday.
Hollingworth wrote about London Earls Court 12-5-1973: "So the kids rushed to the front, and a lot of them were hurt, and kicked-out, but can you damn well blame them? They came to hear and see Bowie. The stage was simple and low. Therefore only humans equipped with Bobby Charlton necks, or giraffian build, were capable of catching a glimpse of what went on. And the sound? Well, if I compared it to playing a transistor full blast in the middle of Victoria Station at 5 pm I would not be inaccurate… I feel sure that David Bowie know nothing of what actually went on around… That he could neither be heard, nor for that matter seen by a good 80 percent of the audience."

19-5-1973 Record Mirror. Article by Val Mabbs: Ziggy's Back.

<u>19-5-1973</u> Edinburgh, Empire Theatre (2 shows) Great atmosphere. The crowd went wild. Gives you chills all over your body. You can almost feel Bowie standing in front of you, when you listen to the tape. A very nice version of The prettiest star (faster than on the single and Album).	2 CDR 2 CDR Tape	*A lad in Edinburgh (Old Gold Records OGCD 027A/B)* *Edinburgh 1973 (No label, no number)* quality 6, 80 min.
<u>21-5-1973</u> Norwich, Theatre Royal. Matinee. Attendance: 1.200.	NT	
<u>21-5-1973</u> Norwich, Theatre Royal. Evening. Attendance: 1.200.	NT	

22-5-1973 Daily Mirror. Article by Deborah Thomas: Has the star gone too far?

| <u>22-5-1973</u> London, Romford Odeon (Odeon Theatre).
Attendance: 1.000. Promoter: Mel Bush.
Tickets: GBP 1,80. Started at 20.00 h. | NT | |

DATE / EVENT	AUDIO / VIDEO	TITLE
<u>23-5-1973</u> Brighton, Brighton Dome (2 shows). Attendance: 2.100. The audience ripped up the seats and Bowie was banned from ever appearing at the venue again by the management. It was one of them great Ziggy concerts. A lot of energy and the band played very well. Every song almost floating into the next one. During Moonage daydream he sings: "Freak out in a teddy-bear dream-dream." Ziggy at his best!	2 CDR 1 CDR 2 CDR 1 CDR Tape	*Brighton 23 May 1973 (BowieHobby)* *Brighton Rock (Old Gold Records OGCD 028)* *Did you see the suits and the platform boots? (Downunder Discs)* *Ziggy & The Spiders live at the Brighton Dome* (No label, no number) quality 7, 80 min.
<u>24-5-1973</u> London, Lewisham Odeon. Sound check. 1. Wild eyed boy from Freecloud (instrumental) (2.08). 2. Wild eyed boy from Freecloud / All the young dudes / Oh! you pretty things (medley) (6.46).	*1 CDR* 1 CDR *2 CDR* 2 CDR Tape	*5 Minutes Mr. Bowie (Down Under Disc)* Soundcheck (Old Gold Records OGCD 390) *Complete Lewisham* Zig the wonderkid (No label, no number) 17 min.
<u>24-5-1973</u> London, Lewisham Odeon. Concert attended by Boy George (it changed his life). Very good concert (I understand Why it changed the life of Boy George!). First concert in which the medley is changed into another one (a pity). Cracked actor substituted Quicksand.	1 CDR *1 CDR* 2 CDR *2 CDR* 2 CDR Tape	Ziggy was a young man too (Old Gold Records OGCD 407) *Zig the wonderkid (A Dutch Connection CD240573)* Zig the wonderkid (No label, no number) *Complete Lewisham* Lewisham Odeon 1973 (Mastertrax) quality 7, 80 min.

25-5-1973 George O'Dowd (who would later become Boy George) went to Haddon Hall. Angie told him (and the other fans) to "Fuck off." George was very happy he had met other people like him (Take it like a man - The Boy George biography 1995).

| <u>25-5-1973</u> Bournemouth, Winter Gardens. Attendance: 2.600. Filmed by the BBC but never shown. BBC's Nationwide films backstage and makes interviews, by Bernard Falkman. Broadcast 5-6-1973 (12 min.) | Tape | quality 8, 15 min. |
| 25-5-1973 Bournemouth, News Report. | *Video* | *Stolp Tapes vol. 10 (12 min)* |

26-5-1973 Record Mirror. Article by James Craig: Bowie goes north.

26-5-1973 Sounds. Article by Martin Hayman: Life and times of David Bowie.

26-5-1973 New Musical Express. Article by Charles Shaar Murray: Total sensory overload.

DATE / EVENT	AUDIO / VIDEO	TITLE
<u>27-5-1973</u> Brighton, Guildford, Civic Hall. Matinee. Attendance: 1.200. During the intro to Quicksand on a sign of Bowie the band stops playing. "We got a problem here. Wild eyed boy or Quicksand." The crowd chooses very clearly for the Quicksand medley.	CD 4 CD 1 CDR 1 CDR Tape	*Heaven or maybe Hell* (complete concert) (Artie Fartie CD001) *The North American Tours* (Pearls Before Swine PBS 1037 / 1038 / 1039 / 1040) *Live in Guildford* (Old Gold Records OGCD 030) *Raw Guildford 73* (A Dutch Connection) quality 7, 70 min.
<u>27-5-1973</u> Brighton, Guildford, Civic Hall. Evening. Attendance: 1.200.	NT	
<u>28-5-1973</u> Wolverhampton, Civic Hall. Attendance: 1.780. Philip Cato (writer of the book Crash course for the ravers) attended the gig. He can't remember too much about the gig except hordes of screaming girls in Bowie t-shirts and Ziggy haircuts and Mick Ronson's extremely loud Gibson and a stormy version of White light white heat as an encore.	NT	
<u>29-5-1973</u> Hanley, Victoria Hall. Attendance: 1.580. A good concert. During the last song Rock 'n' roll suicide Bowie starts improvising: "Don't let anybody turn away the difference, cause you're wonderful. Cause you'll have to make it on your own."	1 CDR 1 CDR 1 CDR 1 CDR Tape	*Hanley 29 May 1973* (BowieHobby) *Ode to Hanley* (Old Gold Records OGCD 031) *Incestuous and vain* (Downunder Discs) *Spitting Sentry Horned and Tailed* (KTLA CD50) quality 7, 70 min.
30-5-1973 London, Earl's Court. *Cancelled.*		
<u>30-5-1973</u> Oxford, New Theatre.	NT	
<u>31-5-1973</u> Blackburn, King George's Hall. Attendance: 1.800.	NT	
June 1973 The Russell Harty Show of 17-1-1973 repeated.		
June 1973 BBC. Steve Dickson. David talks about what prompted him to write the various songs on Aladdin Sane, lost tapes and a Russian tour.	3 CDR Tape	*Hot Shit!* (Old Gold Records OGCD 026/A/B/C) (7.16 min) 20 min

DATE / EVENT	AUDIO / VIDEO	TITLE

June 1973 German radio. Rockspeak. Interview

June 1973 Radio Show? — Tape — 60 min.

June 1973 Top Gear? — Tape — 60 min.

June 1973 Let it rock. Article by Dave Laing and Simon Frith: Bowie, Zowie: Two views of the glitter prince of rock.
They wrote: Take away Bowie's image, and there's nothing left. The image itself is dense with weird and wonderful things - myths of inner and outer space, intimations of bizarre sexuality - but somehow they never lead anywhere except down the hole in the centre of the record.

1-6-1973 Release LP "Raw Power" - Iggy and the Stooges (CBS 32083).
Mixed by David Bowie and Iggy Pop.

Michael Oldfield wrote in 1977 in Melody Maker: "Raw power found them as malevolent as ever, particularly on the title track, Search and destroy, Gimme danger, Shake appeal and Death trip. And yet… a certain sophistication has crept in. The raggedness that gave added bite to their first two albums is replaced by cold calculation, as though Iggy was being told: Go berserk!"

Bowie: "Iggy has natural theatre. It's very interesting because it doesn't conform to any standards or rules or structures of theatre. It's his own and it's just a Detroit theatre that he's brought with him. It's straight from the street."

1-6-1973 Released in the US: Time (3.35) / The prettiest star (3.26) (RCA APBO.0001).

<u>1-6-1973</u> Bradford, St. George's Hall. — NT
Attendance: 1.911.

2-6-1973 Leeds, University.
Cancelled.
(6 hours for the beginning, because David found out he had to walk through the audience).

<u>3-6-1973</u> Coventry, New Theatre. — NT
Attendance: 2.000.

3-6-1973 Los Angeles Times. Article by Robert Hilburn: Aladdin Sane features a broader Bowie.

<u>4-6-1973</u> Worchester, Gaumont. Bowie talkative and introduces most songs. Before White light white heat he says: "Lou Reed is a man that I admire very much."	1 CDR	*Worcester 4 June 1973 (BowieHobby)*
	1 CDR	*The wild eyed Ziggy (Old Gold Records OGCD 032)*
	Tape	quality 6, 75 min.

5-6-1973 David with Lulu in the lobby of a Sheffield Hotel.

5-6-1973 UK TV. BBC. Nationwide. Documentary. — 2 CDR — The final stand (Old Gold
Bournemouth Winter Gardens. — Records OGCD 215A/B)

DATE / EVENT	AUDIO / VIDEO	TITLE
Interview by Bernhard Falkman and footage of 25-5-1973 concert in Bournemouth (Watch that man, Hang on to yourself, Time).	Video	Various 20 (12 min)
6-6-1973 Sheffield, City Hall. Attendance: 2.292. Lulu attended the concert (invited by Bowie, who met her in the lobby of the hotel). After the concert Lulu had to rush to do her act in a nightclub and then returned to the hotel. In Bowie's room Lulu, David, Mike Garson and Mick Ronson watched video recordings of the Japanese tour (David Bowie - Dave Thompson 1986).	Tape Tape	quality 3, 50 min. quality 6, 67 min.
7-6-1973 Manchester, Free Trade Hall. Matinee. Attendance: 2.500. A good concert. The last encore: Round and round (2.58).	CD 2 CDR Tape	*The Width of Ziggy* (Old Gold Records OGCD 408) *Quaaludes and red wine* (KTLA CD52 1/2) quality 7, 75 min.
7-6-1973 Manchester, Free Trade Hall. Evening. Attendance: 2.500.	Tape	quality 6, 75 min.
8-6-1973 Newcastle, City Hall. Matinee. Attendance: 2.186. Great crowd response during the medley Wild eyed boy from Freecloud / All the young dudes / Oh! you pretty things (6.00).	CD 1 CDR Tape	*Newcastle City Hall 73* (No label, no number) *Ziggy's oddity* (Old Gold Records OGCD 412) 50 min.
8-6-1973 Newcastle, City Hall. Evening. Attendance: 2.186.	NT	

9-6-1973 New Musical Express. Article by Susan Mensah: David Bowie: a construction of selves.

9-6-1973 Melody Maker. Article by Robert Matthew - Walker: Rock and roll suicide?

9-6-1973 Preston, Guildhall. Attendance: 2.146.	Tape	
10-6-1973 Liverpool, Empire Theatre. Matinee. Attendance: 2.550. Tickets: GBP 1,—. Started at 6.30 h.	NT	
10-6-1973 Liverpool, Empire Theatre. Evening. Attendance: 2.550.	NT	
11-6-1973 Leicester, Demontfort Hall. Attendance: 2.556. A very good concert. A pity there is only a short tape available.	3 CDR 2 CDR 1 CDR	*Hot Shit!* (Old Gold Records OGCD 026/A/B/C) *Then we went to Glasgow* (Downunder Discs) "Leave them to hang"

DATE / EVENT	AUDIO / VIDEO	TITLE
	1 CDR	*The rising son (7 songs) (KTLA CD42)*
	Tape	quality 6, 25 min.
	Tape	quality 7, 20 min.
<u>12-6-1973</u> Chatham, Central Hall. Matinee. Attendance: 730. A good concert. "On piano there's Mike Garson and on lead guitar Suzie Quatro." A pity I could not see Mick Ronson's face, when listening to this introduction.	1 CDR	*Chatham Daydream (Old Gold Records GCD 413)*
	1 CDR	*Ziggy & The Spiders (A Dutch Connection CD 120673)*
	1 CDR	Central Hall Chatham 1973
	2 CDR	*Zig the wonderkid* (No label, no number)
	Tape	quality 7, 60 min.
	Tape	quality 7, 40 min.
<u>12-6-1973</u> Chatham, Central Hall. Evening.	Tape	quality 7, 60 min.
<u>13-6-1973</u> London, Kilburn Gaumont.	NT	
<u>14-6-1973</u> Salisbury, City Hall. Attendance: 1.120. "We think you're great. Mick thinks it's great. Personally I think I've broken my ankle. Not really, but it hurts a bit. If you wanna make this next one work, you've gotta work together because I'm gonna do this one sitting down. This is an old one by Chuck Berry and it's called Round and round."	2 CDR	*A lad in Edinburgh (Old Gold Records OGCD 027A/B)*
	1 CDR	41 Minutes of Salisbury
	2 CDR	*Quaaludes and red wine (KTLA CD52 1/2)*
	1 CDR	*Salisbury 14 June 1973 (BowieHobby)*
	Tape	quality 6, 45 min.
	Tape	quality 7, 54 min.
	Video	5 min. (Panic in Detroit).
<u>15-6-1973</u> Taunton, Taunton Odeon. 1st Show. Attendance: 1.270.	NT	
<u>15-6-1973</u> Taunton, Taunton Odeon. 2nd Show. Attendance: 1.270.	NT	
<u>16-6-1973</u> Torbay, Town Hall. Matinee. Attendance: 1.200.	Tape	
<u>16-6-1973</u> Torbay, Town Hall. Evening. Attendance: 1.200.	Tape	
<u>18-6-1973</u> Bristol, Colston Hall. Matinee. Attendance: 2.120.	Tape	
<u>18-6-1973</u> Bristol, Colston Hall. Evening. Attendance: 2.120.	Tape	

DATE / EVENT	AUDIO / VIDEO	TITLE

19-6-1973 Portsmouth, Guildhall.
Cancelled.

<u>19-6-1973</u> Southampton, Guildhall. NT

20-6-1973 UPI. Article by Robert Musel: Journey through Siberia.

<u>21-6-1973</u> Birmingham, Town Hall. Matinee. NT
Attendance: 1.540.

<u>21-6-1973</u> Birmingham, Town Hall. Evening. NT
Attendance: 1.540.

22-6-1973 Chronicle. Article by Paul Le Petit: The night Bowie came to Kilburn.

22-6-1973 Release Life on Mars? (3.47) / The man who sold the world (3.56) (RCA 2316).

22-6-1973 Release in Spain: Life on Mars? (3.47) / Drive-in Saturday (RCA 3-10936).

Bowie in 1971 about Life on Mars?: "A sensitive young girl's reaction to the media."
In 1996 / 1997: "I think she finds herself let down. I think she finds herself disappointed by reality. I think she sees that although she's living in the doldrums of reality, she's being told that there's a far greater life somewhere, and she's bitterly disappointed that she doesn't have access to it. I guess I would feel sorry for her now. I think I had empathy with her at the time."

<u>22-6-1973</u> Birmingham, Town Hall. Matinee. NT
Attendance: 1.540.

<u>22-6-1973</u> Birmingham, Town Hall. Evening. NT
Attendance: 1.540.

23-6-1973 Released: The prettiest star / Love around - Simon Turner (UK 44). A-side written by Bowie.

23-6-1973 Brighton, Gliderdrome.
Cancelled.

<u>24-6-1973</u> Croydon, Fairfield Hall. 1st Show. NT
Attendance: 1.800.

<u>24-6-1973</u> Croydon, Fairfield Hall. 2nd Show. NT
Attendance: 1.800.

<u>25-6-1973</u> Oxford, New Theatre. Matinee. Tape 75 min.
Attendance: 1.700.

<u>25-6-1973</u> Oxford, New Theatre. Evening. NT
Attendance: 1.700.

DATE / EVENT	AUDIO / VIDEO	TITLE

<u>26-6-1973</u> Oxford, New Theatre. Matinee.   NT
Attendance: 1.700.

<u>26-6-1973</u> Oxford, New Theatre. Evening.   NT
Attendance: 1.700.

<u>27-6-1973</u> Doncaster, Top Rank Suite.   NT
Attendance: 2.000.

28-6-1973 Beckenham & Penge Advertiser. Article by Barry Shinfield: The prettiest star.

<u>28-6-1973</u> Bridlington, Royal Spa Pavilion (Spa Ballroom).   NT
Attendance: 3.000.

<u>29-6-1973</u> Leeds, Rolarena (2 shows).   *1 CDR*   *Leeding man (Old Gold*
Medley: Wild eyed boy from Freecloud / All the young   *Records OGCD 414)*
dudes / Oh! you pretty things (6.34). Great crowd response   *1 CDR*   *Aladdin Leeds*
when Bowie introduces Mick Ronson.   *(KLTA CD53)*
    Tape   quality 6, 85 min.

30-6-1973 Earls Court.
Cancelled.
A Promo for Life on Mars? was made in Earls Court.

July 1973 Circus. Article by Howard Bloom: Bowie foresees the States in flames. Inside story of Aladdin Sane.

July 1973 Stereo Review. Article by Lester Bangs: Iggy and the Stooges: The apotheosis of every parental nightmare.

July 1973 Music Scene. Bowie voted "World's Best Male Singer."

July 1973 BBC. The Russell Harty Show.   Tape
David and Angie together (interview).

1-7-1973 DeFries made a new record-deal with RCA that ran 5 years from 1-1-1973. Advance per album: USD 60.000 in 1973, USD 100.000 in 1974, USD 150.000 in1975, USD 200.000 in 1976. 15% Of sales above 750.000 copies for Bowie.

<u>2-7-1973</u> London, Hammersmith Odeon.   *1 CDR*   *The night before (Old Gold*
Attendance: 3.000.   *Records OGCD 010)*
Attended by Neil Tennant (later Pet Shop Boys).   Tape   quality 7, 65 min.
"This is something that we haven't done for a long long   Tape   75 min.
long time since we first started. Let's try and do it."
A splendid version of My death really touches the audience
and is highly appreciated.
At Hammersmith Odeon rock photographer Dennis
O'Regan made his first photo's (he borrowed a camera

DATE / EVENT	AUDIO / VIDEO	TITLE

from his uncle) (Freddie Mercury The Definitive Biography - Lesley-Ann Jones 1997).

<u>3-7-1973</u> London, Hammersmith Odeon. Attendance: 3.000. Tickets GBP. 2,—.
Concert announced by Barry Bethel. Promoter: Mel Bush. Support: Mike Garson (his nickname was: Garson the Parson), who played a 15 minute instrumental medley (Changes / Life on Mars? / Ziggy Stardust) on piano. Final concert is filmed by D.A. Pennebaker (film was broadcast on US TV in mid. Oct. 1974 (The Mike Douglas Show?). Later released as Ziggy Stardust and the Spiders from Mars (in Europe also as A London Show) on 9-12-1983.
Concert is recorded by RCA.
"No no, it can't be Suzi Quatro. On lead guitar Mick Ronson."
"This is Mick" (Jagger) before the start of Let's spend the spend the night together.
Before White light white heat: "This one is written by a guy who tonight is in London somewhere, making an album and I think he is a friend of mine."
Before Jean Genie: "We invited a friend of ours to join us and do a couple of numbers. I know what kind of welcome you're gonna give to Jeff Beck."
Guitarist Jeff Beck jams on stage with Mick Ronson.
And before Rock 'n' roll suicide… The farewell speech: "Of all the shows on the tour this one will stay with us for the longest because not only is it the last show of the tour but it's the last show we'll ever do."

The concert was attended by Mick Jagger, Lou Reed, Ringo Starr, Ian McCulloch, Pete Burns, George O'Dowd, Holly Johnson, Marc Almond, Pete Shelley, Neil Tennant, Tony Curtis, Mick Rock, Barbra Streisand.
After the show a party in Inn on the Park.

The American tour was cancelled. The retirement speech was just a publicity-stunt, that gave DeFries time to think about the next move.

Intro (Incorporating Beethoven's Ninth Symphony arranged and performed by Wendy Carlos. The music was also used for the soundtrack A clockwork orange. Bowie and the Spiders were very impressed by Walter Carlos' groundbreaking LP Switched on Bach.
1. Hang on to yourself (2.56).
2. Ziggy Stardust (3.09).
3. Watch that man (4.10).

	2 CD	Ziggy Stardust the motion picture
	2 CD	Ziggy Stardust the motion picture, 30th Anniversary Special Edition
	CD	His masters voice/ First farewell tour
	CD	The Axeman Cometh (DB 003)
	CD	His Master's Voice (Living Legend Records LLRCD 116)
	2 CD	Last beat (Shout to the top STTP 158/159)
	CD	David Bowie & Jeff Beck live in London 1973 (Super Golden Radio Shows No. 001 SGRS 001)
	CD	MissinglinksoneZiggy (2 songs) (Icon One)
	CD	Spaced out (PB81998)
	CD	Pinups 2 (12) (BOWPU02)
	2 CDR	The final stand (Old Gold Records OGCD 215 A/B)
	2 CDR	We're all working together
	1 CDR	Not Only
	1 CDR	The Wizardo
	1 CDR	For the last time (EgoDisc 008)
	2 CDR	Cyberstation (1 song) (STATIONTOBOWIE)
	1 CDR	Ziggy rarities… to victory (No label, no number) (1 song)
	2 CD	Ziggy's final farewell 1973 (Rattle Snake RS 131/32)
	1 VCD	TVC12 (VCDB01)
	2 VCD	Ziggy Stardust the motion picture (No label, no number)
	1 VCD	8MM Ziggy (No label, no number)
	1 VCD	I keep a good friend vol. 3 (No label, no number)
	1 DVD	Ziggy meets Jeff Beck '73 (Amazona)
	2 LP	Ziggy Stardust the motion picture

DATE / EVENT	AUDIO / VIDEO	TITLE
4. Wild eyed boy from Freecloud / All the young dudes / Oh! You pretty things (6.35).	LP	Live in London (WRMB 306)
5. Moonage daydream (6.18).	LP	London July 3, 1973 (Wizardo WRMB 306 A/B)
6. Changes (3.34).	2 LP	The beat goes on (Toasted Records 2 S-916 TAKRL 1905/1935 - 2 S-916)
7. Space oddity (4.51).		
8. My death (5.42).		
2nd Intro (Incorporating The William Tell Overture by Rossini, performed by Wendy Carlos). This intro is taken from the original motion picture soundtrack album "A Clockwork Orange."	LP	The last time I saw Ziggy (Audio Rec. Corp. ARC 1002)
	4 LP	The beat goes on
9. Cracked actor (2.51).	LP	Stardust from the 70's (BO-16)
10. Time (5.12).	LP	His masters voice (TAKRL 1935)
11. The width of a circle (9.36).	LP	His masters voice (Musikinitiative RE Bodo aus RE A 7374)
12. Let's spend the night together (3.09).		
13. Suffragette city (3.02).		
14. White light white heat (4.06).	LP	Golden years of Bow (Gold Records DB 6791) (2 tracks)
15. Jean Genie / Love me do (original by The Beatles in 1962) (8.21).	Single	His masters voice (Panic in Detroit / Rebel rebel)
16. Round and round.		
17. Farewell Speech.	Tape	quality 7, 50 min.
18. Rock 'n' roll suicide (4.20).	Tape	95 min.
Final (Pomp and Circumstance by Edward Elgar, music was used for the soundtrack A clockwork orange).	Video	60 min.
	Video	quality 10, 95 min.
	Video	Various 14 (1 min)
	Video	Stolp tapes no. 18 (10 min, Jean Genie, Round and round)

John Hutchinson: "I couldn't hear it too well but he said something about retiring. Everybody in the band was looking at each other and saying, 'What?' Trevor and Woody seemed to take it worse because they felt double-crossed, they hadn't been told. "What's happening? Oh fuck it!' That was the style."

3-7-1973 At 22.00 h. Radio Luxembourg made Bowie's decision known to its listeners.

4-7-1973 A party at Cafe Royal in Regent Street.
Guests: a.o. Paul + Linda McCartney, Ringo + Maureen Starr, Keith Moon, Barbra Streisand, Sonny Bono, Cat Stevens, Lulu, Britt Eklund, Spike Milligan, Peter Cook, Hywel Bennett, The Goodies, Mick and Bianca Jagger, Lou Reed, Tony Curtis, Jeff Beck, Elliot Gould, Ryan O'Neil, Dudley Moore, D.A.Pennebaker.
Live music by Dr. John the Nighttripper. The party later became known as: The Last Supper.
A woman called Laurita showed her breasts to a surprised Barbra Streisand and Peter Cook did a dirty revue act (Loving the alien - Christopher Sandford 1996).
Mick and Bianca Jagger arrived when Bowie stood near the entrance, talking to Lou Reed. David was afraid Mick would start to fight because of his sexual relationship with Bianca Jagger. To his surprise Mick kissed him on the cheek and before the evening was over David danced with Mick and Angela danced with Bianca and they all sat at each other's laps (David Bowie - Jerry Hopkins 1985).

4-7-1973 Evening Standard. Article by Andrew Bailey: Tears as Bowie bows out.

DATE / EVENT	AUDIO / VIDEO	TITLE

4-7-1973 Daily Mail. Article by Tim Ewbank: Pop idol Bowie gives last show.

4-7-1973 Daily Mirror. Article by Don Short: David Bowie out in a Pop Finale.

Other headlines:
The fall of Ziggy Stardust.
Bowie says it: 'No more gigs.'
Bowie kills concert career.
Ziggy played guitar.

5-7-1973 David Bowie to Disc reporter Ray Fox Cumming: "All I can say, is that at this time I do not want to do live concerts again for a long, long time. Not for two or three years at least."

6-7-1973 David and Angie attend the premiere of the James Bond film Live and let die.

7-7-1973 New Musical Express. Article: Bowie Quits.

7-7-1973 Daily Express. Article by David Wigg: Bowie's last Binge.

7-7-1973 Bowie visits Lou Reed in the studio. He is recording the album Berlin.

9-7-1973 Begin recording Pin-Ups in Paris. The Chateau d'Herouville (Strawberry Studios). There were 2 studios in the Chateau, the one they used called: George Sand Studio. Recordings lasted only 3 weeks. Visitors: Nico, Jean Millington.
Marc Bolan advised Bowie to record in these studio (David Bowie Theatre of Music - Robert Matthew - Walker 1985). Bolan had recorded his album The Slider there.

July 1973 Recording of The man who sold the world (3.50), Watch that man (4.57) and Can you hear me (5.32) by Lulu and Bowie in The Chateau d'Herouville.
Can you hear me never released. The recordings were finished in Willesden (Zomba Studios). This was the first time Bowie worked with Carlos Alomar, who was a member of the band Main Ingredient.

14-7-1973 Radio Luxembourg. Broadcast of interview by   Tape
Kid Jenson (at the Chateau d'Herouville).

14-7-1973 New Musical Express. Article by Ray Fox-Cumming: Bowie bows out.

14-7-1973 New Musical Express. Article by Derek Johnson: Final Bowie gig filmed.

14-7-1973 Sounds. Article by Martin Haymann: Farewell to the genie!

14-7-1973 Melody Maker. Article by Roy Hollingworth: Is Bowie really quitting?

Half July 1973, recording demo with Ava Cherry.

19-7-1973 Rolling Stone. Article by Ben Gerson: Aladdin Sane.
Gerson wrote: A lightning bolt streaks across David's face; on the inside cover the lad is air-brushed into androgyny, a no less imposing figure for it. If by conventional light Bowie is a lad insane, then as

DATE / EVENT	AUDIO / VIDEO	TITLE

an Aladdin a conjurer of supernatural forces, he is quite sane.

24-7-1973 Daily Mirror. Article by Liz Smith: Keeping up with Miss Jones.

27-7-1973 Chicago Sunday Mirror. Article about Bowie.
Angie about David asking her to marry him: "I was quite shocked. It was so romantic. I suppose if I hadn't married David I'd now be a fat Greek type lady with a large family in Cyprus."

August 1973 Release in US, Sweden and Holland: Let's spend the night together / Lady grinning soul (RCA APBO.0028).

August 1973 Disc. Article: Bowie special, poster plus a history of David Bowie.

August 1973 Circus. Article by Steve Gaines: Bowie divines doom in Moscow.

August 1973 Creem. Article by Nick Kent: David Bowie: Best dressed Mainman at the Twilight Zone Ball.

4-8-1973 Sounds. Article by Martin Hayman: David Bowie in search of lost time.

Mid Aug. 1973 Rented a villa in Rome, working on musical 1984. Mick Ronson, Suzi Fussey, Angie and Zowie also stayed there.

16-8-1973 Rolling Stone. Article by Paul Gambaccini and Andrew Bailey: Big private party caps Bowie's final night on stage.

20-8-1973 Rolling Stone. Article by Ed McCormack: New York Confidential.

August / September 1973 Mick Jagger invited Bowie and Scott Richardson (singer Detroit band SRC) to see the Rolling Stones concert in Newcastle. Mick rented them a hotel room.
After the show Mick and his wife Bianca took them to a casino. They stayed till dawn and Mick and David competed to see who would lose the most money (Stardust - Henry Edwards and Tony Zanetta 1986).

September 1973 The Bolan's visited the Bowie's in Haddon Hall.
A naked girl climbed through an open window, entered the dining room and asked Bowie if she could kiss his foot. Bowie said: "You can kiss my boot."
This incident was the last drop for the Bowie's, they decided to move.

September 1973 Release in Italy: Let's spend the night together / Watch that man (RCA N1681).

September 1973 Release in Japan: Let's spend the night together / Drive-in Saturday (RCA 552279).

8-9-1973 Re-release The laughing Gnome (3.01) / The gospel according to Tony Day (2.48), which sells over 250.000 copies in England (Deram DM123).

28-9-1973 Release Sorrow (2.48) / Amsterdam (3.19) (RCA 2424).

28-9-1973 Release in Spain: Sorrow (2.48) / Lady grinning soul (RCA APBO 9056).

DATE / EVENT	AUDIO / VIDEO	TITLE

29-9-1973 Voted top male singer in British section of 1973 Melody Maker poll with Jean Genie and Drive-in Saturday voted top two singles. Second to Robert Plant in world vocal section. Also voted top producer and top composer in international section.

October 1973 After Dark. Article by Henry Edwards: A growing boy who gets better and better.

October 1973 Hi Fidelity / Musical America. Article by Henry Edwards: Rock and rouge.

October 1973 The Bowie's moved to Oackley Street on the Chelsea side of Albert Bridge, close to Cheyne Walk where Mick Jagger lived.
Angie's latest boyfriend Scott Richardson moved in for a while. This way Bowie had a friend with the same interest: Cocaine (Living on the brink - George Tremlett 1996).

6-10-1973 Los Angeles Times. Article by Robert Hilburn: Pop poll points to new leadership.

6-10-1973 Melody Maker. Article by Michael Watts: Bowie, the darling who put glam into rock.

8-10-1973 Rock. Article by Martin Hayman: Outside David Bowie.

19-10-1973 Release LP Pin-Ups (RCA APL.I.0291).
150.000 Advance orders in England.
The sleeve photo was originally destined for the cover of Vogue. Vogue hesitated to use the photo (they always used photos of only women). Then Bowie decided to use the photo for the cover of Pin-Ups.
Twiggy: "I told the circulation manager of English Vogue he was crazy. I know it doesn't really look like me, in fact there are still a lot of people who don't know that it's me. It's still one of my favourite pictures."
The inside sleeve showed Bowie in a suit. Baggies with a 6" turn-up, white silk button down shirt with big knotted blue tie, plus a double-breasted bum freezer with high-cut pockets and a red silk hankie.

Greg Shaw for Rolling Stone: "While well-equipped to cover the material with Mick Ronson's obvious brilliance in the genre, as evidenced by his one-man Yarbirdmania on The Jean Genie, the album was an overall disappointment."
Iggy Pop for Phonograph: "Sounds damn good. Mick Ronson is getting better sound than ever. I mean, he's getting one of the best rock 'n' roll rhythm guitar sounds on the album I've heard in two or three years. I really like what he's playing too, especially on Rosalyn, I wish you would, I can't explain and Anyway, anyhow, anywhere. It's simple and to the point, with a lot of authority, which is how I like to hear guitar."

RCA / MainMan Radio Promo by Cherry Vanilla: Ad for Hunky dory / Space oddity / The man who sold the world / Ziggy Stardust / Aladdin Sane / Pin Ups (1.00).

October 1973 New Zealand. Released Rosalyn (2.27) / Where have all the good times gone (2.44) (RCA Promo 1).
Fan Club release (both sides 3 times interrupted by DJ Tom who tries to persuade the listeners to buy the album Pin Ups).

<u>18,19 + 20-10-1973</u> London, Marquee Club. Recording The Midnight Special for NBC (US TV).	CD	*1980 Floor Show (3,4,5,6,7,8,) (Chapter One CO 25155)*

DATE / EVENT	AUDIO / VIDEO	TITLE
Attended by a 200-strong Fan Club Audience. Also present: Mary Hopkins, Angela and Zowie, Lionel Bart, Dana Gillespie, Wayne County (wearing New York street drag of a red negligee bought in Piccadilly and a snowball wig, carrying a metal handbag engraved with the word 'Campus Queen') (Black Book - Barry Miles 1980). Leee Childers arrived in a black Nazi SS coat. The director refused him on the set (Presenting David Bowie! - David Douglas 1975).	CD	Absolutely Rare (8 songs) (No label, no number)
	CD	RarestOneBowie (2)
	CD	The Axeman Comet (2,4,6) (DB 003)
	CD	Ziggy with soul (Dancing Horse DH-001)
	CD	From the vaults of Mainman (8 songs) (U.R. 00)
18-10-1973 in Studio. Performance Marianne (Evelyn) Faithfull (born 29-12-1946) (As tears go by, 20th Century blues), Carmen (Burlerias, Shouts of Ole from their first LP Fandangos in Space), rehearsal Spiders.	2 CD	Last beat (Shout to the top STTP 158/159)
	CD	NBC Midnight Special (2xS)
19-10-1973 Bowie, The Troggs (Wild thing, I can't control myself, Strange Movie).	CD	Pinups 2 (3) (BOWPU02)
20-10-1973 Sorrow and dance choreography. Bowie's make-up lady was Barbara Daley (She later did the make-up for Lady Diana on her wedding day). Broadcast 16-11-1973.	1 CDR	Dollars in drag (The Amazing Kornyfone Records Label TAKRL 1935)
	1 CDR	Friends (8) (No label, no number)
They had to do various concessions to the NBC-people. For Jean Genie Bowie wore a kind of fish net, with two hands on his chest. The third hand was placed between his legs and had to be removed. On one of the recordings you could see some of Bowie's pubic hair. Panic! They did a second recording (on which they played so bad, they were forced to use the first recording) (David Bowie - Jerry Hopkins 1985).	2 CDR	Waiting in the wings (A Barling Spaniel Recording 2002 BS738/739)
	1 CD	The Midnight Special (Switch On! S.O. 2002-27-1)
	1 CD	1980 Floor Show Outtakes
	1 CD	The 1980 Floorshow (DB 1980A/B)
	2 CD	In 1973 I was down the Marquee
1. Sorrow (2.58). 2. Time (5.22). 3. Everything's alright (original by The Mojos in 1964) (2.36). 4. Space oddity (5.27). 5. I can't explain (original by The Who in 1965) (2.09). 6. The Jean Genie (6.13). 7. 1984/Dodo (5.34). 8. I got you babe (with Marianne Faithfull) (original by Bob Dylan in 1965) (4.11).	VCD	NBC Midnight Special (2xS)
	VCD	The Midnight Special (No label, no number)
	LP	1984 Floor Show / Good enough to eat (Ruthless Rhymes 208 A/B)
	LP	Dollars in drag 1973 (Boss Two PE 3 PE Bowie I/II)
	LP	All the young dudes
Rehearsals: Dialogue Bowie & Amanda Lear (3.07). Time (Take 1) (1.59). Time (Take 2) (5.31). Everything's alright (Take 1) (1.50). Everything's alright (Take 3) (3.24). Everything's alright (Take 4) (2.45). Space oddity (Take 2) (5.46). I can't explain (Take 1) (2.14).	4 LP	The beat goes on
	LP	Dollars in drag (Pigs Eye PE # 3 PE Bowie I/II)
	LP	Dollars in drag (The Amazing Kornyfone Records Label TAKRL 1935)
	LP	Make up do's and dont's
	Single	1984 (1984)
	Single	I can't explain

DATE / EVENT	AUDIO / VIDEO	TITLE
The Jean Genie (Take 2) (2.45).	Video	Various 8 (36 min)
The Jean Genie (Take 3) (5.58).	Video	Stolp tapes, vol 1 (4 min)
1984 (Take 1) (0.16).	Video	Stolp tapes, vol 10 (3 min)
1984 (Take 2) (1.49).	Video	Stolp tapes, no. 13 (52 min)
1984 / You didn't hear it from me (Take 3) (3.34).	Video	Various 26 (36 min)
1984 / You didn't hear it from me (Take 4) (5.36).	Video	Various 27 (6 min, Outtakes)
I got you babe (take 2) (4.03).		

There was a recording studio and control room on Wardour Street (near by the Marquee). The studio was also used as a dressing room. Amanda Lear (by then she was still called Dooshenka) stripped in front of the control room.
David said to Ken Scott: "She's not bad, is she? Would you believe a couple of months ago that she was a man?" (Strange fascination - David Buckley 1999).

21-10-1973 Bowie visited Marianne Faithfull in her flat. They started an affair which lasted through the winter.
Angie Bowie: "He wanted to get in her pants. She'd been Mick's, so he had to have her as well" (Bowiestyle - Mark Paytress 2000).
Through Marianna Faithfull Bowie had met Amanda Lear.

27-10-1973 Melody Maker. Article by Chris Welch: Bowie free for all.

27-10-1973 Disc. Article: Bowie 1984 A.D.
Tony Ingrassia: "We are currently writing scripts. We have not fully acquired the rights to the book yet and it is still possible we will have to call it 1983, or something like that."

31-10-1973 UK TV. Top of the Pops. Bowie's performance of Sorrow is cancelled.

November / December 1973 Barnes, Olympic Studios.
Dodo (full length version) with Lulu recorded (4.29).
End October he recorded an alternate take of 1984 / Dodo (5.27) with Ken Scott at Trident Studios, released on the Sound and Visionbox 1989 / 1990.
In November 1973 Growin' up (3.26) was recorded with Ron Wood playing lead guitar. Bruce Springsteen recorded the original version in 1973.

November 1973 Plans to launch Amanda Lear in the movie Oktobriana (an anti-Soviet cartoon strip), with music by Bowie (Cancelled) (Backstage passes - Angela Bowie and Patrick Carr 1993).

November 1973 God only knows recorded (never released).
The original version was by the Beach Boys in 1966.

November 1973 Barnes, Olympic Studios. I'm in the mood for love recorded with Ava Cherry and the Astronettes (original version by Frances Langford in 1935). Released in US 16-5-1995, in Europe September 1995.

12-11-1973 Mott the Hoople starts a 20-date tour in Great Britain. Support act: Queen.
Bowie helped Queen to secure the tour, but turned down the offer to produce Queen's debut LP (he did not have enough time). In Southend Freddie, Brian and Roger of Queen joined Mott the Hoople on All the young dudes (Freddie Mercury The Definitive Biography - Lesley-Ann Jones 1997).

DATE / EVENT	AUDIO / VIDEO	TITLE
16-11-1973 US TV. NBC. Midnight Special (recorded 18 to 20-10-1973).	Video	Various 26 (36 min)

17-11-1973 William Burroughs and journalist Craig Copetas met Bowie in his home in London. Later on they had lunch together in Bowie's home, a Jamaican fish dish.
In 1939 Burroughs was diagnosed schizophrenic. Despite his homosexuality he married in 1937. In the early 50's he thought he was possessed by demons (Living on the brink - George Tremlett 1996).

21-11-1973 London, Bush Theatre. Performance "Mermaids" by Lindsay Kemp.
Bowie videos the event.

December 1973 Circus. Article by Steve Demorest: Bowie salutes the sixties stars.

3-12-1973 Barnes, Olympic Studios. Start recording first part recording LP People from bad homes - Ava Cherry and the Astronettes.
Before Ava Cherry met Bowie, she used to work as a cocktail waitress at the discotheque Genesis.

4-12-1973 Watford. Palace Theatre. Attends A patriot for me, by John Osborne. Marianne Faithfull was the star (as Anna) and Bowie visited her backstage.

6-12-1973 Rolling Stone. Article by Mick Rock: David Bowie returns - On T.V.

8-12-1973 Disc.
They wrote: "David Bowie is now working on two stage musicals, '1984' and a 'Ziggy Stardust Show' though which of them will be staged first remains anybody's guess."

14-12-1973 London, Odeon Theater, Hammersmith. Mott the Hoople.
Attended by David Bowie and Mick Jagger.

22-12-1973 Disc. Article by Ray Fox-Cumming: Good luck for 1984.

22-12-1973 UK TV. Top of the Pops: Ten years of pop music 1964-74, presented by Jimmy Saville. Broadcast of Starman (3.32), recorded 14-4-1972.

Ava Cherry lived in Oackley Street until Christmas 1973, then she was installed by DeFries in a flat in King's Road
Ava Cherry: "Angie and I were having this tension between us. I felt badly. I was starting to love the guy and really didn't know what to do. When David wasn't there I was at Angie's mercy. Then Angie started to go away and that was the best part. I was in heaven, and when she came back it would start all over again."

One morning Angela served Bowie and Jagger breakfast.
As a result of the way Angela described the scene in a TV interview for the Joan Rivers Show in 1979, a lot of reporters wrote Angela had caught them in bed, making love. In later interviews she said they only slept in the same bed, as far as she knew.

Christmas 1973 at Cheyne Walk (invited by Mick Jagger).
Other guests: Ron Wood, Gary Glitter (complete with chest wig and gold costume?). Bowie gave

DATE / EVENT	AUDIO / VIDEO	TITLE

Mick Jagger a video-recorder.

End 1973 Recording song "1984." Longer version than on the album. Recorded with Mick Ronson and Trevor Bolder.

End 1973 End December 1973. London, Trident Studios. Recording demo Rebel rebel (flamenco version).

31-12-1973 At special luncheon RCA present him with plaque to mark the fact that for 19 weeks he has had 5 different LP's in the charts at the same time.

Late 1973 Recording To know him is to love him with Steeleye Span.
Steeleye Span bass guitarist Rick Kemp had rehearsed with the Spiders begin 1972. He asked David to contribute some saxophone. The original version was by The Teddybears in 1958.

<u>1973 / 1974</u> Bowie plays sessions with Adam Faith   NT
and Ian Anderson (Jethro Tull).

1974 Released in Brasil: Disco De Ouro (same as The world of David Bowie) (Bra London SC 15002).

1974 Popular Music and Society. Article by David F. Fandray: David Bowie: Diamond Dogs.

1974 Book published: Diary of a rock 'n' roll star - Ian Hunter (Panther Books, ISBN 1-89-7783-09-4). In 1996 reprinted by Independent Music Press.

1974 Book published: The David Bowie story - George Tremlett (Futura, ISBN 0 8600 7051 4).

1974 Book published: David Bowie - A portrait - Various contributors (Wise Publications).

1974 Book published: Pop Today - Gavin Petrie (Hamlyn, ISBN 0.600.370801).

In 1974 Mickey (Sparkey) King (a rent boy with Celtic eyes and auburn hair, who sang on Rupert the Riley) was stabbed to death. He had been blackmailing a colonel, who sent a couple of his lads to resolve the situation (Backstage passes - Angela Bowie and Patrick Carr 1993).

1974 The Merv Griffin Show (Angie) with clips of Bowie 1973 not shown on ANC, including him doing Watch that man.

1974 US TV. NBC. The Tonight Show (Angie).

1-1-1974 Barnes, Olympic Studios. Recording demos Can you hear me and Candidate (5.05). Engineers Keith Harwood and Andy Morris.

14-1-1974 Barnes, Olympic Studios. Recordings for Lp People from bad homes - Ava Cherry and the Astronettes.

In the first part of 1974 Corinne Schwab became Bowie's personal assistant.

<u>1974</u> Paris. Bowie did 20 min. of songs in a bar.   NT

DATE / EVENT	AUDIO / VIDEO	TITLE

Early 1974 Pat Wadley of MainMan's New York publicity staff visited David and Angie in their Chelsea home. David put his arm around her and took her back to her hotel (The Park Lane Hotel) and stayed the night.

Begin 1974 MainMan had 3 offices in New York. The newest at 405 Park Avenue.
The office in 18th street was run by Cherry Vanilla (head of MainMan film unit). Cherry Vanilla had the floors, the furniture and everything else done cherry.
All MainMan employees did spend a lot of money. The Los Angeles assistant Susie Ha-Ha had her breasts lift on MainMan's account (Leee Black Childers interview).
MainMan artist Dana Gillespie: "MainMan paid for everything. I had a secretary, BMW, tickets all over the world. I was as happy as a pig in shit while I was in it" (Dutch Fanzine The Voyeur).

January 1974 MainMan received GBP. 16.358 from Chrysalis.

January 1974 Soho Weekly News. Article by Michael Goldstein.
Bowie said: "I'm an awful liar. I'm not sure whether it's me changing my mind or whether I lie a lot. It's somewhere between the two. I don't exactly lie, I change my mind all the time."

5-1-1974 In Sounds poll voted No.1 composer, No.1 record producer, No.2 musician, No.2 male vocalist, with Aladdin Sane voted 4th best LP of the year, and it's sleeve second.

5-1-1974 Melody Maker. Bowie voted No.1 male singer.

8-1-1974 Bowie went to see Fritz Lang's 1926 film Metropolis, Robert Wiene's Cabinet of Dr. Caligari and Murnau's Nosferatu in Hampstead (together with Amanda Lear and George Underwood).

9-1-1974 Bowie visited a lot of London Bookshops in search of studies about Fritz Lang.

10-1-1974 UK TV. Top of the Pops. Lulu performs The man who sold the world.
Bowie helps to record the backing track.

11-1-1974 Release: The man who sold the world (3.50) / Watch that man (4.57) - Lulu (Polydor 2001 490). Produced by Bowie and Ronson. Bowie backs on vocals and plays sax.

14-1974 Barnes, Olympic Studios. Recording demo for Big Brother.

15-1974 Barnes, Olympic Studios. Recording Rock 'n'roll with me, Candidate, Big Brother, Can you hear me and Diamond Dogs.

16-1974 Barnes, Olympic Studios. Recording We are the dead.

Rumoured early title for the album Diamond Dogs: Bowie-ing Out.
Bowie had trouble mixing the album. He phoned Tony Visconti, who was just building his own studio. Visconti agreed he could come over and a few hours later they mixed the first track. The next day Bowie had ordered a lot of furniture for the new studio and they started mixing the rest of the album. During this period Bowie read out passages from The wild boys - William Burroughs (Bowiestyle - Mark Paytress 2000).
Tony Visconti: "David called me in the middle of the night. I could tell he was on something, probably

DATE / EVENT	AUDIO / VIDEO	TITLE

cocaine, because he was speaking quickly, rambling really. He said could we get together soon?"
The album opened with the intriguing Future legend, including a misshapen version of Bewitched, bothered and bewildered (musical Pal Joey, 1941) and ending with applause taken from the Faces LP Coast to coast - Overture and beginners.
Harlan Ellison's Nebula-winning story A boy and his dog (about Vic and his telepathic dog Blood, who are trying to survive in a post-World War 3 wasteland) was an inspiration for the album.

25-1-1974 Release single Love me tender / Slaughter on 10th avenue - Mick Ronson (RCA).

25-1-1974 Released in US. Promo. Slaughter on 10th Avenue / Growing up and I'm fine / All cut up on you / Andy Warhol (RCA LPBO. 5009).

31-1-1974 Downbeat. Article by Ray Townley: Lester... who?

February 1974 Bowie to Disc journalist Fox Cumming: "I haven't walked in the light of day for ages except from my front door to the car and again from the car into the studios" (Black Book - Barry Miles 1980).

February 1974 MainMan began filming a documentary about Mick Ronson (never released).

February 1974 Crawdaddy. Article by James Graig: Pin ups.

In February 1974 Bowie and Lou Reed went into town, to some clubs, then to Bowie's hotel and Lou's apartment. Lou was in a bad mood and started to quarrel. They were both stoned and Lou threw whiskey over the table. They started to shout to each other and Reed hit Bowie in the face. This cooled down the friendship for quite some years (Lou Reed - Victor Bockris 1994).

Begin February 1974 Bowie stayed at the Amstel Hotel in Amsterdam.
Tibor Benkhard, manager press-promotion of RCA Inelco had asked Bowie in January in London to visit Holland for a few days. Benkhard waited in Hook of Holland for the large Cadillac with the Bowie family to arrive from Harwich. Benkhard drove in his old Simca 1000 in front of the Cadillac with David, Angela, Zowie, Freddie and Coco, to show them the way to the hotel. (Dutch Fanzine The Voyeur, August 2000).

6-2-1974 Dutch TV. Toppop. Receives Edison Award for Ziggy album out of the hands of Ad Visser, who also offers him a glass of Schelvispekel.
A large press conference was given at the Amstel Hotel in Amsterdam for the complete Dutch music press. Interviews and photo sessions.

7-2-1974 Dutch TV. AVRO. Toppop. Rebel rebel (playback).	VCD Video Video	Various 1 (4.18 min) Stolp Tapes vol 10 (3 min.) Various 26 (4 min)

13-2-1974 Hilversum (Holland), L. Ludolf Studio. Bowie recorded an alternative take of Rebel rebel (single version in US, May 1974) (2.58). Alan Parker gave him some advices to complete the riff for Rebel rebel in January 1974. Bowie sorted it out for the biggest part, but Parker's advices completed it.

15-2-1974 Release Rebel rebel (4.20) / Queen bitch (3.13) (RCA LPBO. 5009).

DATE / EVENT	AUDIO / VIDEO	TITLE

Creem Magazine: Rebel rebel will amaze and delight even the people who were never in the Bowie camp in the past.

Jayne/Wayne County claims Bowie used the line 'Can't tell whether she's a boy or a girl' from his 1973 song Queenage Baby.

15-2-1974 David and Angela joined the audience at the 12th Grand Gala du Disque Populaire which was held at the Rai Congrescentrum, Amsterdam.

21-2-1974 Top of the Pops. Pre-recorded performance of   CD   *Absolutely Rare*
Rebel rebel (4.39) was cancelled. The film arrived to late.   *(No label, no number)*

22-2-1974 London, Rainbow Theater. Performance by Mick Ronson. Attended by bowie.

28-2-1974 Rolling Stone. Article by Graig Copetas: Beat godfather meets glitter MainMan: William Burroughs say hello to David Bowie.
Bowie said: "A song has to take on a character, shape, body, and influence people to the extent that they use it for their own devices. It must affect them not just as a song but as a lifestyle."

March 1974 Released in Japan 2LP Best of David Bowie.

1-3-1974 Released LP Slaughter on 10th Avenue, Mick Ronson (RCA Victor APLI 0353).
Including Growing up and I'm fine (written by Bowie) (3.12), Hey ma get papa (lyrics by Bowie) (2.17), Music is lethal (lyrics by Bowie, to the music of the original version by Lucio Battisti) (5.12). Bowie suggested Mick Ronson the LP title, based on Richard Rodgers and Lorentz Hart's stage show.

RCA / MainMan Radio Promo ad # 1: Slaughter on 10th Avenue Single and LP out (1.00).
RCA / MainMan Radio Promo ad # 2: Slaughter on 10th Avenue Single and LP out (1.00).
RCA / MainMan Radio Promo LP ad: Slaughter on 10th Avenue (Background music Love me tender) (1.00).
RCA / MainMan Radio Promo LP ad: Slaughter on 10th Avenue (Background music Slaughter on 10th Avenue) (1.00).

1-3-1974 Bowie moves to Kensington.

15-3-1974 Release LP Now we are six - Steeleye Span (Chrysalis CHR1053).
Bowie plays sax on To know him is to love him (2.24) (original in 1958 by the Teddy Bears)

18-3-1974 Premiere The Man Who Fell To Earth, at London Leicester Square.

22-3-1974 Release LP Weren't born a man - Dana Gillespie (RCA APL 1 0354).
Produced Gillespie / Cable / Bowie / Ronson.
Includes Andy Warhol (3.02), Backed a loser (4.51), Mother don't be frightened (4.15).

RCA / MainMan Radio Promo: LP ad # 1 Weren't born a man (1.00).
RCA / MainMan Radio Promo: LP ad # 2 Weren't born a man (1.00).
RCA / MainMan Radio Promo: LP ad Weren't born a man "Her first LP out now" (0.30).

30-3-1974 Bowie and George MacCormack travelled to Paris for a 4-day stay at the Raphael Hotel.

DATE / EVENT	AUDIO / VIDEO	TITLE

3-4-1974 Bowie and MacCormack by train to Cannes. They stayed a few hours in the Carlton Hotel, before they travelled by SS France to New York.
There was a brief stop at Madeira and they arrived in New York on 11-4-1974.
On the SS France they dined with harmonica player Larry Adler (he entertained the guests).
Bowie stayed at The Sherry-Netherland Hotel in Oackley Street / 5th Avenue.
Later he moved to The Pierre Hotel for the rest of the year.
His assistant Corinne Schwab was almost always at his side. Stui George still was his bodyguard and Jim James drove his limousine.

Bowie gave a party. He unzipped his pants to show Wayne County he had shaved his pubic hair (Man enough to be a woman - Jayne County with Rupert Smith 1995).

April 1974 Mick Ronson gave an interview to Allan Jones.
He talked about Bowie's drug-problems. The relation with Bowie cooled down. Begin April 1974 Mick Ronson was rehearsing for his first UK solo tour, which started at 10-4-1974 in Preston Guildhall. His backing band included Trevor Bolder and Mike Garson.

April 1974 Beat Instrumental (UK). Article: Bowie's Equipment Secrets.

April 1974 Rock Magazine.
Bowie: "Lulu's got this terrific voice and it's been misdirected all this time, all these years. She's got a real soul voice, she can get the feel of Aretha."

11-4-1974 RCA's New York Studios. First day of the Young Americans sessions. The recordings only started 11-8-1974 at Sigma Sound Studios.
They recorded a new version of Rebel rebel (2.58) (released in the USA, May 1974).
For this version Bowie overdubbed and remixed the original version. Geoff MacCormack added castanets and congas and Bowie added some additional vocals.

11-4-1974 Release Rock 'n' roll suicide (2.58) / Quicksand (4.54) (RCA LPBO 5201).
Part of the lyrics for Quicksand was inspired by the 1888 black order The Hermetic Order of the Golden Dawn.
Bowie: "Quicksand is about creativity being stifled by ego. It's the germ of ideas being sucked into a pit and suffocated by ego."

Half April 1974. New York. Bowie went to see: The Temptations, Marvin Gaye and The Spinners in the Apollo. Roxy Music and Todd Rundgren at the Carnegie Hall (where he attended the post-concert party). Television. Leather Secrets.
He had an affair with a Puerto Rican drag queen.

20-4-1974 New Musical Express. Article by Clive James: Bringing some of it all back home.

23-4-1974 Venice (California). Chris Burden is nailed to the top of a Volkswagen. This impressed Bowie and July /August 1977 he wrote Joe the lion, inspired by the event.

24-4-1974 Release LP Diamond Dogs (RCA APL.I.0576).

Bowie about the album: "This one again has a theme. It's a backward look at the sixties and seventies

DATE / EVENT	AUDIO / VIDEO	TITLE

and a very political album. My protest. These days you have to be more subtle about protesting than before. You can't preach at people anymore. You have to adopt a position of almost indifference. You have to be super cool nowadays. This album is more me than anything I've done previously" (Black Book - Barry Miles 1980).
About the song Big Brother: "I wanted to have the machine say 'Brother,' but it got stuck and kept repeating 'Bro,' which sounded much better!"

Diamond Dogs Radio Promo: LP ad # 1 (1.00).	1 CDR	Cracked in the past
Diamond Dogs Radio Promo: LP ad # 2 (0.33).		(No label, no number)
	Video	Various 26 (35 sec)
Diamond Dogs Radio Promo: LP ad # 3 (0.32).	1 CDR	Cracked in the past
		(No label, no number)

Costs of the American Diamond Dogs advertising campaign: USD 400.000,—.

Billboard: "A subtler, more aesthetic Bowie comes to the forefront here. The album should reinforce his musical presence in the 70's."

Eric Emerson in Rolling Stone: "Most of the songs are obscure tangles of perversion, degradation, fear and self pity. It's difficult to know what to make of them. Are they masturbatory fantasies, guilt-ridden projections or terrified premonitions?"

Bowie about one of his inspirations for the characters he created for Hunger City: "Dr. Barnardo and Lord Shaftesbury had once gone onto the roofs of the city of London and had found all these urchins living up there. That always stayed in my mind as being an extraordinary image, all these kids living on the roofs of London. So, I had the Diamond Dogs as living on the streets."

End April 1974 Bowie had a meeting with John Dexter (director of the National Theatre in London and Metropolitan Opera in Mew York), to discuss his plans for the musical 1984.

End April 1974 Keith Christmas got a phone-call out of the blue (he hadn't seen or spoken Bowie for some years) to join Bowie for the Diamond Dogs tour.
Keith Christmas: "He hold court surrounded by freaks. It was straight out of Fellini. David took me to a couple of gay clubs. He loved to tease the boys, but wanted to fuck the girls. One day he slashed his razor into a huge chunk of coke. Sometime around then it dawned to me I wasn't going to be on the tour."

Earl Slick: "They played me a couple of tracks from Diamond Dogs, took the guitars out of the mix, told me what key it was in and told me to play!"

<u>April and May 1974</u> Rehearsals in New York City.   NT
RCA Studio Complex.

May 1974 Stereo Review. Article by J. Tiven: Darling David Bowie.

May 1974 David and Marc Bolan went to a press-party for Gary Glitter.

Marc Bolan: "We sat in David's hotel room and watched A Clockwork Orange about four times. We just got back into what we were like when we were kids. David and I have always been the closest of

DATE / EVENT	AUDIO / VIDEO	TITLE

friends. None of the feuding that was reported was real. We sat down in that room and decided our futures."

May 1974 Release in US Promo single: Rebel rebel (2.58) / Lady grinning soul (3.46) (RCA APBO 0287).

May 1974 US TV. Advert for Diamond Dogs.   *Video*   Various 20 (1 min)

Bowie about the cover of the album Diamond Dogs: "It's a painting of me changing into a dog, right, and they're a bit worried that it's cock shows. But apart from the cock, everything's all right" (In his own words - Miles 1980).
Guy Peellaert disgned the cover.

4-5-1974 Sounds. Article by Martin Kirkup:
Kirkup wrote: "Diamond Dogs has the provoking quality of a thought-out painting that draws on all the deeper colours."
Bowie: "Ever since I got to New York I've been going down to the Apollo in Harlem. Most New Yorkers seem scared to go there if they're white but the music's incredible. I saw The Temptations and The Spinners together on the same bill there and next week it's Marvin Gaye. Incredible! I love that kind of thing."

11-5-1974 New Musical Express. Article by Ian MacDonald: A boy and his dog.

11-5-1974 Melody Maker. Article by Chris Charlesworth: Bowie gets the Spector sound.
Charlesworth wrote: "For most of the tracks, he's adopted a wall of sound technique, borrowed from Phil Spector."

17-5-1974 Re-release Hang on to yourself (2.51) / Man in the middle (4.08) - Arnold Corns (Mooncrest 25).

18-5-1974 New Musical Express. Article by Steve Turner: The scruffy little failure who became David Bowie.

18-5-1974 Melody Maker. Article by Michael Watts: Bowie's MainMan.

June 1974 David visits a performance of Roxy Music in New York.

June 1974 Creem. Article by Charles Shaar Murray: Angie: Life with David or when will those clouds all disappear?

The Diamond Dogs Tour:
David Bowie (vocals).
Mike Garson (piano, mellotron).
Earl Slick (lead guitar).
Herbie Flowers (bass guitar).
Tony Newman (drums).
Pablo Rosario (percussion).
David Sanborn (alto sax, flute).
Richard Grando (baritone sax, flute).

DATE / EVENT	AUDIO / VIDEO	TITLE

Michael Kamen (electric piano, moog, oboe).
Geoffrey MacCormack (aka W. Peace) (backing vocals).
Gui Andrisano (backing vocals / dog).

A year earlier David Sanborn and Michael Kamen were both members of The New York Rock Ensemble. Earl Slick was their roadie.

<u>8-6-1974</u> Rye (Port Chester), Capitol Theatre.   CD   *Dawn of the Dogs*
Dress rehearsals.   *(A Paranoid Production*
1. Moonage daydream (2.05).   *BOW74 PP-001)*
2. Sweet thing (7.15).   CD   *The band was altogether*
3. Changes (5.13).   *(No label, no number)*
4. Suffragette city (6.05).   CD   *Port Chester 8.6.74 (11 songs)*
5. Aladdin Sane (4.32).   *(No label, no number)*
6. All the young dudes (4.18).   1 CDR   *Dress rehearsal*
7. Diamond Dogs (6.55).   *(Old Gold Records OGCD 135)*
8. Panic in Detroit (5.57).   2 CDR   *A Sweet Thing (5)*
9. Big brother (5.27).   *(No label, no number)*
10. Time (3.56).   1 CDR   *Port Chester Musician's Show*
11. The Jean Genie (3.03).

<u>9-6-1974</u> Rye (Port Chester), Capitol Theatre.   NT
Dress rehearsals.

<u>10-6-1974</u> Rye (Port Chester), Capitol Theatre.   NT
Dress rehearsals.

11-6-1974 Left New York for a 600-mile drive to Montreal.

14-6-1974 Release Diamond Dogs (5.56) / Holy holy (2.20) (RCA APBO.0293).

<u>14-6-1974</u> Montreal, The Forum.   NT
Attendance: 16.000.   *Video*   *Stolp tapes no. 17 (7 min)*
First time the whole cast worked with a complete set.
During the show the bridge crashed to the ground.
Chris Charlesworth reviewed this show for the Melody
Maker of 22-6-1974.

Choreographer Toni Basil: "It was the greatest set I have ever seen. Nobody knew if the bridge was going to crash or the pole he sat out on was going to crash. The show was phenomenal and David was absolutely brilliant."

Lightning director Jules Fisher: "For Diamond Dogs he had an understanding of German expressionist art and film. He wanted that image and I'd seen all of those films. He saw a town, like the one in Robert Wiene's 1919 classic The Cabinet of Doktor Caligari. David wanted power and Fritz Lang's 1926 film Metropolis."

<u>15-6-1974</u> Ottawa, Civic Center.   1 CDR   *Ottawa 74*
A CDR of this date circulates, but it is the same recording   *(No label, no number)*

DATE / EVENT	AUDIO / VIDEO	TITLE
as Subway. The American guy I got this one from insist he taped this one himself in Ottawa. He claims to be sure, because it is the only Bowie concert he went to in the 70's. If this date is correct, it means the other releases under the name Subway come from the same date. I have no proof at all this is correct, except the man's word.	1 CDR LP LP LP	*Subway 1974* (No label, no number) *Subway 1974* (FW 8211 A/B) *Subway* (FLAT 8211 A/B) *Subway* (BEBOP FW 8211 A/B)
16-6-1974 Toronto, O'Keefe Auditorium. Matinee. Attendance: 1.750. During Sweet thing The audience went wild. Drive in Saturday was acoustic. Space oddity was sung while he was sitting in a chair, high above the heads of the audience. A great show. A pity we did not get to see it in Europe.	2 CD 2 CD 2 CDR 3 CDR 2 CDR 2 LP Tape Tape 1 VCD	*Halloween Jack Spooks 'em in Toronto (almost complete)* *Toronto 74 1st show (Bewlay Muzak Production)* *Toronto, 1st Show, 16 June 1974 (BowieHobby)* *Magic in Toronto (Old Gold Records OGCD 033A/B/C)* *Cracked in the past* (No label, no number) *Halloween Jack Spooks 'em in Toronto (DB 1972)* quality 8, 85 min. quality 9, 83 min. *8MM Ziggy* (No label, no number)
16-6-1974 Toronto, O'Keefe Auditorium. Evening. Attendance: 1.750. The start of the show was 45 minutes delayed because David had laryngitis. Despite the laryngitis it was a good show.	2 CDR 1 CDR 2 CD 3 CDR 2 CDR 2 CDR 1 CDR VCD Tape Tape	*Toronto, 2nd Show, 16 June 1974 (BowieHobby)* *Diamonds in space* (No label, no number) *Toronto 74 2nd show (Bewlay Muzak Production)* *Magic in Toronto (Old Gold Records OGCD 033A/B/C)* *Cracked in the past (1 song)* (No label, no number) *A Sweet Thing (1 song)* (No label, no number) *Just a hint of mayhem* *Various 1 (3.20 min.)* quality 8, 100 min. quality 7, 95 min.
16-6-1974 Owen Sound-Sun Times. They wrote: "Perfect showmanship."		
17-6-1974 Rochester, Memorial Auditorium. Attendance: 9.200. A very good concert. The recordings prove the audience was very amazed and had never seen a spectacular show	2 CDR 1 CDR	*Rochester 17 June 1974 (BowieHobby)* *Future legend (Old Gold Records OGCD 113)*

DATE / EVENT	AUDIO / VIDEO	TITLE

like this before. Just listening to the crowd response makes this recording a treasure to have in your collection.

                                                                                  2 CDR   *You're knocking me dead (Old Gold Records OGCD 111A/B) (3songs)*

Tape   quality 7, 90 min.

<u>18-6-1974</u> Cleveland, Public Auditorium.   Tape
Attendance: 4.000. Produced by WMMS & Tormey-Hooks Productions. Tickets: USD 7.00.

<u>19-6-1974</u> Cleveland, Public Auditorium.   2 CDR   Cleveland Ohio'74
Attendance: 4.000. Produced by WMMS & Tormey-Hooks Productions. Tickets: USD 7.00.   1 CDR   *A Guided Show (Old Gold Records OGCD 110)*
Great show. On my tape somebody gives a full description of the set and tells now and then what happens on stage.   2 CDR   *Cleveland Public Auditorium 1974 (No label, no number)*
Very responsive crowd. Great guitar play in Space Oddity. Everything fits and proves once more this tour is one of the best tours Bowie ever did.   2 CDR   *You're knocking me dead (Old Gold Records OGCD 111A/B) (3songs)*
The well known tape has comments by David Fletcher and his friend Tom Ward.   2 CDR   *Live Cleveland 1974 (No label, no number)*

Tape   quality 7, 85 min.

<u>20-6-1974</u> Toledo, Sports Arena.   NT
Attendance: 7.500.

21-6-1974 Detroit, Ford Auditorium.
Cancelled. Relocated to Cobo because the Detroit stage was too small.

<u>21-6-1974</u> Detroit, Cobo Arena.   Tape
Attendance: 6.000.

22-6-1974 Melody Maker. Article by Chris Charlesworth: Bowie: Birth of the new rock theatre. About the Montreal concert of 14-6-1974: "A few thousand lucky Canadians witnessed a completely new concept in rock theatre last weekend when David Bowie opened his North American tour in Montreal on Saturday."

22-6-1974 Detroit, Ford Auditorium.
Cancelled and relocated to Cobo.

<u>22-6-1974</u> Detroit, Cobo Arena.   1 CDR   *Detroit 22 June 1974 (BowieHobby)*
Attendance: 6.000.
A good concert, but Bowie was not talkative.   2 CDR   *You're knocking me dead (Old Gold Records OGCD 111A/B)*
The mean age of the crowd was 17.
Sanborn's sax solo sounded King Curtis-style.
David danced stiff and jerky.   3 CDR   *Halloween Jack live (Old Gold Records OGCD 034A/B/C)*
First he accepted a glass of wine from and then a whole bottle of wine from somebody in the crowd.
(Psychotic reactions and carburator dung - Lester Bangs 1988)   2 CDR   *Live Detroit 22/6/1974 (No label, no number)*

DATE / EVENT	AUDIO / VIDEO	TITLE
	2 CDR	*No more big wheels*
		(No label, no number)
	Tape	quality 8, 25 min.

<u>23-6-1974</u> Columbus, Mershon Auditorium. NT

<u>24-6-1974</u> Dayton, Harra Arena. NT
Attendance: 7.500.

<u>25-6-1974</u> Akron, Civic Theatre. NT
Attendance: 2.918.

<u>26-6-1974</u> Pittsburgh, Syria Mosque. NT
Attendance: 3.500. Video

<u>27-6-1974</u> Pittsburgh, Syria Mosque. NT
Attendance: 3.500.

<u>28-6-1974</u> Charleston (West Virginia), Civic Center. NT

29-6-1974 New Musical Express. Article by Lisa Robinson: Cracked actor zaps Cannock the spians.

<u>29-6-1974</u> Nashville, Municipal Auditorium. NT
Attendance: 9.000.
Paul and Linda McCartney in town to record the ill-fated
Nashville Diary album, come to the show.

<u>30-6-1974</u> Memphis, Mid-South Coliseum. NT
Attendance: 12.000.

July 1974 Released in US 1984 (3.27) / Queen bitch (3.13) (RCA ABPO 10026).

July 1974 Circus. Article by Michael Gross: David Bowie's Diamond Dogs.

July 1974 New York. Line Club. First live appearance of Bowie-clone Jobriath (In 1946 born as Bruce Campbell in the Town King of Prussia in Pennsylvania).
Not long afterwards his second album Creatures of the Street was released (Young Americans funk).
Peter Frampton played guitar on Jobriath's self-titled debut album.
He performed without much success and retired from rock in 1975. He renamed himself to Cole Berlin and lived in the Manhattan's Chelsea Hotel. He died of AIDS in 1983.

July 1974 Bowie to Tony Visconti: "I've got this great idea. I'll make a prophecy that America is going to go black. Black music is taking over. I want to make a black album. I want to make a soul album and there's a place in Philadelphia called Sigma Sound and that's the place to do it. I'll get Willie Weeks on bass" (David Robert Jones: The discography of a generalist - David Jeffrey Fletcher 1979).

<u>1-7-1974</u> Atlanta, Fox Theatre. 2 CDR *Atlanta 1 July 1974*
Attendance: 3.930. *(BowieHobby)*
Again a good show. No surprises in the song order. 2 CDR *Atlanta Fox Theatre '74*

DATE / EVENT	AUDIO / VIDEO	TITLE
Bowie, band and background singers work well together.	3 CDR	(No label, no number) Halloween Jack live (Old Gold Records OGCD 034A/B/C)
	2 CDR	Live Atlanta Fox Theatre 1/7/74 (No label, no number)
	2 CDR Tape	Savage Jaw quality 8, 85 min.
<u>2-7-1974</u> Tampa, Curtis Hixon Convention Hall. Attendance: 7.400.	2 CDR	Tampa 2 July 1974 (BowieHobby)
On the way to the show, a road accident leaves the entire stage set in a swamp between Atlanta and Tampa. The show goes on without it.	2 CD	Tampa (No label, no number)
Nice piano-bridge between Sweet thing and Changes. During Aladdin Sane Bowie adds a few lines of On Broadway.	2 CDR	1974 (Remastered) (A Dutch Connection CD101074) (First 16 songs)
"Good evening Tampa. Well we thought it wasn't going to happen, because as you probably heard we had a bad	2 CD	David Bowie '1974' (Fire Power FP-0050-A/B) (14 songs)
road accident and we're still upset about it. I'd like to thank you for being here." All the young dudes follows. Bowie did not sing Drive in Saturday (a pity).	2 CDR	The Legendary Soul Tour (David Bowie on Stage DBOS 101074) (14 songs)
At the end a standing ovation (20 min). And for the only time this tour Bowie played an encore.	2 CDR	The return of the Diamond Dogs
Get the remastered recording if you can!	3 CDR	Halloween Jack live (Old Gold Records OGCD 034A/B/C)
	1 CDR	Subway (5 songs) (Old Gold Records OGCD 038)
	LP	Subway (Flat Records 8211)
	LP	Live in Tampa (TP House Production DRJ498)
	LP	Live in Tampa 2 (TP House Production DRJ496) Tampa 1+2 is complete
	LP	The return of the Diamond Dogs (Slat Records 974JU02)
	LP Tape	Stardust from the 70's (BO-16) quality 9, 90 min.
3-7-1974 West Palm Beach, Auditorium. *Cancelled.*		
<u>3-7-1974</u> Casselberry (Orlando), Seminole Jai-Alai Fronton. Attendance: 5.895.	NT	
<u>4-7-1974</u> Jacksonville, Exhibition Hall.	NT	

DATE / EVENT	AUDIO / VIDEO	TITLE

5-7-1974 Charleston SC, Municipal Auditorium.   NT

6-7-1974 Charlotte, Park Center.   NT
A group of wealthy Texans chartered a jet to see the show.
They wore outfits that looked it had been stolen from
NASA: helmets, antennae, ray guns (Presenting David
Bowie! - David Douglas 1975).

7-7-1974 Norfolk, Scope Convention Hall.   NT
Attendance: 13.000.

8-7-1974 Philadelphia, Tower Theatre.   Tape
Attendance: 3.000.

9-7-1974 Philadelphia, Tower Theatre.   Tape
Attendance: 3.000.

10-7-1974 Philadelphia, Tower Theatre.   Tape
Attendance: 3.000.

When the band found out there would be made recordings for a live album, they refused to play.
Herbie Flowers became their spokesman. He demanded USD 5.000,— for every musician. DeFries
refused and David decided to pay the money himself. This would be Herbie Flowers' last tour with
Bowie (Alias David Bowie - Peter & Leni Gillman 1986).

11-7-1974 Philadelphia, Tower Theatre.
Attendance: 3.000.
1. 1984 (3.20).
2. Rebel rebel (2.40).
3. Moonage daydream (5.10).
4. Sweet thing (8.48).
5. Changes (3.34).
6. Suffragette city (3.45).
7. Aladdin Sane (4.57).
8. All the young dudes (4.18).
9. Cracked actor (3.29).
10. Rock 'n' roll with me (4.18).
11. Watch that man (4.55).
12. Knock on wood (original by Eddie Floyd in 1966) (3.08).
13. Diamond Dogs (6.32).
14. Big brother (4.08).
15. The width of a circle (8.12).
16. The Jean Genie (5.13).
17. Rock 'n' roll suicide (4.30).
18. Here today, gone tomorrow (3.32).

2 CD	*David Live*
CD	*Spaced out (PB81998)*
2 CDR	*A Sweet Thing*
	(No label, no number)
1 CDR	*Rock Concert*
	(No label, no number)
2 LP	*David Live (RCA 2.0771)*
1 LP	*Rock Concert*
Single	*Knock on wood / Panic in Detroit (RCA 2466)*

12-7-1974 Philadelphia, Tower Theatre. Matinee.
Cancelled.

DATE / EVENT	AUDIO / VIDEO	TITLE
<u>12-7-1974</u> Philadelphia, Tower Theatre. Evening. Attendance: 3.000. Another great version of Sweet thing (8.35). After Aladdin Sane: "Hallo Philadelphia… ooh it's so hot in Philadelphia. You couldn't sleep last night so you spent your evening on your wonderful… " Great guitar solo during Panic in Detroit.	2 CDR 2 CDR 2 CDR 2 CDR 2 CD Tape	*Philadelphia, evening, 12 July 1974 (BowieHobby)* *David Bowie is Alive and Well and Living only in Theory (No label, no number)* *Philly Dog (Old Gold Records OGCD 108 A/B)* *New Haven '74 (8 songs) (Old Gold Records OGCD 195A/B)* *The Tower PA July 12th 1974 (A Dutch Connection CD 120774)* quality 7, 90 min.
<u>14-7-1974</u> New Haven (Cape Cod), Coliseum. Attendance: 7.200. Again a great version of Sweet thing (8.31). The song also had a nice middle-part, with the saxophone. Beautiful piano part at the begin of Changes.	2 CDR 2 CDR 2 CDR Tape	*New Haven '74 (Old Gold Records 195A/B) (with bonus tracks)* *New Haven '74 (Old Gold Records 195A/B) (without bonus tracks)* *Candidate (No label, no number)* quality 9, 90 min.
<u>15-7-1974</u> Waterbury (Providence), Palace Theatre.	NT	
<u>16-7-1974</u> Boston, Music Hall. Attendance: 4.225. A good concert. Bowie and the band played the 20 songs 100% concentrated. Bowie's only talk between songs is to introduce the band. Rock 'n' roll suicide is a good finale to the concert.	2 CDR 3 CDR 2 CDR 2 CDR 2 CDR Tape	*No soul in Boston (Down Under Discs)* *Hunger cities (Old Gold Records OGCD 037A/B/C)* *Knock on Boston* *At the Music Hall Boston (NEO)* *Boston 16/7/74 (No label, no number)*
<u>17-7-1974</u> Hartford, Bushnell Auditorium (Memorial Hall). Attendance: 2.730.	NT	

18-7-1974 Arrived in New York. Bowie and Visconti worked a few days in Manhattan's Electric Lady studios on the mix of the LP David Live.

18-7-1974 In the evening. Jaime DeCarlo Lotts Andrews (vice-president of MainMan) put down his pants, sat on the Xerox machine, spread his cheeks and printed copies of his anus. He dropped one on everyone's desk to welcome the MainMan staff the next morning (Stardust - Henry Edwards and Tony Zanetta 1986).

DATE / EVENT	AUDIO / VIDEO	TITLE
19-7-1974 New York, Madison Square Garden. Sound check at 18.00 h.	NT	
19-7-1974 New York, Madison Square Garden. Attendance: 9.800. Filmed by MainMan, never officially released. Jac Colello did Bowie's hair. A good concert. Sweet thing is really great, with nice guitar work and ending with piano improvisation, that went straight into Changes, superb! After Suffragette city: "Good evening New York, nice to be here. This is a song I wrote for some friends of mine Mott the Hoople." Nice version of Knock on wood.	2 CDR Tape Video	*Halloween Jack in Hunger City (No label, no number)*
20-7-1974 New York, Madison Square Garden. Attendance: 9.800. Promoter: Ron Delsener. A very good concert. Filmed by MainMan, never officially released. The set was unloaded at the front entrance (the truck was to big for the street to the back entrance). Before Jean Genie he says: "I like to congratulate you all. You're a very successful audience." Afterwards a small party at the Plaza Hotel attended by Mick Jagger, Bette Midler, Rudolf Nureyev. Bowie, Jagger and Bette Midler spend about 45 minutes together in a walk-in closet (Backstage passes - Angela Bowie and Patrick Carr 1993). For the road crew there was a party at the Ice Palace Discotheque. Bowie stayed at the Sherry Netherland Hotel.	2 CDR 2 CDR 2 CDR 3 CDR 2 CDR 2 CDR 2 CDR Tape Tape Video	*New York 20 July 1974 (BowieHobby)* *You're wonderful!* *Class of '74 Vol 2 (EgoDisc 004/005)* *Hunger cities (Old Gold Records OGCD 037A/B/C)* *New York 1974 (No label, no number)* *Live N.Y. 20/7/74 (No label, no number)* *Ottawa 74 (2 songs) (No label, no number)* quality 8, 90 min. quality 8, 80 min.

Bowie about the band: "They would be bugging me about coming out in front and I kept telling them that I didn't have any parts for them and stay behind those bloody sheets because it doesn't look like a street. But they started straying out, and how appropriate it was, because the tour started to collapse and we were trying to depict a destroyed city. The city was supposed to fall apart and now the tour did" (David Robert Jones: The discography of a generalist - David Jeffrey Fletcher 1979).

20-7-1974 Village Voice. Article: Dancing at disaster's edge.

27-7-1974 New Musical Express. Article by Lisa Robinson: David Bowie has left the theatre.

End July 1974 Bowie had a conversation with Tony Zanetta about his earnings and the MainMan expenses. Zanetta explained him he only got 50 percent of his own income, from which all expenses would be deducted. The other 50 percent (without deduction of expenses) was for DeFries. Bowie presumed he got 50% of what was left after deducting costs. A bell started to ring and he finally understood why DeFries didn't mind the absurd high costs of the MainMan machine (Stardust - Henry Edwards and Tony Zanetta 1986).

End July / begin August 1974 Philadelphia, Sigma Sound Studios, Ninth 12th Street. Second part of the

DATE / EVENT	AUDIO / VIDEO	TITLE

recordings LP People from bad homes - Ava Cherry and the Astronettes.
David and Ava Cherry went to: Apollo Club in Harlem and various black and Latin clubs. They went to see The Jackson Five at Madison Square Garden.
Ava Cherry and Michael Kamen recorded a souled-up version of Sweet thing.
Bowie stayed at The Barclay Hotel.

August 1974 Creem. Article by Lester Bangs: Swan dive into the mung.
Bangs wrote: D-d-d-decadence, that's what this album's all about, thematically and conceptually.

August 1974 Richmond, The Wick. Recording It's only rock 'n' roll - Rolling Stones (5.08).
David Bowie and Ron Wood did the backing vocals. Bowie and Jagger dubbed the song.
Later on the Stones re-recorded the song but couldn't get it right and decided to keep this version and overdubbed the original version for their album It's only rock 'n' roll.
Around the same time Mick Jagger and David Bowie helped Ron Wood to write the song I can feel the fire for his solo album I've got my own album to do. They also did the backing vocals (According to the Rolling Stones - The Rolling Stones 2003).

August 1974 Recording ballad-version After Today.

August 1974 New York. Bowie attends a Bruce Springsteen concert at Max's Kansas City and The Jacksons at Madison Square Garden.

Tony Zanetta: "He'd discovered cocaine with a vengeance. It was like his year to play drug addict. He was staying up for four or five days" (In other words - Kerry Juby 1986). Norman Fisher was Bowie's dealer in New York.

1-8-1974 Rolling Stone. Article by Ken Emerson: New Bowie: A dog.

6-8-1974 Release Single Andy Warhol (3.02) / Dizzy heights - Dana Gillespie (RCA 2446).
A-side written by Bowie.

11-8-1974 Philadelphia, Sigma Sound Studios.
Begin recording LP Young Americans. Working title of LP: Shilling the rube(s).
11-8-1974 Recording song Young Americans.
Bowie heard on the radio the DJ just had a visit of Bruce Springsteen. Bowie called the radio station and the DJ went out to look for Springsteen. Bruce came by in the studio and they talked for hours. Springsteen slept on the couch and the next day David recorded Springsteen's 1973 song It's hard to be a saint in the city (David Bowie - Dave Thompson 1986).
Bowie stayed at the Berkeley Hotel and had a blue Cadillac limousine.

13-8-1974 Bowie met the Three Degrees.

17-8-1974 Release Single Slaughter on 10th avenue / Growing up and I'm fine (3.12) - Mick Ronson (RCA). B-side written by Bowie.

17-8-1974 Release Promo-EP (RCA DJEO-0259) including: Andy Warhol (3.02) - Dana Gillespie.

22-8-1974 Release Rock 'n' roll with me / The divine daze of deathless delight - Donovan (Epic EPC 2661). A-side written by Bowie and Peace.

DATE / EVENT	AUDIO / VIDEO	TITLE

End August on the last night of the recordings Bowie invited a group of fans in. They had been given the name The Sigma Kids, because they hung around the studio everyday. That Thursday evening they were the first fans to hear the new album. At first they were a little surprised, then they asked to hear the songs again and started to dance (Strange fascination - David Buckley 1999).

August / September 1974. Melody Maker. Article: Bowie on a soul kick.

September 1974 New York. A play called Femme Fatale, directed by Tony Ingrassia.
Wayne / Jayne County made his / her stage debut. Other "actors": Patti Smith (as a mafia dyke) and transvestite Jackie Curtis.

September 1974 In the house of Elizabeth Taylor in Beverly Hills Bowie.
Elizabeth Taylor introduced Bowie (who had a look of genuine admiration in his eyes) to John Lennon. Bowie was very shy and hardly spoke to Lennon. When John Lennon and his girlfriend May Pang left, Taylor and Bowie sat on a couch in a deserted room at the back of the house. They seemed to be long lost friends, sharing the most intimate secrets (Loving John: The untold story - May Pang and Henry Edwards).

September 1974 New York. Radio WNEW. They broadcast a trailer for 'Women's Night,' spoken by John Lennon: "All females admitted at half price. Oh, good, Bowie can get in!"

September 1974 David and Angie stayed at The Beverly Wilshire Hotel in Hollywood.
DeFries was in the Christian Dior suite, Marc Bolan in the Marc Bolan suite. Mick Jagger and the Stones were also there.

September 1974 Crawdaddy. Article by Mick Brown: This man taught David Bowie his moves.

September 1974 George O'Dowd (Boy George) moved to Oxleas wood (Shooters Hill). He covered his walls with pictures of Bowie, T.Rex and David Cassidy. (Take it like a man - The Boy George Biography 1995).

The band for the September concerts:
David Bowie (vocals).
Mike Garson (piano, mellotron).
Carlos Alomar (guitar).
Doug Raunch (bass guitar).
Earl Slick (lead guitar).
Doug Raunch (bass guitar).
Greg Enrico (drums).
Pablo Rosario (percussion).
David Sanborn (alto sax, flute).
Richard Grando (baritone sax, flute).
Michael Kamen (electric piano, moog, oboe).
Geoffrey MacCormack, Ava Cherry, Gui Andrisano, Robin Clark, Anthony Hinton, Dianne Sumler and Luther Vandross (backing singers).

Earl Slick: "In 74 there was a bit of friction between me and Carlos. But Carlos was a perfect team

DATE / EVENT	AUDIO / VIDEO	TITLE

member, because there were different styles that needed to be covered. We were good as a guitar team."

<u>2-9-1974</u> Los Angeles, Universal Amphitheatre. Attendance: 6.250.
Show filmed by BBC (for documentary Cracked Actor). Attended by: Diana Ross, Bette Midler, Michael Jackson, Iggy Pop, Tatum O'Neal, Raquel Welch, Elizabeth Taylor. Marc Bolan and Gloria Jones attended, but left during All the young dudes.
Hysterical crowd. "I'll tell you what we're gonna do is play a couple of things from a new album that we've done. This is called The Young Americans." The song (5.19) was played for the first time live, as was It's gonna be me. The opening of Big Brother was very "vocal" and later on in the song the background singers played a prominent role. A special version (although I prefer to hear Bowie). Nice sound effects during The Jean Genie.
Bowie stayed at the Sunset Marquis.

2 CDR	*Los Angeles 2 Sept 1974* (BowieHobby)
CD	*The band was altogether* (No label, no number)
1 CDR	*Dress rehearsal* (Old Gold Records OGCD 135)
4 CDR	*The west coast shows '74* (Old Gold Records OGCD 035A/B/C/D)
2 CDR	*LA'74 Amphiteatre First Show* (No label, no number)
2 CDR	*Class of '74 Vol 3* (EgoDisc 006/007)
2 CDR	*Cracked in the past* (No label, no number)
Tape	quality 8, 90 min.
Video	20 min.

Gloria Jones (Marc Bolan's girlfriend): "Marc loved soul music, but I think David just went a little deeper into it. He totally changed over to R&B."

Mickey Finn (T.Rex): "The difference between Marc Bolan and Bowie is that Bowie changed with the seasons. He upgraded his material to change his style. Marc had this hit formula but he never moved on."

<u>3-9-1974</u> Los Angeles, Universal Amphitheatre. Attendance: 6.250.
Before the show Bowie was interviewed by Robert Hilburn for Melody Maker (published on 14-9-1974).

Tape

<u>4-9-1974</u> Los Angeles, Universal Amphitheatre. Attendance: 6.250.
A very good concert and a great crowd response. When the concert is over and Bowie has left the stage the audience goes on applauding for a long time.
Bowie stayed at the Sunset Marquis.

2 CDR	*Los Angeles 4 Sept 1974* (BowieHobby)
4 CDR	*The west coast shows '74* (Old Gold Records OGCD 035A/B/C/D)
2 CDR	*Class of '74 Vol 1* (EgoDisc 002/003)
LP	*Stardust from the 70's* (BO-16)
Tape	quality 8, 80 min.

<u>5-9-1974</u> Los Angeles, Universal Amphitheatre. Attendance: 6.250.
A very good concert.
The concert was broadcast on Radio.
The quality of the bootlegs is superb (for that time).
As intro for the show Bowie used sound effects from Mick

2 CD	*Wealth and Authority* (Shout to the top)
2 CD	*The duke of L.A.* (Papillion Records PPL CD 010-2)
2 CD	*Strange fascination*

DATE / EVENT	AUDIO / VIDEO	TITLE
Ronson's 1974 LP Slaughter on 10th Avenue. During the show Bowie now and then talks with an Italian accent. No idea why he does this, but it sounds funny and makes the tapes and CD's of this concert very recognisable. "We did a new song earlier. This is another new song, from an album we just finished: John I'm only dancing." The song never made the LP. Years later it was released as a bonus track on the CD-version of Young Americans, together with It's gonna be me (6.27). Because of the good sound quality this is the most bootlegged show of the 1974 tour. A must for every collector. Bowie stayed at the Sunset Marquis. In Los Angeles Iggy Pop joined them for a couple of days.	2 CD 2 CDR 2 CD CD CD CD CD 2 CDR 2 CD 2 CD CD CDS 2 CDR 1 CDR 2 LP LP Single Single Single Single Tape	(BOW 001/2) Strange fascination (TOM 001/2) A Sweet thing (No label, no number) A portrait in flesh (070459-1) Cracked actor (Oil Well RSC CD 056) Big Brother (Oil Well RSC CD 057) In concert 1974 part one (Super Golden Radio Shows SGRS No. 011) In concert 1974 part two (Super Golden Radio Shows SGRS No. 012) Class of '74 Vol 2 (3 songs) (EgoDisc 004/005) Class of '74 Vol 3 (3 songs) (EgoDisc 006/007) Bowie 1974 (BOW 741/742) Pinups 2 (1 song) (BOWPU02) Bowie 74 Live (WR 201) Cyberstation (1 song) (STATIONTOBOWIE) This is your life (3 songs) (PD 81997) Strange fascination (A Lomart Production C DB A/B) The missing link (Shelter 252570) (2 tracks) Bowie 74 Live (WR 201) (3 tr.) Bowie 1974 (BOW 1) (3 tracks) *Cracked actor / Cracked actor (CD Various Singles - 1)* Cracked heroes / Sexy actor (Cracked actor) (Slat Records TM)
<u>6-9-1974</u> Los Angeles, Universal Amphitheatre. Attendance: 6.250. Nice concert, very similar to the previous days. A pity of the bad quality of this (short) tape with only 7 songs.	1 CDR Tape	Los Angeles, 6 Sept 1974 (BowieHobby) quality 6, 29 min.
<u>7-9-1974</u> Los Angeles, Universal Amphitheatre. Attendance: 6.250.	Tape	

DATE / EVENT	AUDIO / VIDEO	TITLE
<u>8-9-1974</u> Los Angeles, Universal Amphitheatre. Attendance: 6.250.	Tape	
BBC Video Cracked Actor Working title was: The Collector. Cracked actor, Sweet thing, Moonage daydream, Time, Space oddity, Rock 'n' roll suicide, Diamond dogs, John I'm only dancing (again). Partly filmed in Los Angeles Universal Amphitheatre, period 2 to 8-9-1974.	1 CDR VCD LP LP	*The Cracked actor doc. 1993* *Cracked Actor (No label, no number)* The Cracked Actor (SNJS 38 MW 7 A/III) Stardust from the 70's (BO 16) not complete
<u>11-9-1974</u> San Diego, Sports Arena. Attendance: 15.000. They stayed at The Hilton Inn Hotel. A very good concert. Not a negative thing I can write down about this concert.	2 CDR 2 CD 4 CDR 2 CDR Tape	*San Diego 11 September 1974 (BowieHobby)* *The Strangest living curiosities (No label, no number)* *The west coast shows '74 (Old Gold Records OGCD 035A/B/C/D)* Pulsars Unreal quality 8, 90 min.

13-9-1974 Release Knock on wood (3.03) / Panic in Detroit (5.52) (RCA 2466).

| <u>13-9-1974</u> Tucson, Convention Center. | NT | |

14-9-1974 Melody Maker. Interview by Robert Hilburn (in Los Angeles before the concert of 3-9-1974): Bowie finds his voice.

<u>14-9-1974</u> Phoenix, Arizona Veteran's Memorial Coliseum. Attendance: 15.000.	NT	
<u>16-9-1974</u> Los Angeles, Anaheim Convention Center. Attendance: 15.000. Concert attended by Elizabeth Taylor, Raquel Welch, Diana Ross, Tatum O'Neal.	NT	
<u>17-9-1974</u> Los Angeles, Anaheim Convention Center. Attendance: 15.000.	NT	

According to Tony Zanetta (MainMan) a total of seven shows was cancelled between 16th September and 5th October. I have no further info about dates and places.

| <u>Last two weeks September / begin October 1974</u>, Los Angeles. Rehearsals. | NT | |

During one of these rehearsals Elizabeth Taylor and her boy friend Henry Weinberg were present. Taylor was drinking Jack Daniels, while slapping her thigh at the rhythm (Presenting David Bowie! - David Douglas 1975).

DATE / EVENT	AUDIO / VIDEO	TITLE

October 1974 Released album It's only rock 'n' roll - Rolling Stones (Rolling Stones Records 450202 2). Includes: It's only rock 'n' roll (5.08). Backing vocals by Ron Wood and David Bowie.

October 1974 Release in US Rock 'n' roll with me (4.00) / Panic in Detroit (RCA PB.10105).

Geoff MacCormack: "We wrote it in Oakley Street. David was fiddling around on a tiny piano. He got up and I started fiddling around with a chord sequence and stuff that I had just written. My contribution was round the verse part."

October 1974 That what it's all about. Interview with Mike Garson about Aladdin Sane.	1 CDR Video	25 Years of Ziggy Stardust (No label, no number0 Various 14 (4 min)
October 1974 Philadelphia. Philly WMMR 93.3. Hosted by Rd Sharkey. Interview with Angie, talking about RCA, Pin-ups 2, studio work with Bruce Springsteen.	Tape	quality 9, 35 min.

The Philly Dogs Tour (Soul Tour):
David Bowie and the Mike Garson Band:
David Bowie (vocals).
Mike Garson (piano, mellotron).
Carlos Alomar (guitar).
Earl Slick (lead guitar).
Emir Ksasan (bass guitar).
Dennis Davis (drums).
Pablo Rosario (percussion).
David Sanborn (alto sax, flute).
Richard Grando (baritone sax, flute).
Michael Kamen (electric piano, moog, oboe).
Geoffrey MacCormack, Ava Cherry, Robin Clark, Jean Fineberg, Anthony Hinton, Dianne Sumler and Luther Vandross (backing singers).

<u>5-10-1974</u> St. Paul, Civic Center. Attendance: 15.000.	NT	
<u>8-10-1974</u> Indianapolis, Indiana Convention Center. Attendance: 10.536.	NT	
<u>10-10-1974</u> Madison, University of Wisconsin. Somebody up there likes me is added to the song list. After Moonage daydream Bowie speaks he first words: "Ah Madison, it's a privilege to be here" and he starts singing Rock 'n' roll with me. A very good concert and Bowie works very hard and with a lot of feeling to make the songs sound at their best. This is probably my favourite concert of the Soul Tour. Maybe also because of the excellent	1 CDR CD CD	1974 (Remastered) (A Dutch Connection CD101074) Somebody up there likes me (not complete) (DB 371) Dawn of the Dogs (4 songs) (A Paranoid Production BOW 74)

DATE / EVENT	AUDIO / VIDEO	TITLE
quality of the bootleg 1974 Remastered (one of the few good recordings of that time). He announces Can you hear me in a hoarse voice: "This is a song for girls." "Here's a new song… we just recorded her for a brand new album release next year called Young Americans."	1 CDR	Port Chester 8.6.74 (3 songs)
	2 CD	David Bowie '1974' (Fire Power FP-0050-A/B)
	1 CDR	Can you hear me? (Old Gold Records OGCD 003)
	2 CDR	Somebody up there likes me Version 1 (No label, no number)
	2 CDR	Somebody up there likes me Version 2 (No label, no number)
	2 CDR	The Legendary Soul Tour (David Bowie on Stage DBOS 101074)
	LP	Somebody up there likes me (MIW Records 20 MW 20 A/B)
	Tape	quality 7, 85 min.
	Tape	quality 8, 75 min.

10-10-1974 Rolling Stone. Article by Richard Cromelin: Bowie - Time for another Ch-Ch-Change.

10-10-1974 Rolling Stone. Article by M. Damsker: Philly Stopover: Fans and Funk.

<u>11-10-1974</u> Madison, University of Wisconsin or Dane County Coliseum.	NT	

11-10-1974 Los Angeles. The Palladium. Hollywood Street Revival and Dance. Dubbed by Kim Fowley to "Death of Glitter" night. Attended by Iggy Pop, New York Dolls, Silverhead.

<u>13-10-1974</u> Milwaukee, Mecca Arena. Attendance: 11.874.	NT	

Mid October 1974 ABC-TV. Mike Douglas show. Bowie 73. Contains Hammersmith Odeon film clips and Angie's singing debut, also an interview with Angie.	Tape Video	quality 9, 20 min. quality 9, 20 min.

<u>16-10-1974</u> Detroit, Michigan Palace. In Detroit they stayed in The Hotel St. Regis. He heard a radio program about a flying saucer that had crashed in Arizona. One of the attendants had to call the radio station and the Air Force Base that was mentioned (Presenting David Bowie! - David Douglas 1975). Again a very good show The way the speaker introduced Bowie during Space oddity worked out very well. At the start of The Jean Genie Bowie plays a small part of Love me do on his mouth-organ and sings 2 lines of the song. Very nice version of Knock on wood (4.02). One of the	2 CDR	Detroit 16 October 1974 (BowieHobby)
	2 CD	Infected with Soul love (Savage Hippo Records SH112)
	3 CDR	The Soul Tour (Old Gold Records OGCD 036A/B/C)
	2 CDR	David live, The Palace Detroit (No label, no number)
	2 CDR	Plastic Soul (KTLA CD66 1/2)
	2 CD	Chicago Soul 74

DATE / EVENT	AUDIO / VIDEO	TITLE

very few existing live recordings of these song.

		(A Dutch Connection CD 211074)
	2 CDR	Mr. Diamond Dog
	2 CDR	Detroit 74 First Night
	Tape	quality 8, 90 min.

Earl Slick: "All of a sudden it's all change and I become serious unhappy. I'm starting to feel like a fuckin' throwaway. David had gone completely in a direction I didn't like and it wasn't the way I play."

<u>17-10-1974</u> Detroit, Michigan Palace.   Tape
Between songs Bowie told about the news of the flying saucer he had heard the night before and his theories about space in general (Presenting David Bowie! - David Douglas 1975).

18-10-1974 Release LP Butterfly - Barbra Streisand (Columbia PC 33005).
Including a cover version of Life on Mars.
Bowie commented: "Sorry Barbra, but I prefer to listen to my own version." Even in 1999 Bowie still commented on this cover version. He really disliked it!

<u>18-10-1974</u> Detroit, Michigan Palace.   Tape

<u>19-10-1974</u> Detroit, Michigan Palace.   Tape

<u>20-10-1974</u> Detroit, Michigan Palace.   Tape

<u>21-10-1974</u> Chicago, Arie Crown Theatre.   NT
Attendance: 4.500.
A lot of tapes and CDR's circulate with the date 21-10-1974. This should be Detroit, 16-10-1974. As far as I know there is no audio of this concert.

In Chicago Bowie went to the Playboy Mansion, to play pool with Ava Cherry's friends. Here he met her sister Tandalaya Shimek and her friend Claudia Jennings (Playmate of the year).
David and Ava also visited Ava's parents.

<u>22-10-1974</u> Chicago, Arie Crown Theatre.   Tape
Attendance: 4.500.

<u>23-10-1974</u> Chicago, Arie Crown Theatre.   Tape
Attendance: 4.500.

25-10-1974 US TV. NBC.   *Video*   *Stolp tapes no. 18 (10 min)*
Jean Genie and Round and round from 3-7-1973.

<u>28-10-1974</u> New York, Radio City Music Hall.   2 CD   Infected with soul love
Attendance: 6.200. Tickets: USD 10,50 (for a concert of   (complete concert)
only 50 minutes).   (Savage Hippo Records
David performs Footstompin' for the first time.   SH112)

DATE / EVENT	AUDIO / VIDEO	TITLE
The original is by the Flares in 1961. His cousin Kristina is backstage. "When I come to New York, I usually get the flu. Well, I got it again as usually." After Rock 'n' roll suicide: "Hey, you're wonderful. Hey, and I'm wonderful. Yeah, we're all wonderful. All you got to do is win, when you're trying not to loose." Pablo Rosario: "David was doing to much cocaine. He looked like a tiger in a cage, going from side to side of the stage."	4 CD LP Single Single Tape Tape	The North American Tours (Pearls Before Swine PBS 1037 / 1038 / 1039 / 1040) The missing link (Strap Records) John I'm only dancing (again) / Sorrow / Changes (Wild Cat BOW 1 331/1) Rebel rebel / Young Americans / 1984 / Footstompin' (Wild Cat Record Company BOW 2) quality 7, 100 min. quality 8, 100 min.

29-10-1974 New York Times. John Rockwell wrote: "David looked self-consciously uncomfortable without routines to act out and he was in a hoarse voice."

29-10-1974 New York Post. Jan Hodenfeld wrote: "The show was a sumptuous birthday cake, made out of cardboard with a hollow centre."

29-10-1974 Zoo World. Jack Hiemenz wrote: "It was a disaster. Something like a bad night in Las Vegas, totally mediocre."

29-10-1974 Release 2LP David Live (RCA CPL.2.0771).
Culled from performances made on July 10 and 11, 1974 at the Tower Theatre, Philadelphia.

Bowie about the album: "David Live was the final death of Ziggy. God that album! I've never played it. The tension it must contain must be like vampires teeth coming down on you. And that photo on the cover. My God, it looks like I've just stepped out of the grave. That's actually how I felt. That record should have been called David Bowie Is Alive And Living Only In Theory" (David Bowie - An illustrated record - Roy Carr and Charles S.Murray 1981).

29-10-1974 David Live commercial.	*Video*	*Various 26 (30 sec)*
29-10-1974 New York, Radio City Music Hall. Attendance: 6.200.	NT	

29-10-1974 New York. Wide World of Entertainment. Recording Dick Cavett Show. Broadcast 4-12-1974.

30-10-1974 New York, Radio City Music Hall. Attendance: 6.200.	Tape	90 min.
31-10-1974 New York, Radio City Music Hall. Attendance: 6.200.	NT	

November 1974 Elizabeth Taylor invited Bowie to co-star in the film The Blue bird (Bowie turned it down, he thought the script was horrible).

DATE / EVENT	AUDIO / VIDEO	TITLE

November 1974 Creem. Interview by Bruno Stein.
Bowie: "I used to work for two guys who put out a UFO magazine in England about six years ago. And I made sightings six, seven times a night for about a year, when I was in the observatory."
Stein: Ava Cherry and her girlfriend persuaded David to leave with them, to visit a millionaire who lived not far away. It was 2.30 a.m. and the rock star and four giggling black girls made their way through the lobby to the waiting limousine.

DATE / EVENT	AUDIO / VIDEO	TITLE
1-11-1974 New York, Radio City Music Hall. Attendance: 6.200.	Tape	
2-11-1974 New York, Radio City Music Hall. Attendance: 6.200.	NT	
3-11-1974 New York, Radio City Music Hall. Attendance: 6.200.	NT	
6-11-1974 Cleveland, Public Auditorium. Attendance: 8.000. Short concert (only 60 minutes). Tickets: USD 7.50. Produced by WMMS & Tormey-Hooke Productions. Sound problems during the show. After the show Bowie stayed up all night in the hotel bar and danced (with the help of cocaine) a great deal of the night.	NT	
8-11-1974 Buffalo, Memorial Auditorium. Attendance: 18.000. The day before problems with the working papers of the crew had to be solved. Tony Newman (and wife) and Jeffrey McCormack had to wait at the border until the confusion over their visas was clarified.	NT	
11-11-1974 Washington D.C., Capital Center. Attendance: 19.000. Recorded and videotaped by RCA.	Tape Video	quality 10
14-11-1974 Boston, Music Hall. Attendance: 4.225. Halfway Changes: "Hey man, I've never seen that … " One minute later: "All together!" Bowie stopped the intro to Young Americans after 36 sec.: "Good evening Boston. We're gonna do a love song. This is supposed to be one: Young Americans."	2 CDR Video	Young Bostonians (NEO) 70 min.
15-11-1974 Boston, Music Hall. Attendance: 4.225. Average concert. He sang Sorrow (original by The McCoys in 1965). At the start of Changes Bowie stops and says: "I wanna do a fast one, Panic in Detroit."	1 CDR 2 CDR 1 CDR	Boston 15 November 1974 (BowieHobby) Philly Dog (Old Gold Records OGCD 108 A/B) Soul in Boston (Old Gold Records OGCD 546)

DATE / EVENT	AUDIO / VIDEO	TITLE
	1 CDR	Boston 74 2nd Night (No label, no number)
	Tape	quality 8, 40 min.
	Tape	quality 7, 60 min.

<u>16-11-1974</u> Boston, Music Hall.　　　　　　　　　　　2 CDR　　*Young Bostonians*
Attendance: 4.225.　　　　　　　　　　　　　　　　　　　　　　*(NEO)*
During Young Americans: "Manhattan, good evening."
Nice version of Footstompin' (Flares, 1961) (3.21).
"This is a love song… It's called Can your me… it's called
Can you hear me." At the end of the concert: "Thank you,
see you tomorrow." Mistake David, you only had to do
3 concerts in Boston!

16-11-1974 Sounds. Article: Bowie remakes and remodels.

16-11-1974 New Musical Express. Article by Mick Farren: Mr. Bowie has left the theatre.

18-11-1974 The MainMan play "Fame" opened and closed on Broadway (loss USD 250.000,—).
Afterwards there was a party at Sardi's Restaurant.
Clive Barnes wrote in The New York Times: "It was Fame but not fortune. The best part of this limp rag of a comedy based on the life and times of Marilyn Monroe came at intermission."

<u>18-11-1974</u> Pittsburgh, Stanley Theatre (Civic Arena).　　NT
In Pittsburgh they stayed in The William Penn Hotel.

<u>19-11-1974</u> Pittsburgh, Stanley Theatre (Civic Arena).　　NT

22 or 23-11-1974 Philadelphia. Artemis Club.
Bowie, Mike Garson, Warren Peace and Ava Cherry were having a drink. A policeman asked Bowie for his identity papers to prove he was not under aged. Bowie said: "That's quite flattering actually. Everybody knows that I'm at least fifty-two."

<u>24-11-1974</u> Philadelphia, Spectrum Arena.　　　　　　　2 CDR　　*Philadelphia 24 November*
Attendance: 17.500. A good concert.　　　　　　　　　　　　　　　*1974 (BowieHobby)*
A fan threw a pillow with Bowie's face stitched on it in　　　1 CDR　　*It's only rock 'n' roll (Old*
needlepoint. Bowie said: "I've never sat on my own face　　　　　　*Gold Records OGCD 109)*
before." A part of It's only rock 'n' roll during Diamond　　　2 CDR　　*Philadelphia 24 Nov 74*
Dogs. David did the backing vocals for the original　　　　　Tape　　quality 7, 73 min.
Rolling Stones version in 1974.

25-11-1974 Uniondale, Nassau Veterans Memorial
Coliseum.
Cancelled.

<u>25-11-1974</u> Philadelphia, Spectrum Arena.　　　　　　　NT
Attendance: 17.500.

24-11- or 25-11-1974 A backstage party in a bar, also the Sigma Kids were present. Broken up by a

DATE / EVENT	AUDIO / VIDEO	TITLE

police-raid.

26-11-1974 Norfolk, Scope Convention Hall.
Cancelled.

26-11-1974 Uniondale, Nassau Veteran's Memorial.
Attendance: 16.500.
After Moonage daydream: "Good evening. This is a love song. I think it is."
The audience goes wild.

	1 CDR	*Uniondale 26 Nov 1974 (1) (BowieHobby)*
	1 CDR	*Uniondale 26 Nov 1974 (2) (BowieHobby)*
	2 CDR	*Uniondale 26 Nov 1974 (3) (BowieHobby)*
	1 CDR	*Uniondale '74 (Old Gold Records OGCD 113)*
	2 CDR	*New Haven '74 (1 song) (Old Gold Records 195A/B)*
	Tape	quality 5, 85 min.
	Tape	quality 6, 80 min.

28-11-1974 Bowie's limousine broke down and the local police had to take him to Memphis to be on time for the show.

28-11-1974 Memphis, Mid-South Coliseum (Auditorium).   NT
Attendance: 12.000.

30-11-1974 Nashville, Municipal Auditorium.   NT
Attendance: 9.000.

December 1974 Bowie and Bette Midler recorded a demo of the disco song "Do the Ruby."

December 1974 New York. Filming video for Young Americans.

December 1974 Hit Parader. Article by Leee Black Childers: On tour with David Bowie.

1-12-1974 Atlanta, The Omni (Omni Arena).
Attendance: 16.750.
A good concert.
Jean Genie had the "Love me do - intro."
"... of making up underwear... Never give anybody who said that... Jean Genie lives on his back."

	1 CDR	*Atlanta 1 December 1974 (BowieHobby)*
	1 CDR	*Win (No label, no number)*
	CD	*The band was altogether (No label, no number)*
	1 CDR	*Dress rehearsal (Old Gold Records OGCD 135)*
	3 CDR	*The Soul Tour (Old Gold Records OGCD 036A/B/C)*
	Tape	quality 8, 70 min.

1-12-1974 There was a party at the Hyatt-Regency Hotel. The police held a drug-raid and Tony Zanetta was arrested because it was his suite and he was charged for the drugs that were dropped on the floor when the police came (In other words - Kerry Juby 1986).

DATE / EVENT	AUDIO / VIDEO	TITLE

2-12-1974 DeFries bailed out Zanetta.
Bowie went to New York by car, to his suite at The Pierre Hotel.

2-12-1974 Tuscalousa, University of Alabama.
Cancelled.

<u>4-12-1974</u> US TV. NBC. Dick Cavett Show.
Recorded 29-10-1974 in New York for Wide World of
Entertainment (Radio City Residency).
1. Introduction (3.50).
2. 1984 (3.05).
3. Young Americans (5.19).
4. Interview (18.34).
5. Announcement, Footstompin' / Sister Kate (3.24).
Also on the bill: Roy Dotrice (British actress).

During the interview Dick Cavett asked: "What does your mother think about you?"
Bowie: "She pretends I'm not her son. We never had such a close bond, but we have a certain contact with each other."

For more details about this interview read the part I wrote (with the help of Raymond Stolp) about the Cracked actor documentary.

	AUDIO / VIDEO	TITLE
	1 CDR	*The Dick Cavett Show, 29-10-1974 (BowieHobby)*
	CD	*Look back in anger (3)*
		(No label, no number)
	CD	*RarestOneBowie (5)*
	1 CDR	*MoreRareBowie (5)*
		(No label, no number)
	3 CDR	*The Soul Tour (1,2,3,4,5)*
		(Old Gold Records OGCD 036A/B/C)
	1 CDR	*Dick & Dinah*
		(No label, no number)
	CD	*TV-DB-15 (1,2,3,5)*
	CD	*Footstompin' 74, "Live" Dick Cavett Show 29/10/1974) (A Dutch Connection)*
	CD	*Anthology (5)*
		(BOW 1999)
	2 CDR	*Cracked in the past (1,2,3,5)*
		(No label, no number)
	2 CDR	*The European Cannon is here*
	2 CDR	*Deafacating Ecstacy*
		(No label, no number)
	1 CDR	*The Dick Cavett Show*
	1 CDR	*Alternative Young Americans*
	1 VCD	***Various 1 (11.16 min.) (2,3,5)***
	1 VCD	*The Dick Cavett Show*
	LP	*Stowie (BSS 715 A/B)*
	Tape	*quality 10, 15 min.*
	Single	*Footstompin' (Funk House Records 83530)*
	Video	*Stolp tapes no. 1 (12 min)*
	Video	*Stolp tapes no. 1 (15 min)*
	Video	*Stolp tapes no. 23 (2 min)*
	Video	*Various 20 (40 min)*
	Video	*Various 26 (12 min)*

December 1974 New York's Pierre Hotel. Bowie made silent black and white test footage for a Diamond Dogs film. John Lennon attended part of it. Iggy Pop did some acting for the Bowie's. A flying saucer from this footage was used in the sleeve artwork for Earthling in 1996. Confirmed by Angie Bowie in the book The Starzone Interviews by David Currie (1987).

12-12-1974 Senior Scholastic. Article by E.Sparn: Now more mellow, less glitter.

DATE / EVENT	AUDIO / VIDEO	TITLE

December 1974 Young Americans sessions resume at Record Plant Studios in New York.

18-12-1974 The final mixes were completed for Fascination, All you've got to do is win, and the remix of Win (Memo MainMan, 19-12-1974).

Christmas 1974 St. Pierre Hotel with Angie, Zowie, Tony Zanetta and Jaime Andrews.

Late 1974 Las Vegas. Bowie and Ava Cherry visited a Frank Sinatra concert. Sinatra refused to meet Bowie backstage.

1975 US TV. Rena Barret Show. Appearance by Bowie and Angie.

Angie tried to get as much publicity as possible. When she entered the restaurant White Elephant in Curson Street to have dinner with a minister and Michael Caine and Ken Glancey (head RCA London). Angie wore a beautiful dress. Only, she wore the dress backwards. She took of her dress and everybody looked at her breasts.
In the Dick Cavett show she popped out a tit.
Dick Cavett: "Ummmm, yes Angela, it is indeed a bit hot in here, isn't it?"
Angie: "No, you were not talking to me. And now you are, aren't you?" (David Bowie - Jerry Hopkins 1985).

1975 Rock Superstars. Clip of the Spiders doing The Jean Genie.

1975 Recording of 3 songs with Keith Moon: Naked man (3.23), Do me good (2.49), Real emotion (3.01). Seems to have Bowie and various other guests on backing vocal. This is not audible to me, so I have strong doubts if this is correct. Released as bonus tracks in 1997 and 2000.

1975 Cleveland. "Duke" interview.   Tape   quality 8, 15 min.

1975 Suicide. Article by D. Nigro: Death and suicide in modern lyrics.

1975 Article by David Lewin: Will the real David Bowie stand up.

1975 Book published: Presenting David Bowie - David Douglas (New York, Pinnacle, ISBN 0-523-00724-8).

1975 Book published in US: Valentines and vitriol - Rex Reed.

1975 Released I've got my own album to do - Ron Wood. Includes: I can feel the fire. Written by Wood, Bowie and Mick Jagger. Bowie and Jagger also did the backing vocals.

January 1975 Creem. Article by Lester Bangs: Johnny Ray's better whirlpool: The new living Bowie.

January 1975 Creem. Article by R.A. Hull: David Live.

January 1975 Creem. Article by Ben Edmonds: Mick Ronson, One of the Boys.

January 1975 New York. Went to see: Lance Loud's Band in Trude Heller's club (together with

DATE / EVENT	AUDIO / VIDEO	TITLE

Cherry Vanilla), Patti Smith (and support band Television) at CBGB's, Manhattan Transfer at Café Carlyle (together with Mick Jagger).

1-1-1975 Bowie called Mel Ilberman about 5 times, to talk about his MainMan contract.

Begin January 1975 Recording of Fame.

12-1-1975 Young Americans sessions conclude at Record Plant and Electric Lady Studios in New York. Working title LP: One damn song.

2nd Week January 1975 Bowie lived with Angie, Zowie, Corinne and Ava Cherry in a rented house in West 20th Street.
In 1976, a year after Bowie left, the house was on fire and remained deserted until 1985.
Bowie and John Dove started working on the movie Diamond Dogs, but eventually the project was cancelled.

26-1-1975 UK TV. Russell Harty Plus. Interview with Angie (about modelling and living with Bowie).	Video Tape	15 min. quality 7, 15 min.
26-1-1975 Alan Yentob's documentary Cracked Actor broadcast on BBC-TV (first time in UK). Nicolas Roeg saw it and asked Bowie for the role of Thomas Newton in The man who fell to earth.	*Video* *Video*	*Stolp tapes nr. 6 (54 min)* *Various 8 (62 min)*

29-1-1975 With Michael Lippman to RCA's offices on the Avenue of Americanas to meet Ilberman, Hannington and Glancey. Bowie asked for financial support.

February 1975 Midnight Special. Salute to David Bowie. Special by Wolfman Jack. Bowie appeared in this tribute to him.	Tape Video	15 min 10 min.

Begin 1975 RCA set up an office for Bowie in the Algon Quin Hotel, staffed by Pat Gibbons.

February 1975 Stereo Review. Article by Steve Simels: Bowie: three ways, no way.

12-2-1975 New York, Madison Square Garden. Bowie, Mick and Bianca Jagger and Ava Cherry attended a Led Zeppelin concert. Bowie was very interested in their laser show. A few days later Bowie and Angie visited the band at the Plaza Hotel.	3 CDR	*Flying Circus - Led Zeppelin (Remasters)*
21-2-1975 BBC1's Top of the Pops shows live footage of the current single, Young Americans (from Dick Cavett Show, 4-12-1974)	Video	

21-2-1975 Release Young Americans (5.10) / Suffragette City (3.45) (RCA 2523).

21-2-1975 Release in US: Young Americans (3.12) / Knock on wood (3.03) (RCA JB. 10152).

DATE / EVENT	AUDIO / VIDEO	TITLE

22-2-1975 New Musical Express. Article by Bruno Stein: UFO's, Hitler and David Bowie.

28-2-1975 Release LP Play don't worry - Mick Ronson (RCA Victor APLI 0681). Includes White light white heat (4.08) with the instrumental part of the Pinups sessions of July 1973 and his own vocal.

28-2-1975 Meeting Ilberman, Glancey and DeFries.

March 1975 Release in Poland one side picture 'postcard' flexi Young Americans (Tonpress R 0681).

March 1975 US TV. Young Americans advert. Includes playback clip of single Young Americans.	*Video*	*Various 20 (1 min)*

March 1975 New York. Attends a Rod Stewart concert at Madison Square Garden (accompanied by Ava Cherry and Warren Peace). They also visited the backstage party after the concert.

1-3-1975 Bowie presents (17th annual) Grammy Award for the best Female Soul artist, (won by Aretha Franklin) for US TV at The Uris Theatre in New York. Aretha Franklin: "Woow this was good, I could even kiss David Bowie. And I mean that in a beautiful way." She didn't and left the stage at the right side. Bowie left the stage at the left side. John Lennon took him in his arms, kissed him and said: "David, America loves you." Also present: Yoko Ono, Simon and Garfunkel, Roberta Flack, Bette Midler, Stevie Wonder, Sarah Vaughan, Tony Orlando and Dawn, The Hudson Brothers, princess Ann-Margret, David Essex.	Tape *Video*	quality 9, 5 min. *Stolp Tapes no. 6 (5 min)*

Bowie about Lennon: "John Lennon had been through it all. John told me to stick with it, survive. You'll really go through the grind and they'll rip you off right and left. The key is to come out the other side" (Playboy, Vol.23 No.9).

2-3-1975 Alex Bennet Show. Phone-in interview with Bowie, Lennon and Yoko Ono.	3 CDR	Drunk as a lord (Old Gold Records OGCD 039A/B/C)
	1 CDR Tape	*Alex Bennet Show* quality 9, 15 min.

7-3-1975 Release LP Young Americans (RCA APL.I.0998). Working titles for the album: Somebody up there likes me, One damned song, Fascination. Eric Jacobs made the photo for the album cover.

Bowie about the song Young Americans: "A newley-wed couple who don't know if they really like each other. Well, they do, but they don't know if they do or not."
About Somebody up there likes me: "A watch out mate, Hitler is on his way back... It's your rock 'n' roll social bit."
About Across the universe: "I always thought it was fabulous but very watery in the original, and I

DATE / EVENT	AUDIO / VIDEO	TITLE

hammered the hell out of it."

Review by Ian MacDonald: "A transitional piece, created in a melancholy and confused state and compounded by a generous dose of the self-pity of the privileged."

Review by Michael Watts: "The album is designed to cast our hero in the mould of soul superstar. I get persistent picture of nigger patronisation as Bowie flips through his soul take-offs at Sigma Sound like some cocktail-party liberal."

Young Americans ad. (0.23).	1 CDR	*Cracked in the past* (No label, no number)
	Video	*Various 26 (20 sec)*

Earl Slick about the album Young Americans (he played on the album himself!): "It's the most boring thing I've ever heard" (Black Book - Barry Miles 1980).

8-3-1975 Record Mirror. Article: Bowie plans - Angie speaks!

11-3-1975 Los Angeles. Century Plaza Hotel.
Meeting DeFries, Myers, Bowie. They made an agreement, backdated 1-3-1975.
MainMan got 50% of all David's earnings in the period September 1972 - March 1975 and all future royalties on the albums of that period, including the albums Space oddity, The man who sold the world and the Decca recordings. 16% Of gross earnings from all sources in the period 1-3-1975 to 30-9-1982 and 5% of his personal appearances in that period.

After 30-9-1982 David would also have to pay royalties for the older albums, until he sold out DeFries when collecting USD 50 million with the Bowie-bonds in the nineties.

15-3-1975 New Musical Express. Article: Bowie: His final flirtation?

29-3-1975 Music Week. Article: Bowie files suit against MainMan.
They wrote: David Bowie has filed a lawsuit against his management company, MainMan, and its director Tony DeFries which seeks to terminate all management, employment, record and publishing agreements between the artist and MainMan. The action further seeks damages for breach of contract and Bowie will also claim an accounting of all funds, estimated at several million dollars, earned by him for the past five years.

April 1975 A photo was made of Bowie's crucifix before and after consuming coke. The photo was in 1995 used for the inside sleeve of the album Earthling.

April 1975 The special of the week. K-ULA. The famous "I rocked my last roll" interview.	Tape	60 min.

April 1975 BBC-TV. Repeated The cracked actor documentary (first broadcast on 26-1-1975).

5-4-1975 Melody Maker. Article by Allan Jones: Ronson: I'd like to kick sense into Bowie.

14-4-1975 Release Life on Mars? / Down by the stream - King's Singers (EMI 23 05).
A-side written by Bowie.

DATE / EVENT	AUDIO / VIDEO	TITLE

27-4-1975 Rolling Stone. Article by Cameron Crowe: Random Notes.
Bowie quoted: "DeFries never really understood what I wanted to do. The Colonel Tom Parker trip wasn't what I had in mind."

April / May 1975 Michael Lippman became Bowie's manager (for 9 months).

May 1975 Release The London Boys (3.20) / Love you till Tuesday (2.59) (Decca F. 13579).

May 1975 Release The London boys (3.20) / There is a happy land (3.11) (Decca).

May 1975 Release 2LP Images 1966-1967 (compilation) (Deram BP. 61829).

May 1975 Interviewed by Cameron Crowe for Rolling Stone (published 12-2-1976).

<u>May 1975</u> Los Angeles. OZ Studios.   NT
Jam session with Iggy Pop on acoustic guitar.
3 Songs recorded with Iggy Pop:
Turn blue, Drink to me, Sell your love.
Turn blue has different lyric.
Moving on (only Bowie, Iggy Pop had already left).

Bowie: "Again a song, this wasn't what I was waiting for. This way I make a new album every month. I already have two new ones on the shelf. Give me a break! (David Bowie - Dave Thompson 1986).

May 1975 David stayed a while with Glenn Hughes in Los Angeles.

Later he moved to the house of Michael Lippman. He almost drove Michael and Nancy Lippman nuts. He stored his urine in the fridge and held occult rituals (David Bowie - Jerry Hopkins 1985).

Then he lived with the Playboy-centrefold Claudia Jenning.

Later he rented a house at 637 North Doheny Drive in Beverly Hills and had an affair with a black actress named Winona Williams, who was the girlfriend of Alice Cooper's manager Shep Gordon (later she would talk about Bowie's sexual preference for her bottom). He met her when she gave a party at Gordon's house.
Bowie's house was professionally exorcised. Angie called Wally Elmlark in New York City and by phone he instructed Bowie how to exorcise the place (Backstage passes - Angela Bowie and Patrick Carr 1993).
That month Elton John and John Lennon visited him at North Doheny Drive.

Then he moved to 1349 Stone Canyon Drive, Bel Air.

May 1975 Los Angeles. Marc Bolan demoed some songs.
According to some rumours (a wish of a lot of Bolan fans) Bowie played piano and together with Gloria Jones did the backing vocals for Walking through that door (2.39).
It is certain Bowie was not involved.

3-5-1975 New York times. Article by John Rockwell: Hunter / Ronson at the Felt Forum.

Bowie: "I suppose I do fancy blokes quite a bit but I spend more time with chicks, particularly black chicks. The only type of chicks I can't stand are New York feminists. Get them into bed, and after five minutes they want you to do something funny with a light bulb. It's all so academic. And anyway, I love my wife."

June 1975 Creem. Article by Trixie Balm: Diamond wog.

June 1975 Crawdaddy: Article by James Graig: Young Americans.

June 1975 Bowie visited Iggy Pop in the Neuropsychiatric Institute of UCLA (the university of California, Los Angeles). Iggy was there voluntarily. Bowie was accompanied by Dean Stockwell and both were stoned. Bowie wore a space suit and offered Iggy some cocaine.

June 1975 Bowie took the Santa Fe Super Chef Railway to New Mexico.

July and August 1975 filming of The man who fell to earth, in the dessert around Lake Fenton in New Mexico. Directed by Nicholas Roeg.
During the filming the wealthy Sabrina Guiness came by and stayed with David for some time.
Bowie lived some weeks in a trailer, but most of the time he stayed at the Hotel Inn in Albuquerque. During this period Bowie also wrote on his autobiography The return of the Thin white duke (a part of it was published in Rolling Stone 12-2-1976).
Bowie visited the Carlsbad Caces in Artesia, New Mexico. Also a small part in the film for Tony Mascia (as Newton's chauffeur). Tony Mascia took part in a bank robbery (as driver) and went to jail. Just out of jail Bowie offered him a job as chauffeur and bodyguard. Tony Mascia would prove to be a very good choice.

In a rented house in Bel Air Bowie and Paul Buckmaster started to work on the soundtrack for The man who fell to earth. They used a TEAC 4-track tape recorder and a non-programmable drum machine. Bowie also played a Rhodes Fender guitar and Buckmaster a cello (Strange fascination - David Buckley 1999).

In the end they didn't like Bowie's work and someone else got the job to make the soundtrack music.

20-7-1975 Sunday Times. Article by Tina Brown: The Bowie Odyssey (The new face of David Bowie).

20-7-1975 Chicago Sun Times. Interview by David Lewin.
Bowie: "Our street was mainly Jamaicans, some Irish. Dad owned a sort of club for wrestlers until the booze got him and he had half his stomach out. After that he joined Dr. Bernardo's home as a P.R. man. Mum was an usherette in a cinema. I don't think things were particularly easy."
"One night I went out and got drunk because I couldn't face eighteen months more discipline. So I went on the drink for about a year, my period of debauchery, and then stopped that too. I can stop anything. That's the discipline the monks gave me."
"My sister married an Egyptian sixteen years ago. I haven't seen her since. I was not lonely as a child, but a loner. I still am. We had a four-roomed house in Brixton, South London and one room was let out to a girl who I found out later was a prostitute."
It was obvious one of those cocaine influenced interviews, that made him twist reality quite a few degrees.

DATE / EVENT	AUDIO / VIDEO	TITLE

August 1975 On the set of The man who fell to earth.
Interview with Steve Stroyer and John Liftlander for Creem magazine, published in December 1975.

August 1975 During work on The man who fell to earth.   *1 CDR*   *Hendrikse various vol. 6*
Interview.   *(No label, no number)*

August 1975 New Musical Express. Article by Charles Shaar Murray: A mother's anguish - David never comes to see me (interview with Mrs. Margaret Jones).

18-8-1975 Release Fame (3.23) / Right (4.13) (RCA 2579).

18-8-1975 Release in US Fame (3.11) / Right (4.13) (RCA PB. 10320).

18-8-1975 Release in Italy: Fame (3.23) / Space oddity (RCA TBPO 7013).

23-8-1975 New Musical Express. Article by Anthony O'Grady: Dictatorship: the next step? Bowie about rock-and-roll: "It's a toothless old woman. So what's the next step? 'Dictatorship,' says Bowie. 'There'll be a political figure who'll sweep this part of the world like early rock-and-roll did. You probably hope I'm not right. But I am. My predictions are very accurate… always."

28-8-1975 Rolling Stone. Article by Lucian K. Truscott: Dylan Freewheelin' through the Village.

September 1975 Cherokee Studios in Hollywood, recording sessions for LP Station to station. Recording took 2,5 months. Working titles for the LP: Golden Years. The thin white duke.

<u>8-9-1975</u> Los Angeles, Peter Sellers Birthday Party.   NT
David joins Bill Wyman, Keith Moon and Ron Wood for a
couple of blues songs.

14-9-1975 LA Times. Article by Joyce Haber.
Bowie: "When I was asked if I went with boys as well as girls I said "Yes," although I did have a tremor afterwards when I realised the possible results of such a statement. But then I realizes it was the correct decision to tell the truth."

26-9-1975 Release Space oddity (4.33) / Changes (3.33) / Velvet goldmine (3.07) (RCA 2593).

Autumn 1975 UK TV. BBC. Today. Angie Bowie interviewed by Marc Bolan.

October 1975 Let it Rock. Article by Pete Fowler: Fighting off the Martians.

October 1975 Circus-Raves. Article: Who will I be now?

October 1975 Films and Filming (UK). Article: David Bowie The man who fell to earth.

25-10-1975 Melody Maker. Article by Harvey Kubernik: Fame at last for soulful Bowie.

<u>4-11-1975</u> US TV. ABC. Soul Train (part of Dick Clark's   *1 CDR*   *Hendrikse various*
American Bandstand). Broadcasted 12-1-1976.   *(No label, no number)*

DATE / EVENT	AUDIO / VIDEO	TITLE
Bowie turned up drunk. Fame and Golden years (lip synched) and 5 minutes of interview. Bowie in 1999: "I hadn't bothered to learn it, and the MC of the show, who was a really charming guy, took me on one side after the third or fourth take, and he said, 'Do you know there were kids lined up to do this show, who have fought their whole lives to try and get a record and come on here?'"	2 CDR 1 VCD 1 VCD Video Video Video Video Video	*Raw Moonlight on the Shore* (No label, no number) *Various 1 (2.55 min.)* *Bob's Eggs [+extras]* (No label, no number) *Stolp tapes no. 1 (6 min)* *Stolp tapes no. 22 (3 min)* *Stolp tapes no. 23 (1 min)* *Various 10 (2 songs)* *Various 26 (7 min)*
<u>4-11-1975</u> ABC. Soul Train interview with fans questions. Not broadcast on TV. Radio broadcast 4-12-1975. Bowie about soul music: "Back in England… in London, when I was a teenager, popping them, you know… on street corners. We have street corners in London… and we used to go to a lot of clubs… James Brown was very popular in French clubs. About then I was about 17."	Tape	quality 9, 5 min.
15-11-1975 US TV. CBS. Recording for Cher Show. Broadcast 23-11-1975.	2 CDR	*Raw Moonlight on the Shore* (1 song) (No label, no number)

17-11-1975 Release Golden years (3.23) / Can you hear me (5.02) (RCA 2640).

| <u>23-11-1975</u> US TV. CBS. Cher Show. Recorded 15-11-1975. 1. Fame (3.17). 2. Can you hear me (duet with Cher) (4.20). 3. Young Americans medley (with Cher) (6.39): Song sung blue - Neil Diamond (1972). One is the loneliest number - Harry Nilsson (1969). Da doo ron ron - Crystals (1963). Wedding bell blues (I love you so) - Laura Nyro (1966). Maybe - The Chantels (1958). Maybe baby - Buddy Holly + Bob Montgomery (1957). Day tripper - The Beatles (1965). Blue moon - Frankie Trumbauer & Band (1934). Only you - The Platters (1954). Temptation - Bing Crosby (1933). Ain't no sunshine - Bill Withers (1971). Young blood - The Coasters (1957). | CD CD 2 CDR 2 CDR VCD VCD   LP   LP 2 LP Tape Video Video Video Video | *Vintage David Bowie (1,2,3)* (ZIG 1) *TV-DB-15* *The European Cannon is here* *Cracked in the past (1,2)* (No label, no number) *Various 1 (14.02 min.)* *Vapo(u)rware 1 (1)* (VID 000/A) *Lost and forgotten* (Halloween Jack Production Ltd. Gena A-8206 SIII) *The other Bowie (Piar Records)* *The Thin White Duke* (Duke Plates 1001 TWD 1001) quality 10, 15 min. *Stolp tapes no. 1 (15 min)* *Stolp tapes no. 23 (29 min)* *Various 10* *Various 26 (15 min)* |
| 27-11-1975 BBC TV interview by Russell Harty on LWTV, broadcast 28-11-1975. David starts an international debate when he refuses to give up his satellite time to a mourning Spain, after | 1 CDR Tape Video | *Hendrikse various vol. 10* (No label, no number) quality 8, 20 min. *Stolp tapes no. 15 (29 min)* |

DATE / EVENT	AUDIO / VIDEO	TITLE

Franco died. David was in California during the interview.

December 1975 Mick Ronson recorded Soul Love.

December 1975 Release White man, black man - The Spiders from Mars (Pye).

December 1975 The Spiders from Mars (minus Bowie and Ronson) did a small UK tour.

December 1975 Aborted The man who fell to earth soundtrack sessions at Cherokee Studios in Hollywood.

December 1975 Creem. Article by John Lifflander and Stephan Shroyer: David Bowie: Spaced out in the desert.
Interview was given in August 1975 on the set of The man who fell to earth.

December 1975 Circus. Article by Paul Nelson: Preview: The man who fell to earth.

December 1975 Top of the Pops. Broadcast dry mix of Golden years (3.14).

2-12-1975 European tour details released for the Station to station tour in 1976.

Late 1975 Bowie did a screen test for The eagle has landed.

Late 1975 Playboy. Interview by Cameron Crowe.

Years later Bowie told about his salvation by a friend who confronted him with his drug problem: "On a winter's day, three days before Christmas, a friend pulled me over to the mirror and said: Look at us both. If you continue to be the way you are at this moment, you'll never see me again. You are not worth the effort."

A few days before Christmas a confused Bowie called Lippman, who didn't understand a word of what he said.

Christmas 1975 Jamaica. At Keith Richards house.

Between Christmas 1975 and New years eve Bowie fired Lippman, after consulting Stanley Diamond (who had a show business law practice in Hollywood) about a new agreement that Lippman wanted David to sign.

1976 Terry Burns and Olga moved to Penge.

1976 US Radio. Ad for The man who fell to earth.   Tape   quality 9, 5 min.

1976 The Haddon Hall landlord, Mr. Salter, sued Bowie for unpaid rent and damage to the property.

1976 Announcement Ken Russell was to direct Bowie in 3,5 hour film, scripted by William Burroughs (never heard of it any more, probably just made up by Bowie or MainMan).

1976 Playboy. Interview.

DATE / EVENT	AUDIO / VIDEO	TITLE

Bowie talked about his family: "Most of them are nutty. In, just out of, or going into an institution. Or dead."

About his youth: "When I was 14 sex suddenly became all important to me. It didn't really matter who or what it was with, as long as it was a sexual experience. So it was some very pretty boy in class in some school or another that I took home and neatly fucked on my bed upstairs. And that was it. My first thought was. Well, if I ever get sent to prison. I'll know how to keep happy."

About his marriage: "Angie's visa was about to expire and, since she could remain in Britain as Mrs. David Bowie, we got married. I realized that she'd be one of the very few women I'd be capable of living with for more than a week. There's nobody more demanding than me. Not physically, necessarily, but mentally. I'm very strenuous. I scare away most people I've lived with."

1976 Release LP Spiders from Mars - Spiders from Mars (Pye NSPL 18479). Re-released June 2000 by Castle.

1976 Released in Belgium: David Bowie (reissue of Images 1966-1967) (Deram DA 145/146).

1976 Release LP Max's Kansas City: New York New Wave - Various Artists. Includes three tracks by Wayne County and the Backstreet Boys. One of the tracks, called Max's Kansas City had an unnoticed release as a single. Wayne County nicked the riff from Velvet Underground's Sweet Jane.
One of the lines: "There's David Bowie, he's the Queen of Outer Space" (Man enough to be a woman - Jayne County with Rupert Smith 1995).

1976 Film Released: The Tenant by Roman Polanski. The film was inspiration for the album title Lodger (Bowiestyle - Mark Paytress 2000).

1976 Book published: Linda's pictures - Linda McCartney (Jonathan Cape, ISBN 0.224.01370.X).

1976 Guitar Player. Interview with Mick Ronson.
Ronson: "Violin was quite fun, but after about three years I got fed up with it because people used to make fun of you if you carried a violin case."

January 1976 Release Hot - James Brown (Nicked from Fame).

January 1976 Release Futuristic dragon - T.Rex.
Included the song New York City, released as a single June 1975 (Rumoured Bowie on saxophone and backing vocals.
Bowie: "It's just a rumour."
Marc Bolan told what inspired him to write the song: "I was walking with David Bowie in New York City and we saw this 90-year-old lady who is part of Andy Warhol's Factory and who claims to be a witch. She was walking down Park Avenue with this enormous toad in her hand."
This explanation started the rumour Bowie was involved in recording the song.

<u>Begin January 1976</u> New York. Studio Rehearsals.   NT

3-1-1976 Billboard. Article by N.Freedland: David Bowie: It's back to Live Dates, but Fame Singer Won't Fly.

3-1-1976 US TV. CBS. Recording Dinah Shore Show. Broadcast 2-3-1976.

DATE / EVENT	AUDIO / VIDEO	TITLE

<u>7-1-1976</u> To 21-1-1976 Jamaica. Ochios Point.   NT
Keith Richards' Home Studios.
Rehearsing for the 1976 tour.
David went there because Michael Lippman had not
arranged a house or hotel.

10-1-1976 Street Life. Article by Mike Flood Page.
Interview with Nicolas Roeg. During the making of the interview played the Soundtrack Bowie made for The man who fell to earth on a Sony cassette player.

12-1-1976 US TV. Broadcast of Soul Train. Recorded 4-11-1975.

15-1-1976 Rolling Stone. Article by Cameron Crowe: Bowie to tour: No gimmickry.

21-1-1976 David flew from Jamaica to Canada.

23-1-1976 Release LP Station to station (RCA APL.I.1327).
Recorded at Cherokee Studio in Hollywood.
The title track was inspired by the obscure Aleister Crowley text White Stains and the Jewish Kabbalah. In 1975 Bowie read The Kabbalah Unveiled by S.L.MacGregor Mathers (chief of the Hermetic Order of the Golden Dawn) and referred to Kether and Malkuth (The Complete David Bowie - Nicholas Pegg 2000).
Bowie about the album: "I like it. I wish I'd done it differently though. I compromised in the mixing. I wanted to do a dead mix. It should have been a dry mix. All the way through, no echo. All the way through the making of the album I was telling myself I'd do a dry mix. And I gave in. I gave in and added that extra commercial touch. I wish I hadn't" (Changes - Chris Welch 1999).
"I owe a lot to the French and German bands for things like Word on a wing. Station to station is quite German, a very German romantic statement that gave me another character to work with or become" (David Robert Jones: The discography of a generalist - David Jeffrey Fletcher 1979).
Maslin (producer): "David's not terrifically mike conscious and my hardest problem was that he might change to the words of a song from one time to the next, and if you engineer the vocals the way I do, you have to know what he's trying to do to capture in the way you want. He's not as critical as most singers. As a matter of fact he even don't consider himself as a singer."

24-1-1976 Melody Maker. Article by Allan Jones: Bowie stands alone.

27-1-1976 Los Angeles Times. Article by Robert Hilburn: Dylan Revue at Troubadour.

27-1-1976 Lawsuit to Michael Lippman (2 Million Dollar). Bowie represented by Stanley Diamond.

Bowie: "I want to go out like Vince Taylor. He was the inspiration for Ziggy. Vince Taylor was an American rock and roll star from the sixties who was slowly going crazy. Finally he fired his band and went on stage one night in a white sheet. He told the audience to rejoice, that he was Jesus. They put him away."
"It was quite easy to become obsessed with the character. I became Ziggy Stardust" (In his own words - Miles 1980).

February 1976 Angie Bowie went to their new home in Switzerland, a cuckoo-clock of a house with seven or eight bathrooms (Backstage passes - Angela Bowie and Patrick Carr 1993).

DATE / EVENT	AUDIO / VIDEO	TITLE

February 1976 Dutch Radio. KRO. The Theo Stokkink Show. Bowie Story (60 min.).

1-2-1976 Los Angeles Times. Article by Robert Hilburn: RTR/A Different way to go.
Hilburn wrote: "Station to station is impressive and encouraging. It has a tone of artistic and emotional reawakening and rediscovery."

Bowie about the tour: "I wanted to use a new kind of staging and I think this staging will become one of the most important ever. It will affect every kind of rock 'n' roll act from now on because it's the most stabilized move that I've seen in rock 'n' roll. I've reverted to pure Brechtian theatre and I've never seen Brechtian theatre used like this since Morrison and the Doors, and event then Morrison never used white light like I do" (Black Book - Barry Miles 1980).

Bowie: "Somebody asked me if I ever had a gay experience and I said, "Yes of course, I am a bi-sexual." The guy didn't know what I meant. He thought I had a cock and a cunt" (In his own words - Miles 1980).

The Station To Station World Tour:
David Bowie (vocals).
Carlos Alomar (rhythm guitar).
Stacey Heydon (lead guitar).
Dennis Davis (drums, percussion).
George Murray (bass).
Tony Kaye (keyboards, synthesisers).
In March they gave the band the name Raw Moon.

DATE / EVENT	AUDIO / VIDEO	TITLE
<u>2-2-1976</u> Vancouver, Pacific Nat. Exh. Coliseum. Rehearsals.	2 CD	*Transition (BOW007) complete rehearsal*
A good quality film of the rehearsals exist. Included Sister midnight (6.13).	1 CDR	Vancouver rehearsal (Old Gold Records OGCD 294A/B)
	2 CD	Vancouver rehearsals
	2 CD	*The mainman and the mainline* (No label, no number)
	2 CD	*The Return of the Thin White Duke (ODJN 004/05)*
	2 CD	*Raw Moon Rehearsals (Switch On! Devil KWSK S.O. 200-09-1/2)*
	2 CD	*PNE Live Rehearsal 1976 (Shout to the top STTP 084/085)*
	2 CDR	Station to Vancouver (Flying Cat/FLC-045/46)
	1 CDR	*Battle for Bowie (1 song)* (No label, no number)
	2 CDR	*Cyberstation (1 song)* (StationToBowie)

DATE / EVENT	AUDIO / VIDEO	TITLE
	2 CDR	*Raw moonlight on the shore (No label, no number)*
	1 VCD	*Vapo(u)rware 1 (1 song) (VID 000/A)*
	2 VCD	The Vancouver Rehearsals
	LP	Vancouver rehearsals (Haunting KCS 8993 Scrasch SCR 109 S H85161 A/B)
	Single	*Studio outtakes (Fame Gmbh) Vancouver '76 rehearsals CD's + Single compl. reh.*
	Tape	quality 8, 36 min.
	Tape	quality 9, 90 min.
	Tape	quality 9, 65 min.
	Video	*Stolp tapes no. 15 (77 min)*
	Video	90 min.
3-2-1976 US TV. ABC. Good Morning America. David and Angie interviewed by Rona Barrett.	Tape Video	

3-2-1976 Dinner with Alice Cooper (real name Vincent Furnier, son of a preacher from Phoenix) and Ray Bradbury, cooked by Angela (Backstage passes - Angela Bowie and Patrick Carr 1993).

3-2-1976 Seattle, Center Coliseum.   NT
Attendance: 15.000.
Opened with the 1922 film Un Chien Andalou by Salvador Dali and Luis Bunuel.
He used the same stark light as the German director Georg Wilhelm Pabst used to do. Also inspired by the stage version of Cabaret at London's Palace Theatre in 1968 (starring Judi Dench).
During the Station to station tour Bowie used the same clothes as in The man who fell to earth. The box of Gitanes peeking out of his white waistcoat pocket was done earlier by Ron Wood (The Faces).
Tony Mascia was his bodyguard. Barbara de Witt handled the publicity and Corinne Schwab was present as usual. Afterwards there was a party in Bowie's hotel room.
Cheryl Hise (one of the 4 women present): "David was a voyeur. He arranged groups, chose scenes, suggested positions and sat sketching the whole thing" (Loving the alien - Christopher Sandford 1996).

Bowie: "In Japan there are such beautiful looking little boys. They're all queens until they reach 25, then suddenly they become samurai. I love it" (In his own words - Miles 1980).

4-2-1976 Portland, Paramount Theater.   NT

6-2-1976 San Francisco. Before the show. Interviewed by Robert Hillburn for Melody Maker.

DATE / EVENT	AUDIO / VIDEO	TITLE
<u>6-2-1976</u> San Francisco, Cow Palace. Attendance: 14.706. A great concert and a great crowd. After the show promoter Bill Graham gave Bowie a silver cape, guitar and a gold disc for Fame.	Tape	quality 7, 80 min.
<u>8-2-1976</u> Los Angeles, Inglewood Forum. Attendance: 16.000. Iggy Pop joins the entourage. He and David celebrate by writing Sister Midnight with Carlos Alomar. Concert attended by Ringo Starr, Rod Stewart, Steve Ford, Elton John, Britt Ekland, Patti Smith, Christopher Isherwood, David Hockney, Ray Bradbury, Alice Cooper, Carly Simon, Henry Winkler, Valerine Perrine.	Tape	
<u>9-2-1976</u> Los Angeles, Inglewood Forum. Attendance: 16.000. "A very old friend of both yours and mine, Iggy Pop, is gonna do an album with me and this is a song we're doing on the album and it's called Sister midnight." After the show Patti Smith visited David and Angie. She dropped (by accident) her drink over Angie's clothes (TV interview with Angie).	CD 2 CDR LP LP Tape Video	*Wish upon a star* *(Isolar Music ISOLAR 9276)* *Cyberstation (2 songs)* *(STATIONTOBOWIE)* Wish upon a star (Bowie Rec. BR 10001 1/2) Golden years of Bow (Gold Records DB 6791) (1 track) quality 9, 45 min. quality 9, 13 min. (parts of 5 songs).
<u>11-2-1976</u> Los Angeles, Inglewood Forum. Attendance: 16.000. Bowie played It's only rock 'n' roll. After the show Christopher Isherwood introduced Bowie to David Hockney.	NT	

12-2-1976 Rolling Stone. Interview by Cameron Crowe. (Los Angeles May 1975), also a part of Bowie's never published autobiography The return of The thin white duke. Article: Ground control to Davy Jones.
Bowie: "I want to be a Superman. I know my personality is totally different to what it was then. I stripped myself down, chucked things out and replaced them with a completely new personality."
Bowie about Vince Taylor: "Vince was an American and came to England, then went to France. Then he came back to England and we spoke of our findings. He wore a white robe and sandals and we sat in the busy London street with a map of the world."

| <u>13-2-1976</u> San Diego, Sports Arena. Attendance: 15.000. | NT | |

13-2-1976 A removal firm took David's belongings from Stone Canyon Drive to Los Angeles, to be freightened to Vevey in Switzerland.

14-2-1976 Melody Maker. Article by Rick Waddington: Ziggy the crooner.

DATE / EVENT	AUDIO / VIDEO	TITLE

Bowie about drugs: "I haven't been involved in anything heavy since '68. I did acid three times. It was very colourful but I thought my own imagination was already richer" (In his own words - Miles 1980).

DATE / EVENT	AUDIO / VIDEO	TITLE
15-2-1976 Phoenix, Veteran's Memorial Coliseum. Attendance: 15.000.	NT	
16-2-1976 Albuquerque, Civic Auditorium.	NT	
17-2-1976 Denver, McNichols Sports Arena. Attendance: 19.100. A good concert. Bowie changed the song order for this show. Nice version of Five years.	1 CDR	Strange Order (Old Gold Records OGCD 125)
	2 CDR	McNichols Arena, Denver - 1976 (No label, no number)
	2 CDR	I will be king (No label, no number)
	2 CDR Tape	Bo the lion, Denver '76 quality 7, 80 min.
20-2-1976 Milwaukee, Mecca Arena. Attendance: 11.874.	NT	
21-2-1976 Kalamazoo, Wings Stadium. Attendance: 7.200.	NT	
22-2-1976 Evansville, Roberts Stadium (Riverfront). As encore Bowie sang a beautiful version of Golden years while standing on top of the piano.	Tape	quality 8
23-2-1976 Cincinnati, Coliseum (Convention Center). A good show. Started singing to late on Panic in Detroit.	2 CDR	European Cannon (Old Gold Records OGCD 470A/B)
25-2-1976 Montreal, Forum. Attendance: 16.000.	NT	

25-2-1976 Rolling Stone. Article by Cameron Crowe: David Bowie rolling on to rule the world.

DATE / EVENT	AUDIO / VIDEO	TITLE
26-2-1976 Toronto, Maple Leaf Garden. Attendance: 15.760. A good concert. Bowie is talkative and in a very good mood. He makes jokes and looks sober (this did not happen to often during this tour). During Waiting for the man Bowie announces Stacey Heydon: "Do you know what he said to me? Yeah buddy, my home town. Stacey Heydon." "Would you like me to tell you about Jean Genie?" A rocking version of The jean genie follows (The jean genie / Sister midnight / The jean genie Reprise).	2 CDR	Toronto 26 February 1976 (BowieHobby)
	2 CDR	Calling Sister midnight (KTLA CD87 1/2)
	CD	Cocaine adds life (1 nr.) (Seagul Records CD 037)
	3 CDR	Drunk as a lord (Old Gold Records OGCD 039A/B/C)
	1 CDR	One magical moment (Jumping Horse DB-006)
	1 CDR	Toronto Live 1976 Disc one

DATE / EVENT	AUDIO / VIDEO	TITLE
	1 CDR	(No label, no number) Toronto Live 1976 Disc two
	2 CDR	(No label, no number) Toronto 76
	LP	One magical moment (Magstra Records DB 76 A/B)
	Tape	quality 7, 105 min.
27-2-1976 Cleveland, Public Auditorium. Attendance: 8.000.	Tape	quality 8
28-2-1976 Cleveland, Public Auditorium. Attendance: 8.000. A Great concert! The sound quality of the recording is superb!	2 CD	Neo Expressionism (NCO 1/2) complete concert
	2 CDR	Public Auditorium Cleveland 76 (No label, no number)
	2 CDR	Un Chien Andalou
	Tape	quality 9, 105 min.

28-2-1976 Release LP Play don't worry - Mick Ronson (RCA APL 1 0186).

28-2-1976 Melody Maker. Article by Robert Hilburn: Bowie: Now I'm a businessman.

| 29-2-1976 Detroit, Olympia Stadium. Attendance: 16.500. | NT | |

Bowie: "Rock stars are fascists. Adolf Hitler was one of the first rock stars. Look at some of his films and see how he moved. I think he was quite as good as Jagger. He was a media artist. The world will never see his like. He staged a whole country" (In his own words - Miles 1980).

March 1976 Released in Japan: David Bowie Special (reissue of the 2 LP Best of David Bowie from March 1974) (RCA SRA 9412/13).

March 1976 Stereo Review. Article by Mark Giangrande: Take David Bowie for instance: A collector's tale.

March 1976 Creem. Article by Charles Shaar Murray: Won't you come home David Bowie?

| March 1976 Flash Radio. Bowie special, including interview with Lindsay Kemp. | 1 CDR | Helsinki Press Conference (BowieHobby) |

Bowie: "I'm more approachable on stage this time around, unlike the last time when the character I played was a paranoid refugee of New York City" (In his own words - Miles 1980).

1-3-1976 Detroit. Before the concert Bowie was interviewed by Chris Charlesworth in the Pontchertrain Hotel.

| 1-3-1976 Detroit, Olympia Stadium. Attendance: 16.500. | NT | |

DATE / EVENT	AUDIO / VIDEO	TITLE

2-3-1976 Circus. Article by Richard Cromelin: David Bowie.

2-3-1976 US TV. CBS. Dinah Shore Show. Recorded 3-1-1976. 1. Stay (4.43). 2. Five Years (5.13). 3. Interview. Also present during the show: Henry Winkler (The Fonz), Nancy Walker, Natalie Cole and Candy Clarke. Bowie got a karate lesson from Dwayne Vaughn and presented Natalie Cole with a golden record for Insaparatable. At the end Dinah Shore presented the new LP Station to station.	CD CD 4 CDR 1 CDR 1 CDR 2 CDR CD 1 VCD 1 VCD LP Tape Video Video Video	Look back in anger (1,2) (No label, no number) This is your life (1,2) (PD 81997) An American Duke (Old Gold Records OGCD 040) Dick & Dinah (No label, no number) TV-DB-15 (1,2) Raw Moonlight on the Shore (No label, no number) Legendary Lost Tapes Vol. 1 (1,2) (VigOtone 178) Various 1 (13.26 min.) The Dinah Shore Show The passenger (Emir Gema DBIP 111 291) 90 minutes Stolp Tapes vol. 1 (29 min.) Stolp Tapes vol. 10 (40 min.) Various 26 (9 min)

Bowie about Disco music: "I mean, disco music is great. I used disco to get my first number one single" (Fame).

3-3-1976 Chicago, International Amphitheatre. Attendance: 11.956. Open-air concert. During the concert now and then firecrackers can be heard. An average concert. A dull version of Five years.	1 CDR 2 CDR 3 CDR 2 CD 2 CDR 2 CDR Tape Tape	Chicago 3 March 1976 (1) (BowieHobby) Chicago 3 March 1976 (2) (BowieHobby) Drunk as a lord (Old Gold Records OGCD 039A/B/C) An Open-air Show Chicago March 03 1976 (No label, no number) Chicago 76 quality 8, 85 min. quality 7, 80 min.

3-3-1976 Andy Warhol's interview. Article by John Lifflander and Stephan Shroyer: Nick Roeg… and the man who fell to earth.

4-3-1976 Cherry Vanilla TV interview. She talked about: "How we peddled David's ass."	Tape	20 min.

5-3-1976 St. Louis, Henry W. Kiel Auditorium. Attendance: 10.586. Sang Golden years. Very talkative.	Tape	quality 9, 90 min.

DATE / EVENT	AUDIO / VIDEO	TITLE
6-3-1976 Memphis, Mid-South Coliseum. Attendance: 12.000.	NT	
7-3-1976 Nashville, Municipal Auditorium. Attendance: 9.000.	NT	
8-3-1976 Atlanta, The Omni (Omni Arena). Attendance: 16.750. A good concert. Bowie did not say much, but worked very concentrated to make this a good show. A pity of all the cuts in the recording.	2 CDR 1 CDR 2 CD 2 CDR Tape	Omni, Atlanta, Mars 8 1976 (No label, no number) The duke of Atlanta (Old Gold Records OGCD 079) The duke of Atlanta Gothenburg Rebel (Old Gold Records OGCD 101A/B) quality 7, 85 min.
11-3-1976 Pittsburgh, Civic Arena.	Tape	85 min.
12-3-1976 Norfolk, Scope Convention Hall. Attendance: 13.000. Sister midnight first time live. Bowie stayed at the Holiday Inn (he and Iggy Pop played Sister midnight in the Hotel Bar for a "selected" audience).	NT NT	
13-3-1976 Melody Maker. Article by Chris Charlesworth: Bowie: Ringing the ch-ch-changes.		
13-3-1976 Washington, Capitol Center. Attendance: 19.000.	Tape	
14-3-1976 Washington, Capitol Center. Attendance: 19.000.	NT	
15-3-1976 Philadelphia, Spectrum Arena. Attendance: 17.500.	Tape	
16-3-1976 Philadelphia, Spectrum Arena. Attendance: 17.500. An average concert. Before introducing Sister Midnight (7.04) Bowie announces he will be back together with Iggy Pop within 9 months in the Tower Theatre.	2 CDR 2 CD 2 CDR 4 CDR Tape	Philadelphia 16 March 1976 (BowieHobby) High speed line (No label, no number) Philadelphia Spectrum 76 (No label, no number) An American Duke (Old Gold Records OGCD 040) quality 8, 90 min.
17-3-1976 Boston, New Boston Garden Arena. Attendance: 15.510. An average concert. Bowie and the band just did what they	2 CDR 4 CDR	Boston 17 March 1976 (BowieHobby) An American Duke (Old

DATE / EVENT	AUDIO / VIDEO	TITLE

had to do. He sang well, the band played well. Nothing more to say about this concert.

	2 CDR	*Gold Records OGCD 040)*
		Station to North Boston
		(NEO Records)
	2 CDR	*Age of grand delusion*
	2 CDR	*Boston 1976*
		(No label, no number)
	Tape	quality 7, 85 min.
	Tape	quality 9, 80 min.

18-3-1976 Premiere The man who fell to earth in Leicester Square Theatre in London.
Bowie represented by his wife Angela. Also present: John Walters, James Coburn, Lee Remick, John Peel, Rick Wakeman, Stomu Yamashta, Amanda Lear, Alf Martin.

Various TV reviews of the 18-3-1976 premiere:

UK TV, ITV.	Video	4 min.
UK TV. Clapperboard review.	Video	3 min.
Dutch TV.	Video	2 min.
Dutch TV. Clips from science fiction - documentary.	Video	1 min.
French TV. Entrez les artistes.	Video	3 min.
French TV. A tout coeur.	Video	3 min.
French TV. Rendez vous.	Video	2 min.
French TV. Etoile et etoile.	Video	3 min.

<u>19-3-1976</u> Buffalo, War Memorial Auditorium.   NT
Attendance: 18.000.
Despite a bout of flu, David struggles through the show.

20-3-1976 In the morning in bed, in the afternoon by car from Buffalo to Rochester. Before the show interviewed by Al Rudis.
Bowie: "After the tour the first thing I'm doing is I'm gonna finish off some silk screens and lithographs that I've worked on. I did some earlier this year, which I thought were very successful."

<u>20-3-1976</u> Rochester, Memorial Auditorium.	2 CDR	*Rochester 20 March 1976*
Attendance: 9.200.		*(BowieHobby)*
Bowie had flu. An average concert.	2 CDR	*Station to station live in New York, Rochester*
		(No label, no number)
	4 CDR	*An American Duke (Old Gold Records OGCD 040)*
	2 CDR	*I can't believe it!*
	2 CDR	*Rochester New York 1976 (MCW 99)*
	2 CDR	*Live at Rochester '76*
	Tape	quality 7, 85 min.

20-3-1976 Arrested for possession of marijuana, together with Iggy Pop, Dwain A. Vaughn and Chivah Soo in the Flagship Americana Hotel in Rochester. Bail is set at $ 2.000 each. Bowie and the others had to appear in court 25-3-1976 (Living on the brink - George Tremlett 1996).

DATE / EVENT	AUDIO / VIDEO	TITLE
21-3-1976 Radio Luxembourg. Report on drug arrest.	Tape	1 min.

21-3-1976 New York Times. Article by Henry Edwards: Bowie's back but the glitter's gone.

21-3-1976 Springfield, Civic Center. An average concert. Nice versions of Changes and Jean Genie. After listening to so many concerts, the drum solo in Panic in Detroit gets very boring.	2 CDR	Station to Springfield (NEO)
22-3-1976 New Haven, Memorial Coliseum.	NT	

22-3-1976 New York Post. Article about the drug arrest.
Bowie plus three companions ordered to appear in court in Rochester, NY, on Thursday to answer marijuana charges. Arrested at the Flagship Americana Hotel, Rochester, police found 8 oz of marijuana and charged them with criminal possession. James Osterberg and Duane Vaughns, both of 224 Jefferson Ave, Brooklyn left Rochester last night for Springfield, Mass., for a concert. Bowie put up bail for all four persons of USD 2.000,— each. The woman, Chiwah Soo, 20, of Rochester did not travel on. State police said that the hotel had been under surveillance for several hours.

22-3-1976 Radio Luxembourg. Another report on drug arrest.	Tape	1 min.
23-3-1976 Uniondale, Nassau Veteran's Mem. Coliseum. Attendance: 16.500.	CD	Suffragette city (Great Dane Records GDR CD 9023)
Recorded by RCA for broadcast on US radio's The King Biscuit Flower Hour (KBFH).	CD	Resurrection on 84th street (Stoned Records SR0007CD)
Stay (7.24) and Word on a wing (6.10) released as bonus tracks on Station to station. Queen bitch (3.15) on RarestOneBowie.	CD	Recorded live at the Nassau Coliseum February 12, 1976 (Seagull 005/2)
	CD	Live USA (IMTRAT IMT 900.028)
Great opening of Station to station. Beautiful version of Word on wing (very sensitive).	CD	Live in New York City (On Stage CD 12009)
Panic in Detroit has great guitar work and a pumping beat.	CD	The Thin White Duke (Audifon)
If you don't have this concert on CD, just get it!	2 CD	Live at the Nassau Coliseum New York
	2 CDR	Nassau Coliseum 76 (No label, no number)
	CD	Spaced out (PB81998)
	CD	RarestOneBowie
	1 CDR	MoreRareBowie (1 song) (No label, no number)
	2 CDR	More Uniondale (Old Gold Records OGCD 497A/B)
	1 CDR	Panic in New York (Dreaming Boy Record)

DATE / EVENT	AUDIO / VIDEO	TITLE
	2 CDR	*Cyberstation (2 songs) (STATIONTOBOWIE)*
	1 CDR	*Alternative Young Americans*
	CD	*Pioneers in music (8-5-1985)*
	2 CDR	*Raw Moonlight on the Shore (1 song) (No label, no number)*
	2 LP	The Thin White Duke (Duke Plates 1001 TWD 1001)
	LP	A Tasteful Display (Idle Mind Productions IMP 1114 A/B)
	2 LP	Live at Nassau Coliseum, New York 1976 part 1&2 (SS 18 A/D)
	2 LP	Resurrection (Calico / Circuit Records AST 6024)
	2 LP	Resurrection on 84th street (The Amazing Kornyfone Record Label TAKRL 2995)
	2 LP	Resurrection on 84th street (Saturetad Recordworks TAKRL 2995 A/D - 2 S 702)
	LP	Bowie on stage 1976
	Tape	quality 10, 75 min. complete concert
25-3-1976 Bowie and the others appear in court in Rochester, New York for possession of marijuana. Channel 5 filmed Bowie when leaving court.	Video	

25-3-1976 Rolling Stone. Article by Teri Morris: Station to station.

26-3-1976 New York, Madison Square Garden. Attendance: 19.680. David describes the reaction to the show as "The best I ever had." And it was a great concert! After the show a party for David and the crew at the Penn Plaza Club. Nobody was allowed to take photographs.	2 CDR	*New York 26 March 1976 (BowieHobby)*
	2 CDR	MSG 76 (KGCD-32)
	Tape	

April 1976 Creem. Article by Lester Bangs: Chicken head comes home to roost.
Bangs wrote: A great many David Bowie fans felt burned, turned into veritable women when David released Young Americans. Why? Because, interestingly enough, they thought David was trying to turn himself into a nigger. I was not, however, one of these people.

2-4-1976 Women's wear Daily. Article by Julie Kavanaugh: Nicholas Roeg's Time Machine.

5-4-1976 Bowie arrives by boat (Leonardo da Vinci) from New York in Genua (Italy). Zowie, his nanny Marion and Angela joined him during the boat-trip and travelled from Genua to Switzerland. In Genua they spend a few hours in the Colombia Excelsior Hotel and Bowie went by car to Munich (Dutch Fanzine Bowie Now 1984).

DATE / EVENT	AUDIO / VIDEO	TITLE
<u>7-4-1976</u> Munich, Olympia Halle. Attendance: 12.000.	Tape	
<u>8-4-1976</u> Dusseldorf, Philips Halle. Attendance: 6.500. Average concert. Stay was done in an echo version. At the band intro he spoke his first words and he didn't sound sober.	1 CDR 2 CDR 2 CDR 2 CDR Tape Tape Video Video	*Dusseldorf 8 April 1976* *(BowieHobby)* *OneAndaHalf* *(Old Gold Records* *OGCD 126A/B)* Dusseldorf 76 *Dusseldorf Duke* 85 min. quality 8, 60 min. *Stolp tapes no. 12 (4 min)* 7 min. (Stay)

9-4-1976 Bowie, Coco, Tony Mascia, Iggy Pop and the American photographer Andy Kent visited East Berlin, driving Bowie's big, black Mercedes. Bowie was photographed looking at a bust of Hitler and in front of Hitler's bunker (David Bowie - Jerry Hopkins 1985).

10-4-1976 Berlin, afternoon. Bowie interviewed by Stuart Grundy for the David Bowie Story (broadcast May 1976).

| <u>10-4-1976</u> Berlin, Deutschland Halle.
Attendance: 8.000.
A very average concert. Bowie not inspired.
During Station to station he starts singing to late and confuses the band. A strange moment.
Stay has a nice ending, when Bowie starts singing faster and faster. This way he forces the band to go in overdrive.
During Five years Bowie finds the inspiration for the last part of the concert (maybe the dancing girls in the front, who removed their clothes made the difference). | 1 CDR

2 CDR

1 CDR

2 CDR
1 CDR

1 CDR
Tape
Tape | *Berlin 10 April 1976*
(BowieHobby)
OneAndaHalf (10 songs)
(Old Gold Records
OGCD 126A/B)
Station to station Berlin 76
(No label, no number)
Berliner Station
Live Berlin 1976
(No label, no number)
Right is so vague
quality 8, 70 min.
quality 8, 65 min. |

11-4-1974 Berlin Morgenpost. They wrote: "The show unrolled like a perfect super-machine."

11-4-1976 Hamburg, afternoon. Bowie interviewed by Stuart Grundy for the David Bowie Story (broadcast May 1976).

| <u>11-4-1976</u> Hamburg, Kongress Zentrum.
Attendance: 3.000.
Bowie very drunk. Now and then he talked nonsense.
It is obvious he was not in a condition to deliver a top performance. | 2 CDR

2 CDR

2 CDR | *Hamburg 11 April 1976*
(BowieHobby)
Der Graf
(Old Gold Records
OGCD 127A/B)
Live Hamburg 76
(No label, no number) |

DATE / EVENT	AUDIO / VIDEO	TITLE
	Tape	quality 7, 90 min.
12-4-1976 Hamburg, Kongress Zentrum. Attendance: 3.000.	NT	
13-4-1976 Frankfurt, Fest Halle. Attendance: 8.000. An average concert. Nice version of Five years.	*2 CDR* 2 CDR 1 CDR 2 CDR Tape *Video*	*Frankfurt 13 April 1976* *(BowieHobby)* Der Graf (Old Gold Records OGCD 127A/B) Festhalle '76 Frankfurt 76 (No label, no number) quality 7, 65 min. *Stolp tapes no. 12 (4 min)*
14-4-1976 Bowie visited his new home in Switzerland for the first time.		
14-4-1976 Ludwigshafen, Friedrichs-Eberthalle. Attendance: 3.500.	Tape	
16-4-1976 Frankfurt, The Linus Band Show (Night Club). With guest appearance of David Bowie. 1. Blue Monday (2.43). 2. You tell me why (2.12). 3. Almost of all (2.16). 4. Izabella (3.16). 5. I'll be there (2.52). 6. Things won't be the same (7.31). 7. Louie Louie (1.31).	2 CDR Tape	*The Linus Band* *(BowieHobby)* quality 8, 23 min.
17-4-1976 Bern, Festhalle. *Cancelled.*		
17-4-1976 Zurich, Hallen Stadion. Attendance: 3.000. Tickets: Fr. 30,—. Start: 19.00 hours. Promoter: Good News. Bowie drunk again and between the songs (which are sung in a shaky voice) he talks nonsense. "On percussion Dennis Davis. As you can see he is the star of the band. But when it comes to being a lady-killer here's someone who likes ladies, and does very well with them I must tell." Tony Kaye gets bored with Bowie's talk and starts playing some tunes in the hope Bowie will start singing again, but he just goes on talking.	2 CDR 2 CDR 2 CDR 2 CDR 2 CDR Tape *Video* *Video*	*Zurich 17 April 1976* *(BowieHobby)* Zurich 76 *(No label, no number)* Do you speak English? (Old Gold Records OGCD 080) Gothenburg Rebel (Old Gold Records OGCD 101A/B) Zurich April 17 1976 (No label, no number) quality 8, 90 min. *Stolp tapes no. 18 (4 min,* *photos of the concert).* *Stolp tapes no. 19 (7 min,*

DATE / EVENT	AUDIO / VIDEO	TITLE
	Video	*photos of the concert).* 7 min. (Introductions)

18-4-1976 Release LP Live in Cleveland - Rick Derringer (CBS Blue Sky ASZ 265). Includes a cover version of Rebel rebel.

20-4-1976 Flight Berlin - Moscow.

21 and 22-4-1976 Bowie visited Warsaw and Moscow. At the Russian / Polish border the customs confiscated Nazi books that were in Bowie's possession (David Bowie - Jerry Hopkins 1985).

April 1976. Swedish interviews.	Tape	
24-4-1976 Helsinki. Press conference.	1 CDR Tape	*Helsinki Press Conference* *(No label, no number)*
24-4-1976 Helsinki, Nya Masshallen (Messuhalli). 35 Minutes broadcast on FM radio.	Tape	quality 8, 35 min.

26-4-1976 Stockholm, Kunglinga Tennishallen.
Attendance: 5.000. Bowie sober enough to do a good show.
The audience enjoys the show and is quite enthusiastic.
After the show Bowie says: "As I see it, I am the only
alternative for the premier of England. I believe
Britain could benefit from a fascist leader. After all,
fascism is really nationalism." It was an interview with a
Swedish reporter for Skivspegelen Radio (broadcast
30-4-1976 on Capital Radio).
Later Bowie commented on the interview: "The right wing
politics thing was just bullshit, something I said off the cut.
Some paper wanted me to say something and I didn't have
much to say so I made things up. They took it all in" (David
Bowie - The Archive - Chris Charlesworth 1981).

	1 CDR	*Stockholm Primo (Old Gold Records OGCD 081)*
	2 CDR	*Gothenburg Rebel (Old Gold Records OGCD 101A/B)*
	2 CDR	*Stockholm Primo*
	2 CDR	*Stockholm Sweden April 26 76 (No label, no number)*
	2 CDR	*Live in Stockholm 1976 (No label, no number)*
	Tape	quality 7, 85 min.

27-4-1976 Circus. Article by Ben Edmonds: Bowie meets the press.

27-4-1976 Oslo, Ekebergshallen.
Cancelled.

27-4-1976 Stockholm, Kunglinga Tennishallen.
Attendance: 5.000. Promoter: SACS AB.
Started at 19.30 h. Tickets: KR. 70,—.
Recorded for Swedish Radio (when was the broadcast?).
A good concert with great crowd-response. Includes the
medley Queen bitch / Life on Mars? / Five years.
The first word he spoke was after Panic in Detroit, during
the band intro.

	2 CDR	*Stockholm 27 April 76 (1) (BowieHobby)*
	2 CDR	*Stockholm 27 April 76 (2) (BowieHobby)*
	1 CDR	*Stockholm Secundo (Old Gold Records OGCD 100)*
	1 CDR	*Stockholm Secundo (No label, no number)*
	2 CDR	*Gothenburg Rebel*

DATE / EVENT	AUDIO / VIDEO	TITLE
		(Old Gold Records OGCD 101A/B)
	2 CDR	Second night in Sweden
	Tape	quality 7, 85 min.
28-4-1976 Gothenburg, Scandinavium. Attendance: 7.000. Great version of Station to station. During the encores Iggy Pop was dancing on the stage.	2 CDR	*Gothenburg 28 April 1976 (BowieHobby)*
	2 CDR	*Scandinavium 76*
	2 CDR	Gothenburg Rebel (Old Gold Records OGCD 101A/B)
	1 CDR	Gothenburg Live 1976 Disc 1 (No label, no number)
	1 CDR	Gothenburg Live 1976 Disc 2 (No label, no number)
	Tape	quality 8, 88 min.
	Tape	quality 8, 83 min.
29-4-1976 Copenhagen, Falkoner Teatret. Attendance: 3.000. Tickets: Kr. 150,—. Promoter: ICO. Bowie in a bad mood (maybe a long lasting hangover?). Not a good concert. Bowie not concentrated and singing in a "sloppy" way.	2 CDR	*Copenhagen 29 April 1976 (BowieHobby)*
	1 CDR	*Thin white duke meets Ziggy (not complete)*
	2 CDR	Copenhagen 76 (No label, no number)
	2 CDR	The duke in Copenhagen (Old Gold Records OGCD 102)
	2 CDR	First night in Denmark
	2 CDR	Copenhagen Falkoner Teatret
	2 CDR	Almost complete! (Old Gold Records OGCD 105A/B)
	1 CDR	Don't touch that dial
	1 CDR	Thin white duke meets Ziggy
	2 LP	Thin white duke meets Ziggy (Vinyl Sound Records DB 36)
	Tape	quality 7, 87 min.

30-4-1976 Release TVC15 (3.43) / We are the dead (4.56) (RCA 2682).

30-4-1976 Released in Spain: TVC15 (3.57) / We are the dead (4.56) (RCA PB-10664).

30-4-1976 Swedish Skivspegelen Radio. Broadcast interview of 26-4-1976).	Tape	quality 9, 5 min.
30-4-1976 Capital Radio. Broadcast interview of 26-4-1976.	Tape	quality 9, 5 min.
30-4-1976 Copenhagen, Falkoner Teatret. Attendance: 3.000. Totally drunk again.	2 CDR	*Copenhagen 30 April 1976 (BowieHobby)*
	1 CDR	Overboozed

DATE / EVENT	AUDIO / VIDEO	TITLE
His talking is incoherent and makes no sense at all. Even his singing is not very clear. If there were people in the audience who attended their first Bowie concert, this maybe also was their last.	2 CDR 2 CDR 2 CDR 2 CDR Tape Tape	(Old Gold Records OGCD 103) Falkoner Teatret 2nd Show Almost complete! (Old Gold Records OGCD 105A/B) 2nd Night in Denmark Copenhagen 30 Apr 76 quality 7, 85 min. quality 7, 90 min.

May 1976 Creem. Article by Cameron Crowe: Space face changes the station: David Bowie pulls a Lazarus.

May 1976 Creem. Article by Lisa Robinson: Clockwork Orange in black and white.

May? 1976 Recorded Both guns are out there with Keith Christmas (The Complete David Bowie - Nicholas Pegg 2000).

1-5-1976 Melody Maker. Article by Allan Jones: The David Bowie story.

2-5-1976 BBC Radio 1. The David Bowie Story part 1 (of 4). Written and produced by Stuart Grundy.	Tape	
2-5-1976 Bowie arrived at Victoria Station, platform 8. A photograph was taken for The New Musical Express, of Bowie raising (waving) his hand to the fans. One of the waiting fans was Gary Webb (17), who later changed his name into Gary Numan. Some say it was a Nazi salute. Bowie declared the photographer caught him in mid-wave. I have a piece of film that proves Bowie was right. When you pause the film in mid-wave you can "create" a Nazi salute, just like the photographer did! You can also see the fingers of the hand "at ease," in contrary to a Nazi salute.	VCD Video	Various 5 (BowieHobby) Stolp tapes no. 9 (1 min)
2-5-1976 Capitol Radio. Hullaballo Show. Maggie Norton interview. Taped at the train, right outside Victoria Station.	1 CDR Tape Tape Tape	Hendrikse various vol. 6 (No label, no number) 20 min. quality 8, 10 min. quality 7, 15 min.
<u>3-5-1976</u> London, Wembley Empire Pool. Attendance: 8.000. Promoter: John Smith Entertainment. "And this song just about represents everything we're going through in the seventies. This is called Changes." Bowie left the stage in tears, overwhelmed by the emotions of his homecoming (David Bowie Theatre of	2 CDR 2 CDR 2 CDR	London 3 May 1976 (BowieHobby) Atearinmyeye (MARC 351976) Home sweet home (Old Gold Records OGCD 084A/B)

DATE / EVENT	AUDIO / VIDEO	TITLE
Music - Robert Matthew-Walker 1985). Attended by Neil Tennat (Pet Shop Boys), Natasha Kornilof. Marc Bolan and Gloria Jones danced behind the stage.	2 CDR 2 CDR Tape	Live at Wembley Empire Pool (No label, no number) Copenhagen 76 (8 tracks) (No label, no number) quality 9, 90 min.

4-5-1976 London. Bowie interviewed by Jean Rook for the Daily Express.
Jean Rook asked him about his fascist remarks in Sweden.
Bowie: "I've a terrible feeling I did say something like it to a Stockholm journalist, who kept asking me political questions. I'm astounded anyone could believe it. I have to keep reading it to believe it myself. I'm not sinister. I don't stand up in cars waving to people because I think I'm Hitler. I stand up in cars waving to my fans."
Jean Rook: "Does it matter? It's all publicity."
Bowie: "Yes it does. It upsets me. Strong I may be. Arrogant I may be. Sinister I'm not."
About his son: "I tell my son that the make-up is how daddy makes his money."

<u>4-5-1976</u> London, Wembley Empire Pool. Attendance: 8.000. A good concert. Nice version of Word on a wing. During Five years: "I never thought I needed "Ziggy" so many people."	1 CDR 2 CDR 2 CDR 2 CDR 1 CDR Tape	London 4 May 1976 (BowieHobby) Home sweet home (Old Gold Records OGCD 084A/B) Too cool to fool Wembley 4 May 76 Second Night At Wembley Empire Pool (A Dutch Connection) quality 8, 57 min.

5-5-1976 Daily Express. Article by Jean Rook. Waiting for Bowie - and finding a genius who insists he's really a clown.
Rook wrote: Interviewing David Bowie is a scarring experience. To showbiz, he is a super-planet. To rock, a messiah. To his fans, a god. To his pensioned Beckenham mother, an ungrateful little rotter who doesn't even send her postcards from California.

<u>5-5-1976</u> London, Wembley Empire Pool. Attendance: 8.000. Bowie is drunk again, but his singing is good. Only at the beginning of Five years he messes up the lyrics and says some inaudible words. At about 3/4 of the drum solo in Panic in Detroit one can hear Dennis Davis shout: "Party." I wonder if this shout was meant to Bowie, who wasn't back in time. When Bowie returns on stage he starts talking about free drinks. "My name is Winston Churchill and this one is called Changes." Bowie sees the crowd is not amused and after a line he says: "Hold it. I told you a lie. My name is David Bowie. Good evening, this is called Changes."	2 CDR 4 CDR 1 CDR 2 CDR 2 CDR 2 CDR Single Single	London 5 May 1976 (BowieHobby) The duke of Wembley (No label, no number) My name is Winston Churchill (Old Gold Records OGCD 114) Lost in my circle (Old Gold Records OGCD 116A/B) Wembley Empire Pool may 5 1976 (No label, no number) Copenhagen Falkoner Teatret My name is Winston Churchill (Waiting for the man / Changes) Diamond Dogs / Rebel rebel

DATE / EVENT	AUDIO / VIDEO	TITLE
	Tape	quality 7, 90 min.
<u>6-5-1976</u> London, Wembley Empire Pool. Attendance: 8.000.	2 CDR	*London 6 May 1976 (BowieHobby)*
It was a good, but average concert. After the first verse of Life on Mars? Bowie gets bored.	1 CDR	*London '76 (No label, no number)*
He stops singing and continues with Five years.	2 CDR	Bending Sounds (Old Gold Records OGCD 115)
	2 CDR	Lost in my circle (Old Gold Records OGCD 116A/B)
	2 CDR	Wembley 6 May 76
	Tape	quality 6, 90 min.
	Tape	quality 7, 100 min.

6-5-1976 UK TV. BBC 2. Omnibus. Re-broadcast of Cracked Actor.

| 7-5-1976 Suffolk Cable Vision. Rock Around the World. Interviews with Bowie and Iggy Pop. | LP | Rock Around the World |
| | Tape | quality 10, 45 min. |

Marc Bolan about Bowie: "Not too many gay gods have slept with five thousand chicks."

<u>7-5-1976</u> London, Wembley Empire Pool. Attendance: 8.000.	CD	*The Wembley Wizard touches the dial (not complete) (Desperado Records DP5)*
A very good show. Bowie sober and working like hell to make this a remarkable evening.	1 CDR	Don't touch that dial
A somewhat different version of Five years.	2 CDR	*Isolar One (KTLA CD107 1/2)*
Band intro: "Lady killer George Murray on bass guitar… Stacey, I may hold my head up like Mick Ronson, Heydon on guitar… My name is David "Winston" Bowie."	2 CDR	*London 7 May 1976 (BowieHobby)*
	LP	Don't touch that dial (Marc DB 76072)
After the how Bowie and Eno discuss plans to work together again.	LP	Don't touch that dial (Image Disc Inc, ID LP 101 01 A/B)
	LP	The Wembley Wizard touches the dial (WW A A/B)
	LP	The Wembley Wizard touches the dial (Halloween Jack Records CC 1 A/B)
	Tape	quality 7, 80 min.

8-5-1976 New Musical Express. Article by Tony Stewart: Heil and farewell. They printed the photograph of 2-5-1976 over 3 columns.

8-5-1976 Melody Maker. Article by Michael Watts: Bowie: The exile returns to messiah's welcome. Watts wrote: "It's undoubtedly funky, but it remains somehow mechanistic, ferocious in its loudness and intensity, and quite unlike soul, white or black. It was, I think, the most imaginative lightning of a rock concert I have ever seen."

DATE / EVENT	AUDIO / VIDEO	TITLE
8-5-1976 London, Wembley Empire Pool. Attendance: 8.000. Tickets: GBP 3,75. Started at 20.00 h. Promoted by: M.A.M. / John Smith Entertainment / Early Associates. A good concert. During Queen Bitch Bowie messed up the lyrics. Big applause at the first tones of Life on Mars? Band intro: "This is the one with a beautiful girlfriend… George Murray. That's a Canadian over there… Stacey Heydon." Mick Jagger, Keith Richards and Billy Preston backstage.	1 CDR 4 CDR 2 CDR 2 CDR 2 CDR 2 CDR Tape Tape Video Video	*London 8 May 1976* (BowieHobby) *The duke of Wembley* (No label, no number) Lost in my circle (Old Gold Records OGCD 116A/B) *Wembley Empire Pool 8.5.76* (No label, no number) The European Cannon is here Bowie's back (No label, no number) quality 8, 85 min. quality 9, 90 min. 65 min. quality 8, 54 min.
9-5-1976 BBC Radio 1. The David Bowie Story part 2 (of 4). Written and produced by Stuart Grundy.	Tape	

9-5-1976 Sunday Times. Article by Derek Jewell: Bowie and Bassey.
Jewel wrote: Is he sinister? There are, undeniably, visual Nuremberg overtones. Bowie-obsessiveness is sterile. But mostly, I suspect, he's the prisoner of his own publicity, his need to keep changing his image.

9-5-1976 Released in UK film The man who fell to earth.

| 11-5-1976 Brussels, Vorst Nationaal. Attendance: 8.000. A good concert. Exceptional guitar-intro to Station to station. After about 9 minutes in the song Bowie starts singing at the wrong moment. After 2 minutes in Panic in Detroit there is a part that is spoken in a very low voice (hard to understand). Bob Geldof (Boomtown Rats) was backstage. He had hitch-hiked all the way from Ireland to Belgium. | 2 CDR 2 CDR 2 CDR 2 CDR 2 CDR Tape Tape Tape | *Brussels 11 May 1976* (BowieHobby) *Brussels Vorst Nationaal 1976* (No label, no number) Almost complete! (Old Gold Records OGCD 105A/B) Live in Brussel 1976 (Old Gold Records OGCD 104) Brussels 1976 (No label, no number) quality 9, 83 min. quality 8, 85 min. quality 9, 90 min. |

12-5-1976 Bowie left Brussels at 4 p.m. with his Mercedes 600 Pullman with chauffeur Tony Mascia, for the Amstel Hotel in Amsterdam, where he, Coco and Iggy Pop arrived at 7.30 p.m.
In the afternoon, Bowie's staff was waiting for him in the bar of the hotel, including Barbara DeWitt (press agent), James Fisher (RCA London), Eric (his tour manager) and the band members.
2 Members of Bowie's fan club, Jean and Robert, joined Tibor Benkhard of RCA Inelco.
Later that evening Coco Schwab was looking for a doctor because David was ill, with bronchitis. She send out a piccolo by taxi, to get some medicine. Meanwhile in the bar, there was a lot of drinking

DATE / EVENT	AUDIO / VIDEO	TITLE

going on, all paid by Inelco (Dutch Fanzine The Voyeur, November 2000).

<u>13-5-1976</u> Rotterdam, Sport Paleis Ahoy.
Attendance: 5.000. Tickets: from FL. 15,— to FL. 30,—.
Started at 20.00 hours.
The concert was taped by RCA.
"Most of us in this band tonight are very ill with bronchitis. But we wanna try and rock and roll as much as we can. And my name is David Bowie and this is a bronchial version of Changes" (5.34).
After a very good concert Bowie says: "We'll see some of you tomorrow."

2 CDR	*Rotterdam 13 May 1976* (BowieHobby)
CD	*Cocaine Adds Life* (Seagull Records SEA CD037)
CD	*Immersed in Crowley's Uniform* (not complete) (No label, no number)
CD	*Wish upon a star* (Isolar 9276)
CD	*ChangesthreeBowie* (1 nr) (PD 81989)
CD	*Changesthreeandahalf* (1 nr.) (Grace AZL1-1989)
CD	*Legendary Lost Tapes Vol. 1* (2 songs) (VigOtone 178)
2 CDR	*Almost complete!* (Old Gold Records OGCD 105A/B)
2 CDR	*Immersed in Crowley's uniform*
2 CDR	*Dutch Duke* (KTLA CD110 1/2)
2 LP	*Cocaine Adds Life* (Swastika Records 1-8-15-4-DB A/D)
2 LP	*Immersed in Crowley's Uniform* (DB A/D)
LP	*Nazi heroically* (Juden Ausrottung Schallplatten DB)
LP	*What can I do about my Oedipal dreams* (Sister Ray Records 1984/1212(2) DB C/D)
LP	*Lost and forgotten* (Halloween Jack Productions Ltd. Gema A-8206 SIII)
2 LP	*You're the best thing* (DB A/B)
2 LP	*Bowie's back* (DB A/B)
Tape	quality 9, 90 min.
Video	3 min.

<u>14-5-1976</u> Rotterdam, Sport Paleis Ahoy.
Attendance: 7.592.

Tape	quality 6, 30 min.
Video	

After the concert Bowie went to the bar of the Amstel Hotel in Amsterdam and looked very happy and relaxed. Dressed with shirt and jeans he wanted to eat oysters with pal Iggy.
A drunken guy asked: "Are you David Bowie?"
David turned and asked: "Did somebody call my name? I am David Bowie!"
The loaded man gave David his glass of beer and David drank it in one go (Dutch Fanzine The Voyeur, November 2000).

DATE / EVENT	AUDIO / VIDEO	TITLE

The Dutch press:
Het Vrije Volk. Frank van Dijl wrote: "Bowie personality."
Sythof Pers. Yvonne Parre wrote: "Convincing presence of David Bowie."
Volkskrant. Elly de Waard (who once nicked Bowie's jacket during an interview) wrote: "Bowie is more than masterly."
Haarlems Dagblad. Cees Straus wrote: "Dramatic lines hard to understand in heavy rock violence, Bowie: not enough authenticity."

15-5-1976 New Musical Express. Article by Max Bell: The man who fell into Sinatra's suit.

15-5-1976 Melody Maker. Article by Allan Jones: Space oddities.

16-5-1976 BBC Radio 1. The David Bowie Story part 3 (of 4). Written and produced by Stuart Grundy. — Tape

<u>17-5-1976</u> Paris, Pavillion.
Attendance: 7.000. Started at 20.00 hours.
Bowie's voice was good.
"Bon soir Paris. Je m'apelle David Bowie."
Backstage visited by Brian Eno, Mick Jagger and Romy Haag.

- 2 CDR — *Paris 17 May 1976 (BowieHobby)*
- 1 CDR — *Live Paris 1976, Part 1 (No label, no number)*
- 1 CDR — *Live Paris 1976, Part 2 (No label, no number)*
- 2 CDR — Almost complete! (Old Gold Records OGCD 105A/B)
- 2 CDR — Station to station - Paris 76
- 2 CDR — Station to Paris
- 1 CDR — Pavillion de Paris (Old Gold Records OGCD 106)
- Tape — quality 8, 85 min.

<u>18-5-1976</u> Paris, Pavillion.
Attendance: 7.000.
The last concert of the tour was a very good concert. Bowie and the band were glad the tour was over and did their very best one more time.

- 2 CDR — *Paris 18 May 1976 (BowieHobby)*
- 1 CDR — *1976 Finale (Old Gold Records OGCD 107)*
- 2 CDR — Almost complete! (Old Gold Records OGCD 105A/B)
- 2 CDR — Paris Finale (KTLA CD112 1/2)
- Tape — quality 8, 86 min.

19-5-1976 French TV. Natascha. Meeting Bowie in Paris. — Video — 2 min.

19-5-1976 Paris, Pavillion.
Cancelled (Very poor ticket sales).

19-5-1976 Bowie visited The Alcazar Club in Paris.
The police did a drug-raid later in the evening. Bowie was already back in his Hotel, in bed with Romy

DATE / EVENT	AUDIO / VIDEO	TITLE

Haag, a Dutch woman impersonating a female impersonator (Backstage passes - Angela Bowie and Patrick Carr 1993).
She was the owner of the transvestite revue Chez Romy Haag at the Luftzower Lampe in the Charlottenburg district in Berlin.
She did a mime to Bowie's song Amsterdam. The song was speeded up so it got a female range. She ended her act with "This is my life." Every girl would come out on to the stage, step to the front, take of her wig and smear her lipstick across her face (the inspiration for Bowie's video clip Boys keep swinging) (Man enough to be a woman - Jayne County with Rupert Smith 1995).
Karmeen was the mistress of the house. Club acts (and friends of Bowie): Viola Scotty (who later committed suicide), Daisy, Clare Shenstone (she stayed a close friend long after his Berlin-period) (Bowiestyle - Mark Paytress 2000).

20-5-1976 Release LP ChangesOneBowie (RCA APL.I.1732).
Cover portrait taken by Tom Kelly (he also took the photo for the famous Marilyn Monroe nude calendar).

22-5-1976 Melody Maker. Article by Allan Jones: Bowie's raw power.

23-5-1976 BBC Radio 1. The David Bowie Story part 4   Tape
(of 4). Written and produced by Stuart Grundy.

28-5-1976 David hires out the Casino in Montreux, Switzerland and narrates Jack & The Beanstalkers for his son Joe (his fifth birthday) and his friends. Bowie videoed the children (In other words - Kerry Juby 1986).

End May 1976 arrived in Vevey: Lippman, Levenberg, Diamond and James Wilson in Hotel Trois Couronnes. The proceedings began on 1-6-1976 and lasted 45 minutes.

4-6-1976 Release LP Live at the Roxy - Toni Basil.
Includes cover versions of Suffragette city and Aladdin Sane.

13-6-1976 Sunday News. Article by Rex Reed: David Bowie: He is FAR-Out.

End June 1976 Bowie stayed in Corsier-sur-Vevey (near Montreux).

End June 1976 Paris. Meeting M. Lippman and Bowie.
Lasted 10 minutes and ended in a big row. Bowie stormed out of the room.
Later the dispute was settled. Both parties gave in a little bit.

June / July 1976 Modern Hi-Fi. Article by Susan Ahrens: David Bowie.

Late June to end July 1976 The most of The Idiot recorded at Château d'Herouville Studios by Pop and Bowie.
Bowie played some guitar for the song Dum dum boys. It took him a long time to get it right. When he got cramp in his fingers he shouted to Iggy Pop: "Why dammed am I doing this all for you, asshole!" (David Bowie - Dave Thompson 1986).

Summer 1976 Sight & Sound. Article by Tom Milne: The man who fell to earth.

DATE / EVENT	AUDIO / VIDEO	TITLE

Max's Kansas City held an auction to cover the legal costs of a lawsuit against Wayne County for beating up Dick Manitoba (singer of the Dictators). One of the things they auctioned was a pair of David Bowie's platform boots from the Marquee special in October 1973 (Man enough to be a woman - Jayne County with Rupert Smith 1995).

9-7-1976 Release Suffragette City (3.25) / Stay (6.07) (RCA 2726).

9-7-1976 Released in Germany: Suffragette City (edit) (3.19) / Stay (6.07) (RCA XB-01015).

July 1976 Release in US: Stay (3.21) / Word on a wing (3.09) (RCA PB.10736).

15-7-1976 Rolling Stone. Article by Paul Nelson: Bowie film falls flat: Too much of nothing.

August 1976 The work on 'The Idiot' was completed at Musicland Studio in Munich
Toni Visconti later mixed the album in Hansa Studios in Berlin (a mixing studio in Nestor Strasse, that was part of the Hansa Studios).

22-8-1976 New York Times. Article by Mel Gussow: Roeg: The man behind The Man Who Fell to Earth.

September 1976 Trevor Bolder replaces John Wetton in Uriah Heep.

September 1976 Creem. Article by Trixie A. Balm: Persona non grata ad astra.

September 1976 Playboy. Article about Bowie.
Bowie: "When I started writing I couldn't put more than three or four words together. Now I think I write very well. I have an excellent knowledge of the art. I became a bloody good actor, I'll tell you."
"My plastic rock 'n' roller was much more plastic than anybody's and that was what was needed at the time. Most people still want their idols and their Gods to be shallow, like cheap toys."

September 1976 Stereo Review. Article by Steve Simels: He lost me (again) at the movies.

September 1976 Release Laser love - Marc Bolan and T.Rex (3.20).
Bowie was not involved. Herbie Flowers and Tony Newman played the song live with Bolan.
Jeff Dexter: "I convinced Marc that the band David Bowie had used was the right one. It was good for him and everybody hoped it would make him work harder with that calibre of musician behind him."

1-9-1976 Beginning recording Low at Chateau d'Herouville Studios in Pontoise.
Bowie and Eno had worked out the first ideas at Conny Plank's studio in Cologne.
Angie's boyfriend came over. He and Bowie had a fight.
After a meeting with Michael Lippman Bowie was ill for 3 days and they called the recording sessions to a halt.
Later they moved to Hansa by the Wall Studio, 38 Kothener Strasse in Berlin-Kreuzberg. This time they used the main studio.
Working title for the album: New music, night and day.
The first song they recorded was Sound and vision on which Bowie commented: "It's the ultimate retreat song. Actually the first one done, it was about getting out of America, that depressing era I was going through. It was wanting to be put in a little cold room with omnipotent blue on the walls and

blinds on the windows" (David Robert Jones: The discography of a generalist - David Jeffrey Fletcher 1979).

Tony Visconti: "In the bedroom there was a darker corner of the room that even if you shone a torch in the corner, it sucked the light into it. There was another bedroom in the back where Brian Eno slept and every night he woke up by a tap on the shoulder or a voice in his ear. We just seemed to bring it out of the place" (In other words - Kerry Juby 1986).

Brian Eno (full name Brian Peter George St. Baptiste de la Salle Eno, born 15-5-1948 in Woodbridge, Suffolk): "The way he worked impressed me a lot, because it reminds me of me. He'd go out into the studio to do something, and he'd just come back hopping up and down with joy. And whenever I see someone doing that I just thrust that reaction. It means that they really are surprising themselves" (A chronology - Kevin Cann 1983).

For this (and the next two) album they used a deck of cards: Oblique Strategies. Put to paper by Brian Eno and Peter Schmidt in 1975 (500 copies). Several thousand were sold in revised editions in 1978 and 1979. Each band member took a card with a short message.
Examples:
Would anybody want it?
Go slowly all the way round the outside.
Don't be afraid of things because they're easy to do.
Only a part, not the whole.
Turn it upside down.

Begin September 1976 Bowie lived at The Hotel Gehrus in Berlin, later he moved to Hauptstrasse 155 in Schonberg district.
He rented an apartment on the first floor with 7 rooms. Coco lived in a flat downstairs in the same block of flats. The immediate neighbours were Bucherhalle (bookshop), Amazonia Schmuck & Perlen (jewellery) and a garage.
In Berlin he and Iggy Pop often breakfasted in the gay bar Anderes Ufer (just next door) and the Nemesis Café. Supper at the Ax Bax Restaurant. Lunch at Ganymed Restaurant. Discotheques they visited: The Roxy, The Exxess, The Harlekin, The Tolstefanz, The Dschungle, So-36 Club.
Bowie got to know Zazie de Paris (a French transsexual), Rosalia di Kulessa (a fashion model) who had breast cancer (after one of her breast was removed she posed for a photograph with Iggy Pop, naked to the waist), Gerrit Meijer (of a punk band), Artur Vogdt (from who he bought 2 expressionist works: The three kings of Emil Nolde and a woodcut of 3 horses by Erich Heckel), Leopold Reidermeister (Alias David Bowie - P. & L. Gillman 1986).
Some years later the French-Jewish transsexual Zazie (Serge) de Paris and Wayne / Jayne County worked for some months in Miss Alice's whorehouse in Berlin (Man enough to be a woman - Jayne County and R. Smith 1995).
A transsexual working in the club Chez Nous called herself Angie Stardust.
According to Tony Visconti they visited East Berlin and had dinner at the British Consulate in a restaurant next to the Brecht Theatre. That moment started Bowie's fascination with Berthold Brecht and Kurt Weill.

4-9-1976 Melody Maker. Article by Chris Brazier: Bowie: beauty before outrage.

5-9-1976 Sunday News. Article by Richard Townsend: Remembrance of Things Past.

DATE / EVENT	AUDIO / VIDEO	TITLE

6-9-1976 People. Article by Fred Hauptfuhrer: Rock's space oddity David Bowie falls to earth and lands his feet in film.

22-9-1976 Release LP Luther - Luther Vandross (Cotillion 9907).
Luther Vandross did the backing vocals for Bowie's album Young Americans and the song Funky music was the basis for Bowie's song Fascination.

October 1976 Berliner Morgen Post. Interview with Bowie.

20-10-1976 Radio Luxembourg. David Bowie Special (60 min.).

November 1976 St. Martin's Lane, Little Theatre. Angie in lunchtime show Krisis Kabaret.
Later they made a single Soul house / What's going on - Soul House Company (Track Records 2094 132). Soul house was a poem she wrote, with music written by Roy Martin.

8-11-1976 New Yorker. Article by Pauline Kael: Notes on evolving heroes, morals, audiences.
She wrote: Nicolas Roeg's The man who fell to earth, which stars David Bowie, is The little Prince for young adults; the hero, a stranger on earth, is purity made erotic. He doesn't have a human sex drive; he isn't even equipped for it.

10-11-1976 Bowie collapsed at his apartment in Berlin after a row with Angie and was brought to the British Military Hospital in West Berlin (exhausted).
Bowie was drinking quite heavily. He was a regular visitor to a bar called Joe's Beer House. Often he drank there a lot of Konig Pilsner Beer (David Bowie - Jerry Hopkins 1985).
Uwe Herz remembers holding him more then ones up by his belt, while he vomited in the alley next to the Beer House.
A spokesman of the Berlin British Military Hospital: "In the early morning the hospital received a call from a lady in some distress saying her British husband had had a heart attack. Though we don't usually admit non-military personnel, as an act of mercy we sent out an ambulance to get him. He'd just overdone things, and was suffering from too much drink. We ran various tests and proved he hadn't had a coronary."

19-11-1976 New Satesman. Article by A. Curtis: It's only rock 'n' roll.

December 1976 Circus. Article by Ron Ross: David Live: Bowie throws a bone to his Dog fans.

December 1976 Bowie visited Oona Chaplin (former actress Oona O'Neill) quite a few times.

End 1976 The American Academy of Science choose David as best actor in the category 'Fiction, Fantasy and Horror'.

1976 / 1977 Article by Chris Hodenfield: Bad boys in Berlin. David Bowie and Iggy Pop. The terrible thing an audience can make you do.

1977 Article by Bob Gallagher: Bowie's brave new world.

1977 Released in Australia and Holland, Promo-single: Breaking glass (2.47) (RCA 103295).

1977 Released Single: Criminal world - Metro.

DATE / EVENT	AUDIO / VIDEO	TITLE

1977 Book published: The Songs of David Bowie - Pearce Marchbank (Wise Publications, ISBN 0.86001.004.X).

1977 Book published: David Bowie - His private and public lives, his music, his films, his future. A portrait in words & pictures. Written by Vivian Claire (Flash Books, ISBN number 0.7119.0285.2).

1977 Book published: D.Bowie - A biography in words and pictures - Ed Kelleher (New York, Sire Books).

1977 Book published: The king of glitter rock (mostly photo's) - Vivian Claire (Flash Books).

1977 Edinburgh Festival. First performance of The elephant man. Text by Bernard Pomerance. Produced by Foco Novo.

1977 Rumours that Ingmar Bergman offered Bowie a role in The Serpent's Egg.

1977 Interview Superstar Series.	CD	*An evening with David Bowie*
1977 Japanese Interview.	1 CDR	*Hendrikse various vol.6* *(No label, no number)*
1977 Melbourne Radio 3XY Phone call.	1 CDR	*Hendrikse various vol.6* *(No label, no number)*
1977 Capitol Radio Phone call to Stockholm.	1 CDR	*Hendrikse various vol.6* *(No label, no number)*
January 1977. German radio. Pop Shop. 3 One-hour specials on Bowie's music (part 1).	Tape	

January 177 Release Low promotional single (RCA).

8+9-1-1977 David's 30th birthday party. A two-night talk with super fan Jeff Gold who brings his rare Bowie tracks including the Italian version of Space Oddity. Gold is interviewed by Rodney Bingenheimer who add his comments about David's 1971 trip to America. One interesting anecdote concerns how David forgot the words to Diamond Dogs and had to call Gold for the lyrics.	Tape	120 min.

8-1-1977 Bowie celebrates his 30th birthday in Berlin at The Roxy. Guests: Iggy Pop, Romy Haag. A reporter took a picture. Bowie smashed his camera and raged at Romy Haag.

8-1-1977 Release Fascination / We just want to play for you - Fat Larry's Band (WMOT K 11002). A-side written by Bowie.

Stuart Mackenzie (paratrooper in a British regiment in Berlin): "One night in January I came across

DATE / EVENT	AUDIO / VIDEO	TITLE

David with Iggy Pop and Coco Schwab in Joe's Beer House. Bowie was being mobbed. I sorted him out. Two other paras showed up and we formed a Close Protection Squad. We were Bowie's Boys for a week"(Loving the alien - Christopher Sandford 1996).

Bowie before the release of Low: "I hope it doesn't sell. I hope RCA cancels my contract" (David Robert Jones - The discography of a generalist - David Jeffrey Fletcher 1979).

14-1-1977 Release LP Low (RCA APL.I.2030).
Bowie about Low: "The lyrics on Low reflect that I was literally stuck for words. I was making a new musical language for my new life" (Changes - Chris Welch 1999).
Brian Eno about Bowie: "David works very fast. He's very impulsive and works like crazy for about two hours and then takes the rest of the day off" (Changes - Chris Welch 1999).
Bowie about Eno: "Of all the people that I've heard who write textures, Brian Eno's textures always appealed to me the most. Brian isn't interested in context. He's a man with peculiar notions, some of which I can come to terms with very easily and are most accessible and some of it is way above my head in terms of his analytical studies of cybernetics and his application of those things to music" (Changes - Chris Welch 1999).
Visconti about Low: "Music to cut your throat to" (The Starzone Interviews - David Currie 1987).
"The reason there are not that much lyrics is that he had absolutely nothing to say; there was nothing outside himself. So I think for the first time in his lyrics he's really saying something about himself… His mood was far from optimistic when we were recording at the Chateau. It was absolutely the worst. A lot of things were happening to him."

In an interview Bowie explained the Subterraneans was written with the hidden Jazz scene of East Berlin in mind. The description he gave is lifted straight from the book The Subterraneans by Jack Kerouac from 1958. The only difference is the location. The jazz lovers and beat poets, who listened to Stan Kenton's record Yes daddy yes and John Coltrane's and Charlie Parker's music and read Baudelaire, met at a place called the Mask in San Francisco.

Ian MacDonald reviewed the album for the New Musical Express: "Bowie produces totalitarian music. Mass-production epitomized for the marching morons of TVC15, this is music while you work."

22-1-1977 Melody Maker. Article by Michael Watts: Low.

29-1-1977 Melody Maker. Article by Michael Watts: Bowie: Funeral in Berlin.
About Bowie being the keyboard player for Iggy Pop's touring band.

January / February 1977 Release Sister midnight - Iggy Pop (RCA).

February 1977 Bowie spent a weekend with Marc Bolan in Britain.

February 1977 Cherry Vanilla starts her first concert tour in the UK.

February 1977 Bowie send a letter to Melody Maker: "I would like to correct the misconception that Iggy Pop is managed by myself. Iggy looks after his own business affairs. I would appreciate a printed correction. David Bowie, Berlin."

11-2-1977 Release Sound and vision (3.00) / A new career in a new town (2.50) (RCA PB.0905).

DATE / EVENT	AUDIO / VIDEO	TITLE

16-2-1977 Release LP It's a game - Bay City Rollers (Arista AL 7004). Includes a cover version of Rebel rebel.

23-2-1977 Release LP Eater - Eater (Label Records TLR001). Includes cover version of Queen bitch.

25-2-1977 Circus. Article: Bowie-from Europe with love.

The Idiot World Tour:
Iggy Pop (vocals).
David Bowie (keyboards and backing vocals).
Ricky Gardiner (guitar).
Tony Sales (bass).
Hunt Sales (drums).

<u>Second half February 1977</u> Berlin (Babelberg). Screening Room, UFA Studios. Rehearsals.	CD 1 CDR	*Idiot Sessions* Chatteau a Gogh Gogh (No label, no number)

March 1977 Daily Express. Interview with Angie. She tells she and David are broke and robbed blind.

March 1977 Book published: Book of rock - Bob Hart (Sun Books, ISBN 0.214.20364.6).

<u>1-3-1977</u> Aylesbury, Friars Club. Sound check. After the sound check Bowie, Pop and friends had a drink in the Gun bar of the Bell Hotel.	NT	
<u>1-3-1977</u> Aylesbury, Friars Club. Attendance: 2.000. Support act: the Vibrators.	NT	
<u>2-3-1977</u> Newcastle, City Hall 7. Attendance: 2.168. Support act: the Vibrators.	Tape	quality 6, 65 min.
<u>3-3-1977</u> Manchester, Apollo Theatre. Attendance: 2.494. Support act: the Vibrators.	Tape	quality 7, 65 min.
<u>4-3-1977</u> Birmingham, Hippodrome. support act: the Vibrators.	Tape	quality 7, 25 min.

4-3-1977 After the show they drove to London, where they stayed in the Montcalm Hotel.

<u>5-3-1977</u> London, Rainbow Theatre. Attendance: 3.000 (Sold out). Support act: the Vibrators. Slight crowd trouble. Seats were damaged and security men ejected fans, watched by 60 journalists.	NT	
<u>7-3-1977</u> London, Rainbow Theatre. Attendance: 3.000 (Sold out). Support act: the Vibrators.	CD Tape	*Live London '77* *(No number, no label)* quality 7, 70 min.

DATE / EVENT	AUDIO / VIDEO	TITLE

In London Bowie had lunch with Marc Bolan at Toscanini's in the Kings Road. They left the restaurant slightly drunk. They also worked about 4 days in Marc Bolan's flat on a film. They wrote a part of the script and the soundtrack (A chronology - Kevin Cann 1983).

10-3-1977 Bowie and Pop flew from Heathrow to the US. On arrival in New York Bowie was interviewed by Lisa Robinson.

11-3-1977 Bowie, Pop, David Johansen and his wife Cyrinda Foxe went to the Lower Manhattan Ocean Club to a performance of Patti Smith. Pop joined her on stage for a wild version of 96 Tears.

12-3-1977 Melody Maker. Article: Music-hall humorist.
Marc Bolan talks about Bowie: "David is a great singer. When he was in The Lower Third he used to go to gigs in an ambulance. He was playing saxophone then and singing. I suppose it was a blues band. When he had Space oddity he was on tour with me in Tyrannosaurus Rex. He had a mime act and used to open up the show. He didn't sing at all but had a tape going and he'd act out a story about a Tibetan boy. It was quite good actually."

12-3-1977 Melody Maker. Article by Chris Welch: Bowie: Myths and mystique.

Date / Event	Audio / Video	Title
<u>13-3-1977</u> Montreal, Le Plateau Theatre. Support act: Blondie.	1 CDR Tape	quality 8, 70 min.
<u>14-3-1977</u> Toronto, Seneca College. Support act: Blondie.	Tape	quality 7, 70 min.
<u>16-3-1977</u> Boston, Harvard Square Theatre. Support act: Blondie.	NT	

18-3-1977 Release LP The Idiot - Iggy Pop (RCA Victor PL 12275).
Produced / arranged by Bowie. All songs co-written by Bowie.
Heckel's painting Roquairol (1917) was inspiration for the cover. The painting was named after the incurable insane Roquairol in Jean Paul's novel Titan.
The album was named after Fyodor Dostoevsky's book The Idiot (in September 1958 published in an English translation by Bantam Books).

Kris Needs (Zigzag): "It's two o'clock in the morning and I'm playing The idiot for the fifth time running. Can't stop, it's so compelling… but very VERY strange."

Nick Kent (New Musical Express): "No longer decadent punk, but the full-blooded scream of damnation itself. As such, it's damn unhealthy, depressing, perverse, harrowing and strangely addictive. Certain, so called Iggy fans will mutter morosely about the lack of heavy metal rock action, but that's only because they can't see that The idiot is really only the next logical step from the hell-fire tinglings of Raw power in order to keep the Pop's demon-in-residence biting back on vinyl."

John Swanson (Rolling Stone): "The Idiot steeped in so-called minimalist ambience currently so fashionable amongst young bands who've spent too much time listening to Iggy and taking him seriously, is the most savage indictment of rock posturing ever recorded. The idiot is a necrophiliac's delight."

DATE / EVENT	AUDIO / VIDEO	TITLE
<u>18-3-1977</u> New York, Palladium. Attendance: 3.387. Support act: Blondie. During the concert there was a minor riot. For the second encore he choose China girl. He sang the song with a stagehand holding a light under him for dramatic Fu Manchu effect, pulled his face taut with his hands to make slits of his eyes and began to hop in a bizarre imitation of some bound coolie (Psychotic reactions and carburator dung - Lester Bangs 1988). Attended by Mick Jagger and Keith Richard.	1 CDR Tape	*New York 18 March 1977* *(BowieHobby)* quality 8, 60 min.
<u>19-3-1977</u> Philadelphia, Tower Theatre. Attendance: 3.000. Support act: Blondie.	Tape	quality 7, 10 min.
<u>21-3-1977</u> Cleveland, Agora Ballroom. Attendance: 1.000. Support act: Blondie. Attended by Devo. They gave a demo tape of their music to Bowie and Pop.	NT	
<u>22-3-1977</u> Cleveland, Agora Ballroom. Attendance: 1.000. Support act: Blondie. TV Eye, Dirt and Funtime later included on TV Eye. 1. Raw power (4.45). 2. 1969 (2.59). 3. Turn blue (6.58). 4. Sister midnight (4.05). 5. I need somebody (4.43). 6. Search 'n' destroy (3.35). 7. TV eye (4.18). 8. Dirt (5.18). 9. Funtime (3.22). 10. Gimme danger (4.30). 11. No fun (3.21). 12. I wanna be your dog (4.16). 13. China girl (3.28).	CD CD CD CD CD CD CD LP 2 LP LP LP LP Tape Tape	*Stowaway D.O.A. (12,7,8,9,3)* *(Living Legend LLRCD 112)* *TV Eye (7,8,9)* *Suck on This* *Alarm (13)* *(La Dolce Vita Productions)* *Sister Midnight 2* *Nights of the Iguana vol.1* *Wild Animal 1976 / 1977* *(No label, no number)* Wild Animal (Revenge) Stowaway D.O.A. (Ruthless Rhymes IP 100) Suck on this (Ruthless Rhymes IP 200) Alarm (1 song) (Gravedigger Records A-8149) Why does David Bowie like dressing up in ladys clothes Zowie and a couple of kooks quality 10, 70 min. 60 min.
25-3-1977 Amsterdam, Paradiso. Punk Rock Festival. Performances by Wayne County & The Electric Chairs and Cherry Vanilla.		
<u>25-3-1977</u> Detroit, Masonic Temple Auditorium. Attendance: 4.865. Support act: Blondie.	1 CDR	*Live Detroit 77* *(No label, no number)*

DATE / EVENT	AUDIO / VIDEO	TITLE
	Tape	quality 8, 70 min.
27-3-1977 Chicago, River Theatre. Support act: Blondie.	NT	
28-3-1977 Village Voice. Article by Lester Bangs: Iggy Pop: Blowtorch in bondage.		
28-3-1977 Village Voice. Article by Frank Rose: Four conversations with Brian Eno.		
28-3-1977 Chicago. Radio WKQX. Midnight Mantra Studios with Iggy Pop. Presented by Mitch Michaels. 1. Raw power (4.18). 2. TV Eye (4.13). 3. Dirt (5.11). 4. 1969 (2.52). 5. Turn blue (6.54). 6. Funtime (3.10). 7. Gimme danger (4.30). 8. No fun (3.13). 9. Sister Midnight (3.54). 10. I need somebody (4.38). 11. Search and destroy (3.31). 12. I wanna be your dog (4.29). 13. China girl (6.51).	CD CD CD CD CD CD CD LP LP LP LP LP Tape	Kiss away the darkest day / Liquor & Drugs (No label, no number) Alarm (9,13) (La Dolce Vita Productions) Jesus this is Iggy (Lust for life LFL 069) Mantra Studios (No label, no number) The Leacherling (No label, no number) The Bolan/Pop Sessions (9) (No label, no number) Mantra 1977 Kiss away the darkest day (Jonas / Igor) Alarm (Gravedigger Records A-8149) (9,13) Why does David Bowie like dressing up in ladys clothes Zowie and a couple of kooks The Leacherling quality 10, 55 min.
28-3-1977 Chicago, Aragon Ballroom. Support act: Blondie. Recording I wanna be your dog (4.16) for LP TV Eye.	CD NT	TV Eye (11)
29-3-1977 Pittsburgh, Leonia Theatre. Support act: Blondie.	NT	
30-3-1977 Columbus, Agora Ballroom. Support act: Blondie.	Tape	

31-3-1977 London. Angie models a GBP 700,— wedding dress for designer Yuki.

April 1977 Creem. Article by Billy Altman: Bowie on the brink: Waiting for the gift of Sound and Vision.

April 1977 Crawdaddy. Article by James Graig: Low.

DATE / EVENT	AUDIO / VIDEO	TITLE

1-4-1977 Milwaukee, Oriental Theatre.
Support act: Blondie.
NT

4-4-1977 Portland, Paramount Theatre.
Attendance: 2.960. Support act: Blondie.
NT

7-4-1977 Vancouver, Vancouver Gardens.
Support act: Blondie.
NT

9-4-1977 Seattle, Paramount Theatre.
Attendance: 2.980. Support act: Blondie.
The band performs a medley of 1969, No fun and 96 tears (2.22). They also did China girl (3.40).

	1 CDR	*Iggy & Ziggy (38.00 min)* (No label, no number)
	CD	*Iggy & Ziggy (66.01 min)* (DBPOP)
	LP	Iggy & Ziggy (Duck Records DB POP)
	Tape	quality 8, 70 min.

13-4-1977 San Francisco, Berkeley Theatre.
Support act: Blondie.
Bowie and Pop sang Fame. They shouted the lyrics to each other.

	NT	
	LP	Lebensgross

15-4-1977 Recording Sister midnight and Funtime for the Dinah Shore Show. Broadcast 6-5-1977.

15-4-1977 Santa Monica, Civic Auditorium.
Attendance: 3.000. Support act: Blondie.

	LP	The Stooge turns Pop
	Tape	quality 5, 70 min.
	Tape	quality 7, 25 min.

16-4-1977 San Diego, Civic Auditorium.
Support act: Blondie.

	CD	*Wake up! Suckers (2 songs)* (Skydog SKY 62267-2)
	Tape	quality 7, 70 min.

21-4-1977 Rolling Stone. Article by John Milward: Low.
Bowie about his Los Angeles period: "I had a more than platonic relationship with drugs. Actually I was zonked out of my mind most of the time. You can do good things with drugs but then comes the long decline. I was skeletal. I was destroying my body. I was surrounded with people who indulged my ego, who treated me as Ziggy Stardust or one of my other characters, never realising that David Jones might be behind it."

End April 1977 Start recording Lust for life at Hansa by the Wall Studios in Berlin. The recordings were finished in two and a half weeks. Bowie played the piano and sang the backing vocals.

April / May 1977 Bowie renewed relations with Mick Jagger.
They spend the night with a black cabaret singer and her sister. They had breakfast with Iggy Pop.

May 1977 Released in Germany and US: Starting Point (Deram material) (London Collector's Edition LC 50007). On the back cover of the Lp James Sina wrote something about every song.

DATE / EVENT	AUDIO / VIDEO	TITLE

May 1977 Creem. Article by Simon Frith: How Low can you get?

6-5-1977 Re-released LP Raw power - The Stooges (Embassy).

6-5-1977 Release I got a right (3.20) / Gimme some skin (2.41) - Iggy Pop and James Williamson (Holland-Siamese Records PM001). Mixed by Bowie. Special fan club issue.

6-5-1977 Release Single China girl (5.08) / Baby (3.24) - Iggy Pop (RCA PB 9093).

<u>6-5-1977</u> US TV. CBS. Dinah Shore Show. 2 Numbers with Iggy Pop. Recorded 15-4-1977.	Tape	quality 9, 8 min.
Intro, Funtime (4 min).	Video	*Stolp tapes no. 8 (23 min)*
Interview with Iggy Pop and David Bowie (11 min).	Video	*Stolp tapes no. 3 (1 min)*
On stage interview with Iggy Pop (4 min).		
Sister midnight (4 min).		

19-5-1977 Downbeat. Article: Low.

June 1977 Sounds. Interview with Freddy Mercury. Talked about Bowie's success.

June 1977 in Paris. A video for Be my wife shot. It took years before the first broadcast on TV.

Bowie: "I'm not a big fan of disco music at all. I loathe it. I really get so embarrassed that my records do so well in disco's."

17-6-1977 Release Be my wife (2.55) / Speed of life (2.47) (RCA PB.1017).

17-6-1977 Smash Hits. Article by Tom Hibbert: The most preposterous David Bowie interview ever!

24-6-1977 Attended French premiere of The man who fell to earth at The Gaumont Champs Elysees in Paris, accompanied by Sydne Rome.
Afterwards he managed to fight off a would-be mugger in the street.
Later he visited Paris nightspot Chez with Bianca Jagger.

27-6-1977 French TV. Midi Premiere. Interview by Danielle Gilbert.	Tape	
27-6-1977 French TV. TFI Actualities. Interview by Yves Mourousi.	Tape	

Summer 1977 The band Feedback changed it's name to The Hype (after Bowie's early band). Later they would change their name into U2! The first single and album Larry Mullen bought were Space oddity and Ziggy Stardust.

July 1977 Stereo Review. Article by Paul Kersh: Rock person's guide to Peter and the Wolf.

June 1977 BBC's TV Top of the Pops: Be my wife (Playback).

DATE / EVENT	AUDIO / VIDEO	TITLE

Early July 1977 Bowie and Pop were seen in New York's Ocean Club.

Late July 1977 in Paris Bowie dined with Bianca Jagger. After Bianca Jagger finished her work for the film Flesh Coloured they went to Spain for a short holiday.

July 1977 UK. Radio interview. An evening with Johnny Rotten. Rotten talked negatively about Bowie.

July 1977 Paris. Bowie interviewed for magazine Rock et Folk by Phillip Manoeuvre and Jonathan Farren.
Bowie: "At the moment I'm incapable of composing in Los Angeles, New York or in London or in Paris. There's something missing. Berlin has the strange ability to make you write only the important things."
Bowie about the Sex Pistols: "If Ziggy Stardust had had a son before he died… Johnny Rotten!"

5-7-1977 Release Promo LP Rock around the world - Iggy Pop (Suffolk cablevision program 143). Includes Bowie on keyboard, USA 1977.

July-August 1977 Recording of LP Heroes at the Hansa Studios in Berlin (in Studio 2).
The album sleeve was partly inspired by the 1921 painting Selbstbildnis in Hiddensoe by Walter Gramatte (Bowiestyle - Mark Patress 2000).

For Sense of Doubt they worked with the Oblique Strategies cards.
Eno: "It was like a game. We took turns working on it: he'd do one overdub and I'd do the next. The idea was that each was to observe his Oblique Strategy as closely as he could. And as it turned out they were entirely opposed to one another. Effectively mine said, "Try to make everything as similar as possible," and his said, "Emphasize differences"" (Eno at Edge of Rock - O'Brien).

Bowie and Visconti visited the club Luftzower Lampe (the porter was a guy in drag called Daisy).

August 1977 Release Demon queen - Marc Bolan. It did not feature Bowie, as stated by the record-company. Probably only to get more promotion for the record.

3-8-1977 Bowie and Pop interviewed over the phone for Japanese radio.

16-8-1977 Bowie was in Kenya.

September 1977 Hit Parader. Article by Lisa Robinson: Mick and Patti and David and Iggy and Bryan. Bowie: "Berlin makes me feel uneasy, very claustrophobic. I work best under these sort of conditions."

Bowie: "The Thin White Duke was a very nasty character indeed" (In his own words - Miles 1980).

9-9-1977 Release LP Lust for life - Iggy Pop (RCA PL 12488).
7 Songs co-written by Bowie. Co-produced by Bowie.
For the song Lust for life Bowie used the begin tune of the news at the British Army channel in Germany. The album was named after a book about Vincent van Gogh titled Lust for life.

Iggy Pop about the song Lust for life: "He wrote that one in Berlin, in front of the TV, on a ukulele. He heard the rhythm on this army forced network theme, which was a guy tapping out the beat on a Morse code key. David picked up the nearest available instrument and started strumming."

DATE / EVENT	AUDIO / VIDEO	TITLE

9-9-1977 Bowie and Bolan in a Manchester Hotel called The Post House, rehearsal Madman and Sleeping next to you. Rumoured they also wrote Skunk City and Casual pop. This were just rumours. Gloria Jones (Marc Bolan's girlfriend) and Herbie Flowers can be heard on the track Skunk City.

Tape — 20 min.

9-9-1977 Rehearsals for the Marc Bolan TV show.
1. Sleeping next to you (version 1) (instrumental) (3.18).
2. Sleeping next to you (version 2) (instrumental) (4.05).
3. Jam (2.04).
4. Sleeping next to you (version 3) (long vocal) (4.34).
5. Sleeping next to you (version 4) (short vocal) (0.50).
6. Madman (version 1) (vocal) (1.45).
7. Madman (version 2) (vocal) (2.30).
8. Madman (version 3) (instrumental) (2.49).
9. Sleeping next to you (finished version) (1.10).

- CD — *5 Minutes Mr. Bowie (Down Under Disc)*
- 1 CDR — Soundcheck (Old Gold Records OGCD 390)
- 1 CDR — Reaction (Old Gold Records OGCD 159)
- 1 CDR — *Marc Bolan David Bowie Roy Wood The Complete Sessions (The Collectors Series)*
- 1 CDR — *Battle for Bowie* (No label, no number)

When people in the Bowie-camp got to know Herbie Flowers (who demanded more money to make the album David live) was in Bolan's backing band, they worried David would refuse to play with him. David just made fun with Marc Bolan and ignored Herbie Flowers. Shortly after the recordings of the rehearsals, Marc Bolan leaked copies to his fans.

- 1 CDR — *Sleeping next to you (Funny Tunes)*
- 1 CDR — *Bowie and Bolan (mixed media)* (No label, no number)
- Tape — quality 8, 10 min.
- Video — 20 min.

Bowie: "I never had any competition except Marc Bolan back in England. I fought like a madman to beat him, knowing theoretically there was no race, but wanting passionately to do it."

9-9-1977 UK TV. ITV. Recordings for Marc Show. Granada TV studios, Manchester. Broadcast 28-9-1977.
Interview.
1. Heroes (3.29).
2. Madman (1.45).
3. Sleeping next to you (2.12).
with Marc Bolan's band.

Other guests: The Rods, Generation X, Heart-Throb, Lips Service.

After the recording of the show Bowie talked a few hours with Bolan and he and Eddie and The Hot Rods took the train to Euston.
On the train an interview with Tim Lott for Record Mirror. Bowie about side 2 of the LP Low: "It's my reaction to certain places. 'Warszawa' is about Warsaw and the very bleak atmosphere I got from the city. 'Art decade' is West

- 1 CDR — *Kwant Tapes vol. 2* (No label, no number)
- CD — *Alternative Biography (1,3)* (No label, no number)
- CD — *Alarm (2,3)* (La Dolce Vita Productions)
- 3 CDR — *Golden Moments 1978* (Old Gold Records OGCD 088A/B/C)
- 1 CDR — The speed of life (Old Gold Records OGCD 158)
- 1 CDR — Reaction
- CD — *TV-DB-15*
- 1 CDR — *Bowie and Bolan (mixed media)* (No label, no number)
- VCD — Various 1 (3.18 min.) (1)
- LP — Why does David Bowie like dressing up in ladys clothes
- LP — Ziggy 2

DATE / EVENT	AUDIO / VIDEO	TITLE

Berlin - a city cut off from the world, art and culture, dying with no hope of retribution. 'Weeping wall' is about the Berlin Wall - the misery of it. And 'Subterraneans' is about the people who got caught in East Berlin after the separation hence the faint jazz saxophones representing the memory of what it was."

LP — Zowie and a couple of kooks
Single — Heroes (Bo-Bo Recordings 1977A)
Video — Various 10 (9 min)
Video — Various 26 (5 min)

Jeff Dexter:" The guy from the record company and David's management and minders threw everyone out of the TV studio, even the union floor manager. The union called a meeting, and that's why the show never got properly finished" (Bolan - The rise and fall of a 20th century superstar - Mark Paytress, Omnibus Press 2002).

11-9-1977 Elstee Studios. Recording for Bing Crosby's Olde Christmas Show (Broadcast 24-12-1977).

16-9-1977 Marc Bolan is killed in a car crash on Barnes Common in London.

17-9-1977 New Musical Express. Interview with Iggy Pop.
Iggy Pop: "Bowie gave me a chance to apply myself because he thinks I have some talent. Originally we were just going to do Sister Midnight but I think he respected me for putting myself in a looney bin. He was the only guy who came to visit me. Nobody else, not even my so-called friends in L.A."

17-9-1977 Melody Maker. Article by Chris Welch: Bowie and Bolan get it on.

20-9-1977 Bowie flies from Switzerland to attend Bolan's funeral at a synagogue in Golders Green.
David sat in front of Dana Gillespie, who saw him weeping for the loss of his competitor / friend.
After the funeral the taxi had to drive Bowie slowly down Stansfield Road and stop a while up outside number 40.
Then to Haddon Hall in Beckenham, where Mr. Hoy presented him the bill for unpaid rent, which Bowie paid.

Video — Stolp tapes no. 18 (0.1 min)
Video — Various 24 (20 sec.)

23-9-1977 Release Heroes (3.35) / V-2 Schneider (3.10) (RCA PB.1121).
In Spain they released a mispressing with V-2 Schneider on both sides.
The song Heroes was inspired by the painting Lovers between garden walls (1916) by Otto Mueller (Bowie had seen it at Brucke Museum) and Tony Visconti and Tonia Maass walking hand in hand in front of the wall (Interview with Tony Visconti).
To record the song Visconti set up three mikes with electronic 'gates' on them. The gates wouldn't open until David sang above a certain volume. It took about half an hour of David alternating between shouting and whispering, but it came off beautifully when he got the levels just right.

23-9-1977 Release Promo 12-inch single Heroes (long version) (6.07) / Heroes (short version) (3.35) (RCA JD 1151).

24-9-1977 Release: Lust for life (5.12) / Success (4.23) - Iggy Pop (RCA PB 9166).
Co-written, co-produced, backing vocals and keyboard by Bowie.

25-9-1977 Iggy Pop start UK tour in Manchester (without Bowie). Support act: The Adverts.

1 CDR — Manchester 25-9-1977

DATE / EVENT	AUDIO / VIDEO	TITLE

He played That's how strong my love is (original by O.V. Wright in 1964) / Fame (7.36).

25-9-1977 Release in France: Heros (3.35) / V-2 Schneider (3.10) (RCA PB.9167).

25-9-1977 Release in Germany: Helden (3.35) / V-2 Schneider (3.10) (RCA PB.9168).

27-9-1977 Heroes Video Shoot.   *Video*   *Various 20 (20 min)*
Various unedited takes from Heroes, Sense of doubt, Blackout.

28-9-1977 UK TV. ITV. Broadcast Marc Show. Recorded 9-9-1977.

29-9-1977 Bowie sets up a Trust Fund for Bolan's son Rolan Bolan.

30-9-1977 Release single Success (4.23) / The Passenger (4.40) - Iggy Pop (RCA PB 9160) Bowie on keyboard.

September / October 1977 UK TV. Good Morning.   *Video*   10 min.
Interview.

October 1977 German TV. Telecity.   *Video*   *Various 20 (4 min)*
Heroes (German version, playback). Bowie wore a dress.

October 1977 Sounds. Article by Donna McCallister: Villains and Heroes.

Bowie about Heroes: "I suppose it's not the happiest of albums. The lyrics on each track took five or six minutes to write. I don't retake unless absolutely necessary. I get bored so quickly. I'm not one for delicate social niceties. If I take a jump into the pool, I generally swallow all the water" (In his own words - Miles 1980).

<u>1-10-1977</u> Italian TV. RAI. Odeon.   NT
1. Heroes.   Video
2. Sense of doubt (piano version).
3. Interview.

<u>1-10-1977</u> Italian TV. L'Altra Domenica.   *1 CDR*   *Hendrikse various vol. 6 (1)*
1. Interview (9 min).   *(No label, no number)*
2. Sense of doubt.   Video

1-10-1977 Rome. Recording for Radio 21,25. 30 Minute show analysing Heroes.

1-10-1977 Melody Maker. Article by Allan Jones: Heroes.
Bowie: "I totally sympathise with the new wave's indignation. The sad thing about it all is that it's being called a movement. I wish the people involved were being treated as individuals. I'm so worried for them. I'm dissatisfied with them because I can't tolerate people who either want to form, or be part of, movements."

8-10-1977 New Musical Express. Article by Charles Shaar Murray: Glam rock remembered.

DATE / EVENT	AUDIO / VIDEO	TITLE

13-10-1977 Amsterdam. Bowie phones Capitol Radio to confirm an interview later that month.

| 13-10-1977 Dutch TV. AVRO. Toppop
1. Heroes (3.58).
2. Interview (27 min).
Toppop photo session. Golden records for Low and Heroes handed by Ad Visser. | 2 CDR

3 CDR

1 CDR

Video
Video
Video | Hendrikse various vol. 4
(No label, no number)
Golden Moments 1978
(Old Gold Records
OGCD 088A/B/C)
The speed of life (Old Gold Records OGCD 158)
Various 10 (4 min)
Various 11 (4 min)
Stolp tapes no. 8 (51 min.) |

14-10-1977 Release LP Heroes (RCA AFL.I.2522).
Recorded at Hansa by the Wall Studio in Berlin-Kreuzberg.

| Heroes Album Ad # 1.
Heroes Album Ad # 2. | VCD
VCD
Video | Various 2 (1.06 min)
Various 2 (0.34 min)
Various 26 (65 sec) |

Bowie about the time when he recorded Heroes: "I seriously thought I was coming to the end of my tether. I considered everything as a way out - even suicide" (Changes - Chris Welch 1999).

Bowie to writer Michael Watts: "I felt I was getting predictable and that was starting to bore me. I was entering an era of middle of the road popularity with that soul / disco phase which I didn't like, and it was all getting too successful in the wrong ways. I want and need creative success. I want quality, not a rock-and-roll career" (David Bowie - The Archive - Chris Charlesworth 1981).

Bowie about Neukoln (the Turkish part of Berlin): "There's very much an isolated community. It's very sad. It's very, very sad. And that kind of reality obviously contributed to the mood of both Low and Heroes. I mean, having encountered an experience like that it's hard to sing "Let's all think of peace and love…" No… David why did you say that? That was a stupid remark."

| 16-10-1977 French TFI Show: Le Rendez-vous du Dimanche.
Interview by Michel Drucker.
Heroes. | Tape | quality 9, 5 min. |

| 16-10-1977 French Radio. RTC.
Questions from fans on the phone.
Henri Leproux, the owner of the Golf-Drouot rang in and and reminded Bowie of his first show outside England with The Lower Third in 1966.
Bowie: "I remember Golf-Drouot very well indeed. It's the first place that I tried out. I think you remember the sound we were trying out, something which was pretty much like a kind of punk thing?" | Tape | quality 8, 55 min. |

DATE / EVENT	AUDIO / VIDEO	TITLE

In Paris Bowie stayed at the Plaza Athenee Hotel in the Avenue Montaigne.

17-10-1977 Village Voice. Article by J. Piccarella: Riffs: Iggy transformed.

19-10-1977 Bowie arrives at London airport Heathrow.

19-10-1977 UK TV. BBC. Top of the Pops. Heroes (3.31). First appearance at this show since 1972. Sean Mayes on piano, Tony Visconti bass. After performance Bowie and Tony Visconti went to a pub in Soho. During his London stay Bowie was seen in the company of the 19-year-old actress Suzy Bickford.	CD VCD Video	Look back in anger (No label, no number) Various 1 (3.09 min.) quality 10, 4 min.

20-10-1977 Capitol Radio. D.J. Nicky Horne. You're mother wouldn't like it. Interview and a phone-in with questions from fans.
During the phone-in Bowie told a fan: "The Bewlay Brothers were, I suppose, very much based on myself and my brother. My brother was one of the bigger influences in my life." — Tape

20 and 21-10-1977 London, Dorchester Hotel. Press conference.
After press conference to Soho, to watch a film.
Bowie: "The Bewlay Brothers were, I suppose, very much based on myself and my brother. My brother was one of the bigger influences in my life. He sort of introduced me to authors that I wouldn't have read probably. The Jack Kerouac's, the Ginsberg's."

21-10-1977 With Zowie to Kenya, where they stayed overnight at Treetops (a place the British Royal family visited in 1952).

29-10-1977 BBC. Rock On. Interview with Bowie by Stuart Grundy (recorded earlier that month). — Tape — 27 min.

29-10-1977 Melody Maker. Article by Allan Jones: Goodbye to Ziggy and all that.
Jones wrote: "Heroes is the work of an artist who is willing to take risks but is more mature and sure of his intensions and effects and further evidence of Bowie's genius for dramatising the more controlled experiments of others as well as for seizing the real artistic mood of the times."

November 1977 Muziekkrant Oor (The Netherlands).
Interview: Het David Bowie tyfus interview.

November 1977 US TV. NBC. The Midnight Special. Heroes.	CD Video	Midnight Special
November 1977 US TV. Good Morning America. David Hartman has a 5-minute spot with David.	Tape Video	5 min. 5 min.

DATE / EVENT	AUDIO / VIDEO	TITLE

6-11-1977 Dutch TV. Pop Shop.
Interview by Vic Dennis (begin October in Amsterdam).
Bowie: "Some newspapers asserted I moved to Berlin in relation to politics but it's absolutely wrong. I am apolitical and I think a real artist is apolitical, because an artist is a dreamer."
Tape
Video

12-11-1977 Release Some weird sin (3.40) / Tonight (3.38) - Iggy Pop (RCA PB 9244). Produced, co-written and backing vocals by Bowie.

12-11-1977 New Musical Express. Article by Charles Shaar Murray: David Bowie: who was that (un)masked man?
Bowie about the album Low: "A reaction to having gone through that dull greeny-grey limelight of American rock 'n' roll and its repercussions. Pulling myself out of it and getting to Europe and saying for God's sake re-evaluate why you wanted to get into this in the first place."

27-11-1977 Daily News. Article by Susan Toepfer: A terminal case of cool.

End November / begin December. Bowie spends some time in Japan and Thailand.

Bowie: "Solitude, loneliness, and imprisonment… every album. I can't escape it or get out of my mold."

December 1977 Release in US: Promo 12", Beauty and the beast (Disco version) (5.18) / Fame (RCA PB 1190).

December 1977 New York. Bowie provided the narration of Peter and the wolf - Prokofiev.
Bowie was best man at driver / bodyguard Tony Mascia's wedding on Hudson Street. One of the other guests was Iggy Pop.
Good observers saw Tony Mascia as Bowie's driver in the film The man who fell to earth.

December 1977 Melody Maker. Heroes voted album of the year.

December 1977 Bowie gave a two-hour interview to Sony Fox for the King Biscuit Flower Hour.

December 1977 New York, Broadway. Bowie went to see a performance of Dracula.

December 1977 Max's Kansas City. Bowie introduced Devo on stage.

1-12-1977 Manchester-Piccadilly Radio. Broadcast by John Tobler.
French radio interview by Danielle Gilbert about The man who fell to earth.
Bowie: "Coming back to Europe I took a look at what I was writing and the environments that I was writing about and decided I had to start writing in terms of trying to find musical language for myself to write in. I needed somebody to help me 'cause I was a bit lost and too subjective about it all, so I asked Brian Eno if he would help me and that's
Tape   10 min.

DATE / EVENT	AUDIO / VIDEO	TITLE

how really all things started."

3-12-1977 New Musical Express. Bowie voted no. 1 singer and songwriter. Heroes no. 2 album. Interview with Eno (about working with Bowie): "It was much harder working on 'Heroes' than Low'. The whole thing, except 'Sons of the silent age,' which was written beforehand, was evolved on the spot in the studio. Not only that, everything on the album is a first take. We used Oblique Strategies a lot. 'Sense of doubt' was done almost entirely using the cards."

16-12-1977 Release Over the wall we go (2.48) / Beauty queen - Ivor Bird (later changed his name to Paul Nicholas) (RSO 2090 270). A-side written by Bowie.

Just before Christmas 1977. New York. Interview by Mick (40 min). Bowie was preparing to play the role of Egon Schiele. (he was studying all the books he could get).	1 CDR	*Sleeping next to you (Funny Tunes)*

A few days before Christmas 1977 Angie left Switzerland.

<u>24-12-1977</u> UK TV. ITV. Bing Crosby's Merry Olde Christmas Show. Recorded 11-9-1977. 1. Conversation (with Bing Crosby). 2. Peace on earth / Little drummer boy (with Bing Crosby) (4.23). 3. Heroes (3.09).	CD	*Christiane F./Baal/Rarities (Remembering Mark-Feld-Records)*
	CD	*This is your life (3) (PD 81997)*
	3 CDR	*Golden Moments 1978 (Old Gold Records OGCD 088A/B/C)*
	1 CDR	*The speed of life (Old Gold Records OGCD 158)*
	1 CDR	*Friends (2) (No label, no number)*
	CD	*Legendary Lost Tapes Vol. 1 (2,3) (VigOtone 178)*
	1 VCD	*Like the videofilms we saw (No label, no number)*
	1 VCD	*Bob's Eggs [+extras] (2) (No label, no number)*
	1 VCD	*I keep a good friend vol. 3 (No label, no number)*
	1 VCD	VideosOneBowie (No label, no number)
	LP	*Golden years of Bow (Gold Records DB 6791) (2,3)*
	Single	Peace on earth-Little drummer boy / Fantastic voyage (RCA PB 3400)
	Bootleg-Single	Peace on earth-Little drummer boy / Heroes (B&B)
	Video	quality 7, 10 min.
	Video	*Various 26 (8 min)*

DATE / EVENT	AUDIO / VIDEO	TITLE

Christmas 1977 Switzerland. David Hemmings visited David and persuaded him to appear in Just-a-Gigolo.

Late 1977 Bowie confirmed he would play in film Wally (*Cancelled*).

End 1977 Ex-Spider Woody Woodmansey's band U-boat released their first and only (very disappointing) album.

First weeks of 1978 in Berlin with Zowie and his nanny.

1978 Released in Argentine and France: David Bowie (reissue of Images 1966-1967) (Decca 291029).

1978 Released in France: Collection Blanche (reissue of Images 1966-1967) (251011/12).

1978 Release Fame / Golden years (RCA Gold Standard Series 10938).

1978 Book published: David Bowie - Discography - Colin (Subterraneans).

1978 Book published: Toute la musique (photo's) - Claude Gassian.

1978 Book published: The Melody Maker book of Bowie - Ray Coleman.

1978 French Radio. Europe 1. Interview. Questions in French, answers in English. He talks a lot about LP Heroes.	Tape	60 min.
1978 - Sunday meeting. French Radio. Interview. David lip synchs Heroes and talks about 1966 and The Lower Third.	Tape	60 min.

Bowie: "Ziggy Stardust was a plastic rock and roller. Much better than The Monkees. At first I just assumed the character on stage. Then everybody started to treat me as they treated Ziggy as though we were the next big thing, as though I moved masses of people. I became very convinced I was the messiah. Very scary. Almost Nazi-rock! Looking back about Ziggy he was created out of a form of a certain arrogance. The fucker wouldn't leave me alone and that's when it all started going bad and my personality was affected as I started taking Ziggy to interviews" (David Robert Jones: The discography of a generalist - David Jeffrey Fletcher 1979).

Angie Bowie: "By creating Ziggy to go out and front for him, David never had to act like himself in public if he didn't want to" (Backstage passes - Angela Bowie and Patrick Carr 1993).

Mick Ronson: "Falling into that role, David had to become what Ziggy was, he had to believe in him. Yes, Ziggy affected his personality. But he affected Ziggy's personality. They lived of each other. The success was very overnight. It was like waking up one morning and finding that we were suddenly superstars, with no preparation for it at all" (Glam! Bowie, Bolan and the Glitter Rock Revolution - Barney Hoskyns 1998).

1978 UK TV. Hey good looking.	Video	Various 20 (2 min)

DATE / EVENT	AUDIO / VIDEO	TITLE

Reporter talks about Heroes.

January 1978 Released in US: Bowie Now (compilation from Low and Heroes) (RCA DJLI-2697).

January 1978 Interview with Angie Bowie in Sunday Mirror.

January 1978 Zig Zag. Article about Bowie.

January 1978 Crawdaddy. Article by James Graig: Heroes.

January 1978 Bowie and son Zowie moved (with his nanny Marion) from Switzerland to Berlin.

2-1-1978 Vevey. Angie did a suicide attempt (overdose sleeping pills), fell from the stairs and broke her nose. She was brought to the Samaritans hospital (David Bowie - Jerry Hopkins 1985).

3-1-1978 Angie leaves the hospital.

3-1-1978 Daily Mirror. Article by Tony Robinson: Drama at Snow Chalet in Switzerland.
Robinson wrote: It was a sight I will never forget. There, crumpled at the foot of the stairs, lay Angie Bowie. Her face was covered in blood. Angie, wife of pop star David Bowie, had tried to kill herself in a fit of anxiety over her son on Bowie's birthday seven days ago.
She swallowed three handfuls of pills and tried to stab herself with a carving knife and finally threw herself downstairs.
Angie, 28, was unconscious on and off for nearly two days and when she recovered in hospital with a broken nose, two black eyes and cuts and bruises, she revealed to me that she had been expecting her lover's child.
Keeth Paul told me: "If I hadn't been there to help her, she would have died."

6-1-1978 Release Beauty and the Beast (3.32) / Sense of doubt (3.57) (RCA PB.1190).

Early 1978 Bowie asked Adrian Belew to play in his band. He did this after a Frank Zappa show (Belew played in his band). They went to a restaurant to talk it over. Zappa was in the same restaurant and was not friendly to Bowie.

7-1-1978 Melody Maker. Amanda Lear interviewed by Chris Brazier.
Amanda Lear: "With David it was great because it was a kind of symbiosis, an exchange, it wasn't just take, take, take. I introduced him to Germany, to expressionism and to Fritz Lang. I told him about Dali and he used 'Un chien Andalou' on his tour."

8-1-1978 New York. KBHF.   Tape   quality 9, 90 min.
Interview by Dave Hermann (to promote LP Heroes).

9-1-1978 Berlin. Bowie gave a statement to the press to react on Angie's accusations of kidnapping their son.

12-1-1978 Rolling Stone. Article by Charles M.Young: Bowie plays himself.

12-1-1978 Rolling Stone. Article by Bart Testa: Heroes.
Bart Testa wrote: We'll have to wait and see if Bowie has found in the austere Eno a long-term

DATE / EVENT	AUDIO / VIDEO	TITLE

collaborator who can draw out the substantial works and music that have lurked beneath the surface of Bowie's clever games for so long. But Eno has clearly affected a nearly miraculous change in Bowie already.

13-1-1978 Zowie and his nanny Marion travel from Bern into Switzerland.

21-1-1978 Radio Station JJJ (Australian Broadcasting Commission). Brian Eno interviewed by Tony Barrell.

22-1-1978 New York. Radio. Heroes special with a Bowie interview from 1977.   Tape   80 min.

January / February 1978 Filming for "Just a gigolo" started in Berlin. a.o. at the Café Wien on the Kurfurstendamm.

February 1978 Berlin. Snowdon takes photographs of Bowie for September 1978 issue of Vogue.

February 1978 Creem. Article by Trixie A. Balm: Heroes.

February 1978 Creem. Article by Robert Duncan: Anthromorphosis was never like this. Or is David Bowie really Billy Carter.

February 1978 Crawdaddy. Article by Timothy White: Turn and face the strange.

Begin February 1978 Interview by Michael Watts for Melody Maker (issued 18-2-1978).

8-2-1978 Bowie worked on a painting and woodcuts during the evening.

18-2-1978 Melody Maker. Article by Michael Watts: Confessions of an Elitist (interview during filming Just a Gigolo in Berlin).
Bowie: "I've decided I'm a Generalist now. I think that just about covers all grounds. It encompasses anything I wish to do. I find for instance I really want to paint seriously now and not toy with it."

18-2-1978 Melody Maker. Article by Michael Watts: Bowie Today.

18-2-1978 Melody Maker. Article by Michael Watts: From Brixton to Berlin.
Bowie: "I like Kraftwerk as people very much. Florian in particular. Very dry. When I came over to Europe I got myself a Mercedes to drive around in, cause I still wasn't flying at that time, and Florian saw it. He said "What a wonderful car," and I said "Yes, it used to belong to some Iranian prince, and he is assassinated and the car went on the market, and I got it for the tour." And Florian said, "Ja, car always lasts longer." With him it all has that edge. His whole cold emotion / warm emotion. I responded to that."

20-2-1978 London, Dorchester Hotel. Press Conference, announcing the Station to station tour.
Natsasha Kornilof designed Bowie's wardrobe.   Tape

End February 1978 Short holiday in Kenya with son Joe.

DATE / EVENT	AUDIO / VIDEO	TITLE

March 1978 Released in US LP David Bowie with Eugene Ormandy and The Philadelphia Orchestra / Peter and the wolf (RCA Red Seal ARL.I.2743).
Ralph Mace (director of European marketing) had approached Bowie to do the narration (David Bowie Theatre of Music - Robert Matthew-Walker 1985).

March 1978 Released in US one sided Promo LP Peter and the wolf (RCA JD 11306).

15-3-1978 Bowie comes from Kenya and stays 1 day in London.

From 16-3 till 25-3-1978 Rehearsals in Dallas.　　　　　　NT
The band had begun a several days earlier.
Bowie was tanned after a holiday in Kenya.

17-3-1978 Dallas. Bowie and Band visit rock club "Mother Blues."

25-3-1978 Bowie and the band travel to San Diego. They stay at a bowling alley complex.

The Low And Heroes World Tour:
David Bowie (vocals, keyboards).
Carlos Alomar (rhythm guitar).
Adrian Belew (lead guitar).
Dennis Davis (drums, percussion).
Simon House (electric violin).
Sean Mayes (piano, string ensemble).
George Murray (bass).
Roger Powell (keyboards, synthesisers)

29-3-1978 San Diego, Sports Arena.	2 CDR	San Diego 29 March 1978 (BowieHobby)
Attendance: 15.000.	2 CDR	San Diego sailor
Great crowd response. Stay is performed to perfection. Good concert. A pity the quality of the recording is not very good (a little to slow).	Tape	(Old Gold Records OGCD 152A/B) quality 7, 110 min.

29-3-1978 After concert in the hotel a jam-session　　NT
with Guadelajara National Philharmonic (4 girls
making funk-music).
Played about 4 songs (a.o. Sound and vision).

30-3-1978 Interviewed by Lisa Robinson for US magazine Hit Parade.
Bowie: "I'm incredibly happy now, because I'm not ambitious anymore. I do have a strong paternal streak. I'm a born father. I want more children, but no ego children, I'd like to adopt when my house is a little more in order."

30-3-1978 Phoenix, Arizona Veteran's Memorial Coliseum.　　NT
Attendance: 15.000.

April 1978 KULA. The Special of the Month. Interview.　　Tape　　32 min.

DATE / EVENT	AUDIO / VIDEO	TITLE

April 1978 Interviewed by Flo and Eddie for magazine Phonograph Record.

April 1978 Hit Parader. Article by Patti Smith: Heroes: A communique.
Smith wrote: In Sons of the silent age he is a metropolis valentino - very mythic very manic and very misunderstood. I get some kind of anger/anguish out of Blackout.

April 1978 Midnight Special. Flo & Eddie interview. 2 Versions: Short version (NBC TV, broadcast 21-4-1978), long version CBC-TV. A part of the interview is broadcast by Los Angeles radio on 6-4-1978. Bowie about recreating Ziggy: "If I was to do that I should have done that a long time ago. He was really one of the first characters to come along who wasn't fundamentally of the street, or one of the people."	Tape Video Video	*Stolp tapes no. 24 (short version, NBC, 2 min)* *Various 20 (long version, CBC, 12 min)*
2-4-1978 Fresno, Convention Center (Selland Arena). Attendance: 7.410.	Tape	
3-4-1978 Los Angeles. A TV-crew arrived for a brief interview with David before the Show. Featured on Eyewitness News on US TV.	NT	
3-4-1978 Los Angeles, Inglewood Forum. Attendance: 16.000. After the show David went to The Rainbow Club on Sunset Strip.	Tape	
4-4-1978 Eyewitness News with J.J. Jackson.	Tape	quality 8, 5 min.
4-4-1978 Los Angeles, Inglewood Forum. Attendance: 16.000. "We like to play some songs you may, or may not, remember" and they continue with Five years. In Rebel rebel Bowie mixes the lyrics up and sings: "You've got your guitar in a whirl, not sure if you're a boy or a girl."	2 CD 3 CDR 2 CDR 2 LP 2 LP LP LP LP 4 LP Tape	*Slaughter in the air (No label, no number)* Slaughter in the air (Old Gold Records OGCD 086A/B/C) *No Ziggy or Iggy - Just a gigolo (No label, no number)* No Ziggy or Iggy… Just a Gigolo (Omega 912 OMG 912) Slaughter in the air (Slipped Disc Recs SX-TT 979) Platter two (Duke 001 C/D) Bowie at the Los Angeles Forum - April 4, 1978 (Duke 001 A/B) Sampler (Duke 001 D) Unofficial Wembley wizard box file (Moonbeam Records) quality 8, 100 min.

DATE / EVENT	AUDIO / VIDEO	TITLE
5-4-1978 San Francisco, Oakland Coliseum Arena. Attendance: 14.200. No support act. Before the show they played songs from Iggy Pop's album The idiot. At the beginning of the second part of the show Bowie says: "We'll continue with a selection of very old songs." Followed by a selection of Ziggy songs.	2 CDR 2 CDR 2 CDR 2 CDR 2 CDR Tape	Live San Francisco 5/4/1978 (No label, no number) Speed of Frisco (Old Gold Records OGCD 155A/B) Live in California 78 (No label, no number) San Francisco 1978 (H Design) Oakland Coliseum quality 8, 105 min.
6-4-1978 Los Angeles Radio. Broadcast of part of Flo and Eddie interview.	Tape	
6-4-1978 Los Angeles, Inglewood Forum. Attendance: 16.000. A good concert. A pity my tape runs to slow. Before Five years the band intro. Then Bowie says some inaudible words and the crowd cheers.	2 CDR 2 CDR Tape	Protest on the wind (A Dutch Connection DCCD 060478) Slaughter in Los Angeles quality 8, 90 min.
7-4-1978 Release Single I got a right (3.20) / Sixteen (3.27) - Iggy Pop (RCA PB.9213). Produced by Pop / Bowie.		
9-4-1978 Houston, The Summit. Attendance: 16.000. A very good concert. When Bowie announces the selection of Ziggy songs the crowd goes wild.	2 CDR 2 CDR 3 CDR 2 CDR 2 CDR Tape Tape Tape	Houston 9 April 1978 (BowieHobby) The Summit -Houston 1978 (No label, no number) Slaughter in the air (Old Gold Records OGCD 086A/B/C) Houston The Summit April 9 1978 (No label, no number) Electric Dreams quality 9, 105 min. quality 9, 100 min. quality 9, 55 min.
10-4-1978 Dallas, Convention Center. Long Sound check. 4 Songs filmed for British TV. (Whistle Test etc.)	Tape	
10-4-1978 Dallas, Convention Center. Attendance: 9.820. 6 Songs filmed for US TV. 21 Minutes broadcast includes What in the world, Blackout, Sense of doubt, Speed of life, Hang on to yourself, Ziggy Stardust. Complete show filmed for private use. 2 Songs on BBC TV 16-5-1978 (Don Kirshners' Rock	3 CDR CD 1 CDR 1 CDR	From Dallas to Chicago (Old Gold Records OGCD 087) Wild mutation (2 songs. Bad sound quality) (BOW006) Dallas '78 CD One (No label, no number) Dallas '78 CD Two

DATE / EVENT	AUDIO / VIDEO	TITLE
Concert).		(No label, no number)
	2 CDR	The Texan
	CD	Hours… My death (2 songs) (DCCD 2000)
	VCD	Musikladen on stage (B3 CD015)
	VCD	I keep a good friend…. (No label, no number)
	VCD	Videobits Volume 1 (No label, no number)
	Tape	quality 8, 110 min.
	Video	Stolp Tapes no. 1 (18 min)
	Video	Stolp tapes no. 16 (21 min)
	Video	The video archives 1977-1980
11-4-1978 Baton Rouge, Louisiana State University Assembly Center. Attendance: 15.000. It took quite a long time before this concert got into circulation. But now there are at least 6 different good recordings of this very good show.	2 CD	Baton Rouge (Switch On! Devil KWSK 99-06-1/2)
	2 CD	Bowie 1978 (No label, no number)
	2 CDR	Blackout in Baton Rouge (No label, no number)
	2 CDR	Live in Baton Rouge (No label, no number)
	2 CDR	Goodnight Ziggy (Old Gold Records OGCD 136A/B)
	2 CDR	Cyberstation (1 song) (StationToBowie)
13-4-1978 Nashville, Municipal Auditorium. Attendance: 9.000. My tape of this concert is only 74 minutes and the sound quality is very uneven. Band intro: "From Nashville on lead guitar, Adrian Belew. And here are a few songs from Ziggy Stardust."	1 CDR	Neither Country Nor Western (inferior quality) (Old Gold Records OGCD192)
	2 CDR	Smiles like a toilet roll (Old Gold Records OGCD 194A/B)
	Tape	quality 8, 110 min.
	Tape	quality 9, 90 min.
	Tape	quality 8, 74 min.
14-4-1978 Memphis, Mid-South Coliseum. Attendance: 12.000.	NT	
15-4-1978 Kansas City, Municipal Auditorium.	NT	
17-4-1978 Chicago, Arie Crown Theatre. Attendance: 4.500. After the intermission Bowie wants the house light on a little bit more, so he can see the audience. During Five years he went on his knees twice to look at a red T-shirt that was	2 CDR	Chicago 17 April 1978 (BowieHobby)
	3 CDR	From Dallas to Chicago (Old Gold Records OGCD 087)
	2 CDR	I never touch you

DATE / EVENT	AUDIO / VIDEO	TITLE
thrown on stage.	Tape	quality 8, 110 min.
18-4-1978 Chicago, Arie Crown Theatre. Attendance: 4.500. During Breaking glass Bowie jumped of the stage, kissed a girl in the audience and jumped on the stage again. After the Show David joins the party in the Whitehall Hotel.	CDR Tape	Bits and pieces (Old Gold Records OGCD 174) quality 8, 70 min.
20-4-1978 Detroit, Cobo Arena. Attendance: 11.900. "Here's a character I wrote a long time ago. Here are some songs from Ziggy Stardust." David stops during Ziggy Stardust because of a few bouncers. He shouts: "Hold it! You… Go… This is not necessary. Too many fucking people are going fucking hurt in places like this. Don't do it! I ain't playing or singing no more man, unless it's enjoyable." The bouncers are removed from Cobo Arena and the performance starts again with Suffragette City.	2 CDR 1 CDR 2 CDR 4 CDR 4 CDR 2 CDR 2 CDR Tape Tape	Detroit 20 April 1978 (BowieHobby) Too many fucking people (Old Gold Records OGCD 193) Smiles like a toilet roll (Old Gold Records OGCD 194A/B) Cobo Arena Detroit 1978 (A Dutch Connection 1978202178) Breaking glass (No label, no number) Detroit 1978 First Night Swinging an old bouquet (No label, no number) quality 8, 105 min. quality 9, 110 min.

Bowie: "I haven't lived properly in America. I've been in Los Angeles coping with a town that I consider to be the most repulsive wart on the backside of humanity. I'd rather live here in Detroit than in Los Angeles" (David Bowie - The Archive - Chris Charlesworth 1981).

21-4-1978 Detroit, Cobo Arena. Attendance: 11.900. Toilet rolls and other stuff on stage. During Jean Genie Bowie sang: "He smiles like a toilet roll." Great version of TVC15. The crowd went wild. Riots during the concert. Years later Bowie commented on the aggressive Detroit crowds during several of his concerts.	2 CDR 2 CDR 4 CDR 4 CDR 2 CDR 2 CDR Tape Tape	Detroit 21 April 1978 (BowieHobby) Detroit 1978 second night (No label, no number) Cobo Arena Detroit 1978 (A Dutch Connection 1978202178) Breaking glass (No label, no number) Second Night in Detroit (MCW 99) Smiles like a toilet roll (Old Gold Records OGCD 194A/B) quality 8, 105 min. quality 9, 110 min.
21-4-1978 NBC. The Midnight Special.	Tape	

DATE / EVENT	AUDIO / VIDEO	TITLE
Interview by Flo & Eddie (recorded earlier that month).	*Video*	*Stolp tapes no. 24 (2 min)*
22-4-1978 Cleveland, Richfield Coliseum. Attendance: 20.000. At the hotel Swingo's Inn a meeting with the musicians about the next album (Stage). A local band spotted them in the bar. They announced David. He was not amused and just nodded.	1 CDR 4 CDR	*Parts of Cleveland (Old Gold Records OGCD 182)* 1978 Detroit Cobo Arena
24-4-1978 Milwaukee, Mecca Auditorium. Sound check. Strange acoustic, had to remix the piano (We can be heroes - Sean Mayes 1999).	NT	
24-4-1978 Milwaukee, Mecca Auditorium. Attendance: 6.850. Sound problems during Heroes. Very enthusiastic crowd.	2 CDR 1 CDR Tape Tape	*Genuine Stage! (35 min, same as tape, only available recording of this show) (Old Gold Records OGCD 175A/B)* *My kind of Mecca (Old Gold Records OGCD 545)* quality 8, 35 min. quality 7, 40 min.
26-4-1978 Pittsburgh, Civic Arena. Sound check.	NT	
26-4-1978 Pittsburgh, Civic Arena. Attendance: 18.000.	NT	
27-4-1978 Washington, Capitol Center. Attendance: 19.000.	NT	
28-4-1978 Philadelphia, Spectrum Arena. Special Sound check (The show would be recorded).	NT	
28-4-1978 Philadelphia, Spectrum Arena. Attendance: 17.500. "I'm happy to be in Philadelphia tonight. It's one of our favourite cities. Four years ago we recorded our live album David Live here and we liked the results so much, we've decided to record our second live album here over the next two nights." The recordings of this evening were too fast and not used for the double album Stage.	2 CDR 2 CDR Tape	*Genuine Stage! (compl.) (Old Gold Records OGCD 175A/B)* Stage live quality 7, 85 min.
29-4-1978 Philadelphia, Spectrum Arena. A long rehearsal before the show. First night's recording showed everything was going to fast.	NT	

DATE / EVENT	AUDIO / VIDEO	TITLE

<u>29-4-1978</u> Philadelphia, Spectrum Arena.   *CD*   *Stage*
Attendance: 17.500.   *CD*   *Spaced out (PB81998)*
A good concert.

May 1978 Dana Gillespie interviewed for Sounds. She talked about meeting Bowie.

Bowie: "It's an interesting thing that happened about that bi-sexual situation. It was really just a part of my life."

<u>1-5-1978</u> Toronto, Maple Leaf Gardens.   *2 CDR*   *Toronto 1 May 1978*
Attendance: 15.760.   *(BowieHobby)*
In Toronto David meets Lindsay Kemp with a couple   *1 CDR*   *Toronto '78*
of his mime troupe.   *(Old Gold Records OGCD 178)*
A good concert. Not much more to say about this one.   *2 CDR*   *New York hero (3 songs)*
Every concert when the crowd hears the drum part of the   *(Old Gold Records*
beginning of Five years they start to get exited. Good   *OGCD 177A/B)*
choice to do the band intro after the first cheers.   *2 CDR*   *Live at the Maple Leaf Garden*
   Tape   quality 7, 85 min.
   Tape   quality 8, 90 min.
   Tape   quality 7, 110 min.

<u>2-5-1978</u> Ottawa, Civic Center.   *2 CDR*   *Listen Bowie! (Old Gold*
A good concert.   *Records OGCD 179A/B)*
Bowie didn't speak a word, except for the band intro.   *2 CDR*   *New York hero (4 songs)*
         (Old Gold Records
         OGCD 177A/B)
   2 CDR   *Lepper Messiah*
         (KTLA CD130 1/2)
   Tape   quality 6, 100 min.

<u>3-5-1978</u> Montreal, Forum.   *1 CDR*   *Rumblin' Montreal (Old Gold*
Attendance: 16.000.   *Records OGCD 425)*
Before the Show Sean Mayes asks David why he isn't   *Tape*   quality 6, 40 min.
doing Heroes in French.
The single has 2 sides in Canada, English and French.
David says: "I can't remember the words now" (We can be
heroes - Sean Mayes 1999).

<u>5-5-1978</u> Providence, Civic Center.   NT
Attendance: 14.000.   *CD*   *Stage*
A good concert.
Recorded for the live album (Stage).

<u>6-5-1978</u> Boston, New Boston Garden Arena.   *2 CDR*   *The Garden Arena Boston 78*
Attendance: 15.500.   *(No label, no number)*
During the concert, someone threw two huge rocks   *3 CDR*   *Golden Moments 1978*
on stage. A good, but average concert.   *(Old Gold Records*
Recorded for the live album (Stage).   *OGCD 088A/B/C)*
The police removed two topless girls during Jean Genie.   *CD*   *Stage*

DATE / EVENT	AUDIO / VIDEO	TITLE
At the end of Rebel rebel there is no good coordination between Bowie and the band. Someone smuggled in a giant beach ball. The ball was punched around. The idea was later used by Bowie during the Serious Moonlight Tour.	CD 2 CDR Tape	*Pinups 3 (1 song)* *(BOWPU03)* Shared my life quality 9, 95 min.

7-5-1978 New York. Carlos Alomar was throwing a birthday party in the disco "Hurrah's." David put in a brief appearance with Bianca Jagger (first public appearance with Mrs. Jagger). In New York he stayed at the Regency Hotel.

<u>7-5-1978</u> New York, Madison Square Garden. Sound check.	Tape	

Adrian Belew: "During the sound check I'm on stage. Suddenly I hear behind me the trumpeting of elephants. I turn round and there are four elephants standing behind me. Apparently the Ringling Brothers Circus was being housed in Madison Square Gardens. Later in the day we were standing in the buffet-room, the door opens and in comes this chimpanzee on roller-skates."

<u>7-5-1978</u> New York, Madison Square Garden. Attendance: 19.600. Bianca Jagger stands near the stage. Attended by: Andy Warhol, Robert Fripp, Earl Slick, Brian Eno, Dustin Hoffman, members of Talking Heads. Great crowd response and an inspired Bowie. After Fame: "See you in 10 minutes. Thank you for coming." Band intro: "Dennis Davis on percusssssssion. And now some songs from Ziggy Stardust."	2 CDR 2 CDR 3 CDR 2 CDR Tape Tape	*New York 7 May 1978* *(BowieHobby)* New York '78 (Old Gold Records OGCD 434A/B) New York 78 (A Dutch Connection DCCD 07-08059178 One night at The Garden quality 7, 110 min. quality 9, 110 min.
<u>8-5-1978</u> New York, Madison Square Garden. Attendance: 19.600. A good concert. Brian Eno visits the musicians in the dressing rooms. After the show a party at Hurrah's.	2 CDR 2 CDR 3 CDR 2 CDR Tape Tape	*New York '78 - First night at the Garden* *(No label, no number)* New York hero (Old Gold Records OGCD 177A/B) New York 78 (A Dutch Connection DCCD 07-08059178 Second Night At The Garden 105 min. quality 8, 90 min.
<u>9-5-1978</u> New York, Madison Square Garden. After the show a party at Studio 54 and later at CBG's. Brian Eno and Bianca Jagger attended the party. When going home they discovered the tyres of the limo where slashed.	Tape	100 min.

DATE / EVENT	AUDIO / VIDEO	TITLE

10-5-1978 Bowie went to Paris to dub some vocals for the film "Just a Gigolo."

12-5-1978 Release LP TV Eye - Iggy Pop (RCA PL 12796). Produced by Bowie / Pop.

12-5-1978 Release in UK LP David Bowie with Eugene Ormandy & The Philadelphia Orchestra / Peter and the wolf (RCA Red Seal ARL. 12743).

13-5-1978 Sean Mayes, David, and Coco went to an Iggy Pop concert in London. Later in the dressing room Johnny Rotten joined them. They visited the London clubs Mankberry's and Tramps.

Date / Event	Audio/Video	Title
<u>13-5-1978</u> Frankfurt, Fest Halle. Rehearsal.	NT	
<u>14-5-1978</u> Frankfurt, Fest Halle. Attendance: 8.000. At the end of Breaking glass Bowie repeats "I never touch you" and starts laughing. Again a great concert.	2 CDR Tape	*Frankfurt 14 May 1978 (BowieHobby)* quality 8, 92 min.
<u>15-5-1978</u> Hamburg, Kongress Zentrum. Attendance: 3.000. A good concert. Bowie did not talk much, just the band intro. He did some improvisation during What in the world.	1 CDR 2 CDR 2 CDR 2 CDR Tape Tape	*Live in Hamburg (Old Gold Records OGCD 211)* *Hamburg '78 (KTLA CD135 1/2)* *Cosmic waves (Old Gold Records OGCD 212A/B)* *Hamburg 15 May 1978 (BowieHobby)* quality 5, 110 min. quality 8, 90 min.

16-5-1978 Dusseldorf, Philipshalle.
Cancelled.

David and the band visit Fritz Rau in Berlin for a meal. David in a very good mood, making jokes.

Date / Event	Audio/Video	Title
<u>16-5-1978</u> Berlin, Deutschland Halle. Attendance: 8.000. Tickets: DM 22,—. During Station to station bouncers knocked a boy down. David saw this and shouted: "No!" They continued and he stopped the music. David shouted: "No! Nein! Stop!" They stopped and David shook hands with the boy. They continued with Rebel rebel, followed by a complete version of Station to station.	2 CDR Tape	*Leave him alone! (Old Gold Records OGCD 213A/B)* quality 6, 110 min.
16-5-1978 UK TV. BBC2. Arena Rock. Don Kirshners' Rock Concert. Interview by Alan Yentob (8 min) and live clips of Hang on	Tape Video Video	*Stolp tapes no. 2 (1 min)* *Stolp tapes no. 24 (1 min)*

DATE / EVENT	AUDIO / VIDEO	TITLE
to yourself + Ziggy Stardust from Dallas show (10-4-1978).	Video	Various 20 (12 min)
18-5-1978 Essen, Gruga Halle. Attendance: 7.000. "Wie geht's Essen? Gut?" An average concert. Nothing exceptional happened.	2 CDR	Cosmic waves (Old Gold Records OGCD 212A/B)
	2 CDR	Essen 78 (No label, no number)
	Tape	quality 8, 100 min.
	Tape	quality 8, 110 min.
	Video	5 min.
19-5-1978 Cologne, Sport Halle. Attendance: 8.000. Bowie only introduces the band. For the rest he doesn't speak a word. Not in a good mood, I suppose.	2 CDR	Cologne 19 May 1978 (BowieHobby)
	2 CDR	Ein Kolner abend (Old Gold Records OGCD 241A/B)
	1 CDR	Live in Cologne, Germany 1978 - Disc 1 (no label, no n.)
	1 CDR	Live in Cologne, Germany 1978 - Disc 2 (no label, no n.)
	2 CDR	Germany
	2 CDR	Koln 78
	2 CDR	Sportshalle Cologne 1978 (A Dutch Connection CD 19051978)
Interview (Broadcast 30-6-1978 by Arena Rock).	Tape	quality 8, 90 min.
	Tape	quality 8, 115 min.
	Video	Stolp tapes 19 (12 min)
20-5-1978 Munich, Olympia Halle. Attendance: 12.000. A good concert. During What in the world he sings twice: "Something deep inside…" The last word is inaudible, but sounds different from the normal lyrics. After Star: "Thank you now."	2 CDR	Munich 20 May 1978 (BowieHobby)
	2 CDR	Leave him alone! (Old Gold Records OGCD 213A/B) (only encores: 4 songs)
	1 CDR	A Bavarian show (Old Gold Records OGCD 214)
	2 CDR	Olympiahalle Munchen 1978 (A Dutch Connection CDR)
	2 CDR	Munchen 78
	Tape	quality 8, 86 min.

21-5-1978 Bremen. Recording Musikladen Extra. TV Broadcast 30-5-1978. Broadcast on Dutch Radio (including Wild is the wind).

22-5-1978 Vienna, Stadt Halle (Reich Stadion). Attendance: 10.000. Local RCA officials welcomed David and held a small party after the show. To the end the concert gets better and the audience also gets	1 CDR	Wien 78 (Old Gold Records OGCD 242)
	1 CDR	Live Wien 78 Disc One (No label, no number)
	1 CDR	Live Wien 78 Disc Two

DATE / EVENT	AUDIO / VIDEO	TITLE

in a better mood.

		(No label, no number)
	2 CDR	*First stand in Wien 1978*
		(No label, no number)
	2 CDR	Stadthalle Wien May 22 1978
		(No label, no number)
	2 CD	*We can be heroes*
		(Switch On! 2001-11/12)
	2 CDR	Ein Kolner abend
		(Old Gold Records
		OGCD 241A/B)
	Tape	quality 8, 100 min.
	Tape	quality 9, 110 min.

22-5-1978 Vienna, after the show in the hotel. Carlos Alomar produced a cassette of the new live LP (Stage), so the band could listen to it for the first time.

23-5-1978 Cannes. Bowie attends the film festival. Watches a French-dubbed screening of Just a gigolo.

| 24-5-1978 BBC. Newsbeat. Interview. | Tape | 10 min. |

24-5-1978 Paris, Pavillion de Paris.　　　　　　　　NT
Sound check at 16.00 hour.

24-5-1978 Paris, Pavillion de Paris.	1 CDR	*First Pavillion (Old Gold*
Attendance: 7.000.		*Records OGCD 243)*
Keith Richards visits David before the show.	2 CDR	*Second Pavillion (3 songs)*
A good concert.		*(Old Gold Records*
A pity of all the cuts in my tape.		*OGCD 244A/B)*
	Tape	quality 7, 80 min.
	Tape	quality 8, 110 min.
	Video	quality 8, 34 min.

25-5-1978 Paris, Pavillion de Paris.	2 CDR	*Paris 25 May 1978*
Attendance: 7.000.		*(BowieHobby)*
Bowie only introduced the band. For the rest of the concert	2 CDR	*Second Pavillion*
he didn't speak one single word and just did his "work."		*(Old Gold Records*
After the show David invited everybody to The Palace		*OGCD 244A/B)*
(a disco).	2 CDR	Glasgow 1978
	Tape	quality 9, 110 min.
	Video	22 min.
	Video	25 min.

26-5-1978 Paris. A delay at the airport.
They sit in the plane and David and Coco are getting very nervous.
David: "Oh God, that means the pilot's drunk and they're feeding him black coffee" (We can be Heroes - Sean Mayes 1999).

| 26-5-1978 Lyon, Palais des Sports. | 2 CDR | *Modern feeling (Old Gold* |
| Attendance: 11.000. | | *Records OGCD 140)* |

DATE / EVENT	AUDIO / VIDEO	TITLE
A very good concert. Bowie's voice was very good and he was inspired.	2 CDR	Lyon 78 (A Dutch Connection DCCD 260578)
Very good version of Five years.	2 CDR	Glasgow 1978 (Old Gold Records OGCD 141A/B)
	LP	Modern Feeling Part 1 (UFO G 1017 A/B)
	LP	Modern Feeling Part 2 (UFO 1021 A/B) Part 1+2 is almost complete
	Tape	quality 8, 90 min.
27-5-1978 Marseille, Parc Chaneau. *Cancelled.*		
<u>27-5-1978</u> Marseilles, Palais des Sports. Attendance: 7.500. Tickets Kr. 150,—.	2 CDR	Marseille 27 May 1978 (BowieHobby)
A very noisy crowd. After Blackout a noise of speakers farting, then the lights went on. Carlos shouted: Everybody of the stage, the PA blew up.	2 CDR	Blackout! (Old Gold Records OGCD 246A/B)
	2 CDR	Marseilles 78 (No label, no number)
A girl jumped on stage and kissed Bowie.	Tape	quality 6, 85 min.
They left the stage and went to the hotel.	Tape	quality 8, 80 min.
The crowd started to riot, but the gig was saved.	Tape	quality 9, 90 min.
One hour later they drove back from the hotel to the hall and played the second part of the show with all the lights on.	Video	quality 8, 27 min. (5 songs)
<u>30-5-1978</u> German TV. WDR. Musikladen Extra. Recorded in Bremen 21-5-1978. Repeated on 4-8-1978 and 2-2-1979 (minus What in the world). Attended by: 150 Lucky Ones.	CD	*Secret Lounge 1977 Bremen (first 8 songs) (3D Reality Classics 3DC-DB-001 Bremen)*
1. Sense of doubt, Band-intro (3.51).	CD	*Look back in anger (9) (No label, no number)*
2. Beauty and the beast (4.53). 3. Heroes (7.32).	CD	*Musikladen on stage (No label, no number)*
4. Stay (7.01). 5. The Jean genie (6.27).	2 CDR	*Goodnight Ziggy (Old Gold Records OGCD 136A/B)*
6. TVC15 (4.36). 7. Moon of Alabama (4.23).	2 CD	*The return of the Thin White Duke (ODJN 004/05)*
8. Rebel rebel (3.34). 9. What in the world (4.21).	2 CDR	*David we love you! (9) (RDO Records)*
	1 CDR	Live at the Musikladen '78 (No label, no number)
	VCD	*Vapo(u)rware 1 (7) (VID 000/A)*
	VCD	*Musikladen on stage (8 songs) (B3 CD 015)*
	VCD	*TVC12 (3) (VCDB01)*

DATE / EVENT	AUDIO / VIDEO	TITLE
	1 DVD	1978
	LP	You need a tie to get in (7) (Deaf Records DEAF 1094 DK)
	LP	Looking into mirrors (D 12 - A/B)
	LP	Live in Bremen, West Germany (Mod 1010)
	LP	David Bowie live in Bremen '78 (Chameleon Records)
	LP	Bremen '78
	Video	*Stolp tapes no. 8 (44 min.)*
31-5-1978 Copenhagen, Falkoner Teatret. Attendance: 3.000. A very good concert. No exiting song order or a talkative Bowie, just a nice concert to listen to.	2 CDR	*Copenhagen 31 May 1978 (BowieHobby)*
	2 CDR	*Falkoner Teatret Copenhagen 78 (No label, no number)*
	3 CDR	*Golden Moments 1978 (Old Gold Records OGCD 088A/B/C)*
	1 CDR	Wonderful Copenhagen 78 (No label, no number)
	1 CDR	Copenhagen '78 - 1 (No label, no number)
	1 CDR	Copenhagen '78 - 2 (No label, no number)
	1 CDR	Live Copenhagen '78 (No label, no number)
	2 CDR	Dronningens By '78
	2 CDR	Sula vie dilejo (10 songs) (Old Gold Records OGCD 001A/B)
	LP	Recorded live on stage Copenhagen 1978 (MIW Records 25 MW 25 I/II)
	LP	A Scandinavian affair (No label, no number)
	Tape	quality 9, 105 min.
	Tape	quality 10, 30 min.
	Video	*Stolp tapes no. 12 (13 min)*

June 1978 Melody Maker (special edition). Book of Bowie, From idealism to alienation. Written by Ray Coleman, published by IPC.

June 1978 Melody Maker. Article by Michael Watts: Bowie on Bowie.

1-6-1978 Copenhagen, Falkoner Teatret. Attendance: 3.000. Promoter: ICO. A good show, but the only time Bowie spoke was when he introduced the band. After the show David and a few of the band went to	2 CDR	*Copenhagen 1 June 1978 (BowieHobby)*
	1 CDR	*Hang on to Copenhagen (Old Gold Records OGCD 247)*
	2 CDR	*Blackout! (Old Gold Records*

278

DATE / EVENT	AUDIO / VIDEO	TITLE

a big dance hall and had a crazy time playing cowboys and Indians among the crowd.

| | Tape | *OGCD 246A/B* (2 songs) quality 7, 109 min. |
| | Video | quality 9, 13 min. |

Brian Eno: "In 1974 or '75, I absolutely despised funky music. I just thought it was everything I didn't want in music. And suddenly, I found myself taking quite the contrary position. I suddenly found that, partly because of what David Bowie was doing and one or two other things - mostly Parliament and Bootsy and those people - I suddenly realized that if you took this a little bit further it became very extreme and interesting (Eno - Loder).

1-6-1978 Dagens Nyheter. Article by Mia Gerdin: Copenhagen conquered.

2-6-1978 Stockholm, Skansen.
Cancelled.

<u>2-6-1978</u> Stockholm, Kungliga Tennishallen.
Attendance: 5.000.
Started at 20.00 h. Tickets: KR. 95,—.
Breaking Glass is "stretched out" at the end and Bowie keeps repeating: "I never touch you."
The intro to Stay had some unusual guitar play.
A very good concert.

	2 CDR	*Stockholm 2 June 1978 (BowieHobby)*
	2 CD	*Alabama song + Other lovely songs (Seagull SEA CD019/1)*
	2 CDR	*Live in Stockholm (CD-R 78 0001)*
	2 CDR	*The real thing (Old Gold Records OGCD 048A/B)*
	2 CDR	*The real thing (version 2) (Old Gold Records OGCD 085A/B)*
	2 CDR	*Without faking it all (Y2K 100% British)*
	2 CDR	*Stockholm 78*
	2 LP	*Live in Stockholm '79 (ACR 25)*
	Tape	quality 8, 115 min.
	Tape	quality 9, 120 min.

3-6-1978 Melody Maker. Article by Allan Jones: Bowie: It's a blackout.

<u>4-6-1978</u> Gothenburg, Scandinavium.
Attendance: 7.000.
A good concert.
The sound quality of the bootleg Another stage is great!

	2 CD	*Another Stage (compl.concert) (Black Eagle BE 003/004)*
	CD	*Live in Stockholm 78*
	2 LP	*Live in Stockholm 1979 (Audifon ACR 25 A/D)*
	2 LP	*Live in Stockholm 1978 (ACR 25 Great Live Concerts ACR 25)*
	LP	*Golden years of Bow (Gold Records DB 6791) (1 track)*
	LP	*Live in Gothenburg (ACR 25)*
	Tape	quality 9, 108 min.

DATE / EVENT	AUDIO / VIDEO	TITLE
	Video	40 min.
5-6-1978 Oslo, Ekebergshallen. A very good show. It was Bowie's first concert in Norway.	CD	*This is your life (PD 81997)*
	2 CDR	*Oslo '78 (No label, no number)*
	1 CDR	*Live Oslo 1978 Disc One (No label, no number)*
	1 CDR	*Live Oslo 1978 Disc Two (No label, no number)*
	2 CDR	*Sula vie dilejo (Old Gold Records OGCD 001A/B)*
	1 CDR	*Neon Permafrost part 1 (Jumping Horse DB -009)*
	1 CDR	*Neon Permafrost part 2 (Jumping Horse DB -010)*
	2 CDR	*Ekeberg Hallen, Oslo (No label, no number)*
	2 CDR	*OzLow (remastered)*
	LP	*Recorded live on stage in Norway 1978 (MIW Records 30 MW MW 30 I/II)*
	2 LP	*Neon Permafrost (Ekeberg Records Freeze 2001 Sida 1/4)*
	Single	*Heroes / Heroes*
	Single	*Cracked heroes / Sexy actor (Heroes) (Slat Records TM)*
	Tape	quality 9, 90 min.

6-6-1978 Amsterdam. Carlos Alomar, Adrian Belew, Sean Mayes, David and Coco went for dinner in a French restaurant called "Le Bonsoir."
Bowie stayed at the Amstel Hotel in Amsterdam. The band was lodged at the Hilton Hotel in Rotterdam.

7-6-1978 Rotterdam, Sport Paleis Ahoy. Attendance: 7.500. Tickets from FL 15,— to FL. 30,—. Sold out in a few hours. Concert recorded by RCA. Good concert and a great crowd response and sing-a-long during the second part of the concert. A pity the quality of the tape is not so good. During Ziggy Stardust someone throws roses on the stage. Bowie picked out 1 rose. Adrian Belew did a very wild solo in Station to station. Bowie was very amused by the sight of it and had to lean on the piano to prevent falling on his knees with laughter. During the second encore Bowie was dressed in a fake snakeskin jacket (designed by Natasha Kornilof).	2 CDR	*We love you! (Old Gold Records OGCD 426A/B)*
	2 CDR	*David we love you! (RDO Records)*
	2 CDR	*Rotterdam 7 June 1978 (Art by Walter Ego)*
	2 CDR	*Rotterdam 7 June 1978 (BowieHobby)*
	Tape	quality 6, 90 min.
	Tape	quality 7, 110 min.

8-6-1978 De Volkskrant (Dutch newspaper). Article by Elly de Waard.
She wrote: "In the gangway people were embracing each other spontaneously. The audience leaving the

DATE / EVENT	AUDIO / VIDEO	TITLE
sports hall, are a happy audience."		
8-6-1978 Haarlems Dagblad (Dutch newspaper). Article by John Oomkes. He wrote: "Compulsion pathetic, sound wall and worship in Rotterdam."		
8-6-1978 Andy Warhol's Interview. Article by Lisa Robinson: David Bowie.		
<u>8-6-1978</u> Rotterdam, Sport Paleis Ahoy. Attendance: 7.500. Tickets from FL 15,— to FL. 30,—. Sold out in a few hours. Concert recorded by RCA. A very good concert. Bowie commented: "I think this was the best show of my European tour so far."	2 CDR	*Second Pavillion (5 songs) (Old Gold Records OGCD 244A/B)*
	1 CDR	*Ahoy 78 (Old Gold Records OGCD 245)*
	2 CDR	*Sportpaleis Ahoy*
	2 CDR	*Ahoy '78 Second Night (KTLA CD151 1/2)*
	2 CDR	Rotterdam 78 (No label, no number)
	Tape	quality 7, 90 min.
	Video	7 min.
<u>9-6-1978</u> Rotterdam, Sport Paleis Ahoy. Attendance: 7.500. Tickets from FL 15,— to FL. 30,—. Concert recorded by RCA. A very good show. After the show they went by Limousine to the Hotel, where they arrived at 23.00 hours. Then they went to some clubs in Amsterdam (the place they stayed during the Rotterdam concerts). One of the clubs was Bonaparte's.	2 CDR	*Last Ahoy 78 (Old Gold Records OGCD 065A/B)*
	2 CDR	*Ahoy '78 Third Night (KTLA CD152 1/2)*
	Tape	quality 6, 110 min.
	Video	7 min.
	Video	4 min.
11-6-1978 UK TV. BBC2. 22.55 h. Broadcast of the documentary "Cracked actor."		
<u>11-6-1978</u> Brussels, Vorst Nationaal. Attendance: 8.000. A good concert. Bowie didn't say much, except for the band intro. "On all kinds of percussion Dennis Davis." It's something I miss, compared with his later tours. But during the 2002 and 2003 tour he made this up. During some concerts he talked for 2 or 3 concerts. The way he enjoyed himself on stage in 2002 and 2003 must have made every Bowie fan happy.	2 CDR	*Brussel 11 June 1978 (BowieHobby)*
	1 CDR	*Live in Belgium (Old Gold Records OGCD 248)*
	2 CDR	*Blackout! (Old Gold Records OGCD 246A/B) (4 songs)*
	2 CDR	*Brussels 78 First Night (version one) (KTLA CD153 1/2)*
	Tape	quality 9, 90 min.
	Tape	quality 9, 95 min.
	Video	9 min.
<u>12-6-1978</u> Brussels, Vorst Nationaal. Attendance: 8.000. An average concert. Bowie didn't say a word, except for the band intro. Unusual long middle part during Art decade.	1 CDR	*More Belgium (Old Gold Records OGCD 249)*
	2 CDR	*Blackout! (Old Gold Records OGCD 246A/B) (3 songs)*
	1 CDR	*Brussels 78*

DATE / EVENT	AUDIO / VIDEO	TITLE
	2 CDR	*Brussels 78 Second Night (KTLA CD155 1/2)*
	Tape	quality 7, 90 min.

13-6-1978 London. Music Machine. Iggy Pop concert. Attended by Bowie.

| <u>14-6-1978</u> Newcastle, City Hall.
Attendance: 2.168.
Backstage: Trevor Bolder and Stuey George.
Average concert.
During the band intro: "I… Love to be loved." | 2 CDR

2 CDR
Tape
Tape
Tape | *No room to spare*
(Old Gold Records
OGCD 427A/B)
Newcastle, first show
quality 7, 105 min.
quality 8, 100 min.
quality 7, 10 min. |

15-6-1978 Rolling Stone. Article by John Milward: David Bowie: Man of many phases.

| <u>15-6-1978</u> Newcastle, City Hall.
Attendance: 2.168.
A good concert and an enthusiastic crowd.
Bowie did not say much.
No surprises in the song order and nothing extraordinary happened. | 1 CDR

1 CDR

2 CDR

2 CDR
2 CDR

Tape
Tape | *BowieCastle*
(No label, no number)
BowieCastle
(Old Gold Records OGCD 251)
Anybody home?
(Old Gold Records
OGCD 250A/B)
Newcastle, second show
Beauty before outrage
(No label, no number)
quality 8, 105 min.
quality 7, 90 min. |

| <u>16-6-1978</u> Newcastle, City Hall.
Attendance: 2.168.
Iggy Pop arrived and stayed for a week with the group.
At the intermission Bowie asks: "Anybody home?" | 2 CDR

2 CDR

2 CDR
2 CDR
Tape
Tape | *Newcastle 16 June 1978*
(BowieHobby)
Anybody home?
(Old Gold Records
OGCD 250A/B)
Newcastle 78 Third Night
Newcastle, third show
quality 8, 105 min.
quality 8, 115 min. |

| 16-6-1978 UK TV. Northern Light. Interview in Newcastle by Tyne Tees. | Video | 4 min. |

19-6-1978 Glasgow. Interview for TV show Reporting Scotland (broadcast 20-6-1978).

| <u>19-6-1978</u> Glasgow, Apollo, Renfield Street.
Attendance: 3.181. Promoter: MAM.
A good concert. Nice version of Ziggy Stardust. | 2 CDR

1 CDR

2 CDR | *Glasgow 19 June 1978*
(BowieHobby)
The first of four
(Old Gold Records OGCD 253)
Our last night here |

DATE / EVENT	AUDIO / VIDEO	TITLE
	2 CDR	(Old Gold Records OGCD 245A/B)
	2 CDR	Glasgow Apollo 78 First Night (No label, no number)
	2 CDR	First Night in Glasgow 1978 (A Dutch Connection)
	Tape	quality 8, 115 min.
20-6-1978 Glasgow. Interviewed by Jonathan Mantle for Vogue (September edition).		
<u>20-6-1978</u> Glasgow, Apollo, Renfield Street. Attendance: 3.181. Promoter: MAM. Tickets: GBP. 6,—. A very good show. At most songs the audience joins in.	2 CDR	*Glasgow 20 June 1978 (BowieHobby)*
	2 CDR	Glasgow 1978 (Old Gold Records OGCD 141A/B)
	2 CDR	Glasgow Apollo Theatre 20th June 1978 (No label, no number)
	2 CDR	Glasgow Apollo 78 Second Night
	2 CDR	Ice on the cages
	2 CDR	Apollo landing
	2 LP	Glasgow 1978 (KD 1004 A/D) complete except Warszawa
	Tape	quality 8, 110 min.
	Tape	quality 8, 95 min.
20-6-1978 Interview on regional TV Reporting Scotland, including live clip of Hang on to yourself shot 19-6-1978 at Glasgow, Apollo.		
<u>21-6-1978</u> Glasgow, Apollo, Renfield Street. Attendance: 3.181. Promoter: MAM. A good concert. After the 11th song (Beauty and the beast) he spoke his first words: "Thank you!"	2 CDR	*A frantic audience (Old Gold Records OGCD 252)*
	2 CDR	Anybody home? (Old Gold Records OGCD 250A/B)
	2 CDR	Glasgow Apollo 78 Third Night (No label, no number)
	Tape	quality 7, 105 min.
<u>22-6-1978</u> Glasgow, Apollo, Renfield Street. Attendance: 3.181. Promoter: MAM. "This is our last night here, I'm afraid." Bowie lets the audience finish the song Ziggy Stardust.	2 CDR	*Glasgow Apollo (No label, no number)*
	2 CDR	Glasgow Apollo 22.06.1978 (No label, no number)
	2 CDR	Our last night here (Old Gold Records OGCD 245A/B)
	2 CDR	Glasgow Apollo 78 Fourth Night
	2 CDR	Last Night Apollo Theater

DATE / EVENT	AUDIO / VIDEO	TITLE
	Tape Video	Glasgow '78 (No label, no number) quality 8, 120 min. 5 min.

23-6-1978 By train from Scotland to Birmingham.

24-6-1978 Melody Maker. Article by Chris Brazier: Seriously, it's Bowie.

DATE / EVENT	AUDIO / VIDEO	TITLE
<u>24-6-1978</u> Stafford, New Bingley Hall. Attendance: 7.800. Promoter: MAM. A good concert. During Sense of doubt a hard bang can be heard. After Beauty and the beast he spoke the first words.	2 CDR 2 CDR Tape Video	Stafford 24 June 1978 (BowieHobby) Stafford '78 First Night (KTLA CD163 1/2) quality 8, 90 min. 7 min.
<u>25-6-1978</u> Stafford, New Bingley Hall. Attendance: 7.800. Promoter: MAM. During Jean Genie (after 1.15 min) he starts singing to early and repeats the words. The audience sings Five years "en masse."	2 CDR 2 CDR Tape	Staffordism '78 (Old Gold Records OGCD 163A/B) Stafford '78 Second Night (KTLA CD164 1/2) quality 7, 105 min.
<u>26-6-1978</u> Stafford, New Bingley Hall. Attendance: 7.800. Promoter: MAM. An average concert. The crowd sang Five years 'en masse'. Great version of Station to station. After the show a party. A black woman accompanied David.	2 CDR 1 CDR 2 CDR 2 CDR Tape Video	Stafford 26 June 1978 (BowieHobby) Last night in Stafford (Old Gold Records OGCD 162) Staffordism '78 (Old Gold Records OGCD 163A/B) Stafford '78 Third Night (KTLA CD165 1/2) quality 7, 90 min. Super-8

28-6-1978 David attends a performance of Iggy Pop in The Music Machine in Camden (London). Also present was Johnny Rotten. The three went for a drink after the show. Bowie and Rotten did not talk to each other.

DATE / EVENT	AUDIO / VIDEO	TITLE
<u>29-6-1978</u> London, Earl's Court Arena. Attendance: 18.000. Bowie met his mother Peggy Jones. A good concert. Enthusiastic crowd. Concert filmed by David Hemmings for Bewlay Brothers Productions (but never released). Attended by Neil Tennant (Pet Shop Boys), Bianca Jagger, Dustin Hoffman, Iggy Pop, Bob Geldof, Brian May and Roger Taylor, Ian Dury, Clive Donner, Melvyn Bragg.	1 CDR 2 CDR 2 CDR 2 CDR 1 CDR	Back at Earl's court (Old Gold Records OGCD 159) Earls Court London, 29/06/78 (No label, no number) Staffordism '78 (Old Gold Records OGCD 163A/B) Earl of London (A Dutch Connection CD 290678) Earls Court 78

DATE / EVENT	AUDIO / VIDEO	TITLE
	2 CDR Tape Video	Be my wife quality 8, 105 min. quality 8, 105 min.
30-6-1978 UK TV. BBC. The Arena TV Show. Arena Rock. Ziggy Stardust and Hang on to yourself (London 29-5-1978) Interview Cologne 19-5-1978.	Tape *Video*	20 min. *Stolp tapes no. 19 (12 min)*
30-6-1978 (Before the show) Bowie was interviewed by Janet Street-Porter for London Weekend Television. LWT broadcasted a Bowie documentary of 38 minutes.	Tape *Video* *Video* Video	quality 9, 15 min. *Stolp tapes no. 8 (6 min)* *Stolp tapes no. 24 (1 min)* 38 minutes.
<u>30-6-1978</u> London, Earl's Court Arena. Attendance: 18.000. One of the best 1978 concerts! Bowie announced the first song: "This is a piece of music called Warszawa." Before, during and after the concert a lot of it filmed by David Hemmings. Hemmings differed from opinion with David about the quality of the film and it is never shown. Concert recorded by RCA. Interviews with Fans and Michael Watts. During the concert a banner was draped from the balcony: Ziggy Lives.	*1 CDR* 2 CDR 2 CDR 2 CDR Tape Video *Video*	*London Star (Old Gold Records OGCD 160)* Sound & Vision (Old Gold Records OGCD 161A/B) Live in London 30 Jun 78 (No label, no number) London 30 June 1978 (BowieHobby) quality 8, 113 min. *Stolp tapes no. 8*

After the show everybody went to a performance of the show Elvis! David joined Fumble in the dressing room. Together they went to the Alibi Club.

Summer 1978 director Clive Donner asked Bowie to play a part in his movie Wally (about the painter Egon Schiele). The project was cancelled because of money problems.

Summer 1978 The album Peter and the wolf is nominated for a Best Children's Recording Grammy. Kermit the Frog eventually won the Grammy.

July 1978 Release LP Night flights - Walker Brothers.
The album was an inspiration for Bowie and in 1993 he covered the title track.

<u>1-7-1978</u> London, Earl's Court Arena. Sound check.	NT	
<u>1-7-1978</u> London, Earl's Court Arena. Attendance: 18.000. Before the show David arrived with Bianca Jagger. As encore Bowie announced Sound and Vision: "This is something we never have done before." The backing-vocals were off-key. "This is the last night on tour, I'd like to thank Showco for the sound." During Stay Bowie throws his sailor's cap into the crowd.	*2 CDR* *1 CDR* 2 CDR 2 CDR	*London 1 July 1978 (BowieHobby)* *Various TV - vol. 3 (2 songs) (No label, no number)* Stage Earl's Court '78 Sound & Vision (Old Gold Records OGCD 161A/B)

DATE / EVENT	AUDIO / VIDEO	TITLE
Later on they went to a club called Tramp. David Hemmings films the show for a planned live documentary, but only a few clips are subsequently screened. Only time until 1990 that he sang Soul love. Be my wife (2.44), Sound and vision (3.24) on RarestOneBowie.	CD 1 CDR 2 CDR LP Tape Video	RarestOneBowie MoreRareBowie (2 songs) (No label, no number) Live at Earls Court 1978 (No label, no number) Cocaine adds life (Swastika Records 1-8-15-4-DB A/D) quality 9, 110 min.

2-7-1978 The Observer. Article by Dave Gelly: The Hero.

2-7-1978 In Tony Visconti's Good Earth studio in Dean Street they recorded Alabama Song.

3-7-1978 Daily Mail. Article by Bart Mills: A smile on this new face of Bowie.

| 6-7-1978 2 LWT's London Weekend Show (broadcast 8-7-1978). Including clips from Earl's Court 30-6-1978 (Star, Heroes, Hang on to yourself) and interview by Janet Street-Porter. | Video | Stolp tapes no. 8 (38 min) |

8-7-1978 Melody Maker. Article by Michael Watts: Earls Court: Station to station.

Summer 1978 in Berlin a disco called Bowie opened. July 1978 Bowie appeared in the disco.

| 4-8-1978 German ZDF TV's Musikladen. Same as 30-5-1978, minus What in the world. | Video | 4 min. |

12-8-1978 Bowie visits a new Berlin punk-disco called 50 36. Performance of Berlin group PVC.

September 1978 Creem. Article by M.Goerge Haddad: Bowie: No Ziggy of Iggy… just a gigolo.

Early September 1978 Recordings in Montreux for the album Lodger.
Only the (basic) rhythm tracks.
Working titles: Planned accidents, Strange accident, Some desperate lines, Despite straight lines.

Tony Visconti: "I remember when we were doing the backing vocals to Red Sails. There was David, Brian Eno and myself. In the studio is right off a casino. The side door to the studio was left unlocked. In walked these three Swiss waiters, carrying food to somewhere. They had obviously walked through the wrong door. I opened my eyes and said: "Oh my God!"
I was shaking David, but the headphones were so loud they were totally into it. The waiters saw these three maniacs acting like German operatic singers!" (The Starzone Interviews - David Currie 1987).

Adrian Belew: "I remember we were being woken by the voice of Mary Hopkin. She did her early morning vocal exercises at an open window."

Sean Mayes: "They were using this pack of cards that was developed by Brian Eno and a friend called Oblique Strategies'. You would just shuffle the cards and pick one out. A very odd way of working" (In other words - Kerry Juby 1986).

DATE / EVENT	AUDIO / VIDEO	TITLE

September 1978 Vogue (UK version), Interview with Bowie by Jonathan Mantle (Glasgow 20-6-1978) and photographs taken by Snowdon (Berlin, February 1978): A really strange kettle of poisons.

September 1978 Re-release Liza Jane (2.18) / Louie Louie go home (2.12) - David Jones with The King Bees (Decca F13807).

September 1978 Re-release The laughing gnome (3.01) / The gospel according to Tony Day (2.48) (Deram DM 123).

September 1978 Bowie made a public statement. He wanted to leave RCA and was seeking to move to a new label.

2-9-1978 New Musical Express. Article about Bowie.

8-9-1978 Release 2LP Stage (RCA CPL.2.2913).

8-9-1978 Release Promo single: Star (2.47) / What in the world (2.21) / Breaking Glass (1.52) (RCA EP-L3255).

8-9-1978 Covent Garden. Bowie spotted Jubilee market for old photographs.

25-9-1978 Paris. Photo session for the December edition of Italian edition of Vogue.
During the photo session an interview by phone from Sydney for Australian radio series The Golden Years of David Bowie (Broadcast 25-11-1978).

30-9-1978 Melody Maker. Article by Chris Brazier: Stage.

October 1978 Released in US Promo LP: An evening with David Bowie (RCA DJL 1-3016). 4 Live songs and interview.   CD   An evening with David Bowie

October 1978 Released in US: The Robert W.Morgan special of the week (Watermark Series 3). Interview.

8-10-1978 Jacques Brel died.

8-10-1978 Press release by RCA stating that Bowie did not have the intention to leave RCA.

14-10-1978 The Sunday Times. Article by Leslie Fields: Seventies Style.

November 1978 Creem. Article by Penny Valentine: Letter from Britain: Living up to Bowie.

November 1978 Receives from RCA-Australia a reward for outstanding sales.

November 1978 Australian TV. B4 Show. Sound check (Alabama Song).   Video   quality 8, 5 min.

Begin November 1978 Somebody lent them a boat and the band (including David) had a nice day

DATE / EVENT	AUDIO / VIDEO	TITLE

swimming and sun bathing (We can be heroes - Sean Mayes 1999).

<u>5-11 Up to and including 9-11-1978</u> Sydney. Rehearsals. After the last rehearsal David, Coco and Sean Mayes left by limo. The limo had a flat tyre. After the tyre was fixed they went to a couple of clubs. The last club was the Manzil Room.

NT

10-11-1978 By plain to Adelaide.

The Oz Tour:
<u>11-11-1978</u> Adelaide, Oval Cricket Ground.
Attendance: 20.000.
Support act: The Angels.
In the dressing-room (a caravan) David watched TV because he was interested in a TV-programme with a new group called Dire Straits.
He talked about TV-commercials, how funny they are and imitated some of them. One was about shoes (for the real men) and slippers.
Halfway the show David said: "We're just going off for ten minutes, and when we come back… we won't be wearing slippers."
On this date, Roger Powell is playing with his regular band, Utopia, and his place is taken by local musician, Denis Garcia.
After the show they went to a boring nightclub and left early.

2 CDR — *Sense of Adelaide (Old Gold Records OGCD 054A/B)*
CD — *The speed of life (MCDS 0799B)*
1 CDR — The speed of life (Old Gold Records OGCD 158)
2 CDR — Glasgow Apollo Theatre 20th June 1978 (10 tracks) (No label, no number)
3 LP — When gravity fails (Slaughtered Lamb Ziggy A/B Ziggy II A/B DB 6142 A/B)
LP — The Speed of life (DB 6142)
Tape — quality 9, 105 min.

<u>14-11-1978</u> Perth, Showgrounds.
Attendance: 15.000.
Support act: The Angels.
On this date, Roger Powell is playing with his regular band, Utopia, and his place is taken by local musician, Denis Garcia.
After the show David, Coco and Sean Mayes went to a modern disco called Connections.

Tape — quality 8

14-11-1978 Australian TV Show. Countdown. Includes interview and parts of live clips of Alabama Song and Ziggy Stardust.

Video — *Stolp tapes no. 8 (8 min)*

15-11-1978 With a motor launch they all went for a trip up the Swan River.

16-11-1978 By plain to Melbourne.

16-11-1978 Premiere "Just a gigolo" at Gloria Palast, Kurfuerstendamm (Berlin).

Gitta Fuchs: "He seemed so lonely in the Aufnahme. He didn't know how to mix. He was smart and

DATE / EVENT	AUDIO / VIDEO	TITLE

sort of set apart. I think he was unsure of himself, deep down."

17-11-1978 Release Breaking glass (live) (3.27) / Ziggy Stardust (live) (3.32) / Art Decade (live) (3.10) (RCABOW 1).

<u>17-11-1978</u> Melbourne, Cricket Ground. NT
A wet Sound check.

<u>18-11-1978</u> Melbourne, Cricket Ground. 2 CDR Down under 1978 (10 tracks)
Attendance: 20.000.   (Old Gold Records
Support act: The Angels.   OGCD 053A/B)
During the show: Torrential rain. CD *Kiss you in the rain (45 min)*
Bowie says: "If you're crazy enough to stay for this while   *(MCDS 0999B)*
it's raining, we're crazy enough to play." LP Kiss you in the rain (DB 6143)
After the show (in the hotel) David called Sean Mayes and
said: "Quick Quentin Crip's on TV!" (We can be heroes -
Sean Mayes 1999). Sean Mayes didn't like TV at all.

19-11-1978 To the airport for the flight to Brisbane.

<u>21-11-1978</u> Brisbane, Lang Park. Tape quality 8
Attendance: 15.000. Tickets: Aus. $ 12,50.
Support act: The Angels. Started at 20.00 hours.
Promoter: Paul Dainty.
Later Mr. Russ Hinze (a Queenland's minister) complained
about the loud noise that could be heard 6 km away (A
Chronology - Kevin Cann 1983).

22-11-1978 They flew back to Sydney.

22-11-1978 David went to see Peter Frampton in his hotel.

23-11-1978 David, Coco and Sean Mayes went to The State Theatre, to see Bette Midler.

<u>24-11-1978</u> Sydney, RAS Showgrounds. *2 CD* *Forever yours (102 min.)*
Attendance: 20.000. Started at 19.30 h.   *(No label, no number)*
Promoter: Paul Dainty. 2 CDR Down under 1978
Support act: The Angels. Tickets: Aus $ 12.50.   (Old Gold Records
During Stay he sang: "Stay, yes you wanted to stay, and I   OGCD 053A/B)
didn't know what to say, but I wanted you to stay. I didn't 2 LP Forever yours (DB 6894)
know what to say, so I let you go. Yes I let you go, yes I Video quality 10, 4 min.
let you go. Why didn't you stay."

<u>25-11-1978</u> Sydney, RAS Showgrounds. Tape quality 8
Attendance: 20.000.
Support act: The Angels. Ticket price: Aus $ 12.50.
David in a very good mood.
Then he started everyone singing along to a beer
commercial: Have another Tooey, have another Tooey,

DATE / EVENT	AUDIO / VIDEO	TITLE

have another Tooey or two!
"We'll be back next year - I promise!"
For the second encore he came on stage alone.
He sang a line from With a little help from my friends (Beatles, 1967): "What would you do if I sang out of tune - would you walk out on me?" Crowd: No!

25-11-1978 Australian Radio. Radio series The Golden Years of David Bowie. Interview recorded by phone on 25-9-1978 while Bowie was in Paris for a Vogue photo-session.
Bowie: "I only learnt to swim last week (September 1978). I'm very proud of myself. I can do the crawl. I can only do one length."

27-11-1978 They arrived in New Zealand.

| 28-11-1978 Australian TV. Channel 7. Willesee at Seven. Experts of promo video's and interview (11 min) by Mike Willesee. | *Video* | *Various 20 (13 min)* |

| 29-11-1978 Christchurch, QE II Park. | NT | |

30-11-1978 In the hotel they made Thai food especially for David. After the food they all went downstairs to the pinball room and joined the crowd round the machines. There was nothing else to do in Christchurch.

30-11-1978 Rolling Stone. Article by Johnny Rogan: Stage.

December 1978 Italian edition Vogue. Photo session with Bowie (shot in Paris, 25-9-1978).

December 1978 Juke (Australian magazine). Article about Bowie.
They wrote: Rumours that bizarre rocker David Bowie was paid in gold to avoid customs and taxation, have been established as false.

1-12-1978 By plane to Auckland.

2-12-1978 In the morning David, Coco, Rick and Sean took a jeep and went walking over the cliffs.

| 2-12-1978 Auckland, Western Springs Speedway. Second half of the concert they all took their cameras and photographed the crowd. | NT | |

3-12-1978 By plane to Sydney.

4-12-1978 By plane to Tokyo. A TV-crew filmed the arrival.

5-12-1978 By train to Osaka.

| 6-12-1978 Osaka, Koseinenkin Kaikan. A guy called Anthony did David's subtle stage make-up. Show was broadcast on Japanese FM radio. | *CD* | *Reaction (not complete) (DBO-2269)* |
| | *1 CDR* | *Osaka '78 (49 min.)* |

DATE / EVENT	AUDIO / VIDEO	TITLE
During the band-intro: "On a new, Japanese drum set, Dennis Davis. He just got it today. He's very pleased with it." After the show they went to a small, dull disco.	1 CDR	*(No label, no number)* Reaction (Old Gold Records OGCD 159)
	2 CDR	The complete reaction (Old Gold Records OGCD 189A/B)
	2 CDR	*Osaka 6 Dec 1978 (BowieHobby)*
	2 CDR	Isolar II (No label, no number)
	Tape	quality 9, 110 min.
6-12-1978 Japanese TV. Star Sen Ichi Ya. Interview	Video	10 min.
7-12-1978 Osaka, Koseinenkin Kaikan. An average concert. During Jean Genie (at the 2nd sentence) he forgot a part of the lyrics and switched to the part of the lyrics he knew. No applause after Sense of doubt. The audience did not know the song at all! Special ending to Beauty and the beast. Station to station had a very special intro. Only at the end, before the encores the crowd can be heard very clearly.	*2 CDR*	*Osaka 7 Dec 1978 (Bowiehobby)*
	2 CDR	*Osaka 1978 Second Night* (No label. No number)
	1 CDR	Osaka songs (Old Gold Records OGCD 189)
	2 CDR	The complete reaction (Old Gold Records OGCD 189A/B)
	1 CDR	Live Osaka 1978 Disc One (No label, no number)
	1 CDR	Live Osaka 1978 Disc Two (No label, no number)
	Tape	quality 9, 110 min.
8-12-1978 They took a trip to Kyoto to visit temples and shrines.		
9-12-1978 Osaka, Banpaku Kaikan. A good concert. Beauty and the beast had a very nice ending. After the song Bowie says various lines, but they are not audible. After introducing Dennis Davis Bowie says something funny, but again it is not audible on my tape. Great version of Ziggy Stardust. Special effects during Art Decade.	2 CDR	Japanese hero (Old Gold Records OGCD 190A/B)
	2 CDR	Osaka
	2 CDR	*Under Japanese Influence* (No label, no number)
	Tape	quality 8, 105 min.
9-12-1978 Record Mirror. Article: 100 Bowie albums to be won.		
9-12-1978 Melody Maker. Article by Michael Watts: When Bowie's bad, he's bad.		
10-12-1978 By train to Tokyo.		
11-12-1978 Tokyo, Nihon Budokan Arena (NHK Hall). Attendance: 10.000. A very average concert.	2 CDR	*Live at the Budokan '78 First Night* (No label, no number)
	1 CDR	Tokyo 1978

DATE / EVENT	AUDIO / VIDEO	TITLE
Before Five years there was a long drum intro, before Bowie started introducing the band: "On… guitar (starts laughing) Carlos Alomar. Have you seen the papers the other day. There's a calf born with 2 heads. Did you see that?" No crowd response. Long version (16 min.) of Station to station.	2 CDR 1 CDR 2 CDR 2 CDR 2 CDR Tape Tape Video	(Old Gold Records OGCD 191) Japanese hero (Old Gold Records OGCD 190A/B) Is there life in Tour? (No label, no number) Budokan '78 *Live at NHK Hall, 11-12-1978* *(BowieHobby)* Breaking Budokan quality 7, 110 min. quality 9, 110 min. *Stolp Tapes no. 1 (60 min)*
<u>12-12-1978</u> Tokyo, Nihon Budokan Arena (NHK Hall). Sound check.	NT	
<u>12-12-1978</u> Tokyo, Nihon Budokan Arena (NHK Hall). Attendance: 10.000. Recorded for Japanese TV programme The Young Music Show (60 minutes, titled: Low/Heroes Tour). During Five years Dennis Davis wore a gorilla mask. After some songs he took it off. Very long version of Station to station (15.20 min.). The song had an intro of 8,5 minutes. After the show a party called: Just a Gigolo (at the Bee Club). Start of the party: 10.30 pm. Dress: 1920's style optional, black tie.	1 CDR CD CD CD 1 CDR 2 CDR 4 CD 2 CDR 1 VCD 2 VCD LP LP Tape Video	*Tokyo 12 December 1978* *(BowieHobby)* *Wild mutation (BOW 006)* *Hoping for a little romance* *(Ypu J-002)* *TV confessions* *Is there life on tour?* *(No label, no number)* *Live at NHK Hall, 12-12-1978* *(BowieHobby)* *Watch that man in Tokyo* *(BOW 5162/63/64/65)* Beast *Young Music Program* *(No label, no number)* Wild Mutation David Bowie at Judo Arena (Budokan) (IPS IP-C-8881 A/B) Merry Christmas Mr. Bowie (Audio Recording Corp. ARC 1001) quality 9, 60 min. quality 9, 60 min.

December 1978 Bowie attended the Premiere of Just a Gigolo in Japan and the party at the Roppongi disco with a woman called Dewi Sukarno.

14-12-1978 David, Coco and Sean went to a Japanese restaurant. David was in the company of a charming Japanese girl.

15-12-1978 David, Coco and Sean went to Asuka, an old part of Tokyo, where the Sensu-ji Temple of

DATE / EVENT	AUDIO / VIDEO	TITLE

Kannon is.

Christmas 1978 David, Zowie, Coco and Anthony (the make-up man) in Kyoto. David and Zowie stayed in Kyoto the first part of January 1979.

End 1978 German TV. Rock Concert Highlights of the 1978 Tour.

End 1978 / Begin 1979 Rainbow Theatre, Finsbury Park. Part of the movie Breaking Glass was filmed. Bowie was not involved in the project. If you look closely you can see Boy George during a crowd scene (Take it like a man - Boy George biography 1995).

1979 Released in Australia: Chameleon (compilation from Ziggy Stardust to Lodger) (Starcall STAR 101).

1979 Released in US: 1980 All clear (compilation from Space oddity to Lodger) (RCA DJLL-3545).

1979 Released in Italy: La Grande Storia Del Rock (Deram compilation) (Decca GSR 21).

1979 US Radio. Pioneers in Music.   Tape   quality 10, 50 min.
Mott The Hoople live 8-5-1974. Interviews and music by
Ian Hunter, Roxy Music, David Bowie and T.Rex.

1979 Book published: Pop Score - Jip Golsteijn (Teleboek b.v., ISBN 906122703 8). Partly about Bowie.

1979 Book published: Bowie lives and times - Bootleg Records Illustrated (Babylon Books) (No ISBN number).

1979 Book published: Subculture: The meaning of style - Dick Hebdige (Methuen).
Hebdige about Bowie, Roxy Music and Lou Reed: "Extreme foppishness, incipient, elitism and morbid pretensions to art and intellect effectively precluded the growth of a larger mass audience."
Well Mr. Hebdige. If Bowie didn't have a mass audience in the early seventies, who did have?
"Bowie has in effect colluded in consumer capitalism's attempt to create a dependent adolescent class, involved as passive teenage consumers in the purchase of leisure, instead of questioning the value and meaning of adolescence."
If Mr. Hebdige thinks the Bowie fans were just a bunch of passive teenagers in the seventies, I think he hasn't met many!

1979 Book published: Up and down with the Rolling Stones - Tony Sanchez (William Morrow).

1979 Book published: Christiane F (Wir Kinder vom Bahnhof Zoo) - Kai Hermann and Horst Rieck (Stern-Magazin im Verlag Gruner + Jahr AG & Co.). In 1980 in Dutch translation by J.H. Gottmer. ISBN 90 257 2663 1. Bowie mentioned on page 39, 40, 41, 68, 69 and 70. Page 70 refers to the Berlin concert on 10-4-1976. Page 70 and 71 refer to Station to station.

1979 Book published: The Elephant Man (A play by Bernard Pomerance) - Bernard Pomerance (Grove Press Inc.). ISBN 0-394-50642-1.

1979 Book published: The Seventies - D. Wiegel and E. Wil (Almere Projects, ISBN 90.70205.02.5).

DATE / EVENT	AUDIO / VIDEO	TITLE

1979 Book published: Just a gigolo - Rosemary Kingsland (Corgi Books, ISBN 0 552 11005 1). Based on the 1978 film script. Paul Przygodski is a gigolo. In the Lutzower Club in Berlin he met men made up like women and some even with dresses on, some women in severely tailored British-styled suits and cropped hair.

1979 Belgian TV. Follies. Special. Video 11 min.

1979 The London club The Blitz organised a regular Bowie Night (Club for Heroes).

1979 London, Legend (Gay Club).
Marilyn (a friend of Boy George) slid on Bowie's lap and kissed his ear. Bowie was stony-faced and ignored him (Take it like a man - Boy George biography 1995).

January 1979 Creem. Article by Jeffrey Morgan: Stage.

January 1979 Stereo Review. Article by Steve Simels: Stagey Bowie.

February 1979 US TV. Don Kirshner's Rock Concert. NT
Songs recorded 10-4-1978 in Dallas.

February 1979 Swiss TV. Heroes of rock and roll. Video 2 min.
Including Ziggy Stardust from Cracked Actor documentary.

2-2-1979 The Musikladen show of 30-5-1978 is repeated on German television (minus What in the world).

9-2-1979 The Nashville. Bowie attends Human League concert. Bowie very interested in the light and slide show handled by Adrian Wright). Bowie called the concert: "Watching 1980." One of the other observers that night was Gary Numan.

12-2-1979 Thames at Six. Interview with Rita Carter. Tape 5 min.
  Video *Stolp tapes no. 19 (10 min)*

12-2-1979 UK TV. BBC1. The Tonight Show. Interview Video 10 min.
by Valerie Singleton about Just a Gigolo (9 min). Footage Tape 12 min.
of the film. She opened with footage of Aladdin Sane
doing Watch that man on 3-7-1973.

12-2-1979 UK TV. Good Afternoon. Interview by Mavis Video *Stolp tapes no. 19 (9 min)*
Nicholson (about Just a gigolo). Tape 7 min.
Bowie: "I've always dealt with isolation in everything I've
written, I think. So it's something that triggers me off if it
always interests me in a new project."

13-2-1979 London. Before the Capital Radio interview Tape quality 8, 15 min.
there was another (short) interview.

13-2-1979 Capital Radio. Interview by Nicky Horne at Tape quality 9, 120 min.

DATE / EVENT	AUDIO / VIDEO	TITLE

Capitols' Euston Tower for Your mother wouldn't like it. Also questions of fans on the phone.
Bowie acted like a DJ playing a lot of records. He played his and Iggy's China Girl which he calls absolutely romantic. He also played Baby's on fire by Brian Eno, Shapes of things by The Yardbirds, The Batman Theme by Link Wray, White light white heat by Velvet Underground.
Bowie: "I was David Jones from Brixton who wanted to do something artistically important. But I didn't have the courage to show me as myself to the audience."
He also talked about the years 1962 / 1963. He and George Underwood sometimes went to Eel Pie Island, the AA Athletic Ground and the Crawdaddy clubs in Richmond on Friday nights, to see Gary Farr and The T Bones, The Tridents (Jeff Beck's group prior to The Yardbirds). As they had no scooters, they travelled back to Sundridge Park Station on the milk train.

14-2-1979 Daily Express. Article by Jean Rook: Bowie reborn (interview in Dorchester Hotel).
Bowie: "For years I daren't walk out of my front door alone. I was paranoid about it, terrified. It still takes me courage to walk from A to B and not think, "This person walking down the street is David Bowie and everybody's looking at him." Now I look at other people. I even go into shops and, if somebody talks to me, I chat back."

14-2-1979 London. Café Royal in Regent Street. 15-Minute press conference. Short photo-session (during which Bowie kissed Sydney Rome).

14-2-1979 Bowie attends premiere of his latest film Just a Gigolo (Tedderwick Ltd and Leguan Film Prod.) at Prince Charles Cinema, Leicester Square, London W1, accompanied by actress Viv Lynn (both wore kimonos and wooden clogs).
In aid of the Neighbourhood Trust For Cancer Research.

Various TV reviews of the 14-2-1979 premiere:

Dutch TV. TV Clip & comments.	Video	1 min.
Dutch TV. TV Clip & review.	Video	4 min.
German TV. Kennen Sie Kino?	Video	3 min.
UK TV. Film 79.	Video	4 min.

15-2-1979 Bowie went to New York. He saw a Nico concert at CBGB's (he was in the company of David Byrne). Saw in the Greek Theater a Talking Heads concert.

16-2-1979 UK TV. ITV. Afternoon Plus. Interview.	Tape	10 min.

Bowie: "I do fall in love quite quickly. Once upon a time I used to fall in love quite a lot. I think love is very important for my writing."

17-2-1979 Recording Boys keep swinging for the Kenny Everett Show. Broadcast 23-4-1979.

DATE / EVENT	AUDIO / VIDEO	TITLE

21-2-1979 Release LP Just a Gigolo (Jambo Records JAM 1).

21-2-1979 Released in Japan Revolutionary song (3.43) / Charmaine - The Rebels (Jambo MA-185-V).

2-3-1979 Re-release I pity the fool (2.09) / Take my tip (2.14) / You've got a habit of leaving (2.32) / Baby loves that way (3.03) (EMI). Davy Jones & The Lower Third.

March 1979 New York. Bowie wrote the lyrics for Lodger in a week. He also went shopping at Hurrahs with David Byrne.

March 1979 in Berlin, working on the tapes of Lodger. He and Visconti did the mix in New York's Record Plant Studios.

March 1979 New York. Attends Roxy Music concert. Talks backstage with Bryan Ferry.

<u>March 1979</u> New York, Carnegie Hall.   Tape
Steve Reich and Philip Glass Concert, titled:
The first concert of the Eighties.
David Bowie and John Cale join Steve Reich and Philip
Glass to perform the John Cale composition entitled
Sabotage. Gregor Kitzis plays 1st violin.
David played the viola, dressed in a black kimono.

3-3-1979 New York. Bowie, Debbie Harry and her friend Chris Stein spend the evening at Hurrahs. Later they go to a post-concert party of the Ramones at Mudds.

17-3-1979 Article in Melody Maker.
They wrote: "David Bowie, who is in New York finishing work on his next album, recently approached Scott Walker with a view to working on his next album. Bowie was impressed by the European feeling of the last Walker Brothers album Night Flights. It's understood that Scott Walker turned down his help."

Spring 1979 Bowie moved to a loft on the fringe of Chelsea and Greenwich Village.

April 1979 David does a talk-show on WPLJ-FM.
Bowie: "I have to take a city with friction in it. It has to be a city that I don't know how it works. I've got to be at odds with it. As soon as I feel comfortable I can't write in it anymore. You can look back on my albums and tell which city I was in merely by just listening to them."

7-4-1979 London, The Rainbow. Bowie attends concert of Siouxsie and the Banshees with support-act Human League.

10-4-1979 Bowie visits Lou Reed concert in Hammersmith Odeon.
Afterwards they had dinner together in Chelsea Rendez-Vous in South Kensington.
During conversation Reed drags Bowie across the table by the front of his shirt and fetches him a few slaps about the face, screeching: "I told you never to say that!"
Alan Jones of Melody Maker was present and reported it in Melody Maker of 21-4-1979. He tried to ask Bowie what was the reason. Bowie was not in the mood to answer the question.

DATE / EVENT	AUDIO / VIDEO	TITLE

17-4-1979 Had dinner with Bette Midler in an Indian restaurant.

18-4-1979 Capital Radio. Conversations with Bowie.   Tape
Recorded at Tony Visconti's Good Earth Studio in Soho.
Later that day David met Ken Pitt.
Broadcast on 14-5-1979.

19-4-1979 London. Café Un Deux Trois. Bowie spent the evening with friends in the café.
For 1 of these friends Bowie spoke a message in the answering machine: "Hi, I'm David Bowie and I'm here with Three Beatles and Eric Clapton, why not pop around?"

21-4-1979 Melody Maker. Article by Alan Jones: The great white hope versus The Thin White Duke. Alan Jones about the quarrel Reed and Bowie had on 10-4-1979: "The next thing I know, Lou is dragging Bowie across the table by the front of his shirt and fetching him a few slaps about the face. "I told you never to say that," Lou screeches, fetching the hapless Bowie another backhander. Lou looks like an irate father boxing the ears of a particularly recalcitrant child for pissing in his slippers. He gets in a few more whacks before the minders haul him away from Bowie."

<u>23-4-1979</u> UK TV. ITV. The Kenny Everett Show.
Recorded 17-2-1979.
1. Boys keep swinging (3.21).
2. Slapstick with Kenny Everett (who played Angry of Mayfair).
Kenny Everett: "I fought in the war for the likes of you. And I never got one."

1 CDR	Man I need TV (No label, no number)
CD	Sense of Adelaide (Old Gold Records OGCD 054A/B)
1 CDR	Stream without boredom (Vancouver Manoeuvres VM 001)
CD	TV-DB-15
1 CDR	Is there life on tour? (No label, no number)
CD	Legendary Lost Tapes Vol. 1 (1) (VigOtone 178)
VCD	Various 2 (3.13 min)
VCD	I keep a good friend….(1,2) (No label, no number)
VCD	Videobits Volume 1 (No label, no number)
Video	Various 10
Video	Stolp tapes no. 15 (3 min)
Video	Various 26 (4 min)

27-4-1979 Release Promo: Boys keep swinging (3.17) (RCA 1585).

27-4-1979 Release Boys keep swinging (3.17) / Fantastic voyage (2.56) (RCA BOW 2).

Bowie: "I think my voice sounds rather like it did five years ago. Fantastic voyage could quite easily have turned up on Hunky dory. This album seems to contain things from lots of different areas of my career."

28-4-1979 New Musical Express. Article: Riding on the dynamic of disaster. Interview with Peter

DATE / EVENT	AUDIO / VIDEO	TITLE

Gabriel.
Gabriel: "I think Bowie does things wit a lot more style and fashion consciousness than I do. I get the feeling that he's much more calculating. There's not too much coincidence that emanated from things labelled Bowie. I like Bowie a lot."

May 1979 Released in Holland: Yassassin (3.03) / Fantastic voyage (2.56) (RCA PB 9417).

May 1979 Released in Turkey: Yassassin (3.03) / Red money (4.17) (RCA 79014).

Bowie: "We used the Turkish things about the track Yassassin and put them against a Jamaican back beat."

May 1979 Released in Australia: 20 Bowie classics (Decca SCA.059). Images 1966 / 1967 less Karma Man.

May 1979 Smash Hits. Bowie on the cover.

12-5-1979 Recording for Radio 1's Star Special. Broadcast 20-5-1979.
Bowie: "The only thing I never went off was Diamond Dogs. I really enjoyed that album, I still enjoy it. Something I find hard to come to terms with. I enjoy very much the last three albums, Low, Heroes and Lodger. They still have incredible fascination for me."

12-5-1979 Interview with Stuart Grundy for Radio 1's Saturday Afternoon Rock On Show (about Lodger).	Tape	12 min.
14-5-1979 Capitol Radio. Conversations with Bowie. By Nicky Horne. 10 Fans in the studio.	1 CDR	*Hendrikse various vol. 6 (No label, no number)*
Including The Traveller Competition (recorded 18-4-1979 at Tony Visconti's Good Earth Studios in Soho).	2 CDR Tape	Capital Radio Interview quality 9, 90 min.

They played every track of Lodger and Bowie talked about every track.
Bowie about directing films: "I've had two pieces of advise, one from a very good friend who said that I should plunge into it immediately, and go for a full-scale thing. Another person who I also admire very much said it would just be a waste of time and I shouldn't bother."

17-5-1979 Smash Hits (UK). Article about Boys keep swinging. They wrote: "His best in ages."

17-5-1979 Rolling Stone. Article about Bowie and Elvis Costello being in the same restaurant without talking to each other.

18-5-1979 Release LP Lodger (RCA AQL.I.3254).
The 1976 film The Tenant by Roman Polanski was one of the inspirations for the album title Lodger. Lodger won The Grand Prix du Disque (for best international recording) awarded by the French Minister of Culture. Assistant engineer for the album was Eugene Chaplin (son of Oona Chaplin).

Bowie about Lodger: "I was so pleased that the conclusion of these three albums was so up. You never

DATE / EVENT	AUDIO / VIDEO	TITLE

know until you come out of the studio exactly what you've done and it would have been terribly depressing if the third one had been down. At least this one has a kind of optimism" (Changes - Chris Welch 1999).

18-5-1979 London. Shot video's for Boys keep swinging, Look back in anger and D.J.

19-5-1979 Melody Maker. Article by Michael Watts: Bowie's Lodger: Where new music meets Errol Flynn.

20-5-1979 Radio 1, Star Special, presented by Bowie. Bowie spins the discs (2 hours of his favourite music). Recorded 12-5-1979.
Love Street - The Doors, TV Eye - Iggy Pop, Remember - John Lennon, 96 Tears - ? And the Mysterions, A wagon, the nursery suite - Edward Elgar, Inchworm - Danny Kaye, Trial/Prison - Phillip Glass, Sweet Jane - Velvet Underground, Helen Forsdite (New York Band), He's a star - Little Richard, 21st Century schizoid man - King Crimson, Warning sign - Talking Heads, Beck's Bolero - Jeff Beck, Try some, buy some - Ronnie Spector, 20th Century boy - Marc Bolan, Where were you - The Mekons, Big city cat - Steve Forbert, We love you - Rolling Stones, 2HB - Roxy Music, Saint in the city - Bruce Springsteen, Fingertips - Stevie Wonder, Rip her to shred - Blondie, Beautiful loser - Bob Seger, The book I read - Talking Heads, For your pleasure - Roxy Music, Something on your mind - King Curtis, Lies - Staple Singers.

                                  2 CDR *Star Special*
                                  Tape   120 min.

27-5-1979 New York. WPIX Radio. Interview by John Avoge (about Lodger).
Bowie about Lodger: "By the time I finished I realised so many things had to do with travelling… that's how the idea of Lodger came up, because I suddenly thought what kind of person, without being sort of too glamorous about it, what kind of person does a lot of travelling and the lodger, not really knowing why he's working and sort of moving like a snake from place to place."

27-5-1979 New York. Palladium. The Clash concert. Attended by Bowie and Joey Ramone (David left after 20 minutes).

27-5-1979 Melody Maker. Article by Jon Savage: Bowie: Avant-AOR.
Savage wrote: Lodger is a nice enough pop record, beautifully played, produced and crafted, and slightly faceless. Is Bowie that interesting?

End May 1979 Bowie visits Iggy Pop in Rockpile Studio in Monmouthshire (Wales).
They write and record Play it safe (3.05). Backing-vocals by Bowie and Simple Minds. The Simple Minds were recording the album Empires And Dance in the other studio. They asked Bowie to play some saxophone on their album. Bowie refused but asked them to join him for the backing-vocals on Play it safe (David Bowie - Dave Thompson 1986).

End May / Begin June. New York. Bowie seen at: Hurrah's (where he was introduced to Joe Jackson)

DATE / EVENT	AUDIO / VIDEO	TITLE

and Madame Wong's.

June 1979 Save The Children Fund. Auction at Sotheby's.
Bowie gives a lip print with the inscription: The lips part like silence set for alarm - BO. 79. Others who contributed a lip print: a.o. James Hunt, Peter Ustinov, Bette Davis, Jack Nicholson, Candice Bergen, Audrey Hepburn.

June 1979 Released in Germany: Profile (Decca LC 0171). Deram material.

11-6-1979 Sheffield Top Rank. The Damned. They covered All the young dudes.

29-6-1979 Release D.J. (3.20) / Repetition (2.59) (RCA BOW 3).

29-6-1979 Release in US D.J. (3.20) / Fantastic voyage (2.56) (RCA PB.11661).

The closing scene of David Lean's Great Expectations was an inspiration for the video clip for D.J.

July 1979 Circus. Bowie pictorial.

2-7-1979 Village Voice. Article by J.Piccarella: Riffs: David Bowie moves on.

5-7-1979 New York Radio interview by Dave Herman.	Tape	
6-7-1979 UK TV. LWT. The London Weekend Show. Interview. Clips 30-6-1978. Interviews Nicolas Roeg, David Hemmings, Michael Watts.	Video	38 min.

15-7-1979 Book published: David Robert Jones: The discography of a generalist - David Jeffrey Fletcher (F.Ferguson Prod., no ISBN number).

9-8-1979 Rolling Stone. Article by Greil Marcus: The incomplete David Bowie.

20-8-1979 Release in US Look back in anger (3.05) / Repetition (2.59) (RCA PB.11724).

20-8-1979 Britian. Raids by The British Phonographic Industry Ltd. They try to find the makers of the Bowie bootleg The Wembley Wizard Touches the Dial.

27-8-1979 Wales. Rockfield Studios. Demos for the new Iggy Pop album Soldier.	CD	*Old Mule Skinner - Iggy Pop (Imperium IMP 012)*
	Tape	quality 10, 30 min.

31-8-1979 Edinburgh. Film Festival. Showed film Bowie '73 (the retirement concert 3-7-1973).

August / September 1979 Mirror. Article: Pop pirates scuppered (about operation Moonbeam, bootleggers of The Wembley wizard touches the dial busted).

September 1979 Creem. Article by John Pareles: Lodger.

18-9-1979 Record Mirror. Article by Paula Yates: Bob, Blitz & Bowie.

DATE / EVENT	AUDIO / VIDEO	TITLE

Bowie about Gary Numan: "I've seen a few of Numan's videos. To be honest, I never meant for cloning to be a part of the eighties. He's not only copied me, he's clever and he's got all my influences in too. I guess it's best luck to him."

18-9-1979 London. Filmed video's Alabama song and Space oddity. Space oddity was broadcast 31-12-1979 in Dick Clark's end of the year special. The original version of Alabama songs was by Lotte Lenya in 1927.	*Video*	*Various 11 (4 min)*

19-9-1979 Covent Garden. Blitz. Talks to Bob Geldof and his girlfriend Paula Yates (a reporter for Record Mirror).

October 1979 Trouser Press. Article about Bowie.

4-10-1979 Rolling Stone. Article by Chris Hodenfield: Bad boys in Berlin.

<u>15-10-1979</u> New York, Ciarbis Studio. Rehearsals (jam) with John Cale. 1. Velvet couch (2.48). 2. Piano-la (2.13).	*1 CDR* *1 CDR* *1 CDR* 7"	*Rare Tracks 1* *(No label, no number)* Outtakes 74-98 volume 2 (Old Gold Records OGCD 009) *Even a fool learns to love* *(No label, no number)* Two gentlemen in N.Y.

November 1979 Newspaper article in which Drew Blood (Angie's new boyfriend) was quoted: "When I found her, nothing could matter her anymore. She was out of control. You wouldn't have recognised her. She walked around with a plastic bag full of needles. One more day and she might have died."

November 1979 Vacation in Kenya.

19-11-1979 Melody Maker. Article by Chris Bohn: The Rise and Fall of Ziggy Stardust and The Spiders From Mars.

1-12-1979 Australian TV. ABC. Molly's Column. Presented by Ian Molly. Small part of clip DJ. Interview with Iggy Pop (who play backed I'm bored).	*1 CDR* Video	*I keep a good friend…Vol.2* *(No label, no number)* 8 min.

7-12-1979 Release John, I'm only dancing (again) 1974 (3.26) / John, I'm only dancing 1972 (2.43) (RCA BOW 4).

7-12-1979 Release 12" John, I'm only dancing (again) 1974 (extended) (6.57) / John, I'm only dancing 1972 (2.43) (RCA BOW 124).

7-12-1979 Release in US 12 inch John I'm only dancing (again) 1974 (6.57) / Golden years (RCA PD.11886).

7-12-1979 Release in US John I'm only dancing 1972 (2.43) / Joe the lion (3.05) (RCA PB.11887).

DATE / EVENT	AUDIO / VIDEO	TITLE
Mid-December 1979 Bowie arrives in New York.		
15-12-1979 US TV. NBC. Saturday night live.	CD	1980 Floorshow (3 songs)
Broadcast 5-1-1980. Announced by Martin Sheen.		(Chapter One CD 25155)
1. The man who sold the world (3.06).	CD	Alarm (3 songs)
2. TVC15 (3.16).		(La Dolce Vita Productions)
3. Boys keep swinging (2.16).	CD	Naked & wired (3 songs)
Jimmy Destri (Blondie) on keyboards.		(BOW 005)
One of the background singers was Klaus Naomi.	CD	Alternative biography (1)
		(No label, no number)
Great version of The man who sold the world.	2 CDR	First stand in Wien 1978
The presentation (clothes etc.) was smashing.		(No label, no number)
Bowie had two backup singers. They both wore dresses	CD	TV-DB-15 (1,2,3)
(made by Natasha Kornilof).	CD	Monsters to ashes
The way Boys keep swinging was performed (with a		(Canaletto Records SM 7980)
moving doll as Bowie's boy) was very funny.	VCD	TVC12 (1) (VCDB01)
	VCD	Like the videofilms we saw
		(No label, no number)
	LP	The Rare Singles, volume 2
	LP	Why does David Bowie like dressing up in ladies clothes
	LP	Zowie and a couple of kooks
	Video	Stolp tapes no. 6 (10 min.)
	Video	Various 10 (10 min)
	Video	Various 20 (9 min)
	Video	The video archives 1977-1980
16-12-1979 Australian TV. Countdown ends the decade.	Video	Stolp tapes no. 17 (5 min)
Interview in Kew Gardens. Broadcast 31-12-1979.		
16-12-1979 New York. Interview by Flo and Eddie for the talkshow Good Afternoon.		
Christmas 1979 Bowie stays in New York with Zowie.		
Just after Christmas 1979 Bowie sees performance of The Elephant Man in New York and is introduced to director Jack Hofsiss by Robert Boykin (owner of Hurrahs).		
31-12-1979 UK TV. BBC. Kenny Everett's New Years	CD	Scary monsters
Eve Show.	2 CDR	Hendrikse various vol.4
Space Oddity (acoustic) (4.57), recorded early December		(No label, no number)
1979 in Brixton, filmed by David Mallet.	1 CDR	Dancing in the John
Released as B-side of Alabama Song (15-2-1980).		(No label, no number)
	VCD	Various 2 (9.02 min.)
During the recordings Bowie saw Gary Numan watching	VCD	I keep a good friend....
and listening to his performance. Bowie called producer		(No label, no number)
David Mallet over and ordered him to throw out Numan	VCD	Videobits Volume 1
(Strange fascination - David Buckley 1999).		(No label, no number)
	Single	Space oddity / Moon of Alabama (RCA PB 9510)

DATE / EVENT	AUDIO / VIDEO	TITLE
	Video	*Various 10*
31-12-1979 US TV. Salute to the Seventies. Dick Clarke Show. Included on 18-9-1979 in London pre-recorded mimed version of Space oddity.	1 CDR	*Hendrikse various vol. 10* *(No label, no number)*
	Video	*Various 11 (4 min)*
	Video	*Various 26 (4 min)*
31-12-1979 Australian TV. Countdown. Bowie is interviewed about his career and the end of the decade. Recorded 16-12-1979 in Kew Gardens.	Video	*Stolp tapes no. 17 (5 min)*
Interview 1979-1980. John I'm only dancing. David Bowie's retrospective of the music of the 1970's (US radio broadcast).	CD	*Interview (NCB), 39 min. Printed in Denmark (No label, no number)*
	CD	*Let's talk / Drag Cover (No label, no number)*
	CD	*Let's talk / Rare Interview (No label, no number)*
	LP	Let's talk
	LP	Interview (NCB AR 30.009)
	Tape	quality 10, 100 min.

1980 Released in Japan: Golden Double (reissue of the 1974 2LP The Best of David Bowie).

1980 Released: The Elephant man, Promo 7" (xxx 01). 2 Versions (with small picture and big picture).

1980 Book published: The elephant Man - B. Pomerance (Faber & Faber. ISBN 0.394.175.39.5).

1980 Book published: The true history of the Elephant Man - Michael Howell & Peter Ford (Penguin Books). ISBN 0 14 00.5622 X. Good written and very well researched.

1980 Book published: The Elephant Man (film version) - C. Sparks (Ballentine Books, ISBN 0.345.291236.0).

1980 Book published: Baal - Bertolt Brecht (Suhrkamp Verlag. ISBN 3.518.10170.1)

1980 Book published: Black book - Barry Miles (Putnam, ISBN 0-86001.808.3).

1980 Book published: In his own words - Compiled by Miles, designed by Perry Neville (Omnibus Press, ISBN0-86001-645-5).

1980 Book published: Changes (The illustrated David Bowie story) - Stuart Hoggard (Omnibus Press, ISBN 0.86001.772.9).

1980 Book published: Style Wars - Peter Yorke.

1980 Italian TV. Special.	Video	13 min.
1980 Italian TV. Special.	Video	50 min.

DATE / EVENT	AUDIO / VIDEO	TITLE
1980 US TV. Omnibus '80. Presented by Hal Holbrook.	2 CDR Video	*The Elephant Man (12-8-1980)* *(KTLA CD173 1/2)* 10 min.

1980 LP Ashes and Diamonds - Zaine Griff (WEA K 56 834).
Title of this Bowie-look-a-like's LP is obviously inspired by Bowie.

1980 Berlin. Tony Ingrassia directed a play called Sheila. The play was about a neurotic girl, played by Joy Rider, who is hung up on Sara Lee pound cakes. The music was by the German punk band PVC. Some of the players: Romy Haag and Wayne / Jayne County. They rehearsed at Chez Romy. County and Haag had a fight and the play run for only one month.
In 1980 David Bowie, Elton John and Freddie Mercury still frequently visited the club.

Early 1980. ITV. Go for it? Dustin Gee performed Starman in full Ziggy regalia.

Gary Numan about his 1980 album Telekon: "I can't play like Mike Garson, so what I used to do was just shut my eyes and hit any notes that my hands touched" (Strange fascination - David Buckley 1999).

January 1980 Release LP Soldier - Iggy Pop (Arista SPART 1117).
Including Play it safe (3.05), co-written and backing vocals by Bowie.

January 1980 US. Release uncut (uncensored) version of The man who fell to earth.

January 1980 New York. Irving Plaza. Bowie attends Iggy Pop concert. After the show Bowie, Iggy, Patti Smith and Tom Verlaine go to Hurrahs to see James Chance and The Contortions (benefit show organised by Debbie Harry).

1-1-1980 New York. Bowie spent New Year with Mick Jagger, Jerry Hall and friends at Jagger's manager's apartment near Central Park.

1-1-1980 Melody Maker. Publish a special on the eighties. Bowie wrote down his thoughts on the new decade.

5-1-1980 US TV. NBC. Saturday Night Live. Recorded 15-12-1979.

| 8-1-1980 WXRT Radio. Skafish interviews David Jeffrey Fletcher. | Tape | quality 10, 55 min. |

February 1980 Single: What's it all about (Bowie interviewed by Bill Huie).

February 1980 Recorded: Crystal Japan (working title: Fuje Moto San), I feel free (vocal version), I feel free (instrumental version). Rumoured he also recorded two Marvin Gaye songs.

| February 1980. Demo versions Scary monsters recordings.
1. Scream like a baby (3.21).
2. Because you're young (4.52).
3. Kingdom come (4.01).
The original version was by Tom Verlaine in 1979. | CD

CD
1 CDR | *Vampires of human flesh* *(Midnight Beat MB CD 021)* *Glamour (BOW CD 1980)* Cameras in Brooklyn (No label, no number) |

DATE / EVENT	AUDIO / VIDEO	TITLE
4. Up the hill backwards (3.23). 5. It's no game, part 2 (3.55). 6. Is there life after marriage? (4.39). 7. Up the hill backwards (3.20). 8. Teenage wildlife (7.12). 9. Kingdom come (3.58). 10. Scary monsters (and super creeps) (5.12). 11. Ashes to ashes (disco version) (11.44).	CD	*Monsters to ashes* *(Canaletto Records SM 7980)*
February 1980 20/20 Show filmed Bowie while working on his new LP (broadcast 13-11-1980).	Video	12 min.

February 1980 Release: Can't help thinking about me (2.35) - Purple Hearts (Fiction LP 002).

2-2-1980, 13-3-1980 and 2-4-1980. KPFA Radio (Berkeley, California). Six hour interview Brian Eno by Charles Amirkhanian, called Eno at KPFA.

8-2-1980 David and Angela Bowie's divorce settlement is finalised. Bowie retains custody of their son Joe. Settlement: USD 750.000 over 10 years.

15-2-1980 Bowie returned to New York to record LP Scary monsters in Power Station Studios. His son Joe returned to school in Britain.

15-2-1980 Release Alabama Song (3.51) / Space oddity (4.57) (RCA BOW 5).
Alabama Song came from Kurt Weill's opera The rise and fall of the city of Mahoganny, starring his wife Lotte Lenya.
On the vinyl version you can read the scratched words: Sorry Gus.

16-2-1980 New York. Hurrahs. Bowie talked to fans.

| March 1980, TV-Commercial for mineral water Crystal Jun Rock. Music: Crystal Japan. Bowie says only 5 words: Crystal Jun Rock in Japan. | *Video*
 Video
 Video | *Stolp tapes no. 14 (1 min)*
 Stolp tapes no. 19 (2 min)
 Various 26 (1 min) |

Bowie about the commercial: "No one has ever asked me to do it before. The money is a very useful thing and I think it's very effective that my music in on television twenty times a day. I think my music isn't for radio" (A chronology - Kevin Cann 1983).

March 1980 Release 12-inch Atomic / Die young stay pretty / Heroes (live 12-1-1980) - Blondie (Chrysalis).

March 1980 Released in Japan Crystal Japan (3.09) / Alabama song (3.51) (RCA SS.3270).

11-3-1980 The rough mixes for the Scary monsters album were finished, including I feel free (original version recorded by Cream in 1966).

12-3-1980 Macleans. Article by Brian D. Johnson: Golden years.

April 1980 Good Earth Studios, second part of recordings LP Scary monsters.

DATE / EVENT	AUDIO / VIDEO	TITLE

For It's no game Michi Hirota had sung the first part in Japanese, while Bowie sang in English. Bowie thought the song sounded very sweet and asked Michi to sing again, but now in a macho Samurai way.

Bowie: "It's the opposite of what women are like. They think an awful lot with as much strength as any man so I wanted to sort of caricature that kind of attitude by having a very forceful Japanese voice on it, so I had a girlfriend of mine come out with a very sort of Samurai kind of feeling."

<u>27-4-1980</u> Iggy Pop performed at The Metropol, Nollendorfplatz, Berlin.
Iggy dedicated China girl to David Bowie and said: "Hi Dave wherever you are." David jumped on stage and joined the band playing keyboards (two numbers).
Afterwards they all went to the Restaurant The Exile in Kreuzberg, where David played music on champagne-glasses, inspired by the Toronto Glass Orchestra.   Tape

27-4-1980 Chicago. First World David Bowie Convention. Special guests Cherry Vanilla and Ken Pitt.

May 1980 Video for Ashes to ashes shot in Hastings and Beachy Head. Budget GBP. 25.000,—.   *Video*   *Stolp tapes no. 15 (4 min)*
Natasha Kornilof designed the costume.
Bowie called her and said: "Do you know the beautiful clown in the circus? Well, I want to be the most beautiful" (The Starzone Interviews - David Currie 1987).
Oscar Wilde once wrote in Phrases & Philosophies for the Use of the Young: "One should either be a work of art, or wear a work of art."
Friends from Blitz (a London club) played in the video. Bowie chose them.
Boy George who was also in the club (he was forming Culture Club by then) was not chosen (Take it like a man - Boy George biography 1995).
Boy George: "They didn't ask me. That was fine by me. I wouldn't have done it anyway. Everybody thinks I got my dresses from David Bowie. Not true, they were a present from my aunts" (Fanzine Bowie Now, September 1986).
Also the new video for Space Oddity was shot.

Second part of May 1980 London, Hell (a club). Bowie met Boy George. He insulted him by saying: "You look like Klaus Nomi" (A freaky operatic singer from New York). (Take it like a man - Boy George biography 1995).

June 1980 London. Bowie visited the London Hospital (there was a museum dedicated to John Merrick).

June 1980 Bowie was seen around Carnaby Street. He, Pete Townsend, Johnny Rotten and the members of an unknown band were drunk. The police put them in taxis to their Hotels.

June 1980 Bowie seen in the Virgin Megastore, where he bought LP's of Elvis Costello, The Go-Go's,

DATE / EVENT	AUDIO / VIDEO	TITLE

Human League, Q-Tips and Throbbing Gristle.

June 1980 London. Went to see Iggy Pop, with support act Hazel O'Conner.

June 1980 London. The Venue. Performance of The Roches. Attended by Bowie and Robert Fripp.

10-6-1980 Release Single Madman (3.11) / Join the girls - Cuddly Toys (Fresh Purl 7/10).
A-side written by Bowie and Bolan.

July 1980 San Francisco. Bowie attends performance of The Elephant man with Phillip Anglim as Joseph Merrick.

July 1980 San Francisco. Bowie bought a lot of collector's copies of the Eagle comic.

29-7-1980 to 3-8-1980 Denver, Center of the Performing Arts, "The Elephant man", with Bowie as Joseph Merrick. In it's first week it grossed USD 186.466,—.
Other actors: Donald Donnelly and Patricia Elliott. Director: Jack Hofsiss. Make-up artist: Julie Weiss. Tickets: USD 20.00.

Denver Post: "Bowie seems to gave sculpted to play the role."

Chicago Sun Times: "Bowie adds a new dimension to this character, playing the role differently, yet as superbly as Philip Anglim, the original Elephant Man. If Bowie can do this, I quite soberly say, he can do anything."

31-7-1980 Rocky Mountain News. Article by Jackie Campbell: Rock star Bowie convincing as Elephant man.

August 1980 in Chicago. Interviews by Angus MacKinnon of New Musical Express (published 13-9-1980) and by Sunday Times in dressing room of the Blackstone Theatre.

August 1980 Release in US Promo 12-inch: The continuing story of Major Tom (Space oddity segued into the edit LP version of Ashes to ashes) (also called Space Mix) (10.51) (RCA DJLI-3795).

August 1980 Release in US Promo LP David Bowie - RCA radio series (RCA DJLI-3829A). Complete LP Scary monsters and track Space oddity.

1-8-1980 Released in US Ashes to ashes (3.34) / It's no game (4.15) (RCA PB.12078).

1-8-1980 Released in Europe Ashes to ashes (3.34) / Move on (3.16) (RCA BOW 6).
Working title Ashes to ashes: People are turning to gold.
The first 100.000 singles came with a series of nine stamps, designed by Bowie (he used the idea of Jerry Dreva of the glam-art group Bon Bons Hollywood).
The line "I want an axe to break the ice" was inspired by Kafka's line "A good book should be the axe to break the frozen sea in us."
The lines "My mother said. To get things done. You'd better not mess with Major Tom" come from the nursery rhyme "My mother said, that I never should play with the gypsies in the wood."

Bowie to New Musical Express: "Ashes to ashes represents a continuing, returning sense of inadequacy

DATE / EVENT	AUDIO / VIDEO	TITLE

over what I have done. It is an ode to childhood."

Bowie: "I've got such ideas. The technology was capable in putting Major Tom up there and when he did get up there he wasn't quite sure why he had been put there… There was no reason for putting him up there. It was a technological echo which got him up there. I just added more disaster."

3-8-1980 Chicago Tribune. Article by Lynn Van Matra: Driven by change, rock's David Bowie turns actor.
Van Matra wrote: "Bowie is a man for all stages. He can act, and does."

5-8-1980 Chicago. Roy Orbinson concert. Attended by Bowie.

| 5-8-1980 to 31-8-1980 Chicago, Blackstone Theatre, "The Elephant man." | 2 CDR | *The Elephant Man (12-8-1980)* *(KTLA CD173 1/2)* |
| | Tape | 12-8-1980, quality 8, 85 min. |

6-8-1980 Variety. Article about the opening night (29-7-1980) of The Elephant Man.
They wrote: The acting debut on the American stage of rock singer David Bowie was greeted by a standing ovation in Denver when the singer, noted for his flamboyant musical style, took on the role of physically misshapen John Merrick, the human monster with a liking for culture.

9-8-1980 Record Mirror. Article by Gary Brown: Monster Maestro.

19-8-1980 Chicago. Interview by phone for BBC Radio 1. Newsbeat's reporter Andrew Turner.

| September 1980 Released in US LP Scary monsters interview (RCA DJLL-3840). Open-ended interview record, with David answering questions supplied on a printed insert, the idea being that any DJ could 'interview' the man on the air. | CD | *Let's talk / Drag cover* *(No label, no number)* |

September 1980 Released in US: College Radio Series (RCA DJLL-3829) Interview.

| September 1980. German TV. Interview. | Video | *Stolp tapes no. 10 (1 min)* |

September 1980 New Musical Express. Interview with Howard Devoto of Magazine. Talks about albums Low and The Idiot.

1-9-1980 Start rehearsals The Elephant Man with a new cast.

| 3-9-1980 US. ABC TV. Good Morning America. Live interview at 7.30 a.m. About playing in "The Elephant Man." | Video | *Stolp tapes no. 10 (7 min)* |
| | Video | *Stolp tapes no. 3 (6 min)* |

Bowie: "I was petrified. I didn't know what was going to happen, but once I got on stage, the supporting cast were just truly wonderful."

3-9-1980 NBC Studio. Interviewed by Robert Hilburn for New York Times (published 6-9-1980).

DATE / EVENT	AUDIO / VIDEO	TITLE
5-9-1980 US TV. NBC. The Tonight Show with Johnny Carson. Recorded 3-9-1980. 1. Life on Mars? (4.01). 2. Ashes to ashes (3.43) (with Carlos Alomar on guitar). Bowie wore a red jacket (by the way: great haircut). Very nice and different version of Ashes to ashes.	CD	1980 Floorshow (2 songs) (Chapter One CD 25155)
	CD	Alarm (2 songs) (La Dolce Vita Productions)
	CD	Lost in our vaults until now (No label, no number)
	CD	Naked & wired (2)(BOW 005)
	CD	TV-DB-15 (1,2)
	CD	Glamour (2 songs) (BOWCD1980)
	CD	Monsters to ashes (Canaletto Records SM 7980)
	1 CDR	Is there life on tour? (No label, no number)
	LP	Alarm (Gravedigger Records A-8149)
	LP	Lost in our vaults until now (Elephant Records Elp 012)
	LP	Why does David Bowie like dressing up in ladies clothes
	Tape	quality 10, 10 min.
	Video	Various 10 (8 min)
	Video	Stolp tapes no. 15 (8 min)
	Video	Various 26 (8 min)

6-9-1980 New York Times. Interview by Robert Hilburn before recording The Tonight Show on 3-9-1980.
Bowie about playing in the Elephant Man: "I knew from the first night that I was credible. I felt, yes, I was John Merrick tonight. That made me happy."

12-9-1980 Release in Europe and US LP Scary Monsters (and super creeps) (RCA AQL1 3647).
In the Philippines a mispressing of the LP was released, with Bowie on one side only.
LP is recorded at the Power Station in New York and mixed at Good Earth Studio in Soho.
During mixing the record Bowie had a surprise visit by his Buddhist-teacher Chime Rimpoche.
Pete Townsend played guitar on Because you're young.
On the back of a packet of Cornflakes Bowie read: Inside find Scary Monsters and Super Hero.
This was the inspiration for the song (and LP) title.
Sleeve-design was by Duffy (he also designed the Aladdin Sane sleeve). Make-up for the sleeve-photo was designed by Richard Sharah. Clown costume designed by Natasha Kornilof.

12-9-1980 Sun. First of a series of 7 articles based on the book Free Spirit by Angie Bowie (the book was published on 24-10-1980 by Mushroom Books).

13-9-1980 New Musical Express. Article by Angus Mackinnon: The Elephant man cometh and other monstrous tales / The future isn't what it used to be (interview August 1980 in dressing room of Blackstone Theatre in Chicago).
Bowie: "It was the first time I really seriously thought about Christ and God in any dept and Word on a wing was a protection. I really needed this (fingering his crucifix). We're getting into heavy waters. But yes, the song was something I needed to produce from within myself to safeguard myself against some

DATE / EVENT	AUDIO / VIDEO	TITLE

of the situations that I felt were happening on the film set (filming The man who fell to earth)." About the film Just a gigolo: "It was my 16 Elvis Presley movies rolled into one. Every real legitimate actor that I've ever met has told me never to approach a film unless you know the script is good."

20-9-1980 Melody Maker. Article by Patrick Humphries: Scary Monsters.

22-9-1980 The rehearsals for The Elephant Man were attended by John Lennon's ex-lover May Pang.

23-9-1980 Up to 3-1-1981 New York, Booth Theatre, 222 West 45th Street. The Elephant Man. Tickets: USD 25. Bowie plays Joseph Carey Merrick (5-8-1862 - 11-4-1890). He stayed at the Carlyle Hotel. The name is often misspelled as John Merrick. Joseph Merrick claimed his mother was during pregnancy hit by an elephant. This was not correct, the first signs of his disease showed when he was already 21 months old. 23-9-1980 Attended by: his mother, Aaron Copland, Brian Eno, May Pang, Oona Chaplin, David Hockney, W.Burroughs, Andy Warhol, Elizabeth Taylor, Ken Pitt, Christopher Isherwood, Dianne Vreeland, John and Yoko Lennon.	Video Video	Various 26 (7 min) Stolp tapes vol 10 (1 min)

Director Jack Hofsiss: "There was always an interesting array of hair colours in the third row as I recall. The fact that it was on a 78-year-old lady or a 20-year-old girl didn't really matter" (In other words - Kerry Juby 1986).

September 1980 Radio-ad for The Elephant Man (1.07).	CD	Speaking in tongues

24-9-1980 New York Post. Article by Jay Padroff: Star shoots to earth and Broadway.

27-9-1980 French Radio. Interview by Yves Mourousi in New York (later also broadcast on French TV as Mourousi Special).	Tape	
September / October 1980 Interview Billboard Report.	1 CDR	Various Singles - 1 (No label, no number)

29-9-1980 New York Times. Article by John Curry: Play: Bowie in Elephant.

Autumn 1980 The Blitz and Hell (2 clubs frequently visited by Bowie, to get new ideas) were shut down.

October 1980 Japanese TV. De De Music Now.	Video	8 min.
October 1980. Japanese TV. Young Oh Oh. Interview about Elephant man and Scary monsters	Tape Video	quality 7, 5 min. Various 20 (6 min)

October 1980 UK. Film Just a gigolo released on video.

DATE / EVENT	*	AUDIO / VIDEO	TITLE

October 1980 New York. Trax club. The Psychedelic Furs concert. Attended by Bowie. He also went backstage to talk with lead singer Rhett Butler.

Begin October 1980 Beacon Theatre, Broadway, concert for Film Christiane-F and video for Fashion (used the same set). Bowie mimed the songs.
The scene was mixed with footage of an AC/DC concert. David Mallet directed the Fashion clip. Tony Visconti's later wife May Pang appeared in the clip.   *CD*   *Christiane F.*

8-10-1980 Village Voice. Article by T.Carson: Riffs: David Bowie looks back in horror.
Carson wrote: "David commands the stage."

10-10-1980 BBC TV. Friday Night and Saturday Morning. Interview by Tim Rice in Carlisle Hotel 1 week earlier (about The Elephant man and LP Scary monsters). Footage The Elephant man and part clip Ashes to ashes.
Bowie: "I knew of the tale of the Elephant Man from a book called Strange People by Frank Edwards."   *Video*   *Stolp tapes no. 19 (18 min.)*

23-10-1980 New York. Japanese restaurant. Australian TV. Countdown. 80 Minutes. Interview by Ian Meldrum. Bowie handed a platinum record for Scary Monsters.   *Video* Video   *Stolp tapes no. 19 (16 min)* 19 min.

24-10-1980 Release in US Promo single: Fashion (3.21) (RCA JD 12140).

24-10-1980 Release Fashion (3.21) / Scream like a baby (3.35) (RCA BOW 7).

Tony Visconti: "Fashion was originally called Jamaica. He was going to write a little ditty about Jamaica but couldn't think of a single thing to write. It almost got thrown away, until at the very last minute he decided to call it Fashion. He must have been talking to someone!" (The Starzone Interview - David Currie 1987).

Bowie: "Fashion has to do with that dedication to fashion. I was trying to move a little from that Ray Davies concept of fashion; to suggest more of a gritted teeth determination and to be unsure about why one's doing it. But one has to do it, rather like one goes to the dentist and has the tooth drilled. I must say I did feel it when I was in London. I was taken to one extraordinary place by Steve Strange. Everybody was in Victorian clothes."

Bowie about Scream like a baby: "The old symbolic street fighting, probably won't be symbolic as it was, but will become reality in the eighties."

24-10-1980 Book published: Free Spirit - Angie Bowie (Mushroom Books) ISBN 0 907 39403 5.

27-10-1980 Steve Peregrine Took (T.Rex) died after chocking on a cherry stone.

7-11-1980 The Face. Article by Jon Savage: The gender bender Bowie & Beyond.
Savage wrote: David Bowie has lasted. To the public he's beyond Pop Star - he's Star Artist. On a plateau untouchable and mysterious.

DATE / EVENT	AUDIO / VIDEO	TITLE

13-11-1980 Rolling Stone. Article by Kurt Loder: Scary monster on Broadway.
Bowie about Pete Townshend: "He actually does jump up and down in the studio, I mean that floored me. I took him a record I'd just made called Space oddity. I said, "Scuse me, Mr. Townshend, would you play this at your convenience and tell me what you think of it?" Funnily enough, when he came to the studio to work on this track he said, "By the way, I've been meaning to tell you. About that single. I think it should do all right!"
Concetta Tomei (Mrs. Kendal in the play The Elephant Man): "First of all The Elephant Man is a wonderful role, and if you really are concentrated about what you're doing, you almost can't lose, unless you just can't memorize lines and walk on stage. It's a role in which you draw people to you to begin with. David apparently has no acting background to speak of, and consequently he really has no technique, as we know Gielgud and Olivier are having. But Bowie has the technique of magnetizing people, and that is something you just can't learn in a school or out of a book. The guy is an actor, and you can't really water it down. He's not a rock performer going into acting, he's an actor."

Date/Event	Audio/Video	Title
13-11-1980 ABC, 20/20 Show, Profile (US TV Doc.) Presented by Tom Hobing.	1 CDR	Hendrikse various vol. 7 (No label, no number)
Interview with Bowie, Allan Jones, Cherry Vanilla, Charles Murray, Footage of rehearsing Ashes to ashes (recorded February 1980).	1 CDR	Hendrikse various vol. 10 (No label, no number)
	2 CDR	The Elephant Man (12-8-1980) (KTLA CD173 1/2)
Bowie about his early influences: "I never showed any particular leanings towards anything much, until I hit about	Tape	quality 8, 5 min.
nine or ten, and I fell in love with the Little Richard Band.	Video	Stolp tapes vol. 10 (12 min.)
I never heard anything that lived in such bright colours in	Video	Various 11 (15 min)
the air. It really just painted the whole room for me."	Video	Various 16 (14 min)

Half November 1980 RCA Building, Sixth Avenue, New York. Day of interviews.

25-11-1980 The Times. Interview by Patricia Barnes: Bowie's Achievement on the Legitimate Stage. The interview took place at a Japanese restaurant near Boot Theatre.

30-11-1980 Sunday Times. Interview by Gordon Burn: Bowie Holds Court.
Bowie about the flirtation with Nazi ideology: "Infantile. That was quickly blown away by meeting members of the Far Left while I was living in Berlin."

6-12-1980 John and Yoko Lennon interviewed by Andy Peebles for Radio1.
John Lennon: "Then suddenly I was working with Elton, and Bowie was around, and we were talking and that, and he'd say come down. And I found myself doing that, you know, but he's fiddling round, he writes them in the studio now. He goes in with about four words and a few guys, and starts laying down all this stuff and he has virtually nothing, he's making it up in the studio. We took some Stevie Wonder middle eight and did it backwards, you know, and we made a record out of it, right? So he got his first number one (Fame)."
"I was never around when the Ziggy Stardust thing came, because I'd already left England, so I never really knew what he was. And meeting him doesn't give you much more of a clue, you know."

7-12-1980 Radio1 DJ Andy Peebles interviewed Bowie in the RCA building on 6th Avenue in New York (broadcast 5-1-1981).

7-12-1980 German TV. WDR. Muzikscene. David Bowie,   *Video*   *Various 20 (19 min)*

DATE / EVENT	AUDIO / VIDEO	TITLE

all-round kunstler.
Interview (dubbed) about The Elephant Man, clips, promo for Ashes to ashes.

8-12-1980 John Lennon was shot in front of his New York apartment. The killer (Mark Chapman) saw the play The Elephant Man a few days earlier. May Pang called Bowie's home in Chelsea and spoke to Corinne. Corinne invited May Pang to come over and phoned David to tell the news and ask him to come home and comfort May Pang as long as necessary (Stardust - Henry Edwards and Tony Zanetta 1986).

15-12-1980 Release LP The Best of Bowie (comp. 16 tr.) (K-Tel NE 1111) (Including an edit version of Diamond Dogs (5.27).
The first ones had a sticker on the back cover to correct the wrong song order (Breaking glass instead of Drive-in Saturday). There are also pressings with Beauty and the beast instead of Young Americans.

15-12-1980 Released in France: The Best of David Bowie (K-Tel). With Bonus tracks.

25-12-1980 New York Times. Article by John Rockwell: A revolution with Bowie.

25-12-1980 Rolling Stone. Article by Debra Rea Cohen: David Bowie eats his young.

Christmas 1980 Bowie and Oona Chaplin exchanged gifts under the Christmas tree (Bowie's tree was on fire).

Second part of 1980. French TV. TF1. Mourousi Special. Interview. Footage The Elephant man. Part clips Ashes to ashes and DJ (interview also broadcast on French radio 27-9-1980).   *Video*   *Stolp tapes no. 19 (15 min)*

1981 Bowie's former home Haddon Hall was demolished.

1981 Nevilla Wills, guitar player of the Kon-Rads, died.

1981 Released in Canada: David Bowie (reissue of the Pye singles) (PRT PHEP 001).

1981 Released in Spain: Historia De La Musica Rock (reissue of Another Face with Deram material) (Decca9-LP-002).

1981 Released 2 Love forever (Popular love song duets) - Various Artists (Broken Records 724357636421). Includes The man who sold the world - Lulu & David Bowie (3.50).

1981 Released LP Drama Of Exile - Nico (Aura 715). Includes a cover version of Heroes.

1981 French TV. Histoire de la musique pop.   Video   2 min.

1981 Belgian TV. Lindsay Kemp interviewed by Gilles Verlant.
During the interview Kemp told quite a few lies, exaggerating his role in Bowie's life. He told he worked for four years with Bowie, 'invented' the Ziggy Stardust look and that kind of nonsense. I only wrote down the lines that made sense.

DATE / EVENT	AUDIO / VIDEO	TITLE

Lindsay Kemp: "I once heard him on the radio singing something and it sounded as it could have been me singing, if I had that kind of voice. It was a voice that attracted me like a siren. I brought David Bowie a visual beauty that he didn't have before."

1981 Book published: David Bowie: Portrait de l'artiste en rock-star - Gilles Verlant (Paris, Albin Michel).

1981 Book published: David Bowie - An illustrated record - Roy Carr & Charles S.Murray (Avon Books / London, ISBN 0-380-77966-8).

1981 Book published: David Bowie - The archive - Chris Charlesworth (Omnibus Press, ISBN 0-7119.1066.9).

1981 Book published: David Bowie Profile - Chris Charlesworth (Proteus Books, ISBN 0 90607167 4).

1981 Book published: Cool Cats - Tony Stewart (Eel Pie, ISBN 0906008.476).

1981 Book published: Visions of rock - Mal Bruns (Proteus Books, ISBN 0906071.42.9).

January 1981 Creem. Article by Joe Fernbacher: Scary Monsters.

January 1981 Albums Re-released by RCA:
Hunky Dory (RCA International INTS 5064).
Ziggy Stardust (RCA International INTS 5063).
Aladdin Sane (RCA International INTS 5067).

January 1981 Release 10-inch long-play single Don't be fooled by the name: I'm not losing sleep (2.52) / I dig everything (2.45) / Can't help thinking about me (2.47) / Do anything you say (2.32) / Good morning girl (2.14) / And I say to myself (2.25) - Lower Third (PRT).

2-1-1981 Release Scary monster (and super creeps) (3.27) / Because you're young (4.51) (RCA BOW 8).

2-1-1981 Release Scary monsters (and super creeps) (3.27) / Up the hill backwards (3.13) (RCA). The video of Scary monsters was never broadcast in the UK.

3-1-1981 New York. After the last performance of The Elephant Man a party in David's honour. He was presented an Elephant Man sweatshirt.

5-1-1981 BB1. Interview by Andy Peebles in New York Recorded 7-12-1980.   Tape   quality 9, 60 min.

5-1-1980 BBC. Rock Hour. Interview and studio tracks.   Tape   quality 10, 60 min.
LP

10-1-1981 Record Mirror voted Bowie No. 1 male singer, No. 1 best video for Ashes to ashes, No. 2 LP for Scary Monsters, No. 2 single for Ashes to ashes, No. 3 sleeve design for Scary monsters.

Rented his flat in Schoenberg until February 1981. The last 3 years he hadn't lived there anymore.

DATE / EVENT	AUDIO / VIDEO	TITLE
February 1981 PlusFive. Interview by Karen Mecklenburg. Sponsored by Reeves (tele-tape company). Directed by Marcel Peragine. Was simultaneously broadcast on FM radio. Bowie: "I think video is here to be used as an art form as well as a sort of commercial device for illusion and promotion. In fact I fell in love with video in the early seventies when I got a Sony reel to reel. I developed some scenarios for 'Diamond Dogs' and worked with miniature sets."	*Video*	*Stolp tapes vol. 10 (28 min)*
23-2-1981 London. Bowie arrived at Heathrow.		
24-2-1981 BBC TV. British Rock and Pop Awards at New London Theatre. Best Male Singer Award. Presentation by Dave Lee Travis and Lulu. Organised by BBC Nationwide, Radio1 and The Daily Mirror. Attended by Tony Visconti. The only words Bowie spoke: "I'd like to take this opportunity of not saying very much. But thank you very much, I do appreciate it."	*1 CDR* *Video*	*Hendrikse various vol. 7 (No label, no number)* *Stolp tapes vol. 19 (3 min)*
End February 1981 London. Virgin in Oxford Street. Bowie bought singles by Tot Tatler, Simple Minds, Grace Jones, Human Sexual Response.		
March 1981 Re-released The London boys (3.20) / Love you till Tuesday (2.59) (Decca).		
March 1981 Release Time / Suffragette city / Ain't it funny - Hazel O'Connor.		
1-3-1981 London. Official fan club: Bowie Friends.		
20-3-1981 Release Single Up the hill backwards (3.13) / Crystal Japan (3.09) (RCA BOW 9). Part of the lyrics for Up the hill backwards were based on the 1967 book I'm OK, You're OK by Thomas Harris (about relationships and marriage).		
20-3-1981 Release John I'm only dancing (2.24) / Big green car - The Polecats (Mercury). A-side written by Bowie.		
April 1981 Spearhead. Article: Don't condemn pop.		
April 1981 Release Soundtrack Christiane F: Wir kinder vom Bahnhoff Zoo (RCA BL 43606). April 1981 Released in France: Moi, Christiane F. 13 Ans. Droguee, prostituee (RCA). April 1981 Released in Italy: Christiana F. Noi, ragazzi; zoo di Berlino.		
Various TV reviews about film Christiane F.: UK TV. Preview. UK TV. Music News. German TV. Ratschlag fur Kinoganger (Station to station).	Video Video Video	4 min 1 min. 5 min.

DATE / EVENT	AUDIO / VIDEO	TITLE
French TV. Question de temps Christ.	Video	11 min.

23-4-1981 New Society. Article by Simon Frith: The art of posing.

May 1981 Release Another Face (compilation of Deram material + King Bees) (Decca TAB 17).

10-5-1981 Sunday People. Oona Chaplin interviewed by Chris Hutchins.
Oona Chaplin: "It's a purely platonic thing, of course, although I'm crazy about him in a way. Then came this very charming, very intelligent, very sensitive fellow to dinner. He couldn't have been nicer and I got very fond of him."

June 1981 Released in Germany: 2 LP Rock Galaxy (reissue of Hunky Dory and Ziggy Stardust as a double album) (RCA NL 43593).

June 1981 Record Collector. Article by Paul Pelletier: Complete Deram Singles Listing.
Pelletier wrote: "Obviously the releases by the Move and David Bowie are among the most heavily collected, with the Bowie singles fetching the highest prices."

Summer 1981 London, The Barracuda in Bakerstreet (owned by Steve Strange and Rusty Egan) started a weekly night: Club for Heroes.

July 1981 Release: Heroes (6.17) - Nico (Aura LP 715).

July 1981 David visits Queen in The Mountain Studio.
They decided to write and record a single (Under Pressure). Recorded demo for Cool cat (3.32) (with Bowie). Queen recorded final version for Cool cat (3.27) without Bowie. David also recorded vocals for Cat People. Bowie and Freddie Mercury spoke in length about the positive feedback Queen got from EMI.

Brian May: "He often came by for a chat and a drink. One night somebody suggested to go to the studio, play something and just see what was going to happen. We played each others old songs. The next night we listened to the recordings and worked on one specific idea, and that became Under pressure. It was a very long night" (Freddie Mercury The Definitive Biography - Lesley-Ann Jones 1997).

July 1981 Louis Marks and Alan Clark fly to Switzerland, where they meet Bowie and talk about the play Baal. They meet in a Hotel and Bowie agrees to do the play.

July 1981 David spotted at London's Embassy Club.

July 1981 Book published: Yassassin Bowie - Simon Deun & Philippe (Post Scriptum).

First week of August 1981. Baal filmed at BBC Television Centre in London. Filmed in 5 days, songs recorded at the last day. Broadcast at 2-3-1982. Production: Dominic Muldowney and Louis Marks. Director: Alan Clark. Bowie's guests: Debbie Harry and Chris Stein (afterwards	Video	Various 25 (64 min)

DATE / EVENT	AUDIO / VIDEO	TITLE

they had dinner).
Louis Marks: "Baal is someone who lives his life to the full, experiencing everything. He's rather like a rock star of today. Bowie, of course, was ideal. He's a natural for the part. For one thing, he certainly knows his Brecht. Baal is very close to his own nature, one might say."

Begin August 1981 London. Oxford Circus Air Studios. Bowie visits Pete Townsend who is working on a solo LP.

August 1981 Filmed videos for Wild is the wind and The drowned girl. Both videos have Tony Visconti on cello.

September 1981 Baal EP recorded at Hansa Studios in Berlin (the Baal-songs of TV-broadcast were all re-recorded).

September 1981 London. Interviewed by Henry Fenwick for the Radio Times (published 27-2-1982).

September 1981 New York. Madison Square Garden. Rolling Stones Concert. Bowie was backstage and afterwards they went into town for a drink.

9-9-1981 Bowie obtained a tax certificate that he was a Swiss resident (numbered FD617010220).

October 1981 Circus. Article: 1973 (the year of) David Bowie.

November 1981 New Musical Express. Interview with Adam Ant. Talked about Bowie.

2-11-1981 Release Under pressure (4.02) / Soul Brother (Queen only) (EMI 5250).

19-11-1981 Release ChangesTwoBowie (comp.) (RCA BOW LP 3).

19-11-1981 Release Wild is the wind (3.34) / Golden years (3.23) (RCA BOW 10).

19-11-1981 Release 12" Wild is the wind (5.58) / Golden years (4.00) (RCA BOW T10).

November / December 1981 Bulldog. Article: White European dance music.
They wrote: "Perhaps the anti-Communist backlash and the aspirations towards heroism by the Futuristic movement has much to do with the imagery employed by the Big Daddy of Futurism David Bowie. After all, it was Bowie who horrified the music establishment in the mid-seventies with his favourable comments about the National Front."

December 1981 The Hit Factory. Bowie and Visconti mixed Ziggy Stardust: The Motion Picture.

16-12-1981 Soho News. Article: David Bowie against the music.

17-12-1981 UK. Release film Christiane F.

20-12-1981 At 10.15 pm. UK. BBC 2. First TV broadcast of The man who fell to earth (slightly edited).

DATE / EVENT	AUDIO / VIDEO	TITLE

1982 Released in Japan: Bowie (reissue of The world of David Bowie).

1982 Released in Italy: Superstar (compilation of Deram material) (Decca SU 1027).

1982 Released David Bowie - David Bowie (London 800 087-2) (Deram material).

1982 Book published: David Bowie - Kerry Juby (Midas Books).

1982 Book published: A collectors discography 1964 -1982 - Robert Bruna.

1982 Book published: David Bowie: The illustrated discography - Stuart Hoggard (Omnibus Press).

1982 Book published: Electric warrior: The Marc Bolan Story - Paul Sinclair (Putnam).

1982 Book published: Lou Reed and The Velvet Underground - Diana Clapton (Proteus).

1982 Book published: Lou Reed and The Velvet Underground - Mike West (Babylon Books).

1982 Book published: Bryan Ferry and Roxy Music - Barry Lazell and Dafydd Rees (Proteus).

1982 Book published: I need more: The Stooges and other stories - Anne Wehrer (in 1996 reissued by Henry Rollins's publishing house, 2.13.61 Publications).

1982 Book published: The lives and crimes of Iggy Pop - Mike West (Babylon Books).

1982 Bowie-calendar. Cover called Glamour was made by Edward Bell (who also worked on the sleeve design of Scary monsters. Photo's not used for the sleeve, but for this calendar).

1982 Bowie was offered the role of Satan in film Brimstone and Treacle (he turned the offer down). In his place Sting took the role (during the film he rips a Bowie-poster from the wall).

1982 Bowie went to the theatre, to see a play called 5000 Years Of Rock 'n' Roll, directed by Michael Kamen. Sandy Dillon played Janis Joplin and Bowie visited her backstage (David Bowie - Dave Thompson 1986).

1982 Montreux Jazz Festival. Bowie saw Stevie Ray Vaughan perform and was impressed.

1982 German TV. Peter von Zahn Interview.	Video	4 min.
1982 Belgian TV. Ligne Rock TV Special.	Video	22 min.

30-1-1982 New Musical Express voted Bowie No. 1 male singer, No. 3 songwriter.

February 1982 US. Release film Christiane F.

20-2-1982 Release of Baal EP: Baal's Hymn (4.00) / Remembering Marie A. (2.04) / Ballad of the adventurers (1.59) / The drowned girl (2.24) / Dirty song (0.37) (RCA BOW 11).

DATE / EVENT	AUDIO / VIDEO	TITLE

27-2-1982 Radio Times. Short interview by Henry Fenwick (given in September 1981) and article about Baal.
Bowie: "I've got to start writing again. I haven't written anything for over a year. Every album that I've written I've got three of four paintings to go with it as well. In Berlin they are mostly of Turks and here they're mostly of contemporaries of mine."

March 1982 Released in Germany: Die Weisse Serie (reissue of May 1981 Another Face) (Decca 6.25549).

March 1982 London. In the evening Bowie went to: Gossips, with 3 members of The Exploited and Gene October from the group Chelsea. Later to Gaz (nightclub in Soho).

March 1982 UK TV. Did you see? (Baal TV review).   Video   10 min.

1-3-1982 Start filming The Hunger in London.
Shooting will continue on and off until July 1982.
During shooting scene of The Hunger in gay nightclub Heaven, Bauhaus performed Bela Lugosi's dead. Rumours say Catherine Deneuve refused to act in a nude shower scene with Bowie. She asked for a stand-in to take her place. David made a similar request (A chronology - Kevin Cann 1983).
Bowie about Susan Sarandon: "Pure dynamite."

2-3-1982 At 9.25 pm. UK TV. BBC 1. Baal broadcast.   1 CDR   Baal
      1 CDR   Baal & TV is King
      Video   *Various 25 (64 min)*

4-3-1982 Trouser Press. Article: Bowiewatch 82.

6-3-1982 Melody Maker. Article by Patrick Humphries: David's Baal of confusion.
Humphries wrote: "There was none of the dramatic dominance which made The Elephant Man so memorable."

11-3-1982 Release in US as a promo: Cat people (putting out fire) (edit) (3.18) (Backstreet 545-17-67).

11-3-1982 Release Cat people (putting out fire) (4.06) / Paul's Theme (Jogging Chase) (MCA 770).

11-3-1982 Release 12" Cat people (putting out fire) (6.41) / Paul's Theme (Jogging Chase) (MCA MCAT 770).

11-3-1982 Release in Australia (12") Cat people (putting out fire) (6.41) / Cat people (Remix) (9.12) (MCADS12087).

11-3-1982 London. Sadlers Wells. Premiere of ballet Berlin Requiem. Attended by Bowie and Tony Mascia.

15-3-1982 Bowie and MainMan in court.   Video   3 min

April 1982 Release Soundtrack Cat People (MCA MCF 3138). Including Cat People (6.41) and The myth (5.11).

DATE / EVENT	AUDIO / VIDEO	TITLE

Paul Schrader's film Cat people was a remake of the 1942 film by Jaques Tourneurs. The leading roles were played by Natasha Kinski and Malcolm McDowell.

April 1982 Released in Spain: Gigantes Del Pop Volume 28 (reissue of 1981 Historia De La Musica Rock) (Decca 64 95 081).

May 1982 Tottenham Court Road. Roebuck pub. Design for modern living. Attended by Bowie.

May 1982 Release LP Hot Space - Queen. (EMI CDP 746215 2). Includes Under pressure (4.02) (with Bowie).

4-5-1982 Village Voice. Article by J.Hunter: Licks: White cat moan.

4-5-1982 Village Voice. Article by John Pareles: Eno uncaged.

June 1982 Released in Spain: London Boys (compilation of Pye material (the singles) and 6 other tracks performed by A band of angles, Jimmy Powell and Steve Hammond) (PRT ZL-545).

June 1982 Terry Burns threw himself out of a window at Cane Hill. He was taken to Mayday Hospital in Croydon.

June 1982 Shaftsbury Avenue. Lyric Theatre. Summit Conference (performed by the Glenda Jackson / Georgina Hale comedy). Attended by Bowie and Deneuve.

17-6-1982 Luton Hoo. Filming for The Hunger continued.

July 1982 Bowie visited Terry Burns in Mayday Hospital. He gave Terry a radio-cassette-player, books and cigarettes.

July 1982 David and John McEnroe were neighbours in rented flats in London (Belgravia).
David was disturbed by the guitar playing of McEnroe. McEnroe invited him to give him guitar lessons. Bowie learned him to play Satisfaction and Rebel rebel (David Bowie Theatre of Music - Robert Matthew-Walker 1985).

12-7-1982 The Sun. Article: I'm terrified of going mad.

13-7-1982 The Star. Article: I began to doubt my own sanity.

Mid July 1982 Filming for The Hunger completed.

Mid July 1982 London. Bowie visited the Soul Furnace Club.

August 1982 Released in France: Portrait of a star (reissue of Low, Heroes and Lodger as a triple boxed set) (RCA PL 37700).

August 1982 Re-released in Spain: Historia de la musica rock (Decca 9-LP-002). Re-release of Another face.

15-8-1982 BBC Radio 1. Bowie by Gambaccini.   Tape   60 min.

DATE / EVENT	AUDIO / VIDEO	TITLE

September 1982 Creem. Article by Cyril Blight: Bowie plays Baal.

September 1982 Settlement Bowie-MainMan. DeFries from then on would take ONLY 50% of the royalties from Hunky Dory through David Live.

September 1982 Start filming Merry Christmas Mr. Lawrence. Filmed at Cook Islands (Rorotonga), Auckland and Tokyo. Filming continued until early November.
Paul Mayersburg had written the scenario from Laurens van der Post's story A bar of shadow (Published as part of the collection The seed and the sower).
Bowie about director Nagisa Oshima: "It was just as in life, you only get one chance. Once I asked him to do a scene again. He said: 'If you want, but my editor is a very old and tired man. Pointless to do it again, he only looks at the first take' " (David Bowie - Dave Thompson 1986).

6-9-1982 WBCN Radio. Rolling Stone - Continuous Tape quality 10, 60 min. History of Rock and roll.
Interview with Gary Bridges.

Autumn 1982 Bowie first met Nile Rodgers at an after-hours joint called The Continental in New York. They met by accident after Rodgers had a chat with Billy Idol in the same place.

1-10-1982 Release The Manish Boys / Davy Jones and the Lower Third (See For Miles CYM 1). Included I pity the fool (2.09), Take my tip (2.14), You've got a habit of leaving (2.32), Baby loves that way (3.03).

1-10-1982 Release Ziggy Stardust (3.16) / Third uncle - Bauhaus (Beggars Banquet BEG 83T). A-side written by Bowie.

11-10-1982 Just a gigolo broadcasted on German ARD Television (German dubbed version, 102 minutes).

November 1982 End of shooting Merry Christmas Mr. Lawrence. Bowie staged in Ribald Revue for the cast and crew.

November 1982 Release 10" EP Don't be fooled by the name (3 Pye singles and B-sides) (Pye PRT BOW1).

5-11-1982 Release Fashions (limited edition of 25.000 packs of 10 pictured disc singles) (RCA).
Space oddity (4.57) / Changes (edit album version) (3.26) / Velvet Goldmine (3.07) (RCA BOWP-101).
Life on Mars? (3.47) / The man who sold the world (3.56) (RCA BOWP-102).
The jean genie (4.03) / Ziggy Stardust (3.13) (RCA BOWP-103).
Rebel rebel (4.20) / Queen bitch (3.13) (RCA BOWP-104).
Sound and vision (3.02) / A new career in a new town (2.50) (RCA BOWP-105).
Drive in Saturday (4.29) / Round and round (2.39) (RCA BOWP-106).
Sorrow (2.49) / Amsterdam (3.19) (RCA BOWP-107).
Golden years (slightly edited album version) (3.55) / Can you hear me (5.02) (RCA BOWP-108).
Boys keep swinging (3.17) / Fantastic voyage (2.56) (RCA BOWP-109).
Ashes to ashes (3.34) / Move on (3.17) (RCA BOWP-110).

DATE / EVENT	AUDIO / VIDEO	TITLE

18-11-1982 Release Peace on earth / Little drummer boy (2.38) Bowie and Bing Crosby / Fantastic voyage (2.56) (RCA BOW 12).
12" Peace on earth / Little drummer boy (4.23) / Fantastic voyage (2.56) (RCA T12).

December 1982 The Ritz, New York. Tina Turner made her come back. Bowie was backstage.

10-12-1982 Release LP Bowie Rare (RCA PL 45406).

17-12-1982 New York. Bewlay Bros announces world tour in 1983.

First 3 weeks of December 1982 Recording LP Let's dance in Power Station Studios in New York. First song recorded was Let's dance.

Producer Nile Rodgers: "The interesting thing about David is his demos. He was just doing them right there in his house on a 12 string guitar and a simple tape recorded, so basically they sounded awful to me" (In other words - Kerry Juby 1986).

Willie Weeks: "He was without doubt the nicest, most professional, intelligent rock star I ever met."

Christmas 1982 Acapulco Beach in Mexico. Filmed his cameo in Yellowbeard (a character called: Shark).

1983 Re-released in France: David Bowie Coccinelle Varietes (Decca 210.039) (same as The world of David Bowie).

1983 Released in Germany: Die Weisse Serie Extra Ausgabe (compilation of Deram tracks) (Decca LC 0171).

1983 Released Video-EP (with an uncut version of China girl).

1983 Released Film: The Hunger.

Various TV reviews about film The Hunger:

Swedish TV. Nojesnyt.	Video	1 min.
French TV. Temps X.	Video	4 min.
French TV. Antenne 2 (preview).	Video	2 min.
US TV. MTV (preview).	Video	1 min.
US TV. Various TV clips and preview.	Video	4 min.
Italian TV. Telepuglia.	Video	2 min.
UK TV. Film '83.	Video	3 min.
UK TV. Loose Talk.	Video	3 min.
UK TV. South East At Six.	Video	3 min.
1983 WBOS 92. Inside track.	Tape	quality 10, 90 min.
Interview with Lisa Robinson.	3 LP	Inside Track (IT#17)
1983 Friday Night. Interview and songs.	Tape	quality 10, 15 min.

DATE / EVENT	AUDIO / VIDEO	TITLE
1983 Bowie was offered a part in Peter Davison's final Doctor Who adventure (he turned the offer down).		
1983 German TV. Sudwest 3. Beat Club. Showed Rebel rebel (Musikladen 30-5-1978).	*Video*	*Stolp tapes no. 19 (5 min)*
1983 German TV. Musikzene. David Bowie and Lou Reed. Superstar und cultfigur. Interview, clip Let's dance, Ziggy Stardust (live 1978).	*Video* Video	*Various 22, 11 min.* 23 min.
1983 Friday Night Videos. Private Reel. Bowie presents his own video clips.	*Video*	*Various 24 (20 min)*
1983 German TV. Musik Szene. Angie Bowie.	Video	6 min.
1983 German TV. ZDF. Heute Journal (interview).	Video	2 min.
1983 German TV. Ohne Maulkorb. Special.	Video	35 min.
1983 UK TV. Channel 4. The Tube.	Video	9 min.
1983 UK TV. Channel 4. The Tube. Salute Special.	Video	19 min.
1983 UK TV. The Tube. Rare photo session.	Video	2 min.
1983 UK TV. Greatest hits (compilation of clips).	Video	5 min.
1983 Swedish TV. Nojesmaskinen.	Video	5 min.
1983 Swedish TV. SVT. Rapport (queues for tickets).	Video	2 min.
1983 Swedish TV. Dig Lundstrom. Interview.	Video	5 min.
1983 Australian TV. Countdown (introducing China girl).	Video	3 min.
1983 Dutch TV. Toppop. Let's dance photo promo.	Video	4 min.
1983 US TV. Washington interview.	Video	5 min.
1983 US TV. Japanese interview in New York.	Video	2 min.
1983 US TV. People Now.	Video	4 min.
1983 Japanese TV. Merry Christmas Special.	Video	26 min.
1983 Japanese TV. YMO special (with Sakamoto).	Video	7 min.
1983 French TV. The infants of rock.	Video	19 min.

DATE / EVENT	AUDIO / VIDEO	TITLE
1983 French TV. Houba Houba.	Video	17 min.
1983 French TV. Modes et musiques (with Mick Jagger).	Video	4 min.
1983 French TV. Special.	Video	60 min.
1983 French TV. L'Homme de l'annee 83.	Video	8 min.
1983 French TV. Disco d'or (with a French speaking Bowie).	Video	8 min.
1983 Italian TV. Blitz interview.	Video	9 min.
1983 UK TV. The Sohima gang.	Video	25 min.
1983 UK TV. Introduction to "The Snowman."	Video	2 min.
1983 MTV Award (winning song China Girl).		
1983 Dutch Radio. TROS. (Special, including interview with Mike Vernon).	1 CDR	*Hendrikse various vol. 7* *(No label, no number)*

1983 Time. Article: Dancing in the music. David Bowie rockets onward.

1983 Rolling Stone. Article: David Bowie straight.

1983 Ballade Tidsskrift for Ny Musikk. Article by T. Eggen and G. Haugland: You can't say no to the beauty and the beast.

1983 Commonweal. Article by D.E. Finn: Moon and Gloom.

1983 Book published: Bowiepix - Pearce Marchbank (Omnibus Press, ISBN 0.933328.85.0).

1983 Book published: David Bowie: A chronology - Kevin Cann (Vermilion Books, ISBN 0 09 1538319).

1983 Book published: Out of the cool - Philip Kamin and Peter Goddard (Virgin Books, ISBN 0 8369 053 X).

1983 Book published: Rotterdam 1983 - Sytze Annema (Self published, no ISBN number).

1983 Book published: The Pitt report - Kenneth Pitt (Omnibus Press, ISBN 0.7119.0619.X).

1983 Book published: The Hunger - Whitley Strieber.

1983 Book published: A celebration - Kris Needs.

1983 Book published: Loving John - May Pang and Henry Edwards (Transworld Publishers).

DATE / EVENT	AUDIO / VIDEO	TITLE

1983 Book published: Sound Effects - Simon Frith (Pantheon).

1983 Book published: The role of rock - Don J.Hibbard and Carol Kaleialoha (Prentice - Hall).

1983 Book published: The seed and the sower (Merry Christmas Mr. Lawrence) - Laurens v.d. Post (Penguin Books, ISBN 014.00.2402.6).

1983 Book published: The Sound of the City - Charles Gillet (Pantheon).

1983 Book published: Tres decadas de metamorfoses - Cantelha.

1983 Book published: Before I get old: The story of The Who - Dave Marsh (St. Martin's).

1983 Book published: The British invasion - Nicholas Schaffner (McGraw-Hill).

1983 Book published: A Collector Discography 1964 - 1982 - Robert Bruna.

1983 Book published: The Rolling Stone Encyclopaedia of Rock & Roll - John Pareles and Patricia Romanowski (Rolling Stones / Summit Books).

January 1983 Artforum. Article by C.Ratcliff: David Bowie's survival.

January 1983 The Face. Article by Jon Savage: The age of plunder.

January 1983 Carlyle Hotel, New York. Press conference.   *1 CDR*   *Hendrikse various vol. 7 (No label, no number)*

January 1983 the organisation of the Serious Moonlight Tour was founded at 57 Street in New York City.
Members of the David Bowie Production Office:
Bruce Dunbar (business representative).
Gail Davis (director of creative services) and Wayne Forte (who owned International Talent Group Offices) became booking agents and tour coordinators.
Bill Zysblat became the tour director (he was an accountant who owned Sound Advice. He also was The Rolling Stones accountant in 1978).

28-1-1983 New York. Signs 5 years Record contract with Capitol Records (EMI-America) for about USD 17 million (EMI was Bowie advised by Freddie Mercury).   *Video*   *Stolp tapes no. 23 (1 min)*

29-1-1983 UK. BBC. Nationwide. Interview with Bowie.   *Video*   6 min.

31-1-1983 US TV. Live at five. Interview.   *Video*   6 min.

February 1983 Re-released by RCA: Pin Ups (RCA International INTS 5236).

February 1983 Video's Let's dance and China girl shot in Carinda and Sydney, Australia.
In the video for China girl the actress Jee Ling appeared. She was Bowie's lover for the most of 1983. The video was the perfect way for Bowie (rolling naked on the beach, making love) to settle with the

DATE / EVENT	AUDIO / VIDEO	TITLE

"Gay Thing" he started himself in 1972. They played the love scene from the movie From here to eternity.
Bowie about the song Let's dance: "It was to make something that sounded like disco but had the feeling that it was the last dance" (Out of the cool - Philip Kamin and Peter Goddard 1983).
In Sydney he stayed at The Sebel Town House Hotel and appeared backstage at a Psychedelic Furs concert in the nightclub Seelenas.

February 1983 Australian TV. Rock Arena. Interview and clips.	Video Video	Various 19 (31 min) 50 min.
13-2-1983 US TV. Close Encounters. Susan Sarandon interviews David Bowie.	Video	Various 25 (7 min)
22-2-1983 Switzerland. Interview with Angie Bowie.	Tape	quality 10, 5 min.

Spring 1983. Face. Article by David Thomas.
Bowie: "I had every inkling. I knew from when I was about my son's age now exactly what would be happening to me, that I was going to do something very important. I didn't quite know what. At the time, I thought I was going to be a great painter, but that changed in my teens. But really thought it was my task to do something important, and make a statement about something or another."

14-3-1983 Times. Article by Lisa Robinson: A cracked actor makes repairs.

15-3-1983 Leaves Australia.

16-3-1983 London. Bowie arrives on Heathrow at 5 a.m.

17-3-1983 London, Claridges Hotel. Press conference. Filmed by BBC's Newsnight and Channel 4's The Tube.	Single Single Tape Video	Claridges 1983 (London Talk Records 17383 A/B) David Bowie 1983 interviews (No label, no number) quality 8, 30 min. 21 min
17-3-1983 UK TV. BBC. News Night. Interview (press-conference).	Video	12 min.
17-3-1983 BBC. Radio 1. Parts of 16-3-1983 press conference.	Tape	quality 8, 10 min.

18-3-1983 Release Let's dance (4.07) / Cat people (putting out fire) (5.09) (EMI EA 152).
12" Let's dance (7.38) / Cat people (putting out fire) (5.09) (EMI 12EA 152).

22-3-1983 Australian TV. Humdrum-Countdown. Interview and premiere of the clip "Let's dance."	Video	10 min.
22-3-1983 Swiss TV. Ten O'clock Rock. Interviews with Angie Bowie and David Bowie. Angie Bowie performs Touch and Tell in an L.A. store.	Video	Various 25 (5 min)

DATE / EVENT	AUDIO / VIDEO	TITLE

Various clips.

23-3-1983 Bowie Special with Jools Holland. | *Video* | *Stolp Tapes no. 9 (21 min)*
Recorded 17-3-1983. Interview and part of press conference 17-3-1983 in London.

23 to 25-3-1983 Bowie contributed some lino cuts to an exhibition which included the New Expressionist movement in Germany.

24-3-1983 BBC. Radio 1. Kid Jensen Interview (49 min). | *1 CDR* | *Interviews 1983 - 1990*
 | Tape | quality 9, 26 min.

26-3-1983 Melody Maker. Article by Steve Sutherland: The man who fell back down to earth.

April 1983 Released in Italy: The hunger (MGM). | CD | *The Hunger (Varese Sarabande VSD 47261)*
Soundtrack. Bowie was not involved (except for the sleeve photo).

6-4-1983 New York Times. Article by Herbert Mitgang: Author who checkmated Academe.

14-4-1983 Release LP Let's dance (EMI CDP 7 46002 2).

Reviews were very positive, except a few.
Rolling Stone: A functional album that comes to life only through Rodgers touch-of-funk production.
Commonweal: A disturbing failure.

16-4-1983 New Musical Express. Article by Chris Bohn: Merry Christmas Mr. Bowie.

16-4-1983 Melody Maker. Article by Adam Sweeting: Let's dance.

Spring 1983 London. Bowie visited a number of bookshops, The Ballet, Tate Gallery, Hospital in Whitechapel.

26-4-1983 Village Voice. Article by J.Truman: Riffs: Phase IV Bowie damage.

<u>26-4-1983</u> Dallas, Las Calinas. Rehearsals. | *2 CDR* | *Dallas 26 April 1983 (BowieHobby)*
With Stevie Ray Vaughan.
30 Minute FM broadcast on WBCN. | *1 CDR* | *JR is watching you (No label, no number)*
 | LP | *JR is watching you (45 min.) (Scratch SCR 901 A/B)*
 | Tape | quality 9, 85 min.
 | Tape | quality 10, 30 min.

<u>27</u>-4-1983 Dallas, Las Calinas. Rehearsals. | *CD* | *Complete Dallas Rehearsals Vol. 1 (complete) (Star Spangled Music SSM003)*
With Stevie Ray Vaughan.
Carlos Alomar: "Stevie Ray Vaughan's girlfriend was constantly trying to get his attention. At this point David | *CD* | *Complete Dallas Rehearsals Vol. 2 (complete) (Star*
stopped the rehearsal and really bawled her out" (Strange

DATE / EVENT	AUDIO / VIDEO	TITLE
fascination - David Buckley 1999).		*Spangled Music SSM004)*
	2 CD	*The duke and the hawk (Beech-Marten Records BM 045/2)*
	2 CD	*The serious moonlight rehearsals (Musicgien 91CD-030/2)*
	1 CDR	*The serious moonlight rehearsals Disc One (No label, no number)*
	1 CDR	*The serious moonlight rehearsals Disc Two (No label, no number)*
	2 CDR	*Las Colinas Soundstage (No label, no number)*
	LP	*Dallas Rehearsals (45 min.) (Scrash SCR 109S A/B)*
	2 LP	*The Dallas rehearsals (Toast Records DB 1/2/3/4)*
	Tape	quality 9, 85 min.

After the rehearsals in Dallas the band went to New York, to prepare for the European leg of the tour.

End April 1983 Released LP Let's talk. (EMI SPRO-9960-9961). Open-end interview with songs.	2 CD	*Let's talk on air (Strangest living curiosities TSLC 001/2)*
	Single	*Let's talk / Rare interview (No label, no number)*

May 1983 Kevin Cann interviews Ken Pitt for the fanzine Starzone 7.

May 1983 Musician. Article by Timothy White: David Bowie: A fifteen-year odyssey of image and imagination.
Bowie: "I'd written this little thing about Major Tom and gotten it recorded and I was told I had a concert tour if I wanted it! I thought haughtily "I'll go out and sing my song!" not knowing what audiences were like in those days. Sure enough, it was the revival of the Mod thing which had since turned into skinheads. They couldn't abide me. No! No way! The whole spitting, cigarette-flicking abuse thing by audiences started long before the punks of 1977 in my own frame of reference."
About John Lennon: "After meeting in some New York club, we'd spent quite a few nights talking and getting to know each other before we'd even gotten into the studio. That period in my life is none too clear, a lot of it is really blurry, but we spent endless hours talking about fame, and what it's like not having a life of your own anymore."

May 1983 Musician. Article by Steve Waitzman: Bowie's saxophone struggle.

May 1983 Re-released by RCA: Diamond Dogs (RCA International INTS 5068).

May 1983 Release China girl (4.14) / Shake it (3.49) (EMI EA 157).

May 1983 Release 12" China girl (5.32) / Shake it (Remix) (5.07) (EMI 12EA 157).

DATE / EVENT	AUDIO / VIDEO	TITLE

Iggy Pop wrote China girl in 1976 for Mitsu (half Norwegian / half Tai). Later Mitsu died of an overdose in a basement in Warren Street (in the house where Boy George lived at that time) (Take it like a man - Boy George biography 1995).

May 1983 Release LP Merry Christmas Mr. Lawrence (Virgin). Bowie not involved (except for the sleeve photo).

May 1983 Record. Article by J.D. Considine.
Bowie: "There's always a vacillation in my mind between trying to experiment with new sounds but also to find the original earthly enjoyment that I felt for music when I first started playing."

May 1983 The Face. Article by David Thomas: David Bowie.

May 1983 Harper's Bazaar. Article by John Pareles: The rock and roles of David Bowie.

May 1983 Vanity Fair. Article: David Bowie after the glitter.

May 1983. Swedish TV. Unknown programme.   *Video*   *Various 25 (4 min)*
Interview with Tom Conti. Excerpts from Merry
Christmas Mr. Lawrence.

1-5-1983 Sun Day. Bowie on cover and 3-page article.

2-5-1983 Washington Post. Article by Richard Harrington: The fall and rise of David Bowie.

8-5-1983 London, Plaza Theatre. Special Low-key screening of the film The Hunger.

11-5-1983 Antwerp, Lange Leemstraat 57. Zaal V.O.C. Entrance: B.Frs 120,—. David Bowie evening, organised by FM Klub, T.T.T. and V.V.K. Brabo Records. 10 Tickets for one of the Brussels concerts could be won.

12-5-1983 Rolling Stone. Article by Kurt Loder: Straight time.
Bowie about the album Let's dance: "I've never admitted this before, because it's never been true before, but this album is kind of tentative. I mean, I only kind of touched the edge of what I really want to do. I want to go further, much further, with the next one. A protest album I suppose."

About Australia: "As much as I love this country, it's probably one of the most racially intolerant in the world, well in line with South Africa."

Half-May 1983 Bowie was in Cannes, to promote the film   Tape   quality 9, 10 min.
Merry Christmas Mr. Lawrence.

Reports of the Cannes Film Festival:
French TV. Complete press conference.   Video   45 min.
French TV. Mourousi. Documentary.   Video   30 min.
French TV. TF1. Le Journal.   Video   16 min.
French TV. Antenne 2. Midi.   Video   8 min.
French TV. Soir 3. Chapier.   Video   1 min.
French TV. Journal. Bowie portrait.   Video   2 min.

DATE / EVENT	AUDIO / VIDEO	TITLE
fascination - David Buckley 1999).		*Spangled Music SSM004)*
	2 CD	*The duke and the hawk (Beech-Marten Records BM 045/2)*
	2 CD	The serious moonlight rehearsals (Musicgien 91CD-030/2)
	1 CDR	The serious moonlight rehearsals Disc One (No label, no number)
	1 CDR	The serious moonlight rehearsals Disc Two (No label, no number)
	2 CDR	Las Colinas Soundstage (No label, no number)
	LP	Dallas Rehearsals (45 min.) (Scrash SCR 109S A/B)
	2 LP	The Dallas rehearsals (Toast Records DB 1/2/3/4)
	Tape	quality 9, 85 min.

After the rehearsals in Dallas the band went to New York, to prepare for the European leg of the tour.

End April 1983 Released LP Let's talk. (EMI SPRO-9960-9961).	2 CD	*Let's talk on air (Strangest living curiosities TSLC 001/2)*
Open-end interview with songs.	Single	Let's talk / Rare interview (No label, no number)

May 1983 Kevin Cann interviews Ken Pitt for the fanzine Starzone 7.

May 1983 Musician. Article by Timothy White: David Bowie: A fifteen-year odyssey of image and imagination.
Bowie: "I'd written this little thing about Major Tom and gotten it recorded and I was told I had a concert tour if I wanted it! I thought haughtily "I'll go out and sing my song!" not knowing what audiences were like in those days. Sure enough, it was the revival of the Mod thing which had since turned into skinheads. They couldn't abide me. No! No way! The whole spitting, cigarette-flicking abuse thing by audiences started long before the punks of 1977 in my own frame of reference."
About John Lennon: "After meeting in some New York club, we'd spent quite a few nights talking and getting to know each other before we'd even gotten into the studio. That period in my life is none too clear, a lot of it is really blurry, but we spent endless hours talking about fame, and what it's like not having a life of your own anymore."

May 1983 Musician. Article by Steve Waitzman: Bowie's saxophone struggle.

May 1983 Re-released by RCA: Diamond Dogs (RCA International INTS 5068).

May 1983 Release China girl (4.14) / Shake it (3.49) (EMI EA 157).

May 1983 Release 12" China girl (5.32) / Shake it (Remix) (5.07) (EMI 12EA 157).

DATE / EVENT	AUDIO / VIDEO	TITLE

Iggy Pop wrote China girl in 1976 for Mitsu (half Norwegian / half Tai). Later Mitsu died of an overdose in a basement in Warren Street (in the house where Boy George lived at that time) (Take it like a man - Boy George biography 1995).

May 1983 Release LP Merry Christmas Mr. Lawrence (Virgin). Bowie not involved (except for the sleeve photo).

May 1983 Record. Article by J.D. Considine.
Bowie: "There's always a vacillation in my mind between trying to experiment with new sounds but also to find the original earthly enjoyment that I felt for music when I first started playing."

May 1983 The Face. Article by David Thomas: David Bowie.

May 1983 Harper's Bazaar. Article by John Pareles: The rock and roles of David Bowie.

May 1983 Vanity Fair. Article: David Bowie after the glitter.

May 1983. Swedish TV. Unknown programme.   *Video*   *Various 25 (4 min)*
Interview with Tom Conti. Excerpts from Merry Christmas Mr. Lawrence.

1-5-1983 Sun Day. Bowie on cover and 3-page article.

2-5-1983 Washington Post. Article by Richard Harrington: The fall and rise of David Bowie.

8-5-1983 London, Plaza Theatre. Special Low-key screening of the film The Hunger.

11-5-1983 Antwerp, Lange Leemstraat 57. Zaal V.O.C. Entrance: B.Frs 120,—. David Bowie evening, organised by FM Klub, T.T.T. and V.V.K. Brabo Records. 10 Tickets for one of the Brussels concerts could be won.

12-5-1983 Rolling Stone. Article by Kurt Loder: Straight time.
Bowie about the album Let's dance: "I've never admitted this before, because it's never been true before, but this album is kind of tentative. I mean, I only kind of touched the edge of what I really want to do. I want to go further, much further, with the next one. A protest album I suppose."

About Australia: "As much as I love this country, it's probably one of the most racially intolerant in the world, well in line with South Africa."

Half-May 1983 Bowie was in Cannes, to promote the film   Tape   quality 9, 10 min.
Merry Christmas Mr. Lawrence.

Reports of the Cannes Film Festival:
French TV. Complete press conference.	Video	45 min.
French TV. Mourousi. Documentary.	Video	30 min.
French TV. TF1. Le Journal.	Video	16 min.
French TV. Antenne 2. Midi.	Video	8 min.
French TV. Soir 3. Chapier.	Video	1 min.
French TV. Journal. Bowie portrait.	Video	2 min.

DATE / EVENT	AUDIO / VIDEO	TITLE
French TV. A tout coeur.	Video	2 min.
Belgian TV. BRT 1. Premiere.	Video	8 min.
German TV. ZDF. Apropos Film.	Video	9 min.
German TV. ZDF. Aspekte.	Video	10 min.
German TV. Unterhaltung '83.	Video	2 min.
Swiss TV. TV-Report from Cannes.	Video	8 min.
26-5-1983 Danish TV. Redaktionen (with T. Conti interv.)	*Video*	*Various 25, 7 min.*
25-3-1983 Danish TV. Redaktionen (with Oshima interv.).	Video	6 min.
Swedish TV. Filmkronikan.	Video	1 min.
Swedish TV. Filmkronikan.	Video	6 min.
Swedish TV. Report and Interview.	Video	3 min.
Italian TV. Cannes Report.	Video	4 min.
UK TV. Film '83.	Video	4 min.
UK TV. Visions. Press conference.	Video	2 min.
UK TV. Visions.	Video	3 min.
US TV. Festival report by Robin Leach.	Video	2 min.

Bowie about Merry Christmas Mr. Lawrence: "I think it's terribly successful because it understands that the inner tensions in what's supposed to be a war can backfire and can negate everything else and lead to a respect for the differences between people. And it recognizes that those differences are perfectly legitimate and perfectly logical. People are different and are proud of it" (Out of the cool - Philip Kamin and Peter Goddard 1983).

Vogue. Article by Anne Rice: The end of Gender.
She wrote about Bowie's acting: "Bowie, through the alchemy of his subtle strength and yielding beauty, emerges as a new and thoroughly contemporary star."

13-5-1983 Hoogvliet (Holland), De Ouwe Freak. Bowie-evening.

13-5-1983 Earl Slick got an urgent call at his home in California. Bowie and Stevie Ray Vaughan had a row over drugs and Vaughan promoting his own album Texas Flood and doing the support-act. Bowie decided to replace him at the last minute.

S. Ray Vaughan: "I told him to his face he was full of bull, playing us dirt and telling us to dress up on stage like fairies. And what the fuck do you mean, no dope? What the fuck are you on?"

14-5-1983 Earl Slick arrived in Brussels, to replace Stevie Ray Vaughan.

15-5-1983 New York Times. Article by Debra Rae Cohen: David Bowie takes on the challenge of being himself.

Earl Slick: "I basically sat in my hotel room in Brussels for four days and nights with Carlos and went over and over it" (The Starzone Interviews - David Currie 1987).
Earl Slick hadn't worked in a band since he played in Ian Hunter's Overnight Angels.

The Serious Moonlight World Tour:
David Bowie (vocals, guitar, saxophone).
Carlos Alomar (guitar).
Earl Slick (lead guitar).

DATE / EVENT	AUDIO / VIDEO	TITLE

Carmine Rojas (bass).
Tony Thomson (drums).
Dave Lebolt (keyboards).
Steve Elson, Stan Harrison, Lenny Pickett, Frank Simms and George Simms (backing vocals).

<u>15-5-1983</u> Brussels, Vorst Nationaal. Rehearsals.

	1 CDR	*Brussels 15 May 1983* *(BowieHobby)*
	1 CDR	Serious Moonlight Rehearsal Brussel 83 (No label, no number)
	Tape	quality 7, 25 min.

<u>16-5-1983</u> Brussels, Vorst Nationaal. Rehearsals.
Heroes, What in the world.
Joe the lion, Wild is the wind (original version by Johnny Mathis in 1957), Golden years, Red Sails, I can't explain (original by The Who in 1965), Let's dance, Breaking glass.

	Tape	quality 7, 8 min.
	Tape	quality 6, 10 min.
	Tape	quality 8, 45 min.
	Tape	quality 9, 110 min.

<u>17-5-1983</u> Brussels, Vorst Nationaal. Dress Rehearsal.
12 Songs were played.
Carlos: "OK guys, everybody ready?"
George Simms does the vocals.
They made tour photos and also practiced the Tour Getaway after each concert.
George Simms: "I sourced every shop looking for a pair of outrageously ugly eyeglasses. So I eventually found the glasses I considered ugly enough, pulled the stunt (putting the glasses on the skull) and he cracked up during Cracked actor" (The Starzone Interviews 1987).

	1 CDR	Brussels Rehearsals (No label, no number)
	Tape	quality 8, 55 min.
	Tape	quality 8, 35 min. (band only)

<u>18-5-1983</u> Brussels, Vorst Nationaal. Sound check.

| | Tape | quality 9 |

<u>18-5-1983</u> Brussels, Vorst Nationaal.
Attendance: 7.000 (including a few hundred journalists).
Tickets: B.Frs. 670,—. Started at 20.30 hours.
At the left of the stage a pointing hand. At the right the glittering moon.
Intro: It's alright, it's alright (Alan Freed Band).
Bowie did a great version of Wild is the wind, while he sat on a chair. He also sat in it to sing Golden years (two songs that demanded very much of his concentration).
During Let's dance Bowie did some shadowboxing.
Jackie Wilson already did this on stage in 1957.
But it was a good imitation!
During Red Sails Bowie did a piece of mime.
After Space oddity: "Thank you. I like to tell you how much of a pleasure you've made coming back to the rock stage for me." He wiped his face and continued: "I don't

	2 CDR	*Brussels 18 May 1983* *(BowieHobby)*
	2 CDR	Sneak Try-out (Old Gold Records OGCD 091A/B)
	3 CDR	Stick McQuee (Old Gold Records OGCD 089A/B/C)
	2 CDR	Vancouver video star (5 songs) (Old Gold Records OGCD 057A/B)
	1 CDR	*Birmingham NEC Arena Part 2 (No label, no number)*
	2 CDR	*Premier in the moonlight* *(No label, no number)*
	2 CDR	*Serious Moonlight Tour '83*

DATE / EVENT	AUDIO / VIDEO	TITLE
know how much of this is perspiration and how much tears of happiness. But I tell you, I'm very happy to be back." A great tour opening with no less than 31 songs. The Serious Moonlight stage design was made by Mark Ravitz. Mick Haggerty designed the Tour Logo. Bowie's costumes were designed by Peter Hall. Bowie had picked him because he has seen a musical called Zoot Suit and La Boheme at the Met. Peter Hall made the costumes for both.	3 LP LP 3 LP Tape Tape Tape Tape	(No label, no number) (5 songs) Stick McQuee (5 songs) Cocaine adds life (Swastika Records 1-8-15-4-DB) Serious moonlight tour '83 (ETS 2536/7/8) quality 9, 118 min. quality 9, 125 min. quality 9, 130 min. quality 9, 135 min.
19-5-1983 Record Mirror. Article by Val Mabbs: Ziggy's back.		
19-5-1983 Brussels, Vorst Nationaal. Attendance: 8.000. During Let's dance Bowie picked up some roses from the stage and sang: "If you should fall into my arms and tremble like a flower." The singing on China girl was very bad. Bowie heard somebody call for Amsterdam. He laughed and said: "No, Young Americans." After Jean genie the hall lights went on for a few seconds. The lights dimmed again and they ended the concert with Modern love. They played Joe the lion (2.43) and Wild is the wind (4.26).	2 CDR 2 CDR 2 CDR 3 CDR 2 CDR 2 CDR 2 CDR Tape	*Brussels 19 May 1983* *(BowieHobby)* *On the Hammersmith stage* *(No label, no number)* *Brussel '83 - second concert* *Nothin' but a star* *(Old Gold Records OGCD 092A/B/C)* *Sneaking again* *Live in Brussel* *(No label, no number)* *Brussels Vorst Nationaal* quality 9, 130 min.
19-5-1983 Belgian TV's Journaal shows live clip of Heroes from 18-5-1983.	*Video*	*Various 22, 2 min.*
20-5-1983 Noordwijkerhout (Holland), De Ouwe Freak. Bowie-evening.		
20-5-1983 Frankfurt, Festhalle. Attendance: 8.000. Started at 20.00 h. Promoters: Fritz Rau + Hermjo Klein. Recorded by German TV, Tele Illustrierte, interview and live clips of Heroes, broadcast 24-5-1983. A short concert, with a poor sound.	*CD* *CD* *CD* 2 CDR 2 CDR 3 CDR 2 CDR 2 LP	*Live Dance* *(No label, no number)* *Moonlight Special part 1 (50 min)* *(No label, no number)* *Moonlight Special part 2 (50 min)* *(No label, no number)* Frankfurt Festhalle (No label, no number) Serious moonlight tour '83 (TBC The Bubble Company) Nothin' but a star (Old Gold Records OGCD 092A/B/C) Frankfurt 83 Nothin' but a star (105 min.)

DATE / EVENT	AUDIO / VIDEO	TITLE
		(Chameleon No: 0041/0042 FR 01960/2 A/D)
	2 LP	Live Dance (105 min) (Empire & Verzyl FR 2 MB 1/4)
	LP	Moonlight Special part 1 (Bebop)
	LP	Moonlight Special part 2 (Bebop)
	LP	Cat People, Let's Dance (4 A/B) same as Moonlight special part 1
	LP	Modern love for young Americans (4 C/D) same as Moonlight spec. prt 2
	2 LP	Serious Business (4 A/D)
	2 LP	Serious Moonlight (Rab Limited DOW LP 5)
	2 LP	Frankfurt Festhalle (Freitag Records 019 60/2 FR 01960/2 - A/D)
	2 LP	Serious moonlight tour '83 (The Bubble Co, KA003),
	Tape	quality 7, 100 min.
	Video	13 min. (4 songs)
21-5-1983 Munich, Olympia Halle. Attendance: 12.000. Tickets: DM 35,—. An average concert. The crowd crunched the barriers in front of the stage. Afterwards a party at the Hotel. Bowie did not attend the party, he went to a club called Sugar Shack.	2 CDR	*Munich 21 May 1983 (BowieHobby)*
	3 CDR	Munchen '83 (Old Gold Records OGCD 093A/B/C)
	2 CDR	Munchen 83 First night
	Tape	quality 8, 110 min.
	Video	quality 3, 7 min. (silent)
German TV. Concert Report. Munich 21-5-1983.	Video	4 min.
22-5-1983 Munich, Olympia Halle. Attendance: 12.000. Tickets: DM 35,—. A good concert. During Jean Genie Bowie messed up a part of the lyrics.	1 CDR	*Moonlight special Part 1 (No label, no number)*
	1 CDR	*Moonlight special Part 2 (No label, no number)*
	3 CDR	Munchen '83 (Old Gold Records OGCD 093A/B/C)
	LP	Cat People, Let's Dance (4 A/B)
	LP	Modern love for young Americans (4 C/D)
	2 LP	Serious Business (4 A/D)

DATE / EVENT	AUDIO / VIDEO	TITLE
	2 LP	Serious moonlight-Live in Munich 1983 (4 A/D)
	2 LP	The spider and the fly (Disease Discophiles Ltd 4A/D)
	2 LP	David Bowie
	Tape	quality 9, 105 min.
<u>24-5-1983</u> Lyon, Palais des sports. Attendance: 11.800. Promoter: RTL. A great concert with a very good atmosphere. A very good version of Space oddity, despite the fact that his voice was hampered by a cold.	2 CDR	Merci Beaucoup (Old Gold Records OGCD 029A/B)
	Tape	quality 8, 105 min.
24-5-1983 German TV. Tele Illustrierte. Presented by Volker Wilms. Live clip from Festhalle in Frankfurt 20-5-1983: Heroes. Interview. Fans about Bowie.	Video	Various 25 (4 min)
<u>25-5-1983</u> Lyon, Palais des sports. Attendance: 11.800. Promoter: RTL. During China girl he again messes up a part of the lyrics.	CD	Oui... c'est radical chic! (45 min.) not complete (No label, no number)
	2 CDR	Oui... c'est radical chic! (Old Gold Records OGCD 046A/B)
	2 CDR	Lyon 25 May 83
	2 CDR	Lyon 83 Second Night
	2 CDR	Lyon 1983 (No label, no number)
	2 LP	Oui... c'est radical chic! (Tropicana Records SK 1521)
	Tape	quality 8, 105 min.
26-5-1983 Rolling Stone. Article by Ken Tucker: Bowie: Synth pop without the synths.		
<u>26-5-1983</u> Frejus, Les Arenas. Attendance: 14.460. Promoter: RTL. It took a 4 hour drive from Cannes to Frejus. An average concert.	2 CD	Serious Moonlight 83 complete concert (No label, no number)
	3 CDR	Frejus Moonlight (Old Gold Records OGCD 094A/B/C)
	2 CDR	Frejus 83 First Night (Cover art by Ziggy 2000)
	2 LP	Serious Moonlight 83 (? Prod. Records Ltd. SM 083 DB A/D)
	LP	Let's Bowie dance (No label, no number)
	Tape	quality 7, 105 min.
	Tape	quality 9, 105 min.
	Video	65 min.

DATE / EVENT	AUDIO / VIDEO	TITLE
	Video	85 min.
26-5-1983 Danish TV. DR TV. Filmredaktionen. Bowie interview clip from Cannes press conference. Nagaski Oshima interview and various film clips.	*Video*	*Various 25, 7 min.*
<u>27-5-1983</u> Frejus, Les Arenas. Attendance: 14.460. Promoter: RTL. A good concert. Enthusiastic crowd. Attended by Eric Idle and members of Duran Duran. After the concert Bowie met them for a drink.	CD 2 CDR 3 CDR LP Tape Tape Video Video	*Fashion (38 min.)* *(No label, no number)* *Merci Beaucoup* *(LZCD 049/50)* Frejus Moonlight (Old Gold Records OGCD 094A/B/C) Fashion (Blue Shadow Records 824) quality 7, 85 min. quality 9, 110 min. quality 7, 60 min. 50 min.

28-5-1983 Melody Maker. Bowie on cover and 4-page art.

28-5-1983 They left by bus and rolled out through the mist. They drove to Nice where they took the plane for a 23,5 hours journey (with refuelling in Brussels) to Los Angeles. In Brussels they had to pay the fuel (USD 45.000) in cash. After much talk they accepted Bill Zyblat's check.
They landed in Los Angeles and were supposed to fly to Palm Springs. They were to late and could not make Palm Springs in time (the airport closes at 22.00 h.).
Bill Zyblat managed to charter a limo for Bowie, Coco and Tony Mascia, and a bus for the band (David Bowie's Serious Moonlight - Denis O'Regan and Chet Flippo 1984).

29-5-1983 Nantes, La Beaujoire.
Cancelled.

29-5-1983 Melody Maker. Article by Steve Lake: Bowie: Serious Moonlight.

29-5-1983 Melody Maker. Article: Bowie live in Germany.

29-5-1983 Los Angeles Times. Article by Robert Hilburn: David Bowie has dropped his disguises.

29-5-1983 New York Times. Article by Janet Maslin: A rock singer takes off as a movie star.

| <u>30-5-1983</u> San Bernardino, Glen Hellen Park, US Festival. In fact it was a wasteland called Davore. Attendance: 300.000. Started at 12.00 h. Tickets: USD 20,00. Promoter: Unuson Corporation. David receives a fee of $1 million for appearing at the US Festival before 300.000 fans. Other artists that day: The Pretenders, Little Steven, U2. Bowie was on stage at 23.00 hours (three hours later than | 2 CDR

2 CDR

2 CDR | Merci Beaucoup (11 songs)
(Old Gold Records
OGCD 029A/B)

Oui… c'est radical chic! (10 songs) (Old Gold Records
OGCD 046A/B)

Some band intro!
(Old Gold Records |

DATE / EVENT	AUDIO / VIDEO	TITLE

agreed). | | OGCD 198A/B)
The set ended at 1 a.m. 31 may 1983. | 2 CDR | *Moonlight Festival*
It took a 2-hour drive by bus to get back to the plane. | 2 CDR | *Live at the US Festival 1983*
For the Serious Moonlight Tour Bowie used a chartered | | *(No label, no number)*
Boeing 707 Starship (David Bowie's Serious Moonlight - | 2 CDR | *Cool Million*
Denis O'Regan and Chet Flippo 1984). | | *(No label, no number)*
| Tape | quality 8, 90 min.
| Tape | quality 9, 95 min.

30-5-1983 US TV. Entertainment Tonight. | *Video* | *Stolp Tapes 9 (1 min)*
| Video | 4 min.

French TV. Concert Report. Los Angeles 30-5-1983. | Video | 1 min.
US TV. Concert Report. Los Angeles 30-5-1983. | Video | 3 min.

30-5-1983 Times. Article by Michael Watts: Ziggy's rock and role reversal.

31-5-1983 At 5 a.m. they took off for London.

June 1983 Re-released by RCA:
Low (RCA International INTS 5065).
Heroes (RCA International INTS 5066).

June 1983 Release Lifetime Series (RCA), picture-disc pack of 20 singles.
Drive in Saturday (3.59) / Round and round (2.39) (BOW 501).
Life on Mars? (3.47) / The man who sold the world (3.56) (BOW 502).
Rock 'n' roll suicide (2.58) / Quicksand (4.54) (BOW 503).
Diamond dogs (5.56) / Holy holy (2.18) (BOW 504).
Knock on wood (3.03) / Panic in Detroit (5.52) (BOW 505).
Young Americans (5.10) / Suffragette city (3.45) (BOW 506).
Fame (3.23) / Right (4.13) (BOW 507).
Golden years (3.23) / Can you hear me (5.02) (BOW 508).
TVC15 (3.43) / We are the dead (4.56) (BOW 509).
Sound and vision (3.02) / A new career in a new town (2.50) (BOW 510).
Be my wife (2.55) / Speed of life (2.47) (BOW 511).
Beauty and the beast (3.32) / Sense of doubt (3.57) (BOW 512).
Heroes (3.35) / V-2 Schneider (3.10) (BOW 513).
Rebel rebel (4.20) / Queen bitch (3.13) (BOW 514).
The Jean Genie (4.03) / Ziggy Stardust (3.13) (BOW 515).
D.J. (3.20) / Repetition (2.59) (BOW 516).
John I'm only dancing (2.43) / Hang on to yourself (2.38) (BOW 517).
Space oddity (4.33) / Changes (3.33) / Velvet Goldmine (3.07) (BOW 518).
Sorrow (2.49) / Amsterdam (3.19) (BOW 519).
Breaking glass (3.27) / Art decade (3.10) / Ziggy Stardust (3.32) (BOW 520).

June 1983 Rock & Folk (France). Article about Bowie.

<u>2-6-1983</u> London, Wembley Arena. | *1 CDR* | *A London Trilogy 1 (Old*
Attendance: 7.700. Promoter: Harvey Goldsmith. | | *Gold Records OGCD 166)*

DATE / EVENT	AUDIO / VIDEO	TITLE
Station to station did not have the train-intro, but went straight away in Earl Slick's guitar solo. Great! Bowie was very pleased with the result and this was the begin of the song for the rest of the tour. Attended by: Pete Townshend, Koo Stark, Sabrina Guiness, Keith Richards, John McEnroe, Terence Stamp, Jeff Beck, Carrie Fisher, Vitas Gerulaitis, Tom Stoppard, Paul Theroux, Rod Stewart. etc. etc. They stayed at the Carlton Tower Hotel in Cadogan Place. They woke up rudely by construction noise. Eva Strom slipped GBP. 50,— to the construction foreman to make them stop (David Bowie's Serious Moonlight - Denis O'Regan and Chet Flippo 1984).	2 CDR 2 CDR 2 CDR Tape	*A London Trilogy 2* (Old Gold Records OGCD 167A/B) *Wembley Arena 2-6-1983* (No label, no number) The 1st Show (CD-R 83 0006 02) quality 8, 110 min.
2-6-1983 ITV's News at Ten shows clip of Heroes from 2-6-1983.	*Video*	*Stolp Tapes (1 min)*
3-6-1983 London, Wembley Arena. Attendance: 7.700. Promoter: Harvey Goldsmith. A good concert. During Fame Bowie lay on his back on the stage. The globe rolled on stage, right over him. Carlos Alomar played out of tune during Let's dance and China girl.	2 CDR 1 CDR 2 CDR 1 CDR 3 LP Tape	*A London Trilogy 2* (Old Gold Records OGCD 167A/B) Birmingham NEC Arena Part 2 (No label, no number) Serious Moonlight Tour '83 (No label, no number) (1 song) Wembley 3.6.83 (Mixing Desk Moonlight 002) Serious moonlight tour '83 (ETS 2536/7/8) quality 8, 115 min.
4-6-1983 London, Wembley Arena. Attendance: 7.700. Promoter: Harvey Goldsmith. Tickets GBP. 10,—. A good concert. Better then the previous two nights.	2 CDR Tape Tape	*A London Trilogy 3* (Old Gold Records OGCD 168A/B) quality 8, 105 min. quality 9, 110 min.
5-6-1983 Birmingham, National Exhibition Centre. Attendance: 11.000. A very good concert. Bowie relaxed and joking. "On trombone Gregory Arbellovic. Aaah, we don't have a trombone." During Modern love Bowie messes up the lyrics.	2 CDR 2 CDR 2 CDR Tape	*No Trombone* (Old Gold Records OGCD 472A/B) Serious Moonlight Tour '83 (No label, no number) Birmingham 83 First Night (Paul Notkin) quality 7, 110 min.
6-6-1983 Capital Radio. Interview.	Tape	quality 9, 15 min.
6-6-1983 Birmingham, National Exhibition Centre. Attendance: 11.000.	2 CD	*Moonlight exhibition* (2001 WhoCaresRecords wcr-

DATE / EVENT	AUDIO / VIDEO	TITLE
Begin tune: Stick McGee. End tune: Blue moon on Kentucky. A very good concert.		*127)*
	1 CDR	Live Birmingham 83 Disc One (No label, no number)
	1 CDR	Live Birmingham 83 Disc Two (No label, no number)
	3 CDR	Stick McQuee (Old Gold Records OGCD 089A/B/C)
	1 CDR	*Birmingham NEC Arena Part 1 (No label, no number)*
	1 CDR	*Birmingham NEC Arena Part 2 (No label, no number)*
	3 LP	Serious moonlight tour '83 (ETS 2536/7/8)
	2 LP	Moonlight exhibition
	Tape	quality 9, 115 min.
	Video	8 min.
6-6-1983 BBC ITV's Central News Show shows report and live clip of Heroes from Birmingham 5-6-1983.	*Video*	*Stolp tapes no. 9 (3 min)*
8-6-1983 Paris, Hippodrome d'Auteuil. Attendance: 59.200. Promoter: Albert Koski. Started at 21.15 hours. For the first time this tour a video-screen. Attended by Jing Lee (played in the clip China girl). Support act: Dexy's Midnight Runners. Lead singer Kevin Rowland insulted the audience who kept calling for Bowie. He told the audience that Bowie was not that good, they were a lot better and Bowie was full of shit. The audience threw with everything that was by hand. It was a great concert. Afterwards there was a party (attended by Grace Jones). In Paris Bowie met Brian Gysin. They stayed at the Warwick Hotel.	3 CDR	Stick McQuee (Old Gold Records OGCD 089A/B/C)
	2 CDR	Paris 8 June 1983 (BowieHobby)
	2 CDR	The most of Paris
	2 CDR	Paris 8 June 83
	Tape	quality 8, 110 min.
	Video	quality 6, 90 min.
9-6-1983 Paris, Hippodrome d'Auteuil. Attendance: 59.500. There was a strong wind. After a short while they had to take the video-screen down. They stayed at the Warwick Hotel.	*2 CDR*	*Paris 9 June 1983 (BowieHobby)*
	2 CDR	Soir magnific (Old Gold Records OGCD 165A/B)
	2 CDR	Paris 9 June 83
	2 CDR	Live in Paris Hippodrome d' Auteuil (No label, no number)
	Tape	quality 7, 110 min.
9-6-1983 French TV. TF1's. Actualites. Shows clips of The Jean Genie, Star and Heroes from 8-6-1983 concert.	Video	7 min.
French TV. Antenne 2. Concert Report. Paris 8-6-1983.	Video	3 min.

DATE / EVENT	AUDIO / VIDEO	TITLE

Italian TV. Concert Report. Paris 8-6-1983. — Video — 20 min.

<u>11-6-1983</u> Gothenburg, Nya Ullevi Stadium.
Attendance: 61.206 (he broke the Rolling Stones record).
Tickets: KR. 120,—. Support act: Men at Work.
A good concert. The crowd clapped and sang along with a great deal of the songs.
During Golden years the band had a "false start" and had to start again.
They stayed at the Park Avenue Hotel.
During Cracked actor George Simms had to put the glasses on David's ears. Sometimes he missed one ear because of his hair. In the dressing room they joked about it before the show. When George Simms wanted to put the glasses on that evening he and David had quivering lips to prevent laughing. George was trying hard to get it right and, by accident, let go of one of the bows and caught David right in the eye. David couldn't get on singing properly until Ashes to ashes, because he and George kept on laughing (The Starzone Interviews - David Currie 1987).

	2 CD	*Sold out (Sesam Records 830611)*
	2 CDR	*Sold out (MCDS 011 - 99B)*
	2 CDR	*Visions of swastikas (Old Gold Records OGCD 043A/B)*
	2 LP	Sold Out (Sesam Records)
	Tape	quality 9, 110 min.
	Video	12 min.

11-6-1983 Sweden. Interview with Carlos Alomar and Earl Slick. — Tape — quality 10, 15 min.

11-6-1983 Swedish TV. SVT1. Aktuellt.
Presented by Rolf Gustavsson.
Live clip 11-6-1983: Jean Genie-intro / Star. — *Video* — *Various 25 (4 min)*

11-6-1983 Swedish TV. SVT2. Rapport.
Presented by Ingeleif Ohman.
Live clips from 11-6-1983: Jean Genie-intro / Star.
Footage of clips and fans about Bowie. — *Video* — *Various 25 (7 min)*

12-6-1983 Sydsvenska Dagbladet. Article: All of Gothenburg was David Bowie's last night.

<u>12-6-1983</u> Gothenburg, Nya Ullevi Stadium.
Attendance: 60.000. Tickets: Kr. 120,—.
Promoter: EMA, Knud Thorbkornsen & DKB.
Again a very good concert and an enthusiastic crowd.
They stayed at the Park Avenue Hotel. A few days earlier a Swedish newspaper had run an illustration of the floor plan of the hotel, so the hotel was packed with young fans (most of them women). Bowie used the hotel kitchen to get in and out.

	2 CD	*Serious moonlight in Gothenburg (110 min.) (No label, no number)*
	2 CDR	*Pinpoints of Light (No label, no number)*
	2 CDR	*A rock 'n' roll Hamlet (Old Gold Records OGCD 044A/B)*
	2 CD	*Serious moonlight 83*
	2 LP	*Serious moonlight in Gothenburg (MIW Records DB 73)*
	3 LP	*Pinpoints of Light (Red Shoes Records BF-375-4 A/F))*

DATE / EVENT	AUDIO / VIDEO	TITLE
	Tape	quality 9, 110 min.

14-6-1983 Essen, Grugahalle.
Cancelled.

15-6-1983 Essen, Grugahalle.
Cancelled.

15-6-1983 Bochum, Ruhrland Stadium. Sound check. China girl, Stay, Fashion, What in the world, Life on Mars? Stay. Bowie did not attend the sound check.	Tape	quality 7, 35 min.
15-6-1983 Bochum, Ruhrland Stadium. Attendance: 33.843. Promoters: Fritz Rau and Hermjo Klein. Started at 20.30 hours. First of 5 open-air concerts. Dangerous situations because of much crushing and fights. Not a good concert. The whole situation influenced Bowie's performance heavily. He was in a bad mood.	2 CDR 2 CDR Tape	*Zugabe!* *(Old Gold Records* *OGCD 145A/B)* *Bochum June 15th 1983* *(No label, no number)* quality 9, 110 min.
17-6-1983 Bad Segeberg, Freilicht Buhne. Attendance: 12.075. A good concert. During Modern love he sang: "I don't want to stay in and I don't want to go out. And I'll fuck that up." He started laughing and missed a part of the lyrics.	2 CDR Tape	*Golden year '83* *(Old Gold Records* *OGCD 128A/B)* quality 9, 105 min.
18-6-1983 York. University Radio. The David Bowie Story.	Tape	quality 9, 360 min.
18-6-1983 Bad Segeberg, Freilicht Buhne. Attendance: 12.075. Started at 20.00 h. Promoters: Fritz Rau + Hermjo Klein. A very good concert with a highly concentrated Bowie. Lots of frisbees were thrown during the concert. During Stay a frisbee was thrown and hit Bowie's head.	2 CDR 2 CDR 2 LP LP Tape	*Bad Segeberg 83 (SM 001/2)* Event of David Bowie *(Old Gold Records* *OGCD 139A/B)* Event of David Bowie *(Cheat & Fraud Records CAF* *83.06.17 Part 1/4)* The cool genie (PARTS 3/4) quality 9, 115 min.

20-6-1983 In the afternoon the band (without Bowie) went to East Berlin. Bowie went to see the apartment he used in 1977.

20-6-1983 West Berlin, Wald Buhne. Attendance: 22.245. Not a good concert. After the concert they went to a club called: Jungle.	2 CDR Tape	*Back in Berlin* *(Old Gold Records* *OGCD 197A/B)* quality 9, 115 min.
24-6-1983 Offenbach, Bieber Berg Stadium. Attendance: 24.720. Promoters: Lippman + Rau Konzerte.	2 CDR	*Some band intro!* *(Old Gold Records*

DATE / EVENT	AUDIO / VIDEO	TITLE
Started at 20.30 h. Tickets: DM 30,—. "On guitar Carmi… Cal… Carlos Alomar." Bowie had to laugh so much, he could not go on for a short while. Carlos Alomar introduces the rest of the band. Bowie takes over again and says: "And I think I'm David Bowie."	2 CDR Tape	OGCD 198A/B) *Back in Berlin* (Old Gold Records OGCD 197A/B) quality 9, 110 min.
24-6-1983 UK TV. BBC. The Midsummernight's Tube. Part of film Love you till Tuesday, Interv. Clips. Part of film The man who fell to earth. Victoria station 2-5-1976. Part Merry Christmas Mr. Lawrence. With Marc Bolan 28-9-1977. Part documentary Cracked actor. Part of The Hunger.	*Video*	*Stolp tapes no. 9 (17 min)*
<u>25-6-1983</u> Rotterdam, Feyenoord Stadium. Attendance: 50.600. Started at: 21.30 hours. Support-acts: Icehouse and UB40. The first part of the concert (about 30 minutes) there were sound problems. When Bowie sang Space oddity everybody clapped and sang along. Carlos Alomar translated Bowie's band intro into Spanish. Halfway Bowie just said a few words and Carlos Alomar translated with a few sentences. Bowie almost laughed his head off. After the concert Bowie had a drink in the Hilton Hotel in Rotterdam.	2 CDR 1 CDR 2 CDR 2 CDR 2 CDR 2 CDR LP Tape Tape Tape	*Rotterdam 25 June 1983* (BowieHobby) Magic in the moonlight (Old Gold Records OGCD 201) Keep on (Old Gold Records OGCD 095A/B) Hartford fashion (Old Gold Records OGCD 202A/B) Rotterdam 1983 First Night (A Dutch Connection CDR) In de Kuip (Old Gold Records OGCD 589A/B) Magic in the moonlight (Panic Recordings MA 30-145) quality 7, 110 min. quality 6, 120 min. quality 8, 100 min.
25-6-1983 Dutch TV Journaal. 23.00 Hours. Shows live clip of Heroes from the 25-6-1983 concert.	Video	quality 10, 1 min.
Dutch TV. Countdown. Concert Report 25-6-1983.	Video	7 min.
26-6-1983 Rotterdam. Hilton Hotel. In the afternoon. Interview for Dutch TV-programme Cinevisie (broadcast 29-6-1983).	Video *Video*	45 min. *Stolp tapes no. 9 (40 min)*
<u>26-6-1983</u> Rotterdam, Feyenoord Stadium. Attendance: 50.600. Tickets: FL. 40,—. Support-acts: Icehouse and UB40. During the first part of the concert Bowie was not in a good mood. Fashion had to go over into Let's dance smoothly. The drummer did not make clear when to start Let's dance and	2 CD 2 CDR 2 LP	*Keep on (complete concert)* (No label, no number) Keep on (Old Gold Records OGCD 095A/B) Keep on (Rare Music Record Corporation CK 2908 A/D)

DATE / EVENT	AUDIO / VIDEO	TITLE
the transition part went on until Bowie gave Tony Thompson a sign. During Cracked actor Bowie took the skull and started laughing, it had gold teeth and a piece of cellophane on the top of its head (a joke of the Simms brothers).	2 LP LP Tape Video	Hero of Rotterdam complete concert Holland 1983 (FM 83 002A/B) quality 9, 109 min. 7 min.

27-6-1983 Bowie called Tony Visconti to help him correct the sound balance in Edinburgh.

| 28-6-1983 Edinburgh, Murrayfield Stadium. Attendance: 47.444 (biggest rock crowd ever in Scotland). A good concert. Great atmosphere. After Breaking Glass Bowie had to calm down the people in front, because they were pushing too much. Announcing TVC15: "This is a song about the nicer Americans in life." | 2 CDR
2 CDR
2 CDR

Tape
Tape | Murrayfield Stadium
Edinburgh - June 28 1983
(No label, no number)
Scotland forever
(Old Gold Records
OGCD 199A/B)
quality 8, 105 min.
quality 9, 115 min. |
| 29-6-1983 Dutch TV. NOS. Cinevisie. Interview. Recorded 26-6-1983 in the Hilton Hotel, Rotterdam. | Video
Video | 45 min.
Stolp tapes no. 9 (40 min) |

29-6-1983 Posed in Studio Tussauds for wax statue.

29-6-1983 BBC's Scotland Today shows live clip of Heroes from the 28-6-1983 concert.	Video	5 min.
29-6-1983 BBC. Breakfast News. Concert Report Edinburgh 28-6-1983.	Video	1 min.
30-6-1983 London, Hammersmith Odeon. Sound check.	Tape	quality 8, 5 min.
30-6-1983 London, Hammersmith Odeon. Benefit for Brixton Neighbourhood Community Association. Tony Visconti did the sound. Started at. 19.30 h. Tickets: GBP. 25,— (including a donation of GBP. 17,50). David raises GBP 93.000 with this one-off performance. Attended by 2.120 people (among them Princess Michael of Kent). The band did not wear the stage-clothes. Support band: Amazulu (they joined Bowie for the encore Modern love) A lot of stuff thrown on the stage. Among others an inflatable leg, used by Bowie as guitar and saxophone. Paul and Linda McCartney sent a telegram: "Our daughters Heather and Mery went to the Hammersmith Odeon show and if they are to be believed, you are pretty hot stuff. Thanks for thrilling them."	2 CDR 2 CDR 2 CDR LP LP 2 LP LP Tape	*London 30 June 1983* *(BowieHobby)* *On the Hammersmith stage* *(No label, no number)* Hammersmith Resurrection (Old Gold Records OGCD 055A/B) Hammersmith Odeon 30-6-1983 Part one / Songbook (55 min.) Hammersmith Odeon 30-6-1983 Part two / Moonlight Special (40 min.) Part 1+2 compl.concert The duke of Brixton (A1/B1/C1/D1) David Bowie Songbook quality 9, 100 min.

DATE / EVENT	AUDIO / VIDEO	TITLE

30-6-1983 BBC and ITV national news show clips from Hammersmith Odeon 30-6-1983.   *Video*   *Stolp tapes no. 9 (1 min)*

30-6-1983 The Nine O'clock News.
Interview. Live clip 30-6-1983: Look back in anger (20 seconds).   *Video*   *Various 25 (1 min)*

30-6-1983 UK TV. News at Ten, presented by Keith Hetfield.
Interview. Live clip 30-6-1983: Breaking glass (20 sec.).
Footage of Bowie meeting princess Michael of Kent.   *Video*   *Various 25 (1 min)*

July 1983 Creem. Article by Laura Fissinger: As I write this letter…

July 1983 Creem. Article by Cynthia Rose: Letter from Britain: Stayin' hungry.

July 1983 Creem. Article by Frank Rose: After the wall.

July 1983 Playboy. Article by Frank Rose: After the wall.

July 1983 Stereo Review. Article by M.Peel: David Bowie's next big thing.

July 1983 Bowie had ten albums in the UK top 100.

July 1983 Kevin Cann interviews Ray Stevenson for the fanzine Starzone 8.

<u>1-7-1983</u> Milton Keynes, Milton Keynes Bowl.
Attendance: 58.300. Tickets: GBP. 10,—. A good concert. Support acts: Icehouse and The Beat.
A girl fainted and was lifted onto the stage. When she got of the stage, she managed to steal Bowie's jacket.
At the end of Modern love a balloon, that was lifted over the audience with a crane, opened and a lot of small balloons came out of it.
A face stared out, painted on the moon, very reminiscent of a scene from George Melies 'Trip to the moon' (Fanzine Sarzone 8).
Backstage there were Space Invaders video games for the 3 Milton Keynes days (David Bowie's Serious Moonlight - Denis O'Regan and Chet Flippo 1984).

2 CDR — Live at the Bowl (Old Gold Records OGCD 204A/B)
Tape — quality 8, 105 min.
Tape — quality 9, 115 min.
Video — 80 min.
Video — 70 min.

<u>2-7-1983</u> Milton Keynes, Milton Keynes Bowl.
Attendance: 58.300. Support acts: Icehouse and The Beat.
A good concert. Tickets: GBP. 10,—.
"This is a song from the album Pin Ups and it's called Sorrow." Original version was by The McCoys in 1965.
Before China girl: "Come forth Cinderella. Well, I suppose I'll have to sing about China."

2 CDR — *Milton Keynes 2 July 1983 (BowieHobby)*
1 CDR — A bowl of Bowie (Old Gold Records OGCD 205)
2 CDR — Live at the Bowl (Old Gold Records OGCD 204A/B)

DATE / EVENT	AUDIO / VIDEO	TITLE
	2 CDR	Milton Keynes Second Night (No label, no number)
	Tape	quality 8, 115 min.
	Video	Various 11 (69 min)
3-7-1983 Milton Keynes, Milton Keynes Bowl. Attendance: 58.300. Promoter: Harvey Goldsmith. Support acts: Icehouse and The Beat. Tickets: GBP 10,—. 1. Look back in anger (3.04). After Look back in anger no synthesizer intro as we were used to, but a piano part. 2. Breaking glass (2.59). 3. Scary monsters (3.20). 4. Rebel rebel (2.29). 5. Heroes (5.00). 6. What in the world (3.35). 7. Life of Mars? (3.59). 8. Golden years (3.29). 9. Fashion (2.43). 10. Let's dance (4.25). 11. Red sails (3.24). 12. China girl (5.10). 13. White light white heat (4.56). 14. Station to station (8.32). 15. Cracked actor (3.09). 16. Ashes to ashes (3.43). 17. Space oddity (4.59). 18. Band intro (2.00). 19. Young Americans (4.54). 20. TVC15 (3.47). 21. Fame (5.08). 22. Star (2.34). 23. Sorrow (2.39). 24. Cat people (4.11). 25. Stay (8.09). 26. Jean Genie (7.00). During Jean Genie Bowie finds keys on stage. He tells a story about the keys and asks who they belong to. He sings a few lines and then starts explaining that the keys are from a mansion, a Ferrari and the girlfriends' apartment. Again he sings a line and then puts the keys in his pocket. 27. Modern love (3.43).	2 CD 2 CDR 2 CDR 2 CDR LP Tape Video Video	*No religion (compl. concert) (Isolar MK0030783A/B)* *Dedicated to Lennard Holt (2251-556-131)* *Milton Keynes Third Night (No label, no number)* *The Final Europe Show (No label, no number)* *Serious Moonlight (Rab Limited Dow LP 5)* quality 9, 115 min. quality 7, 86 min. 60 min.
3-7-1983 LWT's South of Watford. Clips of Breaking glass and Scary monsters from Milton Keynes 3-7-1983.	Video	*Stolp Tapes 9 (25 min)*
3-7-1983 Dutch TV. Veronica. Countdown. Live clip (1 min.) of Heroes from Rotterdam 26-6-1983.	Video	quality 10, 1 min.

DATE / EVENT	AUDIO / VIDEO	TITLE
4-7-1983 WBPQ Radio New York. Special.	Tape	60 min.

On the chartered Boeing 707 Starship Bowie was very relaxed. He joked: "I have to start the show with The Legendary Stardust Cowboy." Steve Elson (sax) started singing: "I met my true love down in the wrecking yard." Bowie joined him and sang: "I took a trip on a Gemini space ship, and I thought about you-oo" (David Bowie's Serious Moonlight - Denis O'Regan and Chet Flippo 1984).
In 2002 Bowie covered the song for his album Heathen.

DATE / EVENT	AUDIO / VIDEO	TITLE
<u>11-7-1983</u> Quebec City, Le Colisee. Sound check.	NT	
<u>11-7-1983</u> Quebec City, Le Colisee. Attendance: 14.400. A great concert. Announces Young Americans: "This is called Young Canadians." He also sings Young Canadians instead of Young Americans.	1 CDR	Quebec '83 (Old Gold Records OGCD 203)
	2 CDR	Hartford fashion (Old Gold Records OGCD 202A/B)
	Tape	quality 8, 110 min.
	Tape	quality 8, 90 min.
	Video	2 min.

12-7-1983 Journal de Quebec. Article: Les fans de Bowie au 7e ciel.

DATE / EVENT	AUDIO / VIDEO	TITLE
12-7-1983 Montreal, Forum. Attendance: 16.270. Tickets: Canadian Dollars 15,—. "We have a very special guest for you this evening. It's your royal highness Prince Charles of England. No, he's not. Here he is. No, he's here. May I know your names? Joey Salabo. This is for Joey Salabo. It's called Young Americans." The audience didn't understand the joke (neither do I).	*2 CDR*	*Montreal 12 July 1983 (BowieHobby)*
	2 CDR	Sava Montreal? (Old Gold Records OGCD 216A/B)
	2 CDR	Serious Moonlight
	2 CDR	Funk to Forum (KGCD-33)
	2 CDR	Montreal Forum 1st Night (A Dutch Connection)
	Tape	quality 9, 115 min.
	Video	125 min. Steady.
12-7-1983 Canadian News Report. Look back in anger (1 min).	*Video*	*Stolp tapes no. 9 (4 min)*
<u>13-7-1983</u> Montreal, Forum. Sound check (a very long one).	Tape	
<u>13-7-1983</u> Montreal, Forum. Attendance: 16.270. Tickets: Canadian Dollar 15,—. Modern love (3.43) recorded live for the B-side of the studio version of Modern love (released September 1983). A very good concert. "This is a new song. It's a song nouveaux and it's called China girl." During Fame Bowie took the big balloon on his neck, made	2 CD	*Fame (Neverend NE*16.22) complete concert*
	3 CD	*Montreal (Stoned Records SR 008-3 CD 1/2/3)*
	3 CD	*Montreal connection (Papillion Records PPL CD 008/1/2/3)*
	CD	*Live on Mars*

DATE / EVENT	AUDIO / VIDEO	TITLE
a few attempts to fuck it and then broke it into pieces.		*(Golden Stars GZCD 1007)*
	CD	Live on Mars 2
	CD	*The Thin White Duke (P910028)*
	CD	*The Jean Genie (vol. 3) (Banana BAN-004-C)*
	CD	*The Jean Genie (vol. 4) (Banana BAN-004-D)*
	2 CD	The Jean Genie vol. 1&2
	2 CD	*Serious Moonlight (The Swingin' Pig Records TSP-CD-221-2)*
	2 CD	Montreal 1983 (No label, no number)
	2 CDR	Vancouver video star (5 songs) (Old Gold Records OGCD 057A/B)
	2 CDR	Moonlight in Montreal (No label, no number)
	4 LP	Montreal 1983 (No label, no number)
	LP	Recorded live in Montreal Forum 1983
	LP	Tonight David Bowie live on stage (M/W Records 33)
	Single	Cracked heroes / Sexy actor (Cracked actor / Cracked actor) (Heroes / Heroes)
	Single	I can't explain
	Single	Modern love / Modern love (EMI 1A 006-186/62/)
	Tape	quality 9, 120 min.
	Tape	quality 10, 45 min.
Montreal gig broadcast on US radio's Supergroups in Concert. Later broadcast on BBC Radio 1.		
13-7-1983 Canadian TV. News Report. Reporter Danielle Levasseur in Montreal.	*Video*	*Stolp tapes no. 9 (3 min)*
<u>15-7-1983</u> Hartford, Civic Center. Attendance: 15.000.	2 CDR	Glad to be back (Old Gold Records OGCD 473A/B)
	Tape	quality 8, 110 min.
<u>16-7-1983</u> Hartford, Civic Center. Attendance: 15.000. Bowie messes up the lyrics in a few songs. At the end of the concert (during Modern love) out of the big balloon come a lot of small balloons.	2 CDR	Hartford fashion (Old Gold Records OGCD 202A/B)
	Tape	quality 7, 110 min.
	Tape	quality 9, 85 min.

DATE / EVENT	AUDIO / VIDEO	TITLE

<u>18-7-1983</u> Philadelphia, Spectrum Arena.
Attendance: 17.000.
Great crowd, very good concert.
Before Young Americans: "I dedicate this song to the Sigma Kids."
Before the show EMI Records delivered a big cake with the picture of Bowie on it.

2 CDR — First Philly night (Old Gold Records OGCD 474A/B)
Tape — quality 8, 110 min.

18-7-1983 US TV. CBS. Entertainment this week.
Video — *Stolp tapes no. 9 (1 min)*

18-7-1983 Time. Article by Jay Cocks: Dancing to the music - David Bowie rockets onward.
Tony Visconti to Jay Cocks about David's marriage to Angela: "Thursday was gay night. David would go to a gay club, Angie to a lesbian club, and they would both bring people home they found. We had to lock our bedroom doors because in the middle of the night these people they brought home with them would come climbing into new beds, looking for fresh blood."
Bowie: "My admission of bisexuality was a major miscalculation."

18-7-1983 Newsweek. Article by Jim Miller: David Bowie's new look.

<u>19-7-1983</u> Philadelphia, Spectrum Arena.
Attendance: 17.000.
Enthusiastic Bowie and crowd.
After Space oddity: "Good evening, glad you could come."
Before Fame: "What's you name? Corinne? Hello Corinne. How old are you? 28?"
A lot of improvising during Fame and Stay.
"A wide world of Fame… Fame in the back… Fame on the chair… Hey you!… Hey you!… What's you name?"

2 CDR — *Philadelphia 19 July 1983* (BowieHobby)
2 CDR — Second Philly (Old Gold Records OGCD 475A/B)
4 CDR — Serious Moonlight at the Spectrum (A Dutch Connection)
2 CDR — *Walk talk act fine*
Tape — quality 7, 105 min.
Tape — quality 9, 105 min.

Carlos Alomar: "I was the only one who could talk back to Coco. She could have everybody else fired, but I couldn't be fired and that was extremely frustrating for her. She hated my fuckin' guts."

<u>20-7-1983</u> Philadelphia, Spectrum Arena.
Attendance: 17.000. Very responsive crowd.
Live shots made for Modern love video.
After Space oddity a girl climbs up the stage and smashed (by accident) Bowie's guitar. Bowie says: "Oh my god, oh man." To hide his disappointment he says: "I don't care." When you look at his face, you can see this is not true. Then he jokes about the incident: "I want to apologize for my mother!"

2 CDR — The Sigma Kids
2 CDR — *Live in Philadelphia 20th July 1983* (No label, no number)
Tape — quality 6, 110 min.

<u>21-7-1983</u> Philadelphia, Spectrum Arena.
Attendance: 17.000.
Bowie and the audience really enjoy themselves.
A long talk about the time Bowie was recording in Philadelphia. The audience feels Bowie's mood and they

2 CDR — *Philadelphia 21 July 1983* (BowieHobby)
2 CDR — Spectrum moonlight (Old Gold Records OGCD 330A/B)

DATE / EVENT	AUDIO / VIDEO	TITLE
appreciate it and scream like hell.	4 CDR	Serious Moonlight at the Spectrum (A Dutch Connection)
	2 CDR	*Philly bye ta ta* *(No label, no number)*
	Tape	quality 6, 110 min.
	Tape	quality 9, 110 min.

23-7-1983 Syracuse, Carrier Dome. *Rescheduled.*

24-7-1983 New York Daily News Magazine. Article by Susan Shapiro: Down by the Old Mainstream.

| 24-7-1983 US TV. CBS. Entertainment Tonight. Interview and live clips What in the world, Heroes, Fashion, Let's dance, from Philadelphia concerts. | Video | 11 min. |

24-7-1983 US TV. Billy Joel's HBO Special. Special guest: David LeBolt.

25-7-1983 New York Post. Article by Lisa Robinson: Bowie: I am not an alien freak.

| <u>25-7-1983</u> New York, Madison Square Garden. Sound check 16.30 h. George Simms was singing: "New York, New York, it's a hell of a town." | NT | |

<u>25-7-1983</u> New York, Madison Square Garden. Attendance: 19.250. A very good concert. Small part of Lavender blue (dilly dilly) (Mary Martin, 1948) during Heroes. Bowie adds Red Sails to the song list. When Bowie introduces the band, he says they all come from New York. The audience appreciates it. Glenis Daly did Bowie's make-up. Production manager: Eric Barrett. Attended by Raquel Welch (she wore a white outfit that seemed to be a bit too small), Keith Richards, Patti Hansen, John McEnroe, Mike Nichols, Ron Wood, Mick Jagger, Jerry Hall, Yoko Ono, Richard Gere, Grace Jones, Robert Benton, Mike Nichols, James Goldman, David and Leslie Newman, Martin Bregman, Robert Evans, Paul Newman, Dino DeLaurentis, Robert Altman, Lester Persky, Howard Koch, Gene Kirkwood, Diana Sokolow, Gene Simmons, Les Garland, Caroline Prutzman, Tina Turner, Susan Sarandon, Dustin Hoffman, Chip and Gaynor Rachlin. Who (of the celebrities) wasn't there? Down the hall there was a hospitality room, where Bowie paid a brief visit to greet a few of the VIPs. Ron Delsener (who promoted his 1972 concert at Carnegie Hall) delivered a special pasta dinner to the dressing room.	2 CDR	*New York 25 July 1983* *(BowieHobby)*
	2 CDR	The return to M.S.G. (Old Gold Records OGCD 331A/B)
	2 CDR	*Psychodeltcate boy*
	2 CDR	Lavender Blue (KGCD-18)
	4 CDR	New York Moonlight (A Dutch Connection)
	Tape	quality 9, 113 min.

DATE / EVENT	AUDIO / VIDEO	TITLE
Ian Hunter was backstage. Coco gave Tina Turner a place at the right side of the stage, so she could watch the concert on a monitor. During the break in the show Nile Rodgers arrived to congratulate Bowie. They stayed at the Berkshire Place Hotel, East 52 Street (David Bowie's Serious Moonlight - Denis O'Regan and Chet Flippo 1984).		
25-7-1983 US TV. News 4 New York. Clip of Star from 25-7-1983 concert and reporter Rolonda Watts at Madison Square Garden in New York.	*Video*	*Stolp tapes no. 9 (3 min)*
26-7-1983 The New York Times. Article by Robert Palmer: Rock Concert: David Bowie. Palmer wrote: "A flawless show."		
<u>26-7-1983</u> New York, Madison Square Garden. Attendance: 19.250. A good concert. Bowie to Mick Jagger: "Ah, it's your birthday today." Mick Jagger got 40 that day. Bowie sings I can't explain (original by The Who in 1965). They stayed at the Berkshire Place Hotel, East 52 Street.	*2 CDR* *2 CDR* *2 CDR* *4 CDR* Tape Tape	*New York 26 July 1983* *(BowieHobby)* *Who's birthday?* *(Old Gold Records OGCD 332A/B)* *Beauty and the beast* New York Moonlight (A Dutch Connection) quality 9, 115 min. quality 9, 110 min.
27-7-1983 New York Post. Article by Brian Chin: Bowie sprinkles stardust at the Garden. Chin wrote: "Bowie is subtler, more ferocious, more moving and more dazzling than ever before."		
27-7-1983 Daily News. Article by Ernest Leogrande: Bowie wows the Garden.		
<u>27-7-1983</u> New York, Madison Square Garden. Attendance: 19.250. At the beginning of Space oddity: "I want to dedicate this to a little boy called Sean" (John Lennon's son). After the show EMI-party at Café Seikoyen in Manhattan's warehouse district. Guests: Andy Warhol, Raquel Welch, Keith Richards with his son and father, Mike Nichols, Billy Idol, Yoko Ono, David Byrne, Richard Gere, Lorne Michaels, Susan Sarandon, Dustin Hoffman, Mick Jagger. They stayed at the Berkshire Place Hotel, East 52 Street.	*2 CDR* *2 CDR* *2 CDR* *2 CDR* Tape	*Madison Square Garden NY 1983 (No label, no number)* *Farewell to New York (Old Gold Records OGCD 333A/B)* *New York '83 (No label, no number)* *Moonlight Blueshirts (No label, no number)* quality 9, 115 min.
<u>29-7-1983</u> Richfield (Cleveland), Richfield Coliseum. Attendance: 20.000.	*2 CDR* Tape Tape	Fragments of Cleveland (Old Gold Records OGCD 476A/B) quality 8, 90 min. quality 9, 110 min.

DATE / EVENT	AUDIO / VIDEO	TITLE
	Tape	quality 8, 115 min.
<u>30-7-1983</u> Detroit, Joe Louis Arena. Attendance: 18.600. During Jean Genie Bowie sings "poor Iggy" instead of "poor Genie." He also sings Detroit's a go go instead of New York. Detroit is Iggy Pop's hometown. Various fans say Jean Genie was inspired on Iggy Pop. Years later Bowie denied this.	2 CDR 2 CDR 2 CDR Tape	*Detroit 30 July 1983* *(BowieHobby)* Detroit fashion (Old Gold Records OGCD 334A/B) *Detroit 83* *(A Dutch Connection)* quality 9, 105 min.
30-7-1983 UK TV. South East News. Reporter Tom Brook. Interview before the show at 30-7-1983 in Detroit.	*Video*	*Stolp Tapes 9 (2 min)*
<u>31-7-1983</u> Detroit, Joe Louis Arena. Attendance: 18.600. Not a good concert. Promoter: Belkin & Prism. "This is the world. It's yours if you're welcome to it. here's a song I wrote and recorded for the Young Americans album and it's for you and it's called Young Americans." At the end of Fame Bowie starts a sing-a-long with the audience. During Jean Genie he sings Chicago's a go go.	2 CDR 2 CDR Tape	Farewell to Detroit (Old Gold Records OGCD 401A/B) Detroit '83 (No label, no number) quality 9, 110 min.

August 1983 Release LP Golden Years (Compilation) (RCA BowLP 004).

August 1983 Release Promo-LP Lifetimes (Compilation) (RCA Lifetimes 1).

August 1983 Release LP A second face (compilation of Deram material) (Decca TAB 71).

August 1983 Release Prime cuts (Decca). Re-release of Images 1966 / 1967 plus Liza Jane and Louie Louie go home.

August 1983 Creem. Article by Michael Davis: Let's dance.

August 1983 Record Collector. Article by Steve Scott: David Bowie: The songs he gave away, the records he produced and the sessions he played from 1966 to present.

August 1983 Mother Jones. Article by Simon Frith: Only dancing: David Bowie flirts with the issues.

| <u>2-8-1983</u> Chicago, Rosemont Horizon. Attendance: 18.100. Started at 20.00 hours. Promoter: Jam. Tickets: USD 14.—. Not a good concert. Bad sound. Uninspired band. Tony Thompson ran off stage and hit a pole. They stayed at Chicago's Ambassador East Hotel. At this hotel there was an after-show party. | 2 CD 2 CD 2 CDR 2 CDR 4 CDR | *Live at Rosemont Horizon* *(No label, no number)* Montreal Rosemont Horizon (Old Gold Records OGCD 142A/B) *Live at the Rosemont Horizon (MCDS 022 99B)* Hot Chicago |

DATE / EVENT	AUDIO / VIDEO	TITLE
	3 LP	(No label, no number) Live at Rosemont Horizon (984 DB 103 A/E)
	3 LP	David Part 1 (984 DB 103)
	3 LP	Nothing for free
	Tape	115 min.
3-8-1983 Chicago, Rosemont Horizon. Attendance: 18.100. At the beginning of Look back in anger the drums are to late, this makes this version sound very odd. During the concert Bowie's microphone is out of order. He throws him down and leaves the stage. They find him another microphone and he continues if nothing happened. During Cracked actor he misses the first line.	2 CDR Tape	*Second Night At The Horizon* (No label, no number) quality 7, 110 min.

3-8-1983 Chicago. Interviewed by Gabrielle Sneddon-Pike from the English magazine No.1.

4-8-1983 Chicago, Rosemont Horizon. Attendance: 18.100. Very good concert! After Heroes: "Ah, it's hot." During Breaking glass: "Don't worry kid, I'll never touch. But you now what… you got problems." During Let's dance someone throws a rose on stage. Bowie picks it up and uses it as a fiddle. Cracked actor had a very long instrumental intro. The Jean Genie was really swinging!	2 CDR 4 CDR Tape	*At his best!* (No label, no number) Hot Chicago (No label, no number) quality 9, 125 min.
7-8-1983 Edmonton, Commonwealth Stadium. Attendance: 57.283. Tickets: Can $ 25,— and 20,—. Benefit: USD 1 Million. Support-acts: Peter Gabriel, The Tubes. "I wrote this one in 1975 and it's from an album called Young Americans. It's called Young Americans."	2 CDR 2 CDR 2 CDR 2 CDR Tape Video	*Edmonton 7 August 1983* (BowieHobby) Dig it! (Old Gold Records OGCD 337A/B) Edmonton 83 (KGCD 32) Edmonton 83 (A Dutch Connection) quality 8, 115 min. quality 8, 113 min.

9-8-1983 Village Voice. Article by C. Cooper: Licks: Serious Bowie.

9-8-1983 Vancouver, British Columbia Place Stadium. Attendance: 53.687. Tickets: Can $ 25,— and 20,—. Benefit: USD 1,3 Million. Support-acts: The Tubes and Peter Gabriel. Started at 19.30 h. After Heroes: "We don't want anybody hurt. Don't push to much down there."	Tape	quality 8, 115 min.

DATE / EVENT	AUDIO / VIDEO	TITLE
	2 CDR	Yokohama Stadium
	Tape	quality 8, 110 min.
26-10-1983 Osaka, Furitsu Taiikukan. Bowie not in a good mood (probably because of his throat problems). Not a good show. That's a pity, because the quality of the recording is superb.	2 CDR	*Osaka 26 October 1983* *(BowieHobby)*
	2 CDR	*Shorter than yesterday* *(Old Gold Records* *OGCD 353A/B)*
	4 CDR	*The Furitsu Taiikukan* *Concerts* *(No label, no number)*
	Tape	quality 9, 105 min.

26/27-10-1983 There was an earthquake in Tokyo. The band was in the hotel (pretty high up). The walls started swaying and they hauled down 20 flights of stairs. (David Bowie's Serious Moonlight - Denis O'Regan and Chet Flippo 1984).

DATE / EVENT	AUDIO / VIDEO	TITLE
27-10-1983 Osaka, Furitsu Taiikukan. Bowie not in a good mood (he still has throat problems). Again a great sound, but not a good concert.	2 CDR	*Osaka 27 October 1983* *(BowieHobby)*
	2 CDR	*Serious Osaka* *(Old Gold Records* *OGCD 354A/B)*
	4 CDR	*The Furitsu Taiikukan* *Concerts* *(No label, no number)*
	2 CDR	*Live in Osaka 27th Oct 83* *(No label, no number)*
	Tape	quality 9, 110 min.
29-10-1983 Nagoya, Kokusai Tenji Kaikan. Attendance: 10.064. "This is a song for all the lovely people here and for the thousands that we have performed before all over this world. Thank you! It's called The Young Americans and it's from 1976." The song is from 1975. He made this mistake more often during the tour. During Jean Genie: "Poor little Iggy keeps all his dead hair for making naughty underwear. He's a strange little Iggy." Bowie is obviously in the right mood again.	2 CDR	*Live in Nagoya 1983* *(CD-R 83 0010 29)*
	Tape	quality 6, 35 min.
	Tape	quality 6, 105 min.
30-10-1983 Osaka, Expo Memorial Park. Attendance: 15.105. A very good concert. At the beginning of Heroes: "Ho ho, Please! Back! Back!" Then he says a few words in Japanese to the pushing and rioting crowd. A Japanese speaker tries to calm down the crowd. After a few minutes they start the song from the beginning.	2 CDR	The dressman & the Nippon girl (Old Gold Records OGCD 355A/B)
	1 CDR	*The dressman and the* *Nippon girl (Zig Dust / Who* *Cares? Record LC* *62-13831030)*
	LP	The dressman and the Nippon girl (LC 62-13831030 LP 99)

DATE / EVENT	AUDIO / VIDEO	TITLE
10-8-1983 Canadian TV. First Choice. Concert Report. Vancouver 9-8-1983.	Video	7 min.
<u>11-8-1983</u> Tacoma (Seattle), Tacoma Dome. Attendance: 27.000. Support-act: The Tubes. "Firstly I'd like to thank The Tubes for their excellent support over the last few days, they have lovely tits. I'd like to introduce my band to you, who have no tits but big talents." Announcing Young Americans: "An old song from the mid-seventies."	2 CDR 2 CDR 2 CDR 2 CDR Tape Video	*Tacoma 11 August 1983 (BowieHobby)* Tacoma 83 (Old Gold Records OGCD 338A/B) Tacoma 11/8/1983 (No label, no number) Tacoma Dome 1983 (A Dutch Connection) quality 8, 115 min. quality 7, 110 min.
US TV. Concert Report. Tacoma 11-8-1983.	Video	2 min.
<u>14-8-1983</u> Los Angeles, Forum. Attendance: 16.480. Started with Look back in anger. During the song: "How we doin' so far?" Attended by: Prince, Michael Jackson, Barbra Streisand, Bette Midler, Mick Fleetwood, Sissy Spacek, Henry Winkler, Toni Basil, Sally Struthers, Irene Cara, Tom Conti, Donald Sutherland, Richard Perry, Giorgio Moroder (who had a number one hit in England in 1972 as a member of Chicory Tip with Son of my father), Cher, David Hemmings, Wyne Forte with Missing Persons, Howard Hesseman. Gail Davis (Bowie's director of creative services) introduced Bowie to Gina Shock and Kathy Valentine from the Go-Go's. In David's dressing room there were massive ice sculptures. He invited Michael Jackson, Cher and Bette Midler back stage. He also met Jaclyn Smith, Henry Winkler and Jim Katz (David Bowie's Serious Moonlight - Denis O'Regan and Chet Flippo 1984).	Tape Tape	quality 8, 110 min. 120 min.
14-8-1983 US TV. CBS. News Report. Interview by Pat Collins.	*Video* *Video* Video	*Stolp tapes no. 9 (1 min)* *Stolp tapes no. 9 (15 min)* 5 min.
<u>15-8-1983</u> Los Angeles, Forum. Attendance: 16.480. Hysterical crowd. "I of course am Michael Jackson." During Sorrow Bowie sings: "You long blond hair and your eyes so blue. The only thing I ever got from you were these flowers… these flowers." The crowd loves it.	2 CDR 2 CDR 2 CDR 2 CDR	*Los Angeles 15 August 1983 (BowieHobby)* The best part (Old Gold Records OGCD 173A/B) Los Angeles LA 83

DATE / EVENT	AUDIO / VIDEO	TITLE
	6 CDR	LA to Washington 1983 (A Dutch Connection)
	Tape	quality 8, 130 min.
	Tape	quality 8, 70 min.
<u>17-8-1983</u> Phoenix, Arizona Veteran's Memorial. Attendance: 15.275. Started at 20.00 h. Good concert. Hysterical crowd.	2 CDR	I'm Steve Wonder (Old Gold Records OGCD 477A/B)
During Cracked Actor Bowie forgets to start singing. After an instrumental part he finally starts.	1 CDR	*Phoenix 1983* *(No label, no number)*
At the end of the song: "You make a guy hot." Band intro: "And I, of course, am Stevie Wonder."	1 CDR	Arizona Moonlight (No label, no number)
In the dressing room Bowie played the video game Asteroids with his son Zowie on a Playboy pinball machine. Shelley Duvall visited David on Jet 24 (private-jet Bowie used during this tour) and flew with him to Dallas and stayed for some days (David Bowie's Serious Moonlight - Denis O'Regan and Chet Flippo 1984).	Tape	quality 9, 110 min.

Because of the threat of the Hurricane Alice they decided to base in Dallas for the next six days. At the departure they have to wait for Carlos Alomar (as usual). They go by bus (the same one they used earlier to drive to Palm Springs). The bus departs at 1.20 h. JET 24 takes off from Imperial Terminal at 2.18 h. At the plane they have lunch (assorted guiche and broccoli). Carlos does a Michael Jackson impersonation. Bowie reads Newsweek. The article is titled: Drugs on the job. He is annoyed and asks the band what this is all about. The plane lands at 3.25 h. (David Bowie's Serious Moonlight - Denis O'Regan and Chet Flippo 1984).

<u>19-8-1983</u> Dallas, Reunion Arena. Attendance: 17.881. Great crowd response.	2 CDR	*Dallas 19 August 1983* *(BowieHobby)*
The doors opened at 18.30 h. and the crowd rushed in. Here and there fights started.	2 CDR	So hologramic (Old Gold Records OGCD 339A/B)
At the beginning of White light white heat there is no good coordination between the band members.	2 CDR	Dallas 19/8/1983 (No label, no number)
A red bandana is thrown on stage. Bowie catches it without even looking.	Tape	quality 9, 115 min.

They stayed at the Mandalay Four Seasons Hotel (the same hotel where they stayed during the 19 days of rehearsals), with it's lobby bar called Aperitif.
In Dallas Tony Mascia bought a big hat for Zowie. He wore the hat while he was skateboarding.

20-8-1983 Premiere Merry Christmas Mr. Lawrence.

Various reviews of Merry Christmas Mr. Lawrence:		
Switzerland TV. Neu im Kino.	Video	11 min.
Swedish TV. Preview.	Video	6 min.
German TV. Ratschlag for Kinoganger.	Video	6 min.
US TV. Review.	Video	2 min.
UK TV. Film '83.	Video	5 min.
UK TV. Riverside.	Video	3 min.

DATE / EVENT	AUDIO / VIDEO	TITLE
UK TV. Visions of cinema.	Video	4 min.

They left the hotel at 14.30 h. On the plane they watched Shelley Duvall's fairy-tale "The boy who tried to find the shivers" on the VCR.

<u>20-8-1983</u> Austin, Frank Erwin Center.	*2 CDR*	*Austin 20 August 1983*
Attendance: 16.148.		*(BowieHobby)*
A good concert.	2 CDR	Run for the shadows
In the hall there is a strong marijuana smoke in the air.		(Old Gold Records
Bowie inhales deep and says: "My, don't you smell good!"		OGCD 340A/B)
"This is probably Austin… right? I'd like to thank you	2 CDR	Austin Texas 1983
personally. Every one of you for coming tonight."		(A Dutch Connection
A note with a phone number is thrown on stage. It says:		CD 20081983)
Even a date can be a special event.	2 CDR	Austin 20/8/1983
In the dressing room there was an interview by Chet Flippo.		(No label, no number)
Joey (Zowie) walked in carrying a board game called	Tape	quality 9, 115 min.
21 Baker Street.		
At 23.26 h. the plane leaves for Dallas. They have dinner		
on the plane. At the hotel there is a pool party.		
(David Bowie's Serious Moonlight - Denis O'Regan and		
Chet Flippo 1984).		
<u>21-8-1983</u> Houston, The Summit.	Tape	quality 8, 115 min.
Attendance: 16.232. Tickets: USD 13,75.		
Started at 20.00 h.		
A great concert and an excellent recording.		

22-8-1983 Release Modern love (3.56) / Modern love (live version) (3.43) (EMI EA 158).

22-8-1983 Release 12" Modern love (4.46) / Modern love (live version) (3.43) (EMI 12EA 158).

24-8-1983 Magazine No.1. 5-Page article about Bowie.

24-8-1983 Norfolk. Before the concert there were TV interviews with Bowie fans. Carmine Rojas and Frank Simms joined the fans and told the reporter that they had seen every Bowie concert of the tour! (Broadcast on 25-8-1983).

<u>24-8-1983</u> Norfolk, Scope Convention Hall.	Tape	
Attendance: 10.685. Promoter: Whisper Concerts.		
Tickets: USD 15,00.		

25-8-1983 Newspaper article: Charismatic Bowie delivers.

<u>25-8-1983</u> Norfolk, Scope Convention Hall.	Tape	
Attendance: 10.685. Promoter: Whisper Concerts.		
Tickets: USD 15,00.		
25-8-1983 Swedish TV. Filmkronikan.	*Video*	*Various 25 (1 min)*
Interview and photo-shoot in Cannes.		

DATE / EVENT	AUDIO / VIDEO	TITLE
27-8-1983 Landover (Washington), Capitol Center. Attendance: 14.736. Great concert, very good sound. "Just a little something we have in here to screw up. By the way, thank you very much for coming. In 1976 I made an album called Young Americans." He sings the title song, which off course is from 1975! No Red sails or I can't explain this evening.	2 CDR 4 CDR 6 CDR 2 CDR Tape	Washington 27 August 1983 (BowieHobby) All the way to Washington (Old Gold Records OGCD 342A/B) LA to Washington 1983 (A Dutch Connection) Washington 83 First Night (No label, no number) quality 9, 120 min.
28-8-1983 Landover (Washington), Capitol Center. Attendance: 14.735. A good concert. Last concert that started with Jean Genie intro-Star. During Young Americans Bowie changes the lyrics: "All the way from Washington." Red sails is back in the set-list.	2 CDR 2 CDR 4 CDR 2 CDR 6 CDR Tape Tape	Washington 28 August 1983 (BowieHobby) The last genie intro (Old Gold Records OGCD 343A/B) All the way to Washington (Old Gold Records OGCD 342A/B) At the Capitol LA to Washington 1983 (A Dutch Connection) quality 8, 120 min. quality 9, 120 min.
29-8-1983 Hershey, Hershey Park Stadium. Attendance: 25.530. Promoter: Electric Factory Concerts. During the intro: "We can't keep on meeting like this. Good evening all you oil millionaires. Let's all go swimming, shall we? Your place. Anybody got a plectrum? This is a song from an album we did in 1975." Young Americans follows. Fast version of TVC15. During Jean Genie: "Tells he's a musician and sells you all kind of shit."	2 CDR 2 CDR Tape Tape Tape	Wet songs (Old Gold Records OGCD 344A/B) Hershey Moonlight 1983 (No label, no number) quality 8, 110 min. quality 9, 80 min. quality 9, 115 min.

30-8-1983 British documentary The Oshima Gang includes interview and clips from Merry Christmas Mr. Lawrence press conference.

31-8-1983 Circus. Article by Philip Bashe: David Bowie man of ch-ch-changes.

| 31-8-1983 WBCN. Bowie A-Z Day. To celebrate Foxboro show. Trafic reports, comments etc. | Tape | quality 10, 90 min. |
| 31-8-1983 Foxborough, Sullivan Stadium. Attendance: 53.359. A good concert. When Bowie enters the stage, it stops raining. At the start of Scary monsters Carlos Alomar plays completely out of tune. Bowie not talkative. | 2 CDR
Tape | Let's Dub (NEO, TFB)
quality 8, 115 min. |

DATE / EVENT	AUDIO / VIDEO	TITLE

September 1983 American Film. Article by Ruth McCormick: Let's act.
Bowie about releasing the film Ziggy Stardust the Motion Picture: "That's something I couldn't look at for years. I was so fed up with him, it… all that. But I dragged it out last year and had a look, and thought, "This is a funny film. This boy used to dress like that for living? My God this is funny. Incredible! Wait till my son sees this!"

<u>3-9-1983</u> Toronto, CNE Grandstand.   *2 CDR*   Sold out again
Attendance: 51.700. Benefit Canadian Dollars 2.277.877,—.   (Old Gold Records
A very good concert. Very good recording.   OGCD 478A/B)
November 1983 Without you (3.08) and Criminal world   *Tape*   quality 9, 115 min.
(4.25) were released as a single in Spain.
The original version of Criminal world was released by
Metro (including Duncan Browne) in 1977.
Bowie met Ronson in Toronto. Ronson had asked Corinne
Schwab for some tickets (Starzone 13, Oct / Nov 1984).

3-9-1983 Canadian (a.o. CFTO News) and US news   Video   2 min.
channels show clips of Look back in anger from the
3-9-1983 concert.

<u>4-9-1983</u> Toronto, CNE Grandstand.   *2 CDR*   *Toronto 4 September 1983*
Attendance: 51.700. Promoter: Chum & Chum.   *(BowieHobby)*
Bowie in a very good mood. At the end of Breaking glass   *2 CDR*   *Boy could he play Earl's*
he keeps repeating: "Oh no, no."   *guitar (Downunder Discs)*
Before the encore Jean Genie: "I was walking through a   *2 CDR*   Toronto 4th September 1983
corridor in Toronto last night and I ran into somebody I   (No label, no number)
haven't met for 8 years and I said: What are you doing   *Tape*   quality 9, 120 min.
tonight? And he said: Not much. So I said: Do you
wanna come and play with us? He hasn't worked with me
for 10 years. I'd like to introduce one of the original
Spiders from Mars: Mick Ronson!"
Ronson borrowed Earl Slick's guitar, not knowing it was
his prize guitar. He trashed the guitar, waving it above his
head, banging into it, swinging it round his head.
Afterwards Bowie said about Earl Slick: "You should have
seen his face" (The Starzone Interviews - David Currie
1987).

Canadian TV. Newsweek. Concert Report 4-9-1983.   Video   2 min.

Canadian TV. News. Concert Report. Toronto 4-9-1983.   Video   2 min.

5-9-1983 Canadian TV. Toronto-dimo safari.   Video   2 min.
About Toronto concert 4-9-1983.

<u>5-9-1983</u> Buffalo, Memorial Auditorium.   *2 CDR*   Buffalo Bowie
Attendance: 18.000.   (Old Gold Records
"This is from the ill fated Low album. It's called What in the   OGCD 345A/B)

DATE / EVENT	AUDIO / VIDEO	TITLE

world." During the band-intro: "Thank God they put an air-conditioning in. Can you imagine what it would be like without it?"

Tape — quality 9, 115 min.
Tape — quality 8, 110 min.
Video — quality 10, 1 min.

5-9-1983 US TV. Pop News. Presented by Bob & Patricia.

Video — 5 min.

5-9-1983 US TV. News Hour Final.

Video — 4 min.

<u>6-9-1983</u> Syracuse, Carrier Dome.
Attendance: 28.820. Started at 20.00 hours.
A very, very good concert. Entrance: USD 13,50.
Attended by Paul Simon.
During Stay Bowie was talking to David Lebolt. He leaned over the piano, while Earl Slick did his guitar solo. Bowie stepped to the microphone and Slick expected him to start singing. Bowie stepped back again, to lean on the piano. Slick was confused and forced to stretch out his solo. Bowie and David Lebolt had a lot of fun.

2 CDR — At the university (Old Gold Records OGCD 346A/B)
Tape — quality 8, 110 min.

6-9-1983 US TV news channels show clip of Look back in anger from 5-9-1983 concert.

Video — 1 min.

6-9-1983 Village Voice. Article by J.Hoberman: Rockers.

7-9-1983 The Syracuse Herald Journal. Article: David Bowie's new look tops concert series for year.

9-9-1983 Commonweal. Article by Deborah Elizabeth Finn: Moon and gloom: David Bowie's frustrated messianism.
Finn wrote: Love is a drug that sometimes brings relief, but often the side effects are quite as severe as the initial pain. Cat people, a new arrangement of the 1982 movie theme song with lyrics by Mr. Bowie, is a track that conveys the rawness of emotion associated with addictive love.

<u>9-9-1983</u> Anaheim (Los Angeles), Anaheim Stadium.
Attendance: 70.089. Promoter: Avalon.
Tickets: USD 17,50.
Support acts: Go-Go's and Madness.
During China girl Bowie sang with a heavy Chinese accent: "Oh baby, just you shut your mouth."
Attended by Sting and his wife Trudy, Iggy Pop.

2 CDR — By demand! (Old Gold Records OGCD 347A/B)
2 CDR — *Los Angeles 9 September 1983 (BowieHobby)*
2 CDR — *Los Angeles 9 Sept 1983 (2) (BowieHobby)*
2 CDR — Los Angeles 83 (No label, no number)
Tape — quality 8, 120 min.

<u>11-9-1983</u> Vancouver, Pacific National Exh. Coliseum.
Attendance: 11.000.
The Serious Moonlight video was shot by David Mallet on 11-9-1983 and 12-9-1983.
50 Young women were selected to stand in the front row.
DJ Terry Mulligan told the crowd how to act when they

2 CDR — *Vancouver 11 September 1983 (BowieHobby)*
2 CD — Serious Moonlight Vancouver (No label, no number)
1 CDR — The stones of Mamaragan (No label, no number)

357

DATE / EVENT	AUDIO / VIDEO	TITLE
were filmed. This "spontaneous" approach was a complete failure and not repeated the next evening.	2 CDR	Dancing in the moonlight (Artwork by Walter Ego)
A great show, as always when Bowie knows he is filmed. Backstage there was a Sushi Bar.	LP	The stones of Mamaragan (DT BUNJIL 1 A/B)
	LP	HBO "Serious Moonlight Show"
	Tape	quality 8, 120 min.
	Video	*The Serious Moonlight*
12-9-1983 Vancouver, Pacific National Exh. Coliseum. Attendance: 11.000.	*1 CDR*	*Vancouver 12 September 1983 (BowieHobby)*
The Serious Moonlight video was shot by David Mallet on 11-9-1983 and 12-9-1983.	2 CDR	Serious Moonlight Vancouver (No label, no number)
Again a great concert. At the end of Fame the balloon is bounced back on the stage. Bowie picks it up, walks to the end of the stage and throws it as far as possible.	2 CDR	Vancouver video star (Old Gold Records OGCD 057A/B)
60 Minutes broadcast on FM radio.	*3 CDR*	*Victorian Connection (No label, no number)*
Backstage there was a Sushi Bar.	2 CDR	Dancing in the moonlight (Artwork by Walter Ego)
	2 CDR	Vancouver PNE Coliseum
	2 CDR	Vancouver 1983 (No label, no number)
	LP	HBO "Serious Moonlight Show"
	Tape	quality 10, 90 min.
	Tape	quality 10, 60 min.
	Video	*The Serious Moonlight*
	Video	88 min.

14-9-1983 Winnipeg Sun. Headline: Tonight is the night: Bowie! (a whole edition about Bowie).

14-9-1983 Winnipeg, Winnipeg Stadium. Attendance: 34.816. Tickets: USD 20,00.	*2 CDR*	*Lill Scob's first show (EgoDisc 010/011)*
250 Security guards. 200 People got hurt. 31 People were arrested. Massive crowd response on a great show. Announcing Young Americans: "This is an old Yugoslavian song you might know."	Tape	quality 8, 100 min.
	Tape	110 min.

15-9-1983 Winnipeg Sun. Headline: Bowie: Now we've heard everything!!!!!

15-9-1983 Wall Street Journal. Article by Julie Salamon: David Bowie confronts Japan: the twain don't meet.

16-9-1983 Bowie played D.J. at a local Radio Station in San Francisco in the middle of the night.

17-9-1983 Bowie had lunch with Nagisa Oshima (director of Merry Christmas Mr. Lawrence).

17-9-1983 San Francisco, Oakland Alameda Stadium.	2 CDR	The last American moonlight

DATE / EVENT	AUDIO / VIDEO	TITLE
Attendance: 57.920. Tickets: USD 20,—. "On bass a well known Dutch painter: Carmine Rojas." "I'd like to thank Keay Fogg's radio station for playing Super Requests earlier in the morning."	2 CDR 2 CDR Tape	(Old Gold Records OGCD 348A/B) Oakland '83 (No label, no number) Live in Oakland 1983 (CDR-83 0009 17) quality 8, 115 min.
17-9-1983 Britons in America (documentary). Includes interview and Look back in anger clip from 17-9-1983 concert.	Video	Stolp tapes no. 10 (7 min)
19-9-1983 Macleans. Article by David Livingstone: An exquisite legend in his own time.		
22-9-1983 Premiere film Yellowbeard.		
25-9-1983 WFNX (101.7 FM). The Golden Year interview with Phil Harvey.	Tape	quality 10, 90 min.
October 1983 Mademoiselle. Article by Frank Rose: Is David Bowie coming to earth?		
October 1983 Re-released by EMI: Let's dance (picture disc) (EMI America AMLP 3029).		
October 1983 Release LP Ziggy Stardust the motion picture (RCA PL 84862).		
October 1983 Release White light, white heat (4.06) / Cracked actor (2.51) (RCA 372).		
October 1983 Japanese TV. Funky tomatoe.	Video	18 min.
October 1983 Japanese TV. The message.	Video	25 min.
October 1983 Japanese TV. Still set to Soul love.	Video	1 min.
1-10-1983 BBC. Radio 1. News on Bowie convention held by Kevin Cann. It was a 2-day convention in The Cunard International Hotel in London, attended by Lindsay Kemp and Ken Pitt, answering questions by fans.	Tape	quality 9, 5 min.
16-10-1983 Tokyo. The tour members arrived.		
Between 16 and 20 October 1983. Tokyo. Rehearsals.	NT	
18-10-1983 TV Asaki interview with Bowie and the cast of Merry Christmas Mister Lawrence. Parts of clips Let's dance, China girl, Modern love, Peace on earth / Little drummer boy. Crystal Japan by R.Sakamoto (live).	Video	Stolp tapes no. 9 (50 min)

DATE / EVENT	AUDIO / VIDEO	TITLE
Tokyo. Akasaka Prince Hotel. Press conference.	Video	2 min.
20-10-1983 Tokyo, Budokan Arena. Attendance: 10.700. Tickets: Yen. 6.000. Bowie welcomes the crowd in Japanese. Attended by Nagisa Oshima, Keiko Matsuzaka, Miyu Takagi and Naomi Akimoto.	2 CD	*Japan 1983* (No label, no number)
	2 CD	Moonlight over Japan (Moonraker 453/54)
	2 CDR	Japan 83 (Old Gold Records OGCD 350A/B)
	2 CDR	Live Tokyo 1983
	2 LP	Japan 1983 (Cako Records Inc. Strema ZP 116 A/D)
	LP	Serious moonlight (Rab Limited Dow LP 5)
	Tape	quality 7, 110 min.
21-10-1983 Tokyo, Budokan Arena. Attendance: 10.700. Tickets: Yen. 6.000. A good concert and a hysterical crowd.	2 CDR	Tokyo star
	Tape	quality 8, 105 min.
	Tape	quality 9, 110 min.
22-10-1983 Tokyo, Budokan Arena. Attendance: 10.700. Tickets: Yen. 6.000. During Breaking glass they have to stop, because Earl Slick has some technical problems. "On saxophone and troublemaker of the band Stanley Harrison."	2 CDR	Are you well? (Old Gold Records OGCD 349A/B)
	Tape	quality 7, 120 min.
	Tape	quality 9, 120 min.
24-10-1983 Tokyo, Budokan Arena. Attendance: 10.700. Started at 18.30 h. Tickets: Yen. 6.000. "This is our last night in Tokyo and that's a shame. I'd like to thank each and everyone of the Tokyo aids, who made our stay here so very warm and very wonderful. Thank you very much indeed. I'd like to introduce you to the members of the band." After the band-intro: "Now we'd like to show you all the clothes that we've bought. No, we'll sing instead." They travelled by train to Yokohama.	2 CDR	*Tokyo 24 October 1983* (BowieHobby)
	2 CDR	Goodbye Tokyo (Old Gold Records OGCD 351A/B)
	2 CDR	Tokyo, 24th October 1983 (No label, no number)
	2 CDR	Budokan Arena, Tokyo, Japan 24-10-1983 (No label, no number)
	2 CDR	Tokyo Budokan Arena 4th Night
	2 CDR	Live Tokyo 1983
	4 CD	*Watch that man in Tokyo* (BOW 5162/63/64/65)
	Tape	quality 9, 110 min.
25-10-1983 Yokohama, Yokohama Stadium. Attendance: 25.989. A Good concert. He started the band intro in Japanese and ended with the words: "What a nice night."	2 CDR	Wait until the crowd cries (Old Gold Records OGCD 352A/B)
	2 CDR	*Live in Yokohama 1983* (CD-R 83 0010 25)

DATE / EVENT	AUDIO / VIDEO	TITLE
During China girl: "My little Nippon girl."	Tape	not complete quality 9, 105 min.
<u>31-10-1983</u> Kyoto, Furitsu Taikukan. Announces What in the world in Japanese. Does the beginning of the band-intro also in Japanese. During Modern love he changes the word Goodbye in Sayonara. The crowd loves it.	2 CDR 2 CDR Tape Tape	Japanese finale (Old Gold Records OGCD 356A/B) *Live in Yokohama 1983* *(5 songs)* *(CD-R 83 0010 25)* quality 7, 115 min. quality 9, 115 min.

November 1983 Spain. Release single Without you (3.08) / Criminal world (4.25). Both songs recorded live in Toronto on 3-9-1983. Cover designed by K. Haring.

November 1983 Vogue. Article by Anne Rice: David Bowie and the end of gender.
Rice about the film Merry Christmas Mr. Lawrence: And finally it is through the sexually charged gesture of kissing the Japanese captain (Ryuichi Sakamoto) before the whole camp that Bowie manages to draw the man's anger away from the British commander who is about to be killed.

November 1983 Penthouse. Article by Robert Palmer: David Bowie.

November 1983 Vanity Fair. Article: Portrait.

November 1983 Video World. Article about Bowie.

November 1983 Australian TV. Perth airport.	Video	5 min.
?-11-1983 UK TV. Entertainment Tonight.	Video	7 min.
3-11-1983 Australian TV. Newsworld 7. Interview and press conference.	Video	4 min.

3-11-1983 Australian TV. Morning Show. Interview and press conference.

3-11-1983 Australian TV. Today Show. Interview and press conference.

<u>4-11-1983</u> Perth, Entertainment Centre. Attendance: 7.680. Started at 20.00 h.	Tape	
<u>5-11-1983</u> Perth, Entertainment Centre. Attendance: 7.680. Started at 20.00 h.	Tape	
<u>6-11-1983</u> Perth, Entertainment Centre. Attendance: 7.680. Started at 20.00 h.	Tape	
6-11-1983 Australian TV. Countdown. Interview, clips.	*Video*	*Various 19 (9 min)*

DATE / EVENT	AUDIO / VIDEO	TITLE
9-11-1983 Adelaide, Oval Cricket Ground. Attendance: 18.409.	Tape	
10-11-1983 The News. Article: The show of the decade.		
11-11-1983 Sydney, Don Lane Show. Interview with Bowie (7.05), who appeared unannounced in the show. In a snack bar he saw on TV it was Don Lane's last show and he decided to go to the studio.	CD	Complete Dallas Rehearsals Vol. 2/2 (Star Spangled Music SSM004)
	1 CDR	Various Singles - 1 (No label, no number)
	2 CDR	Hammersmith Resurrection (Old Gold Records OGCD 055A/B)
	Single	Nothing Pornographic Interview (TH 26 FFF)
	Video	Various 22, 7 min.
12-11-1983 Melbourne, VFL Park Waverley. Attendance: 37.914. Started at 19.00 h. A good concert. Band intro: "Anybody wanna play back gammon?"	2 CDR	I believe all the way (Old Gold Records OGCD 357A/B)
	2 CDR	Just the power to charm (No label, no number)
	Tape	quality 8, 115 min.
16-11-1983 Brisbane, Lang Park. Attendance: 26.757. The show had to end at 22.15 hours. Promoter: Paul Dainty. Sound restricted to 80 dB. Paul Dainty had to pay a bond of USD 50.000 to be sure the show wouldn't be too loud. Major Alderman Roy Harvey (who attended the show himself) was very pleased the way the show was done. The rain poured down during the concert.	2 CDR	Oakland Moonlight (A Dutch Connection)
	3 LP Tape	Brisbane '83
19-11-1983 Sydney, R.A.S. of N.S.W. Showgrounds. Attendance: 30.900. Started at 6.30 p.m. Promoter: The Paul Dainty Corporation. Enthusiastic, but violent crowd. Very average concert and Bowie didn't speak a word, except for the intro.	2 CDR	Live in Sydney Nov 19th 1983 (No label, no number)
	2 CDR	The Stones of Marmaragan (No label, no number)
	Tape	quality 7, 80 min.
	Tape	quality 9, 120 min.
20-11-1983 Sydney, R.A.S. of N.S.W. Showgrounds. Attendance: 30.900. Bowie was joking a lot. The crowd again was enthusiastic, but violent. No band coordination at the beginning of Stay. Right after the show they flew to New Zealand.	2 CDR	Sydney moonlight down under (Old Gold Records OGCD 358A/B)
	2 CDR	Moonlight Downunder (Arwork Saloca 2004)
	Tape	quality 7, 105 min.
	Tape	quality 9, 105 min.
22-11-1983 Soundstreet. NHK Japan interview.	Tape	quality 10, 45 min.

DATE / EVENT	AUDIO / VIDEO	TITLE

24-11-1983 The Toarangtira Tribe of the Maori invited Bowie and the band to a formal tribal ceremony. (David Bowie's Serious Moonlight - Denis O'Regan and Chet Flippo 1984).

<u>24-11-1983</u> Wellington, Athletic Park.   2 CDR   *Now be cool!*
Attendance: 47.838.   *(Old Gold Records*
After Life on Mars? Bowie has to calm down the pushing   *OGCD 359A/B)*
people. After Sorrow he stops again: "There is somebody   2 CDR   *Live in Wellington 1983*
down on the ground. Get that person up. There is   *(CD-R 83 0011 24)*
somebody down on the ground. Put a light up there. To   Tape   quality 8, 120 min.
you left." Some time later Bowie gets angry: "Now be cool.
It's alright. Oke!" After White light white heat the
organiser comes on stage to calm down the crowd again.
A concert with a frightening atmosphere.

25-11-1983 Various articles in Auckland's newspapers about the riots in Wellington.

<u>26-11-1983</u> Auckland, Western Springs Stadium.   *2 CDR*   *Auckland 26 November 1983*
Attendance: 74.480. The biggest rock crowd ever to   *(BowieHobby)*
assemble in New Zealand.   2 CDR   Official finale
After Heroes: "I'd like to say that this is the single biggest   *(Old Gold Records*
crowd ever in the history of Australian concerts."   *OGCD 402A/B)*
Before Modern love Bowie thanks everybody who was   2 CDR   Auckland Moonlight
involved in the Serious Moonlight Tour. He ends his speech   2 CDR   Auckland 83
with "God bless you" and releases two white doves as a   (No label, no number)
statement about the nuclear arms race.   2 CDR   Auckland New Zealand 1983
After the show there was a party with Polynesian dancing   (A Dutch Connection)
girls. They ate a huge cake (shaped like the earth).   Tape   quality 8, 110 min.

27-11-1983 They flew to Singapore.

December 1983 Trouser Press. Article by Mick Farren: Surface noise: The trouble with Bowie.

December 1983 Goldmine. Article by Rick Salierno: David Bowie: a guide to collectibles.

December 1983 Rock Magazine. Article by Ethlie Ann Vare: Backstage and beyond with Bowie: An intimate journal of Bowie's 1983 Serious Moonlight tour.

December 1983 Faces Rock. Article: Absolutely live.

Winter 1983 Recension. Article about Bowie.

1-12-1983 Singapore, Youth Club (owned by Dr. Goh Ponseng). Bowie planned and impromptu guest appearance. The authorities *Cancelled* the concert and the resident band was banned for indecent performance!

2-12-1983 UK TV. The Tube.   *Video*   *Stolp tapes no. 9 (4 min)*
Interview. Part of Ziggy Stardust the motion picture.

DATE / EVENT	AUDIO / VIDEO	TITLE

<u>3-12-1983</u> Singapore.
Attendance: 15.000. Promoter: Dr. Goh Pohseng.
Support act: New Joy (a Californian band).
Heroes (4.12) filmed for Ricochet Video.
Bowie wore 2 pairs of socks because of oversized shoes.
His shirt was held into his pants by elastic thongs round his legs.
He stayed at the Ming Court Hotel (Raffles Hotel).

1 CDR — *Dime Store Mystery* (No label, no number)
2 CD — Serious moonlight
1 CDR — *Stream without boredom (Vancouver Manoeuvres 001)*
2 CDR — *Dancing in the moonlight (Artwork by Walter Ego)*
Tape

The Ricochet video is shot during this part of the tour.
Producer: Bhaskar Bhattachoryia. Director: Jerry Troiner.
In Bangkok they got up at 3.00 in the morning to film in the Bangkok Klongs. They filmed until 11.00 p.m. and looked for a taxi, but it was the day of the King's birthday, so no taxi's were available. They took a scooter taxi with 4 persons (it are two-seaters!). (David Bowie's Serious Moonlight - Denis O'Regan and Chet Flippo 1984).

Bashar Bhattachoryia: "You see the sequence in which an exorcist spits water into his face, which has been misinterpreted as 'the man spat on him,' but it was really a blessing because he went to an exorcist and sought his blessing so that his future travel would be graced" (In other words - Kerry Juby 1986).

Earl Slick: "We were sitting on a plane, going to Bangkok. I went over to David and said why don't we do something as a mark of respect for John Lennon's death on 12 December. David said "Well, if we're going to do it we might as well do Imagine." This was on the 4th and we rehearsed the song couple of times in Bangkok" (The Starzone Interviews - David Currie 1987).

4-12-1983 Landed in Bangkok. Bowie made a daylong gondola tour up the Chao Phraya River.

<u>5-12-1983</u> Bangkok, Army's Stadium.
Attendance: 14.981 (biggest crowd ever in Thailand).
Fame (6.39) and Fashion (2.42) filmed for Ricochet Video.
The show ended with firework.
He stayed at the President Hotel.

2 CD — Serious moonlight
1 CDR — *Stream without boredom (Vancouver Manoeuvres 001)*
2 CDR — *Dancing in the moonlight (Artwork by Walter Ego)*
Tape

<u>7-12-1983</u> Hung Hom (Hong Kong City), Hong Kong Coliseum. Attendance: 20.000. Promoter: Rigo Jesu.
The Hong Kong Urban Council complained they thought Bowie kicking a globe into the crowd was unruliness.
Good version of Look back in anger (2.53).
They stayed at Hong Kong's Harbour View Holiday Inn.

1 CDR — *Dime Store Mystery* (No label, no number)
1 CDR — *Stream without boredom (Vancouver Manoeuvres 001)*
2 CDR — *Dancing in the moonlight (Artwork by Walter Ego)*
Tape

8-12-1983 Hong Kong. Press conference.
Tape — quality 8, 25 min.
Video — 6 min.

<u>8-12-1983</u> Hung Hom (Hong Kong City), Hong Kong Coliseum. Attendance: 20.000.
They opened the concert with Scary monsters.
"Well, well, well. This is handkerchief time for all of us.

2 CDR — *Hong Kong 8 December 1983 (BowieHobby)*
2 CD — *Telling lies (Pearls Before Swine PBS 08/09)*

DATE / EVENT	AUDIO / VIDEO	TITLE
"It's been eight months on the road now. We started in March this year and I think we've done just about every country in the world and it's lovely to be here."	2 CDR	Bungle in your jungle? (Old Gold Records OGCD 403A/B)
"On this day, December the 8th 1980, John Lennon was shot and killed outside of his New York apartment."	CD	From the vault of MainMan (1 song) (U.R.00)
What follows is a beautiful version of Imagine (4.38) (John Lennon's original version was released in 1971).	CD	Pinups 4 (1 song) (BOWPU04)
Look back in anger (2.44) filmed for Ricochet Video.	2 CDR	A Sweet Thing (No label, no number)
During Modern love the crew joined the band on stage and started throwing hats, towels etc. into the crowd. Everybody on stage was dancing and singing.	1 CDR	Stream without boredom (Vancouver Manoeuvres 001)
Because of the complaints of the Hong Kong Urban Council Bowie kicked Two globes into the crowd.	1 CDR	MoreRareBowie (1 song) (No label, no number)
(David Bowie's Serious Moonlight - Denis O'Regan and Chet Flippo 1984).	1 CDR	Friends (1 song) (No label, no number)
	2 CDR	Dancing in the moonlight (Artwork by Walter Ego)
There was a goodbye party at the Hollywood Boulevard disco. There was champagne and Chinese food. Bowie visited the party briefly.	2 CDR	The Sun Rises (No label, no number)
	2 CDR	Imagine (No label, no number)
	CD	Legendary Lost Tapes Vol. 1 (1 song) (VigOtone 178)
	CD	Legendary Lost Tapes Vol. 2 (1 song) (VigOtone 179)
	Single	The Myth (Imagine) (CD Various Singles - 1)
	Tape	quality 7, 110 min.
8-12-1983 Interview about the characters of Space oddity, Ziggy Stardust, Aladdin sane and Diamond Dogs.	Video	Stolp tapes no. 9 (6 min)

9-12-1983 Release film Ziggy Stardust the Motion Picture (in Europe also as A London Show).

Various TV reviews about film Ziggy Stardust the Motion Picture:

2-12-1983 UK TV. The Tube.	Video	4 min.
UK TV. Film '83.	Video	1 min.
Switzerland TV. Preview and Promo excerpts.	Video	6 min.
French TV. TF1. Presse citron.	Video	1 min.

10-12-1983 Melody Maker. Article by Brian Case: The cracked image.

After the Serious Moonlight Tour Bowie, Schwab and Pop holidayed in Bali, Java and Singapore.

23-12-1983 First broadcast of Raymond Brigg's animation film The Snowman on Channel 4, 30-sec. introduction by David Bowie.	Video	Various 10 (1 min)
28-12-1983 Private phone interview with D.A. Pennebaker	Tape	quality 9, 50 min.

DATE / EVENT	AUDIO / VIDEO	TITLE

about Ziggy Stardust film.

1984 The Image received a low-circulation video release.

1984 Bowie seen in New York, attending a performance of the Mike Nicholas play Hurlyburly (he had grown a moustache).

1984 Re-release ChangesOneBowie (compilation) (RCA RS 1055).

1984 Re-release ChangesTwoBowie (compilation) (RCA PL 84202).

1984 Interview by Charles Shaar Murray.

1984 Released in Spain: 30 Anos de Musica Rock (reissue of 1981 Historia De La Musica Rock) (9-LP-002).

1984 Spanish magazine Rock, with Promo-CD Love you till Tuesday (Deram RCD017-2 844 117-2).

1984 Released in Canada: Ziggy '83 (promo from the ABC broadcast of the concert on 13-7-1983).

1984 Released in Italy: Early Bowie (reissue of Pye singles) (PRT PRNL 31722).

1984 Released Promo 2LP Retro Rock (interview with commercials) (No label, no number).

1984 Book published: A rock 'n' roll odyssey - Kate Lynch (Proteus Books). ISBN 0 86276 221 9 (paperback). ISBN 0 86276 221 7 (hardback).

1984 Book published: The Anabas look book series (in words and pictures) - Jim Palmer (Anabas Publishing Ltd. ISBN 1 85099 003 4).

1984 Book published in Holland: De man die naar de aarde viel - Walter Tevis (Prisma Pocket 2338) (Dutch translation of The man who fell to earth). ISBN 90.274 1481 5.

1984 Book published: David Bowie's Serious Moonlight - Denis O'Regan and Chet Flippo (Sidgwick & Jackson) ISBN 0-293-99108-9. Reprinted March 1985 and October 1986. Recommended!

1984 Book published: Ziggy Stardust: David Bowie1972-3 (photo's) - Mick Rock (St. Martin's Press).

1984 Book published: Anthology - Jim Palmer.

1984 Book published: Complete bootlegraphy - Kevin Howard Salt.

1984 Book published: David Bowie - Jean-Paul Bourre.

1984 Book published: The Rolling Stone book of Rock Video - Michael Shore (William Morrow).

1984 Book published: The wild eyed boy - Thomas Kamp.

1984 Book published: David Bowie - Tels qu'ils sont - Var. Authors (ISBN 2-86-676-121-9).

DATE / EVENT	AUDIO / VIDEO	TITLE

1984 Book published: David Bowie - Artiste, musicien, acteur, superstar - Var. Authors (ISBN 2-7021-1325-7).

1984 Billy Gray died. From June 1966 he was guitar player for the Buzz's second line-up.

1984 Pete Burns (singer of Dead or Alive) in an interview: "I don't think nowadays it matters if you are a transvestite or a bi-sexual. But… Ziggy Stardust was a breakthrough. In the docks you could here the men say to each other: "That guy Bowie, he's alright." That was great, but it will never happen again."

1984 UK TV. The Tube. Tina Turner, Cat People (live).

1984 Italian TV. Dee Jay part 1 (video special).	Video	12 min.
1984 Italian TV. Dee Jay part 2 (video special).	Video	12 min.
1984 Italian TV. L'Angelo que cadde.	Video	26 min.
1984 Italian TV. Introducing Band Aid Video.	Video	2 min.
1984 French TV. Les portails du crepuscule.	Video	5 min.

1984 Bowie approached to write the soundtrack of Roger Deakin's 1984 (he turned it down).

January 1984 Release Promo-album Ziggy '83 (RCA). Identical to the Serious Moonlight Video.

January 1984 Named Best British Male Artist at London's Grosvenor House.

January 1984 Voted Playboy's Man of the Year.

January 1984 Theatre Crafts. Article by Patricia MacKay: Serious - and stunning - moonlight.

January 1984 Guitar World. Article: Carlos Alomar: The power behind Bowie.

3-1-1984 Village Voice. Article by Jim Farber: Return of the dudes.

February 1984 Rock & Folk (France). Article: David Bowie L'Homme de l'annee.

February 1984 Jump/Cut. Article by Deborah H.Holdstein: Put on your red shoes and dance the blues.

February 1984 Jump/Cut. Article by Deborah H.Holdstein: Music videos: Messages and structures. Holdstein wrote: The video to David Bowie's Let's dance merges several interesting structures and categories: while not as indebted to the traditional musical as most pop videos, Bowie's tries to make a political statement about the permeation of capitalism, particularly as it both seduces and then rejects those outside the mainstream of society.

9-2-1984 Philadelphia. The Ripley Music Hall, 610 South Street. Started at 21.00 hours. A sneak preview of the Serious Moonlight Video.	LP	HBO "Serious Moonlight Show"

DATE / EVENT	AUDIO / VIDEO	TITLE

Presented by HBO, 94 WYSP and The Ripley.

12-2-1984 Home Box Office. Broadcast a special of the concerts in Vancouver on 11 and 12-9-1983.

12-2-1984 WBCN Radio. The Golden Year.   Tape   quality 10, 45 min.
Interview with Charlie Kendall.

12-2-1984 Amsterdam, Kwak Jongerencentrum. Meeting Dutch fan club Bowie Now.

March 1984 Rock Fever. Article: Who/what is he now?

March 1984 Re-released by RCA:
Aladdin Sane (RCA International NL 83890).
Diamond Dogs (RCA International NL 83889).
Low (RCA International NL 83856).
Lodger (RCA International NL 84234).
Scary monsters (RCA International NL 83647).

April 1984 Re-released by RCA:
Hunky Dory (RCA BOPIC 2).
Ziggy Stardust (picture disc) (RCA BOPIC 3).
Aladdin Sane (RCA BOPIC 1).
Pin Ups (RCA BOPIC 4).
Station to station (RCA PL 81327).

April 1984 Release Fame and Fashion (compilation) (RCA PL84919).

26-4-1984 Weesp (Holland), POC. Bowie-evening.

May 1984 Release film Love you till Tuesday (Polygram).
Sell me a coat, When I live my dream and Love you till Tuesday were remixed.

May 1984 begin recording for LP Tonight in Le Studio, Morin Heights (Montreal), Canada.
Some outtakes of Pop-Bowie songs were recorded.
Bowie's son Joe also stayed in Morin Heights.
Bowie was well prepared and Carlos Alomar commented: "It was the first time in the eleven years that I've been with the damn man that he's brought in anything" (David Bowie Theatre of Music - Robert Matthew-Walker 1985).

Hugh Padgham: "David was an amazing singer. David would go in and sing about a verse for you to get a level on the mike and then he'd sing it twice at the most, and that was the vocal done" (In other words - Kerry Juby 1986).
"My bedroom was next to his and the wall were very thin. He stayed up all night with a girl and there was that going on for bloody hours. In the studio he looked knackered, but nobody was more professional as a singer."

3-5-1984 Christian Science Monitor. Article by David Sterritt: The Furniture Music of Rock Star Brian Eno.

DATE / EVENT	AUDIO / VIDEO	TITLE

13-5-1984 Release LP Love you till Tuesday (songs from the film and other tracks) (Deram BOWIE 1). In 1992 re-released on CD (Pickwick PWKS 4131 P).
Kenneth Pitt (on the cover of the LP): "He was immediately impatient with the songs there were to sing and began write his own… David is very much a product of the fast moving era in which he was spent his time."

June 1984 Beat Box. 4-Page Article about Bowie.

4-6-1984 Amsterdam, Madam Tussaud's. New wax-statue: David Bowie (copy of the London statue).

Summer 1984. Bowie spent it in Switzerland.

Second part of 1984 Bowie was offered the role of Max Zorin in James Bond film A view to a kill (turned it down).

July 1984 Beatbox. Article: David Bowie's serious moonlight tour.

3-7-1984 Attends Jerry Hall's birthday celebration in Mayfair.

25-7-1984 Attends concert of Paul Butterfield at Camden's Dingwalls.

August 1984 Re-release Album David Bowie (Deram DOA 1).

6-8-1984 Attends Dingwalls concert of Jonathan Richmond.

8 and 9 August 1984 shooting of Video Jazzin' for Blue Jean in Shepperton Studios and The Rainbow Room in Kensington.

9-8-1984 Walter Tevis (56) (author of the book The man who fell to earth) died in New York of lung cancer.

12-8-1984 Soho (London, The Wag Club). A special afternoon performance with David Bowie and The Aliens in aid of the MTV Awards 14-9-1984 in New York. Performed 1 song: Blue Jean (3.35).	1 CDR	Man I need TV (No label, no number)
	1 VCD	I keep a good friend… (No label, no number)
	1 VCD	Bob's Eggs [+extras] (No label, no number)
	Video	Stolp tapes no. 19 (3 min.)
	Video	Stolp tapes no. 10 (3 min.)
	Video	Various 10 (4 min)
26-8-1984 US Radio. D.I.R. Broadcasting Corp., 32 East 57th Street, New York (ABC Rock Radio Network). King Biscuit Flower Hour (Serious Moonlight Revisited). 45 Minute broadcast of the 13-7-1983 concert in Montreal.	Tape	quality 10, 45

September 1984 His son Joe entered Gordonstoun School in Scotland.

DATE / EVENT	AUDIO / VIDEO	TITLE

September 1984 Release Blue Jean (3.10) / Dancing with the big boys (3.34) (EMI EA 181).

September 1984 Release 12" Blue Jean (Extended dance mix) (5.16) / Dancing with the big boys (Extended dance mix) (7.28) / Dancing with the big boys (Extended dub mix) (7.43) (EMI 12EA 181).

14-9-1984 Radio City Music Hall. Video Music Awards.   *Video*   *Stolp tapes no. 19 (7 min.)*
Presented by Dan Ackroyd and Bette Midler.
Bowie's Wag Club Blue Jean promo shown (recorded
12-8-1984 in The Wag Club, London) (3.35).
Iggy Pop collects Bowie's award for Best Male Video for
China girl.

21-9-1984 Premiere Video Jazzin' for Blue Jean in London as support for the film The Company of Wolves.

22-9-1984 BBC. Radio 1. Julian Temple interview on Blue   Tape   quality 10, 10 min.
Jean video.

24-9-1984 Release LP Tonight (EMI DB 1).
Dana Gillespie: "I still think he's got it for the eighties, I think he's really great. I'm not sure about the new album though, God only knows sounds like Dudley Moore doing a piss take" (The Starzone Interviews - David Currie 1987).
Bowie in 1987 about the song Neighbourhood threat: "A disastrous recording. That's one I wish I'd never touched, or at least touched differently. It went totally wrong. It sounded so tight and compromised, and it was such a gas doing it. It was the wrong band to do it with. Wonderful band, but it wasn't right for that song."

29-9-1984 Melody Maker. Article by Steve Sutherland: Tonight.

29-9-1984 New Musical Express. Article by Charles Shaar Murray: Sermon from the Savoy.

Bowie about the James Bond film A view to a kill: "Absolutely out of the question. Yes, I was offered that. I think for an actor it's probably an interesting thing to do, but I think that for somebody from rock it's more of a clown performance. And I didn't want to spend five months watching my double fall off mountains."

September / October 1984 Fanzine Starzone No. 13. Kevin Cann interviews Mick Ronson.

October 1984 The second part of the Serious Moonlight Video (called: David Bowie - live) is released (Music Media Entertainment Inc - A Heron Communications Company). Price: USD 39,95 or GBP 19,95.

October 1984 The Face (UK). Article: David Bowie, cracked actor on the set (about Blue Jean).

October 1984 Re-released:
David Bowie (RCA).
Space oddity (RCA PL 84813).
Ziggy Stardust (RCA International NL 83843).
David Live (RCA PL 80771).

DATE / EVENT	AUDIO / VIDEO	TITLE

Young Americans (RCA PL 80998).

9-10-1984 Village Voice. Article by M.Coleman: Riffs: David Bowie tube-age daydream.

14-10-1984 You. Article: Bowie mailer, interview.
Front cover in November 1985 used for a 7-track promo-LP called: Dance. Project cancelled. A handful of proof sleeves found their way to collectors.
In 2001 the Bootleg-album Dance was released, with the promo-sleeve from 1984.

25-10-1984 Rolling Stone. Article by Kurt Loder: Iggy Pop: Bowie's Main Man.

25-10-1984 Rolling Stone. Article by Charles Shaar Murray: Let's talk: A conversation with David Bowie.

27-10-1984 TV Times. Bowie on cover and 3-page article.

November 1984 Re-released by RCA:
The man who sold the world (RCA Internat. NL 84654).
Hunky Dory (RCA International NL 83844).
Heroes (RCA International NL 83857).

November 1984 Release Tonight (3.42) / Tumble and twirl (4.56) (EMI EA 187).

November 1984 Release 12" Tonight (Vocal dance mix) (4.29) / Tumble and twirl (Extended dance mix) (5.03) / Tonight (Dub mix) (4.29) (EMI 12EA 187).

November 1984 Nina Hagen concert in Vredenburg, Utrecht. She sang Golden years and My way.

November 1984 Record Collector. Article by Peter Doggett: David Bowie's UK singles.

November 1984 High Fidelity/Musical America. Article by J. Millman: The concert - video shell game.

4-11-1984 New York Times. Article by John Pareles: David Bowie ponders his newfound popularity.
Pareles about the album Tonight: "He ruminates on whether, or how much, he's compromised; he also vows to please his audience, suggests that sweetness and light are not on the agenda and wonders how long his new fans will stick around."

5-11-1984 Bowie's mother Peggy visited Terry Burns in Cane Hill (his 47th birthday).

8-11-1984 Rolling Stone. Article by Kurt Loder: Tonight.
Loder wrote: This album is a throwaway, and David Bowie knows it.

24-11-1984 New York City. Rockages.   Tape   quality 9, 30 min.
Carlos Alomar interview.

25-11-1984 Recording Do they know it's Christmas (Bowie sang the first two lines).
Bowie was absent in the studio, he send a taped message that Geldof mixed into the B-side.
"It's Christmas and there are more starving folk on this planet then ever before. Please give a thought for them this season and do whatever you can, however small, to help them live. Have a peaceful New

DATE / EVENT	AUDIO / VIDEO	TITLE

Year. David Bowie."
Single version (4.38) and B-side Feed the world, with spoken message (4.14).
Other members of the All-star band: a.o. Paul McCartney, Boy George, Sting, Bono.

December 1984 Record. Article by Charles Shaar Murray: On the set with David Bowie.

December 1984 Musician. Article by David Fricke: David Bowie.

December 1984 Musician. Article by Timothy White: Tonight.

December 1984 Creem. Article by Bill Holdship: Ziggy no Biggie.

4-12-1984 Starzone Party at Wardour Streets, Wag Club in Soho (London).
Performance of Boysie (Featuring Sean Mayes). George Simms sings backing vocals on Rebel rebel.
Guests: Phil Lancaster, Ray Stevenson, Denis Taylor, Martyn Ware (Heaven 17), Natasha Kornilof, George Simms, Tony Visconti.

27-12-1984 Terry Burns attempted suicide at Cane Hill. After overdosing sleeping tablets.
Later (16-1-1985) he did a final attempt and laid down his head on the track of Coulsdon South Station.

31-12-1984 Bowie, Joe, Schwab, Iggy + Suchi Pop into the Swiss resort of Gstaad. A party in Bowie's room.

End 1984 / Begin 1985. Recording single This is not America with Pat Metheney and his group.

1985 Released in Spain: David Bowie (reissue of Pye singles).

1985 Released Cinema Verite - Dramarama (Elektra D2-74819) (including Candidate).

| 1985 Luxembourg TV. Chewing Rock Special. | Video | 12 min. |

1985 Film Into the night by John Landis (Bowie plays Collin).

Various TV reviews of film Into the night:		
Dutch TV. Films & Fans.	Video	3 min.
Dutch TV. VARA's Videonieuws.	Video	1 min.

1985 Film The Breakfast Club (director John Hughes) opened with a quotation of Changes.

1985 In New York Bowie visited Tony Scott, John Landis, Bruce Springsteen, Luther Vandross. He went to Long Island. A long weekend with his cousin Kristine. At Manchester he attends a lecture on screen writing.

1985 Transvestite Jackie Curtis dies from a heroin overdose.

1985 Book published: Bowie - Jerry Hopkins (Macmillan, ISBN 90-325-0256-5).

1985 Book published: David Bowie - Steve Gett (Cherry Lane Books, ISBN 0-89524-288-5).

DATE / EVENT	AUDIO / VIDEO	TITLE

1985 Book published: David Bowie: Theatre of music - Robert Matthew-Walker (Kensal Press, ISBN 0-946041-22-9).

1985 Book published: People stared at the make up on his face - Per Nilsen (Self published, no ISBN number).

1985 Book published: The concert tapes - Pimm Jal de la Parra (P.J. Publishing, ISBN 90-9001005-X).

1985 Book published: An illustrated discography - Hans Lelivelt (Howlpress, no ISBN number).

1985 Book published: Springsteen - Robert Hilburn (Scribners).

1985 Book published: Starlust: The secret fantasies of Fans - Fred and Judy Vermorel (Comedia). Reprinted in 1995 by Comet.

1985 Book published: The death and resurrection show: From shaman to superstar - Rogan Taylor (Anthony Blond).

1985 Book published: Une histoire - Jerome Soligny (Grancher).

1985 Book published: Also sprach Zarathoestra - Friedrich Nietzsche (Wereldbibliotheek, ISBN 90-284-1505-X). Also published in 1905.

1985 Book published: Wild Eyed Boy 1964 - 1984 - Thomas Kemp (ISBN 089019-0860).

1985 Book published: Urban Rhythms: Pop Music and Popular Culture - Ian Chambers (New York, St. Martin's).

January 1985 Creem. Article by Richard Riegel: Tonight.

16-1-1985 Terry Burns commits suicide (age 47).
He lay down in front of the Littlehampton-London Express, shortly after midday.
Peggy Jones called David to tell him about the death of his half-brother.

25-1-1985 Funeral Terry Burns at Elmers End Cemetery in Beckenham. Bowie did not attend the funeral.

26-1-1985 The Sun. Article: David Bowie snubs Brothers funeral.
They wrote: Rock idol, David Bowie, was lashed by his aunt today for snubbing his half-brother's funeral. Grief stricken Pat hit out at the millionaire singer saying 'I hope God forgives David. This is a tragic rejection'.

February 1985 Release This is not America (Bowie and Pat Metheney Group) (3.51) / This is not America (Instrumental) (3.51) (EMI EA 190).

March 1985 Hi Fi News & Record Review. Article by Peter Clarke: A lad insane.

March 1985 Stereo Review. Article by L. Meredith: Bowie jazzin.

DATE / EVENT	AUDIO / VIDEO	TITLE

March 1985 Creem. Article by John Mendelsohn: David Bowie and Dee Snider: The bizarre passions they can't control.

<u>23-3-1985</u> Birmingham, National Exhibition Center, 2 songs with Tina Turner.
"Actually this is a song that David Bowie and Iggy Pop wrote a long time ago and David and I recorded it on his last David Bowie Tonight album and we're gonna do it together. Tonight!"
1. Tonight (4.45).
Bowie: "I'd like to say that this was a privilege to be on the same stage as you tonight. It's about the hottest place in the universe."
2. Let's dance (Chris Montez, 1962) - Let's dance (3.25).

CD — *Dancing in the street (2 songs)*
(Exhibition DB-1985M)
1 CDR — *TracksOneBowie*
(No label, no number)
2 CDR — *TracksBowie*
(A Dutch Connection)
LP — *Tina Turner feat. Bowie*
(Metropol Records Inc. TT-233)
LP — *Duets*
Tape — *quality 10, 20 min.*
Video — *Stolp tapes no. 22 (5 min)*
Video — *8 min.*
Video — *Various 22, 55 min.*

31-3-1985 Schiedam (Holland), De Kreek. Fan-meeting Fanzine Bowie Now.

31-3-1985 Arnhem (Holland). Disco Manhattan. Angie Bowie (and singer Chico) did a 25-minute gig to promote her single Closer to heaven.

March / April 1985 Fanzine Starzone No. 14. David Currie interviews George Simms and Denis Regan. Kevin Cann interviews Dana Gillespie.

April 1985 Release Soundtrack The Falcon and the Snowman (EMI America EJ 2403051). Includes an (edit) instrumental version of This is not America (3.21). John Schlesinger directed the film.

April 1985 Sunday Times. 3 Articles based on research of the Gillman's. Bowie outraged and distanced from the Gillman's.

April 1985 Stereoplay. Article by Matthias Inhoffen: Pop-CDs Spezial: David Bowie.

30-4-1985 Village Voice. Article by J. Hoberman: Scanners: Bowie to go.

May 1985 The Face. Article by Robert Elms: All you have to do is win.
Elms wrote about the mid 70's: "It's all come true. We're a nation living in a disco. When Bowie performed Golden Years on Soul Train all those years ago he was the first English artist to tart up black music and sell it back to the Americans since The Beatles did it in 64."

May 1985 Release Loving the alien (Remixed version) (4.43) / Don't look down (Remixed version) (4.04) (EMI EA 195).

May 1985 Release 12" Loving the alien (Extended dance mix) (7.27) / Don't look down (Extended dance mix) (5.03) / Loving the alien (Extended Dub mix) (7.14) (EMI 12EAG 195).

May 1985 Release: Looking for a friend (3.10) - Man in the middle (4.08) - Arnold Corns (Krazy Kat Past2).

DATE / EVENT	AUDIO / VIDEO	TITLE

8-5-1985 US Radio. Pioneers in Music, presented by Dave Hermon. Career-overview, with various parts from the concert at Nassau Coliseum (23-3-1976).   CD   *Pioneers in music*

June 1985 Recording Absolute beginners (8.00), That's motivation (4.12) and Volare (3.18) (at Abbey Road Studios).
Thomas Dolby and Neil Conti received a letter from EMI. They were invited to do a session with Mister X.
Conti about Bowie: "He was bright, witty and above all ready to experiment. He never told anyone what to play. It was always something like 'Think green' or 'Think Brazilian'. He worked at the speed of light. He wanted to record a moment, not an idea."
Alan Winstanley (producer): "Suddenly he did impersonations of Lou Reed, Bruce Springsteen and Iggy Pop. At the end of the session he made sure the tapes were all given back to him."

June 1985 Re-release The Manish Boys / Davy Jones and the Lower Third (See For Miles SEA 1).

7-6-1985 Jazz Magazine. Article: Echoes d'ecran (bande originale du film The Falcon and the Snowman).

Summer 1985. ITV. Spitting Image. A Bowie puppet appeared.

4-7-1985 London, Wembley. Bowie backstage at a Bruce Springsteen concert.

10-7-1985 Recording 7" version Absolute beginners (5.36).

11-7-1985 Recording single Dancing in the street at 6 o'clock.
They took the rough mix over to the film crew on the other side of town and shot the video at 10 o'clock. Mick Jagger took the master tape to New York and added a horn section and Earl Slick's guitar.

July (a Sunday) Windsor. Bray Studios. Rehearsal 1 for Live Aid. They rehearsed 7 songs.   NT

July (another Sunday) Windsor. Bray Studios. Rehearsal 2 for Live Aid.   NT

July. Elstree Studios. Sound Stage. Rehearsal for Live Aid.   NT
The tape of the Sound Stage was send to each group member. Bowie last words to the band: "Be lucky and wear blue."

July 1985 UK Radio. BBC. Radio 1. Bowie's ad to tune in to 'Live Aid'.   Tape   quality 9, 5 min.

13-7-1985 Early in the day. Bowie spent an hour in the Royal box with the Prince and Princess of Wales.

13-7-1985 London, Wembley Arena. Live Aid.   CD   *Dancing in the street (5 songs)*

DATE / EVENT	AUDIO / VIDEO	TITLE
1. Dancing in the street (original by Martha Reeves and the Vandellas in 1964). 2. TVC15 (4.04). 3. Rebel rebel (3.24). 4. Modern love (3.42). 5. Heroes (7.32). 6. Do they know it's Christmas (Feed the world) (5.01). 7. Let it be (original by The Beatles in 1970) (5.28). 40 Minute documentary was broadcast on French TV. The proceeds of Live Aid were USD 40 million. Bowie arrived by helicopter.	1 CDR 1 CDR 1 CDR 2 CDR CD 1 CDR VCD VCD VCD 1 DVD LP LP 11 LP LP 2 LP Tape Tape Video Video Video Video Video Video	*(Exhibition DB-1985M) Hendrikse various vol. 2 (7) (No label, no number) Live Aid Concert TracksTwoBowie (2,3,4,5,6) (No label, no number)* TracksBowie (2,3,4,5,6) (A Dutch Connection) Death by Live Aid *Friends (No label, no number) Various 2 (8.24 min.) I keep a good friend.... (5) (No label, no number) Videobits Volume 1 (5) (No label, no number)* Greatest Show On Earth The missing link (Shelter 252570) (first 6 tracks) Duets (Tonight Records Duet 1/2) Live Aid - A short shame story (Fast Food Prod. SG6) Rock concert (Emir Gema DB 061291-A/B 257070-A/B) Live Aid-The global Jukebox vol. 1 (ETS 2588 B Stereo 33) quality 10, 20 min. quality 10, 25 min. *Stolp tapes no. 5 (3 min.) Stolp tapes no. 10 (4 min.) Stolp tapes no. 9 (1 min.) Various 19 (18 min)* 25 min. 40 min.
20-7-1985 Ken Pitt interview about his book "The Pitt Report."	Tape	quality 9, 10 min.

July-August 1985 Films movie Absolute beginners at Shepperton Studios. After the filming Bowie and Iggy Pop met in New York.

August 1985 Release Dancing in the street (Bowie and Mick Jagger) (3.14) / Dancing in the street (Dub version) (4.41) (EMI EA 204).

August 1985 Release 12" Dancing in the street (Steve Thompson mix) (4.40) / Dancing in the street (Dub version) (4.41) / Dancing in the street (Edit) (3.14) (EMI 12EA 204).

| 17-8-1985 Mick Ronson & Sandy Dillon interview and songs. | Tape | quality 10, 20 min. |

DATE / EVENT	AUDIO / VIDEO	TITLE

17-8-1985 Interview with Fred and Judy Vernon about their book Starlust (about Bowie fans). — Tape — quality 10, 20 min.

23-8-1985 New Statesman. Article by Simon Frith: Confessions of a rock critic.

24-8-1985 Billboard. Article by T.Seideman: Bowie / Jagger videoclip heads for movie screens.

Autumn 1985. Films Labyrinth at Elstree Studios in Hertz. — CD — *Dracula in the lab*

September 1985 Record. Article by Jane Maslin: Making movies - the long jump from MTV.

10-9-1985 Amsterdam. Antoine Loogman interviews Lindsay Kemp for the Dutch Fanzine David Bowie Now.

October 1985 Released 2LP David Bowie collection (Castle Communications CCSLP 118). Deram and Pye material.

October 1985 Pimm Jal de la Para interview. — Tape — quality 9, 10 min.

13-10-1985 Hilversum (Holland), Gooiland. Fan-meeting Dutch Fanzine David Bowie Now.

November 1985 Record Collector. Article by Dave Thomas: David Bowie's rarest recordings.

November 1985 Bowie visits Iggy Pop in New York.

November 1985 New York, Whitney Museum. Columbia Records held a party in the honour of Bob Dylan. Guest: a.o. David Bowie, Lou Reed, John Cale, Iggy Pop, Yoko Ono, Ian Hunter, Pete Townshend, Roy Orbison.

<u>19-11-1985</u> New York City. China Club. — NT
Steve Ferrone's birthday party.
On stage impromptu jam session. The band consisted of: David Bowie, Iggy Pop, Ronnie Wood, Stevie Winwood, Carlos Alomar, Carmine Rojas and Steve Ferrone.
Played over an hour (a.o. China girl).

23-11-1985 Melody Maker. Article by Steve Gett: David Bowie.

30-11-1985 Brixton. The Fridge. Performances by Angie Bowie Band, Sandy Dillon and Mick Ronson.
David Currie was interviewed about his book Starzone. — Tape — quality 9, 10 min.

End 1985 Westminster Bridge and The Thames Embankment. Video Absolute beginners shot by Julien Temple.

Just before Christmas 1985. A Caribbean cruise with Iggy Pop and his wife and Corinne Schwab. On board Bowie and Pop wrote songs.

DATE / EVENT	AUDIO / VIDEO	TITLE

25-12-1985 Dutch TV. Vara. 90-minute broadcast of Live Aid, presented by Boudewijn Buch and Hanneke Kappen.

Christmas 1985 in Switzerland. Iggy Pop and his wife joined Bowie to ski.

1986 NBC Radio. Legends of Rock. Interview and LP tracks on WBRU.	Tape	quality 10, 80 min.

1986 Media Culture and Society. Article by Simon Frith: Art versus technology: the strange case of popular music.

1986 Released Live Magic - Queen (EMI CDP 7 46413 2). Includes Under pressure (Queen only) (3.50).

1986 Book published: David Bowie - Dave Thompson (Plexus, ISBN 90 6756 204 1).

1986 Book published: In other words... David Bowie - Kerry Juby (Omnibus Press, ISBN 0.7119.1038.3).

1986 Book published: Events of David Bowie - Hans Lelivelt. Included free flexi-disc (Tonight interview 1964).

1986 Book published: The pre Ziggy years 1947-1971 - Guus Hornix.

1986 Book published: Absolute beginners - Colin MacInnes (Penguin Books Ltd). ISBN 0-14-002142-6. First published in 1959 by MacGibbon & Kee.

1986 Book published: O Palhaco de deus - Fernando Luis.

1986 Book published: Written in my soul: rock's great songwriters talk about creating their music - Bill Flanagan (Contemporary Books). ISBN 90-245-1793-1. Bowie mentioned on page 18, 91, 201 and 273.

1986 UK TV. Video Jukebox.	Video	10 min.
1986 UK TV. Private Eyes. Interview by Steve Rapport.	Video	6 min.
1986 Swiss TV. Major Tom, Ziggy Stardust, Thin white...	Video	60 min.

January 1986 Vanity Fair (US). Article by Philip Norman: Beginners luck. Showy Bowie hoofing with Dave.
Norman wrote: The grown-up Bowie, steals this musical Absolute Beginners in a character part revealing still further unexpected sides of his endlessly unpredictable talents.

February 1986 Fanzine Starzone 15. Kevin Cann interviews Les Conn.
Les Conn: "I really believed in his talent and I knew he would make it, but I realised that I couldn't afford to bring it about, it needed money which I was running out of."

DATE / EVENT	AUDIO / VIDEO	TITLE

2-2-1986 Observer. Article: Who's who in Absolute Beginners.

15-2-1986 Release Absolute beginners (5.36) / Absolute beginners (Dub mix) (5.42) (Virgin VS 838).

15-2-1986 Release 12" Absolute beginners (Full length version) (8.00) / Absolute beginners (Dub mix) (5.42) (Virgin VS 12838).

18-2-1986 UK TV. The Tube. Premiere video-clip Absolute beginners.
The clip was inspired by the famous Strand cigarettes-commercial from the sixties. The dancer in the clip was Patsy Kensits.

March 1986 Daily Mirror. A series of articles by Angie Bowie, called: My bitterness.

1-3-1986 Channel 4. Screened: A beginners guide to   *Video*   *Absolute Beginners*
Absolute Beginners (featuring behind the scenes footage
and interviews with the players and the crew).

2-3-1986 London Weekend TV. Spitting Image. With it's own particular brand of humour, pays its own tribute to Absolute Beginners (Sting is a guest).

9-3-1986 Interview for newspaper "Today."
Bowie complained about biographers (He meant the Gillman's): "They drag out long-lost aunts to supply all the details. Aunts I've had absolutely no contact with for maybe twenty years. Who have no knowledge of me, and absolutely unbelievable, blatant lies are told."

9-3-1986 Extra. Article by D.Thomas: Bowie's Profile.
Bowie about the film Absolute beginners: "I can remember the riots. They solved the problem from one day to another and put these people for ten years in jail."
About music: "The music is so awful here. I've dropped out of radio. I play my old record collection. What's the point of me trying to write for teenagers? The only way I could do that would be as some kind of father figure."

16-3-1986 Bowie and Coco attend show "Les miserables" in London.

22-3-1986 Melody Maker. Article by Adam Sweeting: Absolute beginners.

23-3-1986 Interview for UK TV-programme The Tube.

27-3-1986 BBC. Radio 1. Bowie phone-in interview.   Tape   quality 9, 15 min.

April 1986 Release LP Absolute beginners (Virgin V 2386).
Includes Absolute beginners (8.00), That's motivation (4.12) and Volare (original version by Domenico Modugno in 1958) (3.12).

April 1986 Release Rare Tracks (12" Repackage of the Pye singles and B-sides) (Showcase SHLP 137).

1-4-1986 BBC. Radio 2. Mandy Rice-Davis interview.   Tape   quality 10, 30 min.

DATE / EVENT	AUDIO / VIDEO	TITLE

2 or 3-4-1986 Premiere film Absolute beginners, in the presence of Princess Anne, in London. Bowie plays a tap-dancing advertising guy from Vendice Partners.

New Musical Express: "Most of us are familiar with David Bowie from his role as Vendice Partners in the sparkling musical comedy Absolute Beginners, but how many I wonder know that David is also a talented all-round entertainer and singer?"
The New York Times: "Bowie is perfectly cast as the teasing, tempting seducer."

Various TV reviews about film Absolute beginners:

Europe. Sky Channel Special.	Video	60 min.
Music Box special (incl. Jazzin' for Blue Jean).	Video	60 min.
Dutch TV. Veronica Film.	Video	8 min.
Dutch TV. Veronica Countdown.	Video	10 min.
Belgian TV. Premiere Extra.	Video	12 min.
Belgian TV. Villa Tempo.	Video	8 min.
Belgian TV. Premiere (That's motivation).	Video	5 min.

6-4-1986 You (Mail on Sunday Magazine). Article by Peter Gillman: Going straight, a new role for the rebel.

20-4-1986 Schiedam, De Erker. Fan-meeting Dutch Fanzine Bowie Now. Performance by Bowie-imitator Arno van Nooy.

End of April 1986 Bowie walked around Haymarket.

May 1986 Mountain Studio. Recording of Blah-blah-blah. Recorded in 1 month. On the last night Bowie and Pop smoked cigars.	CD	*Old mule skinner - Iggy Pop (Imperium IMP 012) (1 track)*
Demo-versions.	Tape	quality 10, 15 min.
Rough mix.	Tape	quality 10, 35 min.

9-5-1986 Interview for BBC-TV by Alan Yentob.

Summer 1986 Lausanna. Bowie had a bacterial infection.

June 1986 Sky Channel. The Making of Underground.	*Video*	*Stolp tapes no. 10 (6 min)*

4-6-1986 Release Underground (4.23) / Underground (instrumental) (5.54) (EMI EA 216).

4-6-1986 Release 12" Underground (Extended dance mix) (7.51) / Underground (Dub mix) (5.59) / Underground (instrumental) (5.40) (EMI 12EA 216).

4-7-1986 Release in South Africa 12": Underground (pink vinyl) backed with other artist (EMI).

Background singers Underground: Luther Vandross, Chaka Khan, Fonzi Thornton (Chic) and the Radio choir of the New Hope Baptist Church.

<u>20-6-1986</u> London, Wembley Arena. Prince's Trust concert.	1 CDR	*Hendrikse various vol. 2* *(No label, no number)*

DATE / EVENT	AUDIO / VIDEO	TITLE
Together with Mick Jagger: Dancin' in the street (live) (4.01). With the McCartney All Stars Band (Elton John on piano, Eric Clapton on guitar). Bowie meets the 13 year old Louise Balhatchet, she has leukaemia and dies in September 1986 (Fanzine Starzone No. 17 March / May 1987).	2 CD CD CD Tape Video Video	*Boys keep singing* (No label, no number) *The Unreleased Stuff* (No label, no number) *Even a fool learns to love* (RDO one of a kind records) quality 10, 5 min. *Various 19 (2 min)* *Various 19 (4 min)*

21-6-1986 Prince's Trust concert broadcast on TV.

22-6-1986 Telegraph Sunday Magazine. Article about Bowie.

End June / begin July 1986 Bowie visited Richard Branson in Oxfordshire. Branson asked Boy George to come over. Boy George was in his heroin-addicted period, very suspicious, and refused.

July 1986 Release LP Labyrinth (EMI America AML 3104).

3-7-1986 Bowie visits Jerry Hall's birthday celebration at a Chelsea house.

5(?)-7-1986 Bowie visits the wedding of Julien Temple and Amanda Pirie in Oxford.

25-7-1986 Western Mail. Article by Jay Savage: A whirlwind ride to… er, where?

July / August 1986 Music Box. Labyrinth Special.	Video	20 min.

August 1986 He had an affair with a young actress.

August 1986 Rockin' On. Article: David Bowie.

24-8-1986 Bowie attends wedding of Bob Geldof and Paula Yates at their home in Faversham, Kent.

24-8-1986 New York Times Book Review. Article by Milo Miles: Stardust.

September 1986 Record Collector. Article by Richard Jackson: David Bowie: The early years.

September 1986 Creem. Article by John Mendelsohn: Absolute beginners.

15-9-1986 Book published: Alias David Bowie - Peter and Leni Gillman (New English Library, ISBN 0-450-41346-8).

September 1986 Radio Rataplan, Nijmegen (Holland). FM 102,5. Start Bowie Keeps Swinging (Bowie-evening). Every last Monday of the month by D.J. Sjoerd Bunnik.

Autumn 1986 recording LP Never let me down at Mountain Studios, Switzerland.

October 1986 Release LP Blah-blah-blah - Iggy Pop (A&M AMA 5145). Iggy Pop's real name is James Osterberg, born 21-4-1947 in Michigan.

| DATE / EVENT | AUDIO / VIDEO | TITLE |

John Wilde (Sounds): "Iggy Pop is so close back to flaunting, flaming magnificence, the difference is not worth a tinker's cuss. Iggy, the true saint in sin, lashes out like he hasn't done for almost a decade."

1-10-1986 BBC. Radio 1. Iggy Pop interview.   Tape   quality 10, 20 min.

6-10-1986 Book published: Stardust (The David Bowie story) - Henry Edwards and Tony Zanetta (McGraw-Hill Book Company, ISBN 0-07-072797-X).

18-10-1986 Utrecht, C.S.B. building. Fan-meeting Dutch Fanzine Bowie Now.

27-10-1986 Release When the wind blows (3.32) / When the wind blows (instrumental) (3.32) (Virgin VS 906).

27-10-1986 Release 12" When the wind blows (Extended mix) (5.39) / When the wind blows (instrumental) (3.32) (Virgin VS 90612).

27-10-1986 Release Video When the wind blows (cartoon   Video   Stolp tapes no. 10 (4 min) version). Video was made on 19-10-1986.

14-11-1986 Attends concert of Iggy Pop at the Ritz in New York.

November 1986 Release Soundtrack When the wind blows (Virgin V 2406). The film was adapted by Raymond Briggs.

November 1986 Power Station Studios in New York, mixing of the album Never let me down.

2-12-1986 Premiere film Labyrinth in Leicester Square Theatre, in the presence of Prince Charles and Princess Diana.

Melody Maker. Ted Mico wrote: "Eye of newt and tongue of mole, David Bowie has become a troll."

Late in 1986 Bowie visited a lot of New York clubs.

December 1986 Bowie and Schwab joined Mick Jagger and Jerry Hall at their Berch cottage in Mustique. They attended the carol service in Mustique's Anglican Church. They entered just before the doors closed. Bowie and Jagger both joined the singing of the other 45 people in the church.

31-12-1986 UK TV. BBC-2. Interview about problems in drought stricken areas of Africa (Africa Tomorrow).

1987 Releases in US. Promo CDS: Bang bang (live) (4.09) / Bang bang (LP Version) (4.00) / Modern love (4.46) / Loving the alien (7.09) (EMI DPRO 31593).

1987 Released in France: Early years (box set of The man who sold the world, Hunky Dory and Aladdin Sane).

1987 Released Promo LP The Interview (EMI SPRO 79112/3). About Never let me down.

DATE / EVENT	AUDIO / VIDEO	TITLE
1987 Glass Spider Promo.	Video	*Stolp tapes no. 10 (2 min)*
1987 US TV. WEGX. Backstage Bash. Photo footage and video clips.	Video	37 min.
1987 UK TV. Sky TV. Interview. Clip excerpts.	Video	1 min.

1987 Book published: De Superstars van de muziek - David Bowie- nr.1 - Paul de Bruyn (Betapress, no ISBN number).

1987 Book published: Glass idol - David Currie (Omnibus Press, ISBN 0.7119.1182.7).

1987 Book published: Moonage daydream - Dave Thompson (Plexus, ISBN 90 6756 204 1).

1987 Book published: The Starzone interviews - David Currie (Omnibus, ISBN 0.7119.0685).

1987 Published: David Bowie Collector's Price Guide & Discography - Pete Smith.

1-1-1987 Film Ziggy Stardust the motion picture on BBC-TV.

January 1987 Release in US 12": Magic dance (A dance mix) (7.11) / Magic dance (Dub mix) (5.21) / Within you (3.29) (EMI 19217).

January 1987 Interview for Rolling Stone.
Bowie: "Sid Vicious was just a mindless twerp. I didn't find anything at all romantic about him, or even interesting. I always have to look for some kind of light at the end of the tunnel. Having a son does that. You change a lot."

8-1-1987 Bowie held his 40th birthday party at the Swiss Ski resort of Gstaad.

Early 1987 Bowie bought a plot of land up the hill from Mick Jagger and Jerry Hall and architect Arne Hasselqvist and designer Robert Litwiller build there a house for him.

Spring 1987 Bowie signs sponsoring deal with Pepsi for the Glass Spider Tour.

February 1987 Record Collector. Article by Arthur King: David Bowie: The Ziggy Stardust years.

February 1987 Musician. Article by Timothy White and David Fricke: David Bowie.

| 14-2-1987 BBC Radio One. Bowie at the Beeb 1967-1972. With DJ comments. | CD | *Ziggy in wonderland (PROCD 89 001-2)* |

22-2-1987 Andy Warhol died.

March 1987 Guitar World. Article: Adrian Belew: Belew's Menagerie.

The band for the press conference performances:
David Bowie (vocals).

DATE / EVENT	AUDIO / VIDEO	TITLE

Carlos Alomar (guitar).
Peter Frampton (guitar).
Carmine Rojas (bass).
Alan Childs (drums).
Richard Cottle (keyboards).

<u>17-3-1987</u> Toronto, Diamond Club. Press conference. Interview. Day in, day out. 87 And Cry.	Tape	Canada TV, Much Music, quality 7, 45 min. (Complete)
Broadcast on radio by CFNY FM 102 (10 min. interview).	Tape	quality 9, 45 min.
Broadcast on FM radio (interview and 2 songs).	Tape	quality 9, 10 min.
	Tape	quality 10, 40 min.
17-3-1987 Canadian TV. Much Music. City Pulse. Presented by Christopher Ward. Clip 87 And cry and interview from 17-3-1987.	Video	3 min.
17-3-1987 Canadian TV. City TV News. Report, clip 87 And cry, interview from 17-3-1987.	Video	1.33 min.
17-3-1987 Canadian TV. First News. Report, clip 87 And cry from 17-3-1987.	Video	0.21 min.
17-3-1987 Global News. Rock News. Clip Day in day out, Clip 87 And cry, interview 17-3-1987.	Video	3 min.
17-3-1987 The Star Tonight. Advert with clip from press conference 17-3-1987.	Video	18 sec.
17-3-1987 CFNY Radio (102 FM). News on Toronto Press conference 17-3-1987.	Tape	quality 9, 10 min.
<u>18-3-1987</u> New York, Cat Club. Press conference. 1. Interview. 2. Day in, day out (4.52). 3. Bang bang (3.28).	3 CDR	*Jones versus Osterberg (2,3)* *(Old Gold Records OGCD 041A/B/C)*
	CD	*The Glass Spider Tour - Press conferences 1987* *(Wax Records Spider101CD)*
Broadcast on radio by WCCC Hartford (interview and 2 songs). quality 10, 45 min.	CD	*Telltales* *(No label, no number)*
	CDS	Press conference Cat Club, New York, 18-3-1987 (Spider 2 A1/B1)
	CDS	The Glass spider in New York and Amsterdam (TH 42 A/B 20C1)
	LP	Press to play (Mart 001)
	Single	David I love you
	Single	Day in, day out / Bang bang
	Single	Bang bang / 87 And cry

DATE / EVENT	AUDIO / VIDEO	TITLE
	Tape	quality 10, 45 min.
18-3-1987 US TV. Channel 9. USA Tonight News. Report of press conference 18-3-1987, including clip of Day in day out.	Video	1 min.
18-3-1987 US TV. Channel 5. Eyewitness News. Report press conference 18-3-1987.	Video	1 min.
19-3-1987 French TV. TF1. Minijournal. Report press conference 18-3-1987, including clips of Day in day out and Bang bang.	Video	2 min.
19-3-1987 Canal +. Zenith. Report press conference 18-3-1987, including clips of Day in day out and Bang bang.	Video	1.23 min.
19-3-1987 Dutch TV. Half Zes Journaal. Report press conference 18-3-1987, including clip of Bang bang.	Video	1 min.
20-3-1987 London, Player's Theatre. Press conference. Interview. Day in day out. '87 And Cry. Attended by about 200 journalists and a couple of fans.	CD	The Glass Spider Tour - Press conferences 1987 (Wax Records Spider101CD)
Broadcast on radio by Newsbeat Radio 1. quality 8, 6 min.	CD	David Bowie on compact disc (C.I.D. Productions 013)
	CDS	Press conference Player's Theatre 20-3-1987 (Spider 1 A1/B1)
Bowie: "I needed time to decide for myself which audience I would continue to write for. Eventually I decided to be true to myself and write music I enjoyed. It's a progression from Scary monsters rather than my last two albums. It's almost like there's no break between the two."	LP	Press to play (Mart 001)
	LP	The Glass Spider Tour Press Conferences 1987 (Spider 101)
	Single	Day in, day out / 87 & Cry
Frampton: "When we were recording the album it was constantly "Do you remember so and so from school?" But that quickly wore off and it was down to business."	Tape	quality 8, 35 min.
	Tape	quality 10, 40 min.
20-3-1987 Capitol Radio. Interview.	Tape	quality 10, 5 min.
20-3-1987 BBC. Radio 1. Stereo Sequence with Johnny Walker and Stuart Grundy.	Tape	quality 10, 25 min.
20-3-1987 BBC. Radio 1. Newsbeat. Interview.	Tape	quality 9, 10 min.
20-3-1987 UK Radio. Independent News (97.2 FM). Bowie comments on Aids.	Tape	quality 9, 10 min.
20-3-1987 UK TV. Channel 4. The Tube.	Video	7 min.

DATE / EVENT	AUDIO / VIDEO	TITLE

Report press conference 20-3-1987, including clips of
Day in day out and 87 And cry.

20-3-1987 Music Box. Super Channel.   Video   1 min.
Report press conference 20-3-1987.

21-3-1987 UK TV. Good Morning Britain (7.50 h.).   Video   3 min.
Report press conference 20-3-1987, including clip of
Day in day out.

21-3-1987 Paris, La Locomotive. Press conference.   1 CDR   *Bowie Mouroussi (2)*
1. Interview.   *(BowieHobby)*
2. Day in day out.   Tape   quality 10, 55 min.
3. Bang bang.   Tape   quality 9, 35 min.
Part of the press conference was broadcast on 5-5-1987   *Video*   *Various 20 (7 min)*
(Swiss TV programme "Music Time").
Also broadcast on 30-6-1987 (Mouroussi Bowie Special).

21-3-1987 French TV. M6. Le Journal.   Video   1 min.
Report press conference 21-3-1987, including clip of
Day in day out.

21-3-1987 French TV. Le Journal (20.00 h.)   Video   2 min.
Report press conference 21-3-1987, including clips Day in
day out and Bang bang. Long hair interview from
November 1964.

21-3-1987 French Radio. La Séance de 10 heures.   Tape   quality 9, 25 min.
Bowie interview translated in French.

21-3-1987 TVE. Week in Rock.   Video   1 min.
Report press conference 18-3-1987, including clips of
Day in day out and Bang bang.

22-3-1987 BBC. Radio 1. Sunday Live interview with   Tape   quality 9, 20 min.
Simon Bates.

22-3-1987 French TV.   *Video*   *Various 20 (7 min)*
Interviews with Bowie and Pop. Parts of press conference
Paris 21-3-1987.

23-3-1987 Release Day in day out (4.12) / Julie (3.40) (EMI EA 230).

23-3-1987 Release 12" Day in day out (Extended dance mix) (7.15) / Day in day out (Extended dub mix) (7.17) / Julie (3.40) (EMI 12EA 230).

23-3-1987 Release 12" Day in day out (Remix by Paul "Graucho" Smirkle) (6.30) / Day in day out (Extended Dub Mix) (7.17) / Julie (3.40) (EMI 12EAX 230).

DATE / EVENT	AUDIO / VIDEO	TITLE

23-3-1987 Release US Promo 12" Day in day out (7" Dance edit) (3.35) / Day in day out (Extended dance mix) (7.15) / Day in day out (Edited dance mix) (4.30) (EMI SPRO9997/7).

23-3-1987 Madrid, Halquera Plateaux. Press conference. 2 CDR *Madrid 6 July 1987*
Interview, 87 And Cry (22 min.). *(BowieHobby)*
Day in day out, Interview (22 min.). Tape quality 8, 35 min.
  Tape quality 10, 45 min.

23-3-1987 Spanish Radio. Discopolis. Tape quality 8, 15 min.
Press conference of 23-3-1987 (only the talking).

23-3-1987 Spanish Radio. Radio Club 25. Tape quality 8, 25 min.
Press conference of 23-3-1987 (talking and the 2 songs).

23-3-1987 Spanish Radio. Radio Barcelona. Tape quality 10, 15 min.
Press conference of 23-3-1987 (talking and 1 song).

23-3-1987 Spanish Radio. Catalunary Radio. Tape quality 9, 15 min.
Press conference of 23-3-1987 (talking and 1 of the songs).

23-3-1987 Spanish TV. Telediaro. Video 1 min.
Report press conference of 23-3-1987, including clips of
Day in day out and '87 And cry.

23-3-1987 Spanish Radio. Bowie announces Day in day 2 CDR *Madrid 6 July 1987*
out in Spanish and gives a phone interview (20 min.) *(BowieHobby)*

23-3-1987 UK Radio. Mike Smith Show. Tape quality 9, 10 min.

24-3-1987 Bowie arrived at Fluminico.

24-3-1987 Spanish TV. La Tarde. Video 5 min.
About Press Conference in Madrid. Including '87 And cry.

24-3-1987 Midday. Coming up. Video 1 min.
Clip Day in day out from 17-3-1987.

24-3-1987 Midday.
Press conference and interview from 17-3-1987. Film and Video 10 min.
live clips from 1973.

24-3-1987 Music Box. Super Channel. Video 2 min.
Report press conference 20-3-1987, including clips of
Day in day out and 87 And cry.

25-3-1987 Rome, Piper Club. Press conference. 3 CDR *Jones versus Osterberg (2,3)*
1. Interview. *(Old Gold Records*
2. Bang bang and intro (4.57). *OGCD 041A/B/C)*
3. '87 And Cry (3.54). Single Bang bang / 87 & Cry

DATE / EVENT	AUDIO / VIDEO	TITLE
	Tape	(SILU 87 B) quality 10, 35 min.
	Tape	quality 10, 45 min.
25-3-1987 Italian TV. RAI. TG2. Report press conference 25-3-1987, including clip of Bang bang (original by Iggy Pop in 1981).	Video	1 min.
25-3-1987 Italian TV. RAI. Discoring. Report press conference 25-3-1987, including clip of Bang bang. Promo video Day in day out.	Video	5 min.
25-3-1987 Italian TV. Channel 5. Superclassifica Show. TV Sorrisi e Canzoni. Report press conference 25-3-1987. Promo video Day in day out.	Video	8 min.
25-3-1987 Italian TV. RAI. Pinki "In" by Red Ronnie. Report press conference 25-3-1987, including clips of Bang bang and 87 And cry. Arrival at Fluminico 24-3-87.	Video	10 min.
25-3-1987 Italian TV. Jeans. Report press conference 25-3-1987, including clip of 87 And cry.	Video	5 min.
26-3-1987 Italian Radio. RAI Stereo 1 - Marathon. Retrospective look at his career and parts of the press conference in Rome on 25-3-1987.	Tape	360 min.
26-3-1987 Munich, Parkcafe Lowenbrau. Press conference. 1. Interview. 2. Day in day out. 3. Bang bang. 4. 87 And Cry.	Tape Tape Tape Tape	Austria, TV, Ohne Maulkorb, 17 min., Interview Day in day out, Bang bang Germany TV, Music Box, 18 min., Interview, Day in Day out, 87 & Cry quality 10, 45 min. quality 10, 30 min.
26-3-1987 German TV. ZDF. Heute Journal. Report press conference on 26-3-1987, including clip of Day in day out.	Video	3 min.
27-3-1987 Swiss Radio. Broadcast of the Munich press conference on 26-3-1987.	Tape	quality 10, 45 min.
27-3-1987 Swedish TV. Stina Med Flera. Broadcast 3-4-1987. Interview (11.25).	3 CDR	*Jones versus Osterberg (Old Gold Records OGCD 041A/B/C)*

DATE / EVENT	AUDIO / VIDEO	TITLE
27-3-1987 Otto Bisgaard Special. Interview (10.31).	3 CDR	*Jones versus Osterberg (Old Gold Records OGCD 041A/B/C)*
27-3-1987 Exclusive interview by Jools Holland. A go at word association through a mirror. Broadcast by UK TV, The Tube on 29-3-1987.	Video	30 min.
28-3-1987 Melody Maker. Article by Mat Smith: David Bowie.		
<u>28-3-1987</u> Stockholm, Ritz. Press conference. 1. 87 And Cry (3.06). 2. Interview (5.20).	CD	*The Glass Spider Tour - Press conferences 1987 (Wax Records Spider101CD)*
3. Day in day out (2.08). Broadcast on Swedish TV in Stina Med Flera, 3-4-1987 (quality 10, 50 min.).	3 CDR	*Jones versus Osterberg (Old Gold Records OGCD 041A/B/C)*
Broadcast on Swedish TV in Halloj Scandinavien (quality 10, 10 min.).	1 CDR	*Made in Sweden (No label, no number)*
	1 CDR	On Swedish TV (Old Gold Records OGCD 397)
	LP	The Glass Spider Tour Press Conferences 1987 (Spider 101)
	Tape	quality 8, 10 min.
	Tape	quality 9, 15 min.
	Tape	quality 10, 50 min.
28-3-1987 Stockholm. Strandhotellet. Interviews. All the interviewers got 15 minutes. Otto Bisgaard (from Danish TV) was the only one who got 30 minutes.		
28-3-1987 Swedish or Danish Radio. Kuart-i-ekot. Interview.	Tape	quality 10, 10 min.
28-3-1987 Swedish or Danish Radio. Rock Departemeutet. Interview.	Tape	quality 10, 15 min.
28-3-1987 Danish TV. Hallo Scandinavia (21.50 h.). Report press conference 28-3-1987, including clips 87 And cry and Day in day out.	Video	6 min.
28-3-1987 Swedish TV. SVT. Report press conference 28-3-1987, including clip Day in day out. Promo video Life on Mars?	Video	4 min.
28-3-1987 Spanish TV. Informe semanal. Pintor del Rock. Report press conference 23-3-1987, clip of 87 And Cry, interview.		
29-3-1987 German TV. Music Box. About Munich Press conference 26-3-1987, including Day	Video Tape	18 min. 18 min.

DATE / EVENT	AUDIO / VIDEO	TITLE

in day out and 87 And Cry.

29-3-1987 UK TV. The Tube. Interview by Jools Holland, recorded 27-3-1987.

29-3-1987 Austrian TV. Ohne Maulkorb (18.15 h.). Report press conference 18-3-1987, including clips of Day in day out and Bang bang.	Video	2 min.

29-3-1987 Super Channel. Coca Cola Rockfile. Report press conference 20-3-1987, including clips of Day in day out and 87 And cry.	Video	5.24 min.

29-3-1987 Rotterdam, Rijnhotel. Fan-meeting Dutch Fanzine Bowie Now. Performances by Ad Sandtke, Fragment, Arno Gratjes, Bart Peeters.
After the fan-meeting some fans went to Shiphol Airport, to see Bowie arrive in Holland at 18.35 h. (Dutch Fanzine David Bowie Now).

30-3-1987 Austrian Radio. Ohne Maulkorb. About Munich Press conference 26-3-1987, including Day in day out and 87 And Cry.	Video Tape	17 min. 17 min.

30-3-1987 Het Parool. Article: Superster David Bowie in Holland.

<u>30-3-1987</u> Amsterdam, Paradiso. Press conference. 1. Interview (9.04) 2. Day in Day out (5.23). 3. Bang bang.	CD	*The Glass Spider Tour - Press conferences 1987 (1) (Wax Records Spider101CD)*
	CD	*The Glass spider in New York and Amsterdam (TH 42 A/B 20C1)*
Broadcast by Top Pop Radio (quality 9, 6 min). Broadcast by Club Veronica Trend (quality 10, 30 min).	3 CDR	*Jones versus Osterberg (1) (Old Gold Records OGCD 041A/B/C)*
The hall can hold 1.200 people. First the special invited 800 people, like the press etc. could go in.	1 CDR	*Hendrikse Various, vol.2 (1,2) (No label, no number)*
Some 50 fans were waiting outside Paradiso. They were invited in by Corinne (Coco) Schwab and had the day of their lives (Dutch Fanzine David Bowie Now).	LP	*The Glass Spider Tour Press Conferences 1987 (Spider 101)*
Bowie and band stayed at the Sonesta Hotel in Amsterdam, to rest after the press conference.	Flexi Tape	*Paradiso 30-3-1987 Belgian TV, Rox Box, 10 min., only the music*
They had dinner at restaurant Mangerie, where David ordered jugged rabbit and apple sauce (Behind the spider - Simon Deun and Antoine Loogman, October 1987).	Tape Tape	quality 9, 5 min quality 10, 30 min
Later in the evening they left Holland by plane. At 22.00 h. David and Coco looked round in Schiphol's bookshop. Bowie took an interesting book, he wanted to have. Coco ordered him to put it back.	Tape Video	quality 10, 40 min Various 20 (8 min)

30-3-1987 German TV. ZDF. Teleillustrierte (17.15 h.). Report press conference 26-3-1987, including clip of Bang bang. Interview.	Video	5 min.

DATE / EVENT	AUDIO / VIDEO	TITLE
30-3-1987 Dutch TV. Half Zes Journaal. Report press conference 30-3-1987, including clips of Bang bang and Day in day out.	Video	3 min.
30-3-1987 Dutch TV. Jeugd Journaal. Report press conference 30-3-1987, including clip Day in day out.	Video	2 min.
March / April 1987 Arena. Article: People: Bowie, Tim Pope, Danny Lane.		
April 1987 New York. Start of 6-week rehearsals.	2 CD 2 CDR	*New York's a go go (DAV 001/002)* New York Rehearsals 1987 (No label, no number)
April 1987 Italian TV. Pinky (2nd show). Interview by Red Ronnie about the video Day in Day out.	Video	20 min.
1-4-1987 Dutch TV. Veronica. Countdown. Amsterdam Press Conference (30-3-1987). Day in day out (live, 3 min.). Interview by Adam Curry (3 min). Clips China girl and Day in day out.	Tape Video	19 min. *Stolp tapes no. 19 (19 min)*
2-4-1987 Dutch TV. Tros. Pop Formule. Report press conference 30-3-1987, including clips of Bang bang and Day in day out. Exclusive interview by Jeroen Soer.	Video	11 min.
2-4-1987 Luxembourg TV. Report press conference 30-3-1987, including clips of Bang bang and Day in day out.	Video	3 min.
2-4-1987 German TV. Kinderkino Pinnwand Extra. Interview in Munich on 26-3-1987. Underground recording sessions.	Video	2 min.
2-4-1987 Norwegian TV. Veras Vendu Mot Pop og Rock. Parts from press-conference 28-3-1987, including clip Day in day out. Promo video Day in day out.	Video	11 min.
3-4-1987 French TV. Grand Public. Bang bang from Paris press conference (21-3-1987) and an exclusive interview by Sabatier.	Video	28 min.
3-4-1987 Swedish TV. Stina Med Flera. About Stockholm Press conference (28-3-1987) and an exclusive interview (11.25).	Video	50 min.

DATE / EVENT	AUDIO / VIDEO	TITLE
3-4-1987 Dutch TV. Tros Pop Formule. Commented on photo of 30-3-1987 press conference.	Video	12 sec.
4-4-1987 Dutch TV. VARA. Nachtshow. Report press conference 30-3-1987.	Video	1 min.
4-4-1987 French TV. Les Enfants Du Rock.	Video	10 min.
4-4-1987 German TV. WDR 3. Roxy. Report press conference 26-3-1987, including clips of Bang bang and Day in day out. Promo video Day in day out. Portrait of a German Bowie fan (repeated 9-4-1987).	Video	7 min.
7-4-1987 Dutch TV. Avro. Top Pop. Exclusive interview by Leonie Sazias.	Video	18 min.
7-4-1987 Radio SWF. Interview.	Tape	10 min.
9-4-1987 German TV. WDR 3. Roxy. Report press conference 26-3-1987, including clips of Bang bang and Day in day out. Promo video Day in day out. Portrait of a German Bowie fan (previously broadcast on 4-4-1987).	Video	7 min.
10-4-1987. Belgian TV. Rox Box (by Serge Bergli). Parts from press-conference 30-3-1987, including Day in day out and Bang bang.	*Video* Video	*Various 20 (8 min)* 13 min.
11-4-1987 Guardian. Article by Steve Lake: Crock and roller.		
11-4-1987 New Musical Express. Advert for The Glass Spider Tour, promoted by Goldsmith.		
12-4-1987 Observer Magazine. Article by Adam Sweeting: Role over Bowie.		
12-4-1987 Observer. Article: The boy David grows up.		
15-4-1987 WHJY 94 Radio. Fresh Tracks. LP Never let me down and DJ comments.	Tape	quality 10, 30 min.
16-4-1987 Denmark TV. Under Uret Ekstra. Interview by Hans Otto Bisgaard and parts of the Stockholm Press conference 28-3-1987.	Video	30 min.
17-4-1987 The Ann Arbor News. Article by Mary Campbell: Ziggy Stardust Survives (David Bowie returns to his rock roots with another spider).		
17-4-1987 Canadian TV. Good Rockin' Tonite. Exclusive interview by J.D. Roberts and part of Toronto Press conference of 17-3-1987.	Video	16 min.

DATE / EVENT	AUDIO / VIDEO	TITLE

18-4-1987 Melody Maker. Article by Chris Roberts: Never let me down.

18-4-1987 Spanish TV. A Tope. | Video | 15 min.
Exclusive interview with Bowie who announces Day in Day out in Spanish.

19-4-1987 Canadian TV. The New Music Special Edition. | Video | 55 min.
Part 1: Toronto press conference, 17-3-1987.
Part 2: US Festival, 30-5-1983.
Part 3: Comments by Nile Rodgers and Iggy Pop and the interview by J.D.Roberts on 17-4-1987.

20/21/22-4-1987 US TV. NBC. Today show, presented by | *Video* | *Various 24 (26 min)*
Bryant Gumpbel and Jane Pauley.
3 Part interview by Rona Elliot.
Special with live clips and video clips.

23-4-1987 Rolling Stone. Article by Kurt Loder: Stardust memories.

25-4-1987 BBC Radio 1. Bowie talks about Never let me | Tape
down.

27-4-1987 US TV. West 57th Street. | Video | 14 min.
Interviews Tony Visconti, Angie Bowie and David Bowie.

27-4-1987 Release LP Never let me down (EMI AMLS 3117), CD (EMI America CDP 7 46677 2). The title song was written for Coco Schwab and inspired by John Lennon's Jealous guy.

Bowie about the song Beat of your drum: "It's a Lolita number! Reflection on young girls. Christ, she's only fourteen years old, but jail's worth it!"

Released in Japan Special Edition CD Album Never let me down (EMI CP32-5398).
Bonus track (as 6th song on the album) Japanese version of Girls (edit) (4.00).
It also included Too dizzy. This track was on the other CD releases deleted in Bowie's order (another attempt to rewrite his own past).

27-4-1987 Released Never let me down Promo EP. Medley: Time will crawl / Never let me down / Blue Jean / Loving the alien / Shining star (3.16) (EMI).

28-4-1987 The New Music. | Video | 8 min.
Part of press conference 17-3-1987. Clips Day in day out and 87 And cry. Promo video Day in day out.

29-4-1987 MTV's Night Network. | Video | 26 min.
Parts of music, interrupted by interviews with Carlos Alomar, Peter Frampton, David Bowie.

May 1987 Tracks. Bowie on cover and 4-page article.

DATE / EVENT	AUDIO / VIDEO	TITLE
2-5-1987 German TV. Peter Illmans Treff. Exclusive interview with Bowie.	Video	15 min.
4-5-1987 Radio SWF 3. LP Review.	Tape	5 min.
5-5-1987 Village Voice. Article by B.Walters: Music: The new Bruce.		
5-5-1987 Swiss TV. Music Time. Music (2 songs) and interview clips from the Paris press conference 21-3-1987.	Video	quality 10, 10 min.
12-5-1987 20.00 h. Bowie arrived in Holland and went to the Amstel Hotel in Amsterdam.		
13 to 16-5-1987 Aalsmeer. Joop v.d. Ende Studios. Pepsi-commercial (called Creation) (1.04) with Tina Turner. In the studio Dutch fan Roeland Suurmond handed Bowie his very rare LP The man who sold the world with fold-out cover (Dutch Fanzine David Bowie Now).	1 CDR	Rock 'n' roll oddessy (Ulfdub)
17-5-1987 Bowie, Coco and bodyguard Jerry moved to the Hilton Hotel in Rotterdam. They ususally had dinner at Portobello's, opposite het Hilton Hotel.		
19-5-1987 Rotterdam, Ahoy Hall. Rehearsals.	1 CDR	Rotterdam Rehearsals (BowieHobby)
	1 CDR	Rotterdam Rehearsals 1987 (No label, no number)
	1 LP	Rotterdam Rehearsals (The Spiders Mart 02 Rs ltd.)
20-5-1987 Rotterdam, Ahoy Hall. Rehearsals. During this rehearsal they played Big Brother without the drum solo.	1 CDR	Rehearsals Rotterdam, vol. 1 (BowieHobby)
	1 CDR	Rotterdam Rehearsals (BowieHobby)
	1 CDR	Rotterdam Rehearsals 1987 (No label, no number)
	1 LP	Rotterdam Rehearsals (The Spiders Mart 02 Rs ltd.)
	Tape	quality 8, 110 min
	Tape	quality 8, 135 min
	Tape	quality 8, 35 min
	Tape	quality 8, 30 min
	Tape	quality 8, 35 min
21-5-1987 Rotterdam, Ahoy Hall. Rehearsals. Day in day out.	1 CDR	Bowie Mouroussi (French TV) (BowieHobby)
22-5-1987 Dutch Radio. Radio Rijnmond. Interview by Stuart Grundy and Lisa Robinson.	1 CDR	Radio Rijnmond 22-5-1987 (BowieHobby)

DATE / EVENT	AUDIO / VIDEO	TITLE
Worldwide broadcast. Full interview is 39 min.		
22-5-1987 Rotterdam, Ahoy Hall. Rehearsals. When Bowie left the Hall he shouted to a fan: "This show is gonna blow your head off" (Shining star - Marshall Jarman and Friends 1988).	NT	
22-5-1987 WCCC Hartford (107 FM). Glass Spider Tour preview. Via satellite from Rotterdam. With Lisa Robinson and tour dates.	Tape	quality 10, 15 min.
23-5-1987 Rotterdam, Ahoy Hall. Rehearsals. Sons of the silent age, New York's in love, Dancing with the big boys, Time will crawl, Beat of your drum, Zeroes, Let's dance, Fame.	1 CDR	*Rehearsals Rotterdam, vol. 2* (BowieHobby)
	1 CDR	*Rotterdam Rehearsals* (BowieHobby)
	1 CDR	Rotterdam Rehearsals 1987 (No label, no number)
	1 LP	Rotterdam Rehearsals (The Spiders Mart 02 Rs ltd.)
	Tape	quality 8, 30 min.
	Tape	quality 7, 25 min.
24-5-1987 Rotterdam, Ahoy Hall. Rehearsals.	NT	
27-5-1987 Rotterdam, Ahoy Hall. Dress Rehearsals. The last song Modern love was played very slowly. Richard Cottle had to rehearse the saxophone solo.	1 CDR	*Rehearsals Rotterdam, vol. 3* (BowieHobby)
	Tape	quality 8, 50 min.
	Tape	quality 8, 45 min.
28-5-1987 Rotterdam, Ahoy Hall. Dress Rehearsals. During Big Brother they played the guitar intro to Panic in Detroit.	1 CDR	*Rehearsals Rotterdam, vol. 4* (BowieHobby)
	Tape	quality 7, 50 min.

The Glass Spider World Tour:
David Bowie (vocals, guitar, saxophone).
Carlos Alomar (guitar).
Peter Frampton (lead guitar).
Carmine Rojas (bass).
Alan Childs (drums).
Erdal Kizilcay (keyboards, trumpet, congas, violin).
Richard Cottle (keyboards, saxophone).
Melissa Hurley, Constance Marie, Craig Allen Rothwell (Spazz Attack), Viktor Manoei, Stephen Nichols (dancers).

DATE / EVENT	AUDIO / VIDEO	TITLE
30-5-1987 Rotterdam, Feyenoord Stadium. Sound check (between 13.30 and 14.20 h.).	Tape	quality 6, 50 min.
30-5-1987 Rotterdam, Feyenoord Stadium. Support act: Nona Hendryx (30 min.).	2 CDR	*The Glass Spider premiere complete concert*

DATE / EVENT	AUDIO / VIDEO	TITLE

Attendance: 50.000. Tickets FL. 37,50 to FL. 45,—.
Pepsi Cola sponsored the tour.
The dance team was called: Thru The Flames.
Toni Basil arranged the choreography.
Bowie's son Joe was present. It was his 16th birthday.
The audience sang Happy Birthday.
Bowie a little over concentrated. A very average concert.
Bowie entered the stage descending in a silver chair from the top of the spider. After a very good version of Time will crawl Bowie spoke his first words. He also congratulated his son Joe with his 16th birthday.

	AUDIO / VIDEO	TITLE
	2 CD	*(No label, no number)* *Live at 'De Kuip'* *Rotterdam 1987*
	2 CDR	*(No label, no number)* *Caught in the web*
	2 CDR	*Rotterdam 30 May 1987* *(BowieHobby)*
	2 CDR	*Glass spider premiere* *(Old Gold Records* *OGCD 118A/B)*
	2 CDR	*Kick off… Rotterdam 87* *(No label, no number)*
	2 LP	*Glass spider premiere* *(Spider Records 801)*
	Tape	quality 8, 130 min.
	Tape	quality 7, 130 min.
	Video	quality 7, 128 min.
	Video	*Various 22 (1 min)*

30-5-1987 BBC Radio 1. Interview.   Tape

31-5-1987 Dutch Newspaper. Article by Maarten Pennewaard: David Bowie maakt van optreden videospektakel (Bowie makes video spectacle of performance).

31-5-1987 Dutch Newspaper. Article by John Oomkens: David Bowie in nieuwe show is alleen nog maar verpakking.

<u>31-5-1987</u> Rotterdam, Feyenoord Stadium.   Tape   quality 7, 20 min.
Sound check.
A very good version of Time will crawl, with Peter
Frampton singing the intro.

<u>31-5-1987</u> Rotterdam, Feyenoord Stadium.
Support act: Nona Hendryx (30 min.).
Attendance: 50.000. Tickets FL. 37,50 to FL. 45,—.
The concert was a lot better than the first night.
"One hundred years ago there lived in the Zi-Duang province of eastern country a glass-like spider…."
Band intro: "Someone who has been with me for over 13 years, write with me and plays guitar… Carlos Alomar."
Great versions of New York's in love and Time.
"Everyone has done so much to make us feel at home. We really will be sorry to leave here."

	AUDIO / VIDEO	TITLE
	2 CDR	*Rotterdam 31 May 1987* *(BowieHobby)*
	2 CDR	*The second night* *(Old Gold Records* *OGCD 119A/B)*
	Tape	quality 9, 130 min.
	Tape	quality 8, 125 min.
	Video	quality 7, 126 min.
	Video	quality 9, 113 min.

31-5-1987 Dutch TV's Countdown.   Video
Glass Spider clip from the 30-5-1987 concert.

31-5-1987 Austria. Ohne Maulkorb.   Video   17 min.
Bang bang and Day in day out from Munich Press

DATE / EVENT	AUDIO / VIDEO	TITLE

conference 26-3-1987. Bowie's paintings. Interview by Rudolf Dolezal.

June 1987 Italian TV. Videomusic Special.   Video   25 min.
Includes an exclusive interview.

June 1987 Release Time will crawl (4.18) / Girls (4.13) (EMI EA 237).

June 1987 Release 12" Time will crawl (Extended dance mix) (6.11) / Time will crawl (4.18) / Girls (Extended edit) (5.35) (EMI 12EA 237).

June 1987 Release 12" Time will crawl (Chris Lord Alge-Dance-Crew-Mix) (5.43) / Time will crawl (Dub mix) (5.23) / Girls (Japanese version) (4.06) (EMI 12EAX 237).

June 1987 Stereoplay. Article by Matthias Inhoffen: Geldgieriges genie.

1-6-1987 Haagse Courant. Article: Bowie als gijzelaar van zijn roeping (Bowie as prisoner of his own calling).

1-6-1987 Daily Express. Article: Spiderman Bowie spins a web of wonder.

1-6-1987 Dutch TV. RTL Flash.   Video   16 sec.
Clip of Glass spider from 30-5-1987.

1-6-1987 Entertainment Tonight.   Video   1.24 min.
Interview and clip of Glass spider from 30-5-1987.

DATE / EVENT	AUDIO / VIDEO	TITLE
<u>2-6-1987</u> Werchter. Festival terrein. Sound check. 1. Loving the alien (5.35). 2. Bang bang (7.36). 3. Fashion (5.35). 4. Scary monsters (4.45). 5. All the madmen (8.51). 6. Never let me down (4.41). 7. Glass spider (5.53).	1 CDR 1 CDR 1 CDR Tape	*Diamonds in space (4,5,7)* *(No label, no number)* TracksThreeBowie (No label, no number) *Loving the alien* *(No label, no number)* quality 8, 40 min.
<u>2-6-1987</u> Werchter. Festival terrein. Attendance: 40.000. A very good concert. Bowie relaxed, talkative and improvising. During a very good version of Day in day out: "Shootin' her with bullets, drugs, promises and video."	2 CDR 2 CDR 2 CDR Tape Tape Video	Werchter 2 June 1987 (BowieHobby) Werchter 1987 (Old Gold Records OGCD 120A/B) Live in Belgium '87 (No label, no number) quality 9, 125 min. quality 9, 90 min. quality 7, 127 min.
3-6-1987 Belgian TV. TF1.	Video	1.53 min.

DATE / EVENT	AUDIO / VIDEO	TITLE

Clip of Day in day out from 2-6-1987 and audience report.

4-6-1987 Rolling Stone. Article by David Fricke: Live! Twenty concerts that changed rock 'n' roll: David Bowie and the Spiders From Mars US Tour.

4-6-1987 Rolling Stone. Article by Steve Pond: Never say never.

6-6-1987 Berlin. Hansa Tonstudios. Press Conference. After the press conference he took a taxi and had a city-tour.	Tape	
6-6-1987 Berlin, Plats der Republik (Reichstag Gelande). Sound check.	Tape Tape	quality 8, 15 min. quality 9, 60 min.
6-6-1987 Berlin, Plats der Republik (Reichstag Gelande). A good concert, the first part was great. "It's a special evening for us. Wir schicken unsere besten wunschen zu allen unseren Freunden die die anderen Seite der Mauer sind." The first 75 minutes of the show broadcast by the local Berlin radio Rias 2. Attended by Neil Tennant and Chris (Pet Shop Boys).	2 CD 1 CDR 1 CDR 2 CDR 2 CDR 1 CDR 2 LP LP Tape	Bang Bang (84 min.) (No label, no number) Bang Bang (Old Gold Records OGCD 042) Glass idol in Berlin Wham Bam Thank You Ma'am! (Old Gold Records OGCD 209A/B) Cyberstation (1 song) (STATIONTOBOWIE) Bang bang in Berlin 87 (No label, no number) Bang Bang (Bang Bang Productions 2407461) You need a tie to get in (Deaf Records DEAF 1094 DK) quality 9, 125 min.

Carlos Alomar: "I'm responsible for 99,5 percent of the music. David would bring me an initial list of around 30 songs he'd want to perform. I would listen to the original songs and then re-arrange the older material to sound similar in style to the newer ones. Ultimately giving one continuous musical frame."

6-6-1987 German Radio. Rias 2. Broadcast of the first 75 minutes of the 6-6-1987 concert.	Tape	quality 10, 75 min.
6-6-1987 German TV shows Wochenspiegel and 1500 Jahre Berlin. Live clips Glass Spider, Day in day out and the near riots of the 6-6-1987 concert.		
6-6-1987 French TV. Champ Elysee. Bowie interviewed backstage at Werchter (2-6-1987).	Video	12 min.
7-6-1987 Koblenz, Nurnbergring (Rock am Ring). Open-air festival at racetrack. Attendance: 70.000. Tickets: DM 55,— and DM 65,—.	2 CDR	A day in Koblenz (Old Gold Records OGCD 210A/B)

DATE / EVENT	AUDIO / VIDEO	TITLE
Very good versions of Glass spider and Day in day out. During All the madmen a dancer unfolded a sheet. On the sheet projections of Bowie-personas.	Tape *Video*	quality 8, 130 min. *Stolp tapes no. 11 (135 min)*
8-6-1987 German TV. ZDF Heute (19.00 h). Clip Day in day out from 6-6-1987.	Video	quality 9, 3.24 min.
8-6-1987 German TV. ARD. Tagesschau. Report about the 6-6-1987 concert.	Video	quality 8, 1.53 min.
9-6-1987 Italy, Firenze (Florence). Stadio Comunale. A lightning engineer (Michael 'Spider' Clark) was killed when he fell from a scaffold 90 minutes before the start of the concert. He was rushed to the hospital, where he died while the concert was going on (Return of the Spiderman - Peter Frederiksen 1988). Bowie improvised a lot during Bang bang. "The next song is dedicated to a dear friend of mine. Spider get better soon!" Then follows Beat of your drum. During the first encore (Time) the crowd went wild.	2 CDR *2 CDR* Tape Tape	Italian spider (Old Gold Records OGCD 255A/B) *Live Florence, Italy - June 9th (No label, no number)* quality 9, 135 min. Italian TV, 7 min.
9-6-1987 Italian Radio. Radio Livorno. Broadcast interview and 9 songs from 9-6-1987 concert.	Tape	quality 7, 120 min.
9-6-1987 Entertainment Tonight. Berlin affair. Clip Glass spider from 6-6-1987.	Video	quality 8, 2 min.
9-6-1987 German TV. Telegiornale. Showed a photo of the set of 6-6-1987.	Video	30 sec.
9-6-1987 MTV. Week in Rock. Clip Bang bang from 6-6-1987.	Video	1 min
10-6-1987 Milano, Stadio Di San Siro. Attendance: 80.000. A good concert. Great crowd response. When they took up Melissa Hurley from the crowd the audience really went wild. The last time they did New York's in love. Frampton sang very nice again. 2 Songs broadcast on Italian Radio (quality 9, 10 min.).	2 CDR 2 CDR 2 CDR 2 CDR 2 CDR *2 CDR*	Glass spider premiere (Old Gold Records OGCD 118A/B) The second night (Old Gold Records OGCD 119A/B) (3 songs) Werchter 1987 (Old Gold Records OGCD 120A/B) Waiting in the wind (Old Gold Records OGCD 096A/B) Glass Spider finale (Old Gold Records OGCD 099A/B) *A night with the duke*

DATE / EVENT	AUDIO / VIDEO	TITLE
	2 LP	*(MCDS 020 99-B)* *A night with the duke* *(R.O.A.R. Records)*
	LP	*Extramilan (TPHP Records Ltd. DRJ 488 A/B)*
	Tape	quality 8, 130 min.
	Tape	quality 9, 135 min.
10-6-1987 Dutch TV. Veronica. Countdown, presented by Adam Curry. Interview. Live clip Glass spider (1 min) from 30-5-1987. Video clip Time will crawl.	*Video*	*Various 22, 9 min.*
12-6-1987 Italian TV. RAI. Clips Glass Spider, Up the hill backwards and interview from 9-6-1987.	*Video*	quality 9, 7 min.
13-6-1987 Hamburger Morgenpost. Article: Bowie in Hamburg.		
<u>13-6-1987</u> Hamburg, Festwiese am Stadtpark. Support-act: Nina Hagen (from 15.00 to 15.30 hours), and several German rock groups. Backstage Bowie met Prince Joachim and Crown Prince Frederik of Denmark (arranged by the Danish Newspaper B.T.). Thomas Hone (EMI) introduced Bowie. Just before the beginning of the concert the fence was smashed down and thousands without tickets got in. The set was short and Bowie looked a little tired. Very average concert.	*2 CDR* *2 CDR* *2 CDR* Tape Video	*Hamburg 13 June 1987* *(BowieHobby)* *Glad to be back* *(Old Gold Records OGCD 256A/B)* *Live At Stadt Park* *(No label, no number)* quality 9, 120 min. quality 8, 120 min.
13-6-1987 German TV's Hamburger Journal. Glass Spider clip from 13-6-1987 concert.	*Video*	6 min.
14-6-1987 German TV. ARD. Wochenspiel (at 12.45 h.). Day in day out from 6-6-1987 and they mentioned the West affair.	*Video*	quality 9, 6 min.
<u>15-6-1987</u> Rome, Stadio Flaminio. A very good concert and Bowie was in a very good mood. Very good version of Loving the alien. Again a few lines of War (The Temptations, 1970) during Fame.	*2 CDR* *1 CDR* *2 CDR* *2 CDR*	*Waiting in the wind* *(No label, no number)* *Studio outtakes / Demanding Billy Dolls.* *Fashion/All the madmen* *Big Brother/Heroes* *Fame / Time* *Together with Waiting in the wind the complete concert* *Roma 87* *(No label, no number)* *Waiting in the wind* *(Old Gold Records*

DATE / EVENT	AUDIO / VIDEO	TITLE
		OGCD 096A/B)
	2 LP	Waiting in the wind (Cinthia Records Ltd. DRJ 490 / 491)
	3 Singles	Demanding Billy Dolls (Cinthia Records Ltd. 331/1)
	Tape	quality 9, 110 min.
	Tape	quality 9, 125 min.
15-6-1987 Italian TV. RAI. Clip Glass spider from 15-6-1987.	Video	2 min.
16-6-1987 German TV. ZDF. Die Report (at 10.30 h). Clip Glass spider from 6-6-1987 and West / East affair.	Video	quality 9, 6 min.
16-6-1987 Rome, Stadio Flaminio. A very good concert and Bowie was in a good mood. During Never let me down he changed from microphone. There were riots outside the stadium and the police used tear gas. Part of the gas floated over the stage and during Time will crawl he sang: "We only smelt the gas, as we lay down to sleep." After the song: "That was a song about gas. Please excuse my eyes, but we're gonna play until we drop." During Let's dance he sang: "Under the gaslight, the serious gaslight." Time was not played as encore.	2 CDR 1 CDR 2 CDR Tape Tape Tape	Glad to be back (Old Gold Records OGCD 256A/B) Roman gas (Old Gold Records OGCD 257) King of Wales (Old Gold Records OGCD 258A/B) quality 9, 120 min. quality 8, 125 min. quality 7, 105 min.
17-6-1987 Bowie arrived in London and stayed at The Hilton Hotel.		
17-6-1987 London, Wembley Stadium. Rehearsal.	NT	
17-6-1987 UK TV. BBC. Top of the Pops. Time will crawl. Recording shelved and for the first time shown in 1989.	Video	Various 25 (5 min)
18-6-1987 Times. Article by Bryan Appleyard: How Ziggy fell to earth.		
18-6-1987 Stuttgart. *Cancelled.*		
18-6-1987 London, Wembley Stadium. Rehearsal.	NT	

Bowie: "The London dates will be extremely important to me. When you're born in a place, that becomes the big one (Glass idol - David Currie 1987).

19-6-1987 London, Wembley Stadium. Rehearsal. Driving rain during the rehearsal.	Tape	quality 7, 5 min.
19-6-1987 London, Wembley Stadium. Tickets: GBP 16,—. Promoted by Goldsmith Entertainments.	2 CDR	*London 19 June 1987 (BowieHobby)*

DATE / EVENT	AUDIO / VIDEO	TITLE
Attendance: 70.000. It rained and the acoustic was terrible. Bowie tensed and nervous (as always in London). Not a good concert.	2 CDR 2 CDR Tape Tape Video Video	Glass Spider Tour Wembley Stadium 87 first night (No label, no number) quality 8, 120 min. quality 9, 125 min. quality 8, 79 min. quality 7, 117 min.
19-6-1987 UK TV. Newsnight. Interview by Wesley Kerr, backstage in London. Part of Glass Spider live at Wembley 19-6-1987.	Video	4 min.
20-6-1987 London, Wembley Stadium. Sound check (in the afternoon).	Tape	
20-6-1987 London, Wembley Stadium. Attendance: 70.000. Tickets: GBP 16,—. A relaxed and improvising Bowie and a good concert. "When I looked at my China girl. Oh, look at her, she's so fine. Oh, she changed my heart." After Time will crawl: "Rock 'n' roll England. We're enjoying ourselves, ain't we?" Short (album) version of Fame. The encore Time: "Time… he's waiting in the wings. He speaks of senseless things. His script… you got it London… is you and me, boy."	2 CDR 2 CDR 2 CDR 2 CDR Tape Video Video Video Video Video	London 20 June 1987 (BowieHobby) Live London 1987 (No label, no number) Best of Wembley (Old Gold Records OGCD 169A/B) Wembley Stadium 87 Second Night quality 9, 125 min. quality 9, 93 min. quality 9, 118 min. quality 9, 125 min. quality 9, 124 min. quality 9, 130 min.
21-6-1987 Cardiff, Arms Park. Tickets: GBP 15,—. First time he did a concert in Wales. Attendance: 45.000. They played in Richard Cottle's home county. A good concert. Loving the alien had great guitar work by Frampton.	2 CDR 2 CDR 2 CDR 2 CDR 2 CDR Tape Tape	Cardiff 21 June 1987 (BowieHobby) King of Wales (Old Gold Records OGCD 258A/B) Cardiff Arms Park 1987 Live in Cardiff 1987 (CD-R 87 0006 21) Echoes in the Tenement Halls quality 9, 125 min. quality 8, 120 min.

22-6-1987 Western Mail. Article: Bowie's new girl Bow's in.

22-6-1987 Guardian. Article by Adam Sweeting: Serious twilight.

22-6-1987 Article by Neil Jones: Bowie wows 45.000 fans.

DATE / EVENT	AUDIO / VIDEO	TITLE

23-6-1987 Receives award during Children's Charity Lunch out of the hands of The Duchess of York.

<u>23-6-1987</u> Sunderland, Roker Park Stadium.
Tickets: GBP 15,—. Promoter: Harvey Goldsmith.
Support act: Big Country.
An average concert.
Pouring rain. Frampton had problems with his guitar.
"Good evening Newcastle." Mistake Dave, you're in Sunderland!
Band intro: "On half guitar Peter Frampton. This is how to fix it." He ran to Frampton and pretended to jump up and down on his guitar.

2 CDR	*Where am I?* (Old Gold Records OGCD 259A/B)
2 CDR	*Roker Park 1987* (H Design)
2 CDR	Sunderland Roker Park
Tape	quality 9, 130 min.
Tape	quality 8, 120 min.
Tape	quality 9, 115 min.
Video	quality 6, 112 min.

23-6-1987 UK TV. Norther Life.
Glass spider, stage set and audience report of 23-6-1987.

Video	4 min.

24-6-1987 UK TV. NL News.
Interview with promoter Harvey Goldsmith.

Video	3 min.

27-6-1987 Expressen. Article by Mans Ivarsson: B-U-W-I-E.

<u>27-6-1987</u> Gothenburg, Eriksberg festival site.
Sound check.

Tape	quality 8, 40 min.

<u>27-6-1987</u> Gothenburg, Eriksberg festival site.
Support act: Iggy Pop (he played 45 minutes).
Attendance: 45.000.
Was held in a shutdown ship yard. Bowie came by boat across the river behind the stage. He entered the stage at 18.00 hours and performed a good concert.

2 CDR	*Gothenburg 27 June 1987* (BowieHobby)
3 CDR	*Jones versus Osterberg* (Old Gold Records OGCD 041A/B/C)
2 CDR	Swedish Spider (No label, no number)
Tape	quality 9, 115 min.

27-6-1987 Swedish TV. SVT. Aktuellt.
Glass Spider clip from 27-6-1987 concert, Bowie interview and audience report.

Video	3 min.

<u>28-6-1987</u> Lyon, Stade Municipal de Gerland.
Attendance: 60.000. Started at 20.30 hours.
A great concert. Bowie dancing and making jokes.

2 CDR	*Lyon 28 June 1987* (BowieHobby)
2 CDR	Lyon Stade Gerlande June 28th 1987 (No label, no number)
Tape	quality 9, 125 min.

29-6-1987 French TV. M6. Le Journal (18.00 h.).
Glass Spider clip from 28-6-1987 concert.

Video	3 min.

29-6-1987 French TV. France 3. Soir 3 (22.00 h.).
Glass Spider clip from 28-6-1987 concert.

Video	1 min.

DATE / EVENT	AUDIO / VIDEO	TITLE

30-6-1987 DH - Cinq. Article by Florence Tradez: Bowie incognito de Lyon a Paris.

30-6-1987 French TV. A2. Le Journal du Tour. Clip Glass spider from 6-6-1987.	Video	1 min.
30-6-1987 French TV. Mouroussi Bowie Special. Broadcast Day in Day out and interview from press conference 21-3-1987 in Paris. Heroes (Top of he Pops 1977), Oh! you pretty things (Old Grey Whistle Test 1972), parts of doc. Cracked Actor.	1 CDR Video	*Bowie Mouroussi (French TV) (BowieHobby)* 52 min.
July 1987 Italian TV. Estate Rock. Ron Wood and Bill Wyman talk about Bowie. At the end Ron Wood interviews Bowie backstage in Rome. Part of Glass Spider (Florence 9-6-1987).	Video	16 min.

July 1987 The Independent. Article by Marek Kohn.
Kohn wrote: Bowie has the visage of the rock idol with the polish of the Vegas crooner. The star was there, what was in alarmingly short supply was taste. Bowie has built a career on making hollowness inspirational so it's surprising that such a past master should have lost the knack of structuring a spectacle.

July 1987 Mademoiselle. Article by John Pareles: David Bowie ch-ch-ch-changes his tune.

1-7-1987 Vienna, Prater stadion. Attendance: 45.000. Support act: Nazz Nasko. Glass Spider filmed and later released on Never let me down - The Videos. Great version of Time will crawl. "We got, I believe, some friends from Yugoslavia with us here tonight." Then he talked a few words in a fake language that was supposed to sound like Yugoslavian.	2 CDR 2 CDR 2 CDR 2 CDR CD 2 CDR Tape Video	*Wienerblut* (Old Gold Records OGCD 260A/B) *Wienerblut (2)* *Wien* *Vienna 1 July 1987 (BowieHobby)* *Legendary Lost Tapes Vol. 2 (2 songs) (VigOtone 179)* *Vienna '87* (No label, no number) quality 9, 130 min. quality 9, 123 min.
1-7-1987 Austrian TV. Glass spider clip from 1-7-1987, promo videos and interview.	Video	quality 9, 5 min.

2-7-1987 Austrian Newspaper. Article by Alexander Haide: Rockopa ohne Sexappeal.

2-7-1987 Austrian Newspaper. Article by Vera: Uber allen Erwartungen.

2-7-1987 DIR Radio Network Broadcast. Glass Spider Special.	1 CDR	*Rock 'n' roll oddessy (Ulfdub)*

DATE / EVENT	AUDIO / VIDEO	TITLE
3-7-1987 French TV. TF1. Le Journal (13.00 h.). Mourousi gives his comments on Bowie.	Video	1 min.
3-7-1987 Paris, Parc Departement de la Courneuve Seine. Sound check at 14.00 hours (30 minutes, 6 songs).	1 CDR Tape	Hendrikse various vol. 7 (BowieHobby) quality 7, 45 min.
3-7-1987 French TV. TF1. Mini Journal. Preview on the Paris concert.	Video	2 min.
3-7-1987 French TV. France 3. 19/20. Preview on the Paris concert and Glass spider clip from Lyon on 28-6-1987.	Video	1 min.
3-7-1987 French TV. TF1. Le Journal (20.00 h.). Bruno Masure gives his comments on Bowie.	Video	10 sec.
3-7-1987 Paris, Parc Departement de la Courneuve Seine. Tickets: F.Frs. 150,—. In the afternoon Bowie had quite a few drinks. In a lot of the songs he changed a part of the words. For the words he forgot, he just made up new ones. Strangely enough it worked out very well. Bowie was laughing, joking and dancing. It became a great concert, despite the booze! Bang bang had a very long intro. During the intro to Loving the alien Erdal Kizelcay played a panpipe. The longer the show lasted, the weaker Bowie's voice sounded.	2 CD 2 CD 2 CD 2 CDR 3 LP Tape Tape	The glass spider tour (No label, no number) The spider over Paris (Moonraker 451/52) God it's dark (Main Stream MAST-034/035) Stiff on my legend (Old Gold Records OGCD 083A/B) The glass spider tour (DB 7731 - 32 - 33) quality 9, 130 min. quality 9, 120 min.
4-7-1987 German TV. Peter Illmans Treff. Clips Glass Spider and Day in day out. Interview in Berlin 6-6-1987.	1 CDR Video	Hendrikse various vol.2 (No label, no number) 15 min.
4-7-1987 Toulouse, Le Stadium. A good concert, but Bowie's voice sounded weak again. After Time will crawl: "Thank you for keeping the rain away."	2 CDR Tape	Toulousian Spider (Old Gold Records OGCD 161A/B) quality 8, 120 min.
4-7-1987 French TV. Soir 3. Le Journal (22.00 h.). Clip Up the hill backwards and interview from 3-7-1987.	Video	1 min.
5-7-1987 Lavanguardia. Article: David Bowie, escala en Barcelona.		
6-7-1987 Madrid, Estadio Vicente Calderon. Bowie had voice-problems. Again the panpipe intro to Loving the alien.	2 CDR	Iberian Premiere (Old Gold Records OGCD 263A/B)

DATE / EVENT	AUDIO / VIDEO	TITLE
"Excuse my voice this evening, it's… however this is a song called Beat of the drum" he said coughing and misspelling the title. It should be Beat of your drum.	2 CDR	*Madrid 6 July 1987* (BowieHobby)
	2 CDR	Madrid '87 (No label, no number)
	3 CDR	The Glass Spaniard (KG-CD 37)
	Tape	quality 9, 120 min.
<u>7-7-1987</u> Barcelona, Mini Estadio C.F. Bowie stayed at Princesa Sofia Hotel. A doctor visited him because he didn't feel very well. Attendance: 20.000. Tickets: Ptas 3.000. Started at 21.00 h. Not a good concert. On routine Bowie sang his songs and seemed the be glad the concert was over, so he could get back to his hotel.	1 CDR	Todos los locos (Old Gold Records OGCD 264)
	2 CDR	Iberian Premiere (Old Gold Records OGCD 263A/B)
	2 CDR	El Genio (Old Gold Records OGCD 265A/B)
	2 CDR	Two nights in Barcia - The 1st (No label, no number)
	2 CDR	Main Road '87 (Old Gold Records OGCD 266A/B)
	2 CDR	*Live in Barcelona* (No label, no number)
	Tape	quality 9, 125 min.
	Video	quality 8, 125 min.
7-7-1987 Spanish TV. Bon Dia Catalunya. AM (8.23 h.). Glass spider clip from 6-7-1987.	Video	2 min.
7-7-1987 Spanish TV. L'Informatiu. Arrival on the airport and Glass spider clip from 6-7-1987.	Video	2 min.
7-7-1987 Spanish TV. Vincente Calderon. Glass spider clip from 6-7-1987.	Video	3 min.
7-7-1987 French TV. Much Music. Rock Flash. Glass spider clip and interview from 3-7-1987.	Video	2 min.
8-7-1987 Mirador. Article: David Bowie ofereix a Barcelona el que no va donar a Madrid.		
8-7-1987 German TV. Blick ins Land. Clip Glass spider from 7-6-1987.	Video	quality 8, 6 min.
<u>8-7-1987</u> Barcelona, Mini Estadio C.F. Sound check.	NT	
<u>8-7-1987</u> Barcelona, Mini Estadio C.F. Attendance: 20.000. Tickets: Ptas 3.000. Started at 21.00 h. Bowie in a good mood and feeling well again.	2 CDR	El Genio (Old Gold Records OGCD 265A/B)

DATE / EVENT	AUDIO / VIDEO	TITLE
During Fashion a fan on stage who danced a few seconds with our hero. Again Bowie had some microphone problems. He surprised the band by starting Jean Genie (not rehearsed by the band and played for the first time during this tour).	2 CDR 2 CDR 2 CDR Tape	*Barcelona 8 July 1987* *(BowieHobby)* Barcelona 87 Second Night (No label, no number) Two nights in Barcia - The 2nd (No label, no number) quality 8, 130 min.
9-7-1987 Vacaciones. Article: Bowie pone Barcelona a sus pies.		
10-7-1987 Irish TV. Newstime. Interview on the tour bus.	Video	4 min.
10-7-1987 Irish TV. RTE. Visual Eyes. Interview in London's Hilton Hotel and Up the hill backwards / Glass spider clips from 19-6-1987.	Video	26 min.
10-7-1987 The Irish Times. Article: PR men riled, but Bowie smiled.		
Summer 1987 Marie Helvin was his partner for a while.		
<u>11-7-1987</u> Dublin, Slane Castle. Attendance: 55.000. A 20-year old tried to swim across the river and drowned (The return of the Spiderman - Peter Frederiksen 1988). The crowd was enthusiastic and pushed a lot. During Absolute beginners Bowie stopped and tried to calm them down. Then he started the song again from the beginning. After Loving the alien he stopped again and asked the crowd (in an angry voice) to stop pushing. After the band-intro Frampton photographed the crowd, Bowie: "We were in France. Bono asked me to send on his love and best wishes." Young Americans performed for the first time during this tour (a very nice version). They started the intro for Jean Genie 2 times. After a special version of White light white heat: "Delicious, delicious." A very good show. A must for every fan! After the show dinner at Casper and Giuimbini's.	2 CDR 2 CDR Tape Tape Video Video	*He's not an absolute beginner* *(No label, no number)* "They will be hurt" (Old Gold Records OGCD 415A/B) quality 8, 135 min. quality 8, 90 min. quality 6, 133 min. quality 9, 135 min.

Bowie: "Slane was like a holiday. The place is great and the crowd were responsive. There was one moment when I thought the crowd looked dangerous and I had to tell them to stop pushing, but it's been wonderful to be in Ireland" (Glass idol - David Currie 1987).

| <u>14-7-1987</u> Manchester, Football Grounds, Maine Road.
Support acts: Terrence Trent D'Arby and Alison Moyet.
Tickets: GBP. 15,—.
After Time will crawl Bowie ran to the front of the stage and pointed: "That shirt is new. You didn't wear that last | 2 CDR
2 CDR
2 CDR | Manchester heat
(Old Gold Records
OGCD 170A/B)
The Glass Spider at Maine Road
Manchester 14 July 1987 |

DATE / EVENT	AUDIO / VIDEO	TITLE

time."
After the show (at 2 A.M.) Bowie, Coco, Carlos and Gina of Starzone went to the pub of the Hotel. There they met Heidi (a Dutch girl who was pointed out by Bowie during the Turin concert on 18-7-1987). When the pub closed they went to a nearby disco called Applejacks to 4. A.M.

	2 CDR	*(BowieHobby)* Manchester 87 First Night (No label, no number)
	Tape	quality 9, 135 min.
	Video	quality 8, 126 min.
	Video	quality 9, 120 min.
	Video	quality 9, 135 min.
	Video	quality 9, 110 min.

<u>15-7-1987</u> Manchester, Football Grounds, Maine Road.
A good concert.
Nice guitar work during Loving the alien.
During the band intro Frampton takes photographs of the crowd and Bowie asks: "When will we get that back from the chemist?"

	2 CDR	*Main Road '87* (Old Gold Records OGCD 266A/B)
	1 CDR	*We ain't going nowhere* (No label, no number)
	CD	*Legendary Lost Tapes Vol. 2* (1 song) (VigOtone 179)
	2 CDR	*Maine Road Manchester July 15th 1987* (No label, no number)
	Tape	quality 8, 130 min.
	Tape	quality 9, 125 min.
	Video	quality 9, 129 min.
	Video	quality 8, 130 min.

15-7-1987 Italian TV. Bebop a Lula.
Report Rome concert (15/16-6-1987), interviews with fans, exclusive Bowie interview, comments by Lindsay Kemp.

	Video	20 min.

17-7-1987 Manchester Evening News. Article: Mr. Manchester's Bowie diary. Bowie steps out on the town.

17-7-1987 French Newspaper. Article by Jean-Marc Tardy: En concert ce soir a Nice Bowie, gentleman-rocker.

<u>17-7-1987</u> Nice, Stade De L'Ouest.
Tickets: Fr. Frs. 160,—. Started at 20.00 h.
Bowie uninspired and tired during the first part of the show.

	2 CDR	*Le roi de Nice* (Old Gold Records OGCD 267A/B)
	2 CDR	*Nice, July 17th '87* (No label, no number)
	Tape	quality 8, 125 min.
	Tape	quality 9, 135 min.

18-7-1987 Melody Maker. Article by Robert Matthew-Walker: Bowie fan dies.

<u>18-7-1987</u> Torino, Stadio Communale.
A very, very good and long (26 songs) show!
He messed up a part of the lyrics of Absolute beginners.
Bowie invited a Dutch girl (Heidi) on stage.
She had seen all the 1987 shows except Lyon.

	3 CDR	*Goodbye Europe* (No label, no number)
	2 CDR	Goodbye Europe (Old Gold Records OGCD 097A/B)

DATE / EVENT	AUDIO / VIDEO	TITLE
He met her in Manchester, on 14-7 after the concert. "The next song is for her. This one's called Beat of your drum." Zeroes was back again in the song list.	3 LP Tape	Goodbye Europe (Wildcat Record Company MCDS 007-99-B) quality 8, 135 min.
18-7-1987 Italian TV. RAI. Glass spider clip from 18-7-1987.	Video	1 min.
22-7-1987 Treffpunkt (German concert-report).	Tape	10 min.
27-7-1987 Philadelphia, Veterans Stadium. Press conf. A barbeque party.	LP Tape Tape	The Glass Spider Tour Press Conferences 1987 (Spider 101) US TV, All new record guide, 22 min. quality 10, 25 min.
27-7-1987 US TV. Channel 3. Eyewitness News. About press conference 27-7-1987 Philadelphia.	Video	quality 10, 1 min.
27-7-1987 US TV. MTV News. About press conference 27-7-1987 Philadelphia. Clip Time will crawl from Rotterdam 30 or 31-5-1987.	Video	quality 10, 2 min.
27-7-1987 US TV. Channel 29. Sam Riggold. About press conference 27-7-1987 Philadelphia. Clip Hang on to yourself (1973). Pepsi Cola ad.	Video	quality 10, 2 min.
27-7-1987 US TV. CNN. Showbizz Today. About press conference 27-7-1987 Philadelphia. Promo video Day in day out. Pepsi Cola ad.	Video	2 min.
27-7-1987 US TV. Entertainment Tonight News. About press conference Philadelphia 27-7-1987.	Video	1 min.
28-7-1987 Article by Steven M. Falk: Bowie, burgers and boogie.		
28-7-1987 Article by Mike Barnard: Bowie ready to spin web.		
28-7-1987 US TV. CNN Philadelphia. Show Biz Today, presented by Susan Washington. About Philadelphia Press Conference of 27-7-1987. Promo video Day in day out. Pepsi Cola ad.	Video	3 min.
28-7-1987 US TV. Good morning America. (4.22 + 10.00 min.) Exclusive interview. Promo videos. Pepsi ad.	Video Video	10 min. 5 min.
28-7-1987 US TV. All New Record Guide. About Philadelphia Press Conference 27-7-1987.	Video	22 min.

DATE / EVENT	AUDIO / VIDEO	TITLE
28-7-1987 US TV. Channel 4. Eyewitness News. About Philadelphia Press Conference 27-7-1987.	Video	1 min.
28-7-1987 US TV. Channel 2. News, presented by Jill Rappaport. About Philadelphia Press Conference 27-7-1987. Promo videos.	Video	3 min.
28-7-1987 US TV. Entertainment Tonight News. About Philadelphia Press Conference 27-7-1987.	Video	1 min.
29-7-1987 The Gazette. Article: Bowie set to launch extraordinarily expensive tour.		
29-7-1987 US TV. Channel 57. Philly Special. About Philadelphia Press Conference 27-7-1987. Promo videos and comments.	Video	44 min.
<u>29-7-1987</u> Philadelphia, Veterans Stadium. Sound check.	Tape	
30-7-1987 Channel 3. Evening Magazine. About Philadelphia Press Conference 27-7-1987. Live clips 1973. Promo videos. Pepsi Cola ad.	Video	6 min.
30-7-1987 Philadelphia Radio. WMMR. About Philadelphia Press Conference 27-7-1987.	Tape	30 min.
<u>30-7-1987</u> Philadelphia, Veterans Stadium. Support acts: Tommy Conwell, The Young Rumblers, Squeeze. Promoter: Electric Factory Concerts. Tickets: USD 21,—. Bowie not talkative and very concentrated. Rebel rebel was added to the song list. Zeroes and Dancing with the big boys where dropped. Parts of London bridge is falling down (traditional folk song) and War (The Temptations, 1970) during Fame.	3 CDR 2 CDR 2 CDR 2 CDR Tape Tape	*Philadelphia 30 July 1987 (BowieHobby)* Liberty spider (Old Gold Records OGCD 360A/B) Philly 87 First Night (No label, no number) Live in Philadelphia 30th July 87 (No label, no number) quality 8, 130 min. quality 9, 135 min.
30-7-1987 US TV. Channel 3. Glass Spider clip of 30-7-87.	Video	quality 8, 1 min.
30-7-1987 US TV. Channel 6. Glass Spider clip, interview with Toni Basil. Up the hill backwards.	Video	quality 7, 2 min.
30-7-1987 US TV. Eyewitness News. Tonight 3, presented by J. Barton. Glass spider clip of 30-7-1987.	Video	quality 7, 3 min.
31-7-1987 US TV. Channel 10. Local News. Glass spider clip of 30-7-1987.	Video	quality 7, 1 min.

DATE / EVENT	AUDIO / VIDEO	TITLE

31-7-1987 US TV. Entertainment Tonight. Video quality 8, 1 min.
Glass spider clip of 30-7-1987.

31-7-1987 The New York Times. Article by John Pareles: Music: Bowie's Glass Spider Tour.

<u>31-7-1987</u> Philadelphia, Veterans Stadium. Tape quality 8, 130 min.
Bowie not in a good mood. But the first part of the concert Tape quality 9, 135 min.
was very good and Bowie sang very clearly.
For the last time Dancing with the big boys and Zeroes.

July / August 1987 In Fashion (US). Article: Turner & Bowie forever cool.

August 1987 US TV. America's Top of the Pops. Video 5 min.
Never let me down (live).

August 1987 Release Never let me down (3.58) / '87 And cry (3.52) (EMI EA 239).

August 1987 Release 12" Never let me down (Extended Dance remix) (7.03) / Never let me down (Dub mix) (3.57) / Never let me down (A Capella) (2.03) (EMI 12EA 239).

August 1987 Released in Japan: Never let me down (Extended dance remix) (7.03) / Never let me down (7"Remix edit) (3.58) / Never let me down (Dub mix) (3.57) / Never let me down (A Capella) (2.03) / Never let me down (instrumental) (4.02) / '87 And cry (single version) (3.52) (EMI CP20 5520).

The Never let me down video was based on Sydney Pollack's 1969 movie They Shoot Horses Don't They?

August 1987 Musician. Article by Scott Isler: David Bowie opens up - a little.
Isler wrote: "He invariably agrees with opinions. Like James Dean, one of his idols, Bowie prefers to mirror an interviewer rather than open a window to his own personality."

August 1987 Creem. Article by Roy Trakin: Never let me down.

1-8-1987 David, Carmine and Richard visited The China Club in New York.

2-8-1987 The New York Times. Article by Jon Pareles: Bowie creates a spectacle.

<u>2-8-1987</u> East Rutherford, Giants Stadium. 2 CDR *Live in East Rutherford*
Support acts: Squeeze, Lisa Lisa, Cult Jam.   *(No label, no number)*
Great version of Heroes. Sons of the silent age was played 2 CDR *Live At Giants' Stadium - East*
in the first part of the show.   *Rutherford*
"And you are all Young Americans." Tape quality 9, 135 min.
Fame included a part of London bridge is falling down
(traditionnel folk song).
The band stayed in New York.

2-8-1987 US TV. Eyewitness News, presented by Video quality 8, 1 min.

DATE / EVENT	AUDIO / VIDEO	TITLE

Rolonda Watts. Glass Spider clip of 2-8-1987.

2-8-1987 US TV. New York. News (22.00 h.). — Video — quality 9, 1 min.
Glass Spider clip of 2-8-1987.

2-8-1987 US TV. Channel 7. News. — Video — quality 9, 1 min.
Glass Spider clip of 2-8-1987.

3-8-1987 US TV. Channel 4. News. — Video — quality 9, 2 min.
Glass Spider clip of 2-8-1987 and audience report.

3-8-1987 US TV. CNN. Show Biz Today, presented by — Video — quality 7, 3 min.
Liz Wickersham.
Portrait of Carlos Alomar. Glass Spider clip of 2-8-1987.

3-8-1987 Music Performance. Article by Anthony DeCurtis: David Bowie, Giants Stadium.

3-8-1987 Music. Article by Patrick Stearns: Bowie live: Forget theatrics, let's dance.

<u>3-8-1987</u> East Rutherford, Giants Stadium. — 2 CDR — *Giants Stadium New York 87*
Support act: Squeeze. — — *(No label, no number)*
A very average concert. The dance routines were sloppy. — 2 CDR — *Sons of the Spider*
During Up the hill backwards the music stopped for a few — — *(Old Gold Records*
seconds, after which they continued the song. — — *OGCD 361A/B)*
During Bang bang Bowie kept repeating "I know…I know" — 2 CDR — *Glass Spider live at Giants*
for some time. — — *Stadium (No label, no number)*
A reviewer wrote in Rolling Stone: "The show was like the — Tape — quality 9, 125 min.
Glass Spider itself, large and meaningless. When Bowie
cast off the frills and ripped through Rebel rebel and China
girl, he displayed all the authority for which his shows are
renowned. Unfortunately, they only served to make the
excesses more apparent, and the experience of suffering
through them more frustrating."

7-8-1987 KRQR Radio (97.3 FM). — Tape — quality 9, 10 min.
Bowie phone-in to Mercy Hawkes.

<u>7-8-1987</u> San Jose, Spartan Stadium. — 2 CDR — *Okey Jose?*
A great show. One big sing-along! — — *(Old Gold Records*
Young Americans ended with: "La, la, la, la, la." — — *OGCD 362A/B)*
Before Fame: "Thanks for your love. Thanks for your — Tape — quality 8, 135 min.
chewing gum." (The gum was thrown on stage). — Tape — quality 9, 130 min.
 — Tape — quality 9, 5 min.

7-8-1987 US TV. Channel 11. News (8.00 hours), by — Video — quality 8, 3 min.
Brian Beirne. Glass Spider clip of 2-8-1987, New York
rehearsals, interview, London 3-7-1973.

<u>8-8-1987</u> Anaheim (Los Angeles), Anaheim Stadium. — Tape — quality 7, 20 min.

DATE / EVENT	AUDIO / VIDEO	TITLE

Sound check.

<u>8-8-1987</u> Anaheim (Los Angeles), Anaheim Stadium. Support act: Siouxsie & The Banshees. Tickets: USD 22,50. Attendance: 58.000.
"Very impressive, good looking crowd tonight, when we started coming on today. Like a David Lee Roth wet dream or a David Bowie wet dream."
Up the hill backwards did not have the spoken intro, the tape recorder refused. During All the madmen he sang: "Gimme some good old LSD."
After Jean Genie the band started playing Let's dance. The band coordination wasn't right.
Bowie shouted annoyed: "Hold it! This is a song by the Velvet Underground: White light, Black heat."
Earl Slick guest guitarist for White light white heat. Then they tried Let's dance again (and the beginning of the song again didn't sound right).

	1 CDR	*Mighty spider of Anaheim (No label, no number)*
	2 CDR	*Earl's return (Old Gold Records OGCD 363A/B)*
	2 CDR	*Live in Anaheim 8th august 1987 (No label, no number)*
	Tape	quality 8, 135 min.

8-8-1987 US TV. MTV Week in review.
Glass Spider clip and interview of 2-8-1987.

	Video	quality 9, 1 min.

<u>9-8-1987</u> Anaheim (Los Angeles), Anaheim Stadium.
"Time will crawl till the 21st century fall, to the 21st century loose." A little mistake in a splendid song.
Blue Jean had a wildly dancing Tony Basil.
Earl Slick guest guitarist for White light white heat.

	2 CDR	Slick as ever (Old Gold Records OGCD 364A/B)
	2 CDR	Total Young Americans (No label, no number)
	Tape	quality 9, 135 min.

10-8-1987 Los Angeles Times. Article by Robert Hilburn: David Bowie spins a glitzy web.

<u>12-8-1987</u> Denver, Mile High Stadium.
Sound check from 12.00 to 13.15 hours.

	Tape	

<u>12-8-1987</u> Denver, Mile High Stadium.
Good concert. Bowie not talkative, but in a good mood and working very hard. Strange version of Time will crawl.
"We've had everything. Good food, good company and Denver throats. But that's okay, we'll sing on."
He stopped during Let's dance and decided to go on with White light white heat.
In Fame he messed up most of the lyrics! The song also had some notes of Dancing in the street (Martha Reeves and the Vandellas, 1964).

	2 CDR	Absolute '87 (Old Gold Records OGCD 365A/B)
	Tape	quality 8, 135 min.
	Tape	quality 9, 130 min.

13-8-1987 Rocky Mountain News. Article by Justin Mirchell: Bowie warm-up lacked only roar of the crowd.

<u>14-8-1987</u> Portland, Civic Auditorium.

	Tape	

DATE / EVENT	AUDIO / VIDEO	TITLE
Sound check, 3 songs.		
14-8-1987 Portland, Civic Auditorium.	2 CDR	Problems in Portland
An average concert. Attendance: 30.000.	*2 CDR*	*Portland 14 Aug 1987*
They had some sound problems.		*(BowieHobby)*
Bowie talked about taping sound checks.	2 CDR	Live in Portland 14th August 1987
		(No label, no number)
	Tape	quality 8, 135 min.
	Tape	quality 9, 130 min.
15-8-1987 The Vancouver Sun. Article: Bowie extravaganza to start early.		
15-8-1987 Vancouver, B.C. Place Stadium.	Tape	quality 8, 135 min.
Support acts: Georgia Satellites, Duran Duran.	Tape	quality 9, 135 min.
Tickets: USD 39,— to USD 300,—.		
During Day in day out Bowie and the backing-singers started singing different parts of the song!		
During China girl a balloon with the words: David we love you, was lifted from the audience and Bowie started laughing.		
16-8-1987 In the Afternoon the band arrived in Edmonton.		
17-8-1987 Edmonton, Commonwealth Stadium.	NT	
18-8-1987 Radio Los Angeles (102.7 FM).	Tape	quality 9, 15 min.
Interview with Rick Dees (Kiss). Talks about Bowie.		
18-8-1987 Bowie went to the Garrick Theatre in Winnipeg to see "La Bamba." Afterwards David and Joey went to the Ichi Ban Japanese Steakhouse for a late dinner (Return of the Spiderman - Peter Frederiksen 1988).		
19-8-1987 Billboard. Article by D.Wykoff: Box set full of Sound & Vision signifying Bowie.		
19-8-1987 Journal. Article by Helen Metella: Bowie's stage a feat in itself.		
19-8-1987 Winnipeg, Winnipeg Stadium.	NT	
Support acts: Georgia Satellites (30 min), Duran Duran (90 min).		
A great show!		
19-8-1987 After the show some band members (Carmine Rojas, Carlos Alomar and Alan Childs) went to the Blue Note Café. Together with the local musicians Monika Deol from Perfect Kiss and Russ Goozee from Hypnogogo they played 30 minutes of blues songs and a 20-minute funk jam of Fame.	NT	

DATE / EVENT	AUDIO / VIDEO	TITLE

20-8-1987 Minneapolis.
Cancelled.

20-8-1987 Winnipeg Free Press. Article by Randal McIlroy: Show rates as triumph of flash.

<u>21-8-1987</u> Chicago, Rosemont Horizon.   *2 CDR*   *Chicago 21 August 1987*
Not a good show. Bowie looked tired.   *(BowieHobby)*
Riots during the concert.   *2 CDR*   Chicago 87 First Night
                                                                 (No label, no number)
                                                                  Tape   quality 9, 130 min.

<u>22-8-1987</u> Chicago, Rosemont Horizon.   *Tape*   quality 8, 135 min.
An average concert.
During Heroes Bowie sang: "We can be Helden."

<u>24-8-1987</u> Toronto, Molson C.N.E. Stadium.   *Tape*   quality 9, 135 min.
Great concert!   *Tape*   quality 8, 120 min.
When Bowie entered the stage, sitting in his chair, he
waved at the crowd as a prince.

<u>25-8-1987</u> Toronto, Molson C.N.E. Stadium.   *Tape*   quality 8, 130 min.
Support acts: Duran Duran, Northern Pikes.   *Tape*   quality 9, 110 min.
Great concert!   *Video*   quality 8, 76 min.

26-8-1987 The Toronto Globe. Article: Bowie's spectacle dazzles.

<u>28-8-1987</u> Ottawa, Lansdowne Park.   *2 CDR*   *Smiling through the darkness*
Support acts: Duran Duran, Eight Seconds.   *(No label, no number)*
Attendance: 29.000.   *(10 songs)*
Good, but average concert.   *2 CDR*   *Canadian Time*
                                                                  (Old Gold Records
                                                                  OGCD 366A/B)
                                                                  2 CDR   Caught in the soundboard web
                                                                  3 CDR   Live in Ottawa
                                                                  (No label, no number)
                                                                  Tape   quality 8, 130 min.

29-8-1987 Citizen. Article by Greg Barr: 29.000 Fans get caught in Bowie's web.

<u>30-8-1987</u> Montreal, Olympic Stadium (Forum).   *2 CD*   *Never let me down*
Attendance: 75.000. Show sponsored by Toyota.   *(Templar Records*
Show broadcast on BBC Radio 1.   *TCD 18-A/B)*
Show broadcast on KBFH (30-8-1987).   *CD*   *Montreal 87 vol.1*
Released on KBFH CD special in 1988 and 1998.   *(Glass Idol LTD. 870830-1)*
Show broadcast on Radiobroadland (8-7-1988).   *CD*   *Montreal 87 vol.2*
                                                                    (Glass Idol LTD. 870830)
A good show.   *3 CD*   *Montreal connection*
Bowie not talkative, but very concentrated.   *(Papillion Records CD 008)*
When Bowie knows a show will be broadcast he always   *CD*   *The fall of the Glass Spider*

DATE / EVENT	AUDIO / VIDEO	TITLE
works extra hard to do a good show. The Bootlegs of this concert are of a superb quality. If you want a souvenir of the 1987 tour, get the CD The fall of the Glass Spider (for the quality) or Never let me down (this 2 CD is complete).	CD CD CD	*(Dr. GIG DGCD 013)* Let's dance (On Stage 12058) *Montreal 1988 (Red Line Post Script CD 1255)* Unlicensed David Bowie live (SW 93)
Never let me down shown on 19-9-1987 during the MTV Video Music Awards.	2 CDR 2 CD	*Glass idol (PD 81999)* *Glass spider concert special (DIR Broadcasting Corp.)*
1. Glass spider (9.38). 2. Day in day out (4.32). 3. Bang bang (4.09). 4. Absolute beginners (7.10). 5. Loving the alien (7.07). 6. China girl (4.52). 7. Rebel rebel (3.23). 8. Fashion (5.02). 9. Scary monsters (4.56). 10. All the madmen (6.28). 11. Never let me down (3.54). 12. Big brother (4.47). 13. '87 And cry (4.12). 14. Zeroes (5.10). 15. Sons of the silent age (2.59). 16. Time will crawl (5.20). 17. Young Americans (5.04). 18. Beat of your drum (4.35). 19. The Jean Genie (5.21). 20. Let's dance (4.58). 21. Fame (6.46). 22. Time (5.08). 23. Blue jean (3.20). 24. Modern love (4.00).	2 CDR CD CDS 2 LP LP 3 LP Tape Tape Tape Tape Tape	*Spyder Glass (KBFH)* (No label, no number) King Biscuit Flower Hour 1998 (K.B. Radio Corp.) Bang bang, Promo, EMI Bon soir Montreal part one (Dragon Fly Records DFR 1/2) Bon soir Montreal part two (Dragon Fly Records DFR 3) Welcome to the show (DFR 1/2/3 A/B) quality 7, 130 min. quality 9, 130 min. quality 8, 135 min. quality 10, 130 min. quality 10, 40 min. (11 songs)

September 1987 Release Video - Smash hits, various artists compilation (Under pressure, including lots of screaming women).

September 1987 Record Collector. Article by Marshall Jarman: David Bowie: Rare picture sleeve singles 1967-71.

<u>1-9-1987</u> New York, Madison Square Garden. Bowie worked very hard and put his whole soul into the show. Great concert. A lot of flowers on the stage. "It looks like a garden here. Madison Garden I suppose." During Young Americans he missed a part of the lyrics and filled in the gap by singing "La, la, la, la." During Time: "His script is you and me, boy, time, time, time, time and one more time… time." Other parts of the song had a completely different lyric. Strange version!	*2 CDR* 2 CDR 2 CDR 2 CDR	*Broadway Spider* *(No label, no number)* Magic Garden (Old Gold Records OGCD 367A/B) Madison Square Garden '87 (No label, no number) Glass Spider 9.1.1987 (No label, no number)

DATE / EVENT	AUDIO / VIDEO	TITLE
	Tape	quality 9, 135 min.
1-9-1987 US TV. Eyewitness News. Glass spider clip of 1-9-1987.	Video	2 min.
2-9-1987 Article by David Fricke: David Bowie Madison Square Garden, New York City.		
2-9-1987 Article by Mary Campbell: Flamboyant David Bowie is rock's renaissance man.		
<u>2-9-1987</u> New York, Madison Square Garden.	2 CDR	Loving the garden (Old Gold Records OGCD 368A/B)
	2 CDR	Spider at the Madison (No label, no number)
	Tape	quality 9, 135 min.
	Tape	quality 9, 125 min.
	Tape	quality 9, 25 min.
<u>3-9-1987</u> Foxboro, Sullivan Stadium. Tickets: USD 22,50. A good concert, with a lot of improvising in the lyrics and Bowie joined the dancers.	*2 CDR*	*Foxboro 3 September 1987 (BowieHobby)*
	2 CDR	Foxboro '87 (No label, no number)
	2 CDR	Tape will crawl (NEO
	2 CDR	Foxboro says 'Hi' (Artwork by Saloca 2004)
	Tape	quality 9, 135 min.
4-9-1987 The Globe. Article by Jim Sullivan: Bowie's daring risk pays off.		
<u>6-9-1987</u> Chapel Hill, Dean Dome (Dean Smith Centre). Attendance: 15,000. An average concert.	Tape	quality 8, 135 min.
	Tape	quality 9, 135 min.
<u>7-9-1987</u> Chapel Hill, Dean Dome (Dean Smith Centre). A great concert! During Absolute beginners he took some flowers of a girl in the front row and held her hand for the rest of the song. At the end of the concert: "We will do some songs we don't usually do." Bowie took Alomar's guitar and Alomar had to find another one. "This is one of the first rock songs ever written. It's called I wanna be your dog." The original version was by Iggy Pop and The Stooges in 1969.	*2 CDR*	*Tar Heel Spider* (No label, no number)
	2 CDR	I wanna be your dog (Old Gold Records OGCD 369A/B)
	Tape	quality 8, 135 min.
<u>10-9-1987</u> Milwaukee, Marcus Amphitheatre. Sound check. One of the songs: I wanna be your dog.	NT	
<u>10-9-1987</u> Milwaukee, Marcus Amphitheatre. A very good concert. Bowie in a very good mood. "As we have not got any curfew we will do some extra	2 CDR	Wisconsin doggy style
	2 CDR	*Milwaukee 10 Sept 1987 (BowieHobby)*

DATE / EVENT	AUDIO / VIDEO	TITLE
songs. I hope you like it, it's called I wanna be your dog."	2 CDR	Live in Milwaukee Sep 10th 87 (No label, no number)
	Tape	quality 8, 135 min.
	Tape	quality 8, 120 min.
	Tape	quality 8, 140 min.
11-9-1987 Milwaukee, Marcus Amphitheatre. A very good concert. After Time: "We like to make assholes of ourselves sometimes… One of our favourite old songs called White light white heat." After this song: "Clap along and join the chorus. It's a little ditty called I wanna be your dog."	Tape	quality 8, 135 min.
	Tape	quality 8, 140 min.
	Video	quality 6, 11 min.
12-9-1987 Pontiac (Detroit), Pontiac Silverdome. Attendance: 35.000. Tickets: USD 20,—. "We haven't been given any curfews, so we'll see if we can take this show through twelve o'clock. It was written by Iggy Pop and the Stooges and it's called I wanna be your dog."	Tape	quality 9, 135 min.
	Tape	quality 9, 140 min.
13-9-1987 Superchannel: 20 Years of modern music. Part 1: The London Press Conference 20-3-1987. Part 2: The EMI press kit. Part 3: Interview backstage Manchester 15-7-1987.	Video	58 min.
14-9-1987 Lexington, Rupp Arena. Attendance: 9.000. Tickets: USD 18,50. Bowie was caught by the great crowd response, although he did not dance much. Parts of London Bridge is falling down and Lavender blue (dilly dilly) (original by Mary Martin in 1948) during Fame.	2 CDR	Lavender blue (Old Gold Records OGCD 370A/B)
	2 CDR	Lexington '87
	2 CDR	*Rupp!* *(No label, no number)*
	Tape	quality 9, 135 min.
16-9-1987 Recording for Top of the Pops. Never let me down (4.18), broadcast 25-9-1987. Time will crawl, broadcast 4-12-1987.	CD	*Look back in anger (1)* *(No label, no number)*
	2 CDR	*Hendrikse various vol. 4* *(No label, no number)*
	2 CDR	*Hendrikse various vol. 14* *(No label, no number)*
	Tape	quality 10, 5 min.
	Tape	quality 10, 5 min.
	Video	*Various 10 (5 min)*
18-9-1987 Miami, Orange Bowl. Attendance: 50.000. Not a good show. The air conditioning under the stage was out of order. During the concert Bowie commented on the temperature: "Oh you make it hot here… don't you. You make it hot."	2 CDR	"You make it hot" (Old Gold Records OGCD 371A/B)
	2 CDR	Miami 87 (No label, no number)
	Tape	quality 9, 130 min.

DATE / EVENT	AUDIO / VIDEO	TITLE

19-9-1987 TV Week. Article: Out of the spider's web.

<u>19-9-1987</u> Tampa, Tampa Stadium (Auditorium).　　　2 CDR　　Showbizz
Attendance: 32.000.　　　　　　　　　　　　　　　　　　　　　(Old Gold Records
Bowie's voice is very clear, also in the high notes.　　　　　　　　OGCD 372A/B)
Young Americans is done without the band-intro.　　Tape　　quality 9, 135 min.
The band was introduced after the first encore (Time).　Tape　quality 8, 135 min.
　　　　　　　　　　　　　　　　　　　　　　　　　Tape　　quality 9, 125 min.
　　　　　　　　　　　　　　　　　　　　　　　　　Tape　　quality 9, 40 min.

19-9-1987 MTV. Video Music Awards.　　　　　　　Tape
Never let me down (live, from Montreal 30-8-1987).　Video

<u>21-9-1987</u> Atlanta, The Omni (Omni Arena).　　　　2 CDR　　"Talk about fame"
"Okay you guys, you're in trouble now. These are a couple　　　(Old Gold Records
we play when we really want to torture our audience, and　　　OGCD 373A/B)
you're a pretty nice audience, so we're gonna torture you.　Tape　quality 8, 135 min.
It's called I wanna be your dog."　　　　　　　　　Tape　　quality 8, 100 min.
White light white heat is played in the rock version.
During Blue Jean Bowie forgets to start singing and when
he starts, he has forgotten the words, to his own
amusement.

22-9-1987 When they left the hotel to go to the concert they were (as usual) waiting for Carlos Alomar.
The band members all wore T-shirts with different messages printed on it, with funny remarks about
Carlos always being late (Return of the Spiderman - Peter Frederiksen 1988).
The hotel had won the Most Pretentious Hotel Award. Some of the band members were reprimanded
by the hotel management for not wearing jackets in the lounge (Shining star - Marshall Jarman and
Friends 1988).

<u>22-9-1987</u> Atlanta, The Omni (Omni Arena).　　　　2 CDR　　Atlanta Spider
Not a good concert. Bowie's voice was weak.　　　　　　　　　(Old Gold Records
The intro to Jean Genie was played on guitar by Carlos　　　　　OGCD 374A/B)
Alomar (a joke from Carlos?).　　　　　　　　　　　Tape　　quality 9, 130 min.

<u>25-9-1987</u> Hartford, Civic Centre.　　　　　　　　　2 CDR　　*Hartford 25 September 1987*
A very good show. Tickets: USD 21,50.　　　　　　　　　　　*(BowieHobby)*
During All the madmen Constance was sitting at the front of　2 CDR　Hartford 87
the stage. She had a doll in her hands. For a joke they had　　　　(Old Gold Records
given the doll a pair of glasses. Bowie smiled, took the doll　　　　OGCD 375A/B)
out of her hands and showed it to the crowd.　　　　2 CDR　　Hartford 87
　　　　　　　　　　　　　　　　　　　　　　　　　　　　　　(No label, no number)
　　　　　　　　　　　　　　　　　　　　　　　　　Tape　　quality 8, 135 min.

25-9-1987 UK TV. BBC. Top of the Pops. Never let me down (4.18). Recorded 16-9-1987.

25-9-1987 US TV. Channel 3. Eyewitness News.　　　Video　　1 min.
Glass spider clip of 25-9-1987.

DATE / EVENT	AUDIO / VIDEO	TITLE

26-9-1987 The Courant. Article by Roger Catlin: Glittery, garish, and good Bowie.

26-9-1987 US TV. The Record Guide.
Report press conference in Philadelphia on 27-7-1987.
Various Promo videos.
 — Video — 23 min.

28-9-1987 Landover (Washington), Capitol Centre.
Attendance: 19.000.
Enthusiastic crowd, but musically a very dull concert.
"Up until one hundred years ago" and then a part is
not even audible because of the great crowd response!

	2 CDR	*Don't look down Tonight* (No label, no number)
	Tape	quality 9, 135 min.
	Tape	quality 9, 125 min.

29-9-1987 Landover (Washington), Capitol Centre.
A great concert and a great crowd. Attendance: 19.000.
During China Girl: "She said oh David, just you shut
your mouth." Great version of White light white heat.
"Thank you, see you again. Happy Christmas."

	2 CDR	"Merry Christmas!" (Old Gold Records OGCD 376A/B)
	2 CDR	*Capital Spidre* (No label, no number)
	2 CDR	Live at the Capitol Centre Landover 29/9/87 (No label, no number)
	Tape	quality 9, 135 min.
	Tape	quality 9, 130 min.

October 1987 Release 1966 (12" repackage of the Pye singles and B-sides) (Pye PRT PYE 6001 / PYX 6001).

October 1987 Australian TV. The Noise.
Sydney Press Conference and Young Americans and Jean
Genie.
 — Video

October 1987 Published: Behind the Spider - Simon Deun and Antoine Loogman (P.S. Productions).
Self published, no ISBN number.

October 1987 Rock Bill. Article: The Glass Spider Issue.

1-10-1987 Minneapolis, St. Paul Civic Centre.
An average concert.
Bowie and the band not very inspired.
During Young Americans Bowie sings: "Ain't you proud
that you still got faces." During Jean Genie a guitar line
from Satisfaction (Rolling Stones, 1965).

	2 CDR	*An ordinary show* (Old Gold Records OGCD 377A/B)
	2 CDR	*Minneapolis 1 October 1987* (BowieHobby)
	2 CDR	Minneapolis 87 First Night (No label, no number)
	2 CDR	White eyed fish in Minneapolis
	Tape	quality 9, 130 min.

2-10-1987 Minneapolis, St. Paul Civic Centre.
An average concert.
Bang bang had a long instrumental intro and Bowie

	2 CDR	*Minneapolis 2 October 1987* (BowieHobby)
	2 CDR	Tiny wails, tiny cries

DATE / EVENT	AUDIO / VIDEO	TITLE
repeated several times: "Let's go!"	2 CDR	Minneapolis 1987 (A Dutch Connection CD 02101987)
	Tape	quality 9, 135 min.
	Tape	quality 8, 140 min.
4-10-1987 Kansas City, Kemper Arena.	Tape	quality 8, 105 min.

5-10-1987 Article by Brian McTavish: Music accompanies fantastic Bowie visuals.

6-10-1987 New Orleans, Superdome. A very good concert, but a lot of echo in the hall. During Jean Genie Frampton played a few notes of Satisfaction (Rolling Stones, 1965). During Fame Bowie forgot to start singing and the band had to play the intro twice.	2 CDR	On Creole ground (Old Gold Records OGCD 378A/B)
	2 CDR	New Orleans 87 (No label, no number)
	Tape	quality 8, 135 min.
	Tape	quality 9, 125 min.
7-10-1987 Houston, The Summit. Attendance: 16.500. "The last sad time when we came here there was glass in the streets. I think it was in '83 a tornado just came through. That was really sad. But nice to hear the oil prices got up a dollar today." Great version of Jean Genie. For one reason or another at the beginning of the song Bowie shouts: "Oh, church."	2 CDR	Master of Houston (Old Gold Records OGCD 379A/B)
	2 CDR	*Summit, Houston Texas - Oct. 7th '87* (No label, no number)
	Tape	quality 9, 130 min.
8-10-1987 Houston, The Summit. A very good concert.	Tape	quality 9, 130 min.

Wanda Lee Nichols accused Bowie of raping her at a Dallas hotel on 9-10-1987. She was photographed covered in bite marks. Bowie had met her through drummer Alan Childs. 6 Weeks later Bowie admitted having sex with her and agreed to take an AIDS test. February 1990 A grand jury in Dallas dismissed the case.

10-10-1987 Dallas, Reunion Arena. Sound check (late in the afternoon). Loving the alien with Carlos Alomar taking the vocals. With Bowie doing the vocals: Rebel rebel, Jean Genie, Loving the alien, Day in day out, All the madmen, Glass spider, White light white heat (Charlie Sexton on guitar).	NT	
10-10-1987 Dallas, Reunion Arena. Tickets: USD 20,—. Promoter: Race Concerts. "Dallas… Longhorns… Are there any Longhorns here tonight? Here are some of my Longhorns" and he introduces the band. Bowie introduced Charlie Sexton on stage: "He's been hanging out with us for some days, so we figured the least	2 CDR	*Dallas 10 October 1987* (BowieHobby)
	2 CDR	*Glass Spider Tour Dallas 1987* (No label, no number)
	2 CDR	Introducing Charlie (Old Gold Records OGCD 380A/B)

DATE / EVENT	AUDIO / VIDEO	TITLE
we could do is to get him on stage and this song is called White light white heat."	2 CDR Tape Tape	Dallas 10 Oct 87 quality 9, 135 min. quality 9, 140 min.
10-10-1987 Radio special (repeated 17-10-1987). DIR Broadcasting Corp., 32 East 57th Street, New York.	2 CD	*Glass spider concert special* *(DIR Broadcasting Corp.)*
11-10-1987 Schiedam, De Erker. Fan-meeting Dutch Fanzine David Bowie Now.		
<u>11-10-1987</u> Dallas, Reunion Arena. A very good concert. During White light white heat and I wanna be your dog guest appearance by Charlie Sexton.	NT	
<u>13-10-1987</u> Los Angeles, Sports Arena. Bowie very talkative. Beat of your drum was removed from the song list.	2 CDR Tape	The L.A. Spider (Old Gold Records OGCD 404A/B) quality 9, 135 min.
<u>14-10-1987</u> Los Angeles, Sports Arena. A very good concert, and Bowie did a lot of improvising. During the song Big brother Richard Cottle played an unusual keyboard part. He ended Time with: "He speaks of anything." During White light white heat and I wanna be your dog guest appearance by Charlie Sexton.	3 CDR 2 CDR 2 CDR 2 CDR Tape Tape	*Los Angeles 14 October 1987* *(BowieHobby)* "On lead vocal…" (Old Gold Records OGCD 381A/B) *Hollywood spider* *(No label, no number)* Los Angeles 87 (No label, no number) quality 9, 135 min. quality 9, 140 min.
17-10-1987 Radio special (same as 10-10-1987). DIR Broadcasting Corp., 32 East 57th Street, New York.	2 CD	*Glass spider concert special* *(DIR Broadcasting Corp.)*
Bowie had a short break in London. 25-10-1987 Bowie and the band arrived in Sydney.		
<u>27-10-1987</u> Sydney, The Tivoli, 656 George Street. Press conference (started at 13.00 hours). 1. Bang bang. 2. Young Americans. 3. Interview (13.02). 4. The Jean Genie.	CD 2 CDR 2 CDR CDS VCD	*The Glass Spider Tour - Press conferences 1987* *(Wax Records Spider101CD)* *Glass spider* *(No label, no number)* Very Short! (Old Gold Records OGCD 382A/B) Press conference, Tivoli Club, Sydney, Australia, 27-10-1987 (Spider 3 A1/B1) *I keep a good friend…* *(No label, no number)*

DATE / EVENT	AUDIO / VIDEO	TITLE
	VCD	Videobits Volume 2 (No label, no number)
	LP	The Glass Spider Tour Press Conferences 1987 (Spider 101)
	Single	Down Under
	Tape	Australian TV, The Noise, 14 minutes.
	Tape	quality 8, 40 min.
27-10-1987 Channel 28. The Noise. Young Americans, Jean Genie. Interview from 27-10-87.	Video	13.08 min.
27-10-1987 Australian TV. News. Clips of Jean Genie and Young Americans from press conference 27-10-1987.	Video	1.21 min.
27-10-1987 Channel 7. TWT. TV ad. Clips of Jean Genie and Bang bang from 27-10-1987.	Video	1 min.
27-10-1987 Channel 7. TWT. Promo medley. Jean Genie and Bang bang from 27-10-87.	Video	5 min.
27-10-1987 Australian TV. TV News. About Bowie accused of raping. Clips of Jean Genie and Young Americans from press conference 27-10-1987.	Video	4 min.
27-10-1987 Australian TV. Today. TV ad. Clip of Jean Genie from 27-10-1987. Part video clip Time will crawl.	Video	2 min.
27-10-1987 Australian TV. Today. Part video clip Day in day out. Clips of Jean Genie and Bang bang from 27-10-1987.	Video	5 min.
27-10-1987 Eyewitness News. Ten. Report about press conference in Sydney 27-10-1987.	Video	1 min.
27-10-1987 Channel 7. Sound. Bowie ad prizes.	Video	1 min.
27-10-1987 Channel 7. Terry Willesee Tonight. Promo medley. Report about press conference in Sydney 27-10-1987.	Video	5 min.
27-10-1987 Channel 7. News. Report about press conference in Sydney 27-10-1987.	Video	1.30 min.
27-10-1987 Channel 2. ABC News. Report about press conference in Sydney 27-10-1987,	Video	1.28 min.

DATE / EVENT	AUDIO / VIDEO	TITLE

including clip Jean Genie.

28-10-1987 Channel 10. Good Morning Australia. Video 4 min.
Report about press conference in Sydney 27-10-1987,
with clips Bang bang, Jean Genie and Young Americans.

Bowie: "It's very hard to convince people that you can be quite different off stage in rock 'n' roll that you are on stage. One of the principles in rock is that it's the person himself expressing what he really and truly feels, and that applies to a lot of artists. But to me it doesn't. It never did. I always saw it as a theatrical experience."

<u>29-10-1987</u> Brisbane, Boondall Entertainment Centre. NT
Bowie tensed and this made it a very average concert.
Beat of your drum was back on the song list.

30-10-1987 Channel 2. The Factory. Video 9 min.
Report about press conference in Sydney 27-10-1987.

30-10-1987 Channel 2. The Factory (repeated). Video 9 min.
Report about press conference in Sydney 27-10-1987.

30-10-1987 Channel 7. Sounds. Video 4 min.
Promo medley.
Report about press conference in Sydney 27-10-1987.

30-10-1987 Channel 7. News. Video 1 min.
Report and clip of Glass spider from 29-10-1987.

30-10-1987 Article by Philip McLean: Bowie's spider a bit much.

<u>30-10-1987</u> Brisbane, Boondall Entertainment Center. NT
Sound check.

<u>30-10-1987</u> Brisbane, Boondall Entertainment Center. *2 CDR* *Brisbane 30 Oct 1987*
A very nice concert.   *(BowieHobby)*
At the beginning of Heroes Bowie stopped. Later he started *2 CDR* Live in Brisbane 30th Oct 87
again from the beginning.   (No label, no number)
                                                            Tape quality 8, 130 min.
                                                            Tape quality 7, 110 min.

30-10-1987 Australian TV. Channel 7. News. Video 1 min.
Glass spider clip of 29-10-1987.

31-10-1987 New Musical Express. Article by Frank Owen: Fans, fantasy and Bowie.

November 1987 Theatre Crafts. Article by Mark Loeffler: Designer remedies for Bowie's theatre bug. Sometimes it is bleak expressionism. Other times melodrama. Sometimes it is a circus. Other times grand opera. Sometimes it is even rock-and-roll. But, always, it is theatre.

DATE / EVENT	AUDIO / VIDEO	TITLE

<u>3-11-1987</u> Sydney, Entertainment Center.
Attendance: 10.000.
It was very hot and Bowie joked during the band intro: "On air conditioning… nobody."

2 CDR — *Smiling through the darkness (No label, no number) (8 songs)*

2 CDR — Caught in the soundboard web

2 CDR — Sydney (No label, no number)

Tape — quality 9, 130 min.

4-11-1987 Article by Chris Blanche: Bowie rocks in with the spectacular.

4-11-1987 Channel 7. News.
Clip Glass spider from 3-11-1987.

Video — 1 min.

4-11-1987 Channel 9. News.
Clip Glass spider from 3-11-1987.

Video — 1 min.

4-11-1987 Channel 10. News.
Clip Glass spider from 3-11-1987.

Video — 1 min.

4-11-1987 Channel 7. Sounds.
Peter Frampton interview. Clips Jean Genie from 27-10-1987 and Glass spider from 3-11-1987.

Video — 6 min.

<u>4-11-1987</u> Sydney, Entertainment Center.
Attendance: 10.000. A great concert!
During China girl he sang: "I feel tragic, like I'm Billy Idol."
Bowie told a story about meeting Carlos Alomar for the first time and a woman called Shirlie Abagail (she did an English television programme).
During White light white heat and I wanna be your dog guest appearance by Charlie Sexton.
During Modern love they threw a koala on stage and Bowie sang: "I know when to go out. I know when to stay in and feed my koala."

2 CDR — *Smiling through the darkness (No label, no number) (8 songs)*

2 CDR — Caught in the soundboard web

Tape — quality 9, 130 min.

Tape — quality 8, 125 min.

Article by Lynden Barber: Bowie in middle-aged confusion.
Article by Paul Ellis: Frampton comes alive again.
Article by Celie Gannon: Bowie and spider weave a web of joyful jumping.

<u>6-11-1987</u> Sydney, Entertainment Center.
Sound check.

NT

<u>6-11-1987</u> Sydney, Entertainment Center.
Attendance: 10.000.
Recorded and filmed for tour-video + ABC TV Special. Because of the filming the show was split into 3 parts and this was not an improvement. During the breaks they showed videos of Bowie songs. Not much of this evening is used for the official video. It was a poor show.

1 CDR — Spider TV (Old Gold Records OGCD 471)

3 CDR — *Victorian Connection (No label, no number)*

1 CDR — Battle for Bowie (1 song) (No label, no number)

1 CDR — Live in Sydney 1988

DATE / EVENT	AUDIO / VIDEO	TITLE
During the encore White light white heat and I wanna be your dog guest appearance by Charlie Sexton.	1 CDR	(No label, no number) Live Sydney 1987
	VCD	(No label, no number) *Sydney Australia 6/11-1987*
	LP	(No label, no number) Glass spider tour (Starlight Records SL 87008 A/B)
	Tape	quality 8, 130 min.
	Tape	quality 7, 140 min.
	Tape	quality 10, 60 min.
	Video	*Various 11 (104 min)*
<u>7-11-1987</u> Sydney, Entertainment Center. Attendance: 10.000. Recorded and filmed for tour-video + ABC TV Special. This was a good show. Now they had 2 breaks in the show, during which they showed the videos. During Fame Johnny Angel gave David flowers. During White light white heat (3.48) and I wanna be your dog guest appearance by Charlie Sexton. The main part of this concert is used for the tour video. On 3-6-1988 simultaneous radio and TV broadcast of a part of the tour video recordings.	*2 CDR*	*Glass spider* (No label, no number)
	2 CD	Glass idol (PD 81999)
	CD	Pinups 2 (1 song) (BOWPU02)
	1 CDR	Live in Sydney 1988 (No label, no number)
	1 CDR	Live Sydney 1987 (No label, no number)
	LP	Glass spider tour (Starlight Records SL 87008 A/B)
	Tape	quality 9, 130 min.
	Tape	quality 8, 140 min.
<u>9-11-1987</u> Sydney, Entertainment Center. Attendance: 10.000. An average concert. Bowie apologises for his weak voice. A girl threw her bra on stage and Bowie said: "Carlos and I and John Lennon wrote this song in 1975. It's called… ha ha… bra. It's called Fame." He picked up the bra and looked at it in a dumb way and several others bra's followed.	2 CDR	Sydney Routine (Old Gold Records OGCD 268A/B)
	2 CDR	Le roi de Nice (Old Gold Records OGCD 267A/B)
	2 CDR	Sydney 87 Fifth Night (No label, no number)
	2 CDR	The show must go on (No label, no number)
	2 CDR	Glass Spider Tour 1988 (No label, no number)
	Tape	quality 9, 130 min.
<u>10-11-1987</u> Sydney, Entertainment Center. Attendance: 10.000. Not a good concert. Bowie's voice very weak. No encores to spare his voice for the next concerts.	2 CDR	Very Short! (Old Gold Records OGCD 382A/B)
	Tape	quality 9, 115 min.
<u>13-11-1987</u> Sydney, Entertainment Center. Attendance: 10.000. Bowie's voice much better and a happy audience. During White light white heat and I wanna be your dog	*2 CDR*	*Sydney 13 November 1987* *(BowieHobby)*
	2 CDR	Australian Dog (Old Gold Records

DATE / EVENT	AUDIO / VIDEO	TITLE
guest appearance by Charlie Sexton.	2 CDR	OGCD 383A/B) Australian Spider (No label, no number)
	Tape	quality 8, 130 min.
	Video	quality 9, 128 min.
<u>14-11-1987</u> Sydney, Entertainment Center. Attendance: 10.000. A very average concert. They did not do Time for the encores.	2 CDR	Goodbye Sydney (Old Gold Records OGCD 384A/B)
	Tape	quality 8, 130 min.
<u>18-11-1987</u> Melbourne, Kooyong Stadium. Promoter: The Paul Dainty Corporation. A good concert. Started at 20.00 h. Bowie in a good mood and his voice had more power again.	NT	
<u>20-11-1987</u> Melbourne, Kooyong Stadium. There was a limit at 22.30 h. They had to pay 1.000 dollars for every minute they played longer. The decibels were restricted to 60 (which is very low for a concert). Bowie was not happy and after Time will crawl he gave the crowd a long explanation.	NT	
21-11-1987 Theatre Crafts. Article by Mark Loeffler: Designer remedies for Bowie's theatre bug.		
<u>21-11-1987</u> Melbourne, Kooyong Stadium. Bowie had a lot of problems with the high notes. He joked and improvised a lot.	NT	
<u>23-11-1987</u> Melbourne, Kooyong Stadium. Promoter: The Paul Dainty Corporation. Very bad weather. A lot of rain and wind. A lot of people did not turn up because of the weather. Again a sound restriction to 60 dB. "The weather tonight prevents us from doing The Glass Spider show. I'm sorry about that. The good news is we are gonna play some stuff anyway." During Day in day out Bowie started singing at the wrong moment. During Absolute beginners Bowie began to sing during the part of the background-singers. Strange concert!	2 CD	*He never let us down*
	1 CDR	*He never let us down* (Wildcat Record Company)
	1 CDR	*87 And cry* (Seleibenho Records)
	1 CDR	He never let us down (Old Gold Records OGCD 098)
	2 CDR	Glass Spider finale (Old Gold Records OGCD 099A/B)
	2 LP	Bowie Live In Melbourne (Wild Cat Records Bow 5/6)
	Tape	quality 9, 70 min.
	Tape	quality 9, 90 min.
<u>28-11-1987</u> Auckland, Western Springs Stadium. Sound check (in the afternoon).	Tape	quality 9, 10 min.
<u>28-11-1987</u> Auckland, Western Springs Stadium. Support act: Patea Maori Club.	2 CDR	Glass Spider finale (Old Gold Records

DATE / EVENT	AUDIO / VIDEO	TITLE
An average concert. Bowie was tired. After China girl: "That's for you Jee Ling, wherever you are." Jee Ling was the woman in the China girl video clip.	2 CDR Tape Tape	OGCD 099A/B) Auckland 87 (No label, no number) quality 8, 130 min. quality 9, 125 min.
28-11-1987 Australian TV. Willesee at Seven. Presented by Mike Willesee. Interview with Bowie, Angie, Visconti. Photo's and clips.	*Video*	*Various 19 (7 min)*

Gabrels wife Sarah was doing the press for the Glass Spider Tour. At the end of the tour Sarah gave David a tape of the current work of Reeves Gabrels.

4-12-1987 UK TV. BBC. Top of the Pops. Time will crawl. Recorded 16-9-1987.

| 26-12-1987 BBC. Radio 1. Loving the alien. | LP
Tape | Loving the alien
quality 10, 100 min. |

27-12-1987 Thanks giving dinner at Regent Hotel.

December 1987 Bowie played a role in The last temptation of Christ (Ponti Pilate), directed by Martin Scorsese. The film was shot in Morocco.

End 1987 or Begin 1988 Amanda Lear died.

1987 / 1988 Jayne County introduced Angie Bowie to Dick Richards, who booked her at Club Rio in Atlanta. Angie really liked the city and moved with her daughter Stash to Atlanta (Man enough to be a woman - Jayne County 1995).

1988 Released CDS Real wild child - Iggy Pop (A&M Records AMCD 909).
Includes Isolation (4.36) (co-written by Bowie) and Shades (edit version) (5.19) (co-written by Bowie).

1988 Released The London Sound - Var. Art. (London 820489-2).
Includes The laughing gnome - David Bowie.

1988 Demo of Life on Mars? (1971) sold on an auction at Philips for GBP 90,—.

1988 Book published: Return of the Spiderman part one & two - Peter Frederiksen (Self published, no ISBN number).

1988 Book published: Shining star (collectors guide to the Glass Spider Tour) - Marshall Jarman and Friends (Self published, no ISBN number).

1988 Book published: Starmakers and svengalis - Johnny Rogan (Queen Anne Press).

1988 Book published: Psychotic reactions and carburetor dung - Lester Bangs (Vintage Books 1988). ISBN 0-679-72045-6. Reviews and interviews with David Bowie, Iggy Pop and Lou Reed.

1988 Book published: Behind the spider - Simon Dean and Antoine Loogman (Self Published).

DATE / EVENT	AUDIO / VIDEO	TITLE

1988 Book published: London's Rock Landmarks (Omnibus Press). Includes the addresses where Bowie lived, worked, etcetera during his London years.

1988 Book published: Iggy Pop: The wild one (The true story of Iggy Pop) - Per Nilsen and Dorothy Sherman Rosebud Publishing).

1988 Videos released: Glam Rock and Glam Rock 2.

1988 Record collector. Bowie in the poll of the most collected artists at number 3.

1988 Music Maker (Holland). Mick Ronson interviewed by Jan van der Plas.
Ronson about the album Pin Ups: "That album was great to do, because the songs were our favourites when we were teenagers. I started to play guitar because of Duane Eddy, and shortly after that you got The Beatles, The Stones, The Yardbirds. The best music is the music that gets you so excited that you want to pick up and learn to play an instrument by yourself. With Pin Ups we got to record all those songs ourselves."

Early 1988 Bowie made demos of Pretty Pink Rose, Lucy can't dance and Like a rolling stone (original by Bob Dylan in 1965). With Bryan Adams backing band.

8-1-1988 Denmark TV. Bowie Special.   Video   90 min.
Includes an exclusive interview from 1987.

January / February 1988 Sonics, The Music Magazine. Article: Inside the Glass Spider.

March 1988 Released 7" Single Tonight (live) (4.45) / River deep mountain high - Tina Turner (EMI / Capitol 2031797). A-side written by Bowie, sang by Bowie and Turner.

March 1988 Released 5" CDS Tonight (live) (4.45) / Let's stay together / River deep mountain high - Tina Turner (EMI / Capitol 2031802). A-side written by Bowie, sang by Bowie and Turner.

March 1988 Release Live in Europe - Tina Turner (Capitol ESTD 1). Included Tonight (live) (4.45), Let's dance / Let's dance (live) (3.25).

March 1988 Fabiola (Belgium). Article: Homo's & Rock, een niet alledaagse lovestory.

5-3-1988 Haarlem (Holland), Rock-Cafe Beauty and the Beast. David Bowie day.

Spring 1988 London. Bowie attends concert of The Pogues.

May 1988 New York. Bowie and Melissa Hurley attend the play Romance-Romance.

May 1988 Gabrels flew to Switzerland and stayed for almost a month with Bowie.
The first number they rehearsed was Ziggy Stardust.
When Bowie called Gabrels in South Kensington, he thought an American friend was making a joke. A few hours later Bowie called again and said: "What are you doing this weekend?" (Strange fascination - David Buckley 1999).

DATE / EVENT	AUDIO / VIDEO	TITLE

May 1988 Bowie and Reeves Gabrels (4-6-1956) were in a Turkish Restaurant in Switzerland. They talked about demos they had made. After this conversation Bowie decided to be a member of a rock band (something he hadn't been since the sixties).

1-5-1988 Schiedam, De Erker. Fan-meeting Dutch fanzine Bowie Now.

3-6-1988 US TV. ABC. TV-special. Behind the web. 12 Songs of the official tour video, filmed on 6 and 7-11-1987 in Sydney. Presented by Al Stewart.	Video	50 min.
At the same time broadcast on WBCN radio.	Tape	quality 10, 60 min.

30-6-1988 Bowie, Edouard Lock and Priya Khajuria visited Amsterdam.

<u>1-7-1988</u> London, Dominion Theatre.	CD	*This is your life* (PD 81997)
Intruders at the Palace, in aid of Institute for Contemporary Arts. Recorded for BBC broadcast. Tickets: GBP. 15,—.	CD	*Look back in anger* (No label, no number)
Look back in anger (7.22) (first live appearance with Reeves Gabrels), featuring La La La Human Steps.	1 CDR	*Battle for Bowie* (No label, no number)
Percussion provided by a drum machine (first time in Bowie's live career).	CD	*Legendary Lost Tapes Vol. 2* (VigOtone 179)
	Tape	quality 9, 10 min.
	Video	*Various 10* (8 min)

2-7-1988 London, Cafe Munchen, 15th Giles Street. David Bowie party-conference.

8-7-1988 English local radio. Radiobroadland. 40-Minute broadcast of the Montreal concert on 30-8-1987.	Tape	40 min.

9-7-1988 Melody Maker. Article by Chris Roberts: David Bowie with La La La Human Steps. Roberts about the performance of 1-7-1988: "It was purely fantastical. They slap one another across the face, tickle the chin, hurl, whirl and assault. The flickering video shows Bowie and Le Cavalier, monochrome icons freezing with fear and lust."

29-7-1988 Channel 4. Wired. Interview with David Bowie and David Byrne. Footage rehearsing Look back in anger 1-7-1988 Dominion Theatre.	Video	*Stolp tapes no. 17* (4 min)

During recording the next album Bowie decided that it should be called Tin Machine as a project. Gabrels at first did not agree it should be a band-project.

August 1988 Montreux (Switzerland), Mountain Studios. First part recordings album Tin Machine.

Second part a few months later in Compass Point Studios in Nassau (the Bahamas). Status Quo was recording in the same studio. Mixing was in New York.

11-8-1988 Rolling Stone. Article: Glass Spider.

12-8-1988 The painter Jean-Michel Basquiat died.

DATE / EVENT	AUDIO / VIDEO	TITLE

September 1988 Record Collector. Article by Lewis Balfour: David Bowie live.

10-9-1988 US TV. Wrap Around The World.	Tape	quality 9, 10 min.
Recorded in New York 'live' in the studio.	Video	quality 9, 10 min.

22-9-1988 Dutch premiere of the film The last temptation of Christ. The Court decided the film could be shown, despite the complaint of a man called Dorenbos.
A few articles in newspapers:
A lot of people want to see Jezus-film.
Court asked to forbid Jezus-film.

1-10-1988 Essen, Saalbau Essen. Fan-meeting German David Bowie fan club.

November 1988 Release Absolute beginners (Full length version) (8.00) / Absolute beginners (Dub mix) (5.42) (Virgin CDT20).

November 1988 Release Under pressure (Bowie and Queen) (4.09) / Soul brother (Queen only) (3.39) / Body language (Queen only) (4.32) (Parlaphone QUE CD9).

20-11-1988 Schiedam, De Erker. Fan-meeting Dutch Fanzine David Bowie Now.

1988 / 1989 Film UHF with Alan Yankovic. Bowie played a small part.

SELECTED BIBLIOGRAPHY

1984	George Orwell (First published in 1950). Published in Holland by Uitgeverij De Arbeiderspers. ISBN 90 295 3371 4 / CIP
25 Jaar Paradiso	Lutgard Mutsaers (Jan Mets). ISBN 90-5330-091-0.
A rock 'n' roll odyssey	Kate Lynch (Proteus Books 1984). ISBN 0 86276 221 9 (paperback). ISBN 0 86276 221 7 (hardback).
A walk on the wild side	Nelson Algren (Farrar, Straus and Cudahy 1956) (Cat. nr. 56-8623).
A year in the life	Alex Alexander (Self publ. 2001). No ISBN number.
A year with swollen appendices (1995 diary)	Brian Eno (Faber & Faber, May 1996). ISBN 0-571-17995-9.
Absolute beginners	Colin MacInnes (Penguin Books 186). ISBN 0-14-002142-6. First published in 1959
According to The Rolling Stones	Dora Loewenstein and Philip Dodd (BZZToH) ISBN 8-712241-000993.
Against interpretation	Susan Sontag (Laurel Edition 0083, January 1969).
Alias David Bowie	Peter and Leni Gillman (New English Lib. 86). ISBN 0-450-41346-8.
Also sprach Zarathustra	Friedrich Nietzsche (Wereldbibliotheek 1985). ISBN 90-284-1505-X. Also published in 1905.
Backstage passes	Angela Bowie and Patrick Carr (Orion Books 1993). ISBN 1 85797 1086.
Behind the Spider	Simon Deun and Antoine Loogman (P.S. Productions, October 1987). No ISBN number.
Black book	Barry Miles (Putnam 1980). ISBN 0.86001.808.3.
Bowie	Jerry Hopkins (Macmillan 1985). ISBN 90-325-0256-5.
Bowie Lives & Times - Bootleg Records Illustrated	Babylon Books (1979). No ISBN number.
Bowiepix	Pearce Marchbank (Omnibus Press 1983). ISBN 0.933328.85.0.
Bowiestyle	Written by Mark Paytress, co-written by Steve Pafford, designed by Pearce Marchbank (Omnibus Press 2000).

BOOK TITLE	WRITER / PUBLISHER
Brian Eno: His music and the Vertical Color of Sound	ISBN 0-7119-7722-4. Eric Tamm (Faber and Faber) ISBN 0-571-12958-7.
Changes	Chris Welch (Carlton Books Limited 1999). ISBN 1 85868 810 8.
Changes (The illustrated David Bowie story)	Stuart Hoggard (Omnibus Press 1980 / 1982). ISBN 0.86001.772.9.
Christiane F (Wir Kinder vom Bahnhof Zoo)	Kai Hermann and Horst Rieck (Stern-Magazin im Verlag Gruner + Jahr AG & Co 1979). (Gottmer 1980). ISBN 90 257 2663 1.
Crash course for the Ravers: A Glam Odyssey	Philip Cato (S.T. Publishing 1997). ISBN 1 898927 65 0.
David Bowie	Dave Thompson (Plexus 1986). ISBN 90 6756 204 1.
David Bowie	Steve Gett (Cherry Lane Books 1985). ISBN 0-89524-288-5.
David Bowie 1962 - 1968	Alex Alexander and Pete Foulstone (Self published 2002) No ISBN nr.
David Bowie: A Chronology	Kevin Cann (London, Vermilion Books 1983). ISBN 0 09 1538319.
David Bowie - An illustrated record	Roy Carr & Charles S.Murray (Avon Books / London 1981). ISBN 0-380-77966-8.
David Bowie Collector's Price Guide & Discography	Pete Smith (1987)
David Bowie - His private and public lives, his music, his films, his future. A portrait in words & pictures	Vivian Claire (Flash Books 1977). ISBN 0.7119.0285.2.
David Bowie - The archive	Chris Charlesworth (Omnibus Press 1981). ISBN 0.7119.1066.9.
David Bowie Profile	Chris Charlesworth (Proteus Books 1981). ISBN 0 90607167 4.
David Bowie 7" Record Discography	Marshall Jarman (Self published 1993). ISBN 0 952275 0 9.
David Bowie: Theatre of Music	Robert Matthew-Walker (Kensal Press 1985). ISBN 0-946041-22-9.
David Bowie's Serious Moonlight	Denis O'Regan and Chet Flippo (Sidgwick Jackson 1984). ISBN 0-283-99108-9.
David Robert Jones: The discography of a generalist	David Jeffrey Fletcher (F. Ferguson Prod. 15-7-1979). No ISBN number.
De Superstars van de muziek - David Bowie - nr.1	Paul de Bruyn (Betapress 1987). No ISBN number.
Dependence day	Robert Newman (Century. Sept. 1994). ISBN 13579108642. First 9 pages story about Bowie.
Diamond Nebula	Jeremy Reed (Peter Owen Limited 1994). ISBN nummer 0-7206-0891-0

BOOK TITLE	WRITER / PUBLISHER
Diary of a rock 'n' roll star	Ian Hunter (Panther 1974). (Independant Music Press 1996). ISBN 1-89-7783-09-4.
Events of David Bowie	Hans Lelivelt (1986).
Freddie Mercury The Definitive Biography	Lesley-Ann Jones (Hodder and Stoughton 1997). ISBN 90 5501 368 4.
Free spirit	Angie Bowie (Mushroom Books 1980). ISBN 0 907 39403 5.
Glam! Bowie, Bolan and the Glitter Rock Revolution	Barney Hoskyns (Faber & Faber 1998). ISBN 0-571-19542-3.
Glass Idol	David Currie (Omnibus Press 1987). ISBN 0.7119.1182.7.
Iggy Pop	Nina Antonia (Virgin Modern Icons 1997). ISBN 1-85227-698-3.
In his own words	Compiled by Miles, designed by Perry Neville (Omnibus Press 1980). ISBN 0-86001-645-5.
In other words... David Bowie	Kerry Juby (Omnibus Press 1986). ISBN 0.7119.1038.3.
Just a gigolo	Rosemary Kingsland (Corgi Books, 1979). ISBN 0 552 11005 1).
Lasher	Anne Rice (Ballantine Books, sept. 1994). ISBN 0-345-39781-9.
Le scaphandre et le papillon	Jean-Dominique Bauby (Laffont 1997). ISBN 90-5689-042-5.
Living on the brink	George Tremlett (Century 1996). ISBN 0 09 995840 6.
Lou Reed	Victor Bockris (De Kern 1994). ISBN 90-325-0461-4.
Loving the alien	Christopher Sandford (Little Brown and Company 1996). ISBN 0 316 879 789.
Man enough to be a woman	Jayne County with Rupert Smith (Serpents Tail 1995). ISBN 1-85242-338-2.
Marilyn Manson: The unauthorised biography	Kalen Rodgers (Omnibus 1998).
Mick Jagger, Primitive Cool	Christopher Sandford (Victor Gollantz LTD, 993). ISBN 90 6291 802 6.
Mick Ronson: The Spider with the platinum hair	Weird & Gilly (independent Music Press 2003). ISBN 0-9539942-3-6).
Moonage Daydream	Dave Thompson (Plexus 1987). ISBN 90 6756 204 1.
On the road	Jack Kerouac (USA 1957. Published in UK by Andre Deutsch 1958. Published in 1972 by Penguin Books). ISBN 0 1400.3192 8.
Out of the cool	Philip Kamin + Peter Goddard

BOOK TITLE	WRITER / PUBLISHER
	Virgin Books 1983). ISBN 0 8369 053 X.
Outside Tour Ultimate Guide	Alex Alexander (Self published 1997). No ISBN number.
People stared at the make up on his face	Per Nilsen (Self published 1985). No ISBN number.
Pop Score	Jip Golsteijn (Teleboek b.v. 1979). ISBN 906122703 8.
Presenting David Bowie	David Douglas (New York, Pinnacle, 1975). ISBN 0-523-00724-8.
Psychotic reactions and carburetor dung	Lester Bangs (Vintage Books 1988) ISBN 0-679-72045-6.
Return of the Spiderman part one & two	Peter Frederiksen (Self published 1988) No ISBN number.
Rock 'n' roll Comic. Volume 56. David Bowie.	Revolutionary Comics (Feb. 1993).
Rolling Stone Raves: What your rock & roll favorites favor	Anthony Bozza and Shawn Dahl (Rolling Stones Press 1999) ISBN 0-688-16304-1.
Rotterdam 1983	Sytze Annema (Self published 1983). No ISBN number.
Seven years in Tibet	Heinrich Harrer (Pan Books Ltd. 1956). No ISBN number.
Shining star (A collectors guide to the Glass Spider Tour)	Marshall Jarman and Friends (Self published 1988). No ISBN number.
Stone alone	Bill Wyman and Ray Coleman (Viking, London 1990) ISBN 90 5018 119 8.
Stardust (The David Bowie story)	Henry Edwards and Tony Zanetta (McGraw-Hill Book Company 1986) ISBN 0-07-072797-X.
Strange fascination	David Buckley (Virgin Books 1999). ISBN 1-85227-784-X.
Stranger in a strange land	Robert L. Heinlein (G.P. Putnam's Sons 1961). ISBN 0-425-07142-1.
Take it like a man (the autobiography of)	Boy George with Spencer Bright (Sidgewick & Jackson 1995). ISBN 0 283 99217 4.
The Anabas look book series (in words and pictures)	Jim Palmer (Anabas Publishing Ltd. 1984). ISBN 1 85099 003 4.
The best a man can get	John O'Farrell (Doubleday 2000). Page 142.
The Bowie Companion	Elizabeth Thomson and David Gutman (Macmillan 1993). ISBN 0-333-57226-2
The Buddha of Suburbia	Hanif Kureishi (1990, Faber and Faber). ISBN 0-670-83342-8.
The David Bowie story	George Tremlett (Futura 1974).

BOOK TITLE	WRITER / PUBLISHER
The complete David Bowie	ISBN 0 8600 7051 4. Nicholas Pegg (Reynolds & Hearn Ltd. 2000). ISBN 1-903111-16-1.
The complete guide to the music of David Bowie	David Buckley (Omnibus Press 1996). ISBN 0.7119.5301.5.
The concert tapes	Pimm Jal de la Parra (P.J. Publishing 1985). ISBN 90-9001005-X.
The definitive guide	Alex Alexander and Pete Foulstone (Self published 2000). No ISBN number.
The Elephant Man (A play by Bernard Pomerance)	Bernard Pomerance (Grove Press Inc. 1979) ISBN 0-394-50642-1.
The Hunger	Whitley Striber (1983).
The idiot	Fyodor Dostoevsky (Bantam Books 1958).
The illustrated Bowie bootleg file	Christian Frifelt (Self published 1990). No ISBN number.
The illustrated Bowie bootleg file 2	Christian Frifelt (Self published 1997). No ISBN number.
The International Encyclopaedia of Hard Rock & Heavy Metal	Tony Jasper and Derek Oliver (Sidgwick & Jackson Limited 1991) ISBN 0 283 061022.
The man who fell to earth	Walter Tevis (Bantam Books 1963).
De man die naar de aarde viel	Walter Tevis (Prisma Pocket 2338). ISBN 90 274 1481 5.
The Originals	Arnold Rypens (Icarus 1996). ISBN 90.02 20451 5.
The Outsider	Colin Wilson (Houghton Mifflin 1956) (Picador (Pan Books) 1978. ISBN 0 330 25391 3). (insp. for album Outside).
The picture of Dorian Gray	Oscar Wilde (Modern Library. Boni and Liveright Inc. 1891).
The Pitt report	Kenneth Pitt (Omnibus Press 1983). ISBN 0.7119.0619.X.
The Prophet	Kahlil Gibran (insp. for The width of a circle). (New York: Knopf 1923) (Dutch translation: Mirananda 1990). ISBN 90-62710597-9.
The rise and fall of a 20th century superstar (Bolan)	Mark Paytress (Omnibus Press 2002). ISBN 0.7119.9293.2.
The seed and the sower (Merry Christmas Mr. Lawrence)	Laurens van der Post (Penguin Books 1983). ISBN 0 14 00.2402 6.
The show must go on (the life of Freddie Mercury)	Rick Sky (Harper Collins 1992). ISBN 90-6291-772-0.
The songs of David Bowie	Pearce Marchbank. (Wise Publications 1977). ISBN 0.86001.004.X.

BOOK TITLE	WRITER / PUBLISHER
The Sound and Vision Tour book	Peter Frederiksen and Sean Doherty. (Self published 1991). No ISBN number.
The sound of the city: the rise of rock and roll	Charlie Gillett (Outerbridge & Dienstrey). ISBN 90-6213-745-8.
The spark that set the flame	Marieke Groen (Kempen Uitgevers 1993) ISBN 90-74271-42-1.
The Starzone interviews	David Currie (Omnibus 1987). ISBN 0.7119.0685.
The Subterraneans	Jack Kerouac (Grove Press 1958. In 1966 reprinted by Zebra Books). Z-1006S.
The Thief's Journal (Journal du voleur)	Jean Genet (Grove Press inc., Black Cat Edition 1973). ISBN 0-394-17811-4.
The true history of the Elephant Man	Michael Howell & Peter Ford Penguin Books 1980). ISBN 0 14 00.5622 X.
The Wild Boys	William Burroughs (Grove Press inc. Black Cat Edition 1973) ISBN 0-394-17819-X.
Tin Machine 1989-1992 (No miracle jive)	Peter Frederiksen (Self published by Bowie Network Production 1993). No ISBN number.
Vile Bodies	Evelyn Waugh (1930. In 1977 republished by Little, Brown). ISBN 0-316-92616-7.
Warhol	Victor Bockris (Penguin 1989).
We can be heroes	Sean Mayes (Independent Music Press 1999). ISBN 1-89-7783-17-5.
We could be heroes	Chris Welch (Thunder's Mouth Press 1999) ISBN 1 56025 209 X.
Written in my soul: rock's great songwriters talk about creating their music	Bill Flanagan (Contemporary Books 1986). ISBN 90-245-1793-1.
Yassassin Bowie	Simon Deun and Philippe (Post Scriptum Productions, July 1981).
Ziggy lives (comic) (D.B.1 R.F.13)	Michael (Rock Fantasy Comics, september 1990). No ISBN number.
Ziggy Stardust: Classic Rock Albums	Mark Paytress (Schirmer Books 1998). ISBN 0-02-864771-8.

| BOOK TITLE | WRITER / PUBLISHER |

FANZINES

Starzone numbers 2,3,4,5,6,7,8,12,13,14,15,16,17.

Crankin' Out 1,2,3,4,5.

David Bowie Fan Club Magazine, Issue 1 (1973)

Bowie Single Mania (B.S.M.). Austrian Fanzine, limited to 1.000 copies (April 1993).

Zi Duang Provence, Volume 1, Issue 4,6,7.
Zi Duang Provence, Volume 4, Issue 41

Bowie Now 83-2	Yellow. Bowie on cover wearing a hat.
Bowie Now 83-5	Blue. Bowie with glasses on cover.
Bowie Now 84-4	Pink. 3 Photo's from different periods on cover.
Bowie Now 84-6	Orange. Bowie smiling on cover, Japanese lyrics.
Bowie Now 84-8	Yellow. Bowie on cover as Lord Byron.
Bowie Now 84-9	Yellow. Cover sleeve of Tonight.
Bowie Now, March 1985	Grey. Cover is a drawing of Bowie.
Bowie Now, June 1985	White with a red tripe (tie).
Bowie Now, September 1985	Yellow with green. Cover is a drawing.
Bowie Now, December 1985	Blue.
Bowie Now, March 1986	White with pink. Cover Bowie with jacket.
Bowie Now, June 1986	White with orange and yellow. Bowie with hand under chin.
Bowie Now, September 1986	White with green. Cover Labyrinth (alone).
Bowie Now, December 1986	White with yellow. Cover Labyrinth (together).
Bowie Now, 87-1	Black with blue. With microphone.
Bowie Now, 87-2	Black with green. With jacket.
Bowie Now, 29-3-1987 (5-years celebration)	Black with white. Photo special.
Bowie Now	Black with yellow. With Glass Spider hair.
Bowie Now	Black with red. On stage.
Bowie Now	Black with yellow. Young Americans look.
Bowie Now	Red with black. With glasses.
Bowie Now	Red with black. With cap.
Bowie Now	Red with black. With Tina Turner.
Bowie Now 1988	Black with red. Laughing, hair discovering his right eye.

BOOK TITLE	WRITER / PUBLISHER
Bowie Now 1989	White with black. With guitar, Tin Machine.
Bowie Now 1989	White with black. 4 Members of Tin Machine.

Best of Bowie Now, July 1990, no. 0
Best of Bowie Now, 1991 (vol.9 no.2 and 3)
Best of Bowie Now, 1992 (vol.10 no.1 and 4)
Best of Bowie Now, 1993 (vol.10 no.2,3 and 4)
Best of Bowie Now, 1994 (vol.11 no.1 and 2)
Best of Bowie Now, autumn 1995 (vol.11 no.3)

The Voyeur, October 1996 (vol.11 no.4)
The Voyeur, 1997 (vol.12 no.1,2,3 and 4)
The Voyeur, 1998 (vol.13 no.1,2,3, and 4)
The Voyeur, March 1999 (vol.14 no.1)
The Voyeur, July/Aug 1999
The Voyeur, Nov/Dec. 1999
The Voyeur, 31 December 1999
The Voyeur, March 2000
The Voyeur, August 2000
The Voyeur, November 2000
The Voyeur, March 2001
The Voyeur, September 2001
The Voyeur, December 2001
The Voyeur, April 2002
The Voyeur, September 2002
The Voyeur, April 2003
The Voyeur, October 2003
The Voyeur, December 2003
The Voyeur, April 2004

The Great Books of Islamic Civilization

On Qur'ānic Exegesis

by

Shaykh Muḥammad Ṭāhir bin ʿĀshūr

An abridged English rendering
of the Introductions of
Tafsīr al-Taḥrīr wa al-Tanwīr
by
Muhammad al-Ghazali

Reviewed with a Note by
Dheen Mohamed M. Meerasahib

Edited by
Muhammad Modassir Ali

Foreword
Prof. Aisha Yousef al-Mannai
Director, Center for Muslim Contribution to Civilization

HAMAD BIN KHALIFA UNIVERSITY PRESS

Hamad Bin Khalifa University Press
P O Box 5825
Doha, Qatar

www.hbkupress.com

Text Copyright © Muhammad Bin Hamad Al-Thani Center
for Muslim Contribution to Civilization

All rights reserved.

No part of this publication may be reproduced or transmitted in any form or by any means, electronic or mechanical, including photocopying, recording, or any information storage or retrieval system, without prior permission in writing from the publishers.

No responsibility for loss caused to any individual or organization acting on or refraining from action as a result of the material in this publication can be accepted by HBKU Press or the author.

The opinions expressed in this book do not necessarily reflect the opinion of the publisher.

First English edition in 2022

ISBN: 9789927161469

Printed in Doha-Qatar

Qatar National Library Cataloging-in-Publication (CIP)

Ibn 'Āshūr, Muḥammad al-Ṭāhir, 1879-1973, author.

[تفسير التحرير والتنوير]. Selections. English

On Qur'anic exegesis by Shaykh Muḥammad Ṭāhir ibn 'Āshūr : an abridged English rendering of the Introductions of Tafsīr al-taḥrīr wa-al-tanwīr / by Muhammad al-Ghazali ; reviewed with Note by Dheen Mohamed M. Meerasahib ; edited by Muhammad Modassir Ali ; forward Prof. Aisha Yousef al-Mannai. First English edition. - Doha, Qatar : Hamad Bin Khalifa University Press, 2022.

pages ; cm. (The Great books of Islamic civilization. Abridgement series. No. 2)

ISBN 978-992-716-146-9

Includes bibliographical references (pages 197-202).

In English; translated from Arabic.

1. Qur'an -- Commentaries -- Early works to 1800. I. Al-Ghazali, Muhammad, translator. II. Meerasahib, Dheen Mohamed M., reviewer. III. Ali, Muhammad Modassir, editor. IV. Al-Mannai, Aisha Yousef, author of introduction, etc. V. Title.

BP130.4 .I2613 2022
297.1226– dc 23   20222852035x

CONTENTS

MUHAMMAD BIN HAMAD AL THANI CENTER
FOR MUSLIM CONTRIBUTION TO CIVILIZATION..........................7

FOREWORD 9

REVIEWER'S NOTE..11

INTRODUCTORY REMARKS..17

INTRODUCTORY SECTIONS..41

CHAPTER ONE
Of Exegesis and Hermeneutics; Exegesis being a Science 43

CHAPTER TWO
Sources of the Science of Tafsīr 51

CHAPTER THREE
On the Authenticity of Tafsīr without Reliance on Transmitted Reports and the Meaning of Tafsīr based on Opinion 67

CHAPTER FOUR
What ought to be the Aim of the Mufassir? 85

CHAPTER FIVE
On the Occasions of Revelation 101

CHAPTER SIX
Of Recitals 111

CHAPTER SEVEN
Stories of the Qur'ān 121

CHAPTER EIGHT

*The Names of the Qur'ān, its Chapters,
their order and names* *129*

    8.1. Verses of the Qur'ān 133

    8.2. Order of Verses 138

    8.3. Pauses in the Qur'ān 143

    8.4. Chapters of the Qur'ān 145

CHAPTER NINE

Semantic Scope of the Qur'ān *153*

CHAPTER TEN

On the Inimitability of the Qur'ān *163*

    10.1. Innovations of the Qur'ān 188

    10.2. Habits of the Qur'ān 193

Bibliography *197*

MUHAMMAD BIN HAMAD AL THANI CENTER FOR MUSLIM CONTRIBUTION TO CIVILIZATION

The Center was established in 1983, when Sheikh Muhammad bin Hamad Al Thani was the Minister of Education for the State of Qatar. The idea behind its formation emerged as a response to the urgent need to provide publication of accurate and academically sound English translations of the most notable works of the Islamic heritage, illustrative of the civilizational and human contribution of Islam, on a global scale.

In May 2010, Her Highness Sheikha Moza bint Nasser, Chairperson of the Qatar Foundation for Education, Science and Community Development announced the affiliation of the Center to the College of Islamic Studies at Hamad bin Khalifa University.

The efforts of the Center were focused almost entirely on translations from Arabic to English language which saw the publication of 16 notable books of the Arab Islamic heritage in 23 volumes all of which related to various disciplines and were published by Garnet Publishing, United Kingdom.

In 2015, the Center reviewed its objectives which now stand as follows:

1. Raising awareness among Muslims and non-Muslims regarding the civilizational heritage of Muslims.
2. Introducing the contributions of Muslims to human civilization.
3. Participating in the promotion of academic research in the area of Islamic civilizational contribution.
4. Enabling researchers in the field of the civilizational contributions of Muslims to communicate and dialogue with each other, with

a view to turning the Center into a bridge and point of collaboration between them.

5. Highlighting and emphasizing the organized endeavors and role of the State of Qatar in the revival of the Islamic civilizational heritage.

In accordance with its objectives, it subsequently expanded the scope of its work and academic pursuits to include:

1. abridgement of a number of significant works
2. editing of manuscripts
3. translation of books from other languages to Arabic and
4. translation of works from English to other world languages.